NATHANAEL GREENE

Strategist of the American Revolution

*His qualifications for statesmanship were not
less remarkable than his military ability.*

ALEXANDER HAMILTON

NATHANAEL GREENE

Strategist of the American Revolution

by

Theodore Thayer

❦

TWAYNE PUBLISHERS

New York ● 1960

MANUFACTURED IN THE UNITED STATES OF AMERICA
BY UNITED PRINTING SERVICES, INC.
NEW HAVEN, CONN.

Preface

Nathanael Greene has always been considered among the great of the American Revolution. Time, however, has dimmed remembrance of the part he played in the winning of independence and the forging of the new nation. He was considered a military strategist of the first order by the men of his own time and the opinion would appear justified in the light of history. Indeed, it may be no overstatement to say that Greene, while with the army in the North, generally masterminded Washington's campaigns. Very early Washington made known his desire to have Greene his successor should anything happen to him in the course of the war. In Congress, also, he was considered the most eligible to succeed Washington.

In the South, Greene's strategy and daring played a major role in the final undoing of British power in America. At the outset this was implemented by a major stroke of good fortune. Greene sent Morgan to harass Cornwallis' flank at Winnsborough but not to risk a pitched battle with any part of the enemy. Cowpens was a lucky break for Greene. It weakened Cornwallis to such an extent that Greene could turn on him at Guilford Court House and give him such a mauling that he was forced to leave North Carolina. After that good fortune was Washington's when the French fleet sailed into the Chesapeake to seal the fate of Cornwallis at Yorktown.

After Guilford Court House, Greene dazzled the world by invading South Carolina and driving the British into Charleston. Sensational as was the campaign in South Carolina, in reality it may have had little bearing upon the outcome of the war. However, it could have been of the greatest importance had the French fleet failed to arrive off Yorktown. If that had not occurred, Greene's army and his successes in South Carolina could have been the only important obstacle between the British and the complete subjugation of the South.

The British had been heavily reinforced and Greene understood what it would mean if he marched to Virginia leaving the enemy

with a free hand in South Carolina. A little later when he heard that the fleet was coming and Washington and Rochambeau were on their way to Virginia, he feared for a time that Cornwallis might break through Lafayette's lines and march for Charleston. To forestall his being caught between Cornwallis and Stewart, Greene fought the Battle of Eutaw Springs.

By nature Greene was high-spirited and excitable, traits which sometimes made him impetuous. During the war these characteristics no doubt tended to give him a boldness and daring which when combined with military talent acquired from study, experience, and natural aptitude, made him the great general he became. But native traits and military talent alone do not explain his success. A capacity for ceaseless and untiring labor which went into all his endeavors was a factor of great importance. Not to be minimized, either, was a fascinating personality with which he influenced people and won friends and support from all but a few.

Greene was an ardent nationalist with an unusual insight into the political, economic, and constitutional problems besetting America during these years of profound change and evolution. All through the war and after he labored to impress leading citizens everywhere of the urgent necessity of providing Congress with the life-giving power of taxation. No doubt he would have had greater influence on Congress and other governing bodies had he shown more patience and understanding of the difficulties they faced in realizing these aims. Although he did not live to see the great changes he advocated embodied in the Constitution of the United States, he had faith in America and believed that the day was not far off when its citizens would rise "to form a more perfect union."

Acknowledgments

For their kindness and helpfulness while I was pursuing my research for a biography of Nathanael Greene, I wish to thank the staffs of The William Clements Library, The Huntington Library, The New York Public Library, The New York Historical Society, The Rhode Island Historical Society, The New Jersey Historical Society, The Historical Society of Pennsylvania, The New Hampshire Historical Society, The Massachusetts Historical Society, The Connecticut Historical Society, Duke University Library, The University of North Carolina Library, The University of South Carolina Library, The Caroliniana Library, The Morristown National Park Library, The Yale University Library, Houghton Library of Harvard University, Marietta College Library, J. Pierpont Morgan Library, The American Philosophical Society Library, The Rhode Island State Archives, The South Carolina State Archives, The Wadsworth Atheneum, and the Library of Congress.

I am also indebted to Dr. Bernhard Knollenberg of Chester, Connecticut, Henry Greene Jackson and Doris I. Benford of Providence, Donald T. Gibbs of Newport, Martha McPartland of East Greenwich, Rhode Island, Mr. and Mrs. Ben Hough, Mrs. Walter C. White, Mrs. W. Bedford Moore, and Henry Savage, Jr. of South Carolina, Milton F. Perry of West Point, and L. R. Wilson of Washington, D.C.

Finally, I wish to thank the Research Council of Rutgers University for generous grants-in-aid for my study.

THEODORE THAYER
Rutgers University

Table of Contents

MAP I

THE NEW YORK–NEW JERSEY AREA

PENNSYLVANIA

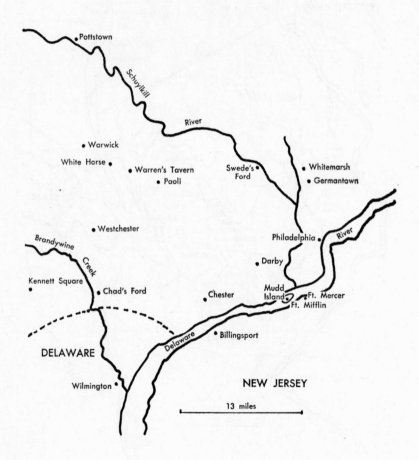

MAP II

THE PENNSYLVANIA CAMPAIGN

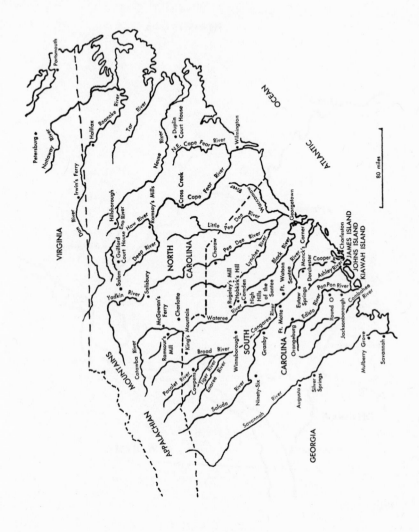

MAP III

THE CAMPAIGNS IN THE CAROLINAS AND GEORGIA

CHAPTER ONE

Potowomut Days

The fateful shots fired at Lexington and Concord on the 19th of April, 1775, raised scores of Americans from obscurity and made their names household words throughout the colonies. Such a man was Nathanael Greene, an anchorsmith by trade and son of a Rhode Island Quaker preacher.[1]

Indeed, there was little in Nathanael Greene's thirty-three years of life prior to the Lexington alarm to indicate he would ever be known outside the narrow confines of his own Rhode Island. True, friends and relatives in later years liked to think they had seen destiny in the eyes of the young Quaker. Some recalled how the astrology-loving Doctor Spencer predicted at his birth that the child would "one day become a mighty man in Israel." But if anyone took the doctor seriously, it was doubtless only to see in Nathanael a soul-stirring Quaker preacher. None in his wildest dreams would have imagined him one day a distinguished general engaged in a war to free America and establish a new nation.

Nathanael Greene's background was, in truth, so limited that only a youth of exceptional talents could have risen above it. Reared in a drab and provincial middle-class Quaker home, Nathanael was taught the simple lessons of toil and plain living. Some schooling he would have, but education beyond the three R's was considered by good Quakers not only superfluous but, like jewelry, fine clothes, and other marks of affectation, an actual snare for the godly. Such were the views on education throughout Kent County where Nathanael was reared, for here nearly everyone was a Quaker or a Baptist of equally simple tastes. To be sure, there were a few, generally Episcopalians, with a college or Latin school background, but Nathanael had little contact with them during his boyhood. Not until he was

15

well into his teens and began going to Newport on business did he come to know something about the world of men and ideas beyond his provincial homeland.

Nathanael Greene was of the fifth generation of Greenes in America. John Greene, the founder of the family, had been a surgeon of Salisbury, England. Like others, he came to the new world in search of a haven where men might be free to worship in their chosen manner. With his friends, the fiery Roger Williams and the eccentric and provocative Samuel Gorton, John Greene believed in "Soul Liberty." But all who held unpopular beliefs in the Massachusetts Bay Colony or the Plymouth Plantations were soon banished. The Gortonists with whom John Greene cast his lot fled to Rhode Island, where after a short and contentious stay at Portsmouth, they were obliged in 1640 to seek a haven in Providence. Here they found Roger Williams tolerant of, though opposed to, their Unitarian doctrines. However, he promised that they might stay as long as they kept the peace.

But within a year some of Gorton's followers became involved in a street brawl. Consequently, the little band of eleven men and their families were forced to flee to Pawtuxet, where friendly Indians provided them with food and shelter. Two years later in exchange for wampum the Gortonists purchased a tract of land called Shawomet (afterwards Warwick Neck) from Miantonomi, the Narragansett sachem. Here, after securing the support of the Earl of Warwick, Samuel Gorton and his followers succeeded in making a permanent home for themselves in the wilderness.

About fifteen years after the Gortonists settled Shawomet, the town fathers bought another tract of land, called Potowomut, for their growing community. At Potowomut three generations later, Nathanael Greene was born. In the Wampanoag tongue, *Potowomut* meant "place of many fires," having apparently once been the site of a sizable Indian village. A pear-shaped neck of land between Potowomut Creek and an arm of Greenwich Bay, Potowomut has remained a part of the township of Warwick. Communication between Warwick and Potowomut in Nathanael Greene's time was still mainly by boat as it was a long way around the perimeter of Greenwich Bay. In the distribution of the purchase, Nathanael Greene's great-grandfather, James Greene, son of John the founder, acquired a large tract of land at the base of Potowomut Neck. Here, in 1684, Nathanael's grandfather, Jabez Greene, established his homestead and built the house in which Nathanael was born. A roomy dwelling fashioned from oak, pine, and cedar, the house stood on a rise where the ground slopes gently down to Potowomut Creek two hundred yards away. Back of the house and away from the creek the Greenes owned several hundred acres of rather poor, sandy soil.

By the time Nathanael Greene was born the farm had its orchards, pastures, woodlots, and cultivated fields. Here, as a boy, before he graduated to the work of the forge and mill, Nathanael learned the hard lessons of primitive New England farming. For him there were never those carefree days so dear to childhood. When only a youngster of five or six, he had the cows to drive, the sheep to watch, and the innumerable chores to do which young hands could perform.

Down in the creek the thrifty Greenes built a dam and in turn constructed a grist and flour mill, a saw mill, and an ironworks. About the time Nathanael was born, his father became sole owner of the forge by buying out his brother's interest and that of another partner. By then he was a wealthy man according to the standards of the day, his iron business being worth £10,000. Indicative of the wealth and circumstance of Nathanael Greene, the elder, was his sedan chair, a rare vehicle in colonial America and, it would seem, a rather worldly possession for a doctrinaire Quaker.

From the Greene homestead at Potowomut a narrow road wound around an arm of Greenwich Bay to the village of East Greenwich two miles away. By the side of the road was an ancient spring from which Nathanael often quenched his thirst in going and coming from the village. Long before, he was told, Roger Williams, who frequently passed that way, had named it "Elizabeth spring" after the wife of his good friend John Winthrop, Junior. Incorporated in 1677, just after the war with the Indians led by King Philip, by Nathanael's time East Greenwich was a seaport of considerable importance as well as the seat of Kent County, in which lay Potowomut, Warwick, Coventry, and most of the places familiar to Nathanael in his early life. In East Greenwich—resting high on the slopes above the bay—Nathanael found friends and relatives with whom to pass some time during his rare leisure moments. On the wide main street, parallel to the bay, stood the busy Court House, built in 1750. Here, as a youth, Nathanael came to listen to the barristers and learn some practical lessons in law. After Arnold's tavern was built in 1770, he often stopped at this bustling hub of community life to hear the news and chat a bit. The only church in town was a Baptist meetinghouse, but just over the hill in a hollow by a little brook called Masquachugh, rested the Quaker meetinghouse. Here father Greene brought his family to sit in silent prayer and contemplation and listen to the testimonies and sermons of the men, and sometimes the women, of the congregation.

Nathanael Greene was born at Potowomut on July 27, 1742 (New Style). His mother was Mary Mott whom his father had married following the death of his first wife. He had two half brothers, Benjamin and Thomas, who died early in life. There was also a sister who died in her infancy. Of the brothers (six in all), Jacob was the eldest, Nathanael was next in age, and after him came William, Elihu, Christopher, and Perry. Of his mother, little is known. She died in 1753 when Nathanael was eleven, and was buried in the family plot behind the house. After her death and until the father married his third wife, Mary Rodman, in November, 1754, the family was cared for by a housekeeper.

Just when Nathanael's forebears became Quakers is not known. It may have been in 1672 when George Fox, the founder of the Society of Friends, visited Rhode Island, then a hotbed of religious radicalism. In any event, Nathanael's father had lost none of the pristine enthusiasm of the Society of Friends. It was his duty, he believed, to raise his sons to be sober, God-fearing men who would live moral and useful lives and this in turn necessitated the faithful application of the precepts of the Society. For more than forty years the senior Greene was recognized as the spiritual leader of the East Greenwich Quaker community. Quakerism naturally left an indelible stamp on the mind of Nathanael Greene who was past thirty before he broke with the faith to become a soldier.

On Sundays, in all weather, father Greene took his family up the long sandy road and over the hill to the meetinghouse beside the brook. When too young to walk, the children were allowed to ride with their parents, but after they were old enough, they walked the three miles with the servants and neighbors who chose to join them. As a youth, Nathanael enjoyed the meetings which afforded respite from the labors of the field and shop and a chance to meet and talk with people. Socially well-adjusted, unlike so many country boys, he was not shy or bashful.

Of special attraction to East Greenwich Quakers were the preachers who came to Rhode Island, often from old England and other faraway places. As a boy, Nathanael hung upon every word spoken by these men and women with their spirtual messages. As his critical powers developed, however, he came to ask that the preachers have something worth-while to say. Otherwise they should sit in silence, like the others, he thought. On a Sunday morning in 1772, we find him in this frame of mind. "Our silence," he wrote, "was interrupted by a vain conceited Minister. His Sermon made me think of a certain Diet called Whistle Belly Vengence, he that eats most has the most Share." His sermon, thought Nathanael, was so light it evaporated like air.[2]

One should not suppose that Nathanael found his father too stern for the natural affection of a son. For all his strictness, the senior Greene was in reality goodhearted and enjoyed most of the simple pleasures of rural life. On occasion, he would even venture a little beyond proper decorum for a Quaker preacher. This occurred one time when he attended a rather convivial meeting at Newport where were gathered all the clergymen of the town as well as the local rabbi. Under the influence of good wine, the men of God became exceedingly liberal and tolerant of each other's views and doctrines. Before long, it was told, preacher Greene became "seized with some mild affliction of the knees, which made the Assistance of a Negro in going upstairs quite convenient." The next day, preacher Greene was moved to make some remarks at the Quaker meetinghouse on the value and beauty of temperance.

Nathanael Greene's formal education was meager although

not unusually so for eighteenth-century rural Rhode Island. East Greenwich did not have a public school until 1826, and apparently the first organized school was an academy, founded in 1802. All of Nathanael's elementary schooling, other than instruction from his parents, was acquired from an unknown itinerant tutor whom the father hired for a short time to teach the boys reading, writing, and ciphering. This was enough schooling to satisfy the father who placed the strictest construction upon the Quaker maxim that education should be entirely utilitarian. In Nathanael —sandy-haired, blue-eyed, and rather plump—the tutor found an apt pupil. For a text, the boy used George Fox's *Instruction for right Spelling and plain Directions for Reading and Writing true English*. Besides the Bible, he in time read the standard Quaker works including Barclay's *Apology* and the writings of William Penn, William Sewel, Thomas Chalkley, and others. But eager as the boy Nathanael was to learn, by far the greater part of his time had to be spent at the plow and the endless chores and work of the farm. As a man, looking back on his early years, he wrote; "My Father was a man of Industry and brought up his Children to Business. Early, very early, when I should have been in the pursuit of Knowledge, I was digging into the Bowels of the Earth after Wealth." His father, he continued, had great piety, humanity, and benevolence, but was prejudiced against learning.[3]

Dominated by his father and kept hard at work most of the time, until late in his teens, Nathanael knew little of the world of secular books and knowledge. As he began to get away from home and meet people other than the staid yeomen of East Greenwich and Potowomut, he gradually became aware of the vast extent of learning in the world at large. He was probably seventeen or eighteen when he met two men who first inspired and then guided him in his quest for higher learning. One of them, the Reverend Ezra Stiles, would leave a lasting imprint on the pages of history. The other, a man named Giles (presumably William Giles who graduated from Yale in 1763), died in a few years after a brief practice of medicine.

Nathanael met William Giles in East Greenwich when the latter was a student at Yale. In the inquisitive and impressionable anchorsmith, Giles found an eager listener for all he had to tell of the marvelous realm of higher education. Inspired by Giles, Nathanael thereafter was seldom seen without a book. Whenever possible, he made his way to Warwick where the library (said to have been one of the largest in Rhode Island) of his kinsman, Judge Philip Greene, was at his disposal. Henceforth, while the grain was grinding in the mill or the iron heating in the forge, the youth snatched time to read and study.

Probably it was not long after he met Giles that Nathanael had the good fortune to come to know the Reverend Mr. Stiles, one day to become president of Yale, but at this time minister of the Second Congregational Church at Newport. According to tradition, Nathanael entered a bookstore at Newport and rather awkwardly made known his desire to buy a book on a certain subject. The bookseller questioned him as to title and author, and the Reverend, who chanced to be in the store, overheard the dialogue. Observing the youth's perplexity, Stiles opened a conversation which presently led into a general discussion of books and authors. It was apparently through Stiles that Nathanael came to read Locke's *Essay on Human Understanding,* a book of unbounded influence on eighteenth-century thought. Nathanael, whose Quaker upbringing and natural turn of mind afforded him a genuine taste for philosophical literature, found the deepest satisfaction in Locke. Meanwhile, Ezra Stiles and Nathanael became fast friends. Thereafter, whenever the youth with the smell of the forge about him visited Newport, he seldom failed to find the good minister for at least a few minutes of precious conversation.

Another who apparently influenced Nathanael in his quest for knowledge and book learning was Lindley Murray, the future grammarian, whom he met several years after meeting Giles and the Reverend Mr. Stiles. Of Quaker background and three years younger than Greene, Murray was then a student of law with John Jay in the office of Benjamin Kissam in New York.* It may be that Murray was the first to awaken in Greene an interest in law, as it was about this time that he purchased and began reading Jacob's *Law Dictionary* and Blackstone's *Commentaries.*

---

* John Jay graduated from King's College in 1764 after which he studied law. This would indicate that Greene met Murray in 1764 or 1765 when he was twenty-two or twenty-three years of age.

In time, Greene acquired a good command of law so that he could handle cases arising from his father's business. In the courts of law he came to know the local lawyers and judges from whom he learned further refinements in the techniques of legal practice and, what was more, a good deal of the art of fine speech and social grace. But with all his enterprise and thirst for knowledge, Nathanael never seemed to have had the least thought of becoming anything other than a learned blacksmith and ironmaster. The barrier between a self-taught country Quaker and the professional world seemed to the youth too great to be bridged.

As much as his father disliked his son's craving for knowledge, he did not feel justified in denying it after the boy had acquired a man's stature and outlook on life. For his part, Nathanael never gave his father cause to complain about neglect of work at the forge or mill. Thus it happened that his father agreed to hire Adam Maxwell, a local schoolmaster, to tutor his son in Latin and mathematics. The youth's powers of persuasion and compelling arguments had won. The elder Greene was not given to changing his mind readily, but he listened when Nathanael spoke. The youth, who had become convinced that the Quakers were wrong in their stand on higher education, may even have raised some doubts in the mind of his father. Years later, while discussing Quakerism, Nathanael told how seventeenth-century Quakers had become disgusted with the pedantry and stuffiness of higher learning which rendered its possessor neither wiser nor better than the untutored. "Friends concluded," he explained, "that a Liberal Education was rather prejudicial than beneficial to Society. Not rightly discovering where the Evil lay, they argued from the abuse to the disuse of the thing."[4]

After spending a few months studying Latin in his spare time with schoolmaster Maxwell, Nathanael found he had little taste for it and give it up. Quakers were right, he no doubt concluded, in feeling that a layman's time could be better spent than in learning the grammar of a dead language. He recognized, however, the value of a knowledge of ancient literature and over the years he built up a shelf of translations of the best known works. In this way, he became as conversant with classical literature as most of the college-bred men he came to know in

later life. Von Steuben's nearsighted French aide-de-camp, Pierre
Du Ponceau, related how Greene led a long discussion on the
Latin poets with Baron von Steuben and himself while they
were en route to the South in 1780.

In order to meet his growing need for book money, Nathanael
began making miniature anchors and other toys of wood and
iron which he sold on his visits to Newport. While sailing his
father's shallop down the bay to Newport, he customarily read
when not engaged in navigating. And on the return trip, with
what avid thirst for the knowledge hitherto hidden from him
did he pore over the new books he had purchased in the Newport
bookstores!

At the time Nathanael was paying his visits to Newport, it was
a thriving seaport of nearly 9,000 souls and, next to Boston, the
largest city in New England. Compared to anything Nathanael
had known, it was a gay town, noted for its families of wealth and
culture who lived in the fine Georgian homes on the hillside
above the bay. Five hundred ships cleared Newport harbor
every year, and the merchants built their houses to look out
over the bay and their profit-laden vessels. The citizens of
Newport were full of civic pride, and were perhaps proudest
of their Redwood Library with its dignified Corinthian portico
and spacious setting. Money for the building had been donated
by many of the town's leading citizens, among the largest con-
tributors being Abraham Redwood and John Collins. Peter Harrison who designed the library also designed Newport's beautiful
Jewish synagogue. What a contrast were these edifices, as well as
the lofty spire of the Anglican church, to the barn-like churches
and meetinghouses back in Kent County. Other landmarks of the
city were its public buildings, taverns, and the Masonic Temple
which served as a mecca for the gentlemen about town.

Through his frequent trips to Newport, Nathanael collected
a sizable library of more than 200 volumes. There were works
on history, government, philosophy, literature, law, and religion.
Books on science, mathematics, and navigation also occupied
a prominent place on his bookshelves. A four-volume dictionary
of arts and sciences, costing £4, answered countless questions
which came crowding into Nathanael's inquisitive mind. A manual on bookkeeping with a glossary of commercial terms, navi-

gation laws, and the rules of trade was as invaluable for his business years as it would be for his service as quartermaster general of the Continental Army. Greene's Roman history was that of the Frenchman, Charles Rollin; his English history was the standard thirteen-volume Tindall edition of the Huguenot, Paul de Rapin. His favorite author was Jonathan Swift, whose style he attempted to imitate. Later, when the war clouds gathered, he added books on tactics and military science to his shelves. Among these were Sharp's *Military Guide* and the works of Marshal Saxe as well as those of Marshal Turenne, whose writings Napoleon once said should be read and reread by every soldier. Prominent among his books was his sheepskin-bound volume of Euclid, one of the first he acquired and which he had kept at his side by the forge until he had mastered every principle of geometry.

Full grown, Nathanael Greene stood five feet ten. His shoulders were broad, his chest full, and his limbs strong. His hair, sandy-colored as a boy, grew darker, until in his thirties it showed signs of greying. Blue-grey eyes looked at one directly from under a high forehead, balanced by a heavy chin. Of somewhat florid complexion, with reddish lips and pink cheeks, as a youth he customarily revealed a happy, exuberant disposition said to have been acquired from Huguenot forebears on his mother's side. Even periods of anxiety and the cares of later years never wholly dimmed his native lightheartedness. He enjoyed a good joke, and when he laughed or even smiled, his blue eyes sparkled. Being fond of elocution, his impersonation of Doctor Slop from Sterne's *Tristram Shandy* never failed to delight an audience. Although he liked to talk, he was a good listener, especially when among men of education.

There was, above all, a certain indefinable air about the Poto-womut anchorsmith that deeply impressed his contemporaries. Something in his frank and open look, his thoughtful and reflective countenance, caused men to believe he was no ordinary person. A quizzical expression found at times in his eyes increased the fascination. His bearing as he gained manhood was ordinarily relaxed yet dignified. For a time, however, he was somewhat restrained in the presence of men of culture and learning. His

self-consciousness, as one would expect, gradually wore away
after he became a general and gained poise and self-assurance.

Greene's vivacious and spirited temperament was conducive to
certain psychological traits which in the long run apparently
contributed to his success. One of these was a tendency to be
impetuous and headstrong on occasion. Although he never
entirely overcame this trait which sometimes brought him trouble,
it presumably had the merit of being one source of the boldness
and daring he displayed as a soldier when the occasion demanded
this kind of action. Inasmuch as a high-spirited individual deeply
feels his disappointments, as a man, Greene was often plunged
into paroxysms of anxiety when confronted by seemingly in-
soluble situations. This, no doubt, was also a factor of his success
as it drove him to overcome difficulties which stood in his way.

During his teens, the youth's spirited make-up found ample expression. At that time he acquired a passion for dancing and
an acute attraction for the fair sex which was well received by
the girls of his acquaintance. Whenever a dance was held, near
or far, he and his cronies would hike to it and after the "hop"
plod their way home at all hours of the night. The boy's interest
in dancing and parties naturally offended the Quaker sensibilities
of his father who sought to curb his worldly-mindedness. Nathanael, however, usually found means to escape his father's
watchfulness. Sometimes he surreptitiously joined his friends
by climbing out of his second-story bedroom and down the
woodshed roof to the ground. Once, by resorting to the time-
honored expedient of padding his breeches, he seems to have
warded off a good whipping from his father who had found
him out and was waiting for his return. It was not long, however,
ere the attraction of dancing waned before his increasing pre-
occupation with reading and studying. Soon his passion for
books overshadowed all other forms of recreation and his interest
in girls narrowed to one. He found too much to be learned and
too few hours to devote to reading.

With the exception of his later years after campaigning in the
fever-ridden South, Nathanael enjoyed good health and a reason-
ably sound constitution. During boyhood he appeared to be a
healthy lad with all the unbounded energy of youth. Neverthe-

less, from an early age he suffered from asthma which caused him much discomfort and many sleepless nights. In a letter of August 1772, he spoke of his suffering during an acute attack of asthma, writing, "I have not slept six hours in four nights, being obliged to sit up the two last nights." On a trip to New York in his early twenties to visit Lindley Murray, Nathanael had himself inoculated for smallpox. The disease was flaring up in many localities and inoculation was still unlawful in Rhode Island. His inoculation took, but the accompanying fever left a blemish in his right eye. The spot never went away and on occasion in later years became infected, causing pain and irritation. Another noticeable defect contracted before he was fully grown was a stiffness in his right knee which caused him to walk with a limp or halting gait. People attributed the limp to his duties at the forge, where for hours he was required to stand on one foot while working the trip hammer with the other. A more plausible explanation, however, may be that the injury resulted from some boyhood accident, quite possibly a fall he was said to have suffered while climbing down the roof to go to a dance.

Through the death of his half brother, Thomas, in 1760, Nathanael became the owner of some land in West Greenwich by which, at the age of twenty-one, he became a freeman with the privilege of voting at the town meetings. Although he appears not to have exercised the right or been overly interested in local politics, from the beginning he was deeply aroused by Parliament's postwar American policies. He understood the threat of the Sugar and Stamp acts of 1764 and 1765, not only to Rhode Island's economy, but also to its cherished political freedom and home rule under its old charter. However, he apparently was not actively involved in the revolutionary movement until 1768 when he undertook to circulate a petition against the obnoxious Townshend duties. Soon he was serving on the Kent County committee, chosen by town meetings to enforce the continental boycott of British goods. One can imagine, during those stirring days, with what approval he read the writings of James Otis, Stephen Hopkins, John Dickinson, and other defenders of the principles of "no taxation without representation." The characteristic moderation of most Quakers found no place in the heart of the Potowomut anchorsmith.

Half of Nathanael Greene's forty-four years of life was spent at Potowomut sharing the blessings of a simple country life with his father and all the family. After he moved to Coventry in 1770 to live four years as a bachelor, he continued to spend much time at Potowomut, especially until his father's death. Even after that, and until he married in 1774, Potowomut, with its memories and attractions, was home to him. Here his kind stepmother would care for him and see to his every need. His coming was marked by mother Greene's best cooking and by the brothers' lingering at the table to hear all that Nathanael had to tell. As Nathanael rode back to Coventry he often drew rein to fondly gaze at Potowomut from the ridges overlooking the blue-green waters of Cowesett Bay. The time, however, was not far off when the shots at Lexington would ring down a curtain upon his life in Rhode Island. Nathanael Greene the Quaker iron-master would suddenly become General Greene and the stage would be set for the future.

CHAPTER TWO

At Coventry

Nathanael Greene's four years at Coventry were to be important ones. New responsibilities and experiences would have their maturing influences and add to his knowledge of life. His interest in politics would increase and he would hold a seat in the assembly, the mark, as it were, of a man of some repute in colonial society. Toward the end of this period, his rise would be aided by his marriage to the niece of William Greene and Samuel Ward as he thereby was brought well within the orbit of Rhode Island society. Lastly, he would become a military leader and find himself almost miraculously lifted into command of Rhode Island's armed forces.

In 1770, Nathanael was twenty-eight when his father put him in charge of the Coventry forge with a share in the profits. The forge, built in 1741, was on the Pawtuxet River about eight miles west of East Greenwich. A share in the ironworks was still held by Nathanael's uncle, John Greene, who, with his son Griffin, lived at Coventry and helped run the business. Near the same age, Nathanael and Griffin became close friends in the days before the war. Often the two were seen traveling far from home as might be prompted either by business or social attractions.

At Coventry, on a long slope above the river and forge, Nathanael built a large, two-story, frame house of eight rooms in the Georgian style of the day. That he hoped to catch a bride to grace his handsome new home sooner than he did was common knowledge. The house had the customary center hall, low ceilings, and large fireplaces found in New England dwellings of the period. In a room to the right of the front door which faced the river, he placed his library and study. In the attic were small rooms for servants, presumably Negroes. On the roof rested a captain's walk from which Nathanael sighted smoke signals at Potowomut announcing the arrival of ships in which the Greenes had an interest.

Visitors were always welcome to "Spell Hall" as Nathanael called his home on the Pawtuxet. Besides Sammy Ward, James Varnum, cousins Griffin and Christopher Greene, his brothers and others, a frequent visitor was David Howell, a tutor at the College of Rhode Island. A future congressman and judge, Howell was impressed by his host. A "very remarkable man," he called Nathanael who found great pleasure in discussing academic questions with his learned friend. Howell was the more impressed when he found the young ironmaster poring over his books in the early morning, long before the others were out of bed.

Greene's ironworks on the Pawtuxet no doubt employed most of the men of Coventry, a village of nearly 100 families. Operating the forge and trip hammers must have demanded the services of a score of relatively skilled workers. In addition, there were many attendant tasks to perform. Iron ore had to be dug in the bogs and ponds nearby; huge piles of charcoal had to be accumulated for smelting and heating the iron; and all required endless carting and hauling. When the anchors, chains, and other iron goods were finished, they were hauled by carts five of six miles to Apponaug, the nearest shipping point on Greenwich Bay. For the return cargo, there was pig iron from Pennsylvania (for mixing with the lower grade Rhode Island iron) or merchandise and other supplies for Coventry.

The Coventry ironworks was probably larger than the older one at Potowomut. The latter was once described as having three forges serving a like number of trip hammers but it is doubtful that it was this large in Nathanael's day. The building housing the ironworks was a large frame structure with a roof sloping almost to the ground on the side away from the creek. A mill race supplied the water for the large, heavy water wheel which furnished the power for the bellows and trip hammers. Quite likely, there was a smelting forge or bloomery as these were common in New England where ore was plentiful. The iron, after being smelted from the ore, was worked in a refinery forge. From the forge the yellowish-hot iron was swung onto a huge anvil to be pounded into shape and tempered by the mas-

sive trip hammer. The long hours handling iron in the forge
with bars and tongs gave Nathanael the strong arms and body
muscles he acquired in his youth.

In 1770, with the permission of the provincial assembly, Nathanael Greene built a dam without a fishway across the Pawtuxet. His petition to the assembly, besides mentioning that the
Browns (of Providence) were allowed a similar dam on the
north branch of the Pawtuxet for their Hope Foundry, declared
that the dam was necessary to provide employment for the men
of Coventry. Water power must be had to keep the ironworks
operating through the spring, the petition explained. The fish,
apparently, would have to bow to progress and seek other habi-
tats for spawning.

After moving to Coventry, Nathanael still enjoyed his frequent
trips to Newport on which he had occasion for mixing pleasure
with the pursuit of business. On the way he sometimes stopped
to visit friends on Hope Island, a small rock-ribbed isle, halfway
down Narragansett Bay. In going and coming, he liked to gallop
over the old dirt roads along which dwelt many friends and
relatives always glad to welcome him should he choose to stop.
From the ridges climbed by the gravel roads, he found pleasure
in viewing the miles of green forest interspersed with farms and
fields. A lover of horses, upon returning to Coventry he customarily went first to his stable to see how his horses were faring.

At Coventry, Nathanael spent much time and effort in founding
a school for the children of the village. He also engaged in an
unsuccessful endeavor to have the College of Rhode Island
moved from Warren to East Greenwich instead of Providence,
where it was transferred in 1770. Participation in public affairs
rapidly multiplied his friends and acquaintances. The most distinguished of his new friends was Samuel Ward, leader of the
southern faction in Rhode Island politics. The owners of a
handsome estate at Westerly near Long Island Sound, the Wards
were related to William Greene of Warwick, a distant cousin
of Nathanael's who would become a wartime governor of the
state. In the year when Nathanael moved to Coventry, Ward
was so disastrously defeated by the Hopkins-Brown-Wanton party
that he retired from active politics. He continued, however, to
be a man of influence and prestige in the province, and when

America was plunged into war, he emerged as one of the most prominent men in the Continental Congress.[1]

In 1770, however, Nathanael was less concerned with political advancement than with preference in the eyes of Hannah Ward, the eldest of Mr. Ward's six daughters. Hannah, now twenty-one, and eight years younger than Nathanael, was an attractive girl of more than ordinary intelligence. Her health, however, was delicate, and she already was showing signs of consumption, the scourge of colonial youth. Unfortunately, only one of Nathanael's letters to Hannah has survived and little is known of his courtship.

Sometimes acting as intermediary between Nathanael and Hannah was her brother Samuel, a boy of fourteen in 1770 but already a Junior in the College of Rhode Island. In Greene's correspondence with Sammy Ward (spreading over four or five years), he occasionally dropped a note for Hannah, or more often simply inquired after her health. But Nathanael, it seems, expected she would read or hear about his letters and become impressed by his erudite discussions of moral philosophy and topics of academic interest. If that—along with satisfying his ego and offering fatherly advice to Sammy—was his aim, he failed miserably: Hannah Ward never fell in love with Nathanael Greene.

Sammy Ward, as one might expect, was most flattered and impressed by the ironmaster's long and sermonizing letters. Occasionally, Sammy rather timidly sought to argue a point or two when Greene's ideas clashed too violently with those he had learned at college. But for the most part he unquestionably accepted the doctrines of his hero.

Sitting at his desk in his comfortable study at Coventry in the early autumn of 1770, Nathanael gave full rein to his philosophical cogitations in a long letter to Sammy. He was concerned with the mainspring of human motivation. Man, said Nathanael, is motivated primarily by self-interest. Even religious worship, he thought, was essentially a selfish expression. It was, in fact, he told Sammy, the most selfish of human practices inasmuch as it arose from a desire to obtain salvation and happiness in the hereafter. People deprive themselves of joys here on earth, he wrote, in the hope that their self-denial will gain them salvation.

Those who pursue the pleasures of the world were, therefore, less selfish than the religious. "Methinks," he told Sammy, "he that neglects the Nobler purposes of Life, by the pursuit of Transitory Pleasures—is not so selfish as he ought to be," as the future rewards for abstinence so outweigh any pleasures to be derived here on earth.

Influenced, it would seem, by the Deistic literature of the period, Nathanael went on to make some observations about country life:

> Thus I compare a Country Life to a Clear Sky and a Serene air, for there and there only it's to be enjoyed and which alone can Qualify our minds properly for Speculation, for here Nature seems to move Gently on undisturbed with Noise & tumult, and here we may Contemplate the beauty and order of the Creation until we arrive to that pitch of Knowledge and understanding (in our Enquiry) that the God of Nature hath Qualified us to Soar to.[2]

In November, Nathanael's father died after an extended illness during which Nathanael spent many hours at his bedside while the days shortened and the air turned frosty. After his father was gone, Nathanael and his brothers continued to operate their ironworks and attendant enterprises as partners. Not until 1778 did they divide the estate which over the years had grown into one of the largest businesses in Rhode Island. Besides the ironworks, they had an interest in several ships engaged in the West Indian and coastwise trade. The ever expanding business of the family kept Nathanael occupied with work nearly the whole year around.

For months after his father's death, Nathanael was so burdened with business that he had no time for social affairs or even letter writing. In March, just before setting out on a voyage to Newport, he wrote Sammy Ward a note of apology for not writing. Not until the summer had passed and work had slackened a bit did he find time to resume his philosophizing with Sammy. A man, Nathanael assured his young friend, was of little account who spent his days in idleness instead of improving himself and using his powers for advancing human welfare. In making his way in the world, man benefited by opposition. It strengthened his character and made him capable of accomplishing greater things in life. Though some of Greene's ideas were little more than a paraphrasing of old shibboleths with a good seasoning of Quaker doctrine, his discourses no doubt benefited the writer if not the recipient. His correspondence with Sammy afforded him an avenue for improving his written expression and developing his powers of reasoning. In their deeper aspects, however, his letters portray a man of twenty-eight striving to answer the age-old questions of the meaning of life and man's existence.

In his letters to Sammy Ward, Greene explained why, contrary to Quaker doctrine, he was a believer in higher education. A liberal education, he wrote, helped to develop "virtuous manners" in an individual which were the foundations of a good society. Education should, therefore, be concerned with "forming the Habits of the Youthful Mind, in forwarding every Passion that may tend to the promotion of the Happiness of the Community, in fixing in ourselves right Ideas of Benevolence, Humanity, Integrity, and Truth." If Greene's observations were sometimes somewhat abstract and a tax upon Sammy's understanding, they were no doubt no more doctrinaire or nebulous than much of the wisdom imparted at the College of Rhode Island. Nathanael was certain, for one thing, that the men of his time were not living according to his rules for "virtuous manners." "Envy Malice, & Detraction," he told Sammy, were the vices of the day.[3] How well he would come to appreciate the truth of his words when he became a general in the war with England!

Greene's interest in moral questions reflected his Quaker upbringing. His piety and ideology remained that of a Quaker throughout his life in spite of being cut off from the influence of the Society of Friends after he became a soldier. Sprinkled through his letters are glimpses of his religious faith. "I feel the Celestial flame to warm my Heart, and Cheer my Soul," he told Sammy Ward in 1772. "Plainess and Simplicity of Manners, stript of all the paint and Ornament of Policy, is what I ever admired, it wins the Affections by the force of its Persuasion."[4]

At times Nathanael feared that Sammy's praise of his book learning was but ridicule in disguise. As yet he could not overcome a feeling of inferiority toward college-bred men. "Like Moses of old I can behold the Beauties of Canaan," he told Sammy, "but Jordan prevents my entrance."[5] Regardless of his complex concerning his academic deficiencies, he nevertheless sought the acquaintance of men with a college background. He customarily attended the commencement exercises of the College of Rhode Island where he would meet the Wards, the Varnums, and other families whose sons attended or had graduated from college.

As time passed, Nathanael came to realize that his courtship was not progressing. Hannah, although by no means frivolous, was not attracted by the preaching and seriousness of her Quaker suitor whose native jollity seems to have failed him in her presence. The thought of losing her, he told Sammy, set him to "brooding over Mischief & hatching Evils." Tormented by these unhappy thoughts, he fought with indifferent success to turn them out of mind and to bury himself in work.[6] But as yet he had not lost hope. He took her to dances and other festivities and did his best to win her heart. As clothes are known to go far to make a man attractive in a woman's eye, he took special pains with his wardrobe, making himself, as it were, a "Shining Figure amongst the Greenwich Bucks."

Nathanael's last hopes, however, were soon dashed. In spite of an inward feeling that he had failed, he mustered enough courage during the summer to propose. He seems to have convinced himself that he was prepared for a refusal, but he was not. He was still quite stunned by her rejection when his Coventry forge caught fire and burned to the ground. Overcome by his double misfortune and weak from loss of sleep and a four-day attack of diarrhea, he sat by the smoldering ruins the next morning and read a long letter from Sammy. The forge could be rebuilt. But was there any chance of persuading Hannah to change her mind? He might have Sammy intercede for him but it hurt his pride to think of it. He would rather suffer his "heart to burst than adopt such an expedient," he assured Sammy.[7]

That Nathanael's courtship was not going well was more than just a suspicion among his friends. One day the once celebrated beauty Susa Harris came to see him at Coventry, perhaps with the intention of kindling in him an interest in herself. Nathanael thought she looked like a gaudy flower, nipped by the pinching frost and destined not to live long. Nonetheless, she "flies Swiftly on the Wings of wild Desire after Matrimony," he unconcernedly reported to Sammy.[8]

Fall and winter found Nathanael no less morbid and unhappy than before. If Coventry had ever been very tolerable, it had now become quite insufferable. "The Trees look as surly, the Bushes as Sour and the Shrubs as Cross, if I happen to put my head out of Doors at any time, as if I had been their sworn Enemy." But if they knew "my pacifick disposition, I am sure they could not apprehend any injury," he told Sammy. About the only solace Greene found at Coventry was in looking at the friendly old oak standing not far from the house. He loved this tree, the only venerable one on his whole plantation.[9]

Fortunately for Greene, the work of reconstructing his forge kept his mind off his troubles to some degree. The Greenes, by special permission of the Rhode Island legislature, were allowed to conduct a lottery to raise £2,500 for rebuilding the forge. Their petition for the lottery described the loss as too great for the partners to bear without help. If the ironworks were not rebuilt, scores of families, the petition read, would lose their livelihood. With the assurance of help from the lottery, which was conducted by William and Christopher Greene, of Warwick, and Charles Holden, the Greenes went ahead with the work of reconstruction. Within five months after the fire, Nathanael had the forge rebuilt and in operation. "The Sound of the Hamer," he wrote, "is once more heard in our land." During its construction he was constantly engaged in supervising and directing the work. Some of the workmen, complained Greene, were the kind who shunned their job but watched for their meals like "old coach Dogs."[10]

In January, Nathanael saw his brother Christopher off on a trading voyage to Virginia. Everyone liked Christopher, next to the youngest of the Greene boys, a fine, good-natured lad on whom good fortune seemed to smile with an easy grace. Already his reputation as a business man was undisputed, and in matters of the heart he never had cause to worry. He was courting Catherine Ward, a girl three years younger than Hannah, and doing so with the confidence of a born winner. Though morose over his own ill-fortune, Nathanael wished his brother all the

happiness in the world. He hoped, he told Sammy, that the
Wards and the Greenes would soon be united by family ties. His
wish was soon realized. Upon Christopher's return the banns were
published, and in a few days Catherine became his bride. About
this time Nathanael heard that Hannah was saying that he had
become unfriendly. This was not so, he assured Sammy, but try
as he would, he could not affect a carefree or indifferent air.
For fear of the "World's dread laugh," he had not dared to tell
anyone but Sammy how things stood between himself and
Hannah.[11]

The winter of 1772-73 was very cold. One day on a trip to
New London, Nathanael suffered through the coldest day of his
remembrance. But in spite of ice and snow, he found more time
than usual for social affairs. At East Greenwich he ordinarily
stopped for a visit with William Greene and his wife Catherine
Ray, who lived in a fine old house on the hill just over the line in
Warwick. William Greene, who with Judge Philip Greene represented the distinguished side of the Greene family, knew all
the important people in Rhode Island and was, like Samuel Ward,
a most valuable friend for a young man to have.

No one in Warwick or East Greenwich entertained more
graciously than William and Catherine Greene. One of their
occasional visitors was Benjamin Franklin who thought Aunt
Catherine one of the most delightful hostesses to be found. Nathanael was equally captivated by Aunt Catherine's good humor
and good cooking. One cold night in January, when he had
the pleasure of spending an evening with the Greenes, they
were joined around the blazing logs in the great kitchen fireplace by Samuel Ward, Henry Marchant (the attorney general),
and one or two others of more than local prominence.

By this time, Nathanael was fast outgrowing his strict Quaker
upbringing. When *The Unhappy Orphan,* the first stage play
to be enacted by local talent, was presented in Providence in
May, 1773, it aroused no qualms in the heart of Nathanael
Greene. Quite to the contrary, his only regret was that he had
been too busy to attend. "Ring the bells backward, Cry fire, the
Church is in danger," he humorously gibed at the pious who were
denouncing the play as "subversive of Morality."[12]

In the general assembly, to which Greene was first elected

from Coventry in 1770, his diffidence in the company of men of superior social attainments and education was noticeable. Since he was a junior member, coming from the soot of forge and furnace rather than from counting house or court of law, it was not surprising that he attracted little attention. During these years he seldom served on committees or in other legislative capacities. All the while, however, he was getting to know the leaders of the colony and by degrees gaining their respect and confidence. He had, it is true, the friendship of two of the most distinguished men of the province, Samuel Ward and William Greene, but their support was founded on their belief that he was a man of unusual promise and worthy of all the assistance they could offer. In the assembly, Nathanael was nominally associated with the old Ward faction, but as the political feud had died down, he found it possible to win friends in all quarters of the colony.

The most provocative episode occurring in Rhode Island prior to the Revolution was that known as the *Gaspée* affair. The *Gaspée*, a British revenue schooner stationed in Narragansett Bay to enforce Parliament's navigation and revenue laws, had earned the hatred of Rhode Islanders. Never very scrupulous as to the means he employed, the *Gaspée*'s commander, a diligent but indiscreet gentleman named Lieutenant William Dudingston, seized ships violating the laws and sent them to Boston for condemnation by Admiralty Court. Armed with the obnoxious writs of assistance, Dudingston occasionally even raided the mainland in search of smuggled merchandise. All Rhode Island was stirred by Dudingston's all-out war on the lucrative smuggling trade. In Providence, Chief Justice Stephen Hopkins was moved to declare that no naval officer had any authority within the borders of the province except by the governor's permission. Governor Wanton agreed. "I do not receive instructions for the administration of my government from the King's Admiral stationed in America," he informed Admiral Montagu who from Boston upheld the actions of his junior officer at Newport.[13]

Provoked as much by the arrogance and testiness of Dudingston as by his zeal, on the night of June 9, 1772, a party from Providence and Bristol rowed quietly toward the *Gaspée* off Namquit Point, Warwick, where she had run aground while chasing a

Rhode Island vessel. The attackers were discovered before reaching the ship whereupon shots were exchanged as the raiders swiftly bore down upon their prey. Lieutenant Dudingston was severely wounded, his ship boarded, and his crew bound and set ashore. The *Gaspée* was fired and during the night burned to the water line.

When the news of the *Gaspée's* destruction reached Boston, Admiral Montagu ordered Governor Wanton to arrest the ringleaders and bring them to trial. Acting from the compulsion of duty, Wanton reluctantly issued a proclamation offering £100 to anyone producing evidence leading to a conviction. Only one man, Aaron Briggs, a mulatto servant who was with the raiders, came forward to collect the reward. The witness named a number of men of prominence, but after several persons testified to the falsity of his statements, his testimony was stricken from the record. The temper of public feeling can be measured by the fact that although the names of most of the participants were generally known—some having openly boasted of it—not another man came forth to expose them.

As this was not the first time Rhode Islanders had attacked the King's revenue ships, the Crown decided to take steps to put an end to it. By orders from England a commission was established consisting of Governor Wanton and four judges from other colonies. The commission was to investigate the whole affair and find the culprits who after being indicted by local authorities would be sent to England for trial. After sitting in January and again in May without accomplishing anything in spite of a handsome reward offered by Admiral Montagu to anyone exposing the ringleaders, the commissioners gave up and went home.

It was in January, while the commission was sitting, that Nathanael Greene heard that an officer of the *Gaspée* had named him as one of the outlaws wanted for the attack. The report threw Nathanael into such a rage that he vowed should he meet his accuser he would put a hole in him big enough to "let the Sunshine through!" It was all a base lie and he could prove it, he exclaimed. Was he not at Coventry that night with his brother Christopher, his cousin Griffin, and an elderly lady named Mrs. Utter? After talking until midnight his guests all stayed overnight. In the morning they rode as a party to Providence and while on the way, saw the smoldering hull of the *Gaspée* not far from shore.[14]

Greene had no fear of being arrested by local authorities regardless of what the "new fangled court," as he called the commission, might report. Chief Justice Hopkins had made it clear he would release anyone brought before him by the findings of the commission which, he declared, had no legal standing in Rhode Island. Greene was not sure, however, but that some way might be found to apprehend individuals and have them delivered to Admiral Montagu for trial in England on charges of treason, piracy, or other high crimes against the Crown.

When aroused, few in Rhode Island were as bold and outspoken as Nathanael Greene. The commission, he warned Sammy, had alarming implications for every "lover of Liberty in America." If this "Mode of Tryal is established into a Precedent it will naturally Affect all the other Colonies." The practice of offering large rewards for information concerning offenses against the Crown encouraged perjury and led to no end of mischief, he declared. Lord North's ministry, it appeared to him, was actually thirsting for "American blood." The Rhode Island Assembly, of which he was a member, was, in his opinion, weak and cowardly for not taking a stand against the illegal directives of Crown officials.[15]

Greene's quarrel with the British authorities had more than just anger arising from the *Gaspée* incident back of it. One of the ships belonging to the Greenes had been seized by Lieutenant Dudingston on charges of smuggling rum and molasses and sent to Boston for condemnation. This action stirred Nathanael to such an extent that he would have willingly put a torch to any revenue boat within reach. Sending his ship to Boston, he maintained, was an illegal and wanton trampling upon his rights as a citizen of Rhode Island. Determined to fight the case to the finish, he made several trips to Boston where he did all in his power to vindicate himself. In Rhode Island, Lieutenant Dudingston admitted in court he had violated the law in the way he seized the ship. The court, thereupon, ordered him to pay the Greenes £295 in damages, but whether or not they ever received the money is not known.[16]

The *Gaspée* affair and Greene's involvement with the revenue officers occurred during the period of comparative quiet in the colonies following the upheavals produced by the Stamp and Townshend acts. The fracas clearly demonstrated that underneath the seeming calm the country was ready to explode wherever Britain endeavored to force its will upon the colonies. The *Gaspée* affair, moreover, had far-reaching repercussions. In Virginia the House of Burgesses resolved the Crown commission in Rhode Island to be a "flagrant attack upon American liberty in general." It then chose a committee of correspondence. When most of the other colonies followed suit, the way was opened for a Continental Congress which followed in a few years.

Although intensive military preparations were not begun until after the Boston Tea Party in 1773, the *Gaspée* incident put new meaning into the periodic gathering of the militia in New England. Greene began to take a deep interest in miltary science and the art of war. Sometime in the spring of 1773 he attended a large military gathering at Plainfield, Connecticut, just over the border from Rhode Island. Sammy Ward, who was there too, complimented him on his military bearing and good showing among the men. From this time on, Nathanael's mind was seldom occupied for long with anything but military affairs—with the exception, one may note, of a growing interest in Catherine Littlefield, a girl of nineteen, who came into his life the year Hannah Ward died of tuberculosis.

In August, the East Greenwich Monthly Meeting had before it a report that Nathanael and Griffin Greene had participated in the military gathering at Plainfield contrary to the teachings of the Society of Friends. The Meeting appointed three Friends to visit the young men to solicit a promise that as good Quakers they would henceforth abide by the pacific teachings of the Society. When the committee finally found an opportunity to talk with the offenders, they discovered that their persuasions were useless. A second visit was no more rewarding than the first. Upon receiving the report of the committee, the Monthly Meeting read the men out of the Society until such time as they chose to conform to the principles of the brotherhood. That time never came.[17]

As Nathanael had come to believe over the years that certain principles of the Society of Friends were ill-conceived, his action on this occasion was not unnatural. Pacifism, though a noble ideal, he had come to look upon as altogether impractical in this kind of a world. After the Revolution, in commenting upon war, he wrote: "To me war was ever a business of necessity. Not that I have a doubt of its being fully authorized from nature and reason, nay necessity, and unavoidable from the plans of our creation; but I am averse to it from its being opposite to my temper and feelings." Like many another Quaker, Greene chose to turn his back on the teachings of the Society of Friends and go to war believing it to be the only course if the "constitutional liberties" of America were to be preserved.[18]

Exciting and far-reaching events followed one another in rapid succession after Parliament's Tea Act was answered by the Boston Tea Party in December, 1773. As word of the destruction of the tea reached England, a storm of indignation swept over the British Isles. Soon Parliament passed the "Intolerable Acts" with the intention of diminishing home rule in Massachusetts. Coupled with these measures was a punitive order to close the port of Boston on June 1st until such time as the city chose to pay the East India Company for the tea destroyed.

The reaction to the "Intolerable Acts" was sudden and violent throughout the length and breadth of America. Even the Quakers condemned the tyranny of the British and resolved to raise funds to relieve the people of Boston. After the closing of the port, provisions and supplies for the beleaguered city poured in from near and far. Soon it was agreed among the colonies that a Continental Congress should be held to devise ways and means for meeting the crisis.

During the fast moving months of 1774, though pressed for time by the demands of both private and public affairs, Nathanael found time for the lighter side of life. In January, he was flattered to be a guest at the wedding of Benjamin Gardner, whose bride, he thought, would have been more attractive if dressed a little more plainly. The wedding party lasted four days, during which all made merry while bitter winds blew outside and piled the snow in huge drifts.[19] After the party, Nathanael amused himself for some days in East Greenwich, where, with the opening of court, the usual flow of lawyers and litigants made life interesting.

Not much is known about Nathanael Greene's courtship of Catherine Littlefield. Apparently it was a swift affair, culminating in marriage a few months after it began. Catherine Littlefield was nineteen, pretty, vivacious, witty, and flirtatious. She loved dancing and merrymaking as much as she disliked schooling. Nathanael was thirteen years her senior, but his boyish, fun-loving nature, now revived under Catherine's spell, together with the young girl's emotional maturity, made the difference in their ages seem slight.

During the courtship, Nathanael made frequent visits to Catherine's home at New Shoreham, or Block Island as it is commonly called. More often, he saw Catherine at her Uncle Samuel Ward's at Westerly or her Uncle William Greene's home near East Greenwich. Nathanael took Catherine to dances, parties, and church affairs. He was an ardent suitor and this time he felt he had found a match. Catherine idolized her Quaker lover and Nathanael was enchanted by Catherine's beauty and charm. His enchantment never wore off.

It was with great exuberance that Nathanael wrote to Sammy Ward that he was to marry Sammy's cousin at Uncle William Greene's house on July 20, 1774. Already banns had been published: for Catherine at her Baptist meetinghouse at New Shoreham and for Nathanael at King's Church in Providence, where the Reverend John Graves was pastor. Only close friends and relatives were invited to the wedding. While Nathanael was occupied with plans for the wedding, his thoughts flitted between Catherine and the great storm gathering over the English-speaking world. The trouble, he thought, was not just a passing phase to be succeeded soon by clear skies, and he wondered whether or not America would have to seek independence as the only means of escape.

When the day of the wedding came, Nathanael and Catherine were married at three in the afternoon by the Elder John Gorton, a Baptist minister. They stood in the cozy southeast room of the old mansion—the room in which Benjamin Franklin liked to sit and look out over the beautiful valley and the hills beyond. After the wedding festivities, Nathanael took Catherine to Coventry, to her new home on the banks of the Pawtuxet.

Now that he was happily married, Nathanael could once again see the humorous side in almost any situation. Writing one day when away on a trip, he asked Kitty (as everyone called Catherine) to remember him to her doctor. "And tell him," he warned Kitty who was ill, "if he don't make a perfect cure, or lay a good foundation for it, I'll put him on board a man-of-war, and send him to England to be tried for the heinous offence of dissaffection to Arbitrary Government and Ministerial tyranny."[20]

Greene was pleased with the appointments of Samuel Ward and Stephen Hopkins as Rhode Island's delegates to the Continental Congress scheduled to meet at Philadelphia in September. They were men, he felt, who would stand firmly by American liberties. By then he expected blood would be shed by the British soldiery who were "insolent beyond measure." He wished to heaven, he told Sammy, that the angel who destroyed the army of the Assyrian Sennacherib, would fall upon the oppressors of Boston.[21] That he was thinking of a more certain remedy in the form of bullets from the guns of the New England Minutemen, one can well imagine.

In September, while the Continental Congress was sitting in Philadelphia, a clash between the British and the Massachusetts militia appeared certain when General Thomas Gage, commander of the King's forces, sent 250 troops toward Cambridge in search of Rebel military supplies. The Redcoats, partially successful in their mission, managed to return before the Americans could gather in numbers sufficient to attack them. By the next morning, however, the countryside was swarming with militia and Minutemen, an object lesson for the British should they hazard a march very far into the country.

Greatly alarmed, General Gage went so far as to send to Quebec for reinforcements after he had called for all the troops which could be spared from New York. By December, he had gathered a force of 3,500 men, enough to hold Boston, but not enough, he believed, to attempt a march against the Rebels in the Massachusetts towns and villages. By this time, Gage was certain that British authority in New England would be wantonly flouted until such time as the rebel leaders could be seized and sent to England for trial and punishment. He was of the opinion that only New England would engage in armed rebellion, but he felt this section would put up a stubborn fight and require at least one hard-fought campaign before the insurrection collapsed. Consequently, he told the Ministry, it was absolutely necessary to send a formidable force to Boston without delay.[22]

By the autumn of 1774 both sides thought that an armed showdown was coming very soon. While the Continental Congress was discussing ways and means to meet the crisis, patriotic groups all over New England were meeting to form volunteer military companies separate from the militia bodies. Their object was to have corps better trained than the militia and therefore capable of fighting the enemy on more equal terms.

One of these units was the Kentish Guards, formed at East Greenwich when about fifty men, mostly of the younger set, met at Arnold's tavern and organized an infantry company. Twenty-six-year-old James Mitchell Varnum, a lawyer of East Greenwich, by virtue of his social position, was the chairman of the meeting although none had been more active in arousing interest and making plans for the company than Nathanael Greene. At a second meeting, the Kentish Guards elected Varnum, captain; Richard Fry, first lieutenant; and Christopher Greene, of Warwick (a distant cousin of Nathanael's), second lieutenant. Soon they obtained a charter from the assembly and were assigned a place in a regiment of volunteer companies.

The Kentish Guards, which soon became known as one of the best volunteer organizations in New England, set about making itself into a fighting force in earnest. Nathanael Greene made his way to Boston where, unnoticed by British or Tory who saw only a plain Quaker of no particular consequence, he hired one William Johnson, a deserter from the British Army, to train the Kentish Guards. For three times a week over a period of four months, Johnson agreed to put the Guardsmen through "the Manual Exercises and Evolutions, Maneuvers with every other movement as taught in the English Army." In addition, he would teach two lads to beat "the English duty" with the drums.[23]

Besides hiring William Johnson as drillmaster, on this or one of his trips to Boston, Nathanael managed to buy a British musket, perhaps one carried away by Johnson. Nathanael hid the gun

under hay in a farmer's wagon, following at a discreet distance
as the farmer drove out of the city. Because of what had recently
happened to another, he was well aware of his danger. Lieutenant
Mackenzie recorded in his diary on March 8th:

A country fellow was detected this day in buying arms from a
Soldier of the 47th Regt. The men of that Regiment immediately
secured him and having provided the proper materials, they
stripped, and then Tarred and feathered him and setting him
upon a Truck, in that manner paraded him, in the afternoon,
through most parts of that town, to the Neck.[24]

As it was freely acknowledged that Nathanael Greene was one
of the best informed men in Rhode Island on military matters,
dissension at once arose in the Kentish Guards when he was not
made an officer. No one was more disappointed than James
Varnum, long one of Nathanael's closest friends. Varnum, generous as well as loyal, declared that Nathanael was better qualified
than anyone to be captain and that he would resign in his favor.
Soon it was reported that Varnum would drop out of the Guards
altogether unless Nathanael was made an officer. Varnum knew
that Nathanael had expected rank in the Guards and that he was
downcast by the decision of his townsmen.

When Greene heard the reason for his failure he was mortified.
Writing to Varnum, he poured out his wounded pride. "I was
inform'd the Gentlemen of East Greenwich said I was a blemish
to the company. I confess it is the first stroke of mortification that
I ever felt from being considered either in private or public life
a blemish to those with whom I associated."[25] The blemish al-
luded to was Greene's limp which some had said was unbefitting
an officer of the Kentish Guards.

Presently Nathanael wrote Varnum that he had about decided
to drop out of the company as he did not want to be an embarrassment to anyone. But though he resigned, he would hold no
resentment. He assured Varnum he would continue to bear his
share of the expense until the company was fully organized and
in the assembly he would give the guards his full support. He
begged Varnum not to do anything rash but to continue as
captain. Otherwise, he was sure, the company would break up,
much to the disgrace of East Greenwich. As it turned out, both
men stayed in the Kentish Guards, Varnum as captain and Na-

thanael Greene as a private. Nathanael, apparently, found comfort enough in the sympathy of his friends to overcome his pride and serve in the ranks.

Nathanael Greene was a member of the assembly during the autumn session at Providence and was put on a committee (along with Colonel James Angell, Colonel Jacob Nightingale, Colonel John Mathewson, and Major David Hitchcock) for revising the military laws of the province. The fact that all but Greene were officers in the militia or military associations bespeaks the high regard the assembly had for his military reputation. His work on the committee removed all doubt, if any existed, that he was one of the most able men in Rhode Island on matters of military science.

When the Rhode Island Assembly sent Samuel Ward and Stephen Hopkins to the Continental Congress, it gave them a free hand. They could "enter into, and adopt, on Behalf of their Colony, all reasonable, lawful, and proper measures for the support, defence, protections and security of the rights, liberties, and privileges, both civil and religious, of all the said colonies, or any of them."[26]

In October, when the Continental Congress adjourned, Rhode Island immediately put its stamp of approval upon the congressional proceedings and recommendations. Following the suggestion of Congress, Rhode Island asked all towns to appoint a committee of safety to enforce the non-importation of British goods and to have the direction of measures for public security. For itself, the assembly chose a special committee to purchase 300 barrels of powder, three tons of lead, 40,000 flints, and several brass cannon for the militia and military associations.

The Revolutionary movement, however, was not without its discord in Rhode Island. A riot was nearly touched off between the men of Warwick and East Greenwich when Judge Stephen Arnold, of Warwick, accused of Toryism, was hanged in effigy in East Greenwich. When a mob in Warwick threatened to burn the rival town, Deputy Governor Sessions sent the Providence Cadets and Light Infantry to restore order in the troubled area. By this time, however, peace had been restored after Judge Arnold signed a paper declaring himself a friend of liberty and no supporter of arbitrary government. Before the incident was closed, Nathanael and William Greene were chosen by the assembly to investigate the affair. Their report, if one was made, is not recorded in the minutes of the assembly.[27]

Small town jealousies and feuds had existed in Rhode Island, as elsewhere, since the days of the founding fathers, and but slight provocation was needed to start something. Plenty of rivalry was generated by the military associations of the various towns. In February, the officers of the Pawtuxet Rangers for no good reason declined an invitation from the Kentish Guards to dine at Arnold's tavern. A little later, a rumor was circulated that the Kentish Guards wanted money from the assembly for loss of time in drilling and other military services. Greene, who was doing his utmost to promote harmony in the colony, made known that the Guards desired no special favors. The organization was self-supporting and would continue to be so, he declared.

During the autumn and early winter of 1774, Nathanael made more trips by horseback to Boston, sixty miles from Coventry. While in the city, he generally stayed at the Bunch of Grapes, a favorite gathering place for revolutionary leaders from all New England. With keen interest he watched the morning and evening parading of the British on Boston Common and before long he had mastered every detail of the art of drilling. With equal concern he watched the fortification of Boston Neck under the direction of the veteran engineer, Captain John Montresor. As much as anything, in the days ahead America would need men with a knowledge of the science of military engineering. As Nathanael looked around him it made him happy to see the way Parliament's Boston Port Bill was being defeated by the patriotism of America in the form of contributions flowing into the city from all parts of the country. Every day supplies brought relief and consolation to the people of Boston, suffering from the closure of their port by British warships since the first of June.

While in Boston, Greene spent what time he could spare at Henry Knox's London Bookstore. Here he purchased precious military manuals and books which he carried back for long hours of study. With the jolly young proprietor of the bookstore, who shared Greene's interest in military science, he discussed the crisis facing America and the problem of defense in the event of war. During these days Greene and Knox laid the foundation for a lasting friendship which would be invaluable to both in the long war to come.

When Greene heard that General Gage was considering the hiring of Indians to attack the New England frontier in an effort to vitiate the rebel strength by a border war, he was not surprised. He was prepared to believe the British capable of almost any outrage or barbarity. Greatly alarmed, Gage was indeed ready to resort to extremes. When the Continental Congress adjourned with resolutions which sounded to him like the demands of a conqueror, he no longer entertained hope of confining the rebellion to New England. In his letters to the Ministry he recommended hiring foreign troops. It would be necessary, he believed, to put a large army in America if the spreading revolt were to be crushed with dispatch. A small force, he declared, would merely encourage the Americans and make the war longer and more expensive.

Preparations for armed resistance moved ahead rapidly during the winter of 1774-75. At his ironworks, Greene set aside orders for anchors and chains to make cannon and shot for the colony. Heavy cannon as well as lighter field pieces were cast and mounted and sent to Providence and Newport. In the towns, "liberty boys" forced shopkeepers to turn over their tea to be burned in the market place. At Providence the people brought their tea voluntarily to the town square, where 300 pounds were burned along with Lord North's speech before Parliament and copies of American newspapers supporting the British.

In England, the ministers of state scoffed at General Gage's appeal for a large army to crush the Americans. Many influential persons were for dismissing Gage at once as a man not firm enough in his dealings with the colonists. But King George would not listen to them. Gage, it was decided, would be reinforced, but by far less than the number he had requested. Soon Generals Howe, Clinton, and Burgoyne were on their way to Boston with several regiments to help Gage and his army. This was Britain's answer to the petition of grievances from the Continental Congress. In February, Parliament declared Massachusetts to be in a state of rebellion. All loyal subjects were called upon to aid the King in stamping out treason and in restoring law and order in America. On April 14th, General Gage received his instructions, drafted by Lord Dartmouth, directing him to use his army to crush the rebellion and punish the leaders of the American insurrection.

Five days after receiving his instructions, Gage set his columns in motion toward Concord, the seat of the Massachusetts Provincial Congress and supply center for the Massachusetts forces. News of the battles of Lexington and Concord and the disastrous retreat of the British was heard for scores of miles over New England before the sun went down that night.

When the report of the fighting reached Coventry toward evening, Nathanael at once mounted one of his fastest horses and rode off in the night toward East Greenwich. On the way he stopped to borrow a few silver dollars from a friend and then hurried on. When he arrived all was excitement in the little village. But since it was late, the Kentish Guards decided to continue their preparations and march in the morning for the scene of battle. At daybreak on the morning of April 20th, they were on their way. The company marched rapidly and by nine o'clock were parading through the streets of Providence amid the cheers of the townspeople. John Howland, who had been watching one after another of the volunteer companies file by, spotted Nathanael Greene by his limp and the sway of his musket on his shoulder among the otherwise even line of guns. The Kentish Guards were a smart outfit; perhaps the best in Rhode Island, he thought. Indeed, the company would produce more officers for the Continental Army than any in the state. More than half of the men would become officers, with Greene, Varnum, and Christopher Greene attaining great renown.[28]

When the Guards reached Pawtucket, about five miles from Providence, a messenger overtook them carrying an order from Governor Wanton to turn about and go back. Wanton had heard or was assuming that they were not needed in Massachusetts where the Minutemen had the situation under control. The Governor, however, was already under suspicion of being lukewarm toward the cause if not actually a Tory. Confronted with the Governor's orders, the Kentish Guards—all but Nathanael Greene, two of his brothers, and a fourth man—retraced their steps to East Greenwich. Nathanael was incensed by the Governor's orders and wanted the Guards to defy them. He would go on, he told his comrades, if he had to go alone. At thirty-two Greene had become a man of unusual determination.

After the Kentish Guards had left, Nathanael and his companions procured horses to carry them the rest of the way as they were becoming very fatigued. But the four had not gone far when they met a messenger from Massachusetts with tidings that the British had been driven into the city and the Minutemen had things under control for the time being. The four plucky Rhode Islanders then turned around and followed their comrades back to East Greenwich.

Three days after the Battle of Lexington-Concord, the Rhode Island Assembly met to consider steps for increasing the military strength of the colony. That day Massachusetts voted to raise 13,600 men for its army. The rest of New England was asked to raise 16,400 to join the Massachusetts forces. In answer to the appeal for help from Massachusetts, Rhode Island within a few days voted to raise a brigade of three regiments numbering 1,500 to be known as the Army of Observation. Volunteers were offered a liberal bounty in addition to a monthly wage. This offer, combined with the attraction of adventure and travel to new places, sufficed to fill most of the quota within a few weeks. The little army, nonetheless, was a considerable drain on the manpower and resources of Rhode Island with her total population (including 4,000 Negroes, mostly slaves, and 1,500 Indians) of only 60,000.

Besides the 1,500 state troops, every man of militia age (unless a pacifist by religious persuasion) was required to be ready to defend the province at any time. So that each town would have powder and lead in case of need, the assembly appointed a committee to supply each community from the provincial stores. It was authorized also to have all small arms repaired and fixed with bayonets at public expense. A significant addition to the defense of the colony and New England was likewise made when the assembly chartered an artillery company for Providence.

Most surprising was the appointment of Nathanael Greene as brigadier general to command the Army of Observation. He was, however, not the first choice of the assembly. According to tradition, the command was first offered to an Episcopalian and then to a Congregationalist. Both men for one reason or another declined the appointment. When it was next offered to Greene, he is said to have exclaimed: "Since the Episcopalian and the Congregationalist won't, I suppose the Quaker must."[29]

With any number of officers in command of military associations or the militia, why the assembly should turn to a private in a volunteer company to lead its army may appear paradoxical notwithstanding Greene's reputation as a man of military talent. It can only be explained by the degree to which Greene had risen in the estimation of the assembly while serving on defense committees. Perhaps too, the influence of friends like William Greene was a help, but Nathanael had no monopoly on friendship. James Varnum, Daniel Hitchcock, Christopher Greene, and many another promising young officer also had friends in the assembly. But Nathanael had impressed the assembly as having the makings of an officer of distinction just as he later impressed Washington and most of the other generals during the war. The keenness of his perception, the power and penetration of his analyses, and the logic of his reasoning, marked him as a man of destiny.

As it was feared the British would soon endeavor to erase their recent humiliation at Lexington and Concord by another attack, Massachusetts asked all New England to hurry troops to Cambridge. In response, the Rhode Island Assembly bade Greene march his brigade at the earliest possible moment. After ordering a uniform for himself from Newport, Greene set out for Hartford with William Bradford to discuss plans with government leaders and officers of the Connecticut line. On his return, he threw himself into the endless work of raising, equipping, and drilling his Rhode Island brigade. As the people saw him grapple with the problems of raising and outfitting his brigade, they felt confident that the assembly had made no mistake in its choice for the supreme command. Greene, of course, was well aware that time was pressing and that no one knew what day the British would choose to throw their forces against the embattled Massachusetts farmers manning the thin lines on the hills surrounding Boston.

CHAPTER THREE

A Fledgling General

The siege of Boston which New England launched in April, 1775, would drag on until the following March when Washington finally had enough cannon to force the enemy to evacuate. During the siege, New England practically dissolved one army and built another in the face of the enemy, a disquieting precedent for the years to come. The siege of Boston, however, went far in convincing the world that America had the will and capacity to wage a general war. Bunker Hill proved Americans could fight, while the long siege demonstrated their tenacity. During this initial period of the war no one rose faster than Nathanael Greene in the estimation of his fellow officers. At Cambridge, it may be said, the army put its stamp of approval upon Rhode Island's choice for its general. Above all, this was a period of building and organizing an army. As no one in the army would display greater talent than Greene for this type of service, his contribution during the siege was of great value.

During the fast moving days before Greene left for Cambridge, he spent many hours working out administrative details with Rhode Island's Committee of Safety, established by the assembly with broad powers over matters of security and defense. With £20,000 in bills of credit voted by the assembly for defense, the Committee set about buying blankets, tents, camp tools, cannon, shot, guns, ammunition, and other things which an army must have. As the existence of an army depends upon its commissary, Greene sought to insure an ample supply of provisions. Together with the committee, he met with Peter Phillips, the commissary, in an effort to solve the innumerable problems attending the gathering, storing, and transporting of supplies.

Some of Greene's time during the hectic days before leaving Rhode Island was spent with a special committee named by the assembly for framing bylaws to govern the army. The committee, headed by lawyer James Varnum, colonel of one of the regiments, drafted a code of fifty-five articles which were adopted by the assembly. These were the rules with which Greene and his staff were to transform their raw recruits into soldiers.

To aid him in making soldiers out of yeomen farmers and artisans, Greene had the assistance of some very able young officers. Although he soon discovered there were others besides Colonel Thomas Church who did not measure up to his standards, the number of good officers was far above the average in the early Revolutionary Army. Naturally, Greene looked to Varnum's regiment to set a standard for the brigade, as many of its officers, such as Major Christopher Greene and Captain Sammy Ward were old friends and were ready and eager to serve him at all times.

While Greene was engaged with the preparations for marching, the Rhode Island Assembly had its troubles with governor-elect Wanton. Conservative by nature and seventy years of age, Wanton made known he would have nothing more to do with revolutionary proceedings. He had voted against the Army of Observation in April after which he returned to Newport on the pretext of being sick. In May he did not appear for the meeting of the new assembly, hoping thereby to prevent the raising of the army. Most urgent were the commissions for the officers which remained unsigned. Having no intention of allowing its will thwarted for long, the assembly presently authorized Henry Ward to issue the commissions under his signature as secretary for the colony. Greene's commission, dated May 8th, like the others was later endorsed by Lieutenant Governor Nicholas Cooke who was named acting governor until Wanton cared to take an oath to support the American cause. This he never did, and Cooke, a prominent Providence merchant and a good friend of Nathanael's, was appointed governor in November by the assembly after declaring the office vacant.*

Ironically, the Rhode Island Assembly called out its Army of Observation to preserve the "Liberties of America" in the name of King George the Third. As commander of the army, Greene

---

* Darius Sessions who was elected Deputy Governor refused to serve, whereupon the Assembly appointed Cooke to the office in May, 1774. David S. Lovejoy, *Rhode Island Politics*, pp. 182-183.

was empowered (with the concurrence of the Committee of Safety) to march out of the colony and in the name of "His Majesty, George the Third" to engage the enemy wherever found.[1] For Americans to call their rebel forces the King's troops and the British Army Parliament's was a most amusing innovation to British officers in Boston. What kind of burlesque, they laughingly inquired, would these rustics think of next?[2]

On May 20th, just a month and a day after the Lexington alarm, Greene ordered Colonels Hitchcock and Church to march their regiments to Massachusetts, leaving Varnum, who was attending to the forwarding of supplies, to follow later. Each man had been paid bounty money for enlisting: those with a gun received forty shillings and those without one got twenty. If the recruit had been an apprentice he received only half the bounty, the rest going to the master for the loss of his services. Just before marching off, Greene supplied each soldier with a knapsack, a blanket, and a month's pay. The officers were also given a month's pay, Greene getting £20, the colonels £15, and the others amounts commensurate to their rank.

According to General John Thomas of the Massachusetts line, Greene's troops came straggling in by companies. The Rhode Islanders are "Coming in Every Day in Small Parteys," he wrote. In marked contrast to most of the New England soldiers, the Rhode Islanders, he noted, were "well dressed and accoutred."[3] High was the praise, too, for Greene's artillery of six three-pounders and twelve heavy cannon. Under the command of the young and able Captain John Crane, the artillerymen made a fine appearance in their leather skullcaps and blue coats faced with red.

After arriving at Cambridge on May 23rd, Greene was promptly escorted to headquarters to meet Artemas Ward, commander of the Massachusetts forces. After an exchange of pleasantries, Greene expressed his desire to serve under Ward. He had no instruction for this but with the war confined principally to Massachusetts, it was generally agreed that leadership belonged to the Bay Colony. General Ward graciously accepted Greene's offer and assigned the Rhode Islanders a place under Major General John Thomas who commanded the right wing of the army at Roxbury.

As part of the right wing, Greene found himself thrust into the most exposed and responsible sector of the American lines circling Boston. As he surveyed the situation and noted the strategic position of the right wing overlooking the British redoubts on Boston Neck, he sensed anew the heavy responsibility of his command. Before Greene's arrival, General Thomas' right wing consisted of Massachusetts troops under Brigadier General William Heath and most of the Connecticut men under Brigadier General Joseph Spencer. Greene's Rhode Islanders brought the number of troops in the right wing to nearly 5,000. Following General Thomas's suggestion, Greene pitched camp on level land known as Jamaica Plain. On each side were low lying hills, very convenient, he thought, for placing his cannon and guard posts. In front of the camp was a pond which he noted would serve as a shield against sudden attack by the enemy as well as a source of water for washing.[4]

While the men were busily engaged in erecting camp, Greene spent as much time as possible away from his desk at his headquarters in the William Pepperrell house riding about to supervise the work. Gun platforms, magazines, storehouses, ovens, and much else had to be made or found. Unlike most of the other camps of the sprawling rebel army, where shelters of boards, tattered sailcloth, earth and stones prevailed, the Rhode Islanders erected an orderly city of tents, row on row. Reverend William Emerson, grandfather of Ralph Waldo Emerson, thought Greene had reason to be proud of his brigade. "Some are your proper tents and marquees and look like ye regular camp of ye enemy," he wrote. "These are ye Rhode Islanders, who are furnished with tent equipage from among themselves and everything in ye most exact English taste."[5] Apparently, very little was done by the Americans toward fortifying their positions before the Battle of Bunker Hill. Greene probably put up redoubts in front of his cannon, and as he was a believer in breastworks, especially for unseasoned troops, he no doubt would have done more in fortifying his position had General Thomas approved it.

At General Thomas' headquarters where there were meetings to attend and business to transact, Greene met scores of new faces among the officers of the Massachusetts and Connecticut lines. Some, he could tell, were obviously misfits and anything but soldiers. Not a few, however, impressed him as being officers of great promise. Later, when Washington arrived and Greene was assigned to a division, many of the officers he was learning to know would be placed in his command.

With his engaging smile and sunny disposition, Greene quickly won new friends throughout the army. Quite understandably, his attitude toward his fellow generals, most of whom were older and with military experience, was one of deference and admiration. So it was with General Thomas, a small-town physician and veteran of both King George's and the French and Indian Wars. Six feet tall and of a commanding presence, he soon came to respect his junior general from Rhode Island, whom he thought displayed an unusual degree of military talent. In turn, Greene learned much in those early days of the war from Thomas, who was perhaps the best of the Massachusetts officers conducting the siege of Boston.

Greene was also favorably impressed with Artemas Ward. The keeper of a general store in Shrewsbury, Ward had been a colonel in the French and Indian War from which he emerged with broken health. He was forty-eight, afflicted with a stone, and almost too stout to ride. Inclined to be slow in making decisions and rather over-cautious, his record was nonetheless favorable during his short term as commander in chief. Contributing, however, to his success was the splendid support of his staff. Without the cooperation of all, little headway would have been made in welding a fighting force out of bands of men as heterogeneous and divided as a feudal army.

While Greene was still occupied with organizing his camp, severe shortages of provisions made it necessary for him to go back to Rhode Island to get at the root of the trouble. Accompanied by a small party, Greene rode to East Greenwich where he conferred with his brother Jacob, a member of the Committee of Safety for Kent County. Probably he saw his wife here, for he scarcely had time to visit Coventry even for a few hours. Early the next morning, accompanied by Jacob, he rode to Providence where the day was spent ironing out difficulties attending the commissary. Just before starting back for camp, he wrote Kitty a note eulogizing America's determination to fight or die. "The cause is the cause of God & man," he confidently

assured his wife. Then all through the night, save for a few hours
when they stopped for sleep and refreshments, Greene and his
companions spurred their horses over the sandy road which led
to Roxbury.[6]

General Greene arrived at Jamaica Plain just in time. To his
dismay, his eyes met a scene of confusion and insubordination.
Some soldiers were preparing to go home, others were wandering
about the camp or idling in their tents in complete disregard for
the orders of their officers. Greene hardly needed to be told the
cause of the commotion. For several days the men had had little
to eat. There had been ugly complaints, too, about moldy bread
and horse meat which had been delivered to the army. While
Greene was gone, some of the boldest of the men had raided
the commissary and stolen practically all the food that remained.
Just how Greene handled the situation is not known, but in any
event, order and discipline were soon restored. The troops would
listen to him and there was something which made them realize they had a commander who could control them. At the
forge and furnace he had acquired the knack of handling men
in a way universally understood by the common soldiers. Food
was on the way, to be sure, but the steady eye of the young brigadier drove mutiny from the minds of the boldest. This was
Greene's first test of authority. He proved, as he would many
times again, that he was the master of his army.

On the day Greene arrived in camp to restore order, he was
summoned to Cambridge where General Ward was holding a
council of war at his headquarters in the home of Abiel Holmes.
For the first time, Greene had an opportunity to discuss problems
facing the army with the assembled staff. As he looked around
the table he saw that all but General Heath were older men
with military reputations. General Ward, in spite of his poor
health, looked the part of a soldier in his well-tailored suit set
off by a pair of shining epaulets. The petulant John Stark,
commanding the New Hampshire men in the absence of Nathaniel Folsom, seemed eager and energetic. David Wooster
who headed the Connecticut line, sat nearby with his brigadiers
Israel Putnam and Joseph Spencer.

Naturally, Greene's eyes often turned to the fifty-seven year old
Putnam, a burly, broad-shouldered man of medium height with

a shock of white hair. Tales of his daredevil adventures as an Indian fighter, wolf killer, and so on, had spread far and wide. Greene recently had heard how Putnam, upon hearing the news of Lexington and Concord, left the stone wall he was building on his Pomfret farm and rode off in his leathern work clothes to battle the Redcoats.

Although Nathanael Greene had been unknown to the assembled officers before he joined the siege, all had heard the high praise he had earned since his arrival at Roxbury. Indeed, Greene was not a little surprised at the attention he received from his fellow officers. "Were I," he wrote Kitty, "to estimate my value by the attention paid to my opinion, I should have reason to think myself some considerable personage."[7] After the meeting, Greene rode back to camp with Heath and Spencer feeling "very much fatigued having slept six hours in two nights," he told Kitty. But he had a pleasant feeling of pride and confidence in himself. That day he had proved himself both master of his brigade and a man of consequence in the eyes of his fellow generals. What more was needed to make a man's sleep untroubled?

Greene now found more time to devote to the drilling and training of his brigade. Patience was required as much as anything, and it was difficult, he explained to Kitty, "to limit people accustomed to much latitude." That this was generally true of the yeoman class throughout America, Greene would discover wherever the fortunes of war were to lead him. Although he avoided the use of punishment as much as possible, he did not hesitate to order it when it was necessary. Punishment in the American army was seldom as severe as in the British. By modern standards, however, it was hard and cruel. Whipping, the most usual form, was administered according to Mosaic law, which prescribed thirty-nine lashes for most offenses. Often, especially in the early stages of the war, American military courts meted out five or ten lashes or suspended sentences for first offenders. Riding the rail or "wooden horse" was a punishment fairly common in the American army. Besides providing the culprit with a lesson he would not soon forget, it afforded entertainment of a sort for troops who witnessed the ordeal.

To his wife, Greene explained the gigantic task confronting

the commanding officers of the American Army. The troops, he felt, had the makings of good soldiers. The army, however, had too few competent officers, especially of the junior grades, to train them. With impatience he awaited the arrival of Colonel Varnum, Christopher Greene, and other officers of the third regiment in whom he placed much confidence. As liquor was a constant source of trouble and disorder, he campaigned unceasingly against it. Before long, at the insistence of all the generals, bylaws were secured from the Massachusetts Provincial Congress which curtailed the sale of liquor to soldiers.

During the weeks immediately following Lexington and Concord, both armies stood in fear of attack by the other—but the British fear was far greater than that of their adversary. Reports of American strength had been magnified to such an extent, declared the British officer James Abercrombie, "that the Rebels are seen in the Air carrying Cannon and Mortars on their shoulders." So great was General Gage's fright, Abercrombie was sure he would have loaded his army on transports and sailed away had there been ships enough in the harbor.[8]

For a while Gage's anxiety was relieved by the convening of the Continental Congress in May. There was a chance, he thought, that Congress might yet turn to reconciliation rather than war. "All acts of hostilities," Abercrombie told Lord Loudoun, "will cease until they determine whether it shall be peace or war." The answer came when Gage learned that Congress had voted to put a formidable army in the field to protect the liberties of America. Rebellion, wrote Abercrombie, thereupon swept through the colonies: the people, worked up to a high pitch by their clergy, "have laid down the Bible & have taken up the Muskett." Anxiously, the British awaited reinforcements from England. On June 12th, with the arrival of the troops, Abercrombie jubilantly wrote, "in four or five days I shall beat the grenadier March and pay General Putnam a Visit." Little did the young British officer realize what was in store for him and his comrades on that fateful day when they would storm Bunker Hill.[9]

With the reinforcements had come William Howe, Henry Clinton, and John Burgoyne—all major generals and considered among the best in the British Army. Howe, forty-six, had served

with distinction in the French and Indian War, leading General
Wolfe's troops up the steep path to the Plains of Abraham where
the fate of France's American empire was decided. Clinton, nine
years younger than Howe, had served on the continent during
the Seven Years' War; Burgoyne who was fifty-three, poet, play-
wright, and man of letters, had a reputation for vigor and dash
on the field of battle. What a contrast to the farmers, lawyers, and
doctors who had acquired the title of general to command the
American Army!

It was largely due to the menace of Indians on the frontier
and the Royal Navy along the coast that only half of the 30,000
New England troops called for by Massachusetts had answered.
Greene, who was a great believer in quality rather than mere
numbers, was apparently not disturbed by the turnout. As it
was, Ward and his generals were having all they could do to
organize and provide for an army of 15,000. More troops at this
time might have served only to make the army more unwieldly
and vulnerable.

Regardless of the strength of the enemy who numbered 10,000,
Greene found that the morale of the Americans remained strong.
By the first of June, confident and spoiling for battle, the New
England men could barely wait for the British to attack. Greene
deprecated the shameful treatment of many defenseless people
in Boston by the British soldiery but he could not deny that it
was a blessing in disguise as it made the Americans more determined than ever to fight. Most of the Whigs had now left Boston,
and Greene for one, had no pity for the Tories who were suffering
along with the British from the land blockade imposed by the
American Army.

The Battle of Bunker Hill, the first major engagement of the
war, was fought on as clear and beautiful a New England day
as men could wish. On Breed's Hill, back of Charlestown, General
Putnam had about 1,700 men behind breastworks under Colonel
William Prescott. During the battle, others joined the fight.
In all, nearly 3,000 Americans participated in the Battle of
Bunker Hill. Against this number General Howe brought 2,500
of the finest troops to be found anywhere in the world.

While the battle raged, Greene was far away in Providence,
again conferring with Governor Cooke and the Committee of

Safety about critical shortages of supplies, especially gunpowder. When word reached him late in the day that the enemy had struck, he mounted his horse and again rode all night back to Roxbury. Arriving at camp early in the morning, in the distance he saw the smoldering ruins of Charlestown, razed by shot and shell from British warships as the redcoats stormed Bunker Hill. Although none of the Rhode Island troops had participated in the battle, Greene learned that some of them under Christopher Greene had gone to help dig entrenchments on Prospect Hill, two miles from the British who occupied Bunker Hill.

As General Howe's troops had finally driven away the stubborn defenders and won Bunker Hill, most patriots considered the battle a defeat for American arms. Attempting to hold hills from which escape could easily be cut off by the enemy was as ill-advised as it was dangerous. General Ward and presumably Dr. Joseph Warren (who had just been made a major general only to die in the battle) had opposed the plan, but Putnam, and the equally brave and impetuous Seth Pomeroy, won the argument. As a result, Breed's Hill (the Bunker Hill of the battle) and the nearby real Bunker Hill were occupied and prepared with breastworks only a few hours before the attack began.

As it turned out, the Battle of Bunker Hill was well-nigh ruinous for the British. Their casualties—828 wounded, 226 killed—constituted forty per cent of the troops engaged. Mortality among the officers averaged even higher as the Americans had taken pains to pick off the men leading the troops. The New England losses were less than 500, with most occurring during the hand-to-hand fighting after the enemy had gained the top of the hill.

Unlike most of his companions in arms, Greene considered Bunker Hill an American victory regardless of their having been driven from the hilltop and forced to retire to a position two miles away. Greene only wished New England could sell more hills to the British at the same price. In a letter to Governor Cooke, he said the battle reminded him of the words of Marshal Saxe of France who once exclaimed on winning a costly victory: "a few such Victories would ruin him."[10] Colonel Abercrombie, severely wounded while leading the Royal Grenadiers, echoed from his deathbed the words of Marshal Saxe in a letter to Lord

Loudoun. "A few such victories would Ruin the Army," he wrote. General Clinton agreed. "A dear bought victory, another such would have ruined us," he declared.[11]

Bunker Hill had the effect of setting the Americans hastily to fortifying their positions. On the day of the battle, Samuel Bixby wrote in his diary: "The Rhode Islanders laid out a piece of ground for entrenchment, and went to work entrenching. Gen. Thomas ordered them to cease work, but they swore they would not, and he thought best to let them go on with the work."[12]

It was not Greene who defied the Massachusetts general, for he was in Providence. Perhaps after thinking it over General Thomas decided that the Rhode Islanders were right. In any event, before the day was much older, he ordered trees cut down and made into barricades across the roads leading from the British works on Boston Neck. The next day Greene was happy to see the Americans entrenching all along the lines. At Roxbury, Cambridge, and other points, forts were started under the direction of Rufus Putnam, a man of considerable engineering talent and a veteran of the French and Indian War. Soon cannon from the newly prepared positions were answering the British whenever powder could be spared.

Viewing the military picture as it now appeared, Nathanael Greene was convinced that the patriot army could hold its own for the foreseeable future. It could not, however, seriously threaten the British or drive them out of Boston until the New England forces had more heavy cannon and much more ammunition. This being the case, Greene advised Governor Cooke against sending more troops, especially raw recruits or militia, until needed. While not altogether opposed to militia when numbers seemed desirable, Greene did not like them occupying space and eating up precious provisions during a siege or long stretches of time between major battles. Rhode Island, however, went right ahead and voted six additional companies for its army on June 18th. If they were not needed in Massachusetts, they could be used in Newport and other towns crying for more protection against ever threatening raids by British warships.

What Greene wanted most of all for the army was more good

officers. Too many of those with the army, he declared, were actually more of a detriment than an asset. "Some captains, and many subordinate officers, neglect their duty, some through fear of offending their soldiers, some through laziness, and some through obstinacy," he complained. Already he had reduced some to the ranks. "I am determined to break every one for the future who shall lay himself open to it," he told Governor Cooke.[13] When Washington arrived, Greene and the commander in chief worked together to improve the caliber of the officers. Greene told Governor Cooke of Washington's criticism of the great number of officers in the Rhode Island brigade and asked him to have the inferior ones removed. Observers, especially from other sections of the country, were agreed that the poor showing of so many of the New England officers was attributable to their belonging to the same social class as their troops. Often they were the friends, neighbors, or relatives of many of the men they commanded. Alexander Graydon, a Pennsylvania officer, thought the officers of New England, and even Virginia, generally came from yeoman stock, as the best families in both sections preferred to let others do the fighting. Washington believed he had a remedy for this problem. He would have Congress choose the officers for the Continental Army from the gentleman class of each colony. But New Englanders would not listen to his proposal. They would have their own home-grown officers or none.[14]

To teach both the officers and soldiers their duties, Greene lectured them in general orders on attention to duty and matters of discipline. After Washington arrived, the tone of the orders issued generally followed the exhortatory orders of the commander in chief, though to Greene preaching came naturally. Following inspection, Greene listed the things wrong or needing improvement. He particularly emphasized matters of daily routine such as promptness, good order in camp and on parade, and the care of weapons, equipment, and all supplies. At parade the soldiers should appear washed and well-groomed, wear shoes if they had any, and as far as possible dress alike. The officers, too, were to wear their uniforms and set a good example for their men in all things.

Two days before the Battle of Bunker Hill, Congress made George Washington commander in chief of the army surrounding

Boston. A month later it officially adopted the army, calling it the Continental Army. Washington's commission required him to seek the advice of his staff on all major decisions and policies. Not until after the disasters of 1776 did Congress see fit to entrust Washington with the sole power to make what decisions he chose.

As long as the British stayed in Boston, the Continental Army remained essentially a New England army. New York, New Jersey, and Pennsylvania, to be sure, sent regiments to join the forces from New England in an abortive attempt to take Canada. But all that were sent to the army surrounding Boston from the colonies to the southward, were 1,200 riflemen authorized by Congress and raised in Pennsylvania, Maryland, and Virginia.

General Washington reached Cambridge on Sunday, July 2nd, accompanied by General Charles Lee, Joseph Reed, his secretary, and Thomas Mifflin, an aide-de-camp, along with other officers and dignitaries. They were escorted by a company of light horse, and as they neared Cambridge, by a throng of citizens on foot, in carriages, and on horseback. The next day, according to tradition, under a tree known as the Washington Elm, General Washington formally took command of the American army.* Very likely only the regiments at Cambridge were drawn up for the occasion, as most of the army had to man the posts and entrenchments all along the eight or ten miles of the American lines. A letter written on the day Washington took over the command said that he would "take a vew of ye Army & that will be attended with a grate deal of grandor. There is at this time one & twenty Drummers & as many feffors a Beating and Playing Round the Prayde."[15] As he addressed his words to the men and officers drawn up on the village green, Washington must have realized the magnitude of his task. James Wilkinson recalled that in the ranks facing Washington there was not "a shade of uniformity in its organization, pay, dress, arms, or exercises." These were the men "destitute of subordination and discipline, and fluctuating from day to day," that Washington had to reckon with.[16]

Nathanael Greene was not present for Washington's reception.

---

* As the story of the Washington Elm first appeared in print in 1837, it has been considered a myth by some historians.

The next day, however, after having received orders from Rhode Island to place himself under the commander in chief, Greene sent a colonel with a detachment of 200 troops to welcome Washington and express his pleasure in serving under him. In return, Greene was invited to headquarters. The following day, accompanied by his aides, he called on Washington. From their first meeting the two men took a great liking to each other. Greene impressed the commander in chief as he did everyone who met him. The rapidity with which he rose in Washington's estimation during the fast moving months ahead is nonetheless remarkable. In less than a year, he would be in charge of Long Island, the most important position in the defense of New York. Alexander Hamilton declared that the "discerning eye" of Washington "marked him out as the object of his confidence. . . . He gained it, and he preserved it amidst all the checkered varieties of military vicissitude."[17]

George Washington was forty-three when he became commander in chief of the American Army—ten years older than Nathanael Greene. Fully aware of the political implications of his appointment, Washington knew that New England had agreed to have General Ward superseded to allay fears of New England domination of Continental affairs and to draw more aid from the other states. His appointment signified continental solidarity and a willingness on the part of New England to abide by the decisions of the thirteen colonies assembled in Congress.

Politics notwithstanding, Greene was aware that Washington was the most logical choice for the office. Charles Lee was English born and bred, and therefore ineligible, as were Horatio Gates and Richard Montgomery. Israel Putnam was as impossible as he was popular; Philip Schuyler was unacceptable to a majority of Congress; and Ward, besides being from Massachusetts was not physically able. None of the younger officers was well enough known or had enough experience to be considered. As the years would tell, only Greene, other than Washington, had the qualities requisite for the tremendous undertaking.[18]

Fearing that Washington's appointment might arouse some resentment in Massachusetts, John Adams sent home from Philadelphia glowing reports and eulogies of the Virginian. With his prestige enhanced by these encomiums, Washington was hailed throughout New England as the country's foremost hero and patriot. Greene's own praise of him was unequivocal. The morale of all was raised and "the spirit of conquest breathed through the whole army," he wrote Samuel Ward at the Continental Congress.

After selecting Washington, Congress appointed Artemas Ward, Charles Lee, Philip Schuyler, and Israel Putnam as major generals. Horatio Gates was made adjutant general with the rank of brigadier. Next, Congress chose eight brigadier generals, the last of whom was Nathanael Greene. Of the fourteen original generals appointed in June, 1775, only Washington, Gates, and Greene were in the Continental Army when the war ended in 1783.

One of the first things Washington did upon taking command was to reorganize the army. Three major divisions were established—the right under Ward, the center under Putnam, and the left under Lee. General Lee's wing consisted of two brigades under Greene and Sullivan numbering four or five thousand men in all. Three of Greene's seven regiments were his own Rhode Islanders under Varnum, Hitchcock, and Church. The others were Massachusetts men led by Colonels Whitcomb, Gardner, Brewer, and Little. Greene's troops occupied Prospect Hill, a strong position between Putnam's center and Sullivan's line to the left.

Nathanael Greene was fortunate in having for his superior the tall, gaunt, slovenly in dress, and anything but handsome, Charles Lee. A veteran of the French and Indian War in which he fascinated the Indians who called him "Boiling Water," Lee subsequently became a general in the Polish Army. Afterward he returned to America and bought a plantation in Virginia. When the war broke out, Lee offered his services to Congress which was glad to have so experienced an officer for its army. To fight for his adopted country, Lee gave up a lieutenant colonelcy and a pension in the British Army. Still, John Burgoyne, who knew him well, was unconvinced that he was motivated by anything more than avarice and personal gratification. Impious, sarcastic, and uncommonly eccentric, Lee nonetheless had more military experience and knowledge of engineering than anyone in the American Army.

During these days, Greene was much attracted to General Lee. Often he was a guest at "Hobgoblin Hall," as Lee dubbed his headquarters at Medford. Greene found Lee's wit and sarcasm amusing, as well as his extraordinary fondness for dogs. A visitor at headquarters described Lee as "a perfect original, a good scholar and soldier, and an odd genius, full of fire and passion, and but little good manners; a great sloven, wretchedly profane, and a great admirer of dogs." He had two dogs with him at dinner that day. "One of them a native of Pomerania," the writer would have "taken for a bear" had he seen him in the the woods.

It was not long before Nathanael Greene and his brigade were flattered with high praise from Washington, Lee, and others. "Though raw, irregular, and undisciplined," observed Washington, Greene's troops "are under much better government than any around Boston."[19] Joseph Reed thought likewise. Greene's Rhode Islanders, he declared, were the best disciplined and appointed in the whole American army."[20] Much of the credit for the high quality of the Rhode Island troops Greene acknowledged was due to the high caliber of many of his officers who more than made up for the shortcomings of some of the others. Besides James Varnum, Daniel Hitchcock, Christopher Greene, and Sammy Ward, there were Israel and John Angell, Stephen and Jeremiah Olney, Simeon Thayer, and others destined to earn fame in the Continental Army during the war. However, it was freely acknowledged that first credit for the quality of the Rhode Islanders belonged to Greene. The high morale of the Rhode Island troops indeed reflected confidence in their commander. "My officers and men are generally well satisfied,—nay I have not heard one complaint," wrote Greene. Observing Greene presiding at a court martial early in the war, Timothy Pickering declared him to be "a man of true military genius."[21] Henry Knox agreed with Pickering. To him, Greene's knowledge and skill seemed almost intuitive. "He came to us," wrote Knox, "the rawest, the most untutored being I ever met with, but, in less than twelve months, he was equal, in military knowledge, to any General officer in the army, and very superior to most of them."[22]

The endless duties and responsibilities incumbent upon the general officers during the early months of the war were staggering even to a man as used to hard work as Nathanael Greene. "I go to bed late," he told Kitty, "and rise early. The number of applications you cannot conceive of, without being present to observe the round of business." Problems in the Commissary and Quartermaster Departments were most vexing. In spite of all Greene's efforts, moldy bread and horse meat continued to turn up in the provisions, much to the disgust of the troops.[23]

One day in August, a messenger brought Washington word that the magazines had only thirty-five half-barrels of powder, enough for no more than nine rounds per man. Washington was so shocked by the disclosure "that he did not utter a word for half an hour." Rush orders to New York, Philadelphia, and Elizabethtown soon relieved the situation, but still not enough arrived to permit the Americans to send more than token shots into the British lines.[24]

On investigating the powder situation, Greene found that not a little was being wasted and some stolen. The men had a yen to fire their guns whenever a chance occurred, wild geese being a favorite target. "It is impossible to conceive upon what principle this strange itch for firing originates," he wrote. In general orders he warned that all soldiers found firing without orders would be tied up and whipped. As a further precaution, he directed officers to limit the number of cartridges to ten or twelve rounds per man (British troops were furnished with sixty) and to put them in the hands of the men only when necessary.[25]

Much improvement was made in supplying the army after Thomas Mifflin was made quartermaster general and Joseph Trumbull, commissary general. Mifflin, Washington's first aide-de-camp and a former Philadelphia merchant, pitched into his stupendous task with buoyant enthusiasm. Before he left the department (not without charges of mismanagement and suspicion of fraud), he did much to put the Quartermaster Corps on a systematic basis. In spite of all the efforts of Mifflin and Trumbull, however, Greene and the other generals still found much of their time had to be devoted to the endless problems attending the devouring needs of the army for supplies and provisions.

Day after day during the long siege of Boston, Washington

and his generals labored to improve discipline in the army and establish proper relations between the officers and the common soldiers. Such things as the sight of a captain shaving one of his privates near the parade ground was inexplicable to Washington.[26] Washington's standards were equally beyond the comprehension of the average New Englander. Even General Putnam at first stood in line with his men for rations and carried his share back to his quarters where he cooked his meals. Greene was fully aware of the shortcomings of the New England soldiery, but he knew it would take time to teach them discipline and that the process could not be hurried. He therefore made allowances when infractions were due to ignorance or misunderstanding. When the men willfully disobeyed military regulations, he dealt firmly with obstreperous individuals by ordering them to be duly punished.

It was not long before Washington's popularity showed signs of fading a bit in New England. Criticism arose not so much from his firm disciplinary measures as from some of his remarks about "Yankees." In a letter to his cousin, Lund Washington, he observed that one might make fair soldiers of them though "they are an exceeding dirty and nasty people." Another time, he declared he had never seen such "a dirty, mercenary spirit" as in New England. Joseph Reed, his secretary, warned his chief against expressing his thoughts too freely but his advice came too late. John Adams, who for a moment may have regretted his enthusiastic sponsorship of Washington, wondered if "every man to the southward of Hudson's River, behaves like a hero, and every man to the northward of it like a poltroon, or not?"[27]

If Washington allowed predilections to color his thinking on this occasion, he soon had cause to reconsider. Joseph Reed, in private life a Philadelphia lawyer and one of Greene's best friends, was sure by September that the real trouble lay not with New Englanders but with recruits from the southward. The riflemen, Reed declared, ever since they arrived from Pennsylvania, Maryland, and Virginia, had been "the pest of the Camp." "We Southern Folk," he confessed, "are quite ashamed of them." General Lee called them "dam'd riff-raff—dirty, mutinous, and disaffected." Not a few riflemen, especially the Irish, deserted to the enemy.[28]

Like everyone, Greene at first had praised the mighty riflemen who came from beyond the Delaware in their hunting shirts, leggings, and moccasins. All along the way people had turned out to cheer the hard-muscled men with the long rifles, tomahawks, and hunting knives, and marveled at their deadly aim. One American wrote a friend in England that Pennsylvania "has raised 1,000 riflemen, the worst of whom will put a ball into a man's head at the distance of 150 or 200 yards; therefore advise your officers who shall hereafter come out to America to settle their affairs in England before their departure."[29]

In August, the first serious brush with the riflemen occurred when a company of Pennsylvanians mobbed a guardhouse holding one of their unruly comrades. The sergeant in charge seized the ringleader and sent him with the prisoner to the main gaol at Cambridge. Soon about thirty riflemen loaded their guns and took off after the guards and their prisoners. A call went out for help and Washington, Lee, and Greene, who were nearby, appeared with a strong detachment from Greene's camp. This was more than the mutineers had bargained for and when they were overtaken, they immediately threw down their rifles and submitted to arrest. Perhaps because of fear of antagonizing the southern interest, the only penalty the mutineers received was a fine of twenty shillings and some fatigue duties.[30]

Though the prestige of the riflemen suffered during the siege of Boston, it was regained in campaigns to follow after they had calmed down and learned something of army discipline. They were, however, always a restless, highly individualistic lot who performed best when engaged in a vigorous campaign or on the battlefield. Among the officers of the riflemen were not a few of high caliber. One who headed a company of Virginians was Daniel Morgan, a former teamster and intrepid frontier Indian fighter. Whether Greene at this time had more than a casual acquaintance with his illustrious subordinate of days to come, is not certain.

To the riflemen, the New Englanders seemed as queer a lot as Gustavus Adolphus' psalm-singing and God-fearing soldiers appeared to the adventurers of the armies of Tilly and Wallenstein. One rifleman declared he had never seen "Such Sermons, such

Negroes, such Colonels, such Boys, & such Great, Great Grand-fathers!"[31]

This description of the New England soldiery was no imaginary one. Their chaplains electrified the air each Sunday with their tremendous sermons defending the American resort to arms, picturing their enemies as tools of Satan. Greene's brigade had for its chaplain the Reverend John Murray, who after being dismissed from a Boston pulpit for his Universalist doctrines, was chosen by Greene upon Colonel Varnum's suggestion to attend the spiritual needs of his men. When the other chaplains with the army protested, Greene brought the matter to the attention of Washington, who quietly confirmed Murray's appointment in general orders. Certainly John Greene, who had followed Samuel Gorton into the wilderness in 1640, would have been proud of the way his free-thinking great-great-grandson challenged New England orthodoxy. On weekdays, one might note, when Murray was not preaching, the soldiers had Nathanael Greene, who like the renowned Gustavus, seldom let an opportunity pass to remind them of their duty to God and their country.

As weeks and finally months went by and there was no attempt to drive the British out of Boston, the inactivity of the American Army naturally evoked criticism. Many chose to ignore the fact that Washington did not have enough cannon or ammunition to warrant fortifying Dorchester Heights, although without this vantage point it was rash to think of attacking Boston. The mounting criticism of Washington and his staff was nonetheless embarrassing to the American generals. Finally, Washington proposed an attack upon the city by crossing the Charles River at night in small boats. The plan, however, was voted down by his staff who thought it was too hazardous. "An attack upon a town garrisoned with 8,000 regular troops, was a serious object," thought Greene whose natural impetuosity was already showing signs of being toned down by the responsibilities of a command.[32]

During the ensuing weeks, Washington continued to press for an attack but on no occasion would his staff go along with him. Greene, Lee, and probably most of the others feared an attack would prove very costly, and the British, by counterattacking, might cut the army to pieces and crush the Revolution at one blow.[33] If the Americans had 20,000 well-trained and equipped troops, Greene thought, they might hazard an attack, but as it was they must be content with continuing the siege. The British, he surmised, wanted the Americans to strike, believing it would be their undoing. America, he declared, should realize that keeping the enemy "hen coopt up" in Boston was very nearly as good as defeating them on the field of battle.

About the time Washington was proposing an attack on Boston, his army was weakened by the departure of numbers of its best men and officers on the ill-fated expedition against Canada. Greene had to part with several of his most able officers, including Christopher Greene, Simeon Thayer, and Sammy Ward. The latter, still only nineteen, seemed too young for the rigors of a winter campaign in the northern wilderness. Greene tried to reason Sammy out of it, "but the heart and zeal of youth, ambitious of distinguishing himself, overcame the cool reasons" of the older man. After the Canadian expedition got under way, Greene anxiously watched the mails for news from the north. If General Richard Montgomery took Canada, he felt confident that with the back door closed, Washington could keep the enemy from entering by the front one. He was destined to disappointment, however, when late in the winter news came of the failure of the expedition and the great losses and suffering borne by his countrymen. Fortunately, Christopher Greene, Sammy Ward, and most of his close friends and relatives who went to Canada, survived.

As fall came and winter approached, the Continental Army was busily engaged in building barracks and huts against the cold. Prospect and Winter Hills, occupied by Greene's division, were especially cold and bleak. Shortages of lumber delayed the completion of the barracks until December. When finally completed the buildings might have been fairly comfortable had they been supplied with enough fuel. But once all the fences, old buildings, orchards, and trees were consumed for miles around, wood had to be hauled long distances. Deliveries in winter were slow and uncertain. Often there was not enough fuel in camp to cook by. Greene wrote:

We have suffered prodigiously for want of wood. Many regiments have been obliged to eat their provisions raw for want of fuel to cook it, and notwithstanding we have burnt up all the fences and cut down all the trees for a mile around the camp, our sufferings have been inconceivable. The barracks have been greatly delayed for want of stuff. Many of our troops are yet in tents, and will be for some time, especially the officers. The fatigues of the campaign, the suffering for want of food and clothing, have made a multitude of soldiers heartily sick of service.[34]

The hardships and privations of camp were often lightened by the American soldiers' sense of humor and love of a good joke. At Greene's headquarters his fat and jolly aide-de-camp, William Blodget, kept everyone laughing with his wit and humor. Stories such as the one about a certain Irishman circulated through camp to give life to the despondent and weary. The Irishman, it seems, being led into camp one night in an intoxicated condition, inadvertently fell into a puddle of water. With a sharp slap of his belt on the back of the unfortunate man, the guard gruffly inquired why he had fallen there. Picking himself up, the Irishman responded, "Why be Jesus, because I hadn't a chance to chuse a better."

With the coming of cold weather, the tempo of camp life gradually subsided. Although Greene was still at his desk or in the saddle the greater part of the day, he managed to find time for some pleasure and relaxation, especially after the arrival of Kitty, who in spite of her pregnancy braved the journey from Coventry to be with her husband. The arrival of the wives, including Martha Washington, Sarah Mifflin, Elizabeth Gates, Lucy Knox, and others, ushered in a season of gay parties and festivities. Elizabeth Gates came clad in her mannish English riding habit which quite scandalized the camp. But Charles Lee continued to be the sensation. At one party given by the Mifflins in December, he astonished all the guests by having his dog Spada mount a chair to offer a paw to Abigail Adams.

During the winter, Martha Washington and Kitty Greene, the first past forty and the latter twenty, became fast friends. Washington, too, was naturally much attracted by Greene's pretty and vivacious wife. At the parties he liked to tease Greene by claiming he was coming to rescue Kitty from her Quaker preacher.

Still another friendship developed between Kitty and Lucy Knox. A great favorite with all the officers, Lucy was jolly and decidedly plump, and was a good match for Washington's 230 pound colonel of artillery. Daughter of the Royal Secretary for Massachusetts, Lucy Flucker had married the handsome, six-foot, twenty-five-year-old Henry Knox the year before. Her parents had objected, but they were now besieged in Boston by the guns of her husband. During the winter, Henry Knox, who had succeeded Richard Gridley as colonel of artillery, was absent from camp for a time superintending the transportation of the Ticonderoga cannon captured by Ethan Allen to Washington's army. While Henry was away, Lucy often stayed with Kitty at the Pepperrell house. No doubt Lucy helped care for Kitty in February when she gave birth to a son, named George Washington Greene.

Before winter set in, the army was visited by a committee from Congress composed of Thomas Lynch, Benjamin Harrison, and the renowned Benjamin Franklin. They came to find out what the army would need for the coming year. After the delegates were shown the camps and fortifications, Washington called his staff together for a meeting with their distinguished visitors. The conference resulted in a decision to ask Congress for a Continental army of 20,000 men. To the disappointment of Greene and most of the officers, Washington opposed a bounty for enlistment; instead he favored a draft to fill the ranks. Throughout the meeting, Nathanael Greene was fascinated by the venerable Franklin. "I had the honor to be introduced to that very great Man, Mr. Franklin, whom I viewed with silent Admiration the whole Evening," he wrote Samuel Ward. "Attention watched his Lips, and Conviction closed his periods," observed Franklin's admirer.[35]

The establishment of the army on an entirely national basis, dependent on the Continental Congress for support, was not altogether popular, especially in New England. There were men in each state who believed parties in other states wanted the Continental system as a means to achieve more power for themselves. To his brother Henry, Samuel Ward wrote: "southern

Gentlemen [meaning anyone outside of New England] wish to remove that Attachment, which the Officers and Men have to their respective Colonies, and make them look to the Continent at large for their Support or Promotion."[36] Already Greene, without success, had tried to convince Samuel Ward of the need of a truly Continental army. Washington, Greene explained, wished to "banish every idea of Local Attachments." For himself, he declared, he felt "the cause and not the place." He would, he assured Ward, as soon go to Virginia to fight as stay where he was. When Congress accepted the recommendation of the general staff and passed the measure, Greene felt encouraged. "This will unite and cement the whole strength of the several colonies.—I think the Continent ought to provide for the security of every Colony," he told Jacob Greene.[37]

Before the winter was far advanced, however, it seemed that Congress must provide bounties or resort to a draft if Washington were to have an army after the first of the year. When the New England men marched off to war following the battle of Lexington and Concord, each colony had given its volunteers a bounty. The coming of cold weather and the accompanying discomforts of camp life made military service increasingly harder to bear, but for many, Greene was sure, the yearning to go home would be overcome with an offer of a bounty. As it was, believing that the states would in the end offer a bounty, nearly all the soldiers disposed to re-enlist waited while the weeks slid by and the end of the year approached.

On December 10, the day the time expired for the Connecticut troops and they left for home, Nathanael Greene wrote Samuel Ward that his Rhode Island men were so homesick and tired of army life that he was afraid all would leave at the end of the month. The day before, Greene had harangued the men from his saddle during parade; if they would not do their duty, he told them, they were surely doomed to slavery. Greene thought his words had some good effect. "They appear of a better disposition to Day; some have Enlisted and others discover a complying Temper."[38] To add to the dismal outlook, from Rhode Island came discouraging reports. Recruiting officers could hardly find a man willing to volunteer for Continental service. As elsewhere in New England, men preferred to join the state troops raised for home guard. "The Regiment raised in the Colony of Rhode Island has hurt our recruiting amazingly; they are fond of serving in the Army at Home and each feels a desire to protect his own family," Greene told Samuel Ward.

Although Greene, like Washington, was very concerned about the loss of the Connecticut troops and the lack of response by his Rhode Islanders, there was some reason to be hopeful. Massachusetts and New Hampshire were sending 5,000 militia to take the place of the departing Connecticut troops. Furthermore, men in Massachusetts were enlisting in encouraging numbers as the state had removed one of the attractions for serving in the state guard by putting it on a calendar basis like the Continental Army, thus abolishing the old lunar system. The failure, however, of all but a few Rhode Islanders to re-enlist became very embarrassing to Greene. He told Ward:

> I feel for the honor of the Colony which I think in a fair way to the conduct of the People at Home and the Troops abroad to receive a wound—it mortifies me to Death, that our Colony & Troops should be a whit behind the Neighbouring Governments in private Virtue or Publick Spirit.[39]

Up to the middle of December, only about 5,000 men had enlisted for service in the Continental Army for 1776. Still Washington clung tenaciously to his resolution not to have a bounty. Men fighting for their homes, in his belief, should not be paid a bounty for defending their lives and property. On this question Greene did not agree with his commander. "The Cement between the Southern and Northern Colonies," he bitterly complained, "is not very strong, if forty thousand lawful [£40,000] will induce Congress to give us up." New Englanders were shedding their blood for all America, and not for just their own section, he maintained. Why then were they not in justice entitled to a Continental bounty? If Congress gave a bounty, he wrote:

> We would then have an opportunity of picking the best men, filling the Army soon, keeping up a proper discipline, and preserving good order and Government in the Camp.—If we had given a good bounty and raised the Troops speedy, it would have struck the Ministry with Astonishment to see that four Colonies could raise such a prodegious large Army in so short

a time. They could not expect to conquer a people so United, firm, and resolutely determined to defend their Rights and Privileges.[40]

Could Greene have had his way, he would have had an army large enough to overawe the Tories and push the British into the sea before they could get a foothold. He believed it possible to raise, by bounties, an army of 70,000. Although initially expensive, in the long run an army of this size would be less costly to the country, he maintained. General Lee agreed wholeheartedly. To depend on militia and provincial forces was to him "childish" and "futile."[41]

Greene's concern during these critical weeks was not wholly focused on the troubles of the army. He worried about the threat of destruction of seacoast towns by the British Navy. Upon hearing of the burning of Falmouth in Maine, he mournfully wrote, "O America! What a black cloud hangs over this once happy land, but now miserable and afflicted people."[42] Realizing that the struggle could not be won without the continued support of the common people, he pleaded with Samuel Ward to do what he could in Congress to keep prices down. Help should be given persons rendered destitute by the stagnation of trade or other loss of employment due to the war, he said. If relief were not found for the unfortunate he feared that necessity would drive them into the lap of the enemy "for they cannot live upon Air."

When General Gage handed over his command to the tall, heavy-set Major General William Howe in September and left for England to answer for his failure in America, the British Army was doubtless stronger (though smaller) than Washington's. But Howe, who well remembered the tragic lesson at Bunker Hill, was not anxious to risk another encounter without unquestionable superiority. Though he probably no longer feared, as earlier, that the Americans might launch an attack led by their accursed riflemen, he was content to hold the city and await reinforcements.

After winter set in, the British suffered as much or more than the American Army. Much of their fuel, after all the old buildings, wharves, fences, and so forth were consumed, had to be brought in by sea. All the food had to be shipped into Boston, and the alertness of the American privateers during the winter severely cut into provisions bound for the city from the outside world. That the British could buy provisions in America, particularly from New York and Philadelphia, was most galling to Greene. If supplies from these ports were cut off, the British, he thought, would have to leave Boston or starve. "If we are to be considered as one people, and they as the common enemy," he asked, "upon what principle are they so differently treated in the different governments?"[43]

Although the British were able to hold off starvation, they were unable to procure enough fruit or vegetables to keep the troops in good health. By January scurvy was prevalent and deaths soon became so numerous that General Howe ordered the church bells not to be rung. "The chapple bell tolled all day for people that died—which was so malincully that the General has stopped the tolling of bells for funerals," explained one Bostonian. At the time, therefore, when Washington was losing thousands by desertion and the expiration of terms, the corresponding strength of the two armies may not have been materially altered.

December 31st, the last day of service for the troops known as "the Eight Months men," was the scene of great confusion and commotion in the American camps. As a shortage of guns was sure to arise if a new army could be raised, Washington ordered the seizure of all muskets from the departing men. As some might manage to get away with their guns, he served notice that anyone doing so would forfeit his pay for November and December. Nevertheless, great numbers slipped away with their guns rather than turn them in for the nominal price allowed by the army.

Happily for the American cause, New England's fundamental patriotism overcame the power of self-interest. When the people realized that there would be no bounty that year and that the men must go back into the army or give up the contest, the tide turned. Before the end of December, Greene reported that many of the Connecticut troops who had recently left for home were returning. "The people upon the Roads," he wrote, "exprest so much abhorrence at their conduct for quitting the Army that it was with difficulty they got Provisions." He wished all troops going home would encounter the same reception.[44]

With the return of many companies to camp before the last had left, and with recruiting picking up nearly everywhere, Greene looked with confidence toward the new year. Although on the night of December 31st he could not have mustered 700 troops in his brigade, four days later he could write that numbers had joined him since the dawn of the new year and he could once again defend himself should the enemy attack.

During the month of January, Washington's army remained too weak to attempt anything against the enemy. Shortages of powder and shot were alarming and not half of the men coming in could be given a musket. Benjamin Franklin, in Philadelphia, wondered why Washington did not resort to bows and arrows, a weapon which he thought had certain advantages over the slow-loading musket. Guns, however, were on the way from Philadelphia and other points of collection. Washington only hoped that the British would continue inactive until his army was ready.

Discouragement, however, still haunted the American Army. Reports were soon received of the failure of the Canadian expedition and the death of the heroic Montgomery. No one was more downcast than Greene by this first serious setback for American arms. "We are all in Mourning for the loss of the Brave Montgomery," he wrote to General Lee.[45] Each letter from the north made the picture darker as the suffering and losses became known. Until Greene received word of the safety of Sammy Ward and other friends, he worried over them and their anxious families back in Rhode Island.

By February the army had at last gained enough strength for Washington to agree with Greene that the worst was past. Before many more days elapsed, both generals were of the opinion that the army would be large enough by the time a French shipment of ammunition arrived from New York to act offensively. Cambridge Bay was freezing over and Washington hoped to take advantage of the ice to cross into Boston and strike the enemy from behind the works on Boston Neck. This time Greene sided with Washington but most of the staff were hesitant although the Continental Army now numbered 10,000 and Howe had but 5,000 effectives.

Greene, however, was confident that a majority of the staff

could be won over to an attack upon Boston. He was eagerly looking forward to the long awaited action when he was seized with a bad case of jaundice. "I am as yellow as saffron . . . my appetite all gone and my flesh too. I am so weak that I can scarcely walk across the room," he wrote his brother Jacob on February 8th. Nonetheless, he was resolved, if able to sit on a horse, to be with his division if it moved against the enemy. But Greene need not have worried, for presently a thaw set in whereupon Washington gave up the plan in favor of fortifying Dorchester Heights. Colonel Knox had brought the cannon of Fort Ticonderoga to camp and there was enough powder and shot to make use of them.

Preparations for fortifying Dorchester Heights were now pushed with great dispatch. Quantities of powder, cannon shot, lumber, bales of pressed hay, barrels, and other material were gathered at Dorchester below the heights to be fortified. As planned by Rufus Putnam, a cousin of Israel Putnam, the breastworks would be made of facsines and gabions (the one bundles of sticks and the other wooden frames filled with dirt) as the ground was frozen to a depth of eighteen inches. The bales of hay were to be set up along the low stretches of Dorchester Neck to prevent the enemy from raking the approaches to the heights with shot and shell. The barrels, made especially strong and filled with dirt on reaching the hilltops, were to be ready to send rolling down the steep slopes upon the enemy should they attempt an assault.

Fearing that the British might be apprised of his plan and anticipate him by occupying Dorchester Heights, Washington decided to wait no longer. March 4th, the anniversary of the Boston Massacre, was selected for fortifying the heights. According to plan, if the enemy launched an attack on the heights, as the Americans hoped, Greene and Sullivan would cross Back Bay with their brigades, land, and attack the British redoubts on Boston Neck from the rear. Simultaneously, other regiments would storm the Neck from Roxbury and together they would attempt to carry the enemy's works. Militia in neighboring towns were to be ready to move into the spaces in the lines vacated by Greene and Sullivan.[46]

To divert the attention of the British, on March 2nd, Washington ordered Knox to begin firing on Boston Neck from Phipp's Farm, Cobble Hill, and Roxbury Heights. On the night of the fourth, while Dorchester Heights was being fortified, the bombardment was stepped up causing "an almost incessant roar of cannon and mortars—on both sides." During the night providential winds carried the sound of the workmen on the heights away from the city, though such good fortune was probably not needed as the cannon presumably drowned out all other sounds.

First to start for Dorchester Heights was a covering party of 800 riflemen and musketeers. They were followed by General Thomas and 1,200 troops with entrenching tools. Behind them came more than 300 ox carts, loaded high with bales of hay, fascines, frames, barrels, and all. During the night most of the carts made three or four trips. Throughout the night low lying fog hid the hills from the sight of the British, while on top of the heights a bright moon shone to light the work for the Americans.[47]

When morning broke, General Howe was amazed to see his enemy strongly fortified on the hills overlooking Boston. Misled, no doubt, by the bastions of fascines and gabions, Howe declared the Americans had done in one night what would have taken weeks for his army to accomplish. The rebels must have had 12,000 men engaged in the work, besides the assistance of the devil himself, he declared. General Thomas, however, accomplished his task without the aid of the supernatural and with only two shifts of about 1,200 men each. In the morning fresh troops marched into the fortifications to be ready for the British in case they launched an immediate attack.

Though Howe was planning to evacuate Boston very soon, he did not relish the thought of being pushed out by the men he had ridiculed. He therefore made speedy preparations for storming the heights with 3,500 of his best troops before the Americans could strengthen their works. The British made ready for the assault with marked lack of enthusiasm and worried looks.

During the day a great throng gathered on distant hills to watch the battle should the British march out. Meanwhile, Greene and Sullivan stood ready to push over the bay for the attack on Boston. But the enemy failed to appear. During the evening at a council of war, Howe apparently was led to change

his mind and call it off. Great was the relief of the rank and
file, unaware of the decision and fully expecting to meet with
a hotter reception than at Bunker Hill, to see a great storm
arise and come crashing down upon them. "The wind blew almost a hurricane from the south," blowing out windows and
driving vessels on shore, according to Heath.

Admiral Molyneaux Shuldham, successor to Admiral Graves,
informed General Howe that inasmuch as his ships in the harbor
were in range of the cannon on Dorchester Heights, the city
must be speedily abandoned. The following day, Howe called
a staff meeting at which it was decided to follow the Admiral's
advice. All Loyalists who wished to sail with the fleet were
asked to be ready at the appointed time.

The British, however, did not move fast enough to satisfy
the Americans. On March 13th, Washington called his staff
together. After a short discussion it was decided to fortify Nook's
Hill looking directly from below Dorchester Heights across the
half-mile span of water to the rear of the enemy lines on Boston
Neck. With the occupation of Nook's Hill, cannonading on both
sides rose to a continuous roar and the bold action had its effect.
Early the next morning, March 17th, the British garrison of
nearly 9,000, along with 1,100 Loyalists, embarked on the eighty
transports in the harbor. There was no firing upon them for
Washington had given his word that the enemy could leave
unmolested in return for a promise not to set fire to the city.
Accompanied by sixteen warships, the fleet moved out of range
of the American cannon and dropped anchor. That night General
Ward with 500 pock-marked men (soldiers who had had the
smallpox) occupied the fever-ridden city. The eleven months
of siege had ended.[48]

The next day Greene was put in charge of the city. During
the few days he was there he was busy taking count of the
supplies left by the enemy. Besides medical supplies, blankets,
camp equipment, and provisions, the British left more than
200 cannon and 150 horses. This was a most welcome windfall
for the Americans. In a sermon preached on Sunday, March 25th,
the Rev. Mr. Bridge expressed the feeling of the people for their
good fortune. From II Kings 7:7, he drew his text: "Wherefore
they arose and fled in the twilight, and left their tents and their

horses, and their asses, even the camp as it was, and fled for their lives."[49]

During Greene's stay in Boston, he found time to visit old friends and attend several dinner parties. On the 28th, the army officers sat down to a sumptuous banquet at the Bunch of Grapes with the city fathers. After dinner they all attended the re-opening of the Thursday lectures at the Old South Church. Here they listened to a sermon by The Rev. Dr. Andrew Eliot whose text was from Isaiah 33: 20: "look upon Zion, the city of our solemnities: thine eyes shall see Jerusalem a quiet habitation, a tabernacle that shall not be taken down; not one of the stakes thereof shall ever be removed, neither shall any of the cords thereof be broken."

For ten days after their evacuation of Boston, the British hovered in the harbor out of range of the cannon on shore. When they finally lifted anchor and put to sea, Greene felt it unlikely that they would return to attempt to surprise the city. He was right. Howe sailed to Halifax to await reinforcements before sailing for New York to begin the second phase of the war.

In the capitals of Europe, British military reputation sunk to an all-time low because of what had happened in Massachusetts during the past year. Everywhere Americans were toasted and looked upon as a kind of supermen. Though Nathanael Greene's part in the long siege had been unspectacular, his value to the army was recognized by all. The confidence that Washington already had in him would presage for him a prominent role in the next campaign.

CHAPTER FOUR

A Desperate Game

When Boston fell, the Americans knew that New York would be the principal target for the British as soon as they could transport the large army being collected in England to America. Formidable as the British would be when they returned to resume the war, few Americans anticipated anything but an easy victory. How desperate would become the American cause before the end of the year was beyond the vision of the victors of the siege of Boston.

Although Washington had information that Howe would sail for Halifax to await the army from England, he was not unmindful that the report might be but a ruse to deceive him while his enemy made straight for New York. To thwart such a move, Washington had sent two brigades and a rifle company under General Heath to New York before Howe sailed from Boston. As an additional precaution, Connecticut's Governor Trumbull was asked to send 2,000 militia to New York to help prepare fortifications being hastily erected to protect the city.

Just after the British sailed for Halifax, word reached Washington that enemy ships had been sighted off Sakonnet Point. Had Howe decided upon Newport for his destination? Greene, about to leave for New York with his brigade, was ordered to hurry to Rhode Island. Sullivan, already on the march for New York, was directed to join him. Leaving heavy baggage behind, Greene reached Providence by forced marches, only to find that some keyed up watchers had mistaken low lying and shifting fog for the sails of enemy ships.

Hearing that Washington was on his way to Providence, Greene made hasty preparations for giving him a grand reception. All men with uniforms were ordered to shave, powder their hair, and be ready to escort his Excellency into town. When Washington and Greene, mounted on fine horses, led the proud paraders through the streets of Providence, it seemed that all Rhode Island had turned out to cheer its heroes.

April 8th was cold and raw when Greene left Providence and headed his brigade toward New London where ships were waiting to take them to New York. Kitty was with him and in the afternoon they reached Coventry. The next morning Nathanael bid fond farewell to Kitty and the friends and relatives gathered to see him off. When he reached New London with his troops, all embarked during a whirling snowstorm (probably in open boats) for passage through Long Island Sound. During the night the ships became dispersed and lost in the storm. It was days before all were reunited and a week before they came through Hell's Gate to land at New York.[1]

Reporting to Washington on the 17th, Greene was given the command on Long Island, the key position for the defense of New York. The responsibility was flattering. But so far as Greene was concerned, the campaign would have little bearing upon his military reputation, for at the final hour a fever removed him from the lines. The defeat which followed shattered the myth of American military invincibility and left the country's nerves on edge. Greene remained calm. America would find the going difficult at times, he believed, but in the end it would be victorious.

When Greene arrived at Brooklyn he found the energetic quartermaster, Thomas Mifflin, had supplies and equipment waiting and more constantly arriving. Not only tents but boards for flooring and bales of straw for bedding were on hand. Into the camp came loads of bricks for ovens, fireplaces, and magazines. Piles of firewood and charcoal were here and there. Entrenching tools, which officers were to account for as meticulously as firearms, were delivered to points along the line. Besides the regiments of Varnum and Hitchcock, Greene had Little's Massachusetts men and a corps of Pennsylvania riflemen under Colonel Edward Hand. With many of them good soldiers by this time, the troops soon had the camp set up and were ready to begin work on the fortifications.

Though the Long Island defenses were far from finished,

Greene found that Lord Stirling had accomplished much in the short time he had been in charge. Plans for the fortifications in the New York area had been made by General Lee who had been dispatched to New York in January upon rumor that Howe was preparing to send a detachment from Boston to strengthen the British garrison on Governor's Island and give encouragement to the Tories.

Lee was in command at New York, but a few weeks before Congress decided that he would be more useful heading the American forces in Canada. Considered by Americans in general as a military genius, some thought Lee might rescue the floundering army staggering back from Canada or perhaps even turn it about and lead it to victory. Lee wrote Washington that if he took the Canadian assignment he would want Greene and Sullivan with their brigades. To this Washington would not agree—he could not weaken his main army to that extent, he replied. Lee, who prided himself on being the only general in the army who spoke and thought in French, was flattered by the offer of the northern command. He was still more elated when Congress changed its mind again and sent him to take command in the Carolinas where Whigs were savagely fighting Tories who momentarily expected the British to come to their aid by sea.[2]

Until Putnam arrived in New York to take Lee's place, William Alexander (known as Lord Stirling since he began sporting a bogus claim to a peerage) was left in charge. Stirling, whom Lee had found a "most zealous, active and accurate officer," had just been made a brigadier general after capturing the British supply ship *Blue Mountain Valley* off Sandy Hook. Although Stirling impressed nearly every man he could find for work on the New York-Long Island defenses, the fortifications were so extensive that progress was irritatingly slow until Washington's army arrived to lend a hand.[3]

After studying the topography and the uncompleted defenses, Greene was convinced that Lee was right in believing Long Island the key to the defense of New York. The Long Island works, which enclosed the village of Brooklyn, consisted of a wall of earthworks, studded by several forts, running from the East River's Wallabout Bay to Gowanus Bay, a small appendage of

New York Bay. The line, which ran north and south, was a mile and a half long. To the westward, facing New York Bay and the East River, stood Fort Stirling and Fort Defiance whose cannon with those on Governor's Island commanded the entrance into the East River. North of Brooklyn at Hell's Gate was another fort with a companion one on the Manhattan side. After the British took Long Island, Montresor described the American works as well planned but poorly executed. The veteran British engineer probably was aware that the man who started the works was Stirling whom he had severely criticized in 1756 for his forts at Oswego. As the defenses were finished by Greene, Montresor's criticism presumably applied to him as well as Stirling.

While Greene was making steady progress on his defenses and training program, he found that some of the soldiers did not measure up to his Quaker standards for deportment. "How can we hope to have the blessings of heaven in our aims if we insult it with impunity?" he asked his soldiers in general orders. Swearing, fast becoming a habit with many of the men, offended Greene very much. In July, too, he was much troubled with soldiers stealing fruit, especially watermelons, from nearby farms. On one occasion some young rascals swimming at Mill Pond ran naked around nearby farm houses, much to the distress of the occupants. Any more insulting the "Modesty of female Decency," Greene warned, would meet with severe punishment. He admonished his countrymen:

> Where is the Modesty, Virtue & Sobriety of the New England People for which they have been so remarkable? Our Enemies have sought to fix a stigma upon New England People as being rude and barbarous in their manners and undisciplined in their Conduct—for Heaven's Sake don't let your behavior serve as an example to confirm their observations.[4]

Regardless of Greene's concern for his men's behavior and spiritual well-being, the American soldiers could not be compared with the freebooters common in British and European armies. One observer thought there were few instances of misbehavior among the Americans considering the number thrown together in strange surroundings. "They have all the simplicity of ploughmen in their manners, and seem quite strangers to the vices of other soldiers," he wrote.[5] To another writer the behavior of the New England men seemed very commendable. At any rate, he noted that they attend their "prayers with the chaplain evening and morning regularly."[6]

In June, accompanied by the strapping Henry Knox, Greene made a trip to the northern end of Manhattan to study the terrain in view of erecting fortifications for controlling the North River and safeguarding an avenue of retreat from New York by way of Kingsbridge over the Harlem. When the question was discussed in council, Israel Putnam proposed fortifying the approaches to Kingsbridge near Roger Morris' house, but Greene, Knox, and Heath insisted this would be ineffectual unless the strategic heights on Mount Washington overlooking the Hudson and Harlem rivers and the heights on the northern side of the Harlem River were strongly fortified as Lee had planned. This was decided and construction of Fort Washington and Fort Independence soon began under the direction of Rufus Putnam.

By 1776, there were few in the army to deny that Greene was of major general caliber. Washington found himself leaning more and more upon the advice of the young general in forming his opinions. So did the staff which was falling under the spell of Greene's analysis of the problems confronting the army. Regardless of his growing prestige, Greene did not wait for Congress to come knocking at his door with a promotion. He was an ambitious man and did not want his merits overlooked.

Writing to Washington on May 21st, Greene observed that doubtlessly there would soon be promotions as the army must be enlarged to cope with the powerful force England was sending to America. In this letter he wrote:

As I have no desire of quitting the service, I hope the Congress will take no measure that will lay me under the disagreeable necessity of doing it. I have ever found myself exceeding happy under your Excellency's command. I wish my ability was equal to my inclination to merit. How far I have succeeded in my endeavors I submit to your Excellency's better judgment. I hope I shall never be more fond of promotion than studious to merit it. Moderation will forever forbid me to apply to that House

[Congress] for any favors. I consider myself immediately under your Excellency's protection, and look up to you for justice. Every man feels himself wounded when he finds himself neglected, and that in proportion as he is conscious of endeavouring to merit attention.[7]

Neither did Greene leave John Adams (with whom he had struck up a correspondence after Samuel Ward's death in March) in the dark as to his expectation of advancement. Congress's reserving the right to promote officers, he told Adams, was a dangerous policy. Congress, he explained, was more apt to be partial than Washington and make promotions which could throw the army into discord. If an officer finds another promoted over his head, it lays him under the necessity of quitting the service "if he has any spirit," Greene said. "For my own part," he firmly declared, "I would never give any Legislative Body an opportunity to humiliate me but once." Congress, he warned, should seek Washington's advice before advancing anyone out of order. "For Rank is of such importance in the Army and so delicate are the sentiments respecting it," that exceptions to seniority should be made only under very strong reasons.

Matters other than personal took up most of the space in Greene's letters to Adams. America, he warned, still had its greatest test ahead and Congress must do more to strengthen the Continental Army if the country were to survive. It would help much, he assured Adams, if Congress would provide a pension for every disabled man as well as for families made fatherless by the war. Such a law would aid recruiting and do much to build morale in the army, thought Greene. It would be only an act of common justice to men risking their lives and fortunes for America.[8] Adams agreed with Greene that something should be done for the war casualties. He was uncertain, though, when Congress could be brought to act. His answer, of course, did not satisfy Greene. If Congress would not provide pensions, then it should demand that each state fill its quota of enlistments, he declared. Otherwise those which sent the most soldiers would have the greatest number of casualties for the state to care for. Fortunately, within two months Congress acceded to the demand of the army for pensions for disabled men and for the

families of those who died in the service. Committees appointed
by the states passed on all applicants for pensions, funds for
which were subtracted by the state from its quota for the United
States.[9]

In his letters, Greene tried to convince Adams that the pay for
officers, "the very soul of an army," did not come near meeting
their expenses. Unless Congress raised their pay, especially for
colonels, "few, if any, of that rank that are worth retaining in
service will continue," he warned. The army, consequently,
would soon be confronted with a serious shortage of officers as
only those with independent means could continue in the service, he concluded. Basically, Greene knew the plight of the army
was attributable to the depreciation of the Continental currency.
However, he thought paper money practical if used with restraint, especially if a system of taxation could be devised for
its redemption. But as it was, unless something were done, the
depreciation, he warned, would "starve the army."

During the spring and early summer, Greene had the company of Kitty in camp. Lucy Knox, Martha Washington, and
many of the wives who had been with the army during the
siege of Boston were there too. Some, including Martha Washington, left for home when the first of the British flotilla entered
New York harbor. Kitty Greene left early too, but as late as
August 7th, Reed noted, ladies in great numbers were still
coming to camp to see their husbands and friends.[10]

The independence movement, culminating in the famous
Declaration of July Fourth, had found its earliest expression
among the officers of the Continental Army. There had been
no indication, however, even in the army, of such sentiment
before the autumn of 1775. Joseph Reed wrote in August, 1775,
that Massachusetts, like the other colonies, would settle for
things as they were before 1765 when Parliament undertook
to tax America. If Britain should agree to this, he thought opposition would cease at once and the colonies would resume
their former peaceful pursuits.[11]

Among the army officers, Charles Lee seems to have been
the first to come out with a recommendation for independence
if Great Britain continued her desperate course. Writing to
Richard Henry Lee, a member of Congress, on September 2nd,

General Lee said Congress should declare independence unless the Ministry recalled the troops at Boston and offered to settle the differences between Great Britain and the colonies by peaceful negotiations. Lee would have a message of this kind sent to England rather than another petition that John Dickinson had persuaded Congress to adopt.[12]

Ten days after Lee penned his letter advocating independence, Greene wrote Governor Cooke from Prospect Hill that he believed the dispute would never be settled so long as Lord North's ministry remained in power. Much as he valued the connection with England, independence, he thought, was likely to be the only solution.[13] At this time Greene and Lee were on very intimate terms and agreed with each other on most things. Perhaps Lee, eleven years older than Greene and much admired, was the initiator of the proposal more than Greene himself. In any event, on October 23rd Greene reminded Ward that he had already hinted that people had begun "heartily to wish a Declaration of Independence."[14]

From this time on Greene was outspoken in his views on independence. At a dinner with Colonel Varnum and the noted Quaker, Moses Brown, on December 12, 1775, he freely expressed his opinion that the time was fast approaching when America must renounce its allegiance to the mother country. Brown demurred, saying he thought everyone should hope for peace and union. Greene replied he had just about given up all hope of reconciliation.[15]

Not many days after Greene's meeting with Brown came reports of the King's latest speech from the throne calling for the suppression of the rebellion with the armed might of the British nation. If Greene needed any more convincing that independence was the only answer for America, this was it. "We are now driven to the necessity of making a declaration of independence," he told his brother Jacob in a letter of December 20th.[16] A fortnight later he appealed directly to Samuel Ward to work for independence. "Permit me then to recommend, from the Sincerity of my Heart, ready at all times to bleed in my country's Cause, a Declaration of Independence; and call upon the World, and the Great God who Governs it, to Witness the Necessity, Propriety, and Rectitude thereof," he begged his friend.

A declaration of independence, Greene knew, would make possible an alliance with the French who, he assured Ward, should be embraced as "brothers." "We want not their Land Forces in America, their Navy we do—Their Military stores we want Amazingly." He was already speculating, too, on the possibility of a European war to "turn Great Britain's Attention that way."[17]

Bold spirits in the army, however, did not represent the thought and feeling of the country on independence, with the exception, perhaps, of New England. Joseph Reed noted in March that independence was inevitable but Congress had to wait for public opinion to crystallize before proceeding. Charles Pettit, a shrewd Trenton lawyer, was sure the time was not ripe for a declaration of independence. If done now, he said, it would split the people to the point of endangering everything, "whereas a few months, perhaps a few weeks, may, like the Sun ripening Fruit, make that pleasant and desirable, which at present appears sour and disgusting."[18]

Powerful forces, nonetheless, were at work, and soon whole sections of the country were turning in favor of independence. The hiring of Hessians and other troops by Great Britain to help put down the rebellion stirred America to its depths. Early in 1776, Thomas Paine's pamphlet *Common Sense* was in everyone's hands and reaping thousands of converts for independence. Still, people gave up the hope for reconciliation slowly, especially in Pennsylvania and New York. In Philadelphia, the moderates, led by John Dickinson, remained in control of the assembly until June and blocked the advance of radicalism as long as they were able.[19] General Lee, with his acid pen, wrote Benjamin Rush in February that anyone who talked of reconciliation "ought to be pelted at with stones by the children when he walks the streets as a common Town Fool." America he declared, should awake to its peril and make an alliance with France at once.[20]

Chafing at Congress's slow pace, early in May the Rhode Island Legislature passed an act discharging its citizens from allegiance to Great Britain. Hearing of the measure, Greene placed his benediction on the act: "Tis nobly done. God prosper you, and crown your endeavors with success."[21] Within a month after the Rhode Island resolution, the way was cleared for action by Congress on the momentous declaration when the Pennsylvania radicals seized the initiative and forced the Pennsylvania Assembly to release its delegates from their instructions to work for reconciliation. About the same time, Richard Henry Lee, acting upon instructions from the Virginia Convention, initiated action in the Continental Congress by offering a resolution for a "free and independent" America. After two weeks of debate, the resolution was carried and on July 4th, Jefferson's declaration was adopted.

News of the Declaration of Independence spread like wildfire through the American camp a few hours after bells began ringing in Philadelphia. On July 9th, Washington read the Declaration of Independence to troops assembled on the New York Commons after which the men cheered amid a running fire from their muskets and the booming of cannon. Thomas Mifflin is said to have jumped on a cannon near Washington shouting, "My lads, the Rubicon is crossed!" and called for more cheering.

That evening in Broadway's Bowling Green, a mob pulled down a lead statue of George the Third after which most of the pieces found their way to Litchfield, Connecticut, where girls ran them into bullets for the army. Greene did not mind the fate of the statue but he disliked soldiers participating in what had all the appearances of a riot. In the future, he warned his men, they were to stay out of all mob actions or suffer the consequences.

The first section of the British army, accompanied by Major General William Howe on the frigate *Greyhound*, arrived in New York Bay on June 29th. During the next six weeks they continued to arrive "like the swarm of locusts escaped from the bottomless pit." On July 12th, Admiral Lord Howe appeared with ten ships of the line and twenty frigates accompanying another large contingent of troops. About two weeks later, Clinton and Cornwallis arrived with 2,500 troops from their ill-fated expedition to Charleston where Colonel Moultrie had riddled the British ships with shot and shell from Sullivan's Island. Eleven days later the Hessians under General Leopold Von Heister came. In all, Howe had 32,000 troops aboard some 400 transports. Six thousand more troops had been sent to Canada to reinforce

General Carleton, who, with Burgoyne, would try without success to join forces with Howe by way of Albany. Never before had America seen such an array of military might.

On July 2nd, Howe, who intended to make New York his base of operations in America and split the colonies by controlling the Hudson, landed and threw up entrenchments on undefended Staten Island. At this, Washington proposed making an attack on the island before the full weight of the enemy was upon them, but his staff was opposed. Greene thought an attack with an army made up mostly of inexperienced troops was trusting too much on the protection of Providence.

Writing to John Adams, Greene reminded him again that America was playing a "desperate game." By desperate, he did not mean hopeless. "I am confident the force of America, if properly exerted, will prove superior to all her enemies, but I would risk nothing to chance. . . ." Adams should not be too confident. "The fate of war is very uncertain; little incidents has given rise to great events. Suppose this army should be defeated, two or three of the leading generals killed, our stores and magazines all lost." In such an event he would not want to be answerable for the consequences, he declared.[22] Although while Greene was writing the size of Washington's army was rapidly increasing and would by the time Howe struck match his regulars in numbers, it remained so scattered as to be open to attack and destruction by detachments. Washington and Greene were aware of the weakness of their positions but there was no alternative if New York were to be held.

Notwithstanding the dangers facing the army, Greene remained as confident as ever as the days came and went. He lamented Congress' failure to provide a larger force of Continentals, but he believed nonetheless that the enemy would meet with defeat so long as the Americans fought from behind breastworks. Greene, it would seem, would not have risked sending out four or five thousand troops to meet the enemy in the open as Putnam did on that fateful day of the Battle of Long Island.

Not all, however, were as optimistic as Greene. Joseph Reed, for one, was at times very pessimistic. A few days after Howe arrived, he wrote that "every man in the army from the general to the private . . . is exceeding discouraged. Had I known the true posture of affairs, no consideration would have tempted me to have taken an active part in this scene, and this sentiment is universal."[23] Two weeks later he was in no better frame of mind. "I very much fear," he wrote, "many of our troops will fail in Spirit especially if taken by Surprise." Eventually foreign aid might tip the scales in America's favor, he thought, but as he looked out over New York harbor with its forest of masts rising from the enemy's ships, his heart sank. "We are playing a very unequal game," he warned his wife, Catherine.[24]

For a time the rapid growth in the size of Washington's army was offset by the thousands who became sick with the "putrid fever" (typhoid and typhus) and the smallpox which hit the camps in July. Heath (who undoubtedly put the number too high) estimated that by August 10,000 lay sick. "In almost every barn, stable, shed, and even under the fences and bushes, were the sick to be seen," he recalled. Smallpox patients were sent to Montresor's Island in the East River. At the time, no inoculations were allowed in the army for fear of spreading the disease. During this trying period, Washington lost more men from the fevers than were to die from British bullets during the approaching battle.

Greene attributed the sickness in the army partly to a diet of too much fresh meat. To remedy this, he tried to get more vegetables, fruit, and milk. All meat was to be roasted rather than boiled. Believing cleanliness essential for good health, he sought to have his men well supplied with soap with which to keep washed, shaved, and dressed in clean clothes. As an additional precaution, he refused to allow his soldiers to stay in swimming more than a half hour or to swim in the heat of the day.

General Howe, it has been said, missed a real opportunity by not attacking Washington at the height of the epidemic. Sickness, however, did not spare his troops who had been weakened by long and enervating weeks on crowded transports, and Howe's army was in no condition to launch an attack at the time. Von Heister's Hessians were, in truth, barely recovered from their voyage when Howe began his campaign late in August. On the transports, the Hessians were so packed together as they slept on the decks that an officer had to give the command for them to turn all at once to relieve their weariness.[25]

Admiral Lord Howe, as dark complexioned and swarthy as his brother, the General, arrived at New York, July 12th, armed with the power to negotiate a reconciliation with America. Disappointed indeed was "Black Dick," as his Lordship was called to learn that Congress had resolved that America was free and independent. But he was hopeful an accommodation could still be reached before any more serious fighting took place. He therefore attempted to open negotiations with Washington whom he addressed simply as George Washington, Esquire. The latter returned the message unopened. After a second attempt, Washington advised Howe to contact Congress if he had anything to say regarding the state of affairs between America and the mother country.[26]

After the Battle of Long Island, Lord Howe tried again to initiate negotiations for peace and reconciliation. Through General Sullivan, captured in the battle, he secured a meeting at Tottenville, Staten Island, with a committee of Congress consisting of Benjamin Franklin, John Adams, and John Rutledge. To his great surprise these gentlemen politely informed him that all America desired from England was recognition of its independence. Instead of coming to Howe with "offers of compromise or submission," the Americans insisted "on the acknowledgement of their Independency as a preliminary article," much to the astonishment of the British. After the meeting, Adams observed that the conference did no harm; it was but "a bubble, an ambuscade, a mere insidious manoeuvre."[27]

Though most Americans were glad to see Congress hold firmly to independency, there were some, including Robert Morris, John Dickinson, and Joseph Reed, who still harbored a lingering hope for reconciliation and were disappointed. Reed, who wondered what America would do for trade should it win independence, was quite dejected. Nonetheless, he admitted that no matter how pleasantly Lord Howe spoke, his instructions held out no hope for an accommodation. Unlike these men, Greene had shut his mind to all thought of reconciliation. No one was happier than he to see Howe's overtures come to a speedy and decisive end.

As the months came and went and the number of New England troops remained far under their quotas, Greene became not a little embarrassed with the seeming lack of patriotism of his native New England. He knew people were saying that since the war had left their doorstep, New Englanders had become indifferent to the fate of the rest of the country. So far, barely a third of the 15,000 quota for New England had been raised. Anxiously Greene wrote to John Adams and Governor Cooke entreating them to do all possible to fill the ranks. Much to Greene's relief, during the last few weeks before the attack on Long Island, more troops arrived from the eastward.

New England's failure to fill its quota, Greene knew, was in no way chargeable to lack of patriotism or indifference. New England had borne the brunt of the Canadian campaign with heavy losses. As Reed phrased it, Canada had been the sinkhole that swallowed up the flower of the American Army. But this was not all. A severe smallpox epidemic in Massachusetts cut enlistments drastically. Out on the New England frontier men could not leave their families threatened by Carleton's bands of Indians led by Tories burning with hatred against their former countrymen. Though not so excusable, many who could have served had succumbed to the mania of privateering and were cruising the ocean in search of British prizes.

Hoping to make the going as difficult as possible for the enemy when the attack came, Washington ordered all farmers in the New York area to remove their livestock, grain, and hay to places out of reach of the invaders. Many on Long Island who would not or could not comply saw their property go up in smoke by orders from Greene. Mills were dismantled by hiding or carting away the grindstones. Greene was particularly harassed by the large number of neutrals and outright Tories on Long Island who required constant surveillance. In spite of all, Loyalists slipped by the guards carrying provisions and information to the enemy. During this time, Howe was joined by many prominent Tories anxious to help him plot the downfall of the rebellion. On one night, three leading Loyalists, Oliver deLancey, William Bayard, and Charles Apthorpe, set out from Bloomingdale and took a boat down the river to join the Howe brothers on the *Asia*.[28]

In executing his ever expanding line of duties, Greene saw precious time which should have been devoted to inspections and supervision in the field consumed by an endless stream of paper work. If for no other reason, he declared, a general should be relieved of this work to give time to think and plan. He wrote Washington:

> It is recommended by one of the greatest generals of the age not only to issue orders, but to see to the execution, for, the army being composed of men of indolence, if the commander is not attentive to every individual in the different departments, the machine becomes dislocated, and the progress of business is retarded.[29]

About a week after he wrote to Washington, Greene was made a major general whereby his desk work was lightened by additional aides and secretaries acquired by virtue of his rank. Greene doubtlessly owed his promotion chiefly to Washington although John Adams (unquestionably the most powerful man in Congress) must also have been largely responsible.

Though appreciating Greene's ability, John Adams by no means accepted all of the young man's opinions. Adams, in fact, had been quite annoyed by Greene's criticism of some earlier promotions, particularly those of Stirling and Mifflin. Greene complained, too, that Congress had discriminated against New England in promotions. Adams pointed out to him quite correctly that all four men made major generals and three of the six raised to brigadiers in August were from New England. As for the promotions of Mifflin and Stirling, there was much to support the action on both. Stirling "was a person so distinguished by fortune, family, and rank and employment he had held in civil life, added to his experience in military life, that it was thought no great uneasiness would be occasioned by his advancement," explained Adams. Mifflin, Adams reminded Greene, was a very important political figure in Pennsylvania and by education, business experience, and ability, well qualified for the rank of brigadier general. Adams furthermore explained to Greene that Congress thought it necessary to keep the number of officers of a given rank somewhere in proportion to the military support rendered by each state.[30]

With the day of battle fast approaching, Washington and his officers bent their energies to last-minute preparations. Scores of Tories who might prove dangerous were rounded up and sent to New Jersey or Connecticut. Passes and furloughs were drastically restricted and guards alerted for spies. From the shores and high points, sentries watched the British day and night. Greene noted that his men were in high spirits and fairly itching for battle. In general orders he congratulated them and expressed his confidence in their bravery. To inspire them, he described the laurels won by the forces of Lee and Moultrie in South Carolina. If his men did as well, he said, he would be most happy.

Though Greene might have prevented the defeat of the American Army on Long Island, or possibly won the victory he expected, fate took him from the lines and gave the command to others. While his men were dying and being cut to pieces by the enemy, he lay sick in bed at the home of John Inglis at Sailor's Snug Harbor, Manhattan. Taken ill on August 14th, he was still able to attend to the most pressing duties until the sixteenth when he went to bed with a raging fever. The next day, his aide, William Livingston, reported to Washington that he had a very bad night and was critically ill. The following day, Major Blodget could report that he had improved a little. Apparently the crisis had passed leaving the General still feverish and very weak. It was at this time that he was moved to New York where his brother Christopher, who chanced to be in New York on business, nursed him back to health. Two weeks later when his defeated troops arrived in New York, he still had no appetite and could scarcely sit up for an hour.

With Greene sick, Washington put Long Island under the command of the unlucky Major General John Sullivan, just returned without laurels from Canada where Sir Guy Carleton had pushed his smallpox-ridden army back to Ticonderoga.*
No improvement was made a few days later when the command passed to Israel Putnam, next in rank to the commander in chief of officers with the main army. "The brave old Man," Reed noted, "was very happy to get over to Long Island to face the enemy."

The mistakes of the Americans on Long Island, the first cam-

---

* Sullivan was in command of the northern army for but a short time upon the death of General Thomas. Gates was appointed to head the northern department in May but Congress made his command very ambiguous by deciding that Schuyler was in command in the Albany area. Late in the season, Carleton was stopped by Benedict Arnold and forced to retire to Canada.

paign in which a knowledge of strategy was required, were so glaring as to seem almost incredible. By the time of the battle, Washington had increased his strength on Long Island to nearly 9,000, one third of his entire army. Putnam thereupon detached about 4,000 under Stirling and Sullivan and sent them forward to guard the roads and passes leading to the Brooklyn fortifications. Thus the Americans established an outer line along a ridge three or four miles long and heavily wooded in places. As the troops were concentrated generally at roads and passes, there were dangerous gaps where few or none were stationed. Worst of all, Sullivan unaccountably left unguarded the Jamaica Pass on the road to Bedford and directly to the rear of the outer line.

Washington and his staff were not expecting Howe to throw his full weight against Long Island. Howe fostered this belief by setting rumors afloat that he was planning to attack New York and Long Island simultaneously. As it turned out, Howe's plans worked so well he had practically his entire army closing in on Sullivan and Stirling before the Americans realized what was happening. Indeed, right up until the enemy pounced upon them, the Americans were confident and fully expecting to slaughter the enemy as at Bunker Hill. Even Reed, who a fortnight before feared all was lost, was optimistic. The enemy, he told his wife, would surely suffer tremendous casualties if they attacked the entrenched Americans.[31] Up until the time when the portly General James Grant threw his 7,000 Regulars, supported by 2,000 Marines, against Stirling's 1,500 men, the redoubtable Stirling answered Grant's boast that he could march 5,000 of the King's troops from one end of America to the other by declaring he would soon find he could not get beyond yonder Mill Pond.

Without opposition Howe landed his army on the shores of Long Island near the village of Gravesend under cover of the guns of warships. The Americans realized they could not prevent a landing on a long coastline any point of which could be brought under the fire of naval guns. Some of Howe's officers had advised him not to do this but to sail into the East River and land at Kip's Bay half way up Manhattan and attempt to trap the whole rebel army in one grand sweep. Rejecting this in favor of General Clinton's plan for throwing a vastly superior force

against the American detachment on Long Island, Howe had
decided to play a more cautious game.[32] Led by Tories, Howe
started his march for the Jamaica Pass with 10,000 troops after
darkness had settled over the land on the evening of August
26th. The veteran James Grant with 5,000 more set out a little
later up the Narrows road straight for Stirling's line while Von
Heister with the Hessians took the Flatbush road on which Sullivan's men were concentrated. Early in the morning Grant encountered stubborn resistance from outlying parties of Stirling's
force which soon would be outnumbered five to one.

About eight in the morning, bright, clear, and warm, Colonel
Samuel Miles, stationed on Sullivan's left, started for the Jamaica
Pass with his Pennsylvania riflemen, having become convinced
that Howe was planning to encircle the army by that route. He
had moved about two miles when suddenly he found himself
surrounded by the enemy. In a matter of minutes Miles and half
his men were prisoners. The others, fleeing through the woods
and headed for the fortifications, were the first to arrive and
give Putnam word of what was happening. Though there was
still time to warn Stirling and perhaps even to get most of Sullivan's men out of the trap, Putnam sent no messages to his commanders in the field.

Reaching Bedford behind Sullivan's lines, at nine o'clock Howe
fired his signal guns for the attack from all sides. Sullivan heard
the shots, as did Stirling, but it was too late. Within a matter
of minutes Sullivan's troops were caught between the British
on one side and Von Heister's Hessians on the other. The latter
paraded up to the Americans with colors flying and without firing
a shot, drove at their victims with the bayonet. Many tried
vainly to surrender but the fierce-looking Hessians who had
boasted that the rebel army would evaporate after their terror
was felt, gave no quarter. The Hessians had been told by their
officers that the Americans were savages who tortured their
prisoners without mercy. Fleeing in any direction which seemed
to offer an escape, some of the men reached the Brooklyn lines.
However, Sullivan and hundreds of others who were lucky
enough to escape the Hessians were captured by the British.

By eleven o'clock only Stirling's two regiments of Delaware
and Maryland men, now virtually surrounded, remained in the

field. Grant had waited after the signal guns for ammunition to come up and the Marines to arrive before driving at Stirling. Why the latter did not take this opportunity to get across the Gowanus marsh to the safety of the Brooklyn lines is hardly explainable. Nonetheless, when the attack came, seldom has a handful of men stood so valiantly against a deluge as did Stirling and his troops that day. Realizing too late that his entire force must soon be cut to pieces, Stirling kept 250 Marylanders under Mordecai Gist and sent the remaining 700 across the marsh toward the forts. Many of these drowned in swimming Gowanus Creek or were hit by the bullets the enemy sprayed upon the fleeing men.

While Grant's troops were shooting at the unfortunate men floundering in the swamp, Stirling led his valiant corps straight against a detachment under Cornwallis advancing on his left. If he could not cut a path through the enemy's ranks for an escape, he could at least prevent the men crossing the swamp from coming under the fire of Cornwallis' men. Six times Stirling's tiny force was driven back by musket fire and grapeshot, each time only to fly back at the enemy. Stirling, though fifty, was still a powerful man. With saber in hand he "fought like a wolf," related Gist. Finally, after the last charge, the heroic band was thrown into confusion and scattered. Soon the survivors, including Stirling, were captured, save Major Gist and nine others who made good their escape through the swamp to the Brooklyn lines.

Washington, who had arrived from New York and was watching the heroic struggle of the Marylanders through his field glass, is said to have exclaimed, "Good God, What brave fellows I must this day lose!" To the right he saw the others making their way through the swamp and Gowanus Creek where they were obliged to swim in deep water with the enemy's cannon and musket fire playing incessantly upon them. In the end, most of them were saved by a regiment of New Englanders who left the fort and with two cannon beat back the British long enough for their comrades to get away. Thus ended the battle of Long Island, and so too ended the illusion that the enemy was no match for Americans. Against the British loss of less than 400, the Americans lost over 1,000 in killed, wounded, or captured.[33]

In the last analysis, Washington, rather than Putnam, was to blame for the defeat on Long Island. Washington was on the spot the day before the battle and should have changed the disposition of the men on the outer lines or brought them all inside the fortifications. In the first place, he should not have put Putnam in charge on Long Island. Alexander Graydon, who was among the captured officers, long afterward summed up the situation. "Even the celebrated General Putnam," he wrote, "riding with a hanger belted across his brawny shoulders, over a waistcoat with sleeves (his summer costume), was deemed much fitter to head a band of sicklemen, or ditchers, than musketeers—he was not what the time required."[34] Looking back upon the scene, one may marvel at the boldness of American generalship which appears the child of inexperience and overconfidence inspired by the success at Bunker Hill.

Finding strength enough to pen a letter to Washington after receiving a report on the battle, Greene wrote, "I have not the vanity to think the event would have been otherwise had I been there, yet I think I could have given the commanding general a good deal of necessary information. Great events, sometimes, depends upon very little causes. . . ." Henry Knox as well as John Adams believed Greene too modest. Had he been there, Knox wrote, "matters would have worn a very different appearance at Present."[35]

CHAPTER FIVE

The Fires Burn Low

The defeat at Long Island was but the beginning of a long succession of defeats and reverses which would end only when the American Army was driven over the Delaware and the British settled down in New Jersey to wait out the winter. Again American generalship, including Greene's, was unimpressive. Though the British strategy was well planned, their moves were too slow to properly take advantage of their enemy's mistakes.

After the defeat of the Americans on the outer lines at Long Island, Howe with difficulty restrained his Grenadiers, flushed with victory, from storming the American fortifications at Brooklyn in a grand effort to annihilate Washington's divisions on Long Island in one day. Had Howe known what confusion and near panic reigned within the American lines, unquestionably he would have given the signal for attack. But remembering the slaughter on that horrible day at Bunker Hill, he ordered his forces to withdraw. Under cover of darkness, he reasoned, in a few days he could erect works parallel to the American lines. From these an assault could be launched in a manner to overpower the rebels with a minimum of losses for his men. This maneuver would also allow Admiral Howe time, he thought, to bring warships into the East River, thus cutting off the only avenue of escape for the Americans.[1]

That the tall, taciturn, good-natured General Howe had no desire to see any more blood spilled than necessary to bring the uprising to a close, was quite apparent. Howe, on numerous occasions, had told friends in England that he would put down the rebellion with a minimum of bloodshed. Although the day's fighting had blasted his hopes of conquering by a mere show of force, he was inclined to think the hardest battle had been fought.

104

It would take another campaign, he thought, to quell the rebellion but for the most part he expected it to be little more than one of parading and maneuvering the British Army. Even after Trenton and the rise of American resistance changed the outlook, Howe refused to countenance ruthlessness as a means of crushing the Revolution and ending the war.

Surprisingly, Washington did not at once realize the mortal danger to his army within the Brooklyn lines. Instead of ordering an immediate evacuation of the island, he called over reinforcements from New York. Mifflin, who arrived with 1,000 men the day after the battle, upon reconnoitering, reported that the American Army must be evacuated at once or face annihilation. Washington called a council of war at which Mifflin, on Washington's suggestion, proposed an immediate withdrawal. The staff, sensing the seriousness of the situation, at once agreed upon evacuation. Fortunately, the weather turned windy and foul and slowed the work on General Howe's parallels and prevented his brother from coming into the East River with his ships. Escape was still possible.

With evacuation determined upon, Washington acted with the utmost dispatch. Behind the entrenchments at Brooklyn were nearly 10,000 troops, the flower of the American Army. If Howe eliminated this army, the rebellion would surely collapse. But under cover of darkness, on the night of August 29th, Washington accomplished what to the British seemed impossible. The whole army with all its baggage, stores, provisions, horses, and cannon were safely on the other side of the river by morning and out of immediate danger. During the early part of the night, northeast winds hindered the stocky Colonel John Glover and his regiment of New England fishermen who manned the boats, but before midnight the wind shifted to the southwest, making the going easy and rapid. Part of the night it rained hard, and after midnight a heavy fog, unusual for that season, settled over the area. Not long after the last American had pushed off from the Brooklyn ferry landing, the fog lifted and the British discovered what had happened. If Washington had displayed no great talents as a strategist in the Long Island campaign, he proved, as he would do many times, that he was a master of the art of stealing a march on the enemy. Any doubts about Washington which may have entered Greene's mind were removed. The retreat was masterful, he declared, worthy of the greatest of generals.

During the first week of September, Greene's strength returned rapidly. On the fifth he resumed his command. His appearance in the field once more gave a measure of reassurance to the whole army, reported William Ellery, a Congressman from Rhode Island.[2]

Two days after Greene resumed his duties, Washington called a council of war at his headquarters at the Mortier house. The principal question demanding a decision was what to do about New York. Congress had gone on record as favoring a defense of the city. Although the army was not bound by this recommendation, Washington and a majority of the staff decided to hold the city for awhile at least. Five thousand troops were to remain while the rest, numbering about 12,000, would move northward and station themselves between Harlem and Kingsbridge. Greene's brigade was among those to occupy the strategic area in the northern part of Manhattan.

Greene was very agitated by the council's decision to hold New York. At the meeting, supported by Reed and Rufus Putnam, he had argued vehemently against it. Scattering the army over the entire length of Manhattan, he said, subjected it to the risk of being beaten by detachments. The army, he insisted, should be concentrated in the neighborhood of Kingsbridge on both sides of the Harlem River. From this point, if threatened by encirclement, it could retire to the hills of Westchester. In private, Greene reminded Washington that he had admitted earlier that New York was untenable if the British took Long Island. Now that they held Long Island and their warships commanded the East River, the thought of what could happen made him shudder. "Part of the army already has met with a defeat, the country is struck with a panick, any capital loss at this time may ruin the cause," he told Washington.[3]

For some time American leaders had debated whether or not New York should be destroyed if evacuated. Washington posed the question to Congress in a letter of September 2nd: "If we should be obliged to abandon the town, ought it to stand as winter quarters for the enemy?" After discussing the matter at length, Congress, in consideration of the patriots of New York, voted against destroying the city.

Greene tried to convince Washington that the city should be burned before it fell into the hands of the enemy. Citing history, he wrote, "Remember the King of France, when Charles the Fifth, Emperor of Germany, invaded his kingdom, he laid whole provinces waste, and by that policy he starved and ruined Charles' army, and defeated him without fighting a battle." Furthermore, he argued, two-thirds of the property of the city and suburbs belonged to Loyalists, so why should Washington put himself in jeopardy by attempting to defend it. Greene's persuasiveness won Washington over to his way of thinking but with Congress opposed he could not order the destruction of New York.[4]

Greene was not the only one who believed New York should be destroyed. Joseph Reed, Washington's adjutant general since June, had advocated burning the city when the British first arrived in July. Now he feared the whole army would be trapped on Manhattan. Reed, indeed, was seized by a bad case of the jitters. Ever since the Battle of Long Island, he had gone to bed, he confessed, with "the utmost anxious Fears for the Fate of tomorrow." Greene, as usual, remained calm. "Don't be frightened," he told Governor Cooke, "our cause is not yet in a desperate state."[5] But Reed's confidence in Washington was shaken. In another six weeks, after nothing but retreat and defeat for the Americans, he was quite prepared to trade Washington for Charles Lee whom he imagined the only man, if anyone, who could save America.

For the first time, criticism of Washington began to appear in the army itself. "We have alarm upon alarm—Orders now issued, & the next moment reversed. Wd to heaven Genl. Lee were here is the Language of Officers and men," wrote Colonel John Haslet, a man who had stood unflinchingly with Stirling against the enemy horde at Long Island.[6] William Duer, a member of Congress, though not so critical as Haslet, hoped Lee would soon arrive from the South. Washington was a great general, he said, but he needed the help of his best officers at this time. Regardless of what others thought, Greene's confidence in Washington remained unshaken. Better than most Americans, he understood the enormous handicaps and difficulties under which Washington labored.

After the disaster at Long Island, Greene never let a chance go by to criticize Congress's reliance upon militia. "The policy of Congress," he declared, "has been the most absurd and ridiculous imaginable—pouring in militia men who come and go every month." If this practice were continued, he could not see how Washington would ever have an army capable of meeting the enemy on anywhere near equal terms. The militia, he said, was not only unreliable (hundreds were deserting every day) but they were in the long run more expensive than regulars. Lee agreed. Congress, he declared, needed military advisors—its resolves were "absurd, ridiculous, and ruinous." "*Inter nos*," he confided to Gates, "the Congress seem to stumble every step. I do not mean one or two of the Cattle, but the whole Stable."[7]

But each day the American troops remained in New York, made Greene the more apprehensive. Finally he could bear the suspense no longer. Breaking with army custom, he presented Washington with a petition for reconsideration of the council's decision to hold New York, signed by himself and six brigadier generals. Feeling that Greene was right, Washington called a staff meeting at General McDougall's headquarters on September 12th. This time Greene won. It was decided that the army would evacuate New York immediately and concentrate itself in the vicinity of Kingsbridge. Washington thereupon moved his headquarters to Morrisania, the country home of Roger Morris on Harlem Heights.

While collecting provisions and making other necessary preparations, General Howe let two weeks go by after Washington's evacuation of Long Island before he made his second move against the American Army. It came, nonetheless, before all the American troops were out of New York and nearly succeeded in trapping a division in lower Manhattan. Led by General Clinton, two divisions of the enemy landed on September 15th, between Kip's and Turtle bays on the East River. Under cover of heavy fire from five warships, Clinton's men met little opposition. In a few minutes his troops, eager for battle, were marching upon the thin line of Connecticut militia holding a ridge above the shore.

At the sight of the enemy advancing upon them, the militia took fright and fled without firing a shot. Neither did General Parson's Continentals, supported by Fellow's Massachusetts Militia, do any better. Unnerved by the panic of the fleeing men, they too, in a moment, turned and joined the flight. Though chased by no more than fifty British in the vanguard of the oncoming divisions, nothing could stop the stampede once it had started.

Washington, Putnam, and Mifflin, having heard the firing at headquarters, arrived at the scene of action to meet the troops fleeing before the enemy. Washington himself struck at the terrified men with his riding whip but to no avail. Left alone for a moment, he would have been taken by the enemy had not two of his aides appeared in time to grab his horse's reins and gallop away to safety. So vexed was the commander in chief "at the infamous conduct of the Troops, that he sought Death rather than life," Greene declared. "Are these the men with which I am to defend America?" Washington exclaimed in his anguish.[8]

While the Americans were fleeing from Clinton's Regulars and taking refuge behind the ranks of Glover's Continentals who had followed Washington, the last of the troops from New York neared the path of the victorious redcoats. They had been warned by Putnam who had galloped all the way to the city from Kip's Bay. By some accounts, the hard-pressed division, which included Knox's invaluable artillery, was saved by the alertness and patriotism of Mrs. Robert Murray, mother of Greene's boyhood friend, Lindley Murray. At her home, she leisurely served cake and wine, the story goes, to Howe, Clinton, Governor Tryon, and other officers, while the British Army waited for orders and the 3,500 Americans, guided by Aaron Burr, slipped by to the safety of Harlem Heights. Perhaps, however, the truth is that the Americans were saved by Clinton's waiting for the landing of his second division before pushing on. The American division, at any rate, had been almost miraculously saved. Even more fortunate for Washington, perhaps, was Howe's decision not to take Clinton's advice to land above Kingsbridge to bottle up the whole American Army on Manhattan. In any event, Greene was glad the army was out of danger for the time being. His only lament was that the troops had been compelled to leave a prodigious amount of baggage and stores behind in New York.

The day after the landing at Kip's Bay, Howe occupied New York. Crowds of joyous Loyalists turned out to cheer and view their liberators as the columns of redcoats marched into the city to the tune of fife and drum. But it was not long before many of the friends of Great Britain began to have cause for doubt. The Hessians, especially, roamed the city, plundering Whig and Tory alike. "They have no idea of the distinction between Whig & Tory," observed Ebenezer Hazard. Neither did they care to learn. When they got into New Jersey, their frightfulness and wholesale vandalism turned many a wavering soul to the patriotic cause.

On the day the British occupied New York, the American Army retrieved some of its honor so miserably sacrificed the day before. On Harlem Heights, a skirmish, starting in the morning, grew into a battle which verged on becoming a general engagement. This time, though, the Americans, part of whom were riflemen (and some those who had run so fast the day before), advanced steadily upon the enemy, pushing them from one position to another.

At the start, the British had sounded fox horns as an insult to the Americans whom they expected would again break and run. "I never felt such a sensation before," wrote Reed. "It seemed to crown our disgrace." Among the enemy were companies of Hessian Jaegers armed with a short, rifled gun used in Germany to hunt boars and thought to be superior to the American rifles. But they were not, as was soon disclosed. At the sight of the Hessians running for cover as the Virginia riflemen got their range, the Americans became exuberant.

Greene, though not in command, soon appeared with Putnam and Reed to furnish an example and give encouragement to the men in the field. This was Greene's first battle at close range, and the sight of the Americans pushing the veterans of European wars from one field to another filled him with pride and satisfaction. On went the Americans but after they had passed the Hollow Way and pushed the enemy up the opposite ridge, Washington called them back. British reserves were approaching and he did not deem it advisable to risk a general engagement.

The terrain over which the men fought that day was ideal for the Americans, being rough, rocky, and wooded. Much of the shooting was at long range but as the riflemen took the major role in the fighting, the British casualties were more than 100, a figure well above the losses suffered by the Americans. An incalculable loss to Washington, however, was the death of the gallant officer, Lieutenant Colonel Thomas Knowlton, a hero of Bunker Hill. Another was the death of Major Andrew Leitch, the brave leader of the Virginia riflemen. Harlem Heights had a magical effect on the drooping spirits of Washington's army. Wrote Reed, "The men have recovered their spirits and feel a confidence which before they had quite lost."[9]

The day following the Battle of Harlem Heights, Washington put Greene in charge of the forces guarding New Jersey. Brigadier General Hugh Mercer, a physician who had served valiantly with Bonnie Prince Charlie at Culloden as well as in the French and Indian War, was retained as second in command in New Jersey. Mercer with his four or five thousand New Jersey, Pennsylvania, and Maryland militia known as the Flying Camp guarded the area near Elizabethtown opposite the British on Staten Island, while Greene made Fort Constitution (soon to be renamed Fort Lee) his headquarters so as to be as near Washington's army as possible. From Fort Constitution, high on the New Jersey palisades and directly opposite Fort Washington, Greene could send reinforcements to Washington or help evacuate the army to New Jersey, if necessary.

Only a few days after Greene took command in New Jersey, the British seized Paulus Hook, a promontory on the Jersey shore opposite New York. With the British navy in control of New York Bay there was nothing Greene or Mercer could do but stand by while the enemy fortified the point. Paulus Hook became an important base for enemy operations against American positions in New Jersey throughout the war.

Greene's assignment to the New Jersey post was proof again of Washington's confidence in the Rhode Islander's military ability. New Jersey was of paramount importance as the land bridge by which the British could march upon Philadelphia. "Greene," wrote Washington's aide Tench Tilghman, "is beyond doubt, a first-rate military genius, and one in whose opinions the General places the utmost confidence." William Duer, to whom the letter was written, answered: "I am much mistaken if he is not possest of the Heaven born Genius which is necessary to constitute a great General."[10]

In Philadelphia, the Continental Congress had suffered a severe shock by the defeat of American arms at Long Island. Indeed, Congress was shocked into adopting some of the measures Greene had been urging since the beginning of the war. One of these was the voting of bounties in money and land for enlistment for the duration of the war. Also, Congress, following the recommendation of Washington and his staff, ordered a substantial increase in the size of the Continental Army.

Greene was exuberant when he heard of the action of Congress. He feared only that the regiments to be raised might be poorly officered unless great care was taken. "For God's sake," he warned Governor Cooke, "let us have good officers from Rhode Island, if you wish to preserve its reputation. We want nothing but good officers to constitute as good an army as ever marched into the field,—our men are infinitely better than the officers." A week later he again urged Cooke to be selective in his appointments. "I don't wish to see one officer in the army, but such as has a regard for their reputation, who feels a sentiment of honor and is ambitious of distinguishing himself. Such will answer the Public Expectation and be an honor to the State that sent him," he concluded.[11]

After waiting a month following the battle of Harlem Heights, Howe landed an advanced division of 4,000 men at Throg's Point in Westchester at the western end of Long Island Sound. Another attempt to encircle Washington's army had begun. At this moment, Greene, who had been occupied reorganizing the hospital service and strengthening the defenses on the New Jersey shore, was contemplating a raid on Staten Island. Believing that the enemy's move against Washington had drained the Staten Island post, Greene and Mercer crossed the Arthur Kill with a sizable force on October 15th. But the British position on Staten Island was too strong to be forced and after taking a few prisoners, the Americans returned to Elizabethtown.

When Howe's forces landed at Throg's Point, Washington still had his army spread out from Harlem Heights to Kingsbridge. A council of war was called at which Stirling and Sullivan, both of whom had been recently exchanged, attended. Surprisingly, some of Washington's officers still thought the army should remain on Manhattan. General Lee, just arrived from South Carolina, insisted that to stay was courting disaster. Lee was also in favor of abandoning Fort Washington whose value was open to question since British warships had run up the river past her guns. The council, though agreeing that the army should move toward White Plains, turned down his suggestion on Fort Washington.

Although Greene was not present at the meeting, everyone knew he was much opposed to evacuating Fort Washington which if properly defended was thought to be almost impregnable. Fort Washington in American hands, he maintained, would require Howe to keep a strong detachment on Manhattan, thus weakening the force of his operations elsewhere. In this Greene was right. Howe left 5,000 men at Harlem to keep watch on Fort Washington while he went on with the rest toward White Plains.

Six days were gained by Washington by the inability of Howe's army to get across a causeway connecting Throg's Point with the mainland. After failing to dislodge American batteries and riflemen blocking his path, Howe embarked his army and went up to Pell's Neck where he succeeded in gaining the mainland. There he met John Glover's brigade which by skillful skirmishing held him back for several days. Finally Howe got into the open and marched toward New Rochelle and White Plains to the north.

During the march to White Plains, Washington's army had so few horses that many of the wagons and cannon had to be pulled by hand. Army nerves were again jittery. Reed declared that if the British made a vigorous, concerted push, he dispaired to think of the consequences. He felt a little relieved by the thought that his estate was too small for the British to make an example of him should the Revolution collapse. He fell to worrying, though, about the possibility of being killed and leaving a widow and children. "When I look around me, I see none but single or childless Persons, & most of them those of such Fortunes that their loss would only be lamented," he wrote his wife. He noted also that whenever a battle appeared imminent many officers, especially those with the New Jersey Militia, wandered away though full of fight when the enemy was far off. This dampened the spirit of those who remained, he declared.[12]

While Washington's army was retiring into Westchester, Greene crossed the Hudson on the evening of the 19th for another conference with Washington. He found the commander in chief still at Morrisania. Most of all, Washington was disturbed by shortages of supplies, especially cartridges. Greene left with the promise that he would do all in his power to get ammunition to the army. Back at Fort Lee, he sent orders for expediting the shipment of cartridges from Philadelphia and other places. Soon he had enough delivered to the army to relieve the shortage and more followed. After this he turned to building a line of magazines through New Jersey in case Howe should cross the Hudson and head for Philadelphia. After studying his maps, he decided to have the supplies collected at Equannock, Springfield, Princeton, and Trenton. Soon at these points were collected the stores which would aid Washington in making his famous retreat to the Delaware.

Having lost his opportunity of trapping the Americans below Kingsbridge, Howe continued to advance slowly against Washington's army at White Plains. Lee's division, the last to reach White Plains, could have been charged upon by Howe, but he held back although he could easily have taken Lee's stores and artillery.

The Battle of White Plains, by no means a general engagement, centered for the most part at Chatterton Hill, a position in advance of the main American line. Before the day (October 26th) closed, the British, with the Hessians doing most of the fighting, pushed the Americans off the wooded hill, but their retreat was orderly and Howe cautiously refrained from following or attempting to draw on a general battle. The next day it rained. On the following morning, Howe discovered that Washington had withdrawn to stronger ground at North Castle, a short distance away. Finding it inadvisable to risk an attack, Howe turned about and headed for Dobb's Ferry and Kingsbridge.

With the pressure off, Washington turned his attention to the menacing problems of supplies, provisions, and army morale. To a Connecticut chaplain, the troops, many of whom were mere boys, were "worried in a manner to death" and "treated with great hardship and fatigue."[13] Greene tried to relieve the suffering by doing all he could to hurry supplies from Philadelphia. Hundreds of soldiers, he knew, were getting sick from want of warm clothing, blankets, and enough food. Many were deserting. Although the situation was not yet critical, it was fast assuming alarming proportions.

That General Howe (Sir William Howe since his victory at Long Island) would probably attempt to take Fort Washington before crossing into New Jersey was quite evident when Howe presently threw his forces against Fort Independence and forced the surrender of this fortified hill overlooking Kingsbridge. Notwithstanding the loss of Fort Independence, Washington at first showed no signs of being concerned for the safety of the rockbound Fort Washington. The immediate problem, as he saw it, was whether or not the outer lines around Mount Washington should be defended or just the area comprising the fort.

On October 30th, Greene received a message from Washington which shed little light on the Fort Washington question. "It depends upon so many circumstances," Washington wrote, "that it is impossible to determine the Point." Greene, he concluded would have to decide by developments whether or not to send reinforcements to Fort Washington. The next day Greene endeavored to get more definite instructions. If the perimeter of Mount Washington, a distance of seven or eight miles, was to be held, more troops would be needed, he pointed out. If only the fort which covered about four acres was to be defended, there were already too many men there, he thought. Greene informed Washington that he was sending another regiment to Colonel Magaw, the commander at Fort Washington, but that he would wait until he heard from Washington before sending more.

Leaving Lee with some 7,000 troops at North Castle and Heath with 4,000 more at Peekskill to guard the Highlands and the approaches to New England, Washington prepared to cross the Hudson with 2,000 of his best troops. He knew that dividing the army in this way was dangerous, but there was no alternative.

Howe was expected to launch an invasion of New Jersey at any time and he must be ready to oppose him.

As the British were in control of the Hudson shore as far north as Dobb's Ferry, Washington was compelled to cross at Peekskill, twenty miles to the north. Leaving White Plains on November 10th, his troops arrived at Peekskill the next day. By the 14th, they had crossed the river, marched to Hackensack, and pitched camp on ground about six miles from Fort Lee. Washington's progress upon reaching New Jersey had been facilitated by Greene who had provisions and fodder at stages along his line of march.

With the threat to New Jersey growing more imminent daily, Greene hurried preparations for meeting the crisis. Following Washington's orders, he had already warned people living in the exposed areas to move their livestock, grain, hay, and valuables back into the country. A few days later he ordered army details to burn all supplies that still remained in the region. Loud were the protests from the farmers, but there was no alternative. Already the enemy was venturing out from Staten Island into Newark Bay to get hay along the shore for their half-starved horses. At the passes in the Orange and Watchung Mountains, Greene prudently set militia to work on fortifications in case Washington found it necessary to retreat into the hills of Morris County to escape encirclement.[14]

Though the situation had grown tense and nerves were taut, most of the officers with Greene, following the example of their commander, remained calm. Greene told his wife how his light-hearted secretary, Major Blodget, kept everyone laughing by his joking and story telling. One of Greene's aides was a more serious minded man who like Greene had been reared a Quaker. This was Thomas Paine who would soon undertake the writing of his immortal essay, *The Crisis*. Another was William Livingston, a diligent youth and son of New Jersey's bellicose and witty war governor. John Clark, a young officer from Lancaster, Pennsylvania, who later became one of Washington's more valuable intelligence agents, was also an aide. Devoted to Greene, he was forever looking for ways to please his chief. On November 8th, he sent Greene a note saying he had a man out fishing in a good place for pike. But if he did not get fish for Greene's table, he hoped the general would not forget to procure some food for thought for his official family by ordering Beccaria's *Crime and Punishment* and Sterne's *Sentimental Journey*.[15]

Before leaving White Plains, Washington had written Greene that he was of the opinion Howe would send a detachment to invest Fort Washington while he crossed into New Jersey with his main force. Again he gave Greene no indication that he thought the fort should be abandoned. On the contrary, he instructed him to give Colonel Magaw all the help required to defend himself. The next day, however, Washington wrote that he had just received word that British warships had again run past the guns of forts Washington and Lee, demonstrating conclusively that American cannon could not control the Hudson. Washington expressed a reluctance to risk the loss of the men and stores on Mount Washington any longer. Still, he did not order the evacuation of the post. Greene was "on the spot," he said, and could best judge what should be done. The only positive order he gave was in directing the removal of surplus stores from Fort Lee to places of safety in the New Jersey backcountry.[16]

The day before Greene received the letter from Washington he had written him strongly advising the defense of Fort Washington to the last. When Washington's letter recommending the abandonment of the fort arrived, he wrote again dwelling at length upon his reasons for holding it. Colonel Magaw, he said, was confident he could hold Fort Washington indefinitely. In any event, Greene felt certain they could evacuate the fort at any time and ferry the men safely to New Jersey. Giving up Mount Washington, he argued, would afford the enemy free and uninterrupted communication between New York and Kingsbridge. On the other hand, a strong American garrison on Manhattan, together with the forces under Lee and Heath to the northward, would oblige Howe to leave a large portion of his army in New York, thus weakening any invasion of New Jersey.[17] Greene was certain Sir William intended to attack Mount Washington in a matter of days. But he was confident right until the day the blow fell that Magaw would prove more than a match for him. Greene, in truth, was banking on another slaughter like the memorable one at Bunker Hill. So far, at least, he had great confidence in the American soldier when fighting from behind breastworks.[18]

On November 14th, two days before the fateful attack on Fort Washington, Washington and Reed rode over to Fort Lee from Hackensack to have a talk with Greene. Finding both Greene and Putnam as confident as ever that Fort Washington could defend itself, Washington hesitated to interfere with their plans. Reed, however, was greatly agitated. Washington, he declared, should order the fort evacuated at once. He had no heart for risking the lives of 2,000 men, a great many of whom were fellow Pennsylvanians.

Washington pondered the question but he could not make up his mind. Greene's reasoning seemed good—yet he could not dismiss the thought that it was very risky. Washington's failure to order the post evacuated put the responsibility squarely upon his own shoulders. He was "on the spot" and directly in charge of all operations. "His Excellency, General Washington," wrote Greene, "has been with me several days. The evacuation of Fort Washington was under consideration but finally nothing concluded on." Moreover, not only did Washington not order the evacuation of the fort but he allowed Greene to send last minute reinforcements for the beleaguered garrison.[19]

With the better part of his army drawn up in the vicinity of Mount Washington and with all the outlying positions including Fort Independence in his possession, Howe was ready to strike. Looking back on the event, historians have sometimes wondered how the American officers could have put so much faith in the fort. Anyone, however, who has viewed the ground will be struck by its Gibralter-like natural bastions of steep cliffs and dizzy heights. From the top Greene was certain the Americans could beat off twice their numbers if necessary. But what if Howe should send three or four times the number on Mount Washington as he did? Greene's answer was simple. In the night the garrison could easily be rescued by boats from the New Jersey shore.

Greene's influence over Washington and the other generals again illustrates the great prestige he had acquired as a general. As yet he had not won a battle nor directed even a minor engagement. Nevertheless, his words commanded the utmost attention. When other officers seemed hopelessly confused and at a loss to know what to do, Greene would have a solution to the problem. His knowledge of military science, his quickness in sizing up a situation, the logic of his conclusions, and his self-assurance, all combined to give him a reputation of being Washington's most astute general. Already it was whispered, Congress would make him commander in chief should anything happen to Washington.

On November 15th, General Howe demanded the surrender of Fort Washington. If Colonel Magaw refused, his garrison, according to the rules of war, could be put to the sword. Magaw at once notified Greene. In answer Greene ordered Magaw to defend Mount Washington as planned. Accordingly, Magaw answered Sir William with the brave words: "Give me leave to assure his Excellency that actuated by the most glorious cause that mankind ever fought in, I am determined to defend this post to the last extremity."[20]

Shortly after receiving Magaw's message, Greene and Israel Putnam went over to Fort Washington for a last minute inspection. Washington, too, when he heard the news, set out from Hackensack for the fort. It was late in the day by the time Washington to got Fort Lee and into a skiff bound for Fort Washington. When part way over he met Greene and Putnam coming back. After being assured that all was well at the fort, all three returned to Fort Lee.

Early in the morning, Washington, Greene, Putnam, and Mercer crossed the river again to Fort Washington. They arrived just in time to hear the battle open on the outer lines as Howe threw 10,000 troops, the flower of his army, against the American stronghold. Greene and Putnam were buoyant and confident. Washington, however, was apprehensive. Reed was worried and fearful of the outcome.

Up at North Castle, General Lee had for days been wondering why Washington had not evacuated Fort Washington. Why should he run the risk of losing at one stroke hundreds of some of the best men in the American Army, Lee asked on the day the fort fell. Lee guessed that Howe would throw practically his entire force against the stronghold to make its capture certain and perhaps less costly. The capture of Fort Washington, Lee concluded, would be well-nigh ruinous to the American cause. It might well be the beginning of the complete dissolution of the American Army.[21]

To have properly manned the outer lines of Mount Washington would have taken at least 10,000 men. The inner works, resting on top of the heights, consisted of open earthworks, a weakness not to be underestimated. Another serious weakness lay in the absence of any water supply, a factor which alone would have doomed the post within a few days of siege. Moreover, Howe, through a deserter, knew all he needed to about the fort—its strength and its weaknesses and how best to assail it.[22]

Magaw decided to defend the outerworks in the hope that the enemy would be defeated there or sufficiently weakened for a final blow when he reached the fort. He no doubt did the right thing. The big mistake, it seems, had already been made by Rufus Putnam, the engineer, in not shortening the line by confining it to the crest of the heights a few hundred yards from the fort. Three thousand men might have held this line or inflicted a decisive blow before retreating to the inner works.[23]

The morning was bright and clear as Sir William opened his attack on Mount Washington from three directions. On the south, General Perry marched up from Harlem Plains against lines held by Lieutenant Colonel Lambert Cadwalader and his Pennsylvania militia. To the eastward, General Matthews, supported by columns under Cornwallis, landed at the foot of Laurel Hill and advanced on Colonel Baxter. On the northeast where the fighting was fiercest, the Hessians under General Wilhelm von Knyphausen, advancing from Kingsbridge, threw themselves against the steep, thickly wooded slopes held by Lieutenant Colonel Moses Rawlings and his Maryland and Pennsylvania riflemen.

For an hour or more Rawling's men held off the Hessians who fought with great bravery. Finally, after many of the rifles became fouled, the Hessians succeeded in driving Rawling's men from their positions at bayonet point. Having paid dearly for their victory, the Hessians, when they got to the fort, wanted to assault it to get at the hated riflemen with their bayonets. But

Howe held back to await an answer to his final offer for the garrison to surrender.

While the battle on the outer lines was developing, the American generals waited anxiously for reports on its progress. During the morning several hundred more troops were brought over from New Jersey but they arrived too late to be of any help. Before long it became apparent that Washington and his staff must either leave or run a great risk of falling into the hands of the enemy. Greene and the other generals expressed their desire to stay for the sake of morale if nothing more. But Washington would not have it. He could not afford to lose them and their capture might very well throw the country into panic and lead to a speedy collapse of the war.[24]

It has been said that Greene at least should have stayed with the doomed garrison on Mount Washington. It was not logical, it has been argued, to leave so important a post in charge of an officer of rank no higher than a colonel. On Greene, it is true, rightfully rested the responsibility of defending the fort. However, the decision of staying or not was with Washington. Greene cannot be censured for following the orders of the commander in chief.

Although closely pursued, most of the Americans from the outer lines succeeded in crowding into the fortified area on Mount Washington. Many came running pellmell into the small enclosure without guns and virtually in a state of panic. Against a scene of rising confusion and insubordination, Magaw tried vainly to quiet the men and make them man the lines. Howe was unaware of conditions inside and to him Fort Washington had too much the appearance of another Bunker Hill to storm it before his cannon were ready. He, therefore, paused and opened negotiations with Magaw while his troops set up batteries and prepared to rush their enemy.

Upon receiving Howe's demand to surrender, Magaw sent a messenger to Washington asking for instructions. Soon after, conditions in the fort deteriorated to such an extent that resistance seemed useless. He thereupon sent Howe word that he would negotiate a surrender. While this was going on, a messenger got through from Washington with a note asking Magaw to hold out until nightfall when rescue would be attempted from New Jersey. Magaw, however, felt he could not in honor break off negotiations after having agreed to surrender. A few minutes later the terms were completed.

General Howe lost about 500 men, killed and wounded, in taking Fort Washington. The American casualties were much lighter, amounting to no more than 150. But the loss of the entire garrison of 2,800, some of them among the best troops in the American Army, was staggering. Many excellent officers were captured, among them Otho H. Williams, one day to become Greene's field commander in the South. Besides the men and officers, the British captured a prodigious quantity of military stores and more than forty cannon.

The fall of Fort Washington brought the total of Americans killed, wounded, or captured by General Howe since his arrival at New York to more than 5,000. In addition, desertion and the expiration of terms was lowering the numbers in the ranks by the hundreds. The loss of Fort Washington, followed swiftly by the capture of Fort Lee and the invasion of New Jersey, accelerated the disintegration of the army to such an extent that it soon appeared to be melting away before the eyes of the American generals.

Naturally Greene was mortified. In an agonized letter to his friend, Henry Knox, he poured out his anguish. "I feel mad, vexed, sick, and sorry,—never did I need the consoling voice of a friend more than now. Happy should I be to see you. That is a most terrible event; its consequences are justly to be dreaded. Pray, what is said upon the occasion?"[25]

Greene blamed Colonel Putnam for the catastrophe by not finishing the redoubts which both he and Knox had strongly urged upon him. He also blamed Magaw to some extent for allowing the troops to crowd into the fort. If they had held the ridge, he believed they could have kept the enemy at bay until nightfall. But most of all, Greene blamed the men themselves for panicking. If they had done their duty, he said, the British would have been repulsed with frightful losses. Two years later, he wrote:

There was men enough there to have defended themselves against all the British army, had they not been struck with a panic, but being most of them [referring to the members of the Flying Camp] irregular troops, they lost all their confidence when the danger began to grow pressing, and so fell a prey to their own fears.[26]

That so many of the troops at Fort Washington were irregulars, places no little of the blame at Greene's door. With a good part of the troops of the Flying Camp, why should he have attempted to hold the fort? Alexander Graydon, one of the officers captured by the enemy, maintained to his dying day that Greene would not have exposed 2,800 men on Mount Washington if they had been New Englanders. If Greene did not know better at the time, he never thereafter exhibited any symptom of rashness, Graydon sarcastically observed.[27]

While examining the fortifications on Mount Washington after the surrender, Nicholas Cresswell, a British officer, concluded that with veteran troops the place was impregnable. Ambrose Serle, another British officer, declared that he marveled at the strength of Fort Washington and the extent of the works. Only American cowardice, he thought, had made it possible for Howe to win the stronghold. Their testimony is strong evidence that Greene erred only in placing too much confidence in a garrison consisting of so many raw and inexperienced troops.[28] Though Fort Washington was a grave error and Greene's worst mistake of his entire military career, it had the good effect of adding caution to his list of attributes. Thus the experiences learned in the hard lessons of war, coupled with his military knowledge and natural ability, were changing the Rhode Island ironmaster into the only great strategist produced by the Revolutionary War.

American opinion at the time, however, was not so kind toward Greene. Tench Tilghman told Robert R. Livingston that the Americans fought well but what could they do "against General Howe's whole army, who poured in upon them from every quarter." The fort would have been evacuated, he wrote, had not Washington listened to Greene who was "positive that our forces might at any time be drawn off under the guns of Ft. Lee." Tilghman lamented the bad effects the loss would have upon Europe as well as America. "We were in a fair way of finishing the campaign with credit to ourselves and I think to the disgrace of Mr. Howe, and had the general followed his own opinion, the garrison would have been withdrawn immediately upon the enemy's falling down from Dobb's Ferry. . . ."[29] In a similar vein, Mifflin wrote to Robert Morris: "Had we adhered to the Fabian plan we should have been . . . in the seat of Honour this winter, the enemy would have come off without Honour & Europe would have given us strong proof of her affection before the Spring."[30]

Reed, though usually one of Greene's admirers, joined in the chorus against him. Washington, he told Lee, thought better than to try to hold the fort "but unluckily, Gen'l. Greene's judg't was contrary, this kept the General's mind in a State of Suspense till the Stroke was struck. Oh! General," he exclaimed, "an indecisive Mind is one of the greatest Misfortunes that can befall an Army."[31] Lee answered, "I lament with you that fatal indecision of mind which in war is a much greater disqualification than stupidity or even want of personal courage. . . ."[32] Washington opened this letter by mistake, saw the character of the contents, apologized to Reed, and made no further comment.

General Lee's stock soared in the army and in Congress as Greene's fame crumbled and fell. If Washington had only put Lee in charge of the forts on the Hudson, nearly 3,000 men now captive would have been saved, was heard on every side. In this vein, Reed wrote to Lee a few days after the event:

> I do not mean to flatter nor praise you at the expense of any other, but I confess I do think that it is entirely owing to you that this Army, the Liberties of America, so far as they are dependent on it, are not totally cut off. You have Decision, a Quality often wanting in minds otherwise valuable, I ascribe to this our Escape from York Island, from Kingsbridge, & the Plains, & I have no Doubt had you been here the Garrison at Mount Washington would now have composed Part of this Army.[33]

For awhile, even Washington's confidence in Greene reached an all-time low. On November 19th, Lee sent Washington a letter announcing he had set aside a list of officers named by Greene for the Rhode Island troops in favor of men more deserving. Lee said that Rhode Island men and troops had reacted violently to Greene's recommendations which, according to Lee, favored his townsmen, relatives, and friends. Washington answered that he approved Lee's action. He even apologized for taking Greene's advice. Not knowing the merits of the men, he was compelled, he explained, to rely on Greene, "hoping . . . that he would make an Arrangement acceptable to his Countrymen; However, I am well satisfied with what you have done and must leave it upon that footing."[34]

That Greene's recommendations were not palatable to all of the Rhode Island troops no one would deny. Any list would be that way. It appears, however, that Lee relished the opportunity to make the most out of the dissatisfaction and further to discredit his most promising rival in the eyes of Washington and the country. Greene, to be sure, named townsmen, friends, and relatives. But in a state as small as Rhode Island it was impossible to do otherwise if the best choices were to be made. Many of the men listed had been members of the various volunteer companies of Rhode Island and had already distinguished themselves on the field of battle.

After a cold, rainy night, the morning of November 20th broke fair and clear along the Hudson. Greene was still in bed at his headquarters at Fort Lee when an excited messenger galloped up to report that the British had landed at Closter's Ferry six miles above the fort, had climbed through the break in the palisades to the road above, and were marching rapidly toward the doomed fort. Cornwallis, Greene's future protagonist in the Carolinas, had stolen a march as Greene had thought that the enemy could only attack Fort Lee by way of Nyack or Haverstraw farther to the north.

The British column, numbering 6,000 veterans, was led by a more enterprising man than Sir William Howe. Tall, handsome, and heavy set, at thirty-eight the Earl of Cornwallis, like Howe, had disapproved of Britain's colonial policies in the days before the war. People were attracted to the Earl by his humorous, good-natured expression and his lively wit. Unfortunately, like Greene, he had a noticeable eye injury. Furthermore, the two resembled each other in appearance and personality. Both had a tendency to be impetuous. But Cornwallis never learned to curb this trait as well as his American rival. Nevertheless, Cornwallis was a dangerous and active opponent and in some ways the best of all the British officers in the war.

As Greene listened to the startling news of the enemy's approach, the frightening thought flashed through his mind that Fort Lee was at least five miles from the New Bridge over the Hackensack while the British could reach it by traveling less than three. Unequivocally, there was no time to lose. Down the road in full flight Greene led his troops until they came upon Washington with a group of aides on his way to help rescue the division. Leaving the troops with Washington, Greene hurried back to the fort to round up several hundred stragglers. Most of them were found quite drunk from rum stolen from sutlers. Though many were hiding in the woods and underbrush, Greene managed to get all but a few over the Hackensack by way of the ferry. The troops with Washington got to the bridge before the British who, misled perhaps by their maps, thought the New Bridge was farther south. The last man, however, was barely over the river when the British appeared. At the last moment the Americans chopped down the timbers holding the bridge, leaving the deep waters of the Hackensack between them and their enemy.[35]

Upon arriving at Fort Lee, the British found the breakfast fires burning and a great quantity of baggage and other belongings scattered over the camp. Greene had been moving stores out of the fort for days but a shortage of wagons and teams had retarded the work. Among other things, the British found more than a dozen mortars and cannon, 1,000 barrels of flour, and 300 standing tents with beds, bedding, and blankets—all of which the American Army could ill afford to lose. Still, Greene was right in claiming that the most important supplies had been removed. Wrote Thomas Paine: "Our ammunition, light artillery, and the best part of our stores had been removed, upon the apprehension that Howe would endeavor to penetrate the Jerseys."[36]

Why Washington had allowed 3,000 men to remain at Fort Lee after the loss of Fort Washington may seem difficult to understand. Both Washington and Greene, however, believed the garrison would have time enough to move out if threatened and the men were needed to help dismantle the fort. Their error came near costing them another catastrophe. Whether the American cause could have stood the shock, coming less than a week after the fall of Fort Washington, is problematical. Providing a semblance of an army could have been kept together, one might wonder whether either Washington's or Greene's reputations could have stood another blow at this time. Would not all America have called for Lee as its last remaining hope?

The day following the loss of Fort Lee, Washington abandoned his dangerous position at Hackensack. That night the army camped just west of the Aquackinack Bridge (spelled a variety of ways) over the Passaic after plodding all day through a pelting rain. This was the first step in Washington's retreat to New Brunswick to cover the main highway leading to Philadelphia. Already he had sent Stirling ahead with his brigade to guard the roads leading from Staten Island and to enlist what men he could for the defense of the state. As full of energy and enthusiasm as before his captivity, Stirling had joined the army in time to participate at White Plains after being exchanged for Governor Montford Brown of Florida.

Washington had expected the New Jersey militia to come flocking to join his army now that their state was invaded. But to his disappointment, few had responded in spite of the urgent appeals of Governor William Livingston. Soon Washington dispatched Reed to urge Livingston to use every possible means to gather the militia without delay, but still few appeared. The term of service expired for the Flying Camp December 1st, and whether any could be coaxed to remain longer was questionable. Only a month later the time would be up for a great majority of the Continental troops. How many of these would sign up again no one could tell. No wonder Washington and his staff saw the shades of December, 1775, appearing. Unless some victory could be secured before the end of the year, what hope could there be that a new army could be raised?

Just before leaving Hackensack, Washington called upon General Lee to cross the Hudson as soon as possible and join the main army in New Jersey. If Lee marched rapidly and the New Jersey militia responded, Washington hoped to make a stand at New Brunswick. Washington's message, according to Heath, was sent by Reed, who, finding himself without paper or pen, found a "light-horseman had a rough piece of wrapping paper in his pocket." After writing "Dear General, we are flying before the British, I pray—" his pencil broke. Not having another, he sent the messenger on with a verbal request for Lee to "push and join us."[37]

In a letter following, Washington informed Lee that the public interest, it seemed, required his joining the main army. To expedite Lee's marching, the removal of the stores at North Castle should be left to the brigades of Fellows and Wadsworth as these would soon be going home. But Washington did not command Lee to join him. As in the case of Greene and Fort Washington, he left it to Lee's discretion and judgment after giving his reasons for advising the move. "Unless therefore some new event should occur," wrote Washington, "or some more cogent reason present itself, I would have you move over by the easiest and best Passage."[38]

On November 23rd, Washington reached Newark where his officers found suitable quarters in the houses along Broad Street and the army sought cover from the cold and rain in stables, barns, and what tents were left and worth setting up. Here the army rested and awaited reinforcements for a week but few came. Much of the time Greene was engaged in directing the removal of supplies farther into the interior. He took occasion, too, to view the work on redoubts at the mountain passes which would need defending in case Washington should be compelled to retreat to Morristown.

In a letter of the 24th to Lee, Washington went over his reasons for wanting him to join the main army. He cautioned Lee to circle Cornwallis at Hackensack by a safe distance. It was as plain by this letter as it was in the first that he expected Lee to come at once although the message contained no positive order. Three days later, however, Washington sharply rebuked Lee for not interpreting his messages as a command to march at once. "My former Letters were so full and explicit, as to the Necessity of your Marching, as early as possible, that it is unnecessary to add more on that Head; I confess I expected you would have been sooner in motion."[39]

When General Lee received Washington's call for help, he at first tried to send General Heath with his division. Heath, however, had been ordered by Washington to remain at Peekskill to guard the Highlands and would not budge. Already Lee had lost most of General Benjamin Lincoln's 3,000 Massachusetts militia whose time expired November 17th. It would hardly pay to march John Fellow's brigade whose term expired on the first

of December. In any event, Lee felt he could not start at once
with hundreds of his men without shoes, blankets, and other
necessaries. Furthermore, he thought he had a chance to strike
a blow against Major Benjamin Rogers and his Rangers, a notorious Tory band which was causing patriots in New England
and New York no end of trouble. Also, Lee hesitated to leave the
gateway into Connecticut open to the British who might still
believe conquest of New England the quickest way to end the
Revolution.

Three days after receiving Washington's letter positively ordering him into New Jersey, Lee crossed the Hudson with
reputedly 5,000 troops. So far, at least, he had done nothing more
than exercise his judgment as Washington had advised. With
Washington's army by this time at New Brunswick and Cornwallis already marching against him from Newark, Lee took the
road to Morristown. His troops, to be sure, were as threadbare as
Washington's. "Many of them were so destitute of shoes that
blood left on the rugged frozen ground, in many places, marked
the route they had taken," wrote Heath.

After capturing Fort Lee, Cornwallis was slow in following
up his gains because of shortages of wagons, teams, and forage
which Greene had systematically removed from the area. After
the British reached New Jersey, the weather, which for weeks
had been clear and beautiful, turned cold and rainy. The roads
became almost impassable, especially for Cornwallis who had
much low ground to traverse on his way to Newark. Howe, too,
was slow in getting under way. Not until November 29th, did
he get his troops in motion from Amboy thus allowing Washington time to make good his retreat along the road to New Brunswick. Howe still believed the war could not be ended that year,
and his plans were to push Washington out of New Jersey and
thus secure an ample supply of provisions and forage for the
British Army during the winter.

If Washington divided his army and posted detachments at
places of questionable value, Howe committed the same error.
Before leaving New York to lead the invasion of New Jersey, he
sent Clinton with 6,000 men to Newport which they occupied
without opposition. Greene correctly surmised that Howe would
reap little benefit from holding Newport. New England would

not be frightened into withholding men and supplies raised for the Continental Army by a force as small as Clinton's, he felt. As it turned out, the only service Clinton rendered was in gathering provisions for Howe's troops in New York and New Jersey. For all their military value, Howe could just as well have sent the troops at Newport back to England. On the other hand, if Howe had used Clinton's force in New Jersey, it might have added enough strength to Howe's army to have sealed the fate of Washington and his dwindling army, Greene thought.[40]

Two days after Washington reached New Brunswick, two brigades of the Flying Camp, their time expired, struck out for home. Greene, perhaps more than Washington (though the latter afterwards called the conduct of New Jersey "infamous"), showed his indignation at the lack of patriotism of these men at such a critical hour. It was bad enough to see the Maryland troops go home, but to see the others, all New Jersey men, march off leaving their state to be conquered seemed to him incredible.[41]

Although Washington still had several hundred New Jersey militia under General Matthias Williamson, very few others came in to offer their services. Washington admitted that one could hardly expect many to join from the region already overrun by the enemy, but he could not understand the backwardness of the militia from the rest of New Jersey. However, the panic in New Jersey was spreading to Pennsylvania and threatening to paralyze America's ability to resist much longer. Sensing the seriousness of the situation, Thomas Paine began writing *The Crisis* at Greene's headquarters in Newark. Soon this memorable essay would be circulating throughout America to help revive the country's determination to fight on.

When the British entered New Jersey, hundreds of inhabitants flocked in to accept the King's forgiveness from General Howe and pledge their allegiance to the Crown. New Jersey seemed on the point of once more becoming a Crown province when the movement was thrown into reverse by the plundering and crimes of the invaders and a little later by Washington's victories at Trenton and Princeton.

Vandalism extended in the British army even to some of the officers. General Erskine no less, was said to have had his baggage wagons piled high with household goods and furniture looted from the better homes along the line of march. Women camp followers helped their soldier friends carry off all they could. Worse still, men, women, and children were beaten and molested and some were murdered. General Howe's "ravages in the Jersey's exceeds all description," Greene told Governor Cooke. Many of the inhabitants fled to the hills where some grew sick and died before finding food and shelter. The worst offenders were the Hessians as had been the case in New York. In Europe armies plundered without much restraint so why, they thought, should rebels in America be spared.[42]

On December 1st, after an exhausting march of twenty miles in a soaking rain, the vanguard of Cornwallis reached the banks of the Raritan opposite New Brunswick. In spite of Washington's hopes that he might make a stand there, resistance was useless. Lee had just crossed the Hudson and was still far to the north. After the departure of the two brigades of the Flying Camp, many others deserted. Washington had no more than 4,000 troops with which to face the enemy who when Howe arrived, would outnumber him three to one.

While the cannon of the two armies played upon each other across the Raritan, Washington paraded his troops and marched them down the road toward Princeton. Some of the baggage and many tents had to be burned before leaving the town as the army did not have enough horses and wagons to transport them. It was, declared Greene, "a very pitiful army to trust the liberties of America upon." One British officer observed that "no nation ever saw such a set of taterdemalions."[43]

After fighting their way into New Brunswick against a small detachment left behind by Washington, Cornwallis, obeying orders from Howe, waited for the rest of the army to arrive. The caution displayed by the British was due to a concern over Lee's crossing the Hudson to threaten their left flank and rear.

Leaving Stirling at Princeton with two brigades, Washington arrived at Trenton with the rest of the army on December 2nd. A day or so later, with most of his baggage and stores over the Delaware, and with some reinforcements already arrived from Pennsylvania, Washington sent Greene back to Princeton with a brigade to help Stirling impede the advance of the enemy.

On reaching Princeton, Greene reported that the British were advancing and that Washington should be ready to transfer the army to the west bank of the Delaware on the shortest notice. If a pontoon bridge could not be thrown over the river, Greene advised having at least forty river boats constantly in readiness.

Before Greene had finished writing, an officer rode up to report that the British would reach Princeton by noon. "I shall make the best disposition I can to oppose them," Greene promised as he hurriedly signed off and dispatched the letter to Washington. Soon, however, with the enemy threatening to outflank him, Greene ordered his troops to retire. Not far out of Princeton, he met Washington coming up with the Pioneers, men skilled with the ax, who were directed to fall in behind the troops to cut down trees and bridges in the enemy's path.

The next day, December 8th, Washington brought his army over the Delaware. The Americans were no sooner across the river than the vanguard of the British appeared with Howe in the lead. Charging recklessly down to the banks of the Delaware without regard for the cannon flying across the water from the American batteries, Howe was much put out to find all of Washington's troops beyond his reach.

Howe ordered Cornwallis to scour the river for boats and rafts for crossing—but none could be found. Everything capable of floating had been taken over the river or destroyed by the vigilant Americans. For a time at least, the British Army was stalled. To make sure, however, that the enemy did not find some way of crossing, Washington sent Stirling to watch the crossings for a dozen or more miles up the river. To the southward, the banks were guarded by the rapidly multiplying Pennsylvania militia supported by a frigate and several gondolas in the Delaware. Washington, nevertheless, was far from sanguine as the British might build boats or cross on the ice if the weather turned cold.[44] After the American Army had crossed the Delaware, Greene thought the situation had taken a turn for the better. Although the New Jersey militia "behaves scurvily," the Pennsylvanians, he noted, were turning out in great numbers now that they had recovered from their first fright and bewilderment. Though Washington tended to take a more somber view of

American prospects, he admitted that the turnout to the south-ward was encouraging.[45]

A few days later, Greene had reason to be further encouraged. The efforts of Thomas Mifflin, John Armstrong, and others, to-gether with the attraction of more bounty, was bringing men from all parts of Pennsylvania. By December 20th, Pennsylvania had 3,000 militia in the field. With Lee momentarily expected to arrive, Washington agreed with Greene that something should be done to retrieve some of America's military prestige which had suffered so since the Battle of Long Island.[46]

General Lee arrived with his division at Morristown on December 4th. Behind him, General Gates was coming with the skeleton of seven regiments released from the Northern Department by General Schuyler who was ordered to seek replacements from New England. Heath, too, on Washington's orders had started out with Connecticut and Massachusetts militia. However, when British naval movements aroused fear that Admiral Howe might try to force the Highlands of the North River, Heath was ordered back to Peekskill where he had left militia under Generals George and James Clinton and Alexander McDougall. Cut down by desertion and sickness, Lee's force numbered only 2,700. At Morristown, however, he found 1,000 militia of Morris and adjacent counties led by Colonel Jacob Ford. Already the New Jerseymen, somewhat recovered from their fright, were menacing Howe's lines of communications on the plains below.[47]

In direct contradiction of Washington's orders, Lee wrote the commander in chief on December 8th that he would take the liberty of hanging on the enemy's flank in the hope of finding an opportunity to harass the British as much as possible. That day he rode down to Chatham to supervise the erection of a post from which New Jersey militia could send out raiding parties. While at Chatham, Lee received another urgent message from Washington calling on him to hurry forward and join the main army.[48] But Lee, who considered Washington's situation far from desperate, still hung back. He would "reconquer the Jerseys" single-handed, he told Heath. It was "really in the hands of the enemy before my arrival," he wrote.[49]

Although of the opinion that Lee's march was unnecessarily

slow, Greene saw merit in his strategy. While at Princeton facing Cornwallis's oncoming columns, he had hoped for awhile that Lee might assist by a flanking maneuver. However, Greene did not trust too much to Lee's cooperation. He should be "confined within the limits of some general plan" considering his fondness for acting independently, he told Washington.[50]

After the American Army had crossed the Delaware, Greene agreed with Washington that Lee should join the army without delay as a flanking movement no longer served any useful purpose. Influenced perhaps by Greene, Washington softened the tone of his letters to Lee. "Were it not for the weak and feeble state of the force I have, I should highly approve of your hanging on the Rear of the Enemy and establishing the posts you mention." But, continued Washington, "I cannot but request and entreat you and this, too, by the advice of all the Genl officers with me, to march and join me with all your whole force, with all possible expedition. The utmost exertions that can be made, will not be more than sufficient to save Philadelphia."[51]

If Lee received Washington's last message before leaving Morristown, he disregarded it like the others. He did not bring the New Jersey Militia with him as ordered nor did he intend to obey Washington's marching orders.* Upon reaching Basking Ridge, eight miles out of Morristown, he revealed his disdain for Washington's military ability in a letter to General Gates. "*Entre Nous,* a certain great man is most damnably deficient. He has thrown me into a situation where I have my choice of difficulties—If I stay in this Province, I risk myself and Army and if I do not stay the Province is lost for ever." But Lee was not asked to risk himself or army and the fate of New Jersey hardly hinged upon his staying in the state.[52]

After breakfast at White's Tavern, Lee traced on a map the route his army would now pursue. Instead of following the road westward to cross the Delaware at an upper ferry as ordered, he sent a message directing Sullivan to march for Pluckemin and Princeton. His object was to strike a blow at the British

---

* On the night of December 11, Col. Jacob Ford struck the enemy's post at Woodbridge driving off more than 400 head of cattle. Rev. James Caldwell to Lee, Dec. 11, 1776, *Lee Papers,* II, 346-347; J. C. Fitzpatrick, *Writings of George Washington,* VI, 341.

post at Princeton and then if necessary circle the British at Trenton and cross the Delaware near Burlington. This was daring to the point of recklessness, but if successful, it might have catapulted Lee into the command of the American Army.[53]

It was 10 o'clock. Lee had just finished his letter to Gates and was about to leave the tavern to join the army bivouacked at Veal's town (now Bernardsville) two miles away. All of a sudden shots rang out and bullets came raining through the doors and windows of the tavern. Colonel William Harcourt with a party of Dragoons, guided by a Tory, had surrounded the building after overpowering the guard. There was no way to escape. Giving himself up, Lee was whisked away without coat, shoes, or hat. At New Brunswick, whither he was taken, the British celebrated his capture that night by a big affair during which they got his horse drunk and the band played all night long.

America was as downcast by Lee's capture as the British and Tories were jubilant; Washington declared that the cause had received a severe blow. "I will not comment upon the melancholy intelligence," he wrote, "only adding, that I sincerely regret Gen. Lee's unhappy fate, and feel much for the loss of my country in his Captivity." Greene called his capture "a great loss to the American states as he is a most consummate general." John Trumbull, the Commissary General, told his father, "This is a misfortune that cannot be remedied, as we have no officer in the army of equal experience and merit."[54] So it went, everyone lamenting Lee's capture and no one sensing that his usefulness to the American cause had ended when he became too enamored with his own importance and indispensability.

After Lee's capture, General Sullivan marched the division to the Delaware which he crossed at one of the upper ferries and joined the main army on December 20th, one month after Washington's first call for Lee to join him. Gates arrived a little later with his 600 equally ragged and half-starved soldiers. All told, Washington had about 10,000 troops. Hundreds, however, were sick or too weak to fight, while others must remain to guard the bases. Washington could count on about 6,000 effectives (until the last day of December) for an offensive against the enemy.

As at the close of the previous year, Greene was more optimistic than Washington who on December 18th, told his brother, John Augustine Washington, that unless "every nerve" was strained to recruit a new army, "I think the game is pretty near up."[55] Greene was far from thinking the cause desperate, he told John Hancock who was in Baltimore whither Congress had fled on Howe's reaching the banks of the Delaware. Still the situation was critical, he acknowledged, as he went on to name some of the things, such as the depreciation of the Continental currency, demanding the immediate attention of Congress.

Many of the difficulties confronting the army, Greene told Hancock, could be directly met if Washington had more power. "Time will not admit nor circumstances allow of a reference to Congress." Greene could see no danger in delegating such powers to the general. He was no advocate of the extension of military power and would not recommend it if the situation were less critical. "Remember the policy of the *Romans*, a people as tenacious of their liberties as any on Earth. When their State was invaded, they delegated full powers to exert their whole forces." Continuing, he reminded Congress that war was so uncertain, depending "upon so many contingencies; a day, nay, an hour, is so important in the crisis of public affairs, that it would be folly to wait for relief from the deliberate councils of legislative bodies." Washington, he assured Hancock, would not exceed his powers. "There never was a man that might be more safely trusted, nor a time when there was a louder call," he concluded.[56]

The feeling that Congress should delegate extraordinary powers to Washington had become widespread. Benjamin Rush, a member of Congress, echoed Greene's sentiment when he wrote: "General Washington must be invested with dictatorial powers for a few months, or we are ruined." Both of Greene's letters to Hancock recommending dictatorial powers for Washington were laid before Congress on the 26th. Before leaving Philadelphia, Congress had relieved Washington of the necessity of seeking the advice of his staff on major decisions. Now Washington was given the power to arrest any person refusing to accept continental currency or otherwise aiding the enemy. Furthermore, he was invested "with full, ample and complete power" to raise sixteen battalions for the army.[57]

During the days when the army waited for reinforcements near the banks of the Delaware, Greene had his headquarters at the home of Samuel Merrick, a short distance from the Keith home near Newtown. While there, Greene had a rising sun painted over the fireplace, symbolizing the birth of the American republic. At the Merricks' Greene lived well, dining on turkey, veal, and all the good food of a well-stocked household. When he finally bid his hosts farewell, he gave a small tea canister to Hannah, the young daughter of the Merricks, who had waited on table and been a little hostess to all the officers who came to see Greene.[58]

While at the Merricks, Greene found time to write and think a good deal. He was sorry, he told Governor Cooke, that Washington could not spare him for duty in Rhode Island as requested by the New England delegates to Congress. He felt sure, though, that Clinton would again find New England a hard country to conquer. Had New Jersey been New England, he declared, the British would not have marched twenty miles into the country before being stopped. But "the fright and disaffection was so great in the Jerseys," he told Cooke, "that in our retreat of one hundred odd miles, we were never joined by more than a hundred men." New Englanders, he told his friends, who thought they had a Tory problem had no idea of conditions to the southward. "You think you are greatly infested with the Tories and disaffected, but there is but the shadow of disaffection with you to what there is here," he wrote. "The Friends or Quakers are almost to a man disaffected. Many have the effrontery to refuse the Continental currency," a situation, he felt, which would soon bring down upon them the wrath of the people.[59]

Though weak and in defeat, the hope was strong in the country that the American Army would take the offensive and strike the enemy. As early as December 14th, Washington told Governor Trumbull that after Lee's men arrived, he hoped "to attempt a stroke upon the Forces of the Enemy, who lay a good deal scattered and to all appearance in a state of Security."[60] Once again one of Washington's closest advisers, Greene knew by December 21st that the blow was coming very soon. "I hope to give the Enemy a stroke in a few days," he told Governor

Cooke four days before the fateful Christmas night.[61] Two days later in answer to a letter from Reed urging an attack, Washington declared it would be a desperate venture, "but necessity, will, nay must justify, my attack."[62] Washington had in mind, of course, that after the first of the year he might find himself with only 1,200 troops and what militia might join him from time to time. Dangerous as the crossing would be, he knew that a "lucky blow" would "have a stunning effect" on the enemy and would greatly revive America's drooping spirits.[63]

On the afternoon of December 24th, Washington rode over and had supper with Greene. That evening Stirling, Sullivan, and some of the other officers joined them. Together they worked out the details on the fateful attack on Trenton. If successful, all agreed, the army might go on to attack Princeton and even New Brunswick where Howe had his treasure chest with its £70,000. None was more optimistic or exhilarated by the prospects than Greene.

CHAPTER SIX

Sir William Takes a Beating

While true that the American Revolution might not have collapsed had the battles of Princeton and Trenton remained unfought, nevertheless the victories did much to revive American courage and carry the country into the new year with something of the spirit and enterprise exhibited earlier in the war. Washington acknowledged he owed much to Greene for the success of the winter campaign. Greene was his "privy councillor," almost constantly at the side of the commander in chief as the campaign unfolded. In the succeeding months he became Washington's spokesman in Congress and his right hand man in the work of building an army for 1777 and preparing for its campaigns.

By not building boats and following the American Army across the Delaware while he had the initiative, Sir William Howe made a fateful mistake. But Howe was satisfied the rebellion would not collapse until New England was cut off from the rest of the country by British control of the Hudson which in any event would take another year. The capture of Philadelphia at this time, to be sure, would be another feather in his cap but he did not think Washington would risk an all out battle to save the city. Howe had crossed the Hudson with a limited purpose, namely, to seize East New Jersey to gain an ample supply of fresh provisions and forage for the winter. When this was accomplished he was content to stack his arms until spring brought a more pleasant season for campaigning. Howe, therefore, went back to enjoy the pleasures of New York, Cornwallis prepared to leave for England, and New Jersey was left in charge of the arrogant Major General James Grant with headquarters at New Brunswick.[1]

For distinguished services at Chatterton Hill and Fort Washington, 3,000 Hessians were given the honor of holding the line along the Delaware facing the American Army on the opposite side. With posts from Staten Island to Trenton and on to Bordentown and Burlington, Howe admitted the line was overextended; but he felt it would cover the state, and with the seemingly invincible Hessians holding the posts on the Delaware, he had no fear.

At Trenton, Howe stationed the cocky Colonel Johann Gottlieb Rall with three regiments—his own blues, Knyphausen's black-clad, and Lossberg's scarlet-coated veterans. In addition there were fifty Jaegers, resplendent in green suits with scarlet lapels, twenty equally flashily dressed British dragoons, and a company of artillery—in all 1,400. They were quartered in taverns, churches, the school and the jail, and in dwelling houses from which many of the owners had fled. The Jaegers and a large number of refugee Loyalists occupied the barracks built during the French and Indian War. Sharing the honor with their fellow countrymen at Trenton, a slightly larger number of Hessians under Colonel Carl von Donop were stationed at Bordentown, Black Horse, and at the time of the Battle of Trenton, at Burlington and Mount Holly, whither von Donop had taken most of his force to drive off New Jersey militia infesting the area.[2]

From the beginning, to their surprise, the Hessians found their positions far from as secure as they had imagined. Patrols from Washington's army and from the Pennsylvania militia crossed the river continuously, where with bands of New Jersey militia, they fired upon outposts and waylaid any of the enemy who ventured beyond the limits of their garrisons. Soon the constant ambushing and sniping unnerved the hitherto dauntless Hessians. One of Rall's officers complained in his diary, "We have not slept one night in peace since we came to this place." The Dragoons, too, became frightened and unwilling to venture out on patrol without a file of infantry to support them. Thus when the hour of battle finally arrived, Hessian fortitude was sufficiently shattered to allow Washington to win a great victory without loss of a single American life during the combat.[3]

Although Colonel Rall was annoyed by the prowling Americans, his contempt for them was in no way diminished. He did, however, appeal to Grant for more troops so as to clear the region of the raiders. Instead of help, Rall received the assurance that he need have no fear. "I will undertake," boasted Grant, "to

keep the peace in New Jersey with a corporal's guard." At first
Rall favored throwing up some defenses for the little town of
some 100 houses in which his brigade was snugly packed. On
further consideration he gave it up because Trenton was open
to attack from so many directions. When Major Frederick von
Dechow and other officers persisted in bringing up the defenseless
state of the garrison, Rall, following the example of Grant,
resorted to ridicule. The enemy ragamuffins with their "pop
guns," he snorted, would not dare cross the Delaware in force
to face again the terror of the Hessian bayonets. When the river
froze, however, the Hessians would cross and sweep everything
before them as they marched to take possession of Philadelphia.

While Washington and his ragged army were descending upon
Trenton, Colonel Rall and several officers entertained themselves
at cards at the home of Abraham Hunt, a local merchant, until
the small hours of the morning. A lover of good wine, lively
music, and buxom women, Rall enjoyed army life. If the next
morning were like the others, he would be leisurely dressing
and eating breakfast long after the sun was high while his
regimental band, standing outside in the cold, serenaded him
with the airs he enjoyed.

During the night while Rall amused himself at Abraham
Hunt's, a Tory from Pennsylvania, having been refused an audience with the colonel by a Negro servant, left a note saying the
Americans were coming. Rall, who knew no English and by that
time probably had too much wine, shoved the note in his pocket
without looking at it. Business could await the morning!

Earlier in the evening there had been an alarm when a party
from Stephen's brigade, scouting in New Jersey for a day or so
unknown to Washington, had fired upon a Hessian outpost. The
resulting excitement in Trenton, however, died down about as
fast as it arose, and soon everyone was back to his drinking and
revelry. As the night became exceedingly cold and blustery, few
patrols were sent out and these returned without going far or
discovering anything unusual. In the morning, the dawn patrol
which should have made the rounds was dismissed by Major
Dechow because of the severity of the storm. Fate was at her
kindest to the Americans that day.

In contrast to Washington who seemed more pensive and

solemn than ever, Nathanael Greene was in his usual lively and buoyant mood on Christmas Day, 1776. Although only the principal officers had knowledge of the plans afoot, Greene was aware that all the army knew that some major action was about to be performed. Late in the afternoon Greene watched 2,400 of the hardiest troops in camp parading behind the low Pennsylvania hills. They would win the day, thought Greene, if anyone could win it. As they took the road to the ferry, each man with three days rations in his knapsack and forty rounds of ammunition for his musket, the short winter day was already drawing to a close. When they arrived at McKonkey's Ferry eight miles above Trenton, it was pitch dark.

As Greene made his way on horseback to the ferry, he wondered how Generals Ewing and Cadwalader were making out with their preparations for crossing the dark and treacherous river. Brigadier General James Ewing with 1,000 Pennsylvania militia was to cross at a point a little below Trenton and close in on the town from the southward. Farther down the river at Bristol, Cadwalader was to cross with Daniel Hitchcock's Rhode Island Continentals and the Philadelphia Associators, in all perhaps 2,000 in number. Cadwalader was to be ready to move against von Donop at Mount Holly and Burlington as soon as Washington, if successful at Trenton, began moving southward.

When Greene arrived, General Glover's regiment of Marblehead fishermen—the men who had saved the army at Long Island—were already poling troops over the ice-clogged river. The boats were the large forty to sixty foot flat-bottomed Durham boats, used on the river to haul grain and iron ore, and each capable of carrying a whole company in one trip. From a spot near the bank, Greene and Washington watched quietly as the boats came and went. Adam Stephen's brigade was put over first with orders to form a ring around the landing place through which no one could enter or leave. His men would lead the march and be ready on entering Trenton to fire the town, if necessary, and drag off the enemy's cannon before the Hessians could bring them to bear upon the Americans.

Greene was not at the river long before he became convinced that the army would not be over the Delaware by midnight as planned. The river was running high and was strewn with floating ice. To retard progress further, about eleven o'clock the wind rose as the snow changed to sleet and rain. The greatest difficulty was experienced in transporting the eighteen cannon and the horses, already nervous and balky, over the river. James Wilkinson thought the crossing would never have been made but for the extraordinary exertions of the giant Colonel Knox who supervised the loading and whose "stentorian lungs" made it possible for everyone to hear his booming commands above the wail of wind and gale.

During the latter stages of the crossing, Washington stood on the New Jersey shore "wrapped in his cloak, superintending the landing of his troops" with the sleet cutting "like a knife." Greene and Sullivan stayed with their divisions, seeing that all remained in their places. According to tradition, the only unnecessary sound during the trip to Trenton occurred when Washington, seeing that his boat was leaning to one side, called to the hefty Henry Knox in the stern to shift his hindquarters and trim the boat. For a moment muffled laughter was heard and then only the sound of the wind and the rain and the oars.

It was four in the morning before all the American Army was over the river and ready to begin the long eight mile march to Trenton. The element of surprise, Greene feared, was lost, but they had to go on to win or be destroyed. Not a word was uttered on pain of death as the men trudged along the rough road shielding their gunlocks as best they could from the driving sleet. During the cruel march two men froze to death, while many, wearing worn-out shoes or cloth tied around their feet, left a trail of blood to mark their progress.

After marching four miles, the army halted a few minutes at Birmingham to rest. It then divided into two columns. The brigades of St. Clair, Sargent, and Glover, led by Sullivan, took the river road. Those of Stirling and Mercer, commanded by Greene, struck out along the Pennington Road about a mile east of the river. Washington was with Greene who was followed by the Frenchman, Matthias Alexis Roche de Fermoy, with orders to veer off to the left near Trenton with his brigade to block the roads leading to Princeton.

At daybreak, Washington's columns had two more miles to reach Trenton. The sleet had changed to a whirling snowstorm which fairly blinded the men as they slipped and staggered over the icy ground. When some of St. Clair's men reported that their guns were too wet to fire, he reminded them of their bayonets, the only weapon likely to prove effective in the snowstorm. About 8 A.M. the American columns neared Trenton still almost miraculously undiscovered. A moment later they burst upon the enemy's outposts and sent the pickets running wildly into town shouting, *"Der Feind! Der Feind! Heraus! Heraus!"*

Only Rall's regiment, the guard of the day, was ready to oppose the Americans when the sound of musket fire on the outskirts of the village brought the Hessians tumbling out of houses and racing down the streets to their stations. After hurriedly dressing, Rall joined his regiment, moving up King Street with band playing. Meanwhile Lossberg's regiment was gathering to try to secure Queen Street. Behind them Knyphausen's men were drawing up at Second and King Streets to form a reserve.

While the Hessians were thus hastily assembling, the Americans converged rapidly upon them. Soon Colonel Knox's artillerymen had their cannon sweeping the main streets and sending the enemy scurrying for cover from the shattering blasts of grapeshot. At the same time, the American infantry came charging through the byways, each company seeming "to vie with the other in pressing forward." For the first time, the Hessians experienced the shock of being on the receiving end of the bayonet. Few shots were fired by the troops on either side as the muskets and rifles soon became too wet to fire. "The storm of nature and the storm of the town," as Greene described it, "exhibited a scene that filled the mind during the action with passions easier conceived than described." Soon the Hessians began dashing hither and yon seeking an avenue of escape. Four hundred succeeded in making their escape by getting on the road to Bordentown before Sullivan's men took command of the bridge. The rest surrendered precipitously after Colonel Rall and Major Dechow fell from their horses mortally wounded. In an epitaph written by one of the Hessian officers, the fullness of the American victory was sadly told.

> *Hier liegt der Oberst Rall*
> *Mit ihm ist alles all!*

Unfortunately for Washington, neither Ewing nor Cadwalader made the crossing to close in on von Donop and complete the destruction of the Hessians. Ewing did not attempt a crossing which he thought impossible in the storm; Cadwalader gave it up when he found no way to land his horses and artillery on the ice-jammed New Jersey shore. Nonetheless, at Trenton Washington won a signal victory. Twenty-two Hessians had been killed, ninety-two wounded, and 950 taken prisoner. Besides all the baggage and horses and a variety of military stores, over 1,000 muskets and six brass cannon were taken. Forty barrels of rum were found but Washington, to the general dismay, ordered all to be emptied on the ground, though not before many brave fellows were staggering for a reason other than the ice underfoot.

In the battle, the only American casualties were four wounded. One of them William Washington, a kinsman of the commander in chief, would become a renowned cavalry officer with Greene in the Carolinas. Another was James Monroe, the future president of the United States.

After the battle, Greene and Knox wanted Washington to "push on" as soon as the men had rested. But Washington, after conferring with his staff, found most of his officers opposed to risking further action with their tired and exhausted army.[4] In a letter to John Hancock, Washington explained his reasons for deciding to retire to Pennsylvania. He wrote:

> I am fully confident that could the Troops under generals Ewing and Cadwalader have passed the River, I should have been able, with their Assistance, to have driven the Enemy from all their posts below Trenton. But the Numbers I had with me, being inferior to theirs below me, I thought it most prudent to return the same Evening, with my prisoners and the Artillery we had taken.[5]

Washington's decision to retire to Pennsylvania with his victorious army has seldom been criticized. Douglas Southall Freeman concludes that the commander in chief did right in not risking all for possible further gain.[6] However, William Gordon, the author of the first history of the American Revolution and a man who talked with many of the participants, was of the opinion that Washington made a great mistake by not advancing against von Donop. Even Washington, he wrote, "has since regretted his not seizing the golden opportunity."[7] If it were a great mistake, Washington alone was responsible, for Congress had made it clear that he was not bound by the opinion of his staff.

On the day of the Battle of Trenton, most of von Donop's troops were still at Mount Holly, eighteen miles below Trenton. If Greene had been in command, after resting his army he would have headed for Bordentown to block the roads from Mount Holly and Burlington. Meanwhile Ewing could get over the river at Trenton Ferry by daylight while the boats carried back prisoners and captured supplies for safekeeping in Pennsylvania. Cadwalader, too, could start crossing (as he did the next day) as soon as he received his orders. If this had been done it is difficult to imagine how any of the Hessians could have escaped.

Greene, Knox, and the other officers who wanted Washington to "push on" could not help feeling disappointed as the army slowly made its way back to McKonkey's Ferry where, after recrossing the river, the men finally staggered into camp late at night. The next day fully half of the troops who had participated in the operation were too sick or exhausted to report for duty. Greene stood the strain without noticeable effects after being out, as he told his wife, "thirty hours in all the Storm without the least refreshment."[8]

Two days after the battle, upon reaching Trenton in advance of General Cadwalader's division, Joseph Reed wrote Washington urging him to invade New Jersey again with his victorious army. Not knowing that von Donop had made his escape, Washington was now ready to follow Greene in a move to beat "up the Rest of their Quarters bordering on and near the River."[9] The next day, however, Greene and Washington learned to their disappointment that von Donop was gone.

But a new thought came to Washington and Greene when they heard that General Mifflin was on his way to join Cadwalader with more Pennsylvania militia. Forgetting, no doubt in their enthusiasm, to weigh all the factors involved, Greene and Washington began to think of driving the enemy entirely out of New Jersey. To Maxwell and McDougall in command of forces at Morristown and Chatham, Washington sent orders to advance upon the rear of the enemy at New Brunswick and Princeton and harass them as opportunities arose. Meanwhile the main army, he assured them, would advance from Trenton. "I think a fair Opportunity," Washington wrote, "is offered of driving the Enemy entirely from, or at least to, the extremity of the province of Jersey."[10]

On December 29th, the army left its camp near Newtown and began crossing the Delaware. Sullivan's division went over by McKonkey's Ferry and Greene's by Yardley's, four miles above Trenton. By promising the Continental troops whose time expired at the end of December a bounty of $10, the greater part, after some hesitation, agreed to stay another six weeks. "God Almighty," wrote Greene, "inclined their hearts to listen to the proposal and they engaged anew." Nathanael Greene was the more pleased because most of the troops affected were New Englanders who had served and fought longer than any others. "This is the greatest evidence of N. E. virtue I ever saw," he glowingly told Governor Cooke.[11]

On New Year's Day, Cornwallis began a rapid advance from Princeton with a formidable army, estimated as high as 8,000 troops. The next day, Washington, who had no more than 5,000 men, sent Greene forward with a detachment to aid Roche de Fermoy and Adam Stephen who were endeavoring to slow down the enemy while Washington prepared to defend a line running along the south bank of Assunpink Creek. One of Greene's soldiers remembered him "dashing up to the company—and calling out in a clear, loud voice, 'Push on boys! push on!'"

The pressure of the enemy, mounting steadily as the day wore on, compelled Greene to fall back for fear of having some of his force cut off. By afternoon the British vanguard was fighting its way into Trenton while the Americans retired over the Assunpink to join their comrades. Knox, who had just become a brigadier general, brought his forty field pieces into play with a cannonade which brought the enemy to an abrupt halt.

To attack Washington successfully, Cornwallis had to outflank the Americans by crossing the creek at one of the upper fords with a strong force. This would take time and it was getting dark. His men were tired from a long march and considerable fighting. Cornwallis, therefore, ordered the campfires to be lit. With the morning, when his men were fresh, Cornwallis was sure he would bag "the old fox" who had eluded him so many times. General Erskine, his quartermaster general, demurred. The Americans, he said, would be gone by morning while an hour or so of maneuvering and fighting might end the war that night.

If Nathanael Greene had not foreseen the peril of crossing the Delaware again in the face of a greatly superior army thirsting for revenge, he realized it now. One officer wrote, "The most sanguine among us could not flatter himself with any hopes of victory had we waited till morning and been reduced to the necessity of engaging a foe so vastly our superior both in numbers and discipline and who could never have a chance of fighting us on more advantageous terms."[12] Truly the American Army was in a tight spot with Cornwallis in front and the Delaware in back. "It appeared to me," wrote Stephen Olney, "that our army was in the most desperate situation I had ever known it."[13] There were not enough boats at Trenton Landing to evacuate the army as Glover had done at Brooklyn even if it were possible. The only way of escaping seemed to be to retreat down along the east bank of the Delaware and hope to get over the river at some point before Cornwallis could overtake them with his army.

Early in the evening, Washington called a council of war at St. Clair's quarters. Washington, it was said, favored risking a battle rather than lose by retreat all the psychological advantages reaped at Trenton.[14] However, most of the staff, including Greene, were of the opinion that ruin faced them if they stayed to fight it out. Not only was Washington's army smaller than the British, but over half were raw recruits who might stampede at the first shot. After a while, someone, probably St. Clair who had been guarding the fords of the Assunpink, proposed an attack on Princeton by bypassing Cornwallis. This was possible, he thought, by taking a new road through the woods running parallel to the creek until it crossed Quaker Bridge and veered off for Princeton.*

Joseph Reed, who knew the country well, agreed that the plan was possible providing they could hide their movement from the enemy. Washington, ready to do almost anything rather than

---

* St. Clair claimed he made the suggestion. Some authors think it was made by Reed. Others ascribe it to Mercer.

retreat, seized upon the proposal. Greene did also. Not only would the army attack Princeton, but, if successful, it might go on to New Brunswick to seize the British Army chest with its £70,000. In any event, the army, Greene knew, could retire to Morristown behind the protective slopes of the Watchung Mountains already guarded by Maxwell and McDougall and the militia of upland New Jersey.

To convince the enemy that he intended to remain and fight, Washington set men at work throwing up breastworks and making as much noise and commotion as possible. Most of the baggage was loaded on wagons and sent off to Burlington. To deaden the sound of the wheels of the gun carriages and the wagons, rags were wrapped around the tires. Everyone, thought Greene, seemed to know just what to do to make the plan a success.

Fortunately, the night became dark and cold, freezing the ground solid after a thaw which had rendered the roads almost impassable. Five hundred men were left behind to feed the fires and continue the digging as the army stole silently away at midnight. At 2 A.M. the ghostly column reached Quaker Bridge. The danger now of meeting an enemy patrol, Greene knew, was unlikely. In six more miles the army would reach Princeton where Cornwallis had left a brigade of about 1,200 troops.

As the day dawned frosty and cold, General Mercer in the lead with his brigade and some of the Pennsylvania militia swung off to the left to secure the bridge over Stony Creek on the main road out of Princeton. Here he came face to face with the first of two regiments led by Colonel Charles Mawhood on his way to join Cornwallis at Trenton. As both sides quickly drew up for battle in a nearby orchard, Mawhood gained the initiative by following a volley with a fierce bayonet charge. Seeing his men breaking and starting to run, Mercer and his officers tried desperately to rally them. A moment later Mercer was wounded but he fought on refusing to surrender. The next instant he was surrounded, stabbed several times with bayonets, and left for dead.

The British charge, however, was soon brought to a halt by the blast of several well placed American cannon. In a moment, Washington, Greene, and several other officers dashed up to the British leading Hitchcock's brigade, Hand's riflemen, and a swarm of Pennsylvania militia who had recovered from their fright. Overwhelmed by the Americans, the British broke and fled for the bridge leading to Trenton. Here some Dragoons held back their pursuers long enough for most of their comrades to get over the creek. "It is a fine fox chase, my boys!" Washington is reputed to have shouted to his exhilarated troops as he dashed after the enemy with Captain Samuel Morris' score of light horsemen from Philadelphia—the only cavalry with the army. After chasing the enemy for about three miles, Washington called it off: but not until many of the enemy were killed or wounded and fifty made prisoners.[15]

Meanwhile, the rest of the American Army under Sullivan closed in upon Princeton where most of the two remaining regiments had taken a position along a ravine on the south side of the town. On being driven from this position, about 200 took refuge in the large stone Nassau Hall while the rest, in great panic, fled down the road toward Kingston. Captain Alexander Hamilton, one of Knox's young artillery officers, had time to fire but one or two cannon balls at the college before some New Jersey militia forced their way into the building whereupon the defenders at once surrendered.[16]

Washington's losses at Princeton were about thirty-five killed and seventy wounded. Though the casualties were comparatively light, the deaths of General Mercer and Delaware's Colonel John Haslet, as well as several other excellent officers, were an inestimable loss. The enemy, according to the American report, had 100 slain and more than 300 captured including the wounded.[17]

After the battle, which lasted less than an hour, Greene was not alone in wishing he had 1,000 fresh troops to march against New Brunswick, seventeen miles away. But the men were tired almost to exhaustion and it would be folly, he knew, to attempt the march with Cornwallis already hurrying toward Princeton. Indeed, the Americans had barely left the town before Cornwallis' rear guard which had been at Maidenhead, only six miles away, reached Stony Creek where they were temporarily halted by the destruction of the bridge.

Before leaving Princeton, Washington held a council with

some of his officers. At first, sentiment favored returning to Pennsylvania by one of the upper ferries. Greene apparently was not present. Knox, however, who was of one mind with Greene on the advantages of marching to Morristown, soon convinced the council that this was the best thing to do.

With Greene already up the road pursuing the enemy in the direction of Kingston, Washington ordered the army to follow. At Kingston, instead of crossing Millstone River over which the enemy had fled, the army continued down along the river to Rocky Hill. After a short rest it marched on to Somerset Court House, fifteen miles north of Princeton. That night, while Cornwallis' bedraggled troops reached New Brunswick in almost a state of panic, most of Washington's army, failing to find shelter, slept in the open around their campfires. Many, especially those of the Pennsylvania militia whose blankets had been sent to Burlington, had no cover but their clothing most of which, fortunately, was quite new.[18]

The next day Washington's army reached Pluckemin where provisions were awaiting the famished men. Here "we got plenty of beef, pork, etc," after having been nearly starved for two days, wrote John Chilton.[19] Two days later, January 6th, the troops reached Morristown. With the New Jersey militia responding with enthusiasm, and more militia led by Israel Putnam on the march from Pennsylvania, Washington was still hopeful that a way could be found to drive the enemy, now confined to New Brunswick, Amboy, and points along the eastern fringe of the state, entirely out of New Jersey. If this could be done, the army would remain at Morristown only long enough to get refreshed and provisioned. But instead, Morristown became the main base and headquarters for the army until spring ushered in another year of campaigning.

Hoping to induce General Howe to draw off some of his troops in New Jersey before he struck again, Washington asked Heath to move down from Peekskill as though he intended to attack New York. Heath eventually moved against Fort Independence (the fort guarding the approach to Kingsbridge from the north) late in January only to withdraw rather ignobly after ordering it to surrender. His maneuvers, which seemed more amusing than threatening to the British, made no change in the number of the enemy in New Jersey. Reinforcements, in fact, soon arrived when troops were brought from Newport to strengthen the British garrisons in New York and New Jersey.[20]

Upon reaching Morristown, a little village of some 300 inhabitants, the army sought shelter wherever it could both in and out of the town. Tents were perhaps found for some, but most of the troops were packed in houses, public buildings, stables, and barns. This was comfort compared with the way the men had lived since leaving Pennsylvania. As soon as Washington decided to winter in the area, a campsite was selected between Morristown and Bottle Hill and huts were built. Greene was satisfied with the Morristown location as it was safe against a surprise attack and the surrounding country could provide the army with enough food and forage. On occasion, shortages did arise during the winter and spring, but this was because of lack of funds and inefficiency in the Quartermaster and Commissary Departments.[21]

Though small, Morristown contained a number of families of means possessing large houses which they willingly offered to share with the American generals and their aides. Washington, however, chose to make his headquarters at Arnold's tavern which faced from the west the long, uneven stretch of village green. Here he had room for his eight or ten aides as well as a place to receive an unending stream of callers and to hold conferences. Among Washington's aides was Tench Tilghman, a most capable Philadelphian who had volunteered without pay. After the first of March, Washington was joined by the brilliant, if somewhat headstrong, Alexander Hamilton. As a member of Washington's official family, Hamilton's relationships with Greene ripened into a lifelong friendship.

With William Blodget, John Clark, and one or two other aides, Greene found lodging at the home of a gentleman named Hoffman, a person of doubtful loyalty in Greene's opinion, but withal a most excellent and good-natured host. His wife was "a great lover of the clergy," and Major Clark, to the amusement of all, found much pleasure in "perplexing her with doubts and difficulties—respecting the purity of manners and principles of the Church of England."

With the tables turned and the Americans victorious, Greene

found that "respect and courtesy flow in upon us from all quarters." What was more, Greene was once again Washington's right-hand man. "I am exceeding happy," he told Kitty, with "the full confidence of his Excellency General Washington." Indeed, Greene had been Washington's closest advisor ever since the beginning of the great offensive. "The more difficult and distressing our affairs grew," he explained to Kitty, the more Washington relied upon him.[22] After Reed resigned as adjutant general early in January, much of the work he had done fell to Greene and when the latter left for Basking Ridge in February, the duties devolved upon St. Clair, Weedon, and other officers until finally in June, Timothy Pickering was appointed adjutant general.

As so often happened during the course of the war, Greene found himself without a mount of his own when his horse gave out due to the strain of the long campaign. But until a replacement was found, Greene had all he could do at his desk to cope with the endless round of administrative detail and letter writing. A sad note was struck when it was learned that General Mercer had died of his wounds at Princeton after showing signs of recovery. Montgomery, Warren, Thomas, and now Mercer, all irreplaceable in Greene's estimation, were dead. Equally sorrowful was the death from pneumonia following fatigue and exposure of his old friend Daniel Hitchcock who had been with him almost constantly since the siege of Boston. If anyone was entitled to first laurels at Princeton it was Hitchcock, who led his brigade against Mawhood to throw the enemy into the flight which won the day.

After the middle of January, Greene knew that it was idle to think of driving the enemy from New Jersey that winter. The British had been reinforced while daily he saw the American Army shrinking because of expiration of terms, desertion, and the failure of recruits to come in to take their places. Soon it seemed that almost everyone was leaving—militia and Continentals alike. "Slept but poorly," one officer recorded in his diary, "on account of the ungodly behavior of our Men. All uproar on account of going home." These were Pennsylvania militia whom Colonel Nixon tried to pacify by giving them his word they would be discharged in ten days. "Some are pleased, some are angry," noted the diarist.[23] On January 19th, Washington told Congress that so many had left only a skeleton of an army remained. For a time, with the Delaware frozen, Howe could have marched straight to Philadelphia for all Washington could have done to stop him. However, Sir William was not convinced that Washington was as weak as he was reported to be. After Trenton and Princeton Howe was taking no chances.[24]

At Morristown, Washington and his staff plunged into the work of raising a new army. This time, to Greene's satisfaction, it was to be raised on a three year basis or for the duration of the war. Congress offered a bounty of $20 plus 100 acres for volunteering for the duration of the war but most men preferred to enlist for three years even though the bounty was but $10. As the states offered additional bounties, soldiers generally went home to enlist or joined up in a state that paid a higher bounty. In some states, too, the bounty and other attractions for duty in the home guards outweighed the benefits received for service in the Continental Army. Many soldiers, Greene was sorry to hear, became bounty jumpers, deserting and then re-enlisting, while not a few officers and recruiting agents found various means of defrauding the public.

To meet the crisis, Washington had to send many of his best officers, among them Greene's friends, James Varnum and George Weedon, back to their home states to assist recruiting. All things considered, insufficient funds more than anything proved the greatest handicap in recruiting. When Greene went to Philadelphia in March, he spent much time rather fruitlessly on the army's financial troubles. Like John Adams, Greene thought the American people were wrong in resisting taxation for the war. Taxation, he maintained, would not only make it possible to raise a formidable army, but would have the tendency to keep prices down and help beat inflation. Had taxation been "adopted in N.E. instead of attempting to regulate the prices of things it would have had a much better effect," Greene wrote to Adams.[25]

More baffling, perhaps than the raising of an army was the problem of desertion. The British claimed that 3,000 Americans deserted to their camp during the first five months of 1777, a number no doubt greatly exaggerated but nonetheless indicating that desertion to the enemy had assumed alarming proportions. Deserters caught by the army were usually punished severely but it finally became necessary to pardon those found at home if they would re-enlist. At one time there were so many deserters that Washington declared it seemed he would have to detach one half of the army to bring the other half back.[26]

Not since the fall of Fort Washington and the occasion of Lee's interference with the Rhode Island appointments had Greene heard from Governor Cooke though he had written the governor several times. As the mails were still open from the eastward, it may be that his failure to hear from Cooke arose from disfavor brought on by the loss of Fort Washington. Although disturbed by the Governor's silence, Greene was much more concerned over the bounty for state troops which apparently was hindering Continental recruiting in Rhode Island.

After Washington wrote Governor Cooke criticizing the Rhode Island measure as injurious to the national interest, Greene followed with a stronger letter of protest. "There is not a State on the continent whose interest and happiness depends so much on a union with the others," as Rhode Island, he told Cooke. It was the most exposed and least capable of defending itself without the help of other states. "Suppose, for instance," he wrote, "every State was to neglect the completion of the Continental regiments, and prepare for their own internal security, where is the State that's able to withstand the enemy's collective force?"

"Divine Providence," Greene assured Governor Cooke, "has given a very favorable turn to affairs at an hour when people least expect it." Now was the hour to press forward and complete the Continental regiments. He was sure the war would be won if Washington had an army. But if men would not volunteer, they must be drafted, he declared. He then went on to paint an optimistic picture of the future. "Our resources are daily increasing; we have now a fine nursery of officers." Military stores were increasing rapidly, and America generally becoming conditioned for war. "If it was prudent to engage in this war without any of these advantages, how foolish must our conduct appear, to despair at an hour when we have much to hope and little to fear," he wrote.

Next Greene turned to the touchy subject of officers and rank.

Greene probably did not know the full story of Lee's tampering with the Rhode Island appointments but he knew enough to be angry. "A general officer," he reminded Cooke, "is in a very disagreeable situation; subject to the censure and reproach of every little dirty politician, ignorant of every circumstance necessary to form a right judgment." The liberality with which Rhode Island bestowed favors upon some and stigmas on others, "must make men of real merit somewhat cautious how they put themselves in a situation where they may be reduced from the highest pitch of glory to the lowest state of contempt. It was ever the policy of the Romans to be cautious whom they trusted, and how they disgraced those they had once honored," observed Greene. He thought the Marquis de Malmedy (someday to be one of his valued officers in the Carolinas) who was made a brigadier general of Rhode Island's state troops might be deserving of the appointment. However, he confessed, he had "not the highest veneration" for the recommendations of General Lee who often based his opinions on mere trifles.* There were men enough in New England, he believed, who would make as good if not better officers than most of the foreign adventurers. But "a novelty of things of foreign growth often makes us rate them above those of more solid worth of our production," he told Cooke.[27]

Nettled by Greene's comments on Rhode Island's military measures, Governor Cooke, at the instance of the assembly, wrote to Washington and Greene, explaining that the state troops were designed as much to serve the nation as for the security of Rhode Island. The only difference, he said, was in their being engaged for fifteen months instead of three years. This was hardly a true representation, but Greene, thinking that nothing would be gained by continuing the dispute, answered that he was glad to learn Rhode Island had kept the national interest uppermost in mind. Rhode Island's policy, however, he let it be known, did not correspond with his own views.[28]

After it became clear that he could not drive the British from New Jersey, Washington adopted a plan offered by Greene for containing the enemy within his posts. A division of the army un-

---

* Congress a little later made Malmedy a colonel in the Continental Army. J. C. Fitzpatrick, *Writings of George Washington*, VIII, 68n.

der the tall, red-haired Scotchman, Arthur St. Clair, would remain in Morristown with Washington. The rest would be spread out like a fan at strategic points between Morristown and the enemy. Accordingly, Sullivan went to Chatham with a force consisting probably of his own brigade. At Turkey (New Providence), three miles south of Chatham, another brigade was stationed. Less than ten miles west of Chatham and Turkey, Greene occupied Basking Ridge with his own and part of Stirling's brigade. Thus with the four advanced brigades Greene was in a position to bring his forces quickly together for striking the enemy should he decide to undertake an offensive or march for the Delaware. If necessary he could easily retreat to Morristown eight or ten miles to the rear.

Beyond the posts at Chatham, Turkey, and Basking Ridge, and below the mountains, Greene set up an advanced line of posts within a few miles of the British at New Brunswick and Amboy. At Bound Brook, twelve miles south of Basking Ridge, General Lincoln was stationed with about 500 troops. A few miles to his left at Quibbletown (New Market), one of Stirling's regiments was stationed. To the right of Bound Brook, at Millstone, on the road to Princeton, was General Dickinson with several hundred New Jersey militia. At least part of the time a detachment occupied Metuchen under the command of Adam Stephen, but whether or not he dared to stay long in a position directly overlooking the road between New Brunswick and Amboy is not known. These posts, forming a semicircle only five or six miles from New Brunswick, kept the British garrison in a constant state of suspense.

The strongest American outpost on the plains below the mountains was at Elizabethtown, only twelve miles north of Amboy. Here and at Newark and Springfield, Brigadier General William Maxwell had his veteran light troops. Maxwell, whose home lay in the hills of Sussex, New Jersey, was one of Washington's best field commanders, fearless and ever on the alert. At the other end of the line at Princeton, was a larger force of Pennsylvania militia commanded by the old warrior, Israel Putnam.

To men of the advanced posts belonged the credit for forcing Howe to delay taking the field until spring was all but gone and the American Army finally assembled. As late as May, the

British horses were in a famished condition and many of their troops still sick with scurvy. Whether enemy foraging parties came out in force or not, the result was invariably disappointing to the British. On February 24th, when a foraging expedition numbering 4,000 came out of Amboy, most of the day was spent fighting Maxwell's troops who waylaid them at every turn. When the British returned at night to their base their wagons were full of dead and wounded instead of provisions and forage. Greene's brigade at Basking Ridge also joined in the work of distressing the enemy. On February 20th, he sent forty wagons to forage the country toward New Brunswick. They returned, loaded with all they could carry.

To formulate plans for coordinating their movements in case of attack, Greene held conferences with the officers commanding the various posts. Meeting with Sullivan and Stirling on February 21st at Bound Brook, it was decided that should the enemy start for Princeton (a move which Greene was expecting), they would, with their combined forces, fall on the enemy's rear or flank, avoiding, however, a general battle unless the prospect appeared most favorable. Every day Greene was sending scouting parties from Basking Ridge down into the lowlands "not so much for the annoyance of the enemy as to get them acquainted with the ground, and to keep them employed." Greene did not rule out the possibility that Howe might attempt a major push against Morristown, the surest way of breaking the American grip on New Jersey. However, Greene hardly thought Howe would hazard a major operation against the American Army protected by the wall of mountains. Should he try it, Greene felt certain the British would be turned back with "bloody noses."[29]

By February, both the American and British armies were hard hit by the smallpox. On first coming to Morristown, Washington had ordered everyone to be inoculated who had not had the disease, but it could not be done all at once or the greater part of the army would be bedridden. To Gates, Washington wrote, "I am much at a loss what step to take to prevent the spread of the smallpox, should we inoculate generally, the Enemy, knowing it, will certainly take advantage of our Situation." The next day, Washington made up his mind. All the troops and the inhabitants likewise were ordered inoculated at once, so fast was the disease spreading. Two weeks later, Washington told Gates that most of his best troops were down with the smallpox either by the natural way or by inoculation. But it turned out to be a great success in the end. On March 3rd, Washington could write that the inoculation had been attended with amazing success. No doubt this was the first mass inoculation in America.

Not since the previous summer had Greene had any correspondence with John Adams. Presumably, as in the case of Governor Cooke, the Fort Washington episode had something to do with the break. But apparently, more than anything Adams was piqued by Greene's outspoken criticism of Congress. Having as great an urge as before, however, to set his views before Congress, Greene undertook to reopen the corrspondence on March 3rd. Washington, too, may have urged him to write as he often found it tactful to present his own views to Congress through one of his generals.

"It is a long time since I wrote to you or you to me; who stands in debt upon the score of letters I cannot tell, therefore I shall begin anew. If you have time and inclination, you will give it an answer; if not, I shall consider it as the ladies do their visits after marriage; if there's no return, the acquaintance drops." After this opening, Greene reviewed the history of the war since General Howe's arrival at New York. He told Adams, as he had others, that no one not actually with the army could conceive the magnitude of Washington's difficulties with an army consisting largely of inexperienced men, confronted by a powerful veteran army supported by a formidable navy. During the campaign of 1776, Howe, Greene explained, tried to bring on a general engagement and avoid skirmishing. "General Washington, as every defender ought, has followed directly the contrary conduct by endeavoring to skirmish with the enemy at all times and avoid a general engagement," he wrote.[30]

Greene then inquired why Congress refused to give General Lee an opportunity to confer with some of its members about his exchange. "Why is he denied his request of having some persons appointed to confer with him? Can any injury arise? Will it reflect any dishonor upon your body to gratify the request of one of your generals?" he asked. So far Howe had refused to treat Lee like other prisoners, claiming he was a traitor who deserved to be executed. However, he had not been treated badly—only kept confined in City Hall's Council Chamber in New York where he could have visitors and each night tumble "jovially mellow" into a comfortable bed. Nevertheless, because Howe refused to treat him like other prisoners, Congress was considering retaliation by similarly treating one of the Hessian officers in American hands. If Lee were executed so would the Hessian meet with a like fate.[31]

Greene and Washington were much opposed to retaliation upon a Hessian. Reprisals, Greene told Adams would upset the good effect of American kindness which already was undermining Hessian desire to fight on. Desertion was spreading among them and one brigade, it was reported, had become mutinous and was withdrawn from New Jersey. "Rancor and hatred prevails between them and the British soldiery," so why, asked Greene, should America heal the breach by retaliating on Hessian prisoners? "If we can alienate the foreign troops from the British service," he wrote, "we inevitably ruin Great Britain, for her own natural strength is totally insufficient to conquer and hold in subjection these States." Washington joined Greene in sending letters to Adams and Robert Morris criticizing the stand Congress had taken. Writing to Adams, Washington said, "I wish, with all my heart, Congress had gratified General Lee, in his request. If not too late, I wish they would do it still."[32]

On this occasion, it would seem, Greene, Washington, and other officers of like mind were not as practiced or astute in politics as was the portly Massachusetts lawyer, John Adams. Lee was being denied his request, Adams told Greene, because he was being duped by the British as Sullivan had been earlier. Adams had reference to reports that Lee hoped to open negotiations by which a reconciliation could be reached between America and Great Britain. If the former conference had been necessary for political reasons, another representation through Lee was not, Adams maintained. Adams, in fact, believed that the former meeting did more harm than good by injuring the American cause in the French Court. Elaborating on this, Robert Morris wrote, "The meeting with Lord Howe at Staten Island last

Summer injured Mr. Deane's Negotiations much and retarded supplies intended for us." General Howe knows this, Adams told Greene, and wants to repeat it.[33]

John Adams's suspicion of Charles Lee was wrong, it seems, only in underestimating the General's capacity for duplicity. He not only was a willing tool (although Howe did not trust him) to a plan for embarrassing Congress by another proposal for peace, but was actually faithless to America by offering the British a plan for subduing the United States in the coming campaign. According to Lee, Howe should take Philadelphia, Annapolis, and Alexandria as early as possible thus sealing off the south and neutralizing Pennsylvania. New England, meanwhile, should be cut off by an invasion of New York from Canada after which the Yankees could be subdued to end the war. Howe probably was not influenced by Lee's suggestions although Lee later claimed that he had hoodwinked Howe into going against Philadelphia by way of Chesapeake Bay so as to give Washington more time to get set for the invasion.[34]

As it seemed imperative to have Congress better informed on the needs and problems of the army, Washington decided in March to send Greene to Philadelphia. He was to inquire into the question of supplies, the touchy subject of appointments and promotions in the army, Lee's request for an interview, and the matter of retaliation on the Hessian prisoners. Above all, he was to try to impress Congress with the necessity of keeping the paymaster supplied with funds or there would be no army of consequence to take the field in the spring. Writing to Congress, Washington explained that he was sending Greene as one intimately acquainted with every detail respecting the army. Greene, he assured Congress, was deserving of "the greatest respect and much regard is due to his opinions in the line of his profession."[35]

On reaching Philadelphia, Greene was called before Congress in Independence Hall for an interview which lasted two hours. After Greene had answered all questions, Congress instructed a committee to meet with him and make a report of its findings and recommendations. Greene sat two evenings with the committee: Samuel Adams, John Witherspoon, James Wilson, Roger Sherman, and several others. The results, Greene thought, looked promising. "I believe the business of the cartel will be settled agreeable to your wishes, that is, General Howe acknowledging General Lee a prisoner of war, and holding him subject to exchange whenever we have an equivalent to offer," he told Washington. Greene was hardly back in camp, however, before Congress had again fouled up the cartel, complicated by questions of the exchange of civilians as well as regular prisoners of war.[36]

Greene was pleased to report to Washington that Congress declared it never intended the commander in chief to be bound by the decisions of his staff when contrary to his own judgment. On questions of money and supplies, Greene, however, met with little success. Congress, it seemed, was afraid to ask the states for more power or to take bolder steps to remedy its financial embarrassment. But there was a brighter ray as several shiploads of goods had just arrived from France. One ship, Greene noted, carried nearly 7,000 muskets and other crucial supplies.

Washington at this time was disappointed in the failure of Congress to give him three lieutenant generals, one of whom would be Greene. Congress felt he could use major generals just as well, not realizing the benefits to be derived from the new rank. In February, Congress had made Stirling, St. Clair, Stephen, Mifflin, and Lincoln major generals. Naturally, there was criticism of Congress's choice both in and out of the army. John Stark resigned from the Continental Army and others did likewise or threatened to leave. Benedict Arnold, chagrined by not being made a major general, wrote Washington of his embarrassment and disappointment. The latter answered that he had expected Arnold to be among those promoted but Congress would allow Connecticut no more than two major generals which it already had.

Greene found John Adams still irritated by his criticism of the promotion of Mifflin and Stirling to brigadier generals the previous summer. He was certainly in no mood to argue about promotions, much less to see Congress give up any of its power over appointments. When a motion was introduced in Congress in February to allow decisions on appointments and promotions in the army to be made by Washington and the senior generals, Adams protested vehemently. Congress, he declared, was too prone "to idolize an image which their own hands have molden." Continuing, he said, "I speak here of the superstitious veneration that is sometimes paid to General Washington."[37]

In answer to Greene's criticism of Congress's promotional policy, Adams replied that it was "justice and sound policy" to have the number of generals from each state somewhere in proportion to the number of troops raised by a state. If some "great men" were thereby left out, Adams sarcastically remarked, he did not "think the public would be ruined."[38] To his wife, Adams revealed his exasperation. "I am wearied to death with the wrangle between military officers, high and low. They quarrel like cats and dogs. They worry one another like mastiffs, scrambling for rank and pay like apes for nuts."[39]

Greene thought Congress had done at least one very commendable thing. Their resolution to set up monuments to the memory of Richard Montgomery at New York when the city was recovered, Joseph Warren at Boston, and Hugh Mercer at Fredericksburg, Virginia, would, he was sure, have a salutary effect on the army as well as the country. He wished Congress would also offer medals for acts of bravery. Medals, he assured John Adams, would exert a great influence on the army with very little expense involved. His suggestion was adopted, and in time Greene and many others became recipients of these honors.

This was Greene's first visit to Philadelphia and he found time to see much of the city and its surroundings besides attending several dinners and other social affairs. After riding around the city and along the Schuylkill, Greene told Washington he believed the city could not be successfully fortified or defended. There were too many approaches and it would be too great a risk to commit a large force to its defense.

Though Greene enjoyed his short stay in Philadelphia, he was glad to get back to his responsibilities with the army. As for Congress, he had found that august body too full of speech makers and too wanting in men of action. "The Congress have so many of those talking gentlemen among them," he wrote, "that they tire themselves and everybody else with their long labored speeching that is calculated more to display their own talents than to promote the public interest." Greene wanted to see more men in Congress acquainted with business who may or may not have had the benefit of a liberal education. For one thing, he thought, Congress should constantly labor to establish a strong federal union, essential to which was free trade between the states. "I wish to see the several states consider themselves as one great body," he declared on more than one occasion.[40]

Washington was glad to see Greene back at his post in Basking Ridge. Reports had come that Cornwallis had learned that Greene was away and was planning to launch an attack before his return. Opinion of Greene's ability was as high in British circles, it would seem, as it was with Washington and his staff. Though the British made no move at that time, it was evident they intended to make one very soon. Not long after his return, Greene heard that the enemy was carting sections of a huge bridge from New York to New Brunswick for spanning the Delaware when the time came.

Cornwallis' attack came at dawn on the morning of April 13th when, with Major General Grant, he led 5,000 troops against Lincoln's little brigade at Bound Brook. Through failure of some militia to guard the river crossings, Cornwallis was able to get over the Raritan and almost upon the Americans before the alarm was sounded. Fortunately, Lincoln was alerted just in time to get away with all but sixty of his 500 men to the safety of the mountains two miles to the north.

When word of the attack reached Basking Ridge, Greene quickly assembled his brigade and by a forced march covered the ten miles to where Lincoln had drawn up his men on the mountain side. By noon, Greene and Lincoln reached Bound Brook, only to find Cornwallis had recrossed the river and slipped back to New Brunswick. Greene and Lincoln dined at Mr. Van Horne's where Cornwallis and Grant had had breakfast but a few hours before. Greene was sorry that Cornwallis had left in such a hurry as he very much desired "to shoot up" his rear guard if nothing more.

When Washington heard of the affair, he was much alarmed by how close the enemy came to capturing all of Lincoln's brigade. He therefore ordered Lincoln to move back within the first range of mountains, leaving but a small detachment at Bound Brook. For awhile Greene and Washington thought of launching a counterattack against New Brunswick but the idea was abandoned. Even if the Americans could drive Cornwallis out of the town, it was unlikely they could hold it for long with the enemy still at Amboy.[41]

Some of the time at Basking Ridge, Greene stayed at Lord Stirling's mansion, a mile and a half from the village. As this house was quite crowded with family and in-laws, Greene's headquarters was probably at White's Tavern in the center of the town. Nathanael found the Stirlings and their guests, Governor Livingston's wife and daughters, most delightful people. Lord Stirling's wife was Livingston's sister. Her sister-in-law, the Governor's wife, had fled to Basking Ridge with her children on the first approach of the enemy in November, leaving her home, "Liberty Hall," to be rifled by the invaders. Writing to Kitty early in April, Greene said, "I am now at Lord Stirling's seat, in a most agreeable family of Governor Livingston's. There are three young ladies of distinguished merit, sensible, polite, and easy. Their manners are soft and engaging; they wish much to see you here." The three young ladies were the daughters of Stirling and Livingston, all about the same age.

Lord Stirling's beautiful plantation, though under obligations of debt and soon to be taken from him, lent an air of grace and enchantment to many a gay party or dinner for officers and their ladies during these days. Slaves worked the land, some of which was planted to orchards and vineyards from trees and vines brought from Europe. Behind the large mansion with its center hall and beautifully decorated rooms was a paved court surrounded by stables, coach house, and other buildings ornamented with cupolas and weather vanes. On warm days Greene liked to sit on the piazza which extended along the front of the house and overlooked a fine lawn sloping down toward the Black River some distance away. Before Greene left Basking Ridge for the summer's campaigning, he saw Stirling's estate in all its beauty with flowers and orchards in blossom and fields and deer park green and lush.

While Greene was staying at Lord Stirling's he received the glad tidings of the birth of his second child, this time a girl to be named Martha Washington in keeping with his first-born,

George Washington Greene. "I read your letter with trembling hand," wrote Nathanael to Kitty. "Some superstitious fears had been hovering round me that something would happen to you. What gave rise to this troublesome train of visitants I cannot tell, unless it was the extreme anxiety I felt for you in your critical condition." God only knew when he would see the little ones, he told Kitty, but at least he had the satisfaction of knowing that his family was at Potowomut, surrounded by kinsfolk and friends.[42]

Successful British raids on Peekskill and Danbury in the Spring of 1777 caused Washington to worry about the safety of the Highlands which guarded America's lifeline between New England and the other states. At this time Greene was of the opinion Howe would first try to take Philadelphia before going against the Highlands. Washington, however, was not certain, and he decided to send Greene and Knox to inspect the forts and other defenses along the high banks of the North River.

It was early May when Greene and Knox set out from Morristown for Peekskill. The days were warm, the countryside beautiful, and there were friends, including Abraham Lott, along the way with whom to spend a night or a few hours of rest. At Peekskill, Greene and Knox were received by McDougall, Wayne, and George Clinton. After dinner, while the generals sat over their cups, Greene listened attentively as each expressed his views on the defense of the Hudson. The next day McDougall took Greene and Knox to Fort Montgomery, guarding the narrows near Bear Mountain. Finding several things there which he thought needed attention, Greene wrote to Clinton for a conference on the question. The next day the three visited Fort Constitution and Fishkill, on the east side of the river a little above Fort Montgomery. From here they crossed to New Windsor to inspect the area around West Point. The following day they rode down along the west bank of the Hudson to the Clove where Greene and Knox left McDougall and headed westward for Morristown.

Before leaving the Highlands, Greene wrote a report for Washington on the results of the inspection. Having been given the power to initiate improvements, Greene ordered a boom and

one or two cables to be put in front of the great iron chain being
suspended across the Hudson from Fort Montgomery to Anthony's Nose on the opposite side. These would break the force
of the blow against the chain, he said, if enemy ships got by the
chevaux-de-frise with their sharp points hidden beneath the
surface of the water. Behind the chain, Greene wanted two ships
and two galleys stationed for firing on British vessels approaching
the barrier. Additional batteries on the banks of the river were
also to be built for firing directly at any ships coming against the
obstructions. Greene concluded his report by stating that he
thought four or five thousand men were enough to guard the
Highlands until it became apparent that Howe intended to throw
the major part of his army against the Hudson River fortifications.[43]

On the way back to Morristown, Greene fell from his horse
on a high ragged mountain trail, cutting his lip badly and otherwise bruising himself. Arriving at Abraham Lott's at Beverwyck
late at night, dreadfully tired, and full of aches, Greene heard
news which made him at once forget all his pain and weariness.
A rumor had come that Kitty had arrived at Morristown! "O how
my heart leaped for joy, notwithstanding I was sure it was impossible! Yet the thought was so pleasing I could not help in-
dulging the sweet delusion!" Thus wrote Greene with the elation
of a schoolboy.

Never did Nathanael Greene find friends more to his liking than
the Lotts. Abraham Lott, Nathanael assured Kitty, was as merry
as a boy of fourteen and his wife charming and fully as vivacious.
The Lotts had five attractive daughters—and Greene always enjoyed the company of young ladies—all accomplished in music
and French. One of the daughters was married to Greene's former
aide William Livingston, son of the Governor. Abraham Lott's
handsome mansion, surrounded by fertile acres and worked by
slaves, stood eight miles northeast of Morristown near Whip-
pany.[44]

For a long time after the birth of Martha, Kitty Greene remained weak and sickly. Greene had been very worried about
her health but seemed to have convinced himself that she
would recover rapidly as soon as warm weather arrived. Just

before leaving for the Highlands, however, Greene received a letter saying that she continued ill in spite of the warm spring sunshine. An anguished Nathanael penned:

> My dear angel, the contents [of your letter] have wrung drops of blood from my heart. Gracious God, how much I wish to come to you! . . . But the General will not permit me to go. I have had exceedingly hard duty this spring. The General keeps me constantly upon the go. . . . There is not a day or night, nay not an hour, but I wish to fold you to my heart.[45]

By then it seemed an age to Nathanael since he had seen his homeland. In a way the old life seemed strange, like a memory of long gone days so much had happened in the two years he had been in the army. "How is Brother Bill? Where is Elihu? My best respects to him and his wife. Pray, is there harmony amongst you? Where is Griffin and his wife?" he queried in a letter to Kitty.[46]

Upon returning to Morristown Greene's hopes were again high as he thought that perhaps the spring had worked a rapid recovery in Kitty:

> I most ardently wish to see you, but the great distance between us, the poor accommodations on the roads, the uncertainty of the motions of the enemy, and the weak state of your health, are obstacles that prevent my pressing you to come, agreeable to my wishes,—I cannot express the recent pleasure I felt at hearing you was come, although I knew it must be false. . . .

Perhaps though he thought he had not made it clear how much he wanted to see her if she could possibly come. A second letter followed on the same day: "If you think your health and strength will endure the journey, my heart will leap for joy to meet you." Lucy Knox, presumably at Boston, would get Kitty all the clothes she needed, Nathanael assured her.

When and if Kitty came, Greene had many friends waiting to receive her. The Lotts, especially, wanted her to come and stay all summer with them. Here she could study music and French with Abraham's daughters. The Hoffmans, too, were equally solicitous for Kitty to stay with them at Morristown. Also Lady Stirling, her daughter Catherine, and the Livingstons were anxious for Kitty to come to Basking Ridge. Then there were

Martha Washington and some of the other wives of the officers at Morristown whom Kitty had known in Cambridge or New York who wanted to see her again.

It may be that Lucy Knox saw Kitty soon after her baby was born as Greene wrote that both Lucy and Henry Knox (who was in New England) were intending to visit Potowomut. Very likely, Lucy was planning to come with Kitty to New Jersey. At any rate, Greene cautioned his wife to mind her spelling when writing to Mrs. Knox as she was a "good scholar." Greene hoped Kitty would not think him unkind in mentioning this. "Nothing but the affection and regard I feel for you," he assured her, "makes me wish to have you appear an accomplished lady in every point of view."[47] As it turned out, Greene did not see his wife for some time to come. Word came from Rhode Island that Kitty had fallen sick with a fever and must postpone her journey indefinitely.

As the spring wore away and summer approached, Greene waited impatiently for recruits to arrive. Howe was getting ready to move and as yet Washington had not nearly enough troops to fight the enemy. "O that the Americans were but spirited and resolute, how easy the attempt to rout these miscreants!" exclaimed Greene. "But their foolish delays and internal disputes," he feared, would greatly prolong the war. Fortunately Howe waited a little longer before starting his campaign. Meanwhile recruits joined Washington in large numbers. As they marched into camp, Greene felt repaid for the untold hours he had spent in the organization of an army to take the field in 1777.

CHAPTER SEVEN

Wandering like the Arabs

A summer of marching and countermarching which was in store for the Continental Army in 1777 was not the kind of campaign which appealed to the Americans. But with transports Howe was able to land his army almost anywhere along the coast, and Washington had little choice but to be wherever danger seemed imminent. In any event, the marching was useful in conditioning the troops for the strain of battle when the time came.

When Greene returned to Morristown from the Highlands, Washington sent him to Bound Brook with orders to lay out an encampment on strong ground overlooking New Brunswick and the area occupied by the enemy. This done, he was to collect the troops from the outlying posts and put them to work fortifying the camp. Arriving at Bound Brook at noon on May 23rd, Greene spent the afternoon searching for a site for the army. He found it at Middlebrook, two miles northwest of Bound Brook where the ground was strong, water available, and retreat possible through a gap in the mountain. Among the first to arrive at Middlebrook was Greene's own division from Basking Ridge, consisting of the Virginia brigades under Weedon and Muhlenberg. John Peter Muhlenberg was the thirty-two year old Lutheran minister who had startled his congregation in Virginia one Sunday by throwing off his vestments to reveal himself in the uniform of a Continental officer. The militant minister then bade the drums to beat and all who would follow him to enlist at the church door. George Weedon, though not so spectacular as the minister, was brave, congenial, and twelve years Greene's senior. He kept a tavern at Fredericksburg, Virginia, which his wife ran while he was in the army. Both men would render invaluable service to Greene and become his lifelong friends.

As the troops came in by brigades, regiments, and companies from the scattered posts, Greene was busy getting them located and supplied with necessities. For a few days many had to sleep in the open but soon General Mifflin had them all in tents. However, moving an army to a location not far from the enemy where provisions had been more or less systematically carried off or destroyed, posed a problem in feeding the army. The commissary, embarrassed by lack of funds and inefficiency within the corps, could not meet the demand. Greene, therefore, was compelled to send foraging parties to scour the country toward Flemington from whence they returned with enough cattle, sheep, and flour to sustain the army until provisions arrived from Pennsylvania.

What gave Greene the greatest cause for alarm, however, was the appearance of camp fever among the troops pouring into Middlebrook. Believing as before that the heavy diet of fresh meat was one of the main causes of the disease, he took measures to have each man supplied with half a pint of vinegar with his daily rations. "Nothing will correct this evil like the free use of vinegar," he told Washington. As not enough cider vinegar could be found, he set about having vinegar made from molasses, flour, and water which he assured Washington would be ready for use in a fortnight. Further precautionary measures against the spread of the disease were taken. All springs were cleaned and rimmed with boards. Over each spring a roof was raised for further protection and to keep the water cool. All slaughtering was ordered to be done at least a mile from camp and the entrails and leavings buried at once.[1]

While Greene was erecting his fortified camp at Middlebrook, the British were not idle. Soon it was reported that they were leveling their works at Amboy and reinforcing New Brunswick in preparation for a push to the Delaware. On May 25th, just two days after Greene arrived at Middlebrook, a large party of horse and some infantry came out of New Brunswick and headed for Middlebrook. They were met by Wayne who drove them back to their lines with a loss of several dragoons. Warning Sullivan who commanded the division at Princeton to be on his guard, Greene wrote, "The Philistines are upon thee, Samson,—take care of yourself."[2]

To guard against an encircling movement, Greene stationed a troop of horse at Millstone and Somerset under Lieutenant

Colonel Francis Barber. Upon returning to Middlebrook from an inspection trip of the outposts on June 1st, Greene found the portly, forty-four year old General Lincoln waiting for him. While at dinner, Greene explained to Lincoln what remained to be done to put the camp in proper condition. Earthworks were being constructed around the camp and Steel's Gap a short distance to the right was being fortified. Greene asked Lincoln to take his brigade and work on the redoubts on the road over the mountain from Bound Brook.

Washington arrived at Middlebrook on May 29th followed by the troops from Morristown. At a council of war it was decided that the army should be ready to march on a moment's notice. Each soldier was to have ready at all times rations for two days and a full supply of ammunition. No details were overlooked. "The music of the army being in general bad," the fife and drum majors were to improve or be reduced to the ranks.[3]

On June 12th, Washington informed his generals that according to intelligence, General Howe had collected nearly his entire force at New Brunswick for the purpose of drawing out and defeating the American Army before marching on Philadelphia. They did not know, however, that Howe had no intention of crossing New Jersey if Washington remained undefeated. Rather than have Washington at his heels, Howe would go to Pennsylvania by sea. In any event he thought he could capture Philadelphia that summer and get back to the Hudson in time to cooperate with Burgoyne in an all-out drive on the Highlands.[4]

June 14th came (the day Congress resolved that America would have a national flag of thirteen red and white stripes and thirteen stars in a field of blue) and Howe began advancing with two divisions, one led by Cornwallis marching toward Princeton and the other, consisting of Hessians under Von Heister, directing its course toward Millstone, six miles west of Middlebrook. If Howe's aim was to catch Sullivan in a pincer movement, Greene knew it was too late as the American force at Princeton had moved to safe ground on Rocky Hill. Fearing, however, that Sullivan might be cut off from joining the main army, Washington directed him to move back twelve miles to Flemington from which position he could circle northward to join the army when necessary.[5]

As one division after another marched out of New Brunswick followed by long lines of baggage and supplies, Howe established a strong line eight or nine miles long between New Brunswick and Somerset with the Raritan River betwixt his army and Middlebrook and the Millstone River shielding his left flank. Like Washington, Greene was not sure whether this was a real thrust for Philadelphia or merely a maneuver to bring the Americans down off the heights. In any event neither Greene nor Washington was of a mind to oblige Sir William by leaving their strong ground for the plains below.

While Howe's army remained facing him, Washington had his troops ready if need be, to retreat. The tents were struck, wagons loaded, and horses harnessed. Meanwhile he sent out detachments to harass the enemy whenever an opportunity occurred. "The militia turn out in a very spirited manner," Washington told Schuyler, "and seem determined, in conjunction with the Continental Troops, to harass and oppose the Enemy upon their march thro' the Country."

Believing that Sir William, after failing to coax the Americans down from their strong position, would attack Middlebrook, Washington ordered Sullivan to send 1,000 Continentals and a like number of militia to strengthen his right flank at Steel's Gap. "As an encouragement to the militia," Washington told Sullivan, "let them know whatever Baggage or Spirits of any kind they can take from the Enemy shall be appropriated to their Benefit."

But to the surprise of everyone, instead of attacking, the British all of a sudden started back under cover of darkness for New Brunswick in great haste. Washington was of the opinion that Howe had been deterred from attacking by the strong ground chosen by Greene as well as "by the spirit that appeared among the Inhabitants who flocked together to join our Army, even beyond my expectation." Washington was right. In a letter to Lord George Germain, Howe explained that he had hoped to draw on a general engagement. Failing, he decided nothing could be gained by staying longer in New Jersey.[6]

Was Sir William after all only trying to draw forces from the Hudson Highlands, preparatory to a British push up the river? Greene asked himself. It was possible, and Washington, to play safe, took Greene's advice to order the brigades of McDougall and Glover which Putnam was sending to Middlebrook back to the Highlands. To strengthen the supposition that Howe's real design was to cooperate with Burgoyne who was slowly inching his way toward Ticonderoga from Canada, on June 21st the British began dispatching all their baggage and stores from New Brunswick overland by wagons and by flatboats down the Raritan to Amboy. Greene was not surprised the next day when the enemy evacuated New Brunswick early in the morning, burning houses and other buildings as they took the road to Amboy.

Although Washington was not unprepared to take advantage of Howe's retreat, orders miscarried and a coordinated attack upon the flanks and rear of the enemy failed to materialize. The night before, General Maxwell had been sent to the vicinity of Metuchen with 1,500 men, but the orders for him to close in on the left flank of the enemy never got through. Sullivan, advancing from Rocky Hill with his division, failed to reach New Brunswick until evening, after the British were safe within their lines at Amboy.

The main body of Americans to go out against the retreating enemy consisted of three brigades under General Greene. Leaving the remainder of the army posted on the slopes of Middlebrook, Greene's troops marched toward New Brunswick in the early morning. Morgan's riflemen and Wayne's brigade in the lead fell upon the rear of the enemy as they crossed the Raritan. After pursuing the fleeing enemy as far as Piscataway, Greene brought his force back to New Brunswick. Although Greene's success on June 22nd was far less than Washington had hoped for, he was not displeased with the outcome. "I fancy the British Grenadiers," he wrote Reed, "got a pretty severe peppering yesterday by Morgan's Rifle Corps."[7]

Upon arriving at New Brunswick, Greene found the town "a desolate village" with "not a house but was not almost entirely ruined." According to reports, the enemy had not been good housekeepers. "Such dog kennels as their huts was my eye never beheld," wrote one American. Even Lord Cornwallis' headquarters literally "stunk."

While Greene was pursuing the British toward Amboy, Washington decided he would follow the next day by marching the army along the border of the mountains toward Quibbletown. However, the next day it rained and the army remained at Middlebrook. With the weather clear again the following day, the army left Middlebrook at daybreak and advanced to Quibbletown, a distance of seven miles, where the troops camped without tents, making their shelters as best they could "with boughs of Trees." Greene's division came up from New Brunswick to form the right flank, camping close to the brook that ran near the town. Meanwhile, Stirling with his brigade had advanced to Metuchen within five miles of Amboy. Still nearer the enemy's lines were "light parties" to watch the British and report anything unusual to Stirling.

Two days passed with no change in the position of either army. Then on June 26th the unpredictable Sir William, hearing that Washington had left Middlebrook, decided he would try once more to engage the American Army before leaving New Jersey. But again Washington would not oblige him. At the first sound of firing, Washington moved back from Quibbletown with Greene leading the way to the slopes of the mountains a short distance away. To help Stirling and Maxwell, Morgan's riflemen and some light troops were sent to their relief.

The British right wing, commanded by the energetic Cornwallis, first fell upon Stirling's men near Metuchen. Twice the forces of Stirling and Maxwell made spirited stands but the pressure was too great and they were compelled to seek the safety of the mountains back of Scotch Plains. Though the day was insufferably hot and humid, Cornwallis, followed by Howe with the left wing, pursued some of the fleeing Americans as far as Westfield. There, dog-tired and parched by thirst (the Americans had plugged every well and spring for miles around with stones), the British made camp. The next day they moved to Rahway and on the following day all returned to Amboy.[8]

On June 30th, the day after Howe returned to Amboy, the British evacuated the town by moving the army with all its stores and baggage to Staten Island. General Charles Scott, the Virginian, whose force lay nearby, immediately moved into the deserted village with a small party to secure any stores left behind and to watch the British from across the Arthur Kill.

Each day it appeared more certain to Greene that General

Howe would do the logical thing and invade the Highlands to help Burgoyne. Two brigades were therefore dispatched under James Varnum and Samuel Parsons to reinforce Putnam. On July 2nd, hearing that Howe was hastily preparing to embark his army at Staten Island, Washington, with Greene's hearty approval, left Middlebrook and headed for Morristown.

Though tired when Morristown was reached, it was the Fourth of July and the army celebrated the event with fireworks and the firing of cannon. In Boston the day was observed by a sermon in the morning by the historian of the Revolution, The Reverend William Gordon. In the afternoon there was a firing of salutes and a big parade of Massachusetts militia. At Philadelphia the Hessian band captured at Trenton furnished music for a stirring celebration which ended with fireworks in the evening.

Soon after reaching Morristown, Greene set out for Abraham Lott's at Beverwyck. He was sent to supervise the collection of provisions and forage along the line of march to the Highlands. But he had another reason for hurrying so fast to Beverwyck. Kitty was there at last and he had not seen her for a year! There is no account of his arrival at Beverwyck and his meeting Kitty after so long a time. But sweet as was the time at Beverwyck, his mission was urgent and his stay was short. General Sullivan had gone ahead to Pompton with his division which was already nearly out of food. Arriving at Pompton, Greene soon had provisions delivered to Sullivan and more waiting along the highway for the rest of the army.[9]

When word arrived at Morristown on July 8th that Burgoyne was nearing Fort Ticonderoga, Washington ordered Sullivan to leave Pompton and march to the Clove, a narrow mountainous defile along the Ramapo River which led to the Highlands. Three days later the army left Morristown and marched to Pompton where Washington waited for further reports of Howe's activities before drawing nearer the Hudson. Greene was back with the army but he found time for a few lingering moments with Kitty each time he passed through Beverwyck.

Just before leaving Morristown, Greene heard the alarming report that St. Clair had given up fortress Ticonderoga, thought to be all but impregnable. "Charity obliges me to suspend all ill-natured reflections, but I fear there has been some misconduct somewhere," he wrote Kitty.[10] He did not know that St. Clair had no more than 3,000 untrained and poorly equipped men to pit against the 7,000 advancing under Burgoyne.

Whether or not St. Clair or Schuyler had done all in their power to hold back the enemy, new blood had to be sent north to satisfy public opinion which seldom took pains to consider the odds against American generals. Washington wanted Greene to go but at the same time he did not want to part with him. Sooner or later, he knew, he would be confronted by Howe's army and would need all the talent he could command. "I can plainly see the General wants me to go," Greene told Kitty, "but is unwilling to part with me; he has set several persons to sound my inclinations." Greene did not care to leave with Kitty nearby. However, if honor and reputation required it, he was sure she would want him to do his duty.[11]

Soon word came that Howe's army was fully embarked and ready to sail. Washington at once made up his mind. He would keep Greene while Benedict Arnold, who had just arrived from Philadelphia, would be sent to command Schuyler's New York militia. Benjamin Lincoln would be sent to lead the New England militia who were joining the northern army in amazing numbers. Greene approved the orders. Lincoln, he knew, was a good choice. Being as he was a Massachusetts man, he could handle his fellow Yankees who sometimes proved balky under strange officers.

Down in Philadelphia there was at least one who would have been happy to see Greene off to the northern army. This was Thomas Mifflin, the quartermaster. He thought Greene was practically directing the movements of the army and was largely responsible for its trek northward to protect the Highlands, thereby leaving the door to Philadelphia wide open for Howe. Although nothing was further from the truth, Mifflin believed that Greene considered the fate of New England before national interests.[12]

With Howe seemingly poised for a push up the Hudson, Washington ordered the army forward and Sullivan to leave the Clove and cross the river to Peekskill. On reaching Smith's Clove, the army rested four days while Greene busied himself with the ubiquitous problem of supplies and provisions. Then on the evening of July 19th, a report arrived that the enemy was sailing up the Hudson! At last, thought Greene, the great struggle for the gateway to the north was at hand. A council of war was called in which everyone agreed that the army must be rushed to the Highlands. Early in the morning with Maxwell's brigade leading and Muhlenberg's bringing up the rear, the army advanced rapidly into the Clove. By sundown, after marching eleven miles, camp was made at Galloway's old log house. Before morning another message came denying the report that the British were sailing up the river. Greene could hardly believe it. He agreed, nonetheless, that the army must wait at Galloway's until further word was received.

As it was possible the army might be in the Clove for some time, he sent Kitty a note suggesting that she pay him a visit. He did not coax her for the accommodations at camp were far from good and everything was so uncertain. However, "if you come," he wrote, "you shall sleep in a room with only myself and I hope you'll have no objection to that." Kitty, however, did not come nor did she hardly have time before the army was on its way back to Morristown.[13]

After five days at Galloway's, word arrived that the British had put to sea with destination unknown. Most of Washington's generals guessed rightly that the enemy had sailed for Philadelphia. Greene was not as sure as the others but he agreed that the army must march rapidly toward that city. Stirling, who had been sent to Peekskill with his brigade, was ordered to recross the North River at once and follow the army. For fear, however, that Howe might be playing a trick and would return as soon as Washington was gone, Sullivan, on Greene's insistance, was ordered to wait a little longer before following Stirling over the river.[14]

On reaching Pompton, Washington received from Putnam an intercepted letter from Howe to Burgoyne. When they learned the strange way the letter had fallen into Putnam's hands, both Washington and Greene agreed this had been Howe's intention. Howe was going to Boston said the intercepted letter. This was proof to Washington that he was sailing for Philadelphia. Greene was inclined to agree yet he was unwilling to rule out altogether the possibility that Howe would come back to the Hudson to go against the Highlands as good military strategy demanded.

As the army tramped the dusty roads to Morristown, Greene and Washington with their aides tarried at Beverwyck where Kitty and the Lotts entertained them as long as they could stay. As pleasant as it was at Beverwyck and as much as Greene wanted to stay longer, the fast lowering afternoon sun signaled their departure. Greene no doubt found it difficult to get his mind back on military problems as he galloped along the road to Morristown with his companions.

After passing the night at Arnold's tavern they caught up with the troops on the march to the Crossroads (now Bedminster). Here Washington and Greene stayed the night while the army marched on a few more miles before making camp. The next day the army camped at Flemington and then reached Coryell's Ferry July 29th, where they camped on both sides of the Delaware.[15]

As Greene followed the army, he could not help wondering if after all they were being led on a wild goose chase. It was hard to believe that Howe would not try to help Burgoyne as much as possible in his invasion of New York. True, Howe had left several thousand troops at Newport and New York, but the number was too small to be of much help to Burgoyne. Those at Newport, Greene knew, were there for the purpose of keeping New England men at home. He doubted that they would have much effect on New England as a whole and thought Howe might better have added them to the force under Clinton at New York or taken them with him if he were going against Philadelphia.[16]

While Greene was trying to figure out Howe's strategy, word came that the British fleet had been sighted off Little Egg Harbor. Washington agreed with Greene that it seemed strange Howe was no farther south if his destination was Philadelphia. Up in the wilderness of New York, Burgoyne, too, was perplexed. Writing to Germain on July 3rd, he said:

I have spared no pains to open a correspondence with Sir William Howe. I have employed the most enterprising characters and offered very promising rewards, but of ten messengers sent at different times and by different routes not one is returned to me, and I am in total ignorance of the situation or intentions of that general.[17]

Six weeks later when Howe entered Chesapeake Bay, he got a letter from Germain, dated May 18th, saying whatever he did should be done in time to cooperate fully with Burgoyne. This Howe intended to do, but Burgoyne, he thought, would not need him until autumn.

Until something more was heard of the whereabouts of Howe, Washington decided to wait at the Delaware, much to Greene's satisfaction. This time, however, he had not long to wait. On July 31st, just two days after he arrived at the Delaware, an express rode in from Philadelphia to announce that Howe's fleet was at the mouth of the river. Apparently the long guessing and waiting was over. Messengers were at once sent to all units of the army to cross the Delaware and march as rapidly as possible to the Quaker city. A fast rider dispatched a command to Putnam to send a division from Peekskill, leaving 2,000 Continentals and the militia to guard the Highlands.

But to the consternation of the foot-weary Americans, they had no sooner reached the vicinity of Philadelphia than the enemy fleet of sixty-seven ships sailed back around Cape May and apparently headed north. Was Howe after all just trying to wear down Washington's army before he made a push up the Hudson? "The enemy have maneuvered us to this place," wrote Henry Knox, "and after all, left us in the lurch."[18]

Having suspected this was Howe's design, Greene was not much surprised. A message was sent to Sullivan ordering him to march back to Morristown if he had advanced from that town. After delivering this order the rider was to go on to Peekskill to have Putnam turn back all troops dispatched to reinforce Washington. Writing from Chester, Pennsylvania, whither he had gone to view the ground, Washington ordered Greene to have the army ready to leave Germantown momentarily. After waiting for more than a week without another sign of the fleet, Washington agreed with Greene that it was time the army moved back toward the Delaware.[19]

The weather which had been distressingly hot for weeks showed no sign of moderating. Greene was very conscious of the great strain put on the troops by marching and countermarching but there seemed no alternative. It would have given the Americans some satisfaction to learn that their enemy in reality was suffering more than they. Packed into the transports and faring on salt rations, drinking foul water, and exposed to the blistering sun on deck or the stifling air below, the British were fast becoming weak and ill.[20]

In the midst of all his perplexities, Washington received more bad news from the north. The inhabitants of upper New York, Schuyler reported, were being thrown into such a state of panic by Burgoyne's Indians that American resistance threatened to become paralyzed. Something had to be done. Greene thought Daniel Morgan's riflemen would do the most good on the New York frontier and Washington reluctantly consented to their going.[21]

Leaving Germantown, the army made a day's march to Neshaminy Creek about halfway between Philadelphia and Coryell's Ferry. Here Greene found time to dash off a few letters. To his old friend James Varnum, now at Peekskill with his brigade, Greene admitted he had opposed coming to Philadelphia so hastily. True, the Quaker city was America's "Diana" and should be defended if possible, but it was far less important in Greene's opinion than the Highlands, the capture of which would seal off New England from the states to the southward like a wall. Greene felt compelled to admit, however, that Washington's rapid march to Germantown may have been the cause of Howe's hasty departure from the bay. In any event, the American Army was left in a "situation not a little awkward—compelled to wander about the country like the Arabs" in search of the enemy.[22]

Writing to his brother Jacob, Greene counselled him not to be despondent over Burgoyne's success in New York. "General Burgoyne's triumphs and little advantages, may serve to bait his vanity, and lead him on to his total ruin." The failure of the American Army at Ticonderoga might in fact, thought Greene, "be a necessary prelude to General Burgoyne's final overthrow." Greene assured his brother that whatever had caused St. Clair to abandon Ticonderoga it was from no lack of bravery as Greene had been in battle with the red-headed Scotchman and knew him to be as fearless as anyone in the army.[23]

To General Varnum, Greene confessed he approved Congress's

recent appointment of General Gates to succeed Schuyler as head of the Northern Department. Schuyler, who was partly blamed for the disaster at Ticonderoga, had lost the confidence of the people. What was more, his officers and soldiers, mostly New Englanders, disliked him. They knew his contempt for New Englanders in general. Greene's attitude was not personal. They were friends, and while Greene had respect for Schuyler's ability, he recognized his limitations.[24]

No sooner had Washington arrived at Neshaminy Creek than an express rode up with a report that the British fleet had been sighted sixteen leagues south of Cape May. What could Howe be doing that far south unless going against Charleston? asked Washington and his generals. The army, however, must wait at Neshaminy to make sure Howe did not turn back for the Delaware, expecting the Americans to be well on their way to the Hudson.

Ten days passed and nothing more was heard of the whereabouts of the fleet. Finally on the morning of August 21st, Washington called a council of war. All agreed that Howe must be sailing for Charleston. The thing to do, said Greene, was to march to the Highlands from where reinforcements could be sent to General Gates. All agreed, and plans were made for marching on the morrow. At the meeting, Greene was pleasantly impressed by Washington's youngest and newest major general, the winsome Marquis de Lafayette. Not yet twenty, Congress had just given him rank without command in honor of the young nobleman and as a token of friendship for the Kingdom of France. After the meeting, Alexander Hamilton was immediately dispatched to Philadelphia to get Congress's approval for returning to the Hudson. Congress offered no objection and Hamilton was soon back with his answer.[25]

On the same day, and probably before Hamilton returned, an express arrived at camp bearing the tidings that Howe's fleet had entered Chesapeake Bay! At first neither Washington nor Greene could find an explanation for this seemingly strange development. "It would appear," wrote Washington, and "(for what reason I am totally unable to account), that Maryland is the object of General Howe's present attention." Orders were now issued for marching back to Germantown instead of to the Hud-

son, and the next evening the army was again at its former
camping grounds.[26]

After a day's rest, the army started for Philadelphia at sunrise
on Sunday morning, August 24th. For a while it rained but by
seven the sun was shining brightly on the columns of marching
men with sprigs of green in their hats as an emblem of hope.
On entering the city, the troops paraded down Front Street and
up Chestnut past Independence Hall where the members of
Congress and city dignitaries were gathered. Buoyed by the
good news of General Stark's victory over the Hessians and British
at Bennington (where Burgoyne lost nearly 1,000 men), the
army paraded with the air of conquerors.

At the head rode Washington with his aides, followed by a
troop of cavalry. Next came the pioneers with their axes slung
over their backs. Greene's division, with Muhlenberg's brigade
leading and marching twelve abreast, were next in the line of
march. Riding in front of his men with his aides, Greene could
not help but notice the pride and satisfaction on the faces of
John Adams and other Congressmen as his horse pranced by
Independence Hall. If the Quakers were absent behind their
closed shutters, there were thousands of others to cheer, he
noted. As the last of the 11,000 troops paraded by Independence
Hall in step with the lively tunes of fifes and drums, Congressman Henry Marchant, Greene's old friend of East Greenwich
days, noted that the parade lasted two hours.[27] John Adams,
seldom at a loss for something to criticize, thought the army
appeared well armed, fairly well clothed, and "tolerably disciplined," though not enough attention was paid by some companies to minor details of dress.[28]

Leaving the city, the army crossed the Schuylkill on the
floating bridge and then marched on to camp at Darby. The
next day, with Greene's division again leading, the army marched
for Wilmington. Meanwhile, Washington, Lafayette, and Greene
rode ahead arriving there a day ahead of the army. Word came
that Howe was landing at the Head of the Elk at the northeast
corner of Maryland, fifty-five miles from Philadelphia. What the
American generals did not know, however, was that 5,000 of the
enemy left the transports too sick for immediate duty.[29]

During the spring and summer while Washington maneuvered against the enemy, his army continued to be shaken by discontent among its highest officers. Just after he arrived at Middlebrook in May, Greene heard a rumor that General Schuyler was going to be made President of Congress while keeping his rank in the Continental Army. Upon hearing of it, Greene wrote to John Adams expressing his abhorrence of the measure: "No free people ought to admit a junction of the civil and military, and no man of good principles would ask it." If General Schuyler cared to become President of Congress let him resign his commission in the army and not attempt to hold two offices "so incompatible one with the other." Rather than serve under a government that violated this great principle, he would resign, Greene told Adams. The blending of the military and civil offices in this way, he concluded, was "incompatible with the safety of a free people. I can assure you, I am not fighting for a change of masters but to have none but the law."[30] In answer, Adams agreed with Greene and declared he would oppose any move to make Schuyler President of Congress if he retained his commission in the army. As it turned out, Schuyler kept his commission but was not elected President of Congress.[31]

By far the most troublesome problem that confronted the army and Congress was the swarm of foreign soldiers who came flocking to America. Never very cordial toward having foreign officers in the army, it was not long before most Americans would have been happy to see all but a few go back from whence they had come. In a letter to Adams, Greene made it clear how he stood on the question:

> I have no wish to see such a large proportion of important officers in the military department in the hands of foreigners. I cannot help considering them as so many spies in our camp, ready to take their measures as their interest may direct. If foreigners are introduced, their command should not be very extensive, then the injury cannot be great, but even in this case it is an injury to America, for the multiplying foreign officers gives us no internal strength. A good nursery of officers, nursed by experience, firmly attached to the interest of the country, is a great security against foreign invaders.

Greene especially feared the power of British gold on these

men, most of whom in Washington's opinion were "but little better than adventurers."[32]

About a week before Greene expressed his opinion on foreign officers to Adams, Washington wrote in a similar vein to Richard Henry Lee. What did Congress expect him to do with so many of them, he asked:

> These men have no attachment or ties to the Country, further than interest binds them, they have no influence, and are ignorant of the language they are to receive and give orders in, consequently great trouble, or much confusion must follow, but this is not the worst, they have not the smallest chance to recruit others, and our officers think it exceedingly hard, after they have toiled in this service, and probably sustained many losses, to have strangers put over them, whose merit, perhaps, is not equal to their own, but whose effrontery will take no denial.[33]

Washington explained that this did not apply to engineers which the army very much needed. Congress, however, should be careful in the selection of engineers as Washington had two of high rank who apparently were but pretenders.

The trouble over foreign officers, whose jealousy of each other was as great as that between them and the Americans, rose to a great storm when the army learned that Silas Deane had engaged the Chevalier Ducoudray to be a major general in charge of artillery and engineers. Ducoudray had been adjutant general for the French Army and had been instrumental in getting the arms from the French arsenals for Beaumarchais to send to America. He was apparently an able officer and a good engineer but when it was found he was to take over the command of the artillery from Henry Knox a storm of indignation swept the army.

Greene at once took up his pen to give John Adams the benefit of his opinion on the proposed appointment. "The impropriety of putting a foreigner at the head of such a department must be obvious to everybody; besides the impropriety, you will deprive the army of a most valuable officer," he told Adams. He also questioned the wisdom of placing so much power in the hands of American ministers to the Court of Versailles. Greene did not know it but Silas Deane had already suggested to Congress that Washington be replaced by the Duc de Broglie![34]

A few days after Greene wrote, Washington addressed a letter to the President of Congress, John Hancock, in which he suggested giving Ducoudray a post not so embarrassing to the army. Command of the artillery, was, in fact, he told Congress, too great a responsibility to be entrusted to any foreigner. On June 5th, General Knox sent a note to Washington intimating that not only would he resign if Ducoudray superseded him, but that many of his officers would do likewise. The next day, Washington wrote President Hancock of his great concern over the possibility of losing many of his best officers because of the Ducoudray affair.[35]

The trouble came to a head in July when a rumor reached camp that Congress had honored Deane's commitment and appointed Ducoudray to command the artillery. Immediately Knox, Sullivan, and Greene sent letters to Congress announcing that if the report were true, they would resign. Greene's letter ended with the words, "I beg you'll acquaint me with respect to the truth of the report and if true, enclose me a permit to retire."[36]

Congress fairly exploded when the letters of the three generals reached Philadelphia. Congress, declared Hancock, considered the communications "highly derogatory to the honor and justice of Congress" and "an attempt to influence its decisions."[37] But no one in Congress was as angry as John Adams who had aided the advancement of all three generals, especially Knox. In a letter to Greene, Adams declared that there was no one in Congress who cared to defend the generals. "It was universally considered," he told Greene, "as betraying the Liberties of the people, to pass them by uncensured." Some were for dismissing all three from the service, others for ordering them to Philadelphia to answer for their offense. The officers, Adams declared, owed Congress an apology. He told Greene:

> It would be far from dictating to you, or giving advice unasked, but I really think, that a Declaration that you had no Intention to influence Congress, to condemn its Authority or infringe the Liberties of the People or the Privileges of Congress, a Declaration that you have the fullest Confidence in the Justice of Congress and their Deliberations for the public good, is the least that you could do, provided you can do this with Truth and Sincerity, if not I think you ought to leave the Service.[38]

If Greene answered Adams, as he implied in a letter written years later, the letter is lost. In any event, this ended the correspondence between the two men until it was resumed four years later after Greene had gone to the South and made a great name for himself on the battlefields of the Carolinas.

After thinking it over, Greene no doubt realized that he had been indiscreet. In a letter to the President of Congress from Ramapo, he sought to sooth the feelings of the delegates and apologize.

> I confess that it was matter of infinite surprise to me that an interpretation of so deep a complexion should have been put upon a meaning so innocent and inoffensive as that contained in those letters. Nor can I be persuaded but that Congress, upon a dispassionate review of the matter, will readily perceive that they have embraced ideas by no means deducible from anything we have done; and will in justice recall a censure equally severe, unmerited, and injurious.[39]

Apparently Washington thought Greene's letter answered Congress's request for an apology, for after informing Congress he had given the resolves to the generals he made no further mention of the incident. Congress read Greene's letter and put it aside without comment. Finally, on August 11th, Congress escaped from its dilemma by making Ducoudray Inspector General of Ordnance and Military Manufacturing with the rank of major general. Soon Ducoudray was assigned the task of improving the defenses of the Delaware where his engineering ability was put to good use until his career was terminated by his accidental drowning in the Schuylkill.

After burning its fingers on the Ducoudray affair, Congress became most circumspect in its handling of assignments and commissions for the foreign officers. When Lafayette appeared for his commission while the Ducoudray case was pending, Congress made him a major general as promised by Deane but dated his commission from the time of appointment and not from the time he made his contract with Deane. Lafayette was given no command and Washington was informed that it was fully understood that his commission was honorary and carried no compensation. A little later when Lafayette signified he expected a command as soon as he had acquainted himself with the American scene, the commander in chief was informed by Benjamin Harrison that Congress never intended him to have a command. Before long, however, both Congress and Washington were convinced, as was Greene, that the amiable young Marquis who had come, as he said, *pour apprendre et non pour enseigner,* was not like so many of the other foreign officers and was deserving of a position of trust and responsibility.

When Washington and Greene heard that General Howe was landing his troops at the Head of the Elk, they were certain at last that Philadelphia was his destination. They did not know that Sir William, upon reaching Cape May, had considered entering the Delaware but being advised that American forts and obstructions might prove embarrassing, had reverted to his original plan of landing at the Head of the Elk.* His decision was predicated on the assumption that by occupying the ground at the Head of the Elk he could shut off help from coming to Washington from the southward. Seemingly, he was using the plan offered so obligingly by his prisoner of war, General Charles Lee.[40] In any event, the summer's marching and countermarching had ended for the Americans. It was with a feeling of relief that they looked forward to the battles which would decide the fate of Philadelphia.

---

* Howe, it has been thought, could have landed without danger at Newcastle, only thirty-six miles from Philadelphia. W. Gordon, *History of the Rise, Progress and Establishment,* II, 493.

CHAPTER EIGHT

Campaign for a Quaker City

It may be that on the fields of Pennsylvania, General Howe
won the battles that lost the war. Nathanael Greene was not
unaware of the opportunities Howe was offering America by
leaving Burgoyne to shift for himself in the northern wilderness,
and his spirit was gay as he accompanied Washington and Lafayette on a ride down to have a look at the enemy and view the
ground between the two armies. Approaching within two miles
of the British camp, the American officers, who were accompanied by their aides and a troop of horse, looked long and
searchingly in the direction of the landing but could discern little
of interest from the slight elevation on which they stood.

On their return, they spent so much time in examining the
countryside that their progress was slow. Greene was confident
they could give the British a warm reception as the ground was
favorable for the Americans. While still far from Wilmington, a
severe thunderstorm in the late afternoon drove them to the
shelter of a farmhouse. As the storm continued, Washington
decided, much against the wishes of Greene, to pass the night
there. Greene could not help thinking about the fate of General
Lee when he chose to pass a night separated from his army at
Basking Ridge. He must have spent sleepless hours as he listened
to the rain and wondered whether they would momentarily be
surprised by the enemy. But the night passed without incident.
Meanwhile, Howe's troops slept in the open with only what
cornstalks and boughs they could find for shelter against the
driving rain.[1]

In the morning all returned to Wilmington. Within a few
hours Washington sent Greene out again with General Weedon
to select ground for making a stand against the enemy. After
studying for a day the land south and west of Wilmington,

189

Greene chose a position at the Cross Roads near Iron Hill, six miles from the Head of the Elk. The ground chosen not only was strong but left the army free to retreat into the hinterland. Furthermore, it was near enough to the enemy to deploy detachments which would make it dangerous for the foe to forage for provisions and horses.

But before Greene's recommendation reached headquarters, Washington held a council of war where it was decided to move forward a few miles to a position between Newport and Red Clay Creek, thus keeping the army directly astride the main road to Philadelphia. This was precisely what Greene had warned against. In this position Washington ran the risk of having his army thrown against the Delaware and surrounded. "You cannot hold your ground," he warned Washington. Furthermore it was not necessary to station the army there as Howe would not think of Philadelphia "until he has beaten this army," he wrote. But the decision had been made and Washington did not relish the embarrassment of reversing himself so soon.[2]

Greene's next assignment was to do all he could in removing and destroying stores in the path of the enemy. Greene said he needed 2,000 men for the work but the army could spare only a few hundred as most of the troops in the five brigades sent forward had to be kept under arms. He was also hampered by a shortage of horses and wagons as most of these were carrying fleeing families westward to places of safety. Much grain and forage had to be burned. Greene disliked doing it and the distress of the people made him sad. "Here are some of the most distressing scenes imaginable," he wrote. "The country all resounds with the cries of the people, the enemy plunders most amazingly."[3]

After Sir William landed his army, the weather continued rainy for several days. Besides the inclement weather, there were other obstacles to forestall immediate marching. In addition to the 5,000 sick, most of the rest of the troops were so weakened as to require several days to recuperate. But before Howe could march he had to get horses as almost all of the several hundred animals on shipboard had died at sea. On the 28th, three days after landing, British units advanced to Elkton where five days were spent in foraging. On September 2nd, forward corps occupied Iron Hill only a short distance from Maxwell's light troops on White Clay Creek. In spite of all that Greene could do, Howe's foraging parties found some cattle and enough horses to get his men moving.

Meanwhile, Washington was getting the army ready for battle and calling upon the militia of Pennsylvania, Maryland, and Delaware to join him. Greene characteristically was not much impressed by the militia. They were, he told Kitty, not much like the seasoned New Jersey militia. "Fighting is a new thing with these, and many seem to have but a poor stomach for the business."[4] On September 7th, word arrived that Howe was disencumbering his troops of all baggage but blankets. Washington did likewise, sending his baggage up the roads toward West Chester. The whole army was commanded to have two days' rations on hand and be ready for marching or fighting at a moment's notice. The next day, Howe marched his army directly toward Washington's and in the late afternoon reached Mill Town, a hamlet only two miles from the American Army back of Red Clay Creek. "We waited for them all day," wrote Washington, "but upon reconnoitering their situation in the Evening, we judged they only meant to amuse us in Front, while they marched by our right flank and gained the heights of Brandywine." A council of war was called, and it was decided that the army must be immediately moved to the high ground on the east side of the Brandywine in the area of Chad's Ford. The position at Red Clay Creek had proved untenable as Greene had predicted.[5]

At 2 A.M., September 9th, the army began marching for Chad's Ford ten miles to the north. In the morning the British marched northward to Kennett Square by a line almost parallel to the American route. The next day Howe advanced to about three miles of Chad's Ford and prepared for battle the following day.

While the American army was marching to Chad's Ford during the early hours of the morning, Greene found time to snatch some rest, if not sleep. He had been constantly in the saddle for the past thirty hours and had not slept in forty. But he could not sleep for a dusty bed brought on his asthma. Nevertheless, in the morning he felt "finely refreshed" and ready for the heavy duties of the day. The army was in fine spirit and Greene felt confident. The Americans would be on strong ground, he knew, and the troops were generally more seasoned and ready for a major battle than at Long Island the year before.[6]

Washington assigned the center of the American line, athwart the main road, to Greene who placed Wayne's brigade with Proctor's Pennsylvania artillery behind breastworks at Chad's Ford. On rising ground behind the front line he stationed the brigades of Weedon and Muhlenberg as reserves. To the right of Greene and extending up along the east side of the Brandy-wine for about two miles were the divisions of Sullivan, Stephen, and Stirling. To the left of Greene, where the banks were steep and rugged, 1,000 Pennsylvania militia were posted under the old Indian fighter, John Armstrong. Far to the right and above Stirling, some Delaware militia and others were placed to watch for a flanking movement by the enemy.

To check the advance of the British while they were still west of the river, Maxwell placed his brigades on high ground on both sides of the Nottingham Road opposite Chad's Ford and threw up a barricade of fallen trees. Some militia were also placed on the west side of the river opposite the upper fords guarded by the main army. Here too, was most of the cavalry under the twenty-nine year old Count de Pulaski, not to be commissioned by Congress until after the battle. In all, Washington had approximately 13,000 men. Howe had about the same number but his army was much superior as a fighting force.[7]

The morning of Thursday, September 11th, was foggy and damp until a blazing sun cleared the sky for a hot and humid day. Very early Maxwell was out scouting for the enemy whose vanguard he stumbled upon about nine o'clock. After several clashes of various degrees of intensity, his men were finally forced to retire over the Brandywine but not until General Knyphausen had brought the full weight of his 5,000 Hessians to bear on the plucky Americans.

Fully expecting the whole front soon to explode, the Americans all along the Brandywine awaited the rush of the enemy. But all that came were shots from the enemy's cannon which did little damage. As the sun passed its meridian, Washington and Greene began to wonder whether or not they were merely being "amused" again while the enemy stole around to their rear. It was thus when a messenger arrived bearing a report that a large section of the British Army had been sighted heading northward at some distance beyond the American right flank.

When the message arrived, Greene was at Washington's headquarters at the McIlwain home near Ridley about a mile back of Chad's Ford.* To both Washington and Greene it seemed incredible that Howe would divide his army. It was a great blunder, they declared, and one that should decide the day. Orders were immediately sent to the whole army, with the exception of the brigades with Stephen and Stirling, to close in on Knyphausen. Howe's flanking column, if the report were true, was ten miles from Greene's center and Stephen and Stirling should be able to hold it off while the rest of the army surrounded and destroyed Knyphausen with twice his number.

Greene's division had begun crossing the creek when another message arrived from Sullivan. Without comment Sullivan relayed a report that a scouting party over the creek had seen nothing of an enemy anywhere on the right flank. Had Howe sent a detachment northward and circled it back to his army in order to make Washington think he had divided his forces? Were they after all marching right into a trap by ordering an advance upon Knyphausen? One would have to be sure. The orders for advancing were therefore countermanded and the army settled down again to await the frontal attack by Howe's whole army. Thus ended, for want of good intelligence, a golden opportunity to give the British Army one of its soundest defeats of the war.[8]

Time passed. Finally at two o'clock a farmer from the north came dashing into headquarters on horseback to announce that he had seen the enemy marching around Stirling's right flank. As there were many Tories in the neighborhood, the American officers were puzzled as to whether to believe him or not. But while they were debating the question, a message from Sullivan removed all doubt. Howe and Cornwallis, after marching fifteen miles, were over the Brandywine and within two miles of Stirling's rear.

Sullivan was at once directed to move the whole right wing

---

* Some accounts place his headquarters at Benjamin Bing's tavern near Ridley. See G. W. Greene, *Life of Nathanael Greene*, II, 461.

to the heights near Birmingham Meeting House, a mile and a half back from the creek. The right wing's new position, declared the British engineer John Montresor, "was remarkably strong, having a large body advanced, small bodies still further advanced and their rear covered by a wood wherein their main body was posted, with a natural glacis for 3/4 of a mile."[9]

However, before Sullivan could get the left wing of the new line placed, it fell under heavy fire. By half-past four in the afternoon the left wing was all but swept away leaving Sullivan's center without support. Though outnumbered two to one, Stirling and Stephen held their line for nearly two hours. General Thomas Conway, a veteran of foreign wars, declared he had never seen "So Close & Severe a fire." The mounting pressure, however, finally compelled the Americans to fall back. By the time help arrived, the retreat had turned into a rout.

Back at headquarters, Washington continued to believe that Howe's attack on Sullivan's lines was but a diversion to draw off American forces after which he would strike at Chad's Ford with his main army. Whether or not Greene shared this view is not known. At five o'clock, Washington wrote the President of Congress, "At half after four o'clock, the Enemy attacked Genl. Sullivan at the Ford next above this and the Action has been very violent ever since. It still continues. A very severe Cannonade has begun here too and I suppose we shall have a very hot Evening."[10] Not long after writing this, Washington learned that the greater part of the enemy had fallen upon Sullivan and that he was in desperate need of help if his troops were to be saved.

Greene was immediately directed to take his division and go to the rescue. Washington and Lafayette galloped ahead to meet and help rally the fleeing right wing. Though wounded in the leg Lafayette stayed on his horse and kept fighting. It was six o'clock by the time Weedon's brigade reached the scene of battle after covering nearly four miles in forty-five minutes. The rest of Greene's troops, consisting of Muhlenberg's brigade and Stewart's Pennsylvanians, arrived a little later.

Arriving upon the scene, Greene ordered his ranks to be opened to allow Sullivan's disorganized troops to fall into the rear and reform. Slowly retreating, Greene brought his division to Sandy Hollow, "a narrow defile flanked on both sides by woods and commanding the road." About sunset Cornwallis threw his forces against Greene's. Twice his men were driven back by a deadly fire. "To the bayonet! to the bayonet!" rang the shouts all along the enemy lines as the Hessians lowered their muskets for what they expected would send the Americans flying for cover.

As the Hessians approached Greene's line, some of the older Anspachers, legend holds, recognized General Muhlenberg riding along his line on his white horse. Muhlenberg had served with them as a boy at Göttingen where he had gained a reputation for being afraid of nothing. *"Hier kommt Teufel Piet!"* they shouted as a warning to their comrades that the battle was not over. Again the Americans poured their lead into the ranks of the charging foe and then stood their ground with the bayonet to push back those who escaped their bullets. Finally Weedon's brigade was forced to withdraw back of Muhlenberg's but by this time it was nearly dark. Meanwhile Sullivan's troops had been able to get away. Greene followed on the road to Chester and the enemy, worn out from a day of marching and fighting, made no attempt to pursue. That Greene's division saved the army from a crippling defeat there can be no doubt.[11]

Across from Chad's Ford, Knyphausen waited until he thought Howe had broken the American right wing before he struck. Howe's strategy at Brandywine was, in fact, so similar to that of Long Island that men have wondered why Washington or his generals did not perceive it earlier. Douglas Southall Freeman blames Washington for the mistake. "Washington conducted the Brandywine operation," he wrote, "as if he had been in a daze."[12] This conclusion hardly seems justified. To the last, Washington and Greene clung to the belief that Howe would not divide his army by sending a major division on a fifteen mile loop around the American Army. There was nothing faulty, therefore, in their analysis. The trouble arose from the breakdown in American intelligence that day.

Though Greene saved Sullivan's troops from being scattered or annihilated, the forces left behind at Chad's Ford came near being trapped as Stirling had been at Long Island. Some of Knyphausen's troops got across a ford below Chad's and came upon the American left flank just about the time a division from Cornwallis' forces, after being lost in the woods for a while, emerged near the American center at Chad's Ford. Fortunately Wayne and Maxwell, unlike Stirling when Cornwallis came upon him at Long Island, got away to some hills to the eastward where they repeatedly fought off the enemy until darkness fell. They then joined the rest of the army trudging through the night toward Chester.

Brandywine was indubitably a defeat for American arms—but not as crushing a one as it came near being. American losses were about 1,200 killed, wounded, and captured. This was double the number lost by the enemy but the vanquished were not discouraged. It was the first major battle since Long Island and though many had never been in combat, most of the men fought long and bravely against very uneven odds.

Of the army which tramped through the darkness toward Chester, the greater part thronged the highway as a mob without the least semblance of order or discipline. Most of the troops reached Chester in time to get a few hours sleep before they were called upon to find their standards and be ready to march again. Washington, Greene, and most of the generals were on hand to help reform and get the army started on a twelve mile march to Germantown. Parties were sent back over all the roads to pick up stragglers and send them to Maxwell at Chester. General Maxwell would follow the army to Germantown the next day.[13]

At Germantown, whither Washington had brought his army to recuperate and procure supplies, there was no rest for Greene. As usual, there were not hours enough in the day for him to attend to any but the most pressing of his duties. The troops, however, not only got some much needed rest, but also some rum for their bravery at Brandywine. Congress, indeed, voted thirty hogsheads of rum for the army, each man to have a gill a day as long as the supply lasted.

Having apparently saved the army from a much greater disaster, Greene's officers were disappointed when Washington made no mention of their services in his general orders or letter to Congress. Greene brought the matter to Washington's attention. Washington, according to some authorities, is said to have replied, "You, sir, are considered my favorite officer: Weedon's

brigade, like myself, are Virginians; should I applaud them for
their achievement under your command, I shall be charged with
partiality; jealousy will be excited, and the service injured."[14]

During the one-day stay at Germantown, orders were issued
for cutting loose the floating bridge over the Schuylkill and
anchoring it on the Philadelphia side. Colonel Du Portail, a
French engineer, was directed to assist General Armstrong in
building redoubts at the fords along the Schuylkill. Messages were
sent to Putnam at Peekskill and Heath at Boston to send all the
Continental troops in their command to Washington. General
William Smallwood, on his way to join the army with over a
thousand Maryland militia, and Colonel Mordecai Gist with a
smaller number of Delaware men were urged to hurry forward.

On September 15th, a day pleasant and warm, Washington's
army crossed the Schuylkill at Levering's Ford and marched west
to the region of Warren's Tavern, about fifteen miles from Germantown. Greene felt as sure as before that Sir William would
not attempt to enter Phildelphia without first doing his best to
destroy the American Army and the move had been made at
Greene's insistence. Greene was confident that another battle
would not end like Brandywine, and he was anxious to engage
the enemy. "We are moving up this Road," wrote Washington,
"to get in between the Enemy and the Swedes Ford and to
prevent them from turning our right flank, which they seem
to have a violent inclination to effect, by all their Movements."[15]

The same day, Howe ordered Cornwallis and Knyphausen to
march rapidly without baggage toward Warren's Tavern. Baron
De Kalb, chiefly engaged in seeking his appointment as major
general from Congress as promised by Deane, agreed with Greene
that Washington had an excellent opportunity to defeat his adversary advancing in three widely separated columns.[16]

Early on the morning of the 16th, scouts from Washington's
army reported the enemy already in the field and advancing for
battle. Wayne and Maxwell with their light troops were sent
forward to skirmish with the enemy and do as much harm as
possible. As Washington drew up his army for battle, Greene
perceived that the position chosen was not entirely suitable.
Back of some of the troops lay low, wet ground which might
bring disaster if the men had to retreat swiftly. When Greene

pointed this out to Washington, the latter seemed unable to make up his mind whether to move or stay. The enemy was coming on, but still Washington debated the question with his officers as the division waited to be placed in line. Finally, Timothy Pickering, the adjutant general, rather boldly asked Washington if he would not come to a decision as the sound of battle was drawing near. "Let us move," answered Washington, at which Greene rode off to get the army to another ridge not far in the rear.

Some days later Pickering told of falling in with Greene on a march and saying, "General Greene, before I came to the army, I entertained an exalted opinion of General Washington's military talents, but I have since seen nothing to enhance it." Pickering commented in his diary that he did not venture to say that his opinion of the commander in chief "was sensibly lowered, though that was the fact, and so Greene understood me, for he instantly answered in these words. 'Why the General does want decision, for my part I decide in a moment.'" If Greene said this, it was the only time on record that he made a statement derogatory to Washington's military ability. Baron De Kalb at this time shared Pickering's opinion of Washington. While most amiable and obliging, he felt Washington lacked certain qualities necessary for a general:

> . . . as a General he is too slow, even indolent, much too weak and is not without his portion of vanity and presumption. My opinion is that if he gains any brilliant action he will always owe it more to failure or to the faults of his adversary than to his own capacity. I will even say that he does not know how to profit by the clumsiest mistakes of the enemy.[17]

While Greene was still engaged in moving the army to the new position, rain began to fall. Presently both armies found themselves caught in a great equinoctial storm borne by a strong northeast wind. Men, horses, and artillery sank into the mud and firearms became too wet to fire. Fearing, however, that Howe might contrive to launch a bayonet charge before the Americans could be supplied with dry powder, Washington marched his men all night through the rain to Yellow Springs, eleven miles to the northeast. The men waded through freshets waist deep; more than 1,000 were barefoot. When they reached Yellow

Springs the rain had stopped. Fires were built and the men warmed themselves as best they could. What shelter they had that night were windbreaks made from blankets and the boughs of trees.

Greene did not arrive at camp until late in the day as he had been along the road doing what he could to bring up the baggage and stores. Officers from each brigade had been dispatched to search buildings along the line of march as hundreds of men had left the ranks in search of shelter against the rain and cold during the grueling night. Not long after Greene arrived Washington sent him with Tench Tilghman toward Warwick Furnace to find strong ground where the army could refresh itself and await provisions and a new supply of ammunition. As nearly as could be ascertained, the army had lost 400,000 rounds of ammunition because of the storm.

At Warwick, Greene chose the side of a range of mountains not unlike Middlebrook in New Jersey where the enemy could not force a general engagement. From the safety of this position, however, Washington could harass the enemy with detachments. In this way Greene would take advantage of Wayne and Maxwell who were hiding on the flank and rear of the enemy ready to strike.

While Greene was selecting ground for strategic maneuvering, Washington called a council of war. Once again, the staff, without waiting to hear from Greene, voted to place the army directly between the enemy and Philadelphia. Developments would show again how wrong Washington was in not following Greene's advice.

On the 19th, clear and sunny again, Washington's army marched east to cross the Schuylkill at Parker's Ford. The water was deep and cold after the rain and the men waded waist deep through the racing river. "The procession lasted the whole night," wrote Muhlenberg, "and we had all kinds of visits from officers wet to the breast, who had to march in that condition the cold, damp night through, and to bear hunger and thirst at the same time."[18]

After crossing the river, the American Army occupied positions at Flatland and Swede's Fords in the path of the oncoming enemy. Sullivan had his men throw trees into the river at the fords to hamper the British in crossing. Greene, however, was not very optimistic about holding them off. There were too many fords for the army adequately to guard them all.

Washington had barely placed his army along the Schuylkill when word came that Howe had turned and was heading northward toward Reading. Did Howe intend to capture Washington's supply base at Reading and then march down the east bank of the Schuylkill? If so he must be stopped. Orders were therefore issued for the army to march northward parallel to the British on the west bank. But the foxy Sir William, with Washington up the river four miles from Potts Grove, wheeled about and marched directly to Gordon's and Flatland Fords. By the morning of September 21st, all were over the river and the way lay wide open to Philadelphia. Washington must have wondered again why he had allowed Greene's well-formed plan to be discarded for one which ended in failure. Four days later Cornwallis with four battalions of Grenadiers and a troop of Dragoons entered Philadelphia. The greater part of Howe's army pitched camp at Germantown.[19]

While Howe's army was crossing the Schuylkill, he won a victory over Wayne which haunted Mad Anthony until he finally reaped revenge at Stony Point. Wayne, while following the enemy, had brought his 1,500 light troops secretly, he believed, to a wooded hill about a mile north of Warren's Tavern. But Howe, apprised of his whereabouts by Tories, sent Major General Grey to wipe out the Americans, if possible.

Anthony Wayne was not surprised by the enemy contrary to what has often been written. He heard the shots fired by his sentries, and he had time to get most of his men in line. He made the fatal mistake, however, of stationing his troops in front of their campfires. With the Americans thus silhouetted against the forest, the enemy had no difficulty in finding their victims, while Wayne's men could not see the British until they were all but upon them. Grey had ordered all flints removed from the guns of his soldiers so that no one could fire his weapon accidently. Victory would be won by the cold steel alone.

In an instant, Grey's men were upon the Americans. Then followed a sickening scene of slaughter. Even then Wayne and about three-fourths of his men made good their escape with all their cannon. With the loss of only six soldiers, however, "No Flint" Grey had crippled Wayne's force and relieved Howe of all worry of being attacked while his back was turned in crossing the river. Chagrined by Wayne's humiliating defeat, Washington made no mention of the "Paoli Massacre" in his letters to Congress. Greene, who respected Wayne's military ability, also refrained from criticizing him. In war such things would happen.*

As it appeared that Howe would sit tight for some time and let the Americans take the offensive if they chose, Greene advised against attacking the enemy until Washington was reinforced and his men refreshed. At this time, Greene was doing his best to get clothing and shoes for the thousands of barefoot and threadbare soldiers.

By easy stages Washington advanced toward the enemy until on October 2nd his army lay encamped at Metuchen Hill, sixteen miles from Germantown. As McDougall and Smallwood had arrived with reinforcements and others were coming, Greene was satisfied that an attack was feasible at the first opportunity. Washington had 8,000 Continentals and 3,000 militia. If the enemy could be surprised, victory should be quite certain, Greene thought.

Sooner than Greene expected an opportunity arose for attacking Germantown. It was learned Howe had sent a large detachment to bring supplies from Elkton. Another detachment had been sent over the Delaware to attack the Americans at Billingsport. With no more than eight or nine thousand troops remaining at Germantown, Greene enthusiastically endorsed Washington's decision to attack.

By seven in the evening of October 3rd, the American Army began moving toward Germantown. For identification each soldier wore a white piece of paper in his hat as the attack was planned to take place before daybreak. The army marched in three main divisions: the center under Sullivan marched by way of the Shippack Road; the left wing under Greene, with the major part of the army, took the Lime Kiln Road; and the right wing, consisting of militia led by Armstrong, took the road

---

* A military court acquitted Wayne with highest honors. According to Baurmeister, 100 Americans were killed, 70 wounded, and 80 taken prisoner. C. L. Baurmeister, *Revolution in America*, p. 115.

nearest the river. The enemy's camp stretched from the Schuylkill near the mouth of Wissahicken Creek for three miles to the center of Germantown and from there over to the Old York Road. The plan was to envelope and destroy the enemy by simultaneously attacking his front, flanks, and rear.

Coming upon the British by way of Mount Airy, Sullivan and Wayne, flanked by Conway, struck the enemy about five in the morning. Soon the Americans had Howe's light infantry in full flight down the road. About six companies of the enemy with four field pieces, however, saw fit to barricade themselves in Benjamin Chew's sturdy stone house where all efforts to dislodge them proved futile.[20] Sullivan and Wayne pushed on with most of the advanced troops but the reserves which had arrived under Stirling, Maxwell, and Nash were deployed in an effort to storm the Chew house. Washington, who was nearby, was urged by Reed to order the reserves forward while the Americans had the initiative. Knox, however, who was ineffectively pounding the house with his cannon, opposed leaving a strong body of the enemy in their rear. Washington agreed and thus rendered a decision which apparently cost him victory when it was all but within his grasp.

It was forty-five minutes after the battle opened before Greene met the enemy as he led his troops down the Lime Kiln Road toward Luken's Mill. Greene was very put out that his guide had lost his way thus leading the division four miles off their route and making him late for the battle. By this time a light mist had turned to a heavy fog which furnished cover for the hard pressed enemy and soon caused confusion and misfortune for the Americans. The next thing to go wrong occurred when General Stephen disobeyed Greene's orders by breaking away with his brigade on the right to race toward the firing at Chew's house. On the way his men bumped into Wayne's who were endeavoring to overtake Sullivan's troops. Both lines fired at each other in the fog and then fled in opposite directions.*

With the brigades of Muhlenberg and Scott, Greene met the enemy at Luken's Mill. Perceiving, however, that he was in

---

* Another version is that Stephen ran into Wayne and after shooting at each other, Stephen was cut off from Greene's division. G. W. Greene, *Life of Nathanael Greene*, I, 476.

danger of being outflanked on his left, Greene swung to the right under cover of the fog and swept all before him as far as the market place. Meanwhile, Sullivan's unsupported troops came up against strong units of the enemy under Grey and Grant. The dense fog was ideal for the British as it allowed them to get close to their enemy before firing and charging with the bayonet. The Americans stood for a moment, then in spite of all their officers could do, turned and fled.

Grey and Grant then turned to meet Greene who with the foe also at his back was soon nearly surrounded. Muhlenberg, in advance of the main body and finding himself cut off by the enemy, made a desperate charge which carried his men right through the British line to rejoin Greene. Colonel George Mathews with the Ninth Virginia regiment was not so fortunate. Some distance ahead of the others with 100 prisoners, he was of a sudden surrounded, wounded by bayonets, and forced to surrender his 400 troops.[21]

Greene retreated through the village, his men firing from fences and walls as they retired. Muhlenberg, it was said, was so exhausted he fell asleep in his saddle while his men were pulling down a fence which his horse refused to jump. He was electrified into consciousness when a musket ball whistled by his head as the enemy appeared just behind him. Wayne joined Greene's troops to help cover the rest of the fleeing army. Here and there the Americans brought their cannon into play to stop the pursuit of the enemy momentarily. Pulaski's red-coated cavalry, who could hardly be distinquished from the enemy dragoons, were quite as demoralized as the infantry. At one place while fleeing from British dragoons, a party of American horsemen rode right through Greene's retreating line, scattering the troops who thought they were the enemy.

Cornwallis, who had come up from Philadelphia with three battalions, took over the chase and followed Greene's tired men for five or six miles. "The enemy kept a civil distance," wrote Thomas Paine, once again one of Greene's aides, "sending every now and then a shot after us and receiving the same from us."

While the Battle of Germantown was fought, American militia on the right and left of the two main divisions failed to close in on the enemy and were pushed back in the general retreat.

As in the Battle of Brandywine, the American loss of over a thousand killed, wounded, and captured was double the casualties suffered by the enemy. Each side lost a general: the Americans, Brigadier General Francis Nash, of North Carolina; the British, Brigadier General James Agnew.[22]

Although the Battle of Germantown turned out to be another defeat for Washington and his forces, Nathanael Greene knew it came near being the ruin of Howe's army. The British officers knew it too. Some even thought that in spite of the American mistakes and the fog, the Americans would have won if Sullivan's division had not run out of ammunition.

For the first time in the war, the Americans in the Battle of Germantown marched out to attack the major part of the British Army. Greene thought it demonstrated that the American Army could at last meet the enemy in a general battle and have a good chance of winning the day. The next time, thought Greene, the Americans would surely have better luck. Wayne agreed: "Upon the whole it was a glorious day. Our men are in high spirits, and I am confident we shall give them a total defeat the next action. . . ."[23]

Some of the American generals, out of consideration for their exhausted troops, wanted to camp after the British stopped following, but Washington made the army march all the way back to Pennypacker's Mill (also spelled Pennebecker) twenty long miles from the scene of conflict. How the men endured it is a wonder. Many of the officers, including Generals Pulaski and Conway, worn out by the strain of battle, were found asleep in buildings along the line of retreat. Major General Adam Stephen, found lying in a fence corner quite intoxicated, was court-martialed and cashiered. Apparently the general, who was brave though sometimes given to exaggerations about his military exploits, had taken too much liquor in an effort to combat fatigue.

As the battle presented a rather confused picture even in the minds of those who had fought it, many accusations were made against various officers. Some blamed Greene for being late. After the battle, however, Reed asked Washington if he were dissatisfied with Greene's conduct. "No, not at all," answered Washington, "the fault lay with ourselves" for stopping at Chew's house when victory was all but won.[24]

Although Sir William Howe had outmaneuvered and outfought the Americans during the past month and was in possession of Philadelphia, the campaign was not ended by the Battle of Germantown. Indeed, Howe's situation was most precarious. Unless the American hold on the Delaware could be broken within a few weeks, the British army would be starved into giving up the city and beating a retreat to New York. If it came to that, Greene was ready to wager that Howe's army would never get across New Jersey without being defeated and most likely destroyed.

Ever since the war began, Pennsylvania had been working on defenses for the Delaware River and the approaches to Philadelphia. After the Battle of Long Island, work was pushed on the fortifications as a march upon Philadelphia by the enemy became daily more threatening. After the victory at Trenton, General Gates was in command at Philadelphia until August. Gates labored to improve the defenses and after him DuCoudray, the French engineer, took over the work until his untimely death in September.

Nathanael Greene had given much thought and attention to the problem of defending the Delaware as well as the Hudson. On his visit to Philadelphia in March he had studied the river and its shore line and given Washington, Gates, and Congress the benefit of his conclusions. In June he supplemented this with a special report to Washington on the defense of Philadelphia and the Delaware.

Greene saw clearly that Fort Mifflin on Mud Island, five miles down the river from the city, was the key to the defense of the Delaware. He advised Washington to concentrate on Fort Mifflin rather than putting too much trust in Fort Mercer at Red Bank on the New Jersey side. As the Delaware channel was narrow, allowing only two ships abreast, Greene put great reliance on the use of fire ships whose blazing hulls could be sent down the river against any enemy ships brave enough to enter the channel or get by the *chevaux-de-frise*.[25]

Though Greene had considered Fort Mercer at Red Bank a secondary point of defense before Philadelphia fell, he now believed it essential to the control of the Delaware. Washington agreed, and Greene instructed General Varnum, just arriving from the Highlands, to send the regiments of Christopher Greene and Israel Angell to Red Bank. In doing so, Greene must have thought of Thomas Mifflin and other Pennsylvanians who accused him of sacrificing their men at Fort Washington the year before. At Red Bank would be Greene's relatives and boyhood friends, among them Sammy Ward and a brother of Kitty's.[26]

Washington drew his army down to its former camping grounds at Metuchen Hill within striking distance of Germantown. The move, which Greene approved, would, he hoped, divert British attention from the river defenses. In any event, it would afford the Americans a better chance to harass the British foraging parties and perhaps another opportunity to strike their army.

But as Greene expected, Howe did not leave Fort Mercer long in suspense. All thoughts were on the 400 Rhode Islanders in the garrison when von Donop appeared with 1,200 Hessians before the Fort to demand its surrender on pain of no quarter if it refused. Greene was exultant when he heard the outcome. Unlike Magaw at Fort Washington, Christopher Greene rejected the demand to surrender and spurned the threat of no quarter. The victory which followed did much to counteract the frustration in the minds of Greene and the others over the recent miscarriage at Germantown. Not since Bunker Hill had the enemy losses, percentagewise, been so large—fully a third of the men engaged. Among the dead was von Donop.

The next day British ships attacked Fort Mifflin only to have two of the largest run aground and burn. Greene again thought there was reason for hope. After all, Howe might be obliged to abandon the city if the river defenses could hold out for another month. Already food was becoming scarce and almost everyone who could get out of Philadelphia was moving away.

After desultory firing upon Fort Mifflin for several days, the British began a heavy cannonade on November 10th. The bombardment came principally from Province Island on whose low marshy flats the British had succeeded in erecting batteries. Was there any possibility, Greene and Washington asked each other, of relieving the fort by a raid on Province Island by way of Darby? Greene thought it might be done and went down to examine the area.

At the house near Darby where Greene stayed were several "sweet Quaker girls" to whom he was much attracted. "If the spirit should move and love invite, who can be answerable for the consequences" he asked his wife in a letter. Of course, Kitty, he said, would not be worried, having as she did, a high opinion of his self-restraint. But, he warned her, "remember the prayer of the Saint. Tempt me not above what I am able to bear."[27] All Pennsylvania Quakers, however, did not please Greene as much as these girls. The Rhode Island Quakers, he thought, were a better order of people than their Philadelphia brethren who had voluntarily loaned Sir William Howe £5000 sterling. If the Rhode Island Quakers were not better, "the Lord have mercy upon 'em," wrote Greene.[28]

Greene would have taken the risk of a raid to relieve Fort Mifflin but Washington held back. To succeed, the force employed would have to be quite large, and the danger of being cut off after crossing the Schuylkill was very real. Finally Washington gave his consent, but before Wayne and Morgan could execute the raid, Fort Mifflin had fallen.

As the days passed and the British failed to make much headway with their heavy bombardment from Province Island, Greene's hopes rose again. It was now the middle of November. The river soon would begin to freeze and every day starvation grew closer for Philadelphia and the British within. But Greene's lingering hopes were soon dashed. The enemy had discovered that the *chevaux-de-frise* had deflected the river's current which had worn a new channel near Mud Island on which Fort Mifflin stood!

Howe now brought warships into the new channel to a point so close to the fort that the crews could throw hand grenades on the heads of the defenders while the ship's broadsides raked the fort from end to end.

Major Simeon Thayer, to whom the command of Fort Mifflin passed after Lieutenant Colonel Samuel Smith was wounded, hoping that help might come, held out to the very last. But if any help came, Greene knew, it must come from Commodore John Hazelwood and the Pennsylvania flotilla. Hazelwood, however, sailed away from the scene of battle. In the night, seeing that speedy annihilation faced the defenders of Mud Island,

Varnum sent over boats to take off the survivors. However, Thayer and forty plucky followers stayed to fire what remained of the barracks and spike the cannon before shoving off for Fort Mercer. Not only had the long defense of Fort Mifflin been magnificent, it had, admitted Howe, broken his campaign. He had gained Philadelphia, it is true, but the important thing, that of destroying Washington's army, remained no nearer to being accomplished than when the campaign opened in the spring.[29]

After the fall of Fort Mifflin there remained small chance that Fort Mercer could hold out for long. But as the fort would have to be taken by infantry and artillery on land, there was still a possibility that another defeat like von Donop's could be inflicted upon the enemy. Washington, therefore, sent Greene with a division over the Delaware to try to help his fellow Rhode Islanders who had fought so bravely.

Cornwallis and Greene crossed the Delaware about the same time, Greene by way of Bristol, Cornwallis near Fort Mercer. Soon Cornwallis was reinforced by 2,500 troops from New York making his total number nearly 6,000. Against him, Greene could muster no more than 3,000, including 700 or 800 New Jersey militia.

Greene had barely entered New Jersey when he received disappointing reports. Fort Mercer had been abandoned and most of the flotilla burned for fear of its falling into enemy hands. In spite of this setback, Greene was not prepared to give up south Jersey as yet. As soon as he had a chance to talk with Varnum, he told Lafayette, who was with him, they could decide upon what to do.

Greene reached Mount Holly on November 22nd where he found Varnum. The latter confirmed Greene's conviction that any advance upon Cornwallis must be made with great caution. Greene wished Captain Harry Lee, who with his cavalry was coming to help, would hurry as he was in dire need of intelligence. Lacking horse, Greene did the next best thing. Daniel Morgan was sent ahead with his Rangers to feel out the enemy and report his findings to headquarters.

While Greene was pondering what he should do, a message arrived from Washington urging him to attack Cornwallis if at all possible. Washington needed another victory now that criti-

cism of his generalship was no longer confined just to Congress
and the politicians.[30] Greene wanted to fight. He knew Washington was being scored as forever a Fabian, one who had
retreated so much that he was incapable of thinking in any other
terms. But Greene did not want to be defeated, which in the end
would harm Washington more than anything else. "The cause is
too important to be trifled with to show our courage," he wrote
Washington, "and your character too deeply interested to sport
away upon unmilitary principles." However, if Washington still
wanted him to advance, he would willingly obey. "I will run any
risk or engage under any disadvantages, if I can only have your
countenance, if unfortunate," he assured Washington. "With the
public, I know," he added, "success sanctifies everything, and
that only."[31]

The next day Greene heard from Colonel Comstock of the
New Jersey militia that Cornwallis was about to ferry his force
over the river to Philadelphia after leveling Red Bank. Comstock
had his information from "a smart young woman" sent into
Gloucester to spy. She returned with no more harm than "a kiss
from a Hessian general," (according to her account) but with
the information desired. With this report, Greene immediately
ordered Varnum, Huntington, and Morgan forward to fall on
the enemy's flank and rear. Greene next discovered that Captain
Lee was at hand. "A detachment from Captain Lee's horse took
nine prisoners yesterday,—the first account I ever had of their
being in this quarter," Greene observed.[32] Independent action by
the cavalry, he would find, especially when he went South, was
nothing unusual for American horsemen.

Soon Greene learned that although Cornwallis was preparing
to cross the river, few, if any, of his troops had as yet left New
Jersey. Varnum now reported that there seemed little chance
of attacking or surprising the enemy as they were closely gathered
at Gloucester under the guns of their warships. Even if an opportunity presented itself, Greene knew that an attack would
be very dangerous in an area spotted with treacherous marshes
and traversed by deep creeks.

Word came from Washington that Greene was needed back
in Pennsylvania at once. Knowing that Washington had divided
his army, Howe was planning, before Greene returned, to bring

Cornwallis back for an attack on the Americans. Some of Washington's generals, too, were clamoring for an attack on Howe while Cornwallis was away. Greene, they said, could cross the Delaware by night, land at Philadelphia, and join in the assault. But when it came to a vote most of the officers joined Washington (who had received Greene's disapproval of the plan) in squelching so reckless an undertaking. Wayne, who wanted to attempt it, complained that the surest way to do nothing was to call a council of war.[33]

Greene marched his division immediately for Burlington upon getting Washington's orders. To cover the country until the British moved out, he left Morgan's Rangers and Lee's light horse. Greene left New Jersey with a heavy heart, but he had done his best. Until the British abandoned Philadelphia, any American force below Mount Holly, he told Washington, would be in the greatest danger.

As usual, Howe was slow in moving against Washington, and Greene had time to get back to the main army. Finally on December 4th, Howe marched out with all his troops and took post on Chestnut Hill. For three days he maneuvered for position while Morgan's riflemen and parties of Pennsylvania militia took a heavy toll of his forward troops. Finding that Washington was on strong ground near White Marsh, all of a sudden Howe wheeled about and marched back to winter quarters in Philadelphia.

Washington soon held a council of war to decide upon his winter quarters. Greene, with the support of Wayne, Lafayette, and several others, favored leaving a detachment east of the Schuylkill while the army moved to the vicinity of Wilmington. Some officers suggested occupying the towns between Lancaster and Easton but this was turned down partly because these places were already overflowing with refugees from Philadelphia.

After considerable discussion, Washington chose Valley Forge for winter quarters. This was pleasing to many Pennsylvanians who wanted as much of the country protected as possible. Barren and with only a few houses in the neighborhood, De Kalb thought it a wretched choice. But the ground at Valley Forge was strong, it was only eighteen miles from Philadelphia, and the enemy, with the Americans so close, would find foraging dangerous in Pennsylvania.

The Pennsylvania campaign had ended, and not ingloriously for the Americans. Wrote the Hessian Baurmeister:

> The last campaign furnished sufficient proof that the stubborn and inexperienced rebels are too lucky. The English army, active as it is, has got no farther than Philadelphia, is master of only some parts of the banks of the Delaware and Schuylkill, and has no foothold whatsoever in Jersey, from whence, as well as Germantown in front and from Wilmington, Darby, and Chester in the rear, it is being watched and constantly harassed by the enemy's main posts.[34]

Howe could boast of capturing the American capital. But he failed to destroy Washington's army and his failure to help Burgoyne ended in the loss of a British army. In general, Washington's army performed well in what turned out to be the hardest fought campaign of the whole war. As the principal architect of Washington's strategy and tactics, Greene's contribution was no less than brilliant. For the first time he had had an opportunity to fully justify Washington's confidence in him.

Saving an Army

During the long months at Valley Forge the American Revolution came as near being lost in the quietude of winter quarters as by any misfortune on the field of battle. Confronted by a complete breakdown of the Commissary and Quartermaster Departments, Washington feared the army would disband. Once again he called upon Greene who answered with his usual command of the emergency. The army was fed and clothed, and when spring came it was again ready to meet the enemy.

As the year 1777 waned, Greene did not lose sight of the progress America was making on the political front. Congress had passed favorably upon the Articles of Confederation and sent them to the states for ratification. Greene hoped the Articles would become the cement for a lasting union as well as the means by which the army could be put on a stronger footing. Apparently he had no foreboding of the suspense and delay which would occur before the Articles were finally ratified. As for the great victory at Saratoga, Greene was fully aware of its international implications, particularly upon the Court of France.[1]

Greene had felt the chill of public displeasure after the fall of Fort Washington and once again he was aware that he was receiving part of the blame for the army's misfortunes during the Philadelphia campaign. That Thomas Mifflin was one of his principal detractors, he had no doubt. Even since summer when Washington had refused to come racing to Philadelphia at the start of the campaign, Mifflin, so Greene believed, had been finding fault with whatever he did. George Lux told him he heard Mifflin condemn Washington for listening to Greene and favoring him over his other generals. Confiding in McDougall, Greene wrote, "General Mifflin and his creatures have been endeavoring to wound my reputation. It is said I govern the General and do everything to damp the spirit of enterprise."[2]

As criticism during a period of reverses is contagious, others besides Mifflin rose to censure Greene's generalship and his influence on Washington. Washington, Wayne told Gates, had several opportunities to win great victories during the Pennsylvania campaign. But "our worthy General," he wrote, "listened too much to some Counsel." James Lovell warned: "The List of our disgusted patriots is long and formidable—and their Resentments keen against the reigning Cabal [Greene, Knox, Lafayette, and others] and their power of opposition not dispicable." By winter, Lovell predicted, the army "will be divided into Greenites and Mifflinians, if things do not take a great turn from their present Situation."[3]

No one in Congress, apparently, was as censorious of Washington and Greene as James Lovell, ex-schoolmaster and Congressman from Massachusetts. Washington, he said, could not get along without his two "privy counsellors" (Greene and Knox). For a few days, at Washington's suggestion, they had stayed away from his table, wrote Lovell, but the chief could not endure their absence and soon they were back. Reed and Cadwalader dined with Washington also, but they were but blinds while Greene and Knox were "at the bottom of every movement," Lovell told Gates. The Mifflinites, John Clark reported, were whispering that Washington planned, if he fell, to have Greene made commander in chief.[4]

Even more than Greene, Washington was the object of criticism, especially after Gates's victory at Saratoga. In comparison to Gates, Washington was held up as a failure. Many looked to Gates as the savior of the country—the man of the hour. Greene suspected that Mifflin was at the bottom of a move to replace Washington with Gates. "This is done by a certain faction," he told McDougall in January, "that is said to be forming under the auspices of General Gates and General Mifflin, to supplement his Excellency from the Command of the Army and get Genl. Gates at the head of it." For this reason, Greene said, Mifflin had thrown out insinuations against him in such a way as to reflect unfavorably on Washington in the eyes of Congress and the army.[5]

As events unfolded, Greene became most certain that Gates was a willing tool of those who wished to oust Washington. "How success wells the vanity of the human heart," wrote Greene. "This Gentleman is a mere child of fortune. The foundation of all the Northern successes was laid long before his arrival there, and Arnold and Lincoln were the principal instruments in completing the work," he told McDougall. He did not want to detract from Gates rightful credit, but he thought, "for the good of the country it should be seen in its true light." However, he knew that Gates was not just sitting by waiting for his plum to fall. In his reports he ignored Washington by sending them directly to Congress. When Daniel Morgan returned from the north, burning with indignation at slights received from Gates, Greene's suspicions were further aroused. Morgan declared that Gates had told him that the army was very dissatisfied with Washington and that many of the best officers would resign unless a change was made in the supreme command.[6]

After Saratoga there was a veritable outburst of comparison between Washington's supposed failure and Gates's success. James Lovell wrote Gates flattering letters praising him for his brilliant generalship and heaping scorn upon Washington.

> We have had a noble Army melted down by ill-judged marches, marches that disgrace their authors and Directors—& which have occasioned the Severest & most just Sarcasm & Contempt of our Enemies. How much are you to be envied my dear General? How different your Conduct & your Fortune! In short this Army will be totally lost unless you come down & collect the virtuous Band, who wish to fight under your Banner, & with their aid save the Southern Hemisphere.[7]

In his next letter, Lovell declared that America had been "Fabiused into a very disagreeable posture" with many of the best officers "discouraged by an overbalance of languid Counsellors." That Greene was as much, if not more than Washington, the author of the Fabian strategy was no secret to Lovell and John Adams. Something could be done right away, Lovell thought, by Gates accepting the presidency of the Board of War. "Good

God, what a Situation we are in! How different from what might have been justly expected!—Come to the Board of War if only for a short Season," he pleaded with Gates.[8]

Joining in the chorus against Washington and Greene were other Congressmen, among them John Adams and Benjamin Rush. If no other good had arisen from Burgoyne's defeat, Adams believed it had accomplished much in convincing many that there were other great men in the army besides Washington. "Now we can allow a certain citizen," he wrote, "to be wise, virtuous, and good, without thinking him a deity or a savior."[9] Still again Adams cried, "O Heaven, grant us one great Soul! One leading mind would extricate the best cause from that ruin which seems to await it for want of it—One active, masterly capacity, would bring order out of this confusion, and save this country." No less critical of Washington than Adams and Lovell was Benjamin Rush, the Philadelphia physician who had recently resigned as surgeon general of the medical corps. "Look at both," he cried, "the one on the pinnacle of military glory—the other out-generaled and twice beaten."[10]

That the civilian armchair generals did not understand what they were attempting to compare, Greene fully realized. "Had our force," he told his brother, Jacob, "been equal to General Howe's, or at least as much superior as the northern army was to Burgoyne, he must have shared the same fate. But, alas, we have fought with vastly superior numbers, and although twice defeated have kept the field!" History afforded but few examples of the kind, he concluded.

Though Washington was quite aware of the criticism he was undergoing, until General Conway made some observations on his generalship he said nothing. It so happened that the talkative James Wilkinson, on his way to Congress with the report of Burgoyne's surrender, stopped at Stirling's headquarters for a convivial hour. To McWilliams, one of Stirling's aides, he repeated a choice bit from a letter Gates had received from General Conway. McWilliams told Stirling who immediately forwarded the disclosure to Washington. As relayed by Stirling, Conway was reputed to have written: "Heaven has determined to save your Country, or a weak General and bad Counsellors would have ruined it."* Greatly irritated, Washington hit back. Without comment he sent the message to General Conway. The latter denied he had written anything like it to Gates. However, persons who had seen Conway's letter knew that he lied. In reality, declared Laurens, it was ten times as bad as Wilkinson reported.[11]

Wilkinson's disclosure was all that was needed to set ablaze a fire which had been smoldering for weeks. Soon the army was buzzing with talk. Greene, McDougall, Tilghman, Knox, and most of those loyal to Washington were sure there existed a cabal to remove him. Had not Alexander Graydon told Wilkinson he heard Conway say that Washington was not fit to command the American Army?[12]

From the beginning, Thomas Conway had not been popular with Washington and Greene. An Irishman who had joined the French Army at the age of fourteen and risen to the rank of colonel, Conway was boastful, sly, and ambitious. For weeks he had annoyed Washington by his intrigues to wring a promotion out of Congress. For a time Congress thought of ridding itself of the annoyance by putting Conway on the Board of War but that would hardly be a pleasing solution to Washington. Congress' next move, however, was no better. Conway complained that De Kalb, a man his junior in the French Army, had been made a major general. Without consulting Washington, Congress thereupon appointed Conway inspector general with the rank of major general. The promotion, which appeared to be a well-studied insult to Washington, touched off a storm which threatened to wreck the army. Nine brigadiers signed a memorial against the promotion and had it sent to Congress.

No one was more disturbed than Greene. Conway's argument that he had more experience than any American brigadier left him unconvinced. Neither was he impressed with Congress's explanation that Conway's appointment was of the "staff" and not of the "line." Though Conway had been praised for his valor at Brandywine and Germantown, and Sullivan held him in high esteem as an officer, Greene had a low opinion of his ability.

---

* In James Wilkinson's *Memoirs of My Own Times,* I, 382-386, there is a slightly different version. It reads: "Heaven surely is determined to save the American cause, or a weak General and bad councils had long since lost it."

"General Conway is a man of much intrigue and little judgment," he told his brother, Jacob.

With the outcry against Conway, Greene did all in his power to mollify the brigadiers. Lafayette and the French officers, he noted with satisfaction, would not speak to Conway, who found the official atmosphere at Valley Forge quite as cold as the surrounding air. Greene blamed Gates for recommending Conway's promotion to Congress. It all tied in with a cabal against Washington, he thought. Gates showed his hand, he believed, when he tried to cover up for Conway after his letter became known. His actions seemed to Greene "too barefaced to deceive anybody." Washington was kinder in his thoughts about the mild-mannered Gates whom he believed was being duped by Mifflin and Conway. Greene, however, thought he was as much a part of the cabal as anyone. All three, in his opinion, were men of "great ambition" without "principles or virtue" who would sacrifice "everything for their private views."[13]

Characteristically, Greene could not withhold from speaking his mind to Congress about a situation which seemed to endanger the very existence of the army. Besides the brigadiers, Congress had stirred the anger of all the colonels in the army by making James Wilkinson a brigadier general for apparently no other reason than that he had brought the report of Burgoyne's surrender, and his promotion was recommended by Gates (forty-seven colonels signed a protest against Wilkinson's promotion). Though Greene's brush with Congress over the Ducoudray affair was barely six months old, he nonetheless sat down and wrote President Laurens on how the army felt about the late promotions.

[The officers] . . . feel the force of the injury in these instances from being superseded by those who had served in subordinate stations. I do not wish to lesson their merit [Conway's and Wilkinson's] but I believe it is generally thought their promotions have been to the prejudice of others at least as deserving as themselves, and had superior claims in every other point of view.

The officers of the army say they engaged in the service of their country, not only from a sense of duty as citizens, but with the fullest confidence that the justice of Congress would assure to them their rank, and the right of promotion according to the rules which prevail in all well-regulated armies. If they conceive these principles to be violated, if they lose their confidence in the justice of Congress, it is easy to foresee the fatal effects that will result. Military ardor will languish; a spirit of enterprise will cease; men of honor will decline the service; art and cabal will succeed, and low intrigue will be the characteristic and genius of the army.[14]

Up until this time he had been happy to think that the American Army had been exceptionally free of favoritism.

As customary, Congress smarted over the protests from the army, made allusions to military dictatorship, and laid the papers on the table. But Congress was not through irritating the army. On its newly created Board of War sat Mifflin, Trumbull, Pickering, and Gates—not a particularly pleasing panel to either Washington or Greene. Congress, however, could justify its choice by pointing out that Mifflin had been quartermaster general; Trumbull, commissary general; Pickering, adjutant general; and Gates, as victor at Saratoga, had the honor coming to him.

It was not long before the Board of War came forth with a proposal for a diversionary expedition against Canada. Greene did not like the idea at all. It would not change the seat of the war, he argued, and it would not provide the army with supplies. Rather, it would drain off what little the army had left. Suspicious of almost anything which came from the board, Greene fancied the scheme had been "cooked up" by Gates and Mifflin to give Conway a command. True it was—the board hoped Conway would be chosen to lead the expedition. His French background, they said, made him the logical choice. But their argument boomeranged. They were quite right, declared Washington, that the commander should be French, and Lafayette was the proper person for the assignment. Congress appointed Lafayette who in turn gave the second place to De Kalb. Conway thus found himself third in the line of command.*

When the three generals finally reached Albany in February, they discovered it was useless to try to launch an expedition against Canada. Greene had sized up the situation in the beginning when he said that neither the troops nor the supplies could be found for the undertaking. Certainly New England

---

* McDougall was Lafayette's first choice but he became sick. E. Burnett, *Letters*, pp. 290-293.

had no stomach for another winter campaign in the north. It was not long after this that Washington at last got rid of General Conway* when Congress took another one of his threats to resign as an actual resignation.[15]

After tempers had cooled down, many Congressmen came to the conclusion that the promotions of Conway and Wilkinson had been a mistake. Were the question of Conway's promotion now before Congress, declared Abraham Clark in February, it would most likely be rejected. "The authority of the Commander-in-Chief must be supported," he concluded. By this time, Lovell, Duane, Rush, and others who had been critical of Washington were aware that he was still very popular throughout the country. "I am glad," wrote George Lux to Greene in May, "that the faction & designing Junto who would sacrifice everything to their insatible Ambition, are alarmed at their unpopularity on accot. of their malevolent machinations, & now deny all their Practices."[16]

Though the evidence indicates that there was no cabal or concerted action to remove Washington, and that Greene and the others jumped at conclusions, it is not improbable that such might have developed had not Washington's friends denounced his traducers in the strongest terms. The outcry, indeed, was so great that Conway and his friends could only console themselves with the thought that they were martyrs to the cause of free speech and stigmatized as something loathsome by the blind worshippers of Washington.[17]

More or less neutral observers such as Timothy Pickering and Richard Peters apparently summed up the "Conway Cabal" quite accurately: "I confess," wrote Pickering, "there appeared but too much colour for them [the belief that there was a cabal], yet I am not satisfied such ill designs were formed: or if they were, certain I am that they must have long since been given over; I should rather suppose they had never existed." Peters agreed: "I hear more of this Party [cabal] from Camp than I see here [York, Penn.] & do not believe it exists. I am not unacquainted

---

* Before Conway left for France he had a duel with John Cadwalader in which he suffered a wound in the neck. Believing himself on his deathbed, Conway confessed that he never had intended Washington any harm and that he sincerely thought him to be a great and a good man.

with some personal Disgusts and cannot but be acquainted from my Situation with a good deal of Secret History, But I am firmly convinced if a Commander in Chief was to be chosen this day, the General would be the Man unanimously elected."[18]

At Valley Forge, Washington had more troops than during the winter before in New Jersey but through failures of the Quartermaster and Commissary Departments and the depreciation of Continental currency, the army suffered more for want of food and clothing. Only during the arctic-like winter at Morristown in 1779-1780 was the suffering greater.

As at the Loantaka encampment near Morristown the winter before, the army built log huts for shelter. Sixteen by fourteen feet with six and a half foot ceilings, the huts housed twelve men. Though windowless, the large clay-lined fireplace opposite the door gave some light and made the building warm and cozy. The main problem arose over how watertight roofs could be quickly constructed. Washington offered $100, with Greene, Sullivan, and Stirling the judges, for the best idea on roofing. Apparently no one came forward with anything better than overlapping boards or shakes.[19]

Like most of the officers, Greene had his headquarters in a log cabin, larger but essentially the same as those occupied by the soldiers. "We are all going into log huts," wrote Greene, "a sweet life after a most fatiguing campaign." But as Greene usually dined with Washington, he was much of the time to be found at his headquarters at Isaac Potts's sturdy stone house above Valley Creek. Nearby on the banks of the creek stood the forge, a constant reminder to Greene of Coventry and Potowomut and of the days when as a youth he toiled and studied and wondered what the future held.

It was early January before all the troops were out of their cold tents and into huts. Fortunately, the weather, though rainy, was mild. Before the huts were finished, however, the army's meager food supply dwindled to the point of exhaustion. After several days of little or nothing to eat, threats of mutiny were heard. But there was no mutiny or disturbance. The men listened to the appeals of their officers and a deep sense of duty and patriotism kept them from disbanding and going home. Nevertheless, the army was so crippled for want of food that Washington was powerless to stop a large British foraging expedition operating with great success in the region of Darby and Chester.

For want of shoes, stockings, and even shirts, hundreds of soldiers were unable to do more than hover around the fires and try to keep warm. At night the men took turns sleeping in what blankets and overcoats they had. The army was worse off, Wayne said, than "Falstaff's recruits" with "not a whole shirt to a Brigade." Soon the hospitals were filled to overflowing. By February, Washington found death taking a frightful toll of his priceless veterans. But few men deserted to the enemy or went home because of privations. When a man did desert it was usually due to an overpowering homesickness.[20]

Hardship at Valley Forge was not restricted to the common soldier. At one time certain officers held a dinner to which no one was admitted who had a whole pair of breeches. Greene, who understood their distress, told Washington it gave him the greatest pain "to hear the murmurs and complaints among the officers for want of spirits. They say they are exposed to the severity of the winter, subject to hard duty, and nothing but bread and beef to eat morning, noon, and night." If the officers complained more than the soldiers, it was that they felt their privations more. Their families, too, were generally used to a higher standard of living and found they could not live on the little money from the officers' pay. On December 27th, fifty officers in Greene's division resigned for this reason. When shown the pleading letters from the wives of the men, what could Greene say? Inflation was sending prices skyward and driving the officers to desperation. Congress must do something to relieve the plight of the officers, declared Greene, or Washington would soon have a leaderless army. Reed agreed: "For heaven sakes after pursuing the game through so many bogs and deserts let us not lose it now."[21]

For a time, after the first bout with privation, conditions improved. Enough food was found near camp to tide the army through January, and the men, better clothed than earlier, rested in warm quarters and gained in health. Then, all at once, the army was hit by a food shortage more serious than the first.

Greene was not surprised: ever since Trumbull had resigned as commissary general in August, the army had lived from hand to mouth. Not only was all the food in the area gone, but the horses needed to haul stores from distant places had either died of starvation or were too weak to work. Knowledge of the condition of supplies often did not reach the upper levels of command until the army was on the brink of disaster. So it was in early February when a delegation of soldiers appeared at headquarters to tell that the troops were actually starving. The men were very civil and spoke in the most respectful terms, Greene related, but "they added it would be impossible to continue in Camp any longer without support." Again Greene took over and found enough food to avert the crisis. It was apparent, nonetheless, that the army could no longer depend on the baffled commissary agents. Another crisis might see the last of the army. On February 12th, therefore, Washington commanded Greene to go out and collect all the livestock, grain, and forage he could find. Notes on the Treasury would be given as Washington had no money.[22]

Greene's assignment presaged his appointment within a few weeks as quartermaster general. The committee from Congress, at headquarters, already had sounded him out on the question. Greene was undecided, but Washington, believing it would be impossible to conduct another campaign without great changes in the supply departments, was of the opinion that as much as he needed Greene in the line, he needed him still more as head of the Quartermaster Department. Confronted by the problems arising from inflation, the army had to have a masterful executive at the head of procuring supplies if the war were to continue.

Greene threw himself into the foraging with his usual vigor and determination. The bottleneck, he knew, was in the shortage of teams and wagons. As he did not expect to find enough of these in Chester and Bucks counties, he sent troops to Lancaster with orders to impress horses and wagons. Meanwhile, he moved out upon his great foraging expedition with several thousand troops. Everything, he ordered, of the slightest value to the army or to the enemy should be taken or destroyed.

The task assigned to Greene was not for one unaccustomed to war. Chester and Bucks counties were notorious for their Tories and uncooperative Quakers. When necessary, Greene was a man of iron. Everywhere he quartered his troops in private homes so they would not suffer or become sick. "You must forage the country naked," he commanded his officers. "Harden your hearts," he told Colonel Biddle, "and dispatch business as fast as possible." Greene would do the same. "The inhabitants cry out and beset me from all quarters," he told Washington, "but like Pharoh I harden my heart." Anyone found hiding things, he gave out, would have his property confiscated and be whipped. When two men were caught carrying provisions to the enemy, Greene ordered them tied up and given 100 strokes with the rawhide, "by way of example." In spite of all, however, some owners hid their property so well that Greene's men, though they scoured the countryside, failed to find it.

Greene returned from his foraging expedition on February 26th, after being out eleven days. The operation was successful, especially that part of it under General Wayne who had collected a large number of cattle and sheep in New Jersey, opposite Marcus Hook. However, as meat would still be in short supply, Greene recommended supplementing the fare of the troops with a course of fermented wheat and sugar. This would be a diet, he said, nourishing and palatable and less expensive than meat.

Though Valley Forge offered a minimum in the way of comfort and convenience, not a few of the wives of the officers again came to camp. Martha Washington arrived early in February, bringing good news of successful recruiting in Virginia. About the same time Lady Stirling and her daughter Catherine joined his Lordship. Kitty Greene came after her long visit with the Lotts at Beverwyck. There she had learned some French from one of Lott's daughters. It was enough at least to enable her to carry on a conversation with the French officers who were delighted to find her as coquettish as any of the belles of France.

Before long, Nathanael seems to have become somewhat embarrassed by Kitty's flirtations with Lafayette, Du Ponceau, and some of the other young gallants from France. Already Lucy Knox was saying that "all was not well with Greene & his lady."[23] Greene himself may have hinted to Jeremiah Wadsworth that his wife was too receptive to the advances of the young officers.

After Greene's death, Wadsworth, who unknown to his wife was having an affair with Kitty, told her that Greene had once complained of her behavior at camp. Wadsworth mentioned this when Kitty, to make him jealous, wrote to her lover: "I believe I forgot to mention my noble lover to you. The Marquis of ——, I forgot what, but he had very serious propositions." If by this she meant Lafayette, the latter, at least, had been very candid about it at the time—even to the point of telling his wife in France how fond he was of Kitty.[24]

At camp Greene found himself called upon to help work out plans for the army with the Congressional committee. The latter "came to camp," he wrote, "with Parliamentary prejudices, but stubborn facts and the condition of the Army had brought a wonderful reformation." Greene had several recommendations, all of them shared by Washington. A pension of half pay for officers was a measure he had long advocated to attract and keep good men. This was not done, but Congress passed an act granting half pay for disabled veterans for seven years, later extended to life. Congress also passed an act which the staff and the committee had recommended for drafting men for a year's service, providing the state did not fill its quota by volunteers encouraged by a Congressional bounty.

More than anything, Greene wanted to see the establishment of a system whereby Congress could tax the states. Many in Congress, he knew, would welcome it but the political climate in the states was such as to block any move in that direction. However, until the end of his life, Greene never gave up trying to persuade leaders everywhere to work for a national system of taxation. Greene chafed at the slow pace of political advancement and never fully understood the difficulties facing Congress. Abraham Clark could write that "Congress Sit day & night taking little rest" but Greene thought it might do better by talking less and doing more.

It was about this time that Greene found another friend among the foreigners who came to America to fight. Baron von Steuben was one of the last to come, but none, save Lafayette, won so high a place in the minds and hearts of Americans. Washington would not have had the services of the Baron had not Franklin (who had been warned by Congress not to send over any more foreign officers) recognized the merits of the picturesque German, schooled in the circle of Frederick the Great's celebrated officers. Though the forty-seven year old Steuben had been but a captain of the general staff, with a little coaching from the Baron, Franklin made him out to have been a lieutenant general in the Prussian Army! Like Lafayette, he came to America professing to render what service he could to the cause of liberty.[25]

After sad experiences with many foreigners trumped up as great military minds, Washington and Greene were skeptical about Steuben. But they liked his frankness and simplicity and impressed by his credentials, they were willing to give him a chance. With Conway off to Canada, here was an opportunity, moreover, for replacing him by making Steuben inspector general. This done, it was not long before Washington and Greene were convinced that von Steuben was a true asset. Greene agreed with Washington, however, that it would be unwise to make him a major general with the brigadiers feeling as they did about Conway's promotion. Greene and Lafayette during these days collaborated with Steuben in writing a manual of arms which remained the standard regulations for the army for the remainder of the war.

At the time the Congressional committee came to camp, it was known that Congress had Philip Schuyler under consideration for quartermaster. Apparently Washington opposed Schuyler while he made known his preference for Greene above all others. As the committee agreed with Washington, it sent Congress a report asking that Schuyler be dropped. Read the report:

> A character has presented itself, which in a great degree meets our approbation, judgment, and wishes. We have opened the subject to him, and it is now under his consideration. When we are at liberty, we shall introduce him to your notice; but delicacy forbids our doing it until he had made up his mind on the subject, and given his consent to the nomination.[26]

After several preliminary meetings, the committee met Greene on February 22nd, while he was directing the big foraging operation. Greene suggested taking the office for a year, without extra pay, while keeping his command in the army. This was turned down by Congress on the assumption that no man could do both and do them well. Some members favored paying the quartermaster a higher salary and doing away with the percentage system. This was also rejected as breeding jealousy among the generals. It was finally decided that Greene would keep his place and rank in the army but not have a command. In his conversations with Washington, Greene understood this to mean that he could take over his command on the eve of battle. This, however, was never clear and became the cause of future misunderstanding and trouble. As was the custom, Greene was to receive a commission of one percent on all expenditures. Congress appointed Greene on March 2nd, but it was understood that his acceptance, among other things, rested upon Charles Pettit and John Cox becoming his assistants.[27]

All through the negotiations, Reed, who was a member of the committee, urged Greene to accept the office as the very existence of the army depended upon it. Washington, Greene knew, was of the same mind. "The General is afraid," he wrote, "that the department will be so ill-managed unless some of his friends undertakes it that the operations of the next campaign will in a great measure be frustrated." What should he do, he asked Knox? "I hate the place, but hardly know what to do." To McDougall, he bemoaned: "All of you will be immortalizing yourselves in the golden pages of history, while I am confined to a series of druggery to pave the way for it." A year later he was in no better frame of mind. He told William Duer:

> There is a great difference between being raised to an office, and descending to one. Had I been an inferior officer, I might have thought myself honored by the appointment. But as I was high in rank in the army, I have ever considered it as derogatory to serve in this office. It was with the greatest difficulty that I could prevail on myself to engage in this business. Nothing but the wretched state that the department was in, and the consequent ruin that must follow added to the general's and the Committee of Congress's solicitations, could have procured my consent. It was not with a view to profit, for the General and the Committee of Congress well remember that I offered to serve a year (unconnected with the accounts of the department) in the military line, without any additional pay to that I had as Major-General.

In similar vein in a letter to Washington, he wrote:

There is a great difference between being raised to an office and descending to one which is my case. There is also a great difference between serving where you have a fair prospect of honor and laurels, and where you have no prospect of either, let you discharge your duty ever so well. Nobody ever heard of a quartermaster in history, as such, or in relating any brilliant action. I engaged in this business as well out of compassion to your Excellency as from a regard to the public. I thought your task too great to be Commander in Chief and quartermaster at the same time.[28]

It was March 23rd before Greene heard that Pettit and Cox had agreed to serve as his deputies. Thereupon, he immediately announced he was taking over the department. Thomas Mifflin, it was said, declared he took the post to keep out of the way of bullets, a rather peculiar accusation for one who had been quartermaster general himself for a time. A more serious charge was the one that Greene had taken the office for its emoluments. The committee had told him he would make a fortune out of it and Greene was a man who admired wealth. "Money becomes more and more the American's object. You must get rich, or you will be of no consequence," he wrote in February, 1778. It cannot be denied that Greene relished the prospect of getting rich. Money meant too much to him to deny it. But consideration for Washington and the pressing needs of the army also went into the making of his decision. Greene convinced himself, at least, that these were the real reasons for accepting the office and perhaps he was right.[29]

If Greene knew Pettit and Cox before they became his assistants, it must have been but slightly. Both were relatives of Joseph Reed and it was upon his recommendation that Greene appointed them for their integrity, industry, and ability. The two men proved all that Reed had said and Greene came to look upon them as indispensable. He divided his commission equally with them whereby each received one third of one percent. Cox was older than Pettit who was about Greene's age. A wealthy merchant of Philadelphia and Trenton, he had invested heavily in the iron business and salt refining. Pettit, a Trenton lawyer and expert accountant, had been secretary to Governor Livingston. Both men felt they were sacrificing much by taking on the quartermaster assignment, and it was with difficulty that Reed got them to accept. In view of Cox's experience, Greene put him in charge of purchasing and examining supplies. Pettit was made auditor and put in charge of the money as it came from the treasurer. Greene himself would attend to the ordering and see that the supplies were delivered to the army.[30]

On the day Greene took over his duties, he wrote Clement Biddle, the foragemaster general, for all the information he could supply. Biddle, who was reared a Quaker, had joined the Philadelphia regiment known as the Quaker Blues. He was a friend of Greene, having been one of his aides during the autumn of 1776 in New Jersey. Through Biddle and others, Greene learned that conditions in the department were fully as bad as had been represented. Equipment, especially wagons, was scattered all over the country and no one knew what had become of many of the horses. In his letters to Congress for the committee, Reed laid bare the deplorable situation.

> We find the property of the Continent dispersed over the whole country; not an encampment, route of the army, or considerable road but abounds with wagons, left to the mercy of the weather, and the will of the inhabitants; large quantities of intrenching tools have in like manner been left in various hands, under no other security, that we can learn, than the honesty of those who have them in possession.[31]

Greene lost no time in getting his department organized and functioning. In the department from Virginia northward were 140 deputy quartermasters and auditors, 115 wagonmasters and 13 wagonmaster generals, 131 deputy commissary generals of forage, 86 foragemasters, 77 clerks, 105 expresses, and one superintendent of artificers. In all, 3,000 men were employed in the Quartermaster Department. Most of the agents, many appointed by Mifflin, were retained, but the right to replace them at any time was cleared with Congress.[32]

Working with Pettit and Cox, Greene soon had estimates before Congress on the amount of money needed to get the army ready for the coming campaign. Not wishing to wait for funds through the usual channels, Greene drew £50,000 on the Treasury for use by Robert Hooper at Easton, urgently in need of money. By June, expenditures had exceeded $4,000,000 (Continental currency worth less than half in specie) but this was "but a breakfast for the department," according to Greene.[33]

As there was a more or less constant shortage of horses and wagons, Greene set about relieving the transportation problem by having boats built for use on the upper waters of the Delaware and Schuylkill. Bad roads were repaired by details from the army. So that hay could be handled more efficiently, screws were ordered for pressing forage into bales. As many agents had purchased horses unfit for heavy work, orders were issued for the purchase of only strong, sound animals. Getting the army out of the huts which had become damp and unhealthful and into tents was another problem which Greene solved in record time.

As much depended upon the cooperation of Pennsylvania in getting the campaign underway, Greene went to Lancaster to see the Executive Council. Being a stranger to most of the officials and perhaps not very much in their favor because of Mifflin, he took along Clement Biddle, whose brother Owen was a man of prominence in the state. Washington also wrote President Thomas Wharton informing him that Greene had something of importance to bring to his attention. Greene desired two things: first of all he wanted more power to impress teams and wagons and secondly, he wanted teamsters and others engaged in the Continental service exempt from militia duty. He succeeded in the last, and although the law governing impressment was strengthened, it still did not grant as much power as desired.

As quartermaster general, Greene had a flow of money coming to him from his commission which soon reached enviable proportions. This income he invested in shipping, privateering, iron manufacturing, and real estate. He was too preoccupied with army duties to handle the investing himself which he left to friends to perform.

One may lament that avarice got the better of Greene and that contrary to his professed high standards for public officials, his conduct as quartermaster was not always above reproach. Most glaring of his aberrations were the favors he granted Jacob Greene and Company of which he was a member. That the company did relatively little business with the army does not excuse him or lessen the impropriety. That the allure of money blinded him and caused him to convince himself that he was doing nothing improper seems a safe deduction. Even to his brother Jacob and cousin Griffin, his partners in business, he never admitted there was anything wrong in what they were doing. "This is a murmuring age and everybody that handles money must expect to be subject to some degree of reproach," he told Griffin. Then he added, "As I know my intentions to be good, I regard the speech of People the less." Later he wrote to Griffin, "If we are not rich, we will be honest."[34]

Soon after becoming quartermaster general, Greene made his brother Jacob an offer to be contractor for the army for Rhode Island. Only Jacob's acceptance appears to have survived. But it was apparently understood from the beginning that Nathanael was to be a partner in the company which would own and operate the Coventry Iron Works and engage in trade, privateering, and supplies for the army. After their father died, all the Greene brothers ran the business as partners. This lasted for several years but not long before Greene became quartermaster, the brothers disagreed and divided the estate. "It grieves me," wrote Nathanael in May, 1778, "that the long harmony is dissolved—The House had got too complex—to go on smoothly long. But the loss of Brotherly affection is a disagreeable circumstance."[35] Thus Jacob Greene and Company came to include only Jacob and Nathanael and their cousin Griffin.

In accepting the contract for purchasing supplies for the Quartermaster Department in Rhode Island, Jacob said that he feared he could be of little assistance as most prizes from which goods were procured came into Boston. As it was against the rules of the Department for contractors to bid against each other by buying outside their territory, he asked Nathanael for permission to join with the contractor at Boston. As ducking was scarce everywhere, he also asked Nathanael if he would compel the Continental agent, who had some, to sell it to Jacob as the agent did not have means for transporting it to the army. About the same time, Griffin, who was in Boston to do the purchasing, complained to Nathanael that the regional quarter-master at Boston was bidding against him for 400 tents. The agent claimed he was serving under orders of the Board of War whose authority, he said, was superior to Greene's. What Greene did, if anything, to help his partners is not known, but in any event, Griffin succeeded in procuring tents, canvass, and other goods for sale to the army.[36]

In May, 1778, Griffin asked Nathanael for passes on a cargo of liquor and clothing which Greene had told Griffin could be sold at a profit to the sutlers with the army. Griffin wanted Greene to allow the goods to pass as army supplies to avoid paying taxes in Connecticut, New York, and New Jersey. General Mifflin, he explained, had profited in this way while he was quartermaster. Cousin Charlie, it seems, made a special trip to see Greene about this but whether or not Nathanael allowed the tax evasion is not revealed. One may suspect that he did inasmuch as he later asked a similar favor of Jeremiah Wadsworth. His friend Abraham Lott, he told Wadsworth, had "purchased a small quantity of rum and salt at Boston, which he cannot get on, owing to State laws. I should be obliged to you to give him such a pass, that his property may come forward; he wants the salt for family use; part of his spirits he proposes for sale.—I am under particular obligation to him, and shall esteem myself so to you, if you will be kind enough to enable him to get forward his property. The propriety and the best forms you are the best judge of, and I therefore submit this matter to your opinion and discretion."[37]

In 1779, Griffin asked Greene if he could get contracts for building some ships, either for the government or private persons. Greene answered that he thought shipbuilding would not be profitable and advised him to speculate in confiscated Tory property. Small orders, however, were appreciated also. Don't you need ten or twelve dozen scythes for the army? queried Griffin. Greene apparently did not order scythes but a few days later he told Griffin that the army needed iron and that he should get in touch with the agent at Springfield, Massachusetts.[38] On another occasion Griffin asked Nathanael to use his influence to get some ships released which were under orders from Congress, so that he could use them to deliver provisions to the Commissary Department. Notwithstanding Greene's aid and advice, the firm of Jacob Greene and Company never seems to have had a very extensive business with the army. Greene, it would seem, was unwilling to go very far in granting favors to the company as it would surely become a public scandal. So far as can be ascertained, the Company received the market price for goods which were of standard quality. Greene tried to convince himself that the business was legitimate and that he clothed his interest in the company with secrecy simply because people liked to gossip. Thus, in most of his letters to Jacob and Griffin, he makes it appear that he is not a partner and that he is only giving them friendly advice.*

For two or more years Greene supplied Jacob and Griffin with large sums of money derived from his commission, most of which was invested in shipping and privateering. During his service as quartermaster, he earned approximately $170,000 in specie from his commission.[39] Unlike some men who handled public funds, Greene never borrowed any of it for his private use. "I make it a standing rule," he wrote, "Never to make up of the Public money for any private purposes whatever."[40] Nevertheless, the extent of his business interests, exaggerated by gossip, made him the target of much criticism. His emoluments by the commission system, it was said, were more than any man deserved and Greene was too grasping, making an immense fortune at public expense.[41]

As Greene's income increased, he sent ever larger sums to Jacob and Griffin, advising them on what he thought would prove profitable investments. In 1779 the company owned part interest in about twenty ships, large and small. Some carried cargoes but all apparently were armed and prepared to engage in privateering whenever an occasion presented itself. In July, 1779, Jacob estimated that the company had earned profits aggregating £45,000. All was reinvested in more speculation. Spurred on by the profits the company was making, Greene offered to put up £10,000 if his partners wanted to invest in one of John Cox's privateers plying out of Philadelphia.[42] A month later he told Griffin he thought there would be great opportunities for trade at Newport as soon as it was evacuated. He offered to send Griffin £20,000 for investment in the Newport trade when it opened. In April, 1780, however came the first bad news from his

---

* The Ledger of Jacob Greene and Company at the Rhode Island Historical Society does not show that Nathanael was a partner or that the company did business with the army after Greene became quartermaster.

partners. The company had suffered a big loss in privateering and more was to follow. By the time Greene left for the South, losses were heavier than Jacob or Griffin cared to admit and Greene tried unsuccessfully in letter after letter to get some account of how the figures stood. When Greene returned from the South very little was left of any of his wartime investments in the North.[43]

In 1779, Greene entered a business partnership with Jeremiah Wadsworth and Barnabas Deane. Greene and Wadsworth each contributed £10,000. Deane, who conducted the business, invested £5,000. The fact that the members often corresponded in code and the firm was referred to as "2030 and Company" has given rise to the suspicion that the company was created for the purpose of secretly supplying the army.[44] A perusal of the Wadsworth Papers at the Connecticut Historical Society and pertinent papers in other collections, indicates, however, that the company was not created for this purpose. Most of the capital was invested, like that with Jacob Greene and Company, in shipping and privateering. Goods were also bought and sold and there was some speculation in bills of exchange from time to time. Occasionally there is a record of sales to the army but only small incidental orders are discoverable.

In letters written by Greene and Wadsworth one can get an idea of the extent of their ventures in privateering and shipping. They invested mostly in small ships, as six sloops with ten guns each cost no more than one thirty-two gun ship and would bring in more prizes. In December, 1779, Deane reported that one of their ships, the *Experiment*, had sailed for Cuba in the dual capacity of a cargo ship and a privateer. The next spring Wadsworth told Greene that they were building a ship which would mount sixteen six-pounders. So far, though, the partners had had little luck. "We are not the children of good fortune," Greene lamented in a letter to Wadsworth. In September, 1780, Wadsworth reported that the company was worth but £5,000 sterling. Bad luck continued to haunt the company and in September, 1782, Deane wrote that they had made and lost a fortune in five months. With the war ended and dull times overtaking the commercial world, the company was dissolved in 1784, Greene getting £960 for his share.[45]

If Barnabas Deane and Company were no more than an ordinary trading and privateering company, why, it may be asked, did the partners resort to so much secrecy? To this Greene offers an explanation. At the time the company was born, he and Wadsworth were already the targets of criticism because of their large receipts from commissions and for their extensive business interests. Greene, therefore, asked Wadsworth if he did not think it wise to use a code for their business letters.

> But in addition will it not be best to take upon us a fictitious name. This will draw another shade of obscurity over the business and render it impossible to find out the connection. The busy World will be prying into the connection and nature of the business, and more especially as a letter of Mr. Deane has lately been intercepted in which it is pretended great things are discovered and dangerous combinations formed.[46]

Furthermore, Greene told Wadsworth that Deane should not let his brother Silas know anything about the company as he might let something drop that would arouse rumors. "While we continue in the office which we hold," said Greene, "I think it is prudent to appear as little in trade as possible. For however just and upright our conduct may be, the world will have suspicions to our disadvantage."[47] For the same purpose Greene often used a code for his military correspondence. It not only helped to prevent information from getting to the enemy but kept it as well from the prying eyes of his countrymen who often started dangerous rumors.

Though the records indicate that Barnabas Deane and Company was primarily concerned in privateering and shipping and was not created for supplying the army, it appears that Greene had an interest in Wadsworth's contracts with both the French and American Armies after the two men had severed their relations with the Quartermaster and Commissary Departments. The contracts made during the period between 1780 and 1783 named only Wadsworth and Carter as partners in fulfilling the terms of the agreements. However, if no other evidence existed, the frequency of Wadsworth's letters to Greene about the business would bring him under suspicion of being a partner.[48]

The most explicit letters which seem to make Greene a partner with Wadsworth and Carter in supplying the armies are two written in October and December, 1782. On October 17th, Wadsworth wrote to Greene: "I know you will be surprised to be told that we have contracted to feed the American Army at three months credit. Our friends are all wondering at it." The letter of December is still more enlightening. He was detained in Philadelphia, Wadsworth told Greene, to close

> our accounts with the French army which are embarked at Boston & to close the Contract with the American Army which expires with this Year—and the Public will then owe us 160,000 dollars. 30,000 payable on ye 1st Feby, 10,000 on the 1 March. 10,000 on the 2d April but whether we shall be then paid is not so clear to us—if we are not we are ruined as our own private Credit is pledged for what we coud not pay down. If you draw on me for any large Sum I beg you to advise me previously as this American contract has exhausted us & if we don't get Paid I shall be unable to answer your draft—.[49]

Greene at this time needed money badly to get his plantations in operation and it would seem that Wadsworth feared he would want to draw from his share in the profits of the Company.*

In New England there were other business houses in which Greene invested while he was quartermaster general. Share holding was usually not very exclusive and the Greenes, Wadsworth, and many others invested with Samuel Otis, Joseph Webb, and other New England promoters. Ordinarily they were allowed to select the ships and cargoes in which they wanted to invest. In September, 1779, for instance, Otis reported to Greene that he had purchased one-sixteenth share in the privateer *Tartar* at a cost of $10,000. Greene was offered half of Otis's share which he accepted. Ordinarily, Greene explained, he would not be interested in privateering as it ran counter to his principles, but as it was a way of crippling the enemy, he approved of it. In the same month, Joseph Webb wrote to Greene from Connecticut that he was building a privateer of eighty tons burden at a cost of £35,000. He was reserving one-eighth interest for Greene, he said, and would let Clement Biddle and Wadsworth also have an interest in the vessel.[50]

Outside of New England, most of Greene's investments were

---

* This was at the time Greene was accused of going into business with John Banks and Company in the South. See Chapter XVII.

with his assistant quartermaster, Charles Pettit. His investments with Pettit were in two categories—ships and iron manufacturing. As with his New England ventures in shipping and privateering, those with Pettit ended with the loss of most of the money. In November, 1779, Pettit and Greene had an interest in several ships, the largest of which was the privateer *Revolution*. Soon Pettit sold their share in this frigate at a handsome profit and then turned about and reinvested in the same ship at an advantageous moment. Some months later, however, came a great disappointment. The *Revolution*, after taking a lucrative prize, ran aground off Virginia and was plundered of most of its cargo of wine by the local inhabitants. Soon there were other losses and finally little was left of his investments with Pettit.[51]

Through John Cox, Greene's other assistant quartermaster, Pettit and Greene invested in ships at Egg Harbor, a favorite rendezvous for privateers on the New Jersey coast. Their Egg Harbor holdings, however, turned out no better than the others. Cox, a man of considerable wealth, could never find time to give his partners' an accounting. Not until after the war did Greene learn to his disappointment that he would salvage little from the investment.

During these years Greene's investments in real estate included purchases of land along the Passaic River in New Jersey and up along the Hudson in New York. In Rhode Island he purchased Patience Island in Narragansett Bay at a cost of $4,700 in specie. The island, according to Griffin, could support twenty-five cows, six oxen, four horses, 100 sheep, and eighteen hogs.

Early in 1779, Charles Pettit purchased one-half interest in the Batsto Iron Works in the bog iron region of southern New Jersey. Greene took one-sixth share in the business and John Cox took a like amount. Greene told Griffin that he bought an interest in the iron works so it could supply their Coventry forge with pig iron.[52] That the owners also planned to make money out of contracts with the Board of War for cannon, shot, shells and bar iron is also a fact. They also expected a good business with shipbuilders and the owners of privateers who would want cannon and shot for their vessels. The contracts with the Board of War were apparently made by Pettit whose connections in Philadelphia were extensive. However, there is no proof that anything other than offering iron at a fair price entered into the transactions with the Board of War.

After Pettit and Greene got into the Batsto enterprise, they soon found that profits were as elusive in this business as in shipping and privateering. Misfortune, indeed, haunted the Batsto venture from the beginning. The first blow fell early in 1780 when a flood destroyed the dam. The flood also destroyed a slitting mill and a rolling mill in which Greene and Pettit apparently held no interest. Pettit reckoned that it would cost £20,000 to rebuild the dam and £40,000 to put the furnace in blast again. So far the furnace had turned out iron worth £150,000. With the high cost of labor and other expenses, however, they were still far in the red.[53]

By August, the Batsto furnace was ready for another blast. Pettit had an order from the Board of War for 100 tons of shot and shells which he estimated would take two months to cast. This had hardly been done when production was again stopped by a fire which burned down the building attached to the furnace. After it was rebuilt, Pettit struggled along trying to make the business pay. But slave labor in Maryland iron plantations and the high cost of labor in New Jersey made the going difficult.

In 1781, Pettit wrote Greene that he had decided to erect a forge for the Batsto works for making rod iron. Pig iron could not be shipped from Batsto at a profit, but if it could be made into rod iron which passed like money in south Jersey, the business would be on a much sounder basis. Already he had purchased 800 more acres of woodland to furnish the charcoal for the forge. He had the millrace dug during the spring and hoped to have the dam built and the forge erected by midsummer. That year they cast a large number of six- and nine-pound cannon at Batsto. Those were apparently for the privateer business and not for the government as Pettit reported to Greene in August that only half the cannon were sold. By December, however, sagging sales and high costs made Pettit very discouraged and he told Greene he would sell out as soon as a buyer could be found. Greene's share, he thought, would bring

£700. After this, and until Greene sold his share in 1784 at a considerable loss, the Batsto enterprise never recovered from its gloomy straits.[54]

At Valley Forge it was late April when the news of the alliance with France reached camp. Greene momentarily wondered if the army could cut down on its expenditures, particularly in his department. A powerful French fleet, already on its way to American waters could alter the course of the war materially. He expected, too, that Spain would join the allies. "I don't doubt all Europe in a few months, not in alliance with Great Britain will declare us free and independent States," he wrote. Regardless of the promising developments, Washington, however, thought it inadvisable to alter plans and ordered Greene to proceed accordingly. That Greene was anxious to cut down expenditures in his department takes the sting out of the accusation that he spent money recklessly to increase his commission.[55]

The French alliance gave the army and America a tremendous boost in morale. For the army, Washington chose May 6th as a day of celebration. In the morning von Steuben paraded the army, led by Lafayette and De Kalb, in honor of France, as Washington, Greene, and other officers stood in review. Behind the latter a huge throng of civilians were gathered to witness the grand parade. As the troops marched and made their turns, anyone acquainted with the army of former years could see the vast improvement wrought by Steuben in a few short months of drilling. The high point of review came when, after the thunder of a score of cannon, the troops shouted "Long live the King of France" and then discharged their muskets in a running fire along the lines. As the roar of cannon and crackling of 10,000 muskets reverberated from the hills of Valley Forge, the watchers became exhilarated by the great display of military power. When someone reported that there was a spy in the throng, an officer replied, "let him be." The more the British heard of the excellent condition and spirit of the Americans, the more they would be disturbed by the news.[56]

After the parade the army retired to its quarters to enjoy

special holiday rations and an extra allowance of rum. While the soldiers ate, drank, and made merry, the officers and their ladies dined with their guests at tables under canopies erected on poles on the parade ground. Just as dinner was called, the junior officers "approached the place of entertainment in several columns, thirteen abreast, closely linked together in each other's arms.—The number of officers composing each line, signified the Thirteen States, and the interweaving of arms a complete union and most perfect confederation." At the center table were George and Martha Washington, Nathanael and Kitty Greene, Lord Stirling and Lady Stirling, and other officers and their ladies. Not wishing to deprive anyone of the joy of the occasion, the next day Washington pardoned all the prisoners in the guard house.[57]

It was just a year since Greene and Knox made their trip to the Highlands to survey the Hudson fortifications. So it was again in May that Greene set off for the Highlands, this time to study quartermaster problems and get magazines established along the roads from Valley Forge to the North River. Apparently Kitty traveled with him on her way to Rhode Island. As usual they stopped at Abraham Lott's where Kitty had spent so many delightful days before coming to Valley Forge.

At Morristown, on his return, Greene received an express from Washington announcing that the stocky Sir Henry Clinton, who had succeeded Howe in command of the British Army, was preparing to leave Philadelphia. Though Washington did not know it, Clinton had instructions to consolidate his army at New York before the French fleet arrived. The British did not relish the thought of being bottled up in the Delaware or running the risk of being attacked by combined American and French forces while divided.[58]

As it was all but certain that Washington's army would fight in New Jersey, Greene strove to hurry the gathering of supplies at Trenton, Princeton, Morristown, and other places in the state. But as Clinton might first attempt a surprise on Valley Forge before leaving Pennsylvania, Greene had the army mobile with a fleet of wagon teams ready on command.

While engaged in his quartermaster duties, Greene heard of Great Britain's new peace offensive. With France now America's ally, and with the war no nearer won, Britain sought to end the struggle on almost any terms short of independence. Lord Carlisle, as peace commissioner, was in Philadelphia ready to guarantee all that the colonies had asked for before the war. Greene had no fear that Congress would take the bait. It had rejected a similar offer in 1776 when skies were darker. Why should it bargain with victory in sight? Lord Carlisle soon discovered, too, that his errand was useless and ere the summer had passed, gave up the quest and sailed for home.

When Greene returned to Valley Forge from his trip to the Hudson, he found General Charles Lee had just arrived with his customary train of dogs. He had finally been exchanged for General Prescott whom the Americans had captured in Rhode Island much in the way Lee was surprised and taken at Basking Ridge. Lee was disgruntled as usual. He was vexed because almost everyone had moved up in rank while he remained stationary. If he had stayed in the Polish Army, he told Congress, he would have been a lieutenant general. Congress, however, made no move to take the hint.[59]

On meeting, Lee was far from cordial to Greene. He had heard that the latter had advised Washington "not to be in any hurry about exchanging him." Sensing that something was wrong, Greene tried to convince Lee that he had not been in favor of how Congress had handled his case. Greene could have been angry, too, when Washington put Lee in command of the division he had led before becoming quartermaster. Greene did not like it for it deprived him of the right to take over the command in event of battle as Lee was his superior in rank. As Greene did not blame Lee, the two men shrugged off their ill-humor and resumed their former friendliness. Later, when Lee became Washington's bitter enemy, Greene expressed his sympathy for the unfortunate Lee.[60]

Just before the campaign of 1778 opened, Greene sat down and wrote Kitty a letter which revealed his yearning for home and family. "I am here in the usual style," he wrote from Moore Hall, his headquarters after Kitty had come to camp, "writing, scolding, eating, and drinking. But there is no Mrs. Greene to retire and spend an agreeable hour with." He was not the only one who missed her, he assured his wife. Martha Washington asked about her every day and so did Lucy Knox, now plumper than ever. Greene closed his letter with the wish Kitty would write a long letter about home—there was nothing "so agreeable." Little Martha, his daughter, Greene had never seen, and George was but a few weeks old when he left for New York in 1776. "Kiss the sweet little children over and over again for their papa," he beseeched. Little did Greene think as he sealed the letter that his labors to put the army in the field again would carry him that summer to Rhode Island.[61]

CHAPTER TEN

As Both Supplier and Fighter

Becoming quartermaster general did not make Nathanael Greene any less Washington's adviser on strategy and military problems. At staff meetings his voice was as telling as ever and Washington continued to keep him as close to headquarters as circumstances would permit. In the double role of quartermaster and staff adviser, no better use could have been found for Greene's military talents in 1778.

Sir Henry Clinton did not have ships enough to take his army and the Loyalists at Philadelphia to New York. But even if he had had them, he probably would have marched across New Jersey as he had little fear of the American Army but a great respect for the French fleet. The Loyalists and some German troops (who were losing their enthusiasm for fighting for the King of England) would go by sea. With the rest, an army of 10,000, Clinton would march for New York. By the morning of June 18th, he had the army over the Delaware and ready to begin the tortuous march through New Jersey.[1]

On the day before Clinton completed his crossing of the Delaware, Washington held a council of war. Greene, Wayne, and Cadwalader were opposed to leaving Valley Forge until the intention of the enemy was fully known. Lee was of the opinion that Clinton would embark and go against Maryland. Greene thought not and said he was quite convinced Clinton would head for New York. Discussion then turned upon what should be done if Greene were right. The latter, with Wayne and Lafayette agreeing, advised giving the British a good mauling, if not a general engagement. However, Lee and most of the other officers talked of only harassing the enemy. Not long after the meeting the news arrived that Clinton was over the river and judging by the number of wagons and horses at Haddonfield, fully intent on crossing New Jersey. Washington acted promptly. Six brigades under Lee were ordered to march immediately for Coryell's Ferry. The next day the army followed.[2]

Greene, it was found, took over the Quartermaster Corps none too soon. In spite of all his exertions it was impossible to keep provisions and supplies with the different units of the army at all times during the march. Everyone, nonetheless, admitted that a great change had been wrought in the Quartermaster Department. Greene's preparations, declared Washington, "enabled us, with great facility, to make a sudden move with the whole Army and baggage from Valley Forge in pursuit of the Enemy."

The work of the quartermaster embraced a multiplicity of duties. The supplies had to be bought and collected and the wagons, teams, and drivers found and hired. Artificers were employed to repair bridges, mend broken wagons, harnesses, guns, and anything needing repair. As the army made its daily marches, Greene picked the camp sites with an eye to water, wood, drainage, and defense. Before the army camped, latrines were dug, wood gathered, straw brought in for bedding, and alarm posts established—all at Greene's direction.[3]

Though there were countless matters demanding attention, Greene never lost sight of the big game being played by the two armies. Knowing Lee's opposition to attacking in force, he set himself to counteracting his influence. At Coryell's Ferry he had a long talk with Washington about strategy but he came away feeling he had not been altogether successful. Washington would not commit himself, he said, until he knew more about Clinton's intentions. He did, however, send out Daniel Morgan with 600 riflemen to aid Maxwell's brigade and Dickinson's New Jersey militia who were already engaged in harassing the enemy.

Marching on to a campsite in Hopewell township five miles from Princeton, Washington called a council of war. After some discussion, it was decided to send forward 1,500 men to aid those already hovering about the enemy. Greene, supported by Lafayette and others, argued for a much larger force but Lee opposed. Thinking that something had been gained, all but Wayne agreed that a general action should be avoided. Perceiving that Lee was not at all pleased with the prospect of commanding a mere detachment, Lafayette (perhaps at Greene's suggestion) offered to lead the troops. Lee seemed willing, and not wanting to have the troops under a man not in sympathy with his assignment, Washington consented.

The decision to send but 1,500 troops troubled Wayne, Lafayette, and Greene so much that each wrote Washington asking for a reconsideration. Greene's masterful letter shows his grasp of the situation.

> I am not for hazarding a general action unnecessarily, but I am clearly of opinion for making a serious impression with the light troops and for having the Army in supporting distance. As I said today in council, I would have two Brigades to support them. The attack should be made on the English flank and rear. If we suffer the enemy to pass through the Jerseys without attacking, I think we shall ever regret it. I cannot help thinking we magnify our deficiences beyond realities. We are now in the most awkward situation in the world and have come to our grief repeatedly—marching until we get near the enemy and then our courage fails and we halt without attempting to do the enemy the least injury. Your Excellency may remember I mentioned the matter at Buckingham. People expect something from us and our strength demands it. I am by no means for rash measures but we must preserve our reputations and I think we can make a very serious impression without any great risk and if it should amount to a general action I think the chance is greatly in our favor. However, I think we can make a partial attack without suffering them to bring us to a general action.[4]

Later in the day or early the next morning, Greene and Hamilton went to see Washington to beseech him to augment Lafayette's force before Clinton got away. "I know what you have come for," Washington is reputed to have said upon seeing them. After a brief discussion, Washington agreed to send forward General Wayne with 1,000 select troops. Thus the army was drawn on to Monmouth.[5]

When General Lee heard that Washington was putting nearly 5,000 men under Lafayette he precipitously announced that he desired to lead them. Otherwise, it would be a disgrace both to Lord Stirling and himself, he told Washington. A "thousand apologies" he offered for the trouble his "rash" answer had occasioned.[6] No doubt Lee had cause to complain and his request was not unreasonable.

Whether or not Washington and Greene had discussed the

possibility that Lee might take offense is not known. It is possible both men gave it some thought but said nothing, preferring to have Lafayette in command and hoping Lee would let it pass. Anyhow, Washington was in a dilemma. A way out was found when Lee and Lafayette agreed upon a face-saving solution. Lee would go forward with two brigades to reinforce Lafayette and take command while the latter would be free to complete any operation already begun. Lafayette, consequently, tried to engage the enemy before Lee arrived but the intense heat and rain wore his men down to a halt. At 8:30 P.M., June 26th, Washington sent Lafayette an order to file off to the left to Englishtown so that Lee could catch up with him. This Lee did the next day.

When Lee joined Lafayette at Englishtown, the head of the main army was about three miles behind. The Americans did not know that Clinton, fearing Gates to the north might join Washington if the British marched for Amboy, had decided to take the road to Sandy Hook. Clinton's army was now resting at Monmouth Court House after toiling through the heat and rain while American sharpshooters swarmed about like hornets. During the march his men were so bitten by mosquitoes that faces were swollen beyond recognition. At one time, too, a third of the Hessians lay by the roadside completely overcome by the heat.[7]

On the evening of Saturday, June 27th, Washington sent Lee orders to attack the enemy the next morning as soon as they started moving away unless there were "very powerful reasons to the contrary." The main army, he assured Lee, would be advancing right behind him. About seven in the morning, 2,000 of Clinton's best troops began marching toward Lee whose troops likewise were advancing. Two hours earlier General Knyphausen's division began filing off toward Sandy Hook with the baggage. About 4,000 more troops were to follow Knyphausen but they were presently called upon to join the battle. Clinton was not seeking a general engagement any more than Washington but he had heard that the Americans were advancing in two bodies to fall on his flanks and make an attempt to capture his baggage. Clinton, therefore, planned to hit the American center while his baggage got safely away.[8]

It was noon when Lee's division made contact with the enemy and the long day of battle began. After skirmishing, General Scott retreated some distance for fear of being surrounded. This necessitated a general withdrawal by Maxwell, Wayne, Lafayette, Varnum, and the others. Soon it became apparent the enemy had received reinforcements. Lee, also concerned about the enemy's superiority in cavalry, then decided to move back to a ridge and await Washington.

Not hearing much firing up ahead, Washington rode forward with some of his aides to see what was wrong. When he came upon Lee's retreating forces, he was amazed as he thought the enemy was but a strong covering party. Coming upon Lee himself, Washington angrily demanded the reason for the confusion and the withdrawal. Stunned by Washington's anger, Lee stammered, "Sir, sir—." Then recovering, he tried to explain the reasons for his action but Washington cut him short. Why did he take the command, he demanded, if he did not intend to carry out the orders? Washington then rode on to see what he could do to check the enemy until his advancing forces were in position.[9]

Washington soon found Wayne smarting over Lee's withdrawal and eager to move forward again to check the enemy's advance. While the fiery Pennsylvanian was successfully executing his assignment, Washington drew up his forces on a ridge, the one Lee had selected for his retiring division. Stirling's division occupied the left wing, while Greene (who had taken over Lee's division after the latter had gone forward to command the light troops) took position to the right of Stirling. Lafayette, much to his chagrin, found himself in command of the second line composed of reserves and the fagged-out light troops who had fought the first phase of the battle.

It should be said for General Lee that after his rough encounter with Washington, he courageously went forward with Wayne and was among the last to retire to the main lines. After that Washington sent him, with those too tired to fight any longer, back to Englishtown. Lee left the field, followed by one of his beloved dogs, never again to command an army. Though the verdict of historians has been hard on General Charles Lee, Nathanael Greene had pity for him. An unfortunate man, he thought, whose vanity and folly had at last brought him to ruin and disgrace.[10]

By the time the second phase of the Battle of Monmouth began, Clinton's army was reinforced by part of Knyphausen's division and some more cavalry. After the enemy had tried in vain to turn Stirling's flank, Cornwallis, in command of the troops facing Greene, ordered a charge. Here again they met a hot reception from men better trained than they had ever encountered in America before. From Comb's Hill, Knox directed the artillery on Greene's side, sending cannon balls and grapeshot tearing through the ranks of the enemy. One shot, it was said, miraculously struck the muskets from the hands of a whole platoon. Driven from the field, Cornwallis did not return to the attack.

After two unsuccessful charges by the Grenadiers, the high point of the battle occurred when Lieutenant Colonel Henry Monckton appeared to lead them in a final charge against Wayne's brigade. Wayne is reputed to have shouted as the enemy came rushing forward, "Steady, steady, wait for the word, then pick out the King birds." Again the American fire was devastating, mowing down scores of the Grenadiers and sending the survivors scurrying from the field, leaving Monckton among the slain.

Clinton then retired to strong ground a short distance away. Exhilarated by the sight of the fleeing redcoats, Washington found his army eager to continue the battle. Calling upon some of the least exhausted troops, he sent them forward, but darkness closed in before the contest could be resumed. During the night and without alarming Washington's tired army, Clinton stole away and soon reached the protection of the hills on the road to Sandy Hook.

All that Sunday while the men fought and died, the heat wave which had enveloped the armies for the past week continued unabated. By noon the temperature was nearly 100 degrees. No wind blew and the smoke at times covered the battle field like a fog. Men died, especially among the heavily clad Hessians, from sheer heat and exhaustion. Fifty-nine of the enemy dead with no wounds were counted after the battle. Washington's white horse, too, died during the battle from exhaustion.[11]

The day following the battle, Nathanael Greene presented to Washington one not enrolled among the fighting men but who had fought like a veteran during the stifling battle. Her name was Mary Hays, wife of one of the gunners, but the men called her Molly Pitcher. During the battle she had carried water from a spring for cooling the cannon, while her husband manned the guns. When he became badly wounded, Molly took his place and helped keep the cannon thundering at the enemy. Washington was so pleased with her courage that he gave her a sergeant's commission and put her on the list for half pay.

General Clinton's losses at Monmouth were somewhere between four and five hundred while Washington's were considerably less. In addition, Clinton lost, during his crossing of New Jersey, over 500, mostly Germans, by desertion.[12] By this time the Hessians had learned much about America, especially from their contacts with the Pennsylvania Germans. The lure of magnificent opportunities in the new world had quite undermined the will of the mercenaries to fight for the King of England. Clinton knew this and took the precaution not to use them unless absolutely necessary. The brunt of the fighting, at Monmouth and from then on, was to be borne by the men from the British Isles.[13]

Nathanael Greene was not displeased with the results at Monmouth. To be sure, the Americans had not won a smashing victory. Nevertheless, for the first time they had more than held their own in a general battle. At Monmouth the opposing sides were about equal in number and to Greene it proved that Brandywine and Germantown would have been more rewarding had the Americans not fought under great disadvantages.

After the Battle of Monmouth, the army marched to Englishtown where the troops were ordered to wash and shave for a grand review. While the men stood rank on rank a prayer of thanksgiving was offered to "the Supreme disposer of human Events for the Victory which was obtained on Sunday over the flower of the British Troops." After this the men were searched by their officers for any articles stolen from the inhabitants.

From Englishtown the army made an exhausting three day march to New Brunswick through the intense heat and over stretches of deep sand "without a drop of water, except at South

River." Arriving at New Brunswick, the army camped and rested for nearly a week in an area east of the Raritan. On July 4th, the military and the town celebrated the second anniversary of the Declaration of Independence. Greene selected ground on the New Brunswick side of the river for the parading. At 5 P.M. the firing of thirteen cannon announced the start of the maneuvers. The parade ended with a *feu de joie*—the running fire from 10,000 muskets and the shouts from as many throats for the perpetual union of the United States. After this the troops, with green leaves in their hats, marched sprightly back to camp where a double portion of rum awaited them. As usual, the officers, ladies, and gentlemen in camp had their social evening over their cups.[14]

Leaving New Brunswick, the army trudged on through the dust and heat to Scotch Plains, Springfield, Newark, and up to Paramus. Fortunately, Clinton made no sign of moving against the Highlands and Washington did not have to hurry his army. Nonetheless, many were overcome by the heat and some died. In New York, Montresor, who noted that so hot a summer had never been known "by the oldest inhabitant," saw people falling dead on the street from heart failure.

All during the march toward the Highlands, Greene was buried in the work of the Quartermaster Department. Many horses died from the heat and had to be replaced. When the army reached the vicinity of Bergen County, he was busy stripping the area of forage and provisions to prevent it from falling into enemy hands and to have enough for the army when it entered the barren Ramapo country.

When Washington reached Paramus he learned that Charles Henri Théodat, Comte d'Estaing, Admiral of the French fleet, had arrived off Sandy Hook with twelve ships of the line and several frigates, manned by 10,000 sailors and marines. Washington sent word to Gates that the allies would now lay siege to New York. On July 15th, the army marched to Haverstraw where Washington wrote the Count that he was sending Alexander Hamilton, a man well acquainted with the New York area, to advise the French. "I would wish," wrote Washington, "you to consider the information he delivers as coming from myself."[15]

Preceding the army, Greene crossed the Hudson at King's

Ferry on the 16th and hurriedly began collecting provisions and supplies. At Croton he found time to dash off a letter to Kitty who had fallen ill after a visit to Boston. She was pregnant and Greene was anxious about her. "Why did you ride in the night? What was your hurry?" he asked. Surely there was no need of this, he scolded. He was happy, however, to hear that people in Boston had treated her with great respect and consideration. "They cannot flatter me more agreeably than by their respect to you. What we love we wish to be regarded," he assured her.

Though surrounded by friends and relatives, Kitty was at times despondent because of her long absences from Nathanael. For comfort, he assured her that at the close of the war he would return to her arms "with the same unspotted love and affection" as at the time he left to serve his country. "Surfeited with the pomp and parade of public life, I shall doubly relish domestic pleasures. To please my love and educate my children will be a most happy employment; my fortune will be small; but I trust by good economy we may live respectably," he wrote.[16]

It was about this time that Washington wrote what seemed to Greene to be a rebuke for not getting things done faster. Washington had sent him over the Hudson with orders to reconnoiter and find strong ground for a camp. When Greene did not return as soon as he had hoped, Washington was annoyed. He wanted Greene to help in the correspondence with d'Estaing and the plans for investing New York. Obviously, he wanted Greene to be in two places at the same time.

Greene explained to Washington that he was unacquainted with Westchester County and had to thoroughly examine the area before deciding upon a proper place to station the army. He also dwelt on the difficulties of managing the Quartermaster Department. He wrote:

> I am very sensible of many deficiences, but this is not so justly chargeable to my intentions as to the difficult[ies] in circumstances attending the business. It is almost impossible to get good men for conducting all parts of so complex a business. It may, therefore, naturally be expected that many things will wear an unfavorable complexion, but let who will undertake the business, they will find it very difficult, not to say impossible, to regulate it in such a manner as not a leave a door open for censure and furnish a handle of reproach.

Furthermore, he reminded Washington of his long service without furlough or respite of any kind and how he had never allowed pleasures to interfere with duty. If he had been neglecting his duties he would have kept quiet and taken the censure. But he had been rebuked for doing what he was ordered to do and his feelings were greatly wounded.[17]

Perhaps Washington did not mean to have his words taken as a rebuke. Or perhaps the heat and strain were wearing him down to a point where no one could satisfy him. Greene, always touchy about criticism, admitted that he himself was very fatigued. But whatever it was, Washington answered Greene in a most friendly tone, disclaiming any intention of rebuking him. "But my dear Sir," wrote Washington, "these must not debar me the priviledges of a friend (for it was the voice of friendship, that spoke to you) when I complained of Neglect; I was four or five days without seeing a single person in your department, and at a time when I wished for you in two capacities, having business of the utmost importance to settle with the Count de Estaign."[18]

About the time that Greene had decided upon White Plains as the most suitable position for the army to take, it was discovered that the French ships drew too much water safely to enter New York Bay. A blockade was still possible from off Sandy Hook but it was decided, as Greene advised, to have the fleet sail for Newport where with General Sullivan's army the city should fall an easy prey to the allies.

Washington now sent Varnum's and Glover's brigades under Lafayette to reinforce Sullivan. Greene was exhilarated by the prospect of what seemed to be a great victory about to fall to Sullivan. In a letter to the good-natured but impetuous Irishman, Greene congratulated him on being the first American general to have the opportunity of conducting a campaign with the French. He should be the happiest man in the world, he assured Sullivan. "What a child of fortune," he exclaimed. With France now an active ally, the balance of power, Greene felt, had definitely shifted to the allies. Naturally, Nathanael Greene yearned to go and help his friend win his laurels.

Greene did not leave Sullivan in the dark as to his advising Washington to send the French fleet to Newport or of his influence in preventing General Gates from taking the command away from Sullivan. If Greene came to help, he would not come "as a northern hero to rob" him of his laurels, but to share them under his command. What an opportunity for both of them, Greene confided in his friend. "Your friends are anxious; your enemies are watching. I charge you to be victorious. The Marquis de la Fayette is coming to join you. Trust to your own judgment for forming the plan, as you have everything at stake; and pray give your orders positive for the execution. The late transactions at the battle of Monmouth make me drop these hints," Greene wrote.[19]

It was not at all difficult for Greene to convince Washington that he would be of more use in Rhode Island than with the main army. Varnum, Christopher Greene, and many other Rhode Islanders in the Continental Army would be there too, and Washington could hardly have disappointed Greene. Besides, Washington no doubt wished to please Greene after having offended him so recently. Accordingly, on July 27th, Washington ordered Sullivan to create two divisions with Continentals and militia in each and put them under Greene and Lafayette.

Lafayette accepted the change with good grace and Washington sent d'Estaing a note introducing Greene as one who would have much to offer. As a native of the state "he is intimately acquainted with every part of it, and with its navigation. From these circumstances, added to his weight and influence in that Country, I have thought that his services might be of material importance in the intended Enterprise against our Common Enemy. I recommend him to your notice and attention, as a brave, Intelligent, worthy Officer, and in whom you may place the utmost confidence," wrote Washington. The Count acknowledged Greene's appointment and in a letter to Sullivan said, "The addition of an excellent general is worth more than several battalions."[20]

Accompanied by William Blodget, Robert Burnet, and his other aides, Nathanael Greene reached Coventry a little past sundown on July 30th. It had been three years (except for an hour or so in 1776) since Greene had been home. George, now age four, and Martha three were waiting up to see the father they had never seen. Kitty, in spite of her pregnancy, was feeling well and was as merry as ever. Jacob and his other brothers and many relatives and friends were there to greet him and ask countless questions about the war. The next day Greene rested and inspected the forge, mills, and stables. Everywhere he went the "little rogues," as he called his children, were tagging at his heels. Writing to Sullivan during the day he made plans to see him soon and told him that forty ship carpenters had been engaged to get the boats ready for crossing the water to Rhode Island.*

The following day he rode to East Greenwich with Kitty and his aides. There he talked with Governor William Greene in the old mansion where he and Kitty were married. Nathanael told Uncle William (he was Kitty's uncle, it will be remembered) that Washington expected the state to put half its able-bodied men in the field. Everything, he told the Governor, was going well. The French fleet had arrived and had trapped eight frigates and several transports in the harbor. As Sullivan was not yet prepared to attack, it was agreed the allies would strike simultaneously on August 10th.

On August 6th, Greene marched his divison from Providence to Tiverton. Lafayette followed a little later. Men of all ages and ranks had joined as volunteers "leaving their farms, their families and amusements—to deliver their holy city from the British infidels," wrote a young officer.[21] The army was not long at Tiverton when it was discovered that the enemy had abandoned his works on the north end of Rhode Island and fallen back to lines about three miles above Newport. Without informing d'Estaing, Sullivan at once ordered his army to cross the water and occupy the abandoned works. This was on the day before the date set by the allies for the attack.

When d'Estaing found that Sullivan had not waited for the appointed time to launch his invasion, he was very annoyed. Sullivan's excuse that it was feared the enemy might reoccupy the works did not seem very plausible. Victory seemed sure, and all were aware that the first one on the ground was likely to reap the most glory. Quite likely, it seems, Greene advised or at least acquiesced in the crossing ahead of schedule.

The French acted swiftly, landing their 4,000 marines on

---

* Rhode Island is the island on which Newport is located and should not be confused with the state.

Conanicut Island from whence they would cross the bay to place themselves under the command of Lafayette. Before all was ready, however, d'Estaing was startled to learn that Admiral Howe's fleet was off Point Judith with reinforcements for General Robert Pigot and his 6,000 defenders of Newport. Count d'Estaing let no time escape in getting his marines back on board his warships. When all were aboard, the ships sailed out into the ocean to meet the enemy fleet. Though Howe had more ships, the French were stronger and the wind was in their favor. Consequently, the British prudently withdrew with the French warships in full chase.

For two days the opposing fleets jockeyed for position off Block Island. Then on the 12th a violent storm blew up which lashed the ships unmercifully. When the storm finally blew itself out, Howe limped back to New York while the French slowly collected their battered ships and made their way back to Narragansett Bay.[22]

During the storm Sullivan's army lay out in the gale and downpour. Tents were blown down or whipped into threads and much of the gunpowder lost. Men hugged the stone walls that studded the land. Some soldiers died during the storm and many horses perished. After the storm it turned cold as the army shivered and dried itself out. Greene afterward said that had the British, who had suffered less, made a concerted attack that day, the Americans would have been helpless.

While the gale raged, Greene was at his headquarters in a farm house two miles from the army. Kitty, who had followed him from Coventry, was at Tiverton on the mainland. After the storm she wrote that she was going home as she did not feel well. A Miss Nancy, with whom Kitty was staying, sent pies and puddings to Greene and his aides who were heartily thankful for her kindness as they had nothing but plain army food.

When Sullivan found to his dismay that Count d'Estaing was going to Boston to refit instead of staying to help take Newport, he was fairly stunned. Hoping he might change his mind, he sent Greene and Lafayette on an evening to see the Count on board his crippled flagship, *Languedoc*. On entering the small boat to carry them to the warship, Greene pessimistically remarked, "If we fail in our negotiations, we shall at least get a good dinner."

He was disappointed in both for he became seasick and nothing could make the Count change his mind. Greene pointed out that the fleet could just as well refit in one of the Rhode Island ports. But d'Estaing would not listen, perhaps for fear of being bottled up in Narragansett Bay by Admiral Howe, who was expecting the arrival of another fleet under Lord Byron. Greene was of the opinion that the Count would have stayed had not the captains balked. "The captains of the French fleet," as Sullivan said, "were so incensed at having d'Estaing [an army man] put in charge that they would do nothing to give him credit." Greene summed it up with the remark that the "Devil" had gotten into the French fleet. The day after the interview the fleet sailed for Boston.[23]

Still hoping they might induce the fleet to return, Sullivan, Greene, Glover, and most of the other generals signed a letter of remonstrance and sent it to d'Estaing on a "fast sailor." After stating nine reasons why the French should not leave, among them that the fleet was in no danger at Rhode Island, the letter ended with an alarming note. It would be "derogatory to the honor of France," for it to leave, "contrary to the intentions of His most Christian Majesty and the interest of his nation, and destructive in the highest degree to the welfare of the United States of America, and highly injurious to the alliance formed between the two nations."[24]

Seeing a great victory slipping from his hands, the unlucky Sullivan lost his head and made a statement in his general orders which could be construed to cast reproach upon the French. Count d'Estaing, a courteous and mild-mannered gentleman, was very angry when he heard of it. More excitable, Lafayette was furious at the insult to his countrymen. Read the order:

> The General cannot help lamenting the sudden and unexpected departure of the French fleet, as he finds it has a tendency to discourage some who placed great dependence upon the assistance of it, though he can by no means suppose the army or any part of it endangered by this movement. He yet hopes the event will prove America able to procure that by her own arms, which her allies refuse to assist in obtaining.[25]

Sullivan's naïveté unleashed a torrent of criticism against the French from Americans both in and out of the army. Lafayette declared he heard remarks of disrespect right in his presence "by a herd of New England Yankees." Seeing the great damage his words were doing to French-American relations, Sullivan tried to smooth it over by declaring in general orders that he did not mean to imply that the French had deserted the Americans.[26] Through all the uproar d'Estaing kept his head, answering Sullivan's letters in words firm but conciliatory. When he got to Boston, he even offered to lead his land force to Rhode Island and put himself under Sullivan's command. This was a grand gesture but as everyone knew only the fleet could have saved the campaign.

Quite naturally Washington, Greene, Hamilton and many others were very disturbed by the strain put on French-American relations by Sullivan's indiscretions. Washington's letter to d'Estaing was one of sorrow for the damage sustained in the storm and assurance that America would do all it could to help repair the damage. Washington also appealed directly to Greene to intercede in the interest of harmony. "I depend much upon your temper and influence to conciliate that animosity which I plainly perceive,—subsists between the American officers and the French in our service." Lafayette, Washington told Greene, would take very kindly to any of his suggestions for restoring amity.[27]

Before Washington had appealed to Greene, the latter had made much progress toward restoring harmony. John Hancock, now head of the Massachusetts militia with Sullivan, likewise was very grateful to Greene without whose intercession "serious consequences," he thought, might have arisen. A letter from d'Estaing reveals the confidence that he had in Greene. "It is from you and what you are, that it is doubtless suitable and flattering to judge of the respectable and amiable qualities of the American general officers whom I have not the honor of knowing by correspondence or personally," he wrote. Later, when Greene had occasion to visit the Rhode Island legislature, he found the assembly about to read dispatches from Sullivan containing more derogatory remarks about the French. These papers must not be read, Greene whispered, whereupon they were laid aside and another embarrassing and dangerous incident was averted.[28]

With the enemy already receiving reinforcements from New York, Sullivan asked Greene for his advice on what to do. Greene

answered that he thought the army should give up the siege and
retreat to the north end of the island. However, he offered a plan
which he thought might possibly succeed. It was a daring thrust
by 300 picked men to break a path through the enemy's lines by
way of Easton's Beach. If successful, the whole army would follow
and take possession of the high ground back of the town. Sullivan,
who yearned for glory, was ready to snatch at anything, but when
the count was taken there were too few troops to take the risk.
Since the sailing of the French fleet, the militia had deserted
in "shoals" as Greene remarked in a letter to Washington.[29]

On the night of August 28th, the army moved back to the
redoubts at the north end of the island. Here the Americans could
wait and hope that the French would return, or if endangered, could retreat to the mainland. The very morning after
the move, General Pigot marched out with his whole force in
two columns, eager to attack his foe. Greene, eating his breakfast
at the home of a Quaker, could hear in the distance the firing as
the enemy came upon the light troops under Lieutenant Colonel
W. S. Livingston and Lieutenant Colonel John Laurens. Not long
after, the latter abandoned Turkey and Quaker Hills and fell
back toward the main lines on But's Hill. The British, meanwhile,
formed on the strong ground vacated by the light troops. Greene,
believing a victory could be won, urged Sullivan to allow him to
advance in force but no one seemed to want to support his plan
of cutting off the enemy's forward troops.

Until about two in the afternoon both sides thundered at each
other with all their cannon while some skirmishing went on between the lines. The enemy then advanced against Greene's right
while several of their warships drew close enough to join in
cannonading the Americans. Twice the enemy was repulsed but
still they came on for a third time to meet Greene, who advanced
with six regiments of Continentals, Livingston's light troops, and
a brigade of militia. "We soon put the enemy to rout," wrote
Greene to Washington, "and I had the pleasure to see them run
in worse disorder than they did at the battle of Monmouth."
Lafayette (who was not present) said that judging by reports
it was the best fought battle of the entire war on the part of the
Americans. Many regiments received special notice and Christopher Greene's Negro and Indian battalion behaved with great

bravery. The day terminated with more cannonading and the next day, though it continued, the Americans crossed to the mainland under cover of darkness. As at Long Island and the Christmas night crossing of the Delaware, they were rowed to safety by John Glover and his renowned regiment of Marblehead fishermen. The same day, Admiral Howe arrived at Newport with reinforcements for General Pigot.[30]

The smoke had barely lifted after the battle before Nathanael wrote Kitty an interesting note.

> We retreated back here last night with an intention to hold this part of the Island. The enemy advanced upon us early this morning, and a pretty smart engagement ensued with nearly the whole right wing. I write upon my horse and have not slept any for two nights, therefore you'll excuse my not writing very legible, as I write upon the field. Colonel Will. Livingston is slightly wounded. My aids all behaved with great gallantry.[31]

The American casualties at the Battle of Rhode Island were heavy for the number engaged, amounting to over 200. British losses were estimated as high as 300. Though the Americans were pushed off the island and the British remained at Newport, Sullivan and Greene found the reaction to the campaign very favorable throughout the country. They had done all that could be done, people said. Greene was happy to hear praise but he took it in his stride. "I remember Cardinal de Retz advice was," he told Sullivan, "that upon any turn of good fortune to prepare for bad." He hoped Sullivan would never meet with great misfortune, but he reminded him that "Fortune is a fickle Jade and often gives us a tumble when we least expect it."[32]

After the battle, Greene again found some time to spend at Coventry with his family and friends. While there, he heard of the destruction of New Bedford, Massachusetts, by General Charles Grey and the British Navy on orders from Sir Henry Clinton. In search of privateers, the British burned seventy ships together with warehouses, wharves, and nearby buildings. "General Clinton deserves to be immortalized for this memorable action. It is highly worthy [of] so great a commander," Greene sarcastically observed. Greene thought Clinton wanted to burn Providence and was making attacks upon other points to draw American forces from Rhode Island. If this was his aim, it failed.

Although Kitty was expecting any day, Nathanael could tarry no longer at Coventry. His endless duties as quartermaster were always haunting him. Soon he was off to Boston where he found prices of everything soaring so high there soon would not be "funds in the universe that will equal the expense" of keeping his department going. He asked the New England states to fix prices by law until higher taxes and interest rates could be levied to combat inflation.[33]

While at Boston, Nathanael was a guest of John Hancock who had just returned with laurels won at Rhode Island as head of the Massachusetts Militia. One thing was now certain: the army would not suffer again during the winter from lack of clothing. Large shipments had arrived from France and not a little had been purchased in New England. Greene reported to Washington that 18,000 suits, 15,000 pair of hose, 12,000 blankets, 8,000 pair of shoes, and other articles of clothing would presently be on the way to the army from Boston and Portsmouth.

Greene was never free from worry lest some of his agents might succumb to the temptation of defrauding the government. Though Greene on occasion placed orders with companies in which he had investments, he expected no overcharging or sale of inferior goods. But Henry Marchant warned him that there was talk in Congress of irregularities in the department, especially in Virginia and Maryland. Although Greene did not deny that fraud to some extent existed, he believed it was greatly exaggerated. He got the best men he could and kept as close a watch over the department as possible, he assured Marchant. His agents, Greene explained, were in about the "same predicament that Lord Chesterfield says ministers of state are. They are not so good as they should be, and by no means as bad as they are thought to be. A charge against a quartermaster-general is most like the cry of a mad dog in England. Every one joins the cry and lends their assistance to pelt him to death. I foresee the amazing expenditure in our department will give rise to many suspicions."[34]

Sometime in October when the leaves were bright with color and Kitty had given birth to a daughter named Cornelia Lott, Nathanael bid farewell to his family and friends and set off for Washington's camp. At Fredericksburg, New York, whither Washington had moved the army, he found his thoughts turning to the question of winter quarters. There was very little fear that Clinton would attempt anything further that year. In November, he sent General Grant with 5,000 troops to the West Indies and 3,000 under Colonel Archibald Campbell to Georgia. After this, there was no need for Washington to wait longer before going into winter quarters.

As usual there were many opinions as to where the army should winter. This time, however, as quartermaster, Greene could practically dictate the choice. With an eye to provisioning as well as defense, he recommended, and Washington adopted, a plan for stationing the army at several places. Three brigades would be at Danbury, to help shield Connecticut from raids from New York; a larger garrison would remain at West Point; smaller posts would be at Elizabethtown, Ramapo, and Fishkill, while the major part of the army would go to Middlebrook, where Greene had so successfully confounded General Howe in 1777.

CHAPTER ELEVEN

Keeping the Wheels Turning

After the hard campaign of 1778, Nathanael Greene was to find his greatest problem for the next two years that of finding the money to prevent the army from melting away or disbanding. Inflation was fast destroying the value of the Continental currency and the states seemed no more willing than before to submit to taxation or support the army. During this time Greene was driven to distraction by an office which to him became daily more unbearable.

Greene set out from Fredericksburg ahead of the army to get things started at Middlebrook where the army would pass the most comfortable winter of the war. At Middlebrook he soon had boards, bricks, wood, and other supplies ready for the troops when they arrived. The latter came in detachments during the first two weeks of December. Though the weather was mild for that time of the year the men found it hard to keep warm in their tents while the huts were being constructed. Some built makeshift fireplaces at the end of their tents, an innovation which helped keep them warm but did great damage to the tents.

Not until the end of December were all the huts built and the army settled down for the winter. Greene then sent many of the 2,500 army horses to other places where forage was more plentiful than at Middlebrook. As he finished the work of getting the army in winter quarters, he had the pleasant feeling of knowing it would be better off than during any previous year. The huts were warm, the men were well clothed, and the magazines were well stocked.[1]

Early in January, Greene set out for Philadelphia to pay his respects to Congress and lay before it the needs of his department. Henry Marchant had warned him he needed to keep his fences mended with Congress and not to put off making an appearance for too long. There were always men with complaints or questions which if not answered would cause trouble. Greene wanted to see Congress himself as his district quartermasters were dissatisfied with the terms of their employment. Unless he could get Congress to make the offices more attractive, he feared most of the agents would resign and the department become completely demoralized. Greene found Congress sympathetic but it took a long time before it got around to improving the terms for the agents. By the time it was done, inflation had again rendered the pay inadequate.[2]

Greene found Philadelphia abounding in extravagance and merrymaking. Franklin's daughter, Sarah, declared that "there never was so much dressing and pleasure going on." Greene thoroughly agreed. "I din'd at one table where there were a hundred and sixty dishes," he wrote in amazement. There was a spirit, too, of "intrigue and cabal," he thought. "The growing avarice and a declining currency," he concluded, were "poor materials to build an independence upon." Though Philadelphia was jarring to Greene's Quaker sensibilities, he nonetheless seemed to enjoy the life he deplored. Parties often lasted until the small hours of the morning and with difficulty he met his early appointments and his daily round of business.[3]

Before Greene left for Philadelphia he was called upon by Congress for suggestions on legislation for the army. In these meetings he found Congress at last convinced that militia was more expensive than continental troops of which there would be more for 1779. As for taxation and the rehabilitation of the currency, he was sad to learn that Congress had made no progress. Most of all he was annoyed by the dilatoriness of Congress and its committees. "All the business they did with me," he complained, "might have been done in a few hours, notwithstanding I was pressing them to a decision every day."[4]

Greene left Philadelphia feeling that his month there had been both the most agreeable and the most disagreeable experience of his life. Back at camp he found that the work of his department had piled up amazingly while he was away. From all over the country his agents were calling desperately for money. New Jersey civil authorities were giving him trouble also, especially those of Monmouth who were non-cooperative in the extreme.

Greene complained to Governor Livingston but it was difficult to overcome local resistance.

Early in December, Nathanael had expected Kitty to start for camp. But she was detained and did not arrive in time to accompany him to Philadelphia. When she finally set out she came in her usual style, riding in a two-horse phaeton with her driver and servants and all the dresses, party shoes, and fancy hats she could bring. By the time she reached camp most of the ladies who customarily visited winter quarters were there—Martha Washington, Lady Stirling, Lucy Knox and the rest, each eager for the season of gayness to begin. At Greene's request Kitty brought little George who was soon sent to Philadelphia where he was inoculated and lived with Dr. Thomas Bond until he recovered.

As all the general officers had houses for headquarters at Middlebrook, the accommodations this year were much superior to Valley Forge or Fredericksburg where Benjamin Rush had found the officers at Washington's table taking turns eating for want of enough knives and forks. Though the officers sometimes had to substitute grog or rum for wine, they fared better than they had for a long time. In January, sled loads of venison arrived to afford a change in the bill of fare.

Greene had his headquarters at the home of Derrick Van Veghten, a mile east of Washington's at the home of John Wallace in Somerville. He also had a house in Pluckemin, away from the whirl of business where he and Kitty could live amid quiet surroundings. Here they entertained at dinner parties and dances. At one affair, in March, the Greenes had thirty guests to their "little hop." Clement Biddle, Greene told Jeremiah Wadsworth, was the favorite with the ladies but if Wadsworth were there "he would depreciate like continental currency." At one party at Middlebrook, Washington is said to have danced three hours with Kitty "without once sitting down," though there were other beauties present such as Miss Cornelia Lott and Miss Betsy Livingston. Apparently Greene had lost his fondness for dancing, preferring conversation with those who strayed from the floor. He was, nonetheless, as proud as ever of Kitty, now twenty-four, dainty, and pretty and sparkling as crystal. How gracefully, he thought, she held her fan, a beautiful piece which Silas Deane had brought from Paris. Her favorite locket, purchased in Philadelphia by Charles Pettit, contained a miniature of Nathanael. Kitty was popular with the ladies as well as the gentlemen. Early in April, she was off to Trenton where Betsey Pettit was having a "tea frolick" (as Greene called it) for the ladies of Philadelphia and the camp.

During the season at Middlebrook two great celebrations were held. The first occurred on February 18th at Pluckemin in honor of the first anniversary of the French Alliance. After a parade the troops repaired to their quarters to enjoy extra portions of rum and rations while a sumptuous dinner was served in the Artillery Hall (a building 50 by 30 feet used for giving lectures on tactics and gunnery) for the officers, visiting gentlemen, and all their ladies. In the evening General Knox put on a brilliant display of fireworks after which a ball was held in the hall. With music furnished by army musicians, Washington led off the dancing with Lucy Knox as his partner.

On May 1st, a similar celebration was held in honor of the arrival at camp of Conrad Alexander Gerard de Rayneval, the French minister to the United States, and Don Juan Marailles, a representative of the King of Spain. At a grand review of the army, Major Henry Lee and the Light Horse rode in front, followed by Washington and his aides. Next came the foreign ministers with their retinue and then Greene and the other generals with the army. In a large stagecoach rode Martha Washington, Kitty Greene, Lucy Knox and several other ladies.

Toward the last of April, Greene made another trip to Philadelphia (this time with Kitty) for the purpose of seeing the Treasury heads about money urgently needed to get the army in readiness for the coming campaign. His trip may have helped some but the strain upon the department was eased but little. Pettit complained that he could not make bricks without straw and he could see no end to the hand-to-mouth existence of the army. Up in the Highlands, Alexander McDougall thought the country needed a dictator to pull it through and there were many in the nation who agreed with him.[5]

By spring, complaints against Greene and his department were increasing. Criticism centered in the large receipts Greene was getting from his commission which they said should be abolished.

Instead of giving it up, it was said, he sat smug amidst his emoluments while the nation sped to ruin. In answer Greene declared that he would not do the drudgery for Congress without reward. Again he tried to resign. Washington, not wanting to lose his services, wrote to Congress explaining the difficulties of a quartermaster. However, if Greene insisted upon resigning he promised him the command in South Carolina if it lay in his power to grant it.[6]

About this time Congress appointed a committee to study the needs and problems of the Quartermaster Department. It also passed a resolution declaring it had full confidence in the integrity and ability of the quartermaster general. Greene did not like this as he thought it cast suspicion upon him. Equally irritating was the resolution that authorized the states to suspend anyone in the Quartermaster Department under suspicion of misconduct. This "folly," as he called it, hardly displayed much confidence in his handling of the department.[7]

A little later New Jersey passed a law taxing the profits of its citizens in the departments supplying the army. To Greene the law seemed discriminatory and aimed principally at Cox and Pettit. Fearing that his deputies would resign, he appealed to Congress. As he expected, Congress laid his message (which one member called a highly insulting letter to the New Jersey legislature) aside.[8]

Besides getting the main army ready for the coming campaign, Greene had his hands full in finding horses, wagons, and supplies for Sullivan's expedition against the Six Nations. Led by Tories, these Indians had terrorized the frontier in 1778, destroying the towns of Wyoming in Pennsylvania and Cherry Valley in New York. In January, Greene had advised a march into the Indian country by way of Wyoming, Albany, and Fort Pitt when their "corn is ripe." Congress agreed and Sullivan was selected to lead the main force of 3,000 Continental troops up the Susquehanna trail and into New York. By May, Greene had 1,500 pack horses and 300 four-horse teams ready to start. Lack of money, however, retarded the preparations. At one time Governor Clinton loaned Greene $100,000 of his private funds for Colonel Hay in charge of supplying Sullivan.[9]

About the first of June, word reached Middlebrook that Gen-

eral Clinton had sailed up the Hudson and was landing a few
miles south of West Point. Washington at once ordered the
army to break camp and head for the Highlands. The command
found Greene ready with the transportation and supplies. Kitty
was with him when he rode ahead to see that provisions were
on hand along the line of march. She stayed at Beverwyck
before leaving for home and Greene went on the next day to
Ringwood Manor, the ironworks which furnished much of the
iron used by the Revolutionary army. Here he had the problem
of collecting enough provisions to carry the army through the
barren country beyond Ringwood. By June 7th, however, he
had the army at Smith's Clove, within fourteen miles of West
Point.

With Washington's army waiting for him, Clinton made no
move to attack West Point. However, it might come, thought the
Americans, for the British had fortified King's Ferry (Verplanck's
Point) and Stony Point directly across the river on the western
bank. As the American Army waited, Greene was busy as usual
rounding up supplies. As there were few houses in the area,
he lived in a leaky tent. For some time he had had a pain in his
chest, contracted, he thought, by so much writing at his desk.

During July, things began to happen. Wayne, remembering his
humiliating disaster at Paoli, successfully stormed Stony Point,
killing 150 of the enemy and taking 600 prisoners. A month
later Henry Lee led a daring raid on Paulus Hook where his
force captured 150 men and got safely away. Soon reports arrived that Sullivan was making steady progress although his
expedition did not prevent Joseph Brant and his Indians from
raiding the frontier again.

Although Clinton did not seem anxious to tangle with the
American Army in a general action, he contrived to give his
enemy as much trouble as possible. Raiding parties burned Fair-
field and plundered New Haven in Connecticut. Greene hoped
that Washington would put him in command of one or another
of the detachments ordered into Connecticut and New Jersey
to protect the states, but he was disappointed. As Congress had
recently left his name off the list of officers in command, he
decided it was time to make an issue of it. To each of the major

generals he wrote a note asking them for their opinion on his right to step in and take command when he so desired. Huntington, Gist, Smallwood, and Robert Howe answered that they considered his right to command was indisputable. Stirling, St. Clair, Wayne, and Woodford, however, thought that so long as Greene was quartermaster he should confine himself to the duties of his office. Furthermore, it would be a great injustice, they felt, for Greene to step in and take command on the eve of battle. "Indeed my own [feelings] would be so much hurt at such an Incident," wrote Stirling, "that I should be ashamed ever to Command the Division again."[10]

When Greene received Washington's opinion on the vexing question, he was startled to find that he agreed with the majority who thought that he had relinquished the right of command while quartermaster. Greene's command at Monmouth and Rhode Island, Washington explained, were special assignments, made because of a vacancy in the one and his usefulness in the other. This was a bitter pill to swallow and it made Greene the more determined to get rid of his irksome office as soon as a way out could be found.

Summer passed and autumn came. In October, Washington received word that Count d'Estaing, after defeating Lord Byron in the West Indies, was coming to help him. Greene was ordered to collect a large number of boats at points on the Hudson, Long Island Sound, and the Connecticut River preparatory to an attack on New York when the French arrived. But they did not come. After failing to take Savannah by a costly assault, d'Estaing put to sea and sailed for France. The French had again disappointed their American allies.

With the days for campaigning in 1779 drawing to a close, Greene wrote Washington that the army should again winter in New Jersey. Washington agreed and Greene arrived at Morristown a week later to find a camp site. He selected one in Jockey Hollow, a few miles to the west of Morristown. It was remote enough not to invite attack and was otherwise suitable.

Up to this time the American Army had been fortunate in experiencing rather mild weather on going into winter quarters. But the good fortune gave out and before all the men were hutted and the stores gathered they were caught in raging blizzards and sub-zero temperatures. This time, too, Greene had trouble finding suitable quarters for the officers at Morristown. General Parsons complained of having only one small room for himself and five aides in a house with an owner "worse than the Devil." Greene soon found himself in much the same predicament. James Abeel had arranged for him to stay at the home of Jacob Arnold and on Greene's instructions had installed a kitchen so as not to discommode the Arnolds.

To Greene's surprise he received a note from Arnold saying that he expected Greene to leave his home as soon as he found other quarters. Greene's answer was firm. He did not want to be arbitrary but as every foot of living space in and around Morristown had to be put to use, there was no alternative. Anyone unobliging would learn that no officers were going to be left in the cold for fear of causing some inconvenience. If the magistrates tried to hinder him, he had Washington's permission, he said, to commandeer any and all quarters not actually needed by the inhabitants.[11]

Early in January and before all the huts were finished, the American Army was confronted by what was perhaps the most serious crisis of its existence. Without money Greene had been unable to gather more than a few days supply of provisions and forage ahead of consumption. Then on January 3rd, came a great blizzard which buried the tents and huts under huge snow drifts. All the roads were blocked and the countryside lay paralyzed. Everyone feared the army must disband or starve and freeze to death. But the storm let up enough to allow Greene to get out teams to break a path through to Hackettstown where some supplies were stored.

In desperation, Washington levied quotas of provisions and forage on all the counties in New Jersey. It was a week, however, before the crisis was past as Greene's efforts to get more provisions were frustrated by one storm after another. Meanwhile, all discipline was abandoned and the soldiers allowed to roam the countryside begging food. A few took to stealing but most of them "received what they got with thankfulness, and did little or no damage."

By the 12th the crisis was over. Food had arrived and the

men were back at their quarters. Washington and his staff then decided that it might be possible to launch a successful attack upon Staten Island not unlike the one on Trenton four years before. So cold was the weather that the water between New Jersey and Staten Island was frozen solid and the way was open for a large scale attack. Lord Stirling was selected to lead the troops while Greene was called upon again to get the raiders off upon their dangerous mission.

Greene sent out orders for 300 horse-drawn sleds from the farms of Morris County. Five hundred farmers answered the call and were ready for loading at Peter Kemble's on the morning of January 14th. That night, 3,000 picked men with six cannon and two mortars were carried down out of the hills by the fleet of sleighs. Though furnished with straw, blankets, woolen caps and mittens, 500 men were frostbitten before the expedition returned to Morristown the next day.

It was after midnight when Stirling crossed the Arthur Kill on the solid ice and headed for the enemy's fortifications on the heights above Richmondtown. When he arrived, he found the enemy had been warned and were prepared to defend themselves. After sizing up the situation, Stirling ordered a retreat as he did not want to run the risk of being cut off should Clinton send out reinforcements from New York. Two hundred cattle brought back by the raiders were considered spoils of war but a great quantity of loot from the houses carried off by the militia and civilian followers constituted an act of vandalism which Washington would not countenance. As much as could be recovered was restored to the owners.[12]

Kitty Greene left Coventry with her son, George, to join her husband about the time the army arrived at Morristown. As she was expecting her fourth baby within two months, she rode slowly, making frequent stops. Apparently she arrived sometime after the great blizzard and but three weeks before a son, to be named Nathanael Ray Greene, was born. As usual, Greene did all in his power to make her comfortable and happy. Clothes were ordered from Philadelphia and Colonel Cox searched the city for oranges and other delicacies for her. After the baby was born, Greene wrote McDougall that he was very happy to have another son even if his family grew faster than his purse.

During January an epidemic of colds and fevers spread through Morristown and the camp. At one time Washington and all eighteen of his aides were stricken with colds. They were to be found crowded into the large kitchen of the Ford house trying to keep warm and so hoarse none could speak above a whisper. By February, the siege of colds had passed and the officers and their ladies were looking to their entertainment. An assembly was opened, each officer contributing to the music and refreshments.

At one of the dinner parties occurred an incident not without its interest. After the dinner given by Clement Biddle, the officers, Washington, Greene, George Olney, and one or two others, remained at the table with their host to drink and talk while their wives retired to the parlor. Presently Olney, one of Washington's aides, excused himself and joined the women in the next room. Sometime later one of the men suggested it might be amusing to command the presence of Olney who seemed to be doing well at entertaining the ladies. The men, jolly over their wine, thereupon sent one of their number to summon Olney to report to the dining room. But the ladies returned word that they would not surrender their captive. Led by Washington, the men then marched into the parlor to take their man by force. A scuffle ensued between the beaming warriors and the defiant ladies. The latter won, and the men retreated ignominiously to their den.

Later Mrs. Olney heard that Kitty Greene had spread a tale that she and her husband had offended Washington at the party. Kitty was said to have made known that Mrs. Olney told Washington during the scuffle, "If you do not let go my hand, Sir, I will tear out your eyes and hair from your head even if you are a general." Kitty denied she had spread the story but insisted that Mrs. Olney had threatened Washington. "You did say," she wrote, "you would tear his hear [hair]." If it were not true, why, asked Kitty, did General Greene take the Olneys into the next room and tell them that Washington was offended and that they should apologize? Mrs. Olney's version was that George had left the men because they wanted to get him intoxicated. General Greene only advised her husband to cultivate a more polite manner of refusing to drink with the commander in chief, she maintained.[13]

With the lull afforded by the winter season, Greene considered it a good time to press his desire to resign and leave the Quartermaster Department. Therefore, he wrote to President Huntington asking why his request to resign remained unanswered. Congress replied by appointing another committee to talk with Greene and try to work out a plan of requisitioning supplies from the states. Greene had little faith in such a plan but most of all he was irritated by finding Thomas Mifflin on the committee. To appoint Mifflin, a man under impeachment for his management of the department, seemed to him incredible.[14]

From Philadelphia Greene received some contradictory advice. Reed thought he should resign as soon as possible. Greene would be blamed, he said, no matter what happened: if he stayed with the department, he would be blamed for its failures: if he left, they would say he got rich and then left the country to flounder. Charles Pettit, on the other hand, thought Greene should not resign before Congress found a successor and was prepared to launch the new system. He tried to convince Greene that the majority in Congress were really his friends and wished him no harm. But Greene who never was one to take criticism very well remained unconvinced.[15]

Greene knew that he had at least one true friend in Congress. This was Philip Schuyler who kept him and Washington acquainted with the course of congressional thinking. Greene's enemies, he said, launched bitter attacks on him whenever quartermaster questions arose. His friends, however, did not remain silent and one of them told Congress "that he was the first of all the Subordinate Generals in point of Military knowledge and ability, that in case of an accident happening to Gen. Washington he would be the properest person to Command the Army, *And that George Washington thought so too.*"[16]

For some time Washington had been urging Greene to go to Philadelphia to talk directly to Congress. Greene put off going just as long as he could, not wishing to give Congress the impression that he wanted to keep the office. It was late in March when he set off with Clement Biddle and Kitty. He left with the feeling that little or nothing would be accomplished so far as bettering the department was concerned. Mifflin, he believed, was cabaling again and doing his best to undermine Washington and all his friends. Perhaps, he thought, he might convince Congress of the need of sending more help to General Lincoln in South Carolina before all was lost in that quarter.[17]

After a round of committee meetings interspersed with dinner parties, Greene and Kitty left Philadelphia for camp. Talking with Greene may have helped Congress in working out a new system for the Quartermaster Department but in reality he had lost his usefulness. He was too blinded by criticism and dislike for Mifflin and some of the congressmen to see all sides of the question. His advice was more negative than constructive, blaming Congress for almost everything and not taking account of its mountainous problems. He had helped the army through many difficulties but he had now outserved his time and it was best for the Quartermaster Department to have a new head.

When Greene got back to Morristown he was sick and tired. His head ached and he was feverish. But he soon recovered and was as hard at work as ever. His experience in Philadelphia left him bitter and pessimistic. Congress, he thought, was "haughtier and more impervious than ever and their subordinate Boards had all the insolence of office." But he was not through with Congress as yet. Soon another committee was chosen, this time headed by Schuyler. The latter made a trip to Morristown where he asked Greene to submit his views on what should be done for the department. Greene agreed, providing the committee would first conduct an investigation into his conduct as quartermaster. This the committee declined to do as Congress had not given it the power. Finally Greene submitted his recommendations wherein everyone was put on a salary basis and the committee departed. Without money or credit, the army was half-starved, ragged, and destitute of medical supplies and other necessities the committee told Congress. The picture was, indeed, most discouraging.[18]

Late in May, mutiny broke out in the Connecticut line and threatened to run through the whole army. On an evening the drums beat and the Connecticut men turned out ready to march home. Instead of following suit as expected, the Pennsylvania troops marched to quell the mutiny. Perhaps the Connecticut officers had just about convinced their men that they should stay for without further protest they marched back to their quarters. A day or two later food arrived after quartermaster agents had finally found wagons and teams to haul it to the army.

To Greene the only remedy for what seemed to be a hopeless situation was for the people of the country to hold a convention for making a constitution which would give Congress "powers of general jurisdiction and control over individual states to bind them in all cases, where the general interest is concerned." Washington spoke the same way. "Unless Congress speak in a more decisive tone, unless they are vested with powers by the several States competent to the great purposes of war, or assume them as matter of right, and they and the States respectively act with more energy than they hitherto have done, our cause is lost."[19] Certainly the two men clearly saw what the country needed but they were far ahead of opinion over the nation as a whole. Washington would live to see such a government established but Greene would not.

Toward the end of May came news from the South that General Lincoln had lost Charleston, surrendering practically the entire southern army. General Clinton was sailing triumphantly back to New York with 9,000 troops to join the 8,000 in New York under General Knyphausen. Before Clinton arrived, however, Knyphausen opened the summer's campaign with a thrust into New Jersey straight for Morristown.

Believing that America was tired of the war and that he might find Washington's army too weak to offer much resistance, Knyphausen thought to gather the laurels of a victory before Clinton arrived. A victory might also open the way for an attack on West Point when Clinton joined him. On the night of June 6th, therefore, Knyphausen marched 5,000 troops from Staten Island over a pontoon bridge to Elizabethtown. By morning the enemy was advancing toward Connecticut Farms. No doubt the hero of Mount Washington planned on a jaunt through New Jersey, as he came riding in a carriage behind a pair of spirited horses.

The British had not advanced far, however, before their van-

guard ran into firm resistance from Colonel Elias Dayton's
regiment which was rapidly being reinforced by New Jersey
militia. When word reached Morristown of the enemy, Greene
loaded the wagons with ammunition and entrenching tools and
sent them down the road toward Springfield. So stubborn was
the American resistance, especially at Connecticut Farms, that
it was afternoon before Knyphausen's men neared Springfield
where several divisions of American troops had gathered. But
Knyphausen did not come any farther. He had found that American resistance was strong and he did not like the idea of a general battle with but 5,000 men at his command. He ordered
his columns back to Staten Island.[20]

Washington waited in the vicinity of Springfield and Connecticut Farms for Knyphausen to make the next move after his
abortive march of June 6th. A week passed and then came
word that Clinton had arrived at New York. Could Knyphausen's
maneuver be part of a plan to keep Washington's army in New
Jersey while Clinton made a push up the Hudson against West
Point? Greene suspected that it was and without waiting longer,
Washington took the road to the northward, leaving Greene
with 2,500 troops and Lee's cavalry at Springfield. Although
Greene was still quartermaster no one offered any objection
to his command and Washington made no explanation.[21]

At daybreak on June 23rd, Knyphausen, on orders from Clinton, entered New Jersey again. As before, he had about 5,000
troops supported by cavalry and fifteen or twenty cannon. Clinton did not intend to keep the field in New Jersey but he
wanted to draw Washington back while he brought West Point
under attack.[22]

As Knyphausen advanced he found mounting resistance with
each mile. At Galloping Hills and Connecticut Farms his army
was stalled for three hours by Colonel Dayton aided by Lee's
cavalry. From his headquarters at Bryant's Tavern in Springfield
at eight in the morning, Greene could hear the fighting up ahead
as well as the thunder of the alarm cannon on the hills signaling
the militia to come to the aid of the army.

The enemy finally dislodged the stubborn defenders at Connecticut Farms and pushed on toward Springfield. At the main
bridge over the Rahway the British met Colonel Israel Angell with

his infantry and artillery under Lieutenant Colonel Thomas Forrest. Here they were held up for two hours in sharp fighting all along the banks of the little river. The enemy's right column met Major Lee's men at the Vauxhall bridge, where their advance was likewise stalled for a while. Finding the men in need of wadding after firing so many times, Reverend Caldwell brought the hymn books from the nearby Presbyterian church, exclaiming as he delivered the hymnals (so tradition holds), "Give 'em Watts, boys!" Finally the enemy got around Lee's corps, at which time Greene ordered a general retreat to the high ground above the mill. Here he posted his reserves under Maxwell and Stark, and Dickinson's militia, none of which had participated in the battle.[23]

After setting fire to many of the houses in Springfield and burning the church, the enemy, as on the former excursion, began retiring late in the afternoon. Greene sent Stark after them but they had too much of a start to be overtaken. During the day's fighting the Americans suffered seventy or eighty casualties but only thirteen were killed. The enemy's losses were probably heavier. Years later, Alexander Hamilton said in reference to the Battle of Springfield: "Knyphausen, at the head of a veteran army, was baffled and almost beaten by a general without an army—or rather embarrassed by small fugitive bodies of volunteer militia, the mimicry of soldiership!"[24]

Not many hours after the battle, word came to Greene that twenty ships had been seen sailing up the Hudson. Leaving Dickinson to guard New Jersey, Greene at once started after Washington who had also been warned of Clinton's move. But it soon was found that Clinton's rapid ascent of the Hudson was no more than a big foraging expedition. Knyphausen's diversion into New Jersey had apparently convinced the British that their strength was insufficient to attempt an all-out drive on the Highlands. Clinton knew, as did Washington, that a French fleet was bringing 6,000 troops to America, a factor of no little importance in any action to be undertaken that year.

The first division of the long awaited French troops arrived at Newport on July 10th. Hoping to blockade the French, commanded by Lieutenant General Comte de Rochambeau, Sir Henry Clinton moved 8,000 troops to Long Island where they could cooperate with the British fleet against Newport. But Washington forced him to recall his troops by crossing the Hudson and marching toward Kingsbridge. Thoughts now turned upon the possibility of storming New York with the help of the French. Greene, however, stoutly opposed it unless the French could wrest command of the seas from the British and get control of the harbor. For the rest of the summer the American Army waited to see if this would happen.

About the time the French arrived at Newport, Greene heard that Congress had at last adopted its new system for the Quarter-master Department. Congress again tried to get Greene who had relinquished all emoluments from the office to continue under the new arrangement. The attempt was useless for Greene had been waiting for the day to arrive when he could send in his resignation. He therefore sent it in effective as of August 1st. Five days later Congress appointed Timothy Pickering to fill the vacancy.[25]

Greene was wrong, however, if he assumed that Congress would take no offense by his resignation. His enemies at once demanded that Washington relieve him of command until all his accounts were settled to the satisfaction of the Treasury. Some even talked of discharging him from the army. Even his friends wished he had offered to run the department until the close of the campaign. President Henry Laurens, who liked him, thought his letter was indiscreet and showed disrespect to Congress.[26] John Armstrong thought that he had never seen Congress so incensed against anyone as they were on this occasion. Members usually moderate in their opinions were said to have denounced him for dictating terms and conditions in a highly offensive manner.

With feeling running so strongly against his favorite general, Washington became worried. If possible, he was not going to allow Congress to do anything rash. Writing to Joseph Jones, a member of Congress, he said:

> If by this it is in contemplation to suspend him from his command in the line (of which he made an express reservation at the time of entering on the other duty) and it is not already enacted, let me beseech you to consider *well* what you are about before you resolve. I shall neither condemn, or acquit Genl. Greene's

conduct for the act of resignation, because all the antecedents are necessary to form a right judgment of the matter, and possibly, if the affair is ever brought before the public, you may find him treading on better ground than you seem to imagine.[27]

But Washington was not only worried about what Congress might do. Unless Greene could be persuaded to carry on in the Quartermaster Department, at least until Pickering could learn the ropes, Washington feared the worst. "We not only must cease the preparations for the campaign," he told Congress, "but shall in all probability be obliged to disperse, if not disband the army for want of subsistence." Schuyler's committee now rose to the occasion and offered to allow Greene to operate under the old system until Pickering took over. Perceiving, no doubt, that he had been too inflexible, Greene agreed and the crisis was averted. Throughout the affair Greene had been kept fairly informed of what transpired in Congress. At one time he told Kitty, in self-righteous indignation, that he believed he would be dismissed by an action as "high handed and arbitrary—[as] ever disgraced the Annals of a free people."[28]

With the darkening skies, talk again turned upon giving Washington dictatorial powers. Some said Washington despaired of victory and was seeking a place in the French Army when the war collapsed. Greene wrote to Gouverneur Morris that unless more authority was given to the central government the country might as well make terms with Great Britain. A dictator, he thought, was impractical in a country as large and disconnected as America. A strong government which could get money to run the war was the only solution, he maintained. "It is a point pretty well established in European politicks," he told Lewis Morris, "that the longest purse will prove the longest sword."[29]

On September 17th, Washington set out for Hartford to meet General Rochambeau and Admiral Ternay to discuss plans. He left Greene in charge of the army with headquarters at New Bridge, near Hackensack. While in command, Greene sent troops out to forage the country toward Newark. He had orders to cross the Hudson if a French fleet should arrive for an attack on New York. "This makes a great man of me for a few days," he jokingly wrote his wife.

On his return, Washington was nearing West Point in the

early morning of September 23rd, when some papers captured from a Major John André were delivered to him. To his amazement, he discovered that the papers contained the details for turning West Point over to the enemy. Benedict Arnold, the man entrusted with this important fortress, was a traitor! It seemed unbelievable. Setting spurs to their horses, Washington and his aides galloped to the Robinson house, Arnold's headquarters, but he was gone. The captors had sent Arnold a report of André's capture and he had fled just in time to the British ship *Vulture* anchored in the river.

Greene received the stunning news of Arnold's treason at Paramus where part of the army was encamped. Like others, he found flaws in Arnold's character which he thought were indicative of a low, cunning nature. Arnold, it was said, had been profiting by selling army supplies sent to the relief of the poor destitute soldiers. "Such acts of little dirty villany as he has been guilty of here were they to be related could astonish you," Greene told Joseph Webb. Forgetting Arnold's rightful claim to bravery on the field of battle, he agreed with Wayne that Arnold's bravery arose from imbibing strong liquor "even to intoxication" before going into battle.[30]

In the days which followed, Greene found himself with the disagreeable assignment of presiding at Major André's trial. If it were not for this he would have felt like a free man once more as Colonel Pickering had arrived to take over his duties as quartermaster. At the trial, after the examination of all evidence, it was ruled that André was a spy and must suffer the consequences. Everyone felt sorry for the talented young officer but there was no way to save him. Tears came to Greene's eyes when he pronounced the sentence and Lafayette, one of the court, declared it was "one of the most painful duties he had to perform." Steuben wished there was some way to save him but the British would not exchange Arnold, the only alternative. Major André asked for a firing squad but Washington, remembering the hanging of Nathan Hale, denied his request. Before the execution, Greene met General Robertson sent by Clinton to try to save André. The meeting took place at Dobb's Ferry and none could have been more polite or useless as the enemy would not surrender Benedict Arnold.

With the office at West Point vacant, Greene asked Washington for the command and received it the next day. He at once set about repairing the fort and stocking it with provisions and supplies. But he was not long at West Point before fate came knocking at his door. General Gates who had been sent south after the fall of Charleston was disastrously defeated at Camden and his army all but destroyed. Gates, it was said, had sped from the battlefield after the rout began and did not stop for long until he had nearly 200 miles between himself and the enemy. His retreat, remarked Greene, was "equal to that of Zenophon, but only a little more rapid." Gates's reputation was not only lost forever, but the South as well, it was thought, unless extraordinary measures were taken to save it.[31] South Carolina was overrun by the enemy and firmly held by a network of forts. Lord Cornwallis with a strong force was at Charlotte, North Carolina, poised for the conquest of the state. Even after word of the severe setback the British received at King's Mountain arrived, Greene and Washington felt the military situation remained desperate in the South. If North Carolina fell the prospect of holding Virginia for very long did not appear promising.

Congress left the appointment of the successor to Gates up to Washington. Everyone in Philadelphia, however, was quite certain whom he would choose. All hands, it seemed, simultaneously pointed to Greene. In Congress the delegates from the South made it known that he was their choice. In the army, Lafayette, McDougall, Knox, and others thought of no one but Greene. As one officer said: "If anything is to be expected from the abilities and exertions of a single person, I think no one will be more likely to answer every reasonable expectation than this amiable officer. There can be no better proof of his worth than the universal regret all ranks among us feel at the idea of parting with him."[32]

Washington offered Greene the command of the Southern Department on October 14th. He accepted, asking only for time to go home to settle affairs which had been at loose ends since he entered the army six years before. Washington answered that although he would like to grant the request, the situation in the South admitted no delay. But before Washington received the letter, Greene wrote that he had changed his mind. Word had come of the sailing of more troops from New York to reinforce the British in the South as well as of the rapid progress of Cornwallis into the interior of the Carolinas.[33]

Greene assured Washington he would leave within a few days during which time he hoped to see his wife who was preparing for her annual visit to camp. Greene had invited her to come to West Point although he had hesitated to encourage her too much because of the poor accommodations at the fort. But rather than lessening her desire to come, the letter had sent her off to Providence to buy clothes and get her carriage repaired. By the time Greene was appointed to the Southern command she was nearly ready to start.

Upon receiving his appointment, Greene wrote Kitty urging her to hurry if she were on her way. An officer, he said, had been sent out to look for her as rumors had come that she was on the road. "My dear Angel, What I have been dreading has come to pass," he began his letter, "His Excellency General Washington by order of Congress has appointed me to the command of the Southern army." How much happier he would be, he told her, to stay with her at West Point but he must do his duty and go where he could be of the most service.

The next day Greene hurried to Fishkill having heard that Kitty was about to reach that village. But she was not there and no one had heard of her whereabouts. He returned to the Manderville house opposite West Point where he dashed off another letter and sent it by a rider over the road to the eastward. "I am rendered unhappy beyond expression," he wrote. "I have waited until the last moment, in hope of your arrival, and have just returned from Fishkill, where I went this afternoon, in hopes of meeting you. But alas, I was obliged to return with bitter disappointment. My longing eyes looked for you in all directions, and I felt my heart leap for joy at the sound of every carriage." Morning came and Greene dashed off a parting letter. "I am at this moment setting off for the southward, having kept expresses flying all night to see if I could hear anything of you,—I have been almost distracted, I wanted to see you so much before I set out." And, he concluded, "If Heaven preserves us until we meet, our felicity will repay all the painful moments of a long separation." It was some days later that Greene learned that his wife had not left Coventry.

Arriving at Preakness, New Jersey, where the main army was camped, Greene conferred with Washington at his headquarters at Colonel Dey's house. Here he saw Knox, Hamilton, and many of the officers with whom he had shared so many joys and sorrows during the past six years. Upon bidding farewell, Washington thanked him for his invaluable services in keeping the army going during his two years as quartermaster and wished him the best of luck in his new venture. With Baron von Steuben, his inspector general, Greene took the road to the south with almost the feeling that he was going to his doom, so hopeless did the war appear in the South.

CHAPTER TWELVE

An Unexpected Victory

Nathanael Greene realized that in the South he would be confronted with a military situation far different from the war in the North. The South produced little in the way of manufactured goods. Consequently, practically everything in this line would have to be brought from the north. The absence of much manufacturing likewise made it hard to find artisans who could join the army as repairmen and mechanics. Food and forage there were, except in the areas ravaged by the armies and in the pine barrens, but lack of transportation facilities rendered it difficult to procure supplies. Population centers were scattered and separated by vast stretches of wasteland. Many communities were composed of Tories, especially in North Carolina. A large slave population further reduced the numbers available for military service.

Two years of almost constant warfare since the British had turned to subjugate the South after the war in the North had drifted into stalemate had left the region exhausted and warweary. General Lincoln had surrendered 5,000 men to the British with the fall of Charleston in May, 1780. In August the debacle at Camden had just about put an end to organized resistance in the South. Even if Greene could raise troops, the South had lost so many experienced officers that it would be most difficult to find men to lead them.

Organized government in South Carolina and Georgia no longer existed, and even in North Carolina it was weak and dislocated. The inhabitants were generally impoverished and those not Loyalist were apathetic or afraid to leave their families. In South Carolina a few partisan bands such as those with Francis Marion and Thomas Sumter still held out in the swamps, but in general the country seemed almost subjugated. The ring of forts by which the enemy covered South Carolina and Georgia made their conquest appear secure. Most of the people had been obliged to take an oath of allegiance and otherwise aid and abet the enemy. Although this dark picture was modified by the victory of the mountain men at King's Mountain, the British hold on South Carolina and Georgia remained unshaken. King's Mountain, however, as well as the coming of Greene, revived the spirit of the people and made it possible to carry on.

The more Greene heard of the military situation in the South, the more disconcerting it appeared. Cornwallis had 8,000 troops in South Carolina and Georgia and more were on the way to join him from the North. In addition, he was planning to enlist great numbers of Loyalists for the subjugation of North Carolina and Virginia. Against this host, Greene would find scarcely 2,000 Americans under arms and many of these would be in no condition for active service. As Greene sized it up he became convinced that in the immediate future he must depend to a large degree upon bands of horsemen. These would keep the enemy from overrunning the country and frightening the people into submission. This part of the war would be one of movements, swift and deadly. Meanwhile, he must do his best to raise an army large and powerful enough to meet and defeat the enemy when the time came. To a surprising degree, Greene succeeded in accomplishing his objectives during the first phase of his command which ended in victory at Cowpens.

Greene and Steuben arrived at Philadelphia on October 27th, where they spent about a week conferring with members of Congress, quartermaster agents, heads of departments, and many others. Although all Continental recruits from the states south of the Mason-Dixon Line were henceforth to come under his command, Greene knew how hard it would be to raise and equip an army in the South. Of no small consolation, however, was the thought that he would have "Lighthorse Harry" Lee and his legion of about 300 infantry and dragoons, the pride of the American Army. Besides Lee's veterans, Washington was sending a corps of artificers under Captain Nathaniel Pendleton who would serve as one of Greene's aides and become his lifelong friend.

After hurrying from place to place and person to person in an effort to raise the supplies without which he could not long keep an army in the field, Greene met with some success. Congress appointed Timothy Matlack, a prominent Philadelphian, to head a committee for procuring clothing, the most needed article for the Southern army and the hardest to get. Greene tried to persuade certain merchants to furnish 5,000 suits on credit but they excused themselves "as having engaged more already than they can perform," Failing in this, he tried to get Congress to draw bills on France to pay for the clothing but Congress felt this would be too embarrassing. Lastly, he wrote to James Wilkinson, clothier general, asking him to do all in his power to get clothing for the Southern army.[1]

From the Board of War Greene received promise of a few muskets but not nearly enough to meet the initial demands. To help out, Joseph Reed agreed to lend Greene some muskets from Pennsylvania's meager supply. Altogether Greene reckoned he might get 1,500 stands of arms from the Board of War and Pennsylvania. Writing to Washington, Greene asked if he could send him four or five thousand muskets from New England as this section of the country was no longer in much danger of attack. Washington answered that guns were scarce in New England but he was sending a thousand muskets from the army in New Jersey. On his order, too, General Knox would send an artillery company with several field pieces.

Means must be found for transporting the supplies to the South and in this he also made headway. Timothy Pickering, the quartermaster, promised to get forty wagons and the teams together for carting. As more wagon teams would be needed, the helpful Reed, used his influence to get the Pennsylvania Executive Council to order out 100 wagons from York County. On departing, Greene left the Dane, Christian Febiger (Colonel of the Second Virginia Regiment), a resourceful young officer, to supervise the gathering of supplies and their shipment to the Southern army.[2]

Unlike Gates, Greene was a believer in cavalry for the fighting in the South, and at Philadelphia he did all he could to increase his cavalry strength. For Lee, he obtained a long overdue promotion to the rank of lieutenant colonel, as well as another officer for his legion. As horse gear would be a crucial factor in putting more dragoons in the field, Greene and Lee stressed the need of shipments of saddles, bridles, and sabers to the Southern army. The 150 dragoons under Lee, added to the 100 under Lieutenant Colonel William Washington with the army near Charlotte, were a good beginning, but Greene wanted double that number not including the several hundred horsemen with the partisan bands under Sumter, Marion, and Andrew Pickens. A small number of dragoons under Colonel Charles Armand—the survivors of Pulaski's Legion—was also in the South but these were so poorly equipped that Greene hardly counted them. Ready to try anything, Greene asked Washington if he could persuade Rochambeau to loan him his cavalry, commanded by Duke de Lauzun. Washington answered that it would be useless to try but that he would do all in his power to help Greene raise a formidable cavalry for his army.[3]

Just before Greene left Philadelphia came news of the amazing victory of the back-country riflemen over the enemy at King's Mountain in South Carolina. Led by colonels Campbell, Cleveland, Shelby, Sevier, and Williams—all great names in the mountain country—mounted militia from the hills of Virginia, North Carolina, South Carolina, and Georgia, had trailed Major Patrick Ferguson with his force of 1,000 Loyalists and 100 Regulars to King's Mountain. Here in a savage battle Ferguson was slain and all but 400 of his men were killed, wounded, or captured. From Charlotte, Cornwallis felt compelled to fall back to Winnsborough to prevent a Whig uprising in South Carolina and to await reinforcements before attempting again the subjugation of North Carolina.[4]

The significance of King's Mountain was not lost on Nathanael Greene. Like the battle of Trenton in 1776, he knew it would revive the Whig cause and make the going infinitely easier for him. But although it should be less difficult to raise men in the South, the problem of clothing and equipping them would still remain. In any event, Cornwallis would soon be back in South Carolina and for awhile the pressure would be off and Greene would have a few precious days to prepare for the coming test of arms.

As Greene and his party left Philadelphia on November 2nd and rode toward Chester talk turned to all that had happened in the city and the prospects ahead. Congress had given Greene

$180,000 in almost worthless bills for traveling expenses for himself, Steuben, and their aides, and there was much joking about what they could do with all the money. Blodget was no longer one of Greene's aides, having retired in June to become chaplain on the frigate *Deane*. His place was taken by Lewis Morris, a talented young man and scion of the famous New York family. With Greene was also Robert Burnet, an invaluable aide who had been with him since 1778. Steuben's aides were Benjamin Walker and the talkative Frenchman, Pierre Du Ponceau. With them rode several fellow travelers. As Greene's command included all the states south of Pennsylvania, his first business would be in Maryland, the only state at that time with any sizable body of Continental troops in the South.

Arriving on the second day at the Head of the Elk, a place Greene remembered well from the days of the Brandywine campaign, the party found lodging for the night at a tavern. Greene spent the evening going over Maryland's quota for the army with Daniel Yeates, a quartermaster. First of all, Greene wanted Maryland to fill and equip its five Continental regiments. The state was also asked to furnish 104 four-horse wagon teams with drivers as well as sixty first-class dragoon horses. In addition, it was to raise twenty-two artificers consisting of ten carpenters, six blacksmiths, four wheelwrights, and two harness makers. Lastly, it was to deliver to Greene £1,000 in specie for use in the intelligence division.[5]

At Annapolis, Greene called upon Governor Thomas Lee and laid before the legislature its quota for the army. He found the governor and the assemblymen anxious to do all in their power but not very optimistic about being able to do much. "They promise me all the assistance in their power," Greene wrote to Washington, "but are candid enough to tell me that I must place but little dependence upon them, as they have neither money nor credit, and from the temper of the people are afraid to push matters to extremity."[6]

General Mordecai Gist, whom Greene met at Annapolis, assured him that it was folly to expect much in the way of supplies from any of the Southern states as they were all but destitute. However, Greene was determined to keep trying. He wrote to Governor Caesar Rodney of Delaware, naming what was expected of his state and stressing the importance of keeping the war as far away from Delaware as possible. Greene left the supervision of raising men and supplies in Maryland and Delaware in the hands of General Gist and then headed for Mount Vernon, a convenient stop on the way to Richmond.[7]

Nathanael Greene and his companions arrived at Mount Vernon about noon on November 13th. Greene had often heard Washington talk of his plantation and he knew it was a very beautiful place, but its beauty, he confessed, exceeded anything he had imagined. At the door they were greeted by Martha Washington, her son Jack Custis, cousin Lund Washington, and the wives of the two men.

After the greeting, Martha wanted to know what Kitty had been doing and all the news from camp where she was going in a few days. After dinner Greene and Steuben and their aides rode around the plantation with Lund and Jack. At the stables they stopped to inspect Washington's prized horses and fine cattle. How they wished they could stay longer at Mount Vernon and enjoy more of Martha Washington's hospitality but they had to be on their way. The next morning Greene was up before daybreak writing letters by candlelight so as not to delay their departure.

The next stop was at Fredericksburg where Greene's former brigadier, George Weedon lived. The latter, however, was near Portsmouth with General Muhlenberg where they were directing the forces gathered to fight off General Leslie, recently arrived from New York with a contingent of 2,500 troops. Mrs. Weedon, left in charge of the tavern, entertained Greene and his company with Southern hospitality. Greene left with her invitation for Kitty to come and stay with her whenever she should come south.

Arriving at Richmond, Greene met the tall, red-haired Thomas Jefferson, Governor of Virginia. As he talked with the governor, he had the feeling that Jefferson was too concerned about safeguarding the rights of the people at a time when their liberty and all were at stake. But everything went well and Jefferson was as obliging as the governors of Maryland and Delaware. However, he was no more optimistic than they about filling quotas for the army. The richest state in the South, Virginia was asked to furnish 10,000 barrels of flour, 5,000 barrels of beef, 200 hogs-heads of rum, a large quantity of hay, and 3,000 cattle to be stall-fed and driven to the army when needed. Besides filling up its regiments for the Continental army it was also to provide forty white or negro artisans. Lastly, the state was asked to furnish Greene with £5,000 in specie.[8]

During his stay, Greene constantly reminded Virginians as he had the people of Maryland and Delaware that the enemy would surely overrun their country if they did not fully support his army. Virginia, he said, should not think of relying upon its militia, for although it was useful as an auxiliary force, only a strong Continental army could keep Cornwallis from conquering the South.

Upon appearing before the Virginia legislature, Greene felt encouraged by the response of its members. The state already had raised about 1,500 of its quota of 3,500 troops for the Continental service. However, without money the clothier could not supply the men with clothing and some were already deserting. Although this was disconcerting, neither Greene nor Steuben realized as yet how difficult it would be to get any considerable number of troops properly clothed and equipped in Virginia. The prospect of getting wagons and teams was no better and before Greene left the state he learned that although armed with press warrants, Jefferson's agents had collected only eighteen wagon teams.

Whether or not Virginia could clothe and equip its recruits, Greene was now certain it could provide very little for its regiments in North Carolina. Before leaving Richmond, therefore, he wrote several letters to the northward pleading for supplies. Unless Congress drew bills on France, he told Timothy Matlack, he could not see how he could keep an army going for very long. It may be disagreeable to do this, he said, but it was better than inviting ruin. Other letters were sent to Febiger, Gist, Pickering, and to Congress, all appealing for supplies. He also squeezed in a letter to Kitty, telling her about Mount Vernon and what had occurred since leaving Philadelphia.[9]

As Greene made his way into the South he came to realize more and more the part played by personal influence in a country where government was weak and in some places non-existent. To Washington, he wrote:

> It has been my opinion for a long time that personal influence must supply the defects of civil constitution, but I have never been so fully convinced of it as on this journey. I believe the views and wishes of the great body of the people are entirely with us. But remove the personal influence of a few and they are a lifeless, inanimate mass, without direction or spirit to employ the means they possess for their own security.[10]

Greene and his aides left Richmond on November 21st, leaving behind Baron Steuben to command in Virginia. Leslie's troops had embarked again on the ships in the Chesapeake, and Greene wondered where they were going. He knew they had not withdrawn from any fear of Generals Muhlenberg or Weedon whose forces were hardly a match for seasoned veterans. But whether or not Leslie left Virginia, Steuben, Greene knew, would have his hands full with supervising the recruiting, training, and equipping of the troops to be sent to him.

At Petersburg, Greene heard that the British had landed again at Portsmouth. The rumor turned out to be false, but before he learned the truth, Greene warned Steuben not to let it interfere with sending troops to North Carolina, as any action in Virginia with so small a force was intended only as a diversion. "Our weak side is not here, and therefore I wish to secure ourselves against the enemies advancing into North Carolina," he told Steuben. To facilitate getting supplies to the south, he asked Steuben to make a survey of river transportation. Greene had just discovered an instance where flour was carted sixty miles by wagons when it could have reached the same place in thirty by boat.[11]

One of the officers who accompanied Greene from Richmond to Hillsborough was Lieutenant Colonel Edward Carrington, a young artillery officer, currently without command, but who would soon become Greene's quartermaster. On the way, discussion turned upon the battle of Camden in which Carrington had participated. After hearing the facts, Greene decided that General Gates was not to blame for the defeat. No one understood better than he how precarious were battles and how easy it was for raw troops to stampede and ruin everything.

As Greene and his companions rode over the red clay roads and through vast stretches of pine and oak in North Carolina, he was impressed more than ever by the great problem of logistics in the South. There were rivers enough in the Carolinas but they tended more to divide the country and make movement difficult than to facilitate transportation. This of course was a handicap to the enemy as well, as the main settlements in North Carolina lay to the west of a broad belt of pine barrens paralleling the coast. With Charleston and the posts in the interior of South Carolina in British hands, this state became the enemy's passageway into North Carolina.

Upon arriving at Hillsborough, a town of several hundred inhabitants, Greene wrote Governor Abner Nash asking him to take immediate steps for raising North Carolina's quota of Continental troops. The same day he wrote General Jethro Sumner whom he wanted to see at once in order to draw up a list of officers for the North Carolina line. Greene realized that although the population of the Carolinas and Georgia was around a half million, the great number of Loyalists, as well as the large slave population, severely limited the manpower available. In some parts of the Carolinas Greene found loyalism so strong that he felt he was fighting in the enemy's country. With Tories so numerous, the Whigs were naturally very hesitant to leave their homes to join the army even for a short period of service.

After surveying the situation, Greene wrote to Steuben saying that what he had feared was true in North Carolina. The state had had shoals of its militia on duty for months prior to his coming and like locusts, the men had practically eaten the state into bankruptcy. North Carolina had spent twelve million dollars on its militia since spring, a lesson, thought Greene, for Virginia to consider well before committing itself to the same folly. Greene's letter arrived just as Steuben was endeavoring to send home sections of the Virginia militia against the will of the legislature. Steuben wanted stocks of food which had been collected for Greene's army rather than have it consumed by ravenous militiamen.[12]

At Hillsborough, Greene found a section of the Continental army left there by Gates who had gone to Charlotte to establish winter quarters. With these troops he found Colonel Thaddeus

Kosciuszko, the Polish engineer. Greene would have much work
for Kosciuszko but his first assignment was to survey the Catawba
for navigation from Mill Creek, below the forks, to Oliphant's
Mill. Although the rivers in this area were not navigable for
large boats, Greene hoped he could use flatboats on the ice-free
waters of North Carolina. On a similar mission, Greene sent out
Brigadier General Edward Stevens, who commanded the Virginia militia, to explore the Yadkin. Lieutenant Colonel Edward
Carrington was also sent to see if the Dan, which followed a west
to east course, could be used for bringing supplies to points
near the upper waters of the Catawba or the Yadkin which
flowed generally southward, the Catawba passing near Charlotte
and the Yadkin not far from Salisbury, two important towns in
the Mecklenburg area where loyalty to the Whig cause was very
strong.

Nathanael Greene arrived at Charlotte, a typical back-country
village of several hundred inhabitants, on December 2nd. Here
he found the army which he had come to lead to consist of no
more than a thousand Continentals and perhaps 1,200 militia.
Six or seven hundred of the best troops were on command in
the direction of Camden. Of those in Charlotte, few were in any
way fit for duty. Ragged, half-starved, and spiritless, these woe-
begone creatures looked more like a collection of scarecrows than
soldiers. Many of the Virginia troops were literally naked except
for breechcloths, and all were living in makeshift huts as they
had no tents. Discouraged and beaten to the point of apathy,
the men stared wonderingly at Greene. What could anyone
do, they thought, to revive a lost cause.

In their new commander, the men of the Southern army saw
a man somewhat corpulent though active and alert. At thirty-
eight, Greene's countenance had a mild, serene look indicating,
thought Henry Lee, "a goodness which seemed to shade and
soften the fire and greatness of its expression." With his foundations laid behind him as best he could, Nathanael set to
work at reconstructing his army. Colonel Thomas Polk, who had
served as North Carolina's commissary general, declared that
by the next morning Greene understood the supply situation
better than Gates during the whole period of his command. As
Lee said, Greene at once turned confusion into order "and in-

fused a spirit of exalted patriotism" which earned him "the durable attachment and esteem of all."[13]

General Gates formally turned over the command of the army to Greene on December 3rd. From the time of Greene's arrival, the relationship between the two generals was most cordial. Many officers feared that it might be otherwise and were surprised by the friendliness of both men. Each seemed to have forgotten the days of the Conway episode and their old suspicions. Greene felt sorry for the fallen hero (whose only son had recently died) and did his best to put him at ease. Congress had resolved that Greene should hold an inquiry into Gates's conduct at Camden and Washington appointed Steuben to be president of the court. Gates welcomed an investigation but Greene said it would be impossible at the time with Steuben in Virginia and witnesses scattered or in the hands of the enemy. Therefore, on December 8th, Gates bid farewell to Greene and his fellow officers and set off for "Travelers Rest," his home in Virginia. No court was ever held for Horatio Gates and although he was to serve again in the North, his prestige as a general was never regained.[14]

On the day Greene took over the command, he wrote to Brigadier General Francis Marion. Greene knew Marion only by reputation but it was the kind of reputation he liked. Of Huguenot extraction, Marion was a small, slender man, forty-eight years of age, simple in his tastes, generous, quiet, and unassuming. He commanded a daredevil force of partisans, numbering from twenty to seventy, depending on the ebb and flow of the war. Some mere boys and some Negroes, his band hid in the swamps of the Pee Dee or the Santee when pursued by superior numbers. Rather than patriotism, many of Marion's men were motivated more by personal hatred and a love of adventure. Some were not loyal even to Marion and deserted to the enemy. In his letter, Greene greeted Marion by declaring that although he had never had the honor of meeting him, he was no stranger to his character or his merit as a soldier. Marion's activities in the Pee Dee—Santee region, said Greene, had been most helpful and he wished him to stay there for the present. From this vantage point he especially wanted Marion to get intelligence without which any general was groping in the dark. Greene wanted to know all he could about the British at Winnsborough, Camden, and Charleston as well as the smaller posts. Spies, he told Marion, should be specific in their information, supplying the names of the corps, the size, officers in charge, and so forth. As fast as information was gathered, he wanted it forwarded to him.[15]

Greene studied his officers as well as his problems in logistics. Carrington, he was sure, would make an excellent quartermaster and upon his acceptance of the post, he hurried him off to Richmond to rush supplies to the army. Being quite sure by then that bateaux could be used on the rivers, Carrington was to get shipwrights and tools and half a ton of nails for building the boats. Equally important was the finding of a capable commissary. Greene found such a man in the person of the twenty-four-year-old William Richardson Davie who became commissary for the army as well as for the state of North Carolina. Born in England and brought to America at the age of seven, Davie was adopted by his uncle, William Richardson, the Presbyterian preacher of the Waxhaw settlement in South Carolina. Since the beginning of the war, Davie, who was an expert swordsman, had alternated between fighting the British and studying law. When Greene offered him the post of commissary general, Davie was engaged in raising a troop of horse for North Carolina. Greene knew from experience how Davie felt about putting aside the sword for the mundane office of commissary and the two became fast friends, each admiring the abilities of the other.[16]

Besides the Quartermaster and the Commissary Departments there were many other offices to fill if the army were to be properly serviced. The details of organization kept Greene confined to his desk a good share of the time after he arrived at Charlotte. Carefully, he appointed the wagonmaster, foragemaster, superintendent of boats, clothier, commissary of prisoners, commissary of hides, and other officers. The commissary of hides, whose services none underestimated, gathered up the army's cow hides and exchanged them for shoes when possible.

One order after another flowed from Greene's desk. A prison camp was to be built at Salisbury with palisades eighteen feet high surrounding a half acre. Inside, the prisoners could build huts for themselves. Although most of the men captured at King's Mountain had been imprudently paroled or taken into the Whig militia, about 130 remained, enough, with the 100 which had just been captured, at Rugeley's Mill by Lieutenant Colonel William Washington, for Greene to open negotiations for an exchange of prisoners with Cornwallis. At Salisbury there was also to be established a hospital under the direction of Dr. William Read, a veteran army surgeon. Hundreds of troops were sick and unless clothing soon arrived there would be many more for the hospital, Greene knew.

From the Chiswell's mine in Virginia, Greene ordered lead to be shipped to the Moravians of Salem where cartridges would be made. From somewhere he got a supply of denim and sheeting which he had sent to Salisbury where Joseph Marbury, one of the quartermasters, would have the women of the town make it into overalls and shirts. Marbury was directed to pay the women in salt (fully as good as money) from the government stores. Horseshoes were ordered from blacksmiths and 1,500 pounds of bar iron, some steel, and sixty camp kettles were ordered from Hunter's iron works at Fredericksburg, Virginia.[17]

Having carefully studied the topography of North Carolina, Greene sent instructions for forming magazines to the North Carolina Board of War. The main magazines he wanted at Salisbury and at Oliphant's Mill on the Catawba. These should be stocked with provisions for one month's consumption—not for longer as it would be lost should the enemy make a rapid march into North Carolina. To ease the pressure on transportation facilities, Greene asked that 3,000 cattle be collected at convenient locations where they could be stall-fed until wanted by the army. All salt (an indispensable commodity) belonging to the state was to be removed from the seacoast and stored in the interior. In stressing the importance of losing no time in gathering provisions, he told the board it "must begin by providing for the belly for that is the main spring of every operation." He made the seriousness of the situation clear to everyone: "If the army was not supplied it must retire to the interior towards Virginia or disperse, and the Enemy must be left in peaceable possession of the two Southern States."[18]

Greene was not long at Charlotte before he ran into some unexpected trouble. Major General William Smallwood, who had been with General Morgan and Colonel Washington at the forward post, came to town to announce that he was Steuben's senior in rank and had the right to be second in command. Although Greene was inclined to think Smallwood competent, he knew him to be unpopular with his officers as well as the troops. Greene's friend, George Lux, called Smallwood dilatory, avaricious, and haughty. He was said to allow no field officers to see him but by appointment, treating them with no more regard than a private soldier. Greene tried to reason with Smallwood but it was useless. As he would serve no longer and was determined to present his case to Congress, Greene empowered him to help General Gist when he got home to Maryland. Upon Smallwood's departure, Greene sent word to Steuben to come forward if possible inasmuch as Brigadier General Isaac Huger, though a good officer and next in line, did not feel equal to the assignment. Events, however, kept Steuben in Virginia and Huger reluctantly accepted the command.[19]

More crippling than Smallwood's departure was the loss of Colonel Charles Armand's and Lieutenant Reed's dragoons which Greene found necessary to send to Virginia because they had no clothes fit for service. "No man will think himself bound to fight the battle of a State that leaves him to perish for want of covering," Greene told Jefferson who apparently was beginning to be annoyed by this Rhode Islander's outspoken ways. Clothing was but a small part of the cost of putting men in the field, he reminded Jefferson, but it was essential, even in the South.[20]

Though Greene was not fully aware of it as yet, it would be some time before there would be more than a few hundred troops from Virginia to help fill the ranks. General Lawson's brigade, which Steuben had hopes of sending, was delayed for lack of clothing and equipment and then discharged by the legislature. Greene agreed with Steuben that they were not much of a loss as their time expired in February. Steuben was having trouble, too, with Muhlenberg's brigade, the officers of which refused to march until paid for past services. Shocked by this disclosure, Steuben went to Muhlenberg only to find him too sick to intercede. Weedon had gone to Fredericksburg where he pretended, said Steuben, to have business. Virginia seemed full of officers on furloughs and all behaving, according to Steuben, as though the war was on another planet. Greene, wrote Steuben, should allow no furloughs without his own consent. However, not all was bad news from Virginia. Steuben had Colonel John Greene's (no relative of Nathanael) 450 Continentals about ready to march. Lee, too, with his legion was near Petersburg and by the first of January should reach Charlotte.

Greene was at Charlotte, but a few days before he saw that the army could not remain there. In October, Cornwallis had ravaged the region to obtain provisions and it would be weeks before supplies could be gathered and delivered to the army from other parts of the state and from Virginia. After considering everything, Greene decided he would not only move but would divide the army as well. He would send Brigadier General Daniel Morgan with the best troops to annoy Cornwallis' left flank, while with the remainder of the army he would move about seventy-five miles to the southeast to a site on the Pee Dee.

Though confronted by a momentous decision, Greene did not call a council of war—a policy to which he generally adhered throughout his campaigning in the South. Too often he had seen the proper move scuttled by Washington's councils of war. Wayne used to say that the surest way to have no action taken was to call a council of war. Greene was not averse to listening to advice in an informal way and he usually sought the opinions of some of his officers. But the responsibility was his and he did not intend to be ruined by the opinions of others. Lee, commenting on Greene's capacity for military leadership, wrote:

> No man was more familiarized to disspassionate and minute research than was General Greene. He was patient in hearing everything offered, never interrupted or slighting what was said; and having possessed himself of the subject fully, he would enter into a critical comparison of the opposite arguments, convincing his hearers, as he progressed, with the propriety of the decision he was about to pronounce.[21]

On this occasion Greene apparently sounded out Morgan on the advisability of offensive action on the enemy's flank and found him opposed. Greene was fully aware that it violated the rules of good strategy and was risky, but he had sound reasons for his decision. Cornwallis would be forced to stay at Winnsborough and perhaps divide his army to protect Ninety-Six and Augusta. In any event, Greene would have a better chance of being un-

disturbed while he labored to build an army at his base on the
Pee Dee. Furthermore, Morgan's move would cover the country
north of Winnsborough and keep the men of that region from
joining the enemy for the sake of protection. Morgan's instructions were to keep the British as closely confined to Winnsborough as possible, to act offensively, to remove food stocks,
cattle, and horses out of reach of the enemy, and to encourage the
militia to help cover the countryside.[22]

Perhaps if General Thomas Sumter had not been incapacitated
from a wound received during a brush with Tarleton, Greene
would have relied upon him to cover the area on the enemy's
flank instead of sending Morgan. Governor John Rutledge had
shown Greene a letter from Sumter asking that a detachment be
sent over the Catawba to cover the country north of Winnsborough and threaten the smaller enemy posts. Greene wrote
Sumter on December 15th, stating that this was precisely what
he had in mind: "The Constitution of the Corps I mean to employ
in that quarter, and the position I intend they shall take, are
part of a plan I have had in contemplation ever since I came to
this ground."[23]

Not long after crossing the Catawba, Morgan got into a dispute
with Sumter who jealously contended that all orders to his
militia must come through him. A native of South Carolina and
owner of a plantation in the High Hills of the Santee, Sumter was
a man in his late forties with a long record for bravery and daring.
As a strategist and tactician, however, he was inferior to Marion,
depending as he did on dauntless courage to carry the day. He
had a reputation of being careless about observing the rules of
war and of having a reluctance to take orders from anyone.
Sumter never forgave Morgan for slighting him, as he thought.
Greene, however, by flattery and cajolery, won over the sensitive
Sumter, although he was never as dependable as Francis Marion.[24]

With 320 Maryland and Delaware Continentals and 200
Virginia riflemen, accompanied by about 100 dragoons under
William Washington, Morgan left Charlotte on his mission the
day after Greene marched for his new camp on the Pee Dee.
Morgan was not well, having contracted rheumatism at Valley
Forge which pained him when riding. He was now forty-four,
taller than Greene and much stronger of limb. Greene found his

rustic wit as amusing as Blodget's broad humor had been. Like Israel Putnam, Morgan was fond of fraternizing with his men, making it a practice of walking among them and offering encouragement before a battle. For a time he had been in retirement at his home in Virginia but after Camden he hurried to Hillsborough to help Gates rebuild the shattered Southern army.

Although Greene was forced to leave Charlotte to feed his army, his selection of a location down the Pee Dee was made for military reasons as well as for the stock of food provided by the region. Following the advice of Kosciuszko who had been sent to look for a site, Greene chose a spot where Hick's Creek joins the Pee Dee opposite Cheraw Hill. Here his army would be in a good position to aid Marion, threaten Camden, and annoy the enemy's communication with Charleston.

Heavy rains delayed Greene's departure by eleven days and when the army finally got under way it had food enough only for the day. After six days of toiling over miry roads and through desolate stretches of pines, subsisting on what could be collected along the line of march, the tired and hungry army reached Hick's Creek on December 26th. The region was no "Egypt," wrote Greene, but it would serve the purpose of his coming. Food stocks were quite plentiful and judging by the number of hogs roaming the woods the army would have pork, providing salt could be procured at Cross Creek. (Cross Creek is now Fayetteville, N.C.) Cheraw was at the head of navigation on the Pee Dee and supplies could also be brought up the river in flatboats from the rice plantations below.

After arriving at Cheraw, the more Greene thought about dividing his army, the more satisfied he felt even though Morgan was 150 miles away.

> I am here in my camp of repose, improving the discipline and spirits of my men, and the opportunity for looking about me. I am well satisfied with the movement, for it has answered thus far all the purposes for which I intended it. It makes the most of my inferior force, for it compels my adversary to divide his, and holds him in doubt as to his own line of conduct. He cannot leave Morgan behind him to come at me, or his posts of Ninety-Six and Augusta would be exposed. And he cannot chase Morgan far, or prosecute his views upon Virginia, while I am here with the whole country open before me. I am as near Charleston as

he is, and as near Hillsborough as I was at Charlotte; so that I am in no danger of being cut off from my reinforcements.[25]

While Greene was moving his army and getting established at Cheraw, Marion was constantly foraging or destroying stores within the enemy's lines. Frequently his men clashed with British patrols on the south side of the Santee. But more could be done, Marion told Greene, if he could send him 100 Continentals. Some of his militia were, indeed, too timid to suit the intrepid "Swamp Fox" as Cornwallis called Marion. But Greene had only 640 Continentals and 450 militia at Cheraw and he did not feel that he could part with any of them. Marion, however, would get all the ammunition that could be spared and Greene hoped he would continue to scour the country for horses and continue his raids. Greene also directed Marion to collect all the boats he could find right down to Georgetown and bring them to a safe place up the river.[26]

Meanwhile Greene was foraging the country bare between Cheraw and Camden, a distance of sixty miles. If Cornwallis invaded North Carolina, logically he would push toward Greene and the fertile Cross Creek region, inhabited by Highland Scotch Loyalists. Camden was directly in the line of march from Winnsborough and nothing would hinder the enemy more than a country stripped of food and forage.

While Greene was getting settled at his "camp of repose" on the Pee Dee, Morgan's division scored a victory over the enemy. Morgan had crossed the Catawba and then the Broad. Hearing that a force of Georgia Tories was nearby, Morgan sent Lieutenant Colonel Washington forward with his dragoons and about 200 mounted militia. Washington surprised the enemy near Hammond's Storehouse where without the loss of a man the enemy was destroyed. One hundred fifty were killed or wounded, forty made prisoners, and only about sixty escaped. Without stopping Washington swept on to Fort Williams, a stockaded log house about fifteen miles north of Ninety-Six. But when Lieutenant Hay, in advance of Washington's main force, came upon the Fort he found it deserted. Leaving the place in flames, Washington then rejoined Morgan.[27]

William Washington's victory over the Georgia Tories at Hammond's Storehouse was his second successful exploit within a few weeks. The first had occurred when Greene arrived at Charlotte to take command. Morgan, Smallwood, and Washington were advanced to keep an eye on Lord Rawdon with his garrison of 700 troops at Camden, when they heard there was a party of Tories in a fortified barn at Rugeley's Mill, thirteen miles to the north. Being so near Camden, an attack on the barn would have to be swift. Therefore Washington was dispatched with his dragoons and some mounted infantry to take the fort, if possible. Washington had been in the South since he joined General Lincoln in 1779. A powerfully built man of twenty-eight, he was a fearless officer who led his charges and fought like a lion in the hand-to-hand contests waged by the dragoons.

Upon arriving at Rugeley's Washington found that it was useless to try to take the fort with only small arms. But Washington was resourceful as well as brave. He ingeniously mounted a pine log on wagon wheels and after pointing it at the fort, summoned it to surrender. Believing the Americans had a cannon, the Tories capitulated and Washington (as in a scene of comic opera, rather than deadly warfare) carried off over 100 prisoners.

While Morgan maneuvered on his flank and Greene foraged the country in front of him, "Corncob" Cornwallis, as his men called him, waited impatiently at Winnsborough for General Leslie to arrive with reinforcements. Cornwallis had at first directed Leslie to join him by way of Wilmington but after Greene arrived in North Carolina, he prudently advised him to come by way of Charleston. Whipped by gales, the ships bearing the British did not arrive at Charleston until December 13th. Want of wagons and horses held up Leslie's march five days but by the 23rd he was as far as Monck's Corners with 1,500 troops. It was Tarleton's opinion that Greene did not know of Leslie's coming at the time he sent Morgan across the Catawba or he would not have done so. Greene, it is certain, was convinced at the time of Morgan's departure that Cornwallis would not attempt an invasion of North Carolina without reinforcements.[28] But a knowledge of Leslie's coming might not have deterred him in detaching Morgan as he did not recall him when he heard of his landing at Charleston.

With Leslie in South Carolina, Greene knew that Cornwallis would soon be in motion. Cornwallis, who now outnumbered him two to one, would most likely bring his army directly against Cheraw to open a way to Cross Creek, Greene thought. Indeed, this was his plan before it was interrupted by Tarleton's defeat at Cowpens. As part of the plan, Major James Craig left Charleston early in January with 300 troops and took post at Wilmington where he was to enlist Tories and be ready to close in on Greene. As Greene pondered the intentions of the enemy he became convinced that when the push came he could do nothing but retreat until such time as sufficient reinforcements joined him to make possible a stand. On December 29th, he instructed Morgan to be constantly on the alert and to come to his assistance whenever Cornwallis started for Cheraw.[29]

A few days later Greene again warned Morgan to keep a close watch on Cornwallis now that Leslie was drawing near. Like Cornwallis and Tarleton, Leslie had the reputation of being an enterprising officer. He might well lead a march upon Cheraw from Camden, thought Greene. But he knew that Cornwallis might first contrive to surprise and attack Morgan in which case he advised him not to place too much confidence in his militia and to have some place designated for a rendezvous in case of defeat.[30]

A disquieting report followed from Morgan. The region from the Pacolet to the Catawba, wherein Morgan was operating, was stripped bare of forage and provisions. It seemed to Morgan that he would have to move back across the Catawba or proceed west into Georgia. Morgan thought the Georgia move seemed the most promising. In either event, the people north of Winnsborough would be left at the mercy of the enemy. For self-protection, Morgan believed the men of the area would be compelled to join the enemy.[31]

In answer, Greene told Morgan he did not want him to go into Georgia where he would be completely out of touch with the main army. Greene was sure the presence of Morgan's troops on the enemy's flanks had kept hundreds of men in South Carolina and Georgia from joining Cornwallis and he did not want this to change. He therefore instructed Morgan to remain where he was. If Cornwallis marched toward Cheraw, he was to harass his rear instead of trying to join Greene as previously directed. Were it possible for Morgan to spare a detachment for a few days, he might try a surprise attack on Ninety-Six. However, it would be of more help, Greene thought, to send raiding parties down along the Congaree to kill the horses before the British rounded them up. Above all, Greene warned Morgan not to get caught by flooded rivers. The Pee Dee had recently risen twenty-five feet in thirty hours, thereby impressing Greene with the danger that lurked in the southern rivers. Finally, Greene cautioned Morgan to fight only under favorable conditions and not to worry about what critics might say. American generals, declared Greene, must not regard the opinion of the day but "look to the long side of the struggle."[32]

Now that the British lion was rising from his lair again, the Tories of South Carolina began mobilizing. Lieutenant Colonel Nisbet Balfour, in command at Charleston, told Germain that many of the principal families of South Carolina had again changed sides. Tory bands were gathering in the swamps along the Santee and Pee Dee and all settlements, whether Tory or Whig, between these rivers would soon be deserted, Greene thought. "The whole country is in danger of being laid waste," Greene told President Huntington, "by the Whigs and Tories who pursue each other with as relentless fury as beasts of prey." Lewis Morris described the rapine and destruction in South Carolina as many times worse than anything seen in the North.[33]

As suggested by Greene, Morgan soon sent Washington with a mounted force of about 300 against the Tories in the region of Ninety-Six on the upper reaches of the Saluda. Hearing that Ninety-Six was threatened, Cornwallis sent a strong force under Lieutenant Colonel Tarleton against Washington. Finding he was pursued, Washington circled back and made good his retreat to Morgan at his camp west of the Pacolet.

Whatever should be the outcome of Morgan's maneuvering on the British flank, Greene was certain that the enemy would begin marching toward his army at Cheraw in a matter of days. By this time Greene was fully aware that he would have to rely mainly on help from the North Carolina militia as the enemy had again invaded Virginia. Clinton had sent Benedict Arnold, to be followed by more troops under General Phillips in March, to Virginia to make a diversion while Cornwallis attempted the destruction of Greene's army and the conquest of North

Carolina. Lafayette was in Virginia helping Steuben, having taken charge of the forces in the field. It was very likely, too, that Greene could get little help from the back-country frontiersmen as they had been out fighting the Indians and conditions were still unsettled along the western border.

While developments were moving swiftly toward a climax in South Carolina, Greene continued to build his defenses and inflict as much harm on the enemy as possible. Colonel Farmer was sent with militia to reinforce General William Davidson at Charlotte. At Rocky River, sixty miles north of Cheraw, General John Lillington, aided by Kosciuszko, was building a stockade. Henry Lee, with his legion in their bright green coats (similar to the ones worn by Tarleton's dragoons), had arrived and had been sent to help Marion in a raid on Georgetown. Another detachment was sent from Cheraw against a Tory concentration under Hector McNeill on Downing Creek, a branch of the Little Pee Dee, about thirty miles southeast of Greene's camp. Greene had also written to Sumter urging him to collect his militia and go to Morgan's aid but that general was either too sick or indisposed to take the field.

Upon Tarleton's return from pursuing Washington, Cornwallis put 1,150 of the best troops under his command with orders to find and destroy Morgan's force. As soon as this was accomplished, Cornwallis planned to start marching against Greene. On January 17, the day of the battle of Cowpens, Cornwallis made a start up between the Broad and the Wateree rivers to cut off any survivors after Tarleton struck his blow. Fortunately for Morgan, Cornwallis did not expect a battle so soon and stopped at Turkey Creek, twenty-five miles short of Morgan's line of retreat. Here he awaited Leslie marching from Camden to join him.

Lieutenant Colonel Banastre Tarleton, Cornwallis' dreaded cavalry officer, approached Morgan's camp at Cowpens on the evening of January 16th with his 350 dragoons and 800 infantry, the flower of Cornwallis' army. At two in the morning, Tarleton had his division in motion. At daybreak, after a tiring march of eight difficult miles, Tarleton came in sight of Morgan's front line. Surely the prospect did not appear very promising for Morgan. Although his force was but slightly smaller than

Tarleton's, he had but half as many dragoons. Furthermore, Tarleton had two cannons while Morgan had none. Morgan, however, had confidence in his men most of whom were, in truth, as good as Tarleton's. The Maryland and Delaware Continentals and Washington's dragoons were tried and seasoned men. Moreover, most of the militia and riflemen which made up the remainder of his force had formerly served in the Continental line.

If Morgan purposely chose Cowpens for his battle ground, as has been said, it should earn him no credit for being a cautious general. On a slight rise in the ground on a wide plain interspersed with pine, chestnut, and oak, where pens had been built for cattle, Morgan drew up his lines. His ends were not protected by swamps or thickets and five miles behind them ran the Broad River. Hardly a better spot could have been chosen for Tarleton's cavalry to operate and, if defeated, Morgan's troops would have little chance of escape.

Daniel Morgan afterward claimed he chose this location so that his militia would have to fight or be cut to pieces. He did not worry about his ends, he said, knowing the kind of battle his enemy would fight would be head-on and bloody. Lee considered, however, that this was an afterthought. Morgan's Welsh blood was up and his choice, he believed, arose not from good judgment but from an "irritation of temper" provoked by Tarleton being cocksure of victory. Very likely neither Morgan's nor Lee's explanation is right. In a letter to General Gates written ten days after the battle, Morgan said that he was planning to move to stronger ground but he did not have time. His scouts came in two hours before the battle to tell him that Tarleton was only five miles away and marching very fast. Therefore, he had to change his plans and prepare for battle where he was.[34]

Finding that Morgan had placed a thin line of riflemen behind trees in front of the militia, Tarleton sent his cavalry to rout them. But the fire of the backwoodsmen was so deadly that the dragoons came flying back and could not be induced to resume the attack. Tarleton then sent his infantry against General Pickens' South Carolina militia, by then joined by the riflemen. Andrew Pickens with his militia from the region north of the Saluda had joined Morgan the night before. Like Sumter and

Marion, the thirty-eight-year-old Pickens was a picturesque character. An elder in the Presbyterian Church, he was as dour as any New England deacon and nearly as silent as the Sphinx. Indeed, so guarded was he in conversation that it was said "he would first take the words out of his mouth, between his fingers, and examine them before he uttered them."

Morgan had told Pickens that all he wanted from his men was two volleys. Then they could file off to the left and reform behind the main line consisting of the Maryland and Delaware Continentals and some Virginia militia. As ordered, Pickens delivered his fire at close range, causing great destruction among the enemy. Then the militia ran for shelter. However, before all of them could get off the field, some of Tarleton's dragoons were upon them. But the latter hardly had their sabers lifted to strike before Lieutenant Colonel James McCall and his Georgia horsemen fell upon them. The force of McCall's charge swept the British from the field with the Americans in hot pursuit.

This action, happening on the left of the American line, did not obstruct Tarleton's infantry who believed they had the whole of Morgan's force on the run. They pressed forward cheering wildly, with band playing and colors streaming. Then, suddenly, they came upon the Continentals who poured a deadly fire into their ranks. As the Continentals kept firing and made no move to retire, Tarleton ordered the Highlanders, led by their bagpipes, to outflank the Americans on the right. Lieutenant Colonel John Howard, in command of the Continentals, ordered his line to be extended to meet the British maneuver but his troops mistook the order and retired a few paces. Believing that the Americans were beaten and quitting the field, the British came rushing forward, losing all semblance of formation as they ran. Washington saw them advancing like a mob and sent word to Morgan to give them one more volley and then he would charge.

After coming over the rise where the Americans had stood, the British came rushing down the other side when Howard ordered his men, still in line, to turn about and fire. The enemy, stunned by the shock of the musketry, were thrown into great confusion. Before they could recover, Howard's men were upon them with the bayonet and Washington's dragoons were cutting down those endeavoring to escape. In a few minutes it was all over in the center. Most of the enemy not killed or wounded threw down their guns and begged for quarter. On the right, however, the Highlanders held out a little longer, but when the full weight of the Americans came upon them, they surrendered.

Tarleton tried in vain to get his 200 cavalry reserves into action but they were too terrified to enter the fray, and when Washington appeared with his dragoons they fled the field. For a moment it seemed that Tarleton might fight a saber duel with the muscular Washington. Instead he fired his pistol but the shot missed Washington and wounded his horse. Then Tarleton wheeled about and joined his fleeing dragoons.

Morgan's victory at Cowpens was as complete as the victory at King's Mountain and scarcely less important. Tarleton was out-generaled and his men out-fought. Only about 150 of Tarleton's force of 1,150 escaped from Cowpens. One hundred were killed, double the number wounded, and 700 were captured. The Americans had only twelve killed and sixty wounded. Besides the prisoners, Morgan took thirty-five wagons full of baggage and supplies, 100 dragoon horses, and sixty Negroes. Eight hundred stands of arms were also taken as well as two brass cannon.[35]

If Greene had known that Morgan would undertake to fight a pitched battle with Tarleton, it is very unlikely that he would have sent him out. Greene did not want Morgan to give battle but to harass the enemy while keeping a safe distance from any large force. Greene knew that it was highly dangerous to divide his army but he felt he had little choice if Cornwallis were to be held off long enough for him to get ready for the British push into North Carolina. By exceeding his orders, Morgan ran the risk of having his force annihilated. If Cornwallis had put more troops under Tarleton and then moved immediately to block Morgan's escape, Greene's light troops would doubtlessly have been destroyed. Greene could well breathe a sigh of relief when he heard the news of Cowpens—and pray that he could reunite his army before the light troops were overtaken by Cornwallis.

CHAPTER THIRTEEN

Cornwallis Foiled

Cornwallis was stunned by Tarleton's almost unbelievable defeat at Cowpens. But the defeat, after he had recovered from the shock, made him determined to avenge his wounded pride at all costs. British opinion expected much of him and he had a reputation at stake. His army was still superior to Greene's and he still had hope that the North Carolina Loyalists would join him once he had routed their enemies from the state. By swift marches he expected not only to recover Morgan's prisoners but also to destroy Morgan and get between Greene and Virginia and then defeat him. That he could fail and be forced to abandon North Carolina never entered Cornwallis' mind as he prepared to come to grips with Greene.

Cornwallis lost two precious days by waiting for Leslie and collecting Tarleton's survivors before marching to head off Morgan who, unknown to him, had already crossed the Broad River. Although Cornwallis moved swiftly when he got started, he took the road to Gilbert Town keeping west of the Broad River. When he discovered his mistake, Morgan was two days ahead and over the Catawba at Sherrill's (Sherrald's) Ford. Cornwallis then swung east and arrived at Ramsour's Mills on the Little Catawba on January 25th.

Just before the British reached Ramsour's Mills the river, swollen from rains which had fallen in the mountains, rose to a depth too high to ford. While waiting for the water to subside, Cornwallis foraged the country for provisions. He also burned all except his most essential baggage and stores, leading off by giving his own luggage to the flames. He even burned his wagons, saving only enough to carry the ammunition, hospital supplies, salt, and some for the sick and wounded. In this way he converted his whole army of about 2,500 men into light troops, capable of very fast marching: fast enough, Cornwallis hoped, to overtake Morgan, destroy his force, recover the prisoners, and go on to rout Greene. Except for warm clothing and good shoes, however, the British, without tents and depending on a daily collection of provisions, would be no better off than the men they were chasing.

From Sherrill's Ford Morgan wrote Greene that he would stay there if possible until he heard from him. General Pickens, who had stayed at Cowpens to look after the wounded before joining Morgan, was going back along the road to hinder the progress of the enemy. Morgan suggested to Greene that a diversion toward Georgia, by circling Cornwallis, might be productive of good consequences if it did no more than cover the country and keep the Tories from getting an upper hand. Greene, of course, would not let Morgan do this.

Morgan was occupied blocking the fords with fallen trees, gathering militia, and collecting pack horses. The prisoners which Colonel Washington had brought over the Catawba at an upper ford were sent on to Salem. So far all was well, he told Greene, except for his rheumatism which had become so painful that he would have to leave the army just as soon as Greene appointed a successor.

Greene did not receive the tidings of the battle of Cowpens until five or six days after it was fought. He was delighted with the victory and only sorry that he did not have the troops to follow it up by a direct attack upon Cornwallis. But great as was the victory, Greene knew Cornwallis was far from beaten and that the battle, in spite of its fortunate ending, had been won at a great risk. "In this command," he wrote James Varnum, now a Congressman, "I am obliged to put everything to the hazard; and contrary to all military propriety am obliged to make detachments that nothing but absolute necessity could authorize or even justify."[1]

Two days went by after Greene received the report of the battle of Cowpens before Morgan's letter arrived from Sherrill's Ford announcing that he would wait at the Catawba as long as possible. Upon reading the letter Greene knew that he must unite his army with all haste after which he could give battle if the militia turned out in sufficient numbers. General Huger was told to prepare at once for marching the army to Salisbury to await the arrival of Morgan's light troops and the militia. Greene, meanwhile, would ride to Sherrill's Ford, eighty miles away, to be on hand, if possible, to personally direct the retreat of the light troops.

Even working as hard as he could, it was two days before Greene could start for Morgan's camp. Meanwhile, good fortune came Greene's way again when "Light Horse Harry" Lee and Marion scored a minor victory in a surprise attack on Georgetown. The high-spirited, twenty-five-year-old Lee, whose ambition was matched only by his vanity, was exultant and confident. If Greene would send him two cannon and some reinforcments, he wrote, he could take the fort at Georgetown and its entire garrison of 300 troops. The prospect was pleasing, but Greene had to tell Lee that his legion must return at once to march with the army. When Greene's instructions reached Lee, he responded to orders as quickly as circumstances would permit. But part of his cavalry under Captain Joseph Egleston was over the Santee destroying stores on the Congaree and it took several days before Lee could unite his legion and start for Cheraw.[2]

Greene did not ask Marion to join Huger as his forces were needed to watch the British garrisons at Camden, Georgetown, and Fort Watson, and prevent, if possible, Cornwallis from receiving reinforcements. Marion might actually be able to capture Fort Watson, a fortified Indian mound on the Santee near Nelson's Ferry, Greene thought. Just before Morgan's letter arrived, Greene, in fact, was considering sending 300 mounted militia to help Marion take the fort.

Following the attack on Georgetown, Marion was engaged in bringing stores up the Pee Dee out of reach of the enemy. He had a party of Negroes to man the boats but the river for some days was too high to navigate. Marion was also searching the country for replacements for his horses, worn out by the great strains they endured. Marion informed Greene that in the future he wished to serve under his old Continental commission rather than as a militia officer. He was prompted no doubt by Sumter's claim to leadership of the South Carolina militia as well as the fact that the Continental army in the South was in competent hands. Greene apparently made no comment. With the enemy pressing upon him there was no time to discuss an officer's status in the army.[3]

Before leaving Cheraw, Greene directed that all the prisoners at Salisbury, as well as those taken at Cowpens, were to be in charge of General Stevens who would march them as rapidly as possible to Virginia. Stevens was to keep a commissary and for-agemaster a day ahead of the prisoners so that no time would be lost on the march. Lastly, Greene sent off more appeals for help to Congress, Virginia, and North Carolina. The North Carolina legislature was sitting at Halifax but without money or credit, Greene hardly expected anything more from the legislature than a call for the militia to turn out. Nevertheless, he urged Governor Nash to draft men for the Continental line and to find some way to raise £1,000 in specie for intelligence and other vital needs of the army.[4]

In letters to Benjamin Harrison and John Mathews, Greene laid bare to Congress the crisis confronting the South. Virginia, occupied in fighting off Arnold, had sent few men or supplies to Greene. The Virginia troops with the army were still, for the most part, miserably clothed. Greene warned Congress not to think that Cornwallis was seriously crippled by his losses at Cowpens. "Our prospects are gloomy notwithstanding these flashes of success," he told Mathews. Unless Virginia built up stores on the Roanoke, he declared, the worst might come to pass and he be forced in a few weeks to disband the army. To General Gist, he wrote that Maryland and Delaware which so far had been fortunate in not being overrun by armies, should realize that the Carolinas had struggled so long that their spirit was broken and their resources exhausted.[5]

Accompanied by a sergeant's guard of dragoons and his aides, Greene left for Morgan's camp on January 28th. The next morn-ing General Huger set the army in motion for Salisbury, seventy-five miles to the north. Upon reaching Morgan's camp on January 30th, Greene was pleased to hear that the prisoners were well on their way to Virginia and altogether beyond the reach of the enemy. Reports, too, on the gathering of the militia were at first encouraging but soon Greene learned that his information was false. General Davidson had been issuing call after call for the militia but few responded. Militia officers galloped through the towns and countryside calling loudly upon all men to turn out to defend their homes. But still for fear of leaving their families to the mercy of the Tories, they did not come.

On the 31st, the day before Cornwallis crossed the Catawba, only 300 militia had joined General Davidson who then had 700— far too few to guard all the fords along the river. Greene added his voice to the call to arms and designated a place twelve miles east of the river as a rendezvous. If they came out and did their duty, he declared, Cornwallis was ruined. If they did not, North Carolina was lost. When they failed to come, however, Greene did not belabor them the way he had the New Jersey militia when the men of that state failed to come to Washington's aid in 1776. The North Carolinians had little faith in the ability of the army to defend their homes and they had seen so many reverses and had suffered so long that Greene could understand their apathy.[6]

Considering Greene's opinion of militia generally, he must not have been very surprised when the Virginia militia with Morgan announced they were leaving for home as their time had expired. That night Morgan's Continentals left Beattie's Ford for Salisbury, while the Virginia militia disengaged itself and struck out for Virginia. As the time was also expiring for the Virginia militia with General Huger, Greene sent an appeal to General Stevens to do everything possible to get them to stay longer. Some few did stay, as did a few with Morgan, but most of them would not listen. Stevens was astonished and mortified that his countrymen would desert the army at the hour of need.

Daniel Morgan was a splendid tactician but no strategist. Despairing of being able to keep out of Cornwallis' reach for long, he desired to retreat with the light troops into the mountains. When Greene emphatically vetoed such a move, Morgan exclaimed that he would not be answerable for what happened if Greene tried to retreat through North Carolina. "Neither will you," Greene is said to have replied, "for I shall take the measure upon myself."[7] Before Greene arrived at the Catawba, Morgan had written him that he could not see how any stand could be made against Cornwallis in North Carolina. Morgan's views, however, as expressed to Greene hardly agreed with his boast in a letter to Horatio Gates that if no one else would fight Cornwallis, he would. It is a pity that this brave general was not above casting a slight upon Greene's Fabian strategy as he well knew that it was impossible to give battle unless the militia turned out in numbers.[8]

From Sherrill's Ford, Greene sent out more orders to his scattered forces. All stores were to be sent north beyond Salisbury to Guilford Court House. General Lillington at Rocky River was to join Huger with his corps of North Carolina militia. Huger was ordered to impress all horses and wagons needed to get the stores away. If Marion could not cross to the west side of the Santee to obstruct the British lines of communication between Charleston and the interior posts, he was to move toward Camden by way of Lynches' Creek and operate in the rear of Cornwallis. Should Arnold leave Virginia and come to Wilmington by sea, Huger was to order all stores out of Cross Creek.[9]

While a detachment made a feint at Beattie's Ford, Cornwallis crossed the Catawba before daybreak on the morning of February 1st at McCowan's Ford, six miles below. General Davidson had about 300 militia guarding the ford but most of his force was a quarter of a mile down the river from the point where the British made the crossing. Wading waist-deep through the cold waters of the wide, swift-running, river, the British found few men to oppose them when they neared the eastern bank. Davidson soon arrived with his main force but during a short exchange of gunfire he was killed, whereupon his militia fled, though not before inflicting thirty or forty casualties upon the enemy.

By the time Cornwallis had his whole army over the Catawba, Morgan's Continentals were thirty miles away nearing the town of Salisbury. Greene, however, had stayed behind and was at Oliphant's Mills, seventeen miles above McCowan's Ford. On hearing that the enemy was over the river, Greene immediately left for David Carr's, the place where the militia had been directed to rendezvous. He was probably still on his way to Carr's tavern, twelve miles from the river, when some 300 of the fleeing militia drew up at Tarrant's tavern seven miles short of the place of rendezvous. Here they were resting and eating lunch when their lookout signaled the approach of the enemy. It was Tarleton who with his dragoons soon came charging upon their intended victims. The militia waited only long enough to send a volley of well-directed fire into the British before they wheeled on their horses and sped away.

Nathanael Greene had known that General Davidson could not stop the enemy from crossing the Catawba for long. There were too many fords up and down the river for twenty miles for a few hundred men to guard. However, Greene did expect them to rendezvous at the place designated and to join the others who were to gather there. But when Greene and his aides arrived at David Carr's there was no militia to greet him. He waited through a cold and rainy night until past midnight, unaware that Tarleton's dragoons had scattered what remained of Davidson's militia at Tarrant's tavern. Finally, a rider came to tell him that the militia had dispersed and the enemy were all across the river. Greene then set out through the rain for Salisbury where he arrived early in the morning.

According to tradition, Greene traveled the distance alone, having sent out his aides on one errand or another. Dr. Read, it is said, met him at Steele's tavern and exclaimed, "What! alone, General?" To which Greene replied, "Yes, tired, hungry, alone, and penniless." But Greene said nothing in his letters about traveling alone and it is very doubtful that he was rash enough to have been without his sergeant's guard. The latter could have been tending their horses at the stables when Greene appeared wet and weary at the door of the tavern.[10]

The story that Mrs. Steele, the mistress of the tavern, heard Greene say he was penniless and brought out and gave him all her savings consisting of two small bags of coins is doubtless true. Likewise it is true that Greene, seeing a picture of George III over her fireplace, wrote on the back of it with charcoal, "O George, hide thy face and mourn" and replaced it with its face to the wall. For years the picture remained as Greene had hung it over the fireplace.[11]

At Salisbury, Greene found 1,700 muskets stored for the militia, all of the guns in miserable condition. And where were the men for whom the guns were kept? Greene answered by exclaiming to Steuben, "O that we had in the field as Henry the Fifth said some few of the merry thousands that are idle at home!"

Cornwallis' march was so rapid that his army all but caught up with the light troops before they got over the Yadkin at Island Ford (Trading Ford). With hundreds of horses freed from pulling wagons, Cornwallis put two men on a horse and covered twenty or more miles a day. With the more or less constant rain which had been falling, he expected to trap his adversary west of the Yadkin which was too high to ford. But he did not know that Greene had ordered boats collected and that some were drawn from one river to the other on wagons. It was, therefore, with high expectations that Cornwallis sent ahead General O'Hara to hold the enemy until the main body arrived. When Cornwallis arrived, to his disappointment all the Americans were over the Yadkin. O'Hara had found only a few stores guarded by a small number of riflemen who fired a volley and then pulled off across the river. Greene had succeeded in getting not only all the troops and stores over the river but a countless number of frightened inhabitants as well. The providential rising of the rivers, the people believed, was surely an act of God, although they gave Greene some credit for having the boats available.

Finding that it was impossible to cross the swollen river, Cornwallis, greatly vexed, ordered his artillery to bombard the American camp on the opposite shore. Protected by a ridge along the river, the Americans were more amused than frightened by the thunderous fire from across the Yadkin. Soon, Cornwallis' gunners sighted the roof of a building above the ridge on which they concentrated their fire. It was the house in which Greene had established his headquarters and soon the shingles and boards went flying from the roof. But Greene kept right on writing his dispatches. "His pen," wrote Dr. Reed, "never rested but when a new visitor arrived, and then the answer was given with calmness and precision, and the pen immediately resumed."[12]

One of Greene's letters was directed to General Huger who had been slowed by rains, bad roads, worn-out horses, and other troubles. Huger was ordered to join Greene at Guilford Court House where he hoped they might yet be able to make a stand against the enemy. Urgent letters were sent to the heads of the surrounding militia requesting them to gather their men and repair to Guilford Court House. If they would turn out, North Carolina might still be saved, Greene wrote, otherwise the heel of the tyrant would surely be upon them. More appeals were also sent to Virginia where Greene wanted 1,500 men to be ready to join him if he crossed the Dan. As Greene could see some hope of giving battle at Guilford Court House, he ordered ammunition, guns, flints, tools, clothing, shoes, and other vital articles to be sent there from points of collection in Virginia and North Carolina. All other stores were to be transported to Virginia and beyond the Dan.[13]

Greene also had new orders for Pickens, Marion, Sumter, and others playing a vital part in the campaign. Pickens was directed to hurry back across the Broad to raise militia and operate in the rear of the enemy. Pickens obeyed and was soon trailing Cornwallis with six or seven hundred troops consisting of Salisbury militia as well as his own South Carolinians. To General Sumter, Greene sent a letter calculated to sooth and flatter. He agreed with Sumter that a force in the rear of the enemy would do much good and he wanted him to head all partisans in South Carolina. Marion was to continue his good work along the Santee. By these measures Greene hoped to prevent the rise of dangerous Tory concentrations in South Carolina and make it impossible for Cornwallis to be reinforced or even to communicate with his base at Charleston.[14]

Although frustrated again at the Yadkin, Cornwallis was no less determined to catch his prey. He decided that Greene could not cross the Dan at the ferries for want of enough boats in the area and by going up the Yadkin to the Shallow Ford he could head off Greene from the fords of the Dan. In this he again guessed wrong, for Greene had his boats at Irwin's Ferry and Cornwallis' march of twenty-five miles up the Yadkin to the Shallow Ford gave Greene time dearly needed to unite his army and get his stores over the Dan. After spending several days gathering provisions, it was February 8th before Cornwallis crossed at the Shallow Ford. The same day Huger joined the Light troops at Guilford Court House, thirty-five miles from the enemy.

As it turned out, the militia of the northern counties of North Carolina responded no better than those of Mecklenberg and Rowan. Greene found that he had but 200 militia at Guilford Court House and about 200 more coming under General Lillington. This was not enough to hazard a general battle with Cornwallis and after having his views confirmed by a council of war, Greene prepared to retreat to the Dan, seventy miles away. Greene had hoped that his call for help from the mountain men of western Virginia and North Carolina would be answered in a manner similar to the way they turned out for King's Mountain but he had no reply from William Campbell or Isaac Shelby. By the time Greene reached the Dan all but a handful of the North Carolina militia had disappeared.[15]

As it would be an all-out race for the Dan and Greene must keep far enough ahead of the enemy to get over the river before Cornwallis was upon him, he again divided his army by setting up a body of 700 light troops selected from the best in the army. Colonel Otho H. Williams, his adjutant general, was put in command since Morgan must leave on his painful journey to his home in Virginia. The light troops consisted of 280 infantry under Lieutenant Colonel Howard (the man who had routed Tarleton at Cowpens), and about 250 dragoons under Washington and Lee, sixty Virginia riflemen, and the infantry of Lee's legion.

In Colonel Otho H. Williams Greene found an excellent commander to take the place of Morgan. As a young man of education, Williams had left Baltimore for Boston in 1775 as a lieutenant in the Frederick County rifle corps. That winter he served in the ill-fated Canadian expedition and the next November, as a major, with Rawling's riflemen who kept Knyphausen at bay so long at Fort Washington. Taken prisoner, after his exchange he marched to South Carolina with De Kalb, as colonel of the sixth regiment of Maryland Continentals. At the battle of Camden, Williams did everything humanly possible to save the army and was among the last to quit the field. Except for being rather vain, Williams was much like Greene—warm-hearted and expansive with an eager, expressive countenance. Like Greene, too, he was a strict disciplinarian, dependable and cooperative as an officer, and clear and concise in expressing himself.

On February 10th, William's light troops and cavalry started along a road in the direction of the upper fords of the Dan while Greene marched for Irwin's Ferry where Kosciuszko had been sent to prepare for the crossing. Greene knew that Cornwallis thought that he could not cross at Irwin's Ferry and that the British at first would veer off toward the upper fords in anticipation of heading off the Americans. Besides having boats waiting for him at the ferry, Greene had other reasons for choosing to cross at this point. It was fifty miles below the upper fords and in a direct line should Arnold undertake to join Cornwallis. Furthermore, it lay nearer the more populous sections of Virginia from which reinforcements could come to Greene.

The red-clay roads were slippery and rutted and it rained a good part of the time. Each army had but a few tents for keeping things dry and depended entirely upon fires to keep from freezing at night. After William's force turned to follow the main body on a parallel road, Greene's men were about a day's march ahead, trudging along in their ragged clothing. Hundreds had no shoes and their cut and bloody feet made their progress most painful. One night Greene and South Carolina's Governor, John Rutledge, found shelter in a house no better than a hovel. During the night they awoke and both accused the other of kicking in his sleep. But the kicking continued and upon examining the bed, they found a hog had joined them to get out of the cold and rain.[16]

Williams kept just ahead of the British after the latter discovered that the Americans were headed for Irwin's Ferry, constantly maneuvering to confuse his enemy and give the main body time enough to get well ahead and finally over the Dan. So that Cornwallis could not steal a march and get between him and Greene, Williams kept half his men patrolling at night while the others snatched some sleep. At 3 A.M. he marched his troops so they could get far enough ahead to have time to cook the food which had to last until the morning of the next day. During the day, Cornwallis' compact column often was in sight of Williams' light troops but they never could overtake them and force a battle. Lee's and Washington's dragoons, better mounted than the British and more agile horsemen, kept Tarleton's cavalry at a respectful distance most of the time.

On several occasions, however, parties of enemy dragoons were severely mauled as they attempted to rush the Americans when crossing streams. But generally, wrote Lee, "the demeanor of the hostile troops became as pacific in appearance, that a spectator would have been led to consider them members of the same army."[17]

At one time just after dark, Williams' vanguard saw a long row of campfires ahead. If it were Greene's camp, and they thought it must be, there would be nothing to do but stand and fight while Greene tried to get away with the main army. But it turned out to be Greene's camp of two days before. Friendly hands had kept the fires burning thinking that perhaps Williams' men could rest there for awhile. But they could not stop even for a moment until the enemy stopped, and as yet the British were still marching.

The next morning a note came from Greene, who had barely slept four hours since leaving Guilford Court House, directing them to follow his route. About noon another message arrived, this time with the glad tidings that Greene's army had crossed the Dan! At once the news spread throughout the whole division and the men with one voice shouted to the top of their lungs with joy. O'Hara, not far behind, heard them and guessed the meaning of the cheering.

Williams sent his cavalry back to delay the enemy and hurried forward with his infantry. They reached the river that evening and within a short time all were ferried to the other side. When Lee and Washington got to the Dan with the British in hot pursuit, they found the boats had returned and were waiting. They leaped into the boats while their horses swam at their sides and reached the other bank just as the first of the enemy arrived at the river.

In a letter to Jefferson, Greene summed up his historic retreat. He was "almost fatigued to death, having had a retreat to conduct for upwards of two hundred miles, maneuvering constantly in the face of the enemy, to give time for the militia to turn out and get off our stores." British praise of Greene's retreat has been as high as American. "Every measure of the Americans," wrote Tarleton, "during their march from the Catawba to Virginia, was judiciously designed and vigorously executed."[18]

Although Greene was not sure at first whether or not he would have to fall back farther, the great retreat had ended. He had saved his army and all his stores while Cornwallis was drawn from his bases and reinforcements. Greene was now close to his supplies and he could expect reinforcments. Soon he would give Cornwallis a mauling that would compel this proud general to leave North Carolina and go on to his doom at Yorktown. If Greene had been destroyed, wrote Henry Lee, in all probability all the territory south of the Potomac would soon have fallen under British control.[19] Greene's retreat was masterful and few have ever been more productive of great consequences.

When Lord Cornwallis arrived at the Dan, Nathanael Greene was of the opinion his pursuer would seek the first opportunity to cross the river. Greene was not very worried, in fact, he was hoping that his Lordship would continue his pursuit. Reports were coming in of militia rising all over southern and western Virginia and Greene thought it would not be long before he could face Cornwallis in battle with a good prospect of winning.

Right after Williams crossed the river, the Dan began falling. In a few hours, Greene observed, the British should be able to cross. He would not try to defend the river: there were too many places where it could be forded and he did not want to divide his army that much. But the next day when Cornwallis made no sign of crossing, Greene changed his mind and concluded that Cornwallis would advance no farther.[20]

Soon it was reported that Cornwallis was collecting a ten days' supply of provisions but was not intending to follow Greene. The latter was quite convinced that Cornwallis would march to Halifax or Hillsborough, North Carolina. If he did so, he would follow at his heels, Greene told Steuben. To protect Halifax, the capital and the center of a rich farming area, Greene sent Colonel Kosciuszko to fortify the town, a measure which many of the citizens felt was useless and might only serve to draw Cornwallis that way.

Greene had worked constantly to build up his cavalry which every day seemed more important to him. He sent Lieutenant

Colonel Washington out to impress dragoon horses with orders to "treat the inhabitants with tenderness" and explain to them the necessity of taking their horses. A few days later Greene received Jefferson's consent to impressing the horses and paying for them with certificates. Greene directed Washington not to take breeding mares or the troublesome stallions, but the dragoons paid little heed to his orders. Soon their actions aroused a great storm of protest in Virginia and greatly embarrassed Greene's efforts to enlarge his cavalry.

Greene set up headquarters at Halifax Court House (Virginia) near the Dan. Word soon arrived from General Richard Caswell, head of the North Carolina militia, that men were collecting under Generals Butler, Lawson, Polk, and other county leaders. Not a few were joining General Lillington who had been detached by Greene on the retreat from Guilford Court House to Cross Creek to protect the stores and be ready to obstruct the roads should Cornwallis march that way or Benedict Arnold show up at Wilmington to cooperate with Cornwallis.

Although Greene was skeptical about help from North Carolina, he sent Brigadier General John Butler orders to collect the Hillsborough militia and for Robert Lawson, another brigadier, to join Butler with his Halifax men and some North Carolina cavalry under the Frenchman, Colonel Marquis de Malmedy, an experienced Continental officer. Colonel Thomas Polk who had replaced the fallen Davidson as head of the Mecklenburg militia, was asked to collect five or six hundred riflemen and repair to Hillsborough. Again Greene asked the North Carolina Legislature to make every effort to complete the regiments of Continentals for which General Sumter was recruiting officers. The war could only be won by a strong regular army, he told the legislature, although militia was useful as an auxiliary force.[21]

Meanwhile, the Virginia militia was gathering, although as usual reports were more promising than the real thing. Notwithstanding, in two or three days about 800 Virginia militia joined Greene under General Stevens with more said to be coming. Jefferson had, in fact, called out one fourth of the militia of the southern, central, and western counties and was prepared to call them all out if Cornwallis crossed the Dan. After they collected, however, many had to be dismissed for want of arms suitable for service. Most of all, Greene wanted the riflemen from the western waters, the ones who had earned fame for themselves at King's Mountain. A thousand under Shelby, Lynch, Crocket, and the Campbells were said to be on their way.[22]

Greene warned Steuben to watch Arnold at Portsmouth lest he endeavor to join Cornwallis with his 1,500 troops by marching overland. French ships in the Chesapeake had blocked his way to Wilmington, Greene learned. Greene's warning was hardly necessary, for Arnold had reports that Cornwallis had crossed the Dan in pursuit of Greene and could be joined when he reached Petersburg.

Though far away, Greene did not lose sight of South Carolina. He asked General Sumter to do all he could to keep men from joining the British. It had been reported to Greene that the enemy intended to draft all the militia and was raising two regiments of Negroes in South Carolina. If they succeeded, Greene told Sumter, South Carolina was lost. Sumter and Marion, however, were not idle. While Greene was conducting his retreat, Sumter had unsuccessfully besieged Fort Granby at the head of the Congaree, then crossed the Santee where he had a brush with Colonel Watson. Thereafter he retreated to his own neighborhood, the High Hills of the Santee. From here, Greene hoped he could raid Camden and destroy the mill without which Lord Rawdon would find it most difficult to feed his troops. Whether Sumter tried or not, the mill was still standing when Greene arrived at Camden four weeks later.[23]

On February 19th, four days after he reached the Dan, Cornwallis turned about and headed for Hillsborough. His Lordship knew it would be courting ruin to pursue Greene into Virginia unless he could first enlist North Carolina Tories by the hundreds, gather the resources of the state, and get supplies from Wilmington.

Greene guessed Cornwallis' intentions and knew there was no time to lose if the Tories were to be kept from rising and the Whigs encouraged to gather under their county leaders. On the same day that Cornwallis marched toward Hillsborough, Greene sent Lee to follow him. General Pickens, who had advanced as far as Guilford Court House, was urged to join Lee without delay. The next day Williams crossed the Dan with the light troops. The following day, February 22nd, Greene recrossed with the main army and six or seven hundred Virginia militia. Many of the latter remained behind, finding one reason or another for not following.

On the day the army crossed the Dan, Greene rode ahead eighteen miles with his aides to get information from Lee and Pickens who had joined forces. That night he caught some sleep wrapped in a blanket borrowed from the taciturn Pickens. By daybreak he was on his way back to the army. The recrossing of the Dan, Greene found, was having its desired effect. The Tories were apprehensive and the Whigs encouraged. If Virginia and North Carolina militia would only join him in the numbers required, he would invite Cornwallis to a showdown.[24]

At Hillsborough, Cornwallis raised his standard and called upon all loyal subjects of King George the Third to join him. Hundreds swarmed into town to take the oath of allegiance though most were reluctant to be mustered into service. Lee believed this was accountable to the presence of his dragoons in the neighborhood. Soon many of the inhabitants began to grow cool toward the British, especially when the commissaries went about seizing what food they could find. Houses were searched for provisions and all livestock, even the oxen, were rounded up for slaughtering. Some of the wavering, finding the British behaving more like an enemy than a friend, left Hillsborough and joined the Whigs.

By cajolery and intimidation, however, Cornwallis succeeded in enlisting seven companies at Hillsborough. One source maintains that he took all the men of the village with him except two who were blind. Cornwallis left Hillsborough on February 24th, two days after Greene had crossed the Dan. For a day he camped nearby on the banks of the Eno after which he marched toward the Haw River on the road to Guilford Court House where he hoped to enlist more men from among the German settlements which were known to be Loyalist. When he arrived in this area, however, he found few who cared to join his army.

The event which hurt Cornwallis' recruiting more than anything else occurred on February 25th while the British were marching toward the Haw. While scouting for Tarleton who happened to be but a mile away, Lee and Pickens discovered that just in front of them was a corps of three or four hundred Tories under Colonel John Pyle marching to join Cornwallis. Just then two countrymen came by who mistook Lee's green-coated dragoons for Tarleton's. Lee's nimble wit seized the occasion to send the men ahead with Colonel Tarleton's compliments and to ask Pyle to draw his men up alongside the road to let the dragoons by.

Soon Lee's horsemen with sabers drawn were alongside the Tories and Lee was just about to shake hands with Pyle when some of the Tories spied Pickens' men coming and fired on them. Lee always maintained he intended to identify himself and demand the surrender of the corps. But it was too late. Lee's dragoons flew at the helpless Tories and in no time 100 were butchered and most of the others badly wounded. Lee declared this had to be done or else his own men would have been killed. This seems hard to believe as the victims had thrown down their guns and were crying for mercy. None of Lee's or Pickens' men were hurt.

Greene looked upon the bloodshed as unavoidable and only wished it could have been Tarleton's corps that was cut to pieces. Many thought it evened up the massacre of Buford's regiment at the Waxhaws the year before by Tarleton. The annihilation of Pyle's corps almost in sight of the British army put a damper on the Tory uprising in North Carolina. Greene declared that this practically brought recruiting for the British Army to a standstill in North Carolina. The British themselves admitted that the massacre was justified from a military standpoint.[25] Hearing that Cornwallis was very discouraged by what had happened, Greene was thinking that he might give up and retreat to Camden. From near and far in North Carolina and Virginia men were marching to join Greene. Would Cornwallis pit his dwindling army against one which would soon be twice the size of his? Greene wondered.

About the time Greene reached Hillsborough, the first of the mountain men joined the army. Hugh Crocket came with 160 men and William Campbell, the hero of King's Mountain, appeared with about 100 more from Botetourt County, Virginia. Arthur Campbell was still gathering men in Washington County but a new Indian alarm was holding them back. When he did arrive, to Greene's disappointment, he had but sixty riflemen.

But more were following. Greene no doubt was depending on his commission to William Campbell, Shelby, and others to negotiate a peace with the Indians to bring the mountaineers flocking to his army. Virginia had recently ceded its western lands to the United States and as commander of the Southern Department, Greene assumed authority to appoint commissioners for treating with the Indians. The westerners, to be sure, liked nothing better than having treaty making in their own hands.

The mountaineers had no sooner joined Otho Williams than they made known they came as volunteers and must be treated as such. They refused to serve under any officer not elected by them and gave out hints they might not go beyond Hillsborough "unless upon an occasion the advantage or necessity of which they will judge." Williams, for one, did not know how he was going to make out with men who talked as though they were all commanding officers.[26]

On the day of Pyle's carnage, Greene camped at County Line Creek, five miles back of his light troops. The next day he moved to High Rock Ford where the road to Guilford Court House crosses Troublesome Creek. Cornwallis had now crossed the Haw and was camped about twenty miles to the south on Alamance Creek. The next morning Greene caught up with Williams, Lee, and Pickens, and the whole army advanced to within fifteen miles of the enemy. Greene was not looking for a major engagement as yet but he wanted to alarm the country and frustrate Cornwallis' efforts to recruit the Tories. Williams, therefore, moved ahead again and camped on the evening of March 1st on the old battlefield where the Regulators fought Governor Tryon before the Revolution. They were within three miles of Cornwallis' camp at the crossroads but separated by the Alamance. Greene had no fear in having his light troops within a short distance of the British because of his superiority in cavalry. He not only had more horsemen but they were better mounted and better fighters than Tarleton's dragoons. One of Greene's constant worries was to keep this superiority without which he feared he could not long hold out against the enemy.

The morning after Williams camped at the Alamance, Lee's dragoons exhibited another display of their bravery and prowess. Coming upon Tarleton's dragoons, Lee's men made a savage

attack that felled over twoscore of the enemy while suffering
only a half-dozen casualties. Following this encounter, Tarleton's
cavalry mistook a party of Tories for Greene's militia. Before he
realized what was happening, his dragoons had run down and
cut to pieces the whole corps. After that it was no wonder that
more and more of Cornwallis' recruits slipped away for home.

Although Greene was pressing Cornwallis, the nervous
strain was still very great. He was tired to the point of exhaustion
and his old eye trouble had flared up again to annoy and pain
him. With his men faring on an uncertain diet of bread and meat,
Greene lived on the same coarse food. More than once his
allowance ran out and his aides had to beg food from the troops
to have anything for Greene's table. No wonder he became an
idol to the men as well as the officers of the Southern army.

Forage was as scarce as food and as all the militia with Greene's
army came mounted, the problem of feeding the horses soon
became very acute. Lee had earlier recommended dismounting
all the militia who did not have sabers and good mounts as so
many horses made for confusion as well as overtaxing the forage
department. The militia naturally did not want to part with
their means of speedy escape from danger and Greene hesitated
to deprive them of their horses for fear they would desert. However, he had no alternative and the order went out for sending
away 1,000 horses. The next day Pickens reported that the Salisbury men were deserting in shoals and many of the mountaineers
had also left because their horses had been taken away.[27]

Hoping to cut off Williams or get Greene's stores, Cornwallis
on March 6th set his troops in motion during a dense fog for
Whitesell's (Wetzell's) mill on Reedy Fork. Williams got word
of the approach of the enemy in time to prevent Cornwallis from
getting between his detachment and Greene. He had orders from
Greene not to risk an engagement with all his troops as Cornwallis
would like nothing better than to defeat Greene detachment by
detachment. Williams, therefore, stationed a corps of riflemen
supported by cavalry at Whitesell's mill while he retired with his
main force. When the British appeared a very warm skirmish
ensued at the mill. The historian Gordon put the American losses
at fifty and the enemy's as greater, but his estimates may be high
as Greene said the American losses were trifling.[28]

Greene then retired to the north side of the Haw, moving his camp every night without telling anyone ahead of time where he intended to camp next. Some of the time he was at High Rock Ford and Speedwell's iron works on Troublesome Creek or at Boyd's where the road crossed Reedy Fork. Greene, it is said, was up at the crack of dawn going the rounds to see that all the sentinels were on duty. Early morning, he knew, was the time Cornwallis liked to launch surprise attacks. Passing the tent of Colonel John Greene one morning, he heard him snoring inside. Greene went in and putting his hand on the sleeper inquired how he could sleep so soundly with the enemy so near. With a drowsy stare, the Colonel replied after a moment, "Why, General, I knew that you were awake." Greene often spoke of this as the greatest compliment he ever received.[29]

Greene was aware that there were people who criticized him for being too cautious. He was a good retreater but retreating did not win wars, they declared. What was needed were more fighters like Morgan. Say what they would, Greene was not going to be rushed into a battle until he was ready. To Jefferson he wrote on March 10th:

> I have been obliged to practice that by finesse which I dared not attempt by force. I know the people have been in anxious suspense, waiting the event of a general action; but be the consequence of censure what it may, nothing shall hurry me into a measure that is not suggested by prudence or connects not with it the interest of the southern department.[30]

Just before reinforcements joined Greene in large numbers from Virginia and North Carolina, he had to dismiss the South Carolina and Georgia militia with General Pickens. Most of the men, Pickens reported, were too ragged and naked to serve and no clothes could be found for replacements. Perhaps Greene would have sent them anyhow as a few days before he had told Pickens he might have to send him back because conditions in South Carolina had deteriorated to such an extent that his services were urgently required by Sumter and Marion.[31]

Reinforcements reached Greene's army in large numbers right after the 10th of March. Two brigades of North Carolina militia and a regiment of eighteen-month state troops, 1,000 in all, came with Generals John Butler and Thomas Eaton. Over 1,000 Virginia militia under Robert Lawson arrived to swell the number with General Stevens to 1,700. Five hundred and thirty Virginia Continentals raised by Steuben arrived under Lieutenant Colonel Richard Campbell and were placed in Huger's division.[32] In addition, the riflemen from the western waters under Colonels Charles Lynch, William Campbell, Hugh Crocket, and others, numbered all of 400.[33] Altogether Greene had an army of about 4,200 men. Cornwallis had but 2,000, but they were all veterans while not half that number with Greene were seasoned soldiers.[34]

At 6 A.M. on the morning of March 14th, Greene's army was cooking its breakfast before marching to the vicinity of Guilford Court House, within eight or nine miles of the enemy. By this move, Greene made it clear he was inviting Cornwallis to a general engagement, so long sought by his Lordship. Providing it did not rain, Greene had little fear of the enemy. But rain would make his muskets useless and give Cornwallis an opportunity to come at him with the deadly bayonet. As a precaution Greene had tents set up nightly where the men of each company could stack their guns.

While Greene's army made its way toward the courthouse, Cornwallis sent off his stores and prepared for battle. He was as anxious to fight as before, knowing that recruiting would remain at a standstill until he had given Greene a good beating. It was altogether necessary, Cornwallis told Clinton, to secure the help of the Loyalists to win and to hold North Carolina. Apparently Cornwallis did not expect the coming battle to be decisive.

March 15, 1781, the day of the battle of Guilford Court House, was clear and mild after an early-morning frost. Cornwallis set his columns in motion at daybreak without waiting for breakfast. It was late morning by the time they had covered the eight miles to the courthouse but Cornwallis gave them no time for rest or refreshment, so anxious was he to win his victory. Meanwhile, Greene's army had breakfast after which the men were each given a gill of rum. From then until the enemy appeared the army prepared itself for battle.

Before Cornwallis reached Guilford Court House, Tarleton's legion in the lead came face to face with Lee's dragoons supported by Campbell's riflemen. For some minutes there was fierce fighting and then Tarleton withdrew with much greater losses than those suffered by his foe. While Tarleton and Lee were thus engaged four miles away, Greene formed his army in a woods about a mile and a quarter from the courthouse. Like Morgan at Cowpens, he put his militia in two lines in front of the Continentals. The first line on the edge of the woods and behind a rail fence facing the field was composed of the North Carolina militia flanked by the riflemen and cavalry. About 300 yards back in the woods were the Virginians and approximately the same distance beyond the Continentals were drawn up.

Greene's battle formation and choice of ground at the crest of a long rise was flawless. Tarleton wrote that Greene's position was extremely well chosen "and the manner of forming his troops unexceptionable." Greene's offering to give battle now, said Tarleton, showed his good judgment. "A defeat of the British would have been attended with the total destruction of Earl Cornwallis' infantry, whilst a victory at this juncture could produce no very decisive consequences against the Americans," wrote Tarleton.[35]

The battle of Guilford Court House opened about midday with a cannonade by each side which lasted for about thirty minutes. The two American cannons facing the field then ran out of shot and Cornwallis seized the occasion to start his columns moving up the long grade to where the North Carolinians nervously awaited. The critical moment had arrived. Would the militia hold and give the enemy two or three well directed volleys before leaving the field? If they did, Greene felt confident that Cornwallis was ruined. Like Morgan before the Battle of Cowpens, Greene had told the front line they could leave the field after delivering two volleys as most of them had no bayonets and the British would by that time be coming at them with theirs. One can picture Greene as he sat on his horse surrounded by his aides giving last-minute orders as he held his right glove in his left hand and rubbed his left forefinger on his upper lip as was his habit when thinking out momentous decisions.

The North Carolinians fired a volley when the enemy's front ranks were 400 feet away, too far to do much damage. This, it would seem, was the fault of their officers. A moment later, the British fired a volley after which the North Carolinians, who were reloading, broke and stampeded through the woods. Lee declared they left before one of them was hurt. In any event, it would seem that they had time to deliver another volley without much danger. The North Carolina officers tried in vain to stop the rout but it was impossible and it was useless for the riflemen to threaten to shoot them. It would seem, as Greene maintained, that the day would have been won and Cornwallis' army destroyed if the North Carolina militia had performed as directed.[36]

The Virginia militia stood the pressure of the British for a long time but finally gave way, leaving the decision with the Continentals. Greene and everyone praised the behavior of the Virginians but it must be remembered that the woods prevented the British from keeping formation and sweeping down on them as they had upon the North Carolinians at the edge of the field. Cornwallis told Germain that the woods hindered his men in their use of the bayonet and made it possible for the Americans to make frequent stands.[37]

The Battle of Guilford Court House lasted for more than two hours. Otho Williams, who had seen about as much fighting as anyone in the war, declared it was the fiercest battle he had ever seen. At one time, to save the day for his army which seemed about to be routed, Cornwallis had his artillery fire directly into a section of the battle field where O'Hara's men and Gunby's Marylanders were struggling hand to hand. O'Hara, lying severely wounded, saw the grapeshot tear through both his own men and the enemy, but Cornwallis had accomplished his purpose. For an instant Greene was in grave danger of being taken by the enemy. Seeking a better view of the battle, he rode through the din and smoke almost into the midst of the British before Major Burnet came shouting at him to turn back. Not long after the enemy broke through the second Maryland regiment to threaten the whole line. Fearing the worst, Greene ordered a general retreat.[38]

According to one of Greene's aides, the Continentals, finding it impossible to get away with a large number of prisoners, bayoneted the helpless men rather than have them recovered by the enemy.[39] But after falling back the retreat became orderly and unhurried as John Greene's Virginians who had been kept in reserve came in to cover the retreat. The army's four cannon, though, had to be abandoned because most of the artillery horses had been killed. Three miles back the army crossed Reedy Fork where it rested and waited to see if Cornwallis wanted to continue the contest. But the enemy did not come and it was no wonder, for after marching all morning and then fighting a two hour battle, they were totally exhausted. After collecting all the stragglers and deserters that could be rounded up, Greene marched his army all night through a pelting rain to Speedwell's iron works on Troublesome Creek, ten miles from the battle ground. Greene wanted another battle but he wanted to go in to it with his powder dry.[40]

Cornwallis, who had had two horses shot from under him during the battle, lost 600 killed and wounded, more than a fourth of his whole army. The British loss in officers, killed and wounded, was twenty-nine, a staggering blow which attested the keen eyes of the riflemen for epaulettes. Greene's casualties were not more than 400 although the greater number were Continentals, the backbone of his army. General Huger was wounded. General Stevens was severely wounded early in the battle.

Tarleton marked the Battle of Guilford Court House as a great disaster for Cornwallis who but narrowly escaped complete destruction. If the North Carolina militia had stood, Cornwallis' fate, he believed, would have been sealed. Even after the flight of the North Carolinians, Greene could have won a complete victory, Tarleton thought, had he brought up his reserves when Colonel John Gunby's charge threw the British into disorder. Greene, of course, could have been unaware of this opportunity as he could not be everywhere at once and he had to rely on reports as they reached him. In any event, Cornwallis was crippled to the point where he could not chance another battle. Not until some hours after the battle when the full returns were in did his Lordship realize how much his army had suffered at the hands of his foe.[41]

Viewing the Revolutionary War in its broadest aspects, the Battle of Guilford Court House led directly to the final collapse of British power in America. Cornwallis had to leave North Carolina or be confined to the Wilmington area. Perhaps he could have gotten to South Carolina to join Lord Rawdon at Camden, but he deemed it inadvisable to attempt it. Instead, he chose the less hazardous route to Wilmington. When he arrived there and found that Greene had seized the occasion to invade South Carolina, he decided it was quite beyond his power to follow and bring help to the stranded posts there. Anyhow, he had convinced himself that Virginia, and not South Carolina, was the key to the conquest of the South. It was, therefore, as a result of the Battle of Guilford Court House that Cornwallis marched to Virginia where his army was soon caught between the forces of Washington and Rochambeau and the French fleet. Thus the long sequence of brilliant maneuvers which culminated in the Battle of Guilford Court House was Nathanael's Greene's principal contribution to the final American victory in the War of Independence.

CHAPTER FOURTEEN

We Fight, Get Beat, Rise, and Fight Again

Though the campaign that led to the Battle of Guilford Court House marked Greene's supreme contribution to the ending of the war, his conquest of most of South Carolina and Georgia in 1781 would have been of the greatest strategic importance had the French fleet not arrived to trap Cornwallis at Yorktown. Thus the South Carolina campaign also supports the claim that Greene was the "strategist of the American Revolution."

The release of nervous tension after the Battle of Guilford Court House and the continuous strain of the past six weeks left Greene weak and exhausted. The night after the battle, having driven himself through another day at his desk and in the saddle, he actually fainted from exhaustion. Two aides, Lewis Morris and Robert Burnet, though considerably younger, were likewise completely fagged and became sick. Like everyone else, Greene had slept in his clothes since the beginning of the great retreat six weeks before. Nothing was so good for army morale as examples like this. "We have little to eat, less to drink, and lodge in the woods in the midst of Smoke," wrote Greene from the iron works on Troublesome Creek.[1]

Although the militia had been widely scattered by the battle, all but five or six hundred rejoined the army by the time it reached the iron works. Few, however, remained for long. Great numbers were soon on their way home, wrote Greene, "to kiss their wives and sweet hearts," leaving the army, as he thought, without enough troops to launch an attack the next day. Unhappy as Greene was with this development, he at least had the satisfaction of knowing there was nothing to fear from the enemy. "I have never felt an easy moment since the enemy crossed the Catawba," he told Reed, "until the defeat [of the British] of the 15th. But now I am perfectly easy, persuaded it is out of the enemy's power to do us any great injury. Indeed I think they will retire as soon as they can get off their wounded."[2]

He was entirely right—three days after the battle, Cornwallis left seventy of his severely wounded at the Quaker meeting-house near the battlefield and made a day's march to Bell's Mill on the Deep River. Having proclaimed himself the victor at Guilford Court House, Cornwallis thought the Loyalists might rise and join him. But he found they were unconvinced and remained hidden from friend or foe. With one third of his remaining force wounded or sick and all as ragged as the Americans, Cornwallis decided he must beat a hasty retreat. The distance to Wilmington was somewhat shorter and much safer than the road to Camden where Marion and Sumter would be in front and Greene closing in from the rear. This time Cornwallis would be the one to worry about getting over the rivers before his enemy was upon him. All this would be avoided in going to Wilmington as the road ran parallel to the Cape Fear River. Furthermore, most of the march to Wilmington, especially down to Cross Creek, would be in friendly country where provisions could be found and help obtained in transporting the sick and wounded. Wilmington, consequently, became Cornwallis' destination.

Upon hearing of Cornwallis' departure, Greene at once set out after him with the intention of forcing a battle. But try as he would, he could not catch up with the fleeing foe. Cornwallis swept the country clean of provisions making it necessary for Greene to stop and wait while food and forage were collected at distant points. At times his men were so famished they could hardly march. Many fainted or became sick and had to be left behind. As usual, Lee was sent ahead with his dragoons but they were unable to delay the enemy for long. At Ramsay's Mill on the Deep River, however, the vanguard of Greene's army nearly caught up with Cornwallis who departed in such haste that his bridge was left standing and his dead unburied. Quarters of beef hanging in the slaughtering pens were pulled down and eaten by Greene's half-starved men. Those who were too late to get any fell to devouring the garbage the British had thrown to the buzzards.

Greene decided it was useless to try to overtake the enemy. There were long stretches of pine barrens ahead and it would take too long to collect provisions to carry the army through the wastelands. Though disappointed in not being able to give the enemy another blow, Greene already had hit upon a plan the possibilities of which fascinated him. He would let Cornwallis pursue his way to Wilmington, followed only by Lillington's militia and a small detachment of horse under Major Emmet (to give the appearance that the army was still following) while he struck out for South Carolina.

Greene reasoned that by the time Cornwallis reached Wilmington and got supplies and reinforcements, he would, with the help of Marion, Sumter, and Pickens, have taken all or most of the interior posts in South Carolina and Georgia. Cornwallis, he believed, would follow him but not until it was too late to save his posts or before reinforcements arrived for the Continental army from Virginia. Although his plan did not work out quite as expected, it nonetheless was attended with remarkable success.

When Greene's move into South Carolina became known, it brought great applause from Americans everywhere and nothing short of consternation to the British. Lafayette thought Greene's move was "a great piece of generalship" and only wished he could learn to emulate him. Richard Henry Lee declared that "like Scipio" he had "left Cornwallis in N. Carolina and pushed into S. Carolina intending no doubt to compel the British general to relinquish his prospects this way, or find his southern conquests wrested from him, if he does not return to defend them."[3]

Virginia, especially, was pleased with Greene's strategy. Washington told Greene that Mr. Custis found him high in the esteem of the Virginia Legislature and the governor, Thomas Jefferson. The latter, writing to Lafayette, said:

> North as well as South Carolina being once in the hands of the Enemy may become the Instruments of our Subjugation and effect what the Enemy themselves cannot. The British may harass and distress us greatly but the Carolinas alone can subdue us. The militia of North Carolina is very nearly as numerous as that of this State. Out of that our Enemy will be able to raise great armies. We therefore think it our first Interest to keep them under in that Quarter, considering the war in our Country but as a secondary Object. For this reason we mean to send our new Levies for the regular Army to General Greene as fast as they

shall be raised, acting with our Militia on the Defensive only in this State.[4]

Thomas Jefferson's explanation of Greene's strategy emphasized one aspect of Greene's invading South Carolina. Greene had shocked the North Carolina Loyalists out of joining Cornwallis and now he intended to break the British grip on South Carolina and Georgia for fear of finding much of the manpower of these states arrayed against him. Although Balfour had momentarily given up enlisting Negroes for the army, he was making dangerous headway in recruiting the South Carolina militia. Greene therefore told Steuben he was determined to invade South Carolina whether Cornwallis followed him, stayed in North Carolina, or marched for Virginia. If successful in South Carolina Greene hoped to return to North Carolina in time to confront Cornwallis should he march northward to join Arnold in Virginia. Writing to General Sumter, Greene cautioned him to keep a secret of his coming to all but a chosen few. Surprise would not only make it easier to take the British garrisons but would have a profound effect upon the minds of both the Whigs and the Tories.[5]

When Cornwallis heard that Greene had marched into South Carolina, he was filled with indignation. In a letter to Clinton he explained how Greene had forced him to retire to Wilmington and then turned and invaded South Carolina. He was powerless to help Lord Rawdon at Camden, 150 miles away and separated from him by large rivers. Should he try to relieve Camden, he was in danger of being caught between the rivers by the enterprising Greene. If he waited for transports to take him to Charleston, he would most likely arrive in South Carolina too late to save the interior forts.[6]

In more detail Cornwallis explained his dilemma to General Phillips:

Greene took the advantage of my being obliged to come to this place, and has marched to South Carolina. My expresses to Lord Rawdon on my leaving Cross Creek, warning him of the possibility of such a movement, have all failed.—I much fear that Lord Rawdon's posts will be so distant from each other, and his troops so scattered, as to put him into the greatest danger of being beat in detail.[7]

As he could not help Rawdon and as Charleston was safe for the time being, he had decided, he told Phillips, to invade Virginia. "I shall, therefore," he wrote, "immediately march up the country by Duplin Court House, pointing toward Hillsborough, in hopes to withdraw Greene."

Cornwallis' failure to hold North Carolina and Greene's invasion of South Carolina were very distressing developments to General Clinton. He told Cornwallis:

> In the disordered state of Carolina and Georgia, as represented to me by Lieutenant Colonel Balfour, I shall dred what may be the consequence of Your Lordship's move unless a reinforcement arrives very soon in South Carolina. Had it been possible for Your Lordship in your letter to me of the 10th *ultimo* to have intimated the probability of your intention to form a junction with General Phillips, I should certainly have endeavored to have stopped you—as I did then, as well as now, consider such a move as likely to be dangerous to our interests in the southern colonies.[8]

As it was, he could do nothing against Washington and Rochambeau until he could draw troops from the South. But what chance was there of this as long as Greene remained undefeated?

Though the import of Greene's strategy was fully understood and appreciated by his contemporaries, not all historians have comprehended it. Some have thought in terms of the smallness of the individual posts in South Carolina and Georgia in contrast to the size of the British Army in Virginia after the arrival of Phillips and Cornwallis. In April, 1781, however, neither of these generals were in Virginia and the enemy forces in South Carolina and Georgia were much more formidable than any in Virginia. Greene, therefore, was marching against the center of British power in the South.

Another criticism is that Greene's move was unwise because it drew him away from his source of supplies. It is true, of course, that the farther he moved from Virginia, the harder it would be to get supplies. But it was not impossible with the roads through North Carolina quite safe from the enemy. Greene, furthermore, counted upon capturing sizable military stores in South Carolina, enough, perhaps, to take care of his needs until he returned to Virginia. In the last analysis, Greene's success is the best vindication for his movement.[9]

Greene, however, had no sooner set out to liquidate the British posts in South Carolina than complications arose to trouble him. The French fleet in the Chesapeake had fought a battle with British warships and although victorious the French set sail for Newport for repairs. This left the way open for Clinton to send reinforcements under Phillips to Virginia in the hope of paralyzing Greene by conquering the heart of the southland. Greene, however, thought that Virginia could take care of Arnold and Phillips.[10]

The report that Clinton was sending reinforcements to Virginia reached Greene just as he was setting out for South Carolina. His response was to send an urgent letter to Lafayette, who was going north, to return immediately and resume command in Virginia. Upon arriving, if he found Cornwallis was following Greene, he was to join the latter with his best troops, leaving the remainder to cope with the British in Virginia.[11] Steuben was directed to order out a large body of Virginia militia and send as many as possible to Greene to insure a speedy victory in the Palmetto State.

Steuben at once set about complying with Greene's orders. But he was soon blocked by the Virginia Council which having heard that Clinton was sending reinforcements to Virginia, refused to allow troops to leave the state. Furious, Steuben let go with verbal blasts at all who stood in his way. Tactless and dictatorial, he had long before lost his popularity in Virginia. As he fell to attacking "the Governor and Council and Assembly in person and by letter," Greene soon realized that the services of the "Dutchman," as Jefferson called him, were severely crippled. But as there was no one to put in his place, he asked him to stay in Virginia and do the best he could.[12]

Greene never forgave Jefferson and the Virginians for withholding help at a most crucial hour. Jefferson understood his strategy but let local interests and pressures control him, Greene declared. To Lafayette he wrote that it was "extremely wrong for a Governor of a State to undertake from partial views to counteract a general plan."[13] He afterward often remarked that no general should feel compelled to undertake a campaign without control of the reinforcements pledged to him.

By this time Greene's differences with Jefferson and the

Virginia Legislature on a number of other things made a very embarrassing situation. Jefferson was irritated because Greene conducted much of his business through the "Dutchman" who appeared ridiculously pompous to the plain and unassuming governor of Virginia. Although Jefferson admired Greene, like John Adams, he sometimes found it hard to take all of the general's preaching, exhortation, and unveiled censorship. Greene, on the other hand, chafed at the slowness and clumsiness of the civil powers and desired the army to have control over recruiting and the gathering of supplies. Jefferson, naturally, looked upon these demands as an encroachment upon the civil powers by the military and resented what he considered to be the aggressiveness of Greene and his officers.[14]

Most unfortunate as well as dangerous to the army was the dispute with Virginia growing out of the seizure of dragoon horses. Jefferson had given Greene permission to impress horses with certain exceptions, but Colonel Washington's men had seized brooding mares and anything else promising in the way of horseflesh. Responding to the great uproar caused by the seizures, the Virginia Legislature resolved that all horses valued at more than £5,000 (perhaps Virginia paper money) must be returned to the owners. Realizing what this would mean to the Southern army, Jefferson asked Greene to write a remonstrance which he would lay before the legislature. Greene did so, as "every measure which is taken to cramp the business of compleating the Cavalry, has a direct tendency to sacrifice the Citizens." The price fixed by Virginians for horses, he told Jefferson, was such that no horses fit for duty could be purchased. "It would not purchase by voluntary sale a horse that I would trust a dragoon upon, and it would be little less than deserting the Men and supplying the enemy with implements to mount them on such Cattle," declared Greene.[15]

With the supply of dragoon horses from Virginia in doubt, Greene turned to Governor Nash. He needed 100 horses at once, he wrote Nash, as most of the cavalry horses must soon be replaced. After the Battle of Hobkirk's Hill, during which only fifty-six of Washington's eighty-seven dragoons could be mounted for want of horses, Greene wrote Jefferson again stressing the urgent need of dragoon horses. If the Virginia law were not changed at once, he feared calamity faced the army. "Are your horses dearer than your liberty?" asked Greene. After Cornwallis reached Virginia, Joseph Reed told Greene that the horses that Virginia had refused to send to the American Army were now being ridden by the enemy on plundering excursions over the state.[16]

Greene used every possible means to keep his supply agents informed of his needs and of how to get military stores to him. There was no end, however, to the interruptions and failures of supplies. At one place in North Carolina where shoes were being made for the army, the cobblers either ran off or were carried away by the enemy. When Greene sent a British cavalry saber to Hunter's Iron Works in Virginia with a request that it be used as a pattern for making swords for his dragoons, he was told that none could be made until it was known where the pay was coming from. For a time Greene also found his supply of lead jeopardized when the miners at Chiswell lost the vein they were working. When it was found again, William Davie assured Greene he would make certain the army was served first. Much lead, he said, had gone to the back country where the people appeared to be more concerned with driving the Indians off the land than with winning the war with Great Britain.

As soon as Greene decided to invade South Carolina, he sent Lee ahead with orders to fall in with Marion and try to prevent reinforcements from reaching Camden from the posts to the southward. Lee and Emmet trailed Cornwallis some distance toward Cross Creek and then Lee swung off toward the Pee Dee leaving Emmet to continue the pursuit of Cornwallis. Lee's first assignment was to gather all the boats to be found along the Pee Dee and hide or destroy them so that Cornwallis could not use them if he decided to follow Greene. Lee was also to take every good horse he could find and give the owner a receipt. As Lee was known for his craving for glory, Greene cautioned him not to overtax his men: "Remember that you Command men and that their Powers may not keep pace with your ambition."[17]

When Greene set out for South Carolina he had but 1,000

Continentals and two or three hundred militia, a pitifully small army with which to confront the British whose troops, although scattered, numbered fully 8,000 in South Carolina and Georgia. The Virginia militia upon which Greene relied soon announced, moreover, that their service began when they left home and that their six weeks were up. Greene tried to convince them that their time began when they joined his army but it was useless. He was confident as yet, however, that Virginia would replace these troops by others in time to help out in the siege of Camden. Thus far North Carolina had sent few men but there were signs which seemed encouraging. For one thing, the state had initiated a draft of all the men who had run away at Guilford Court House.

Cornwallis reached Wilmington about April 10th, twelve days before Greene arrived at Camden. At Cross Creek Cornwallis had found the Loyalists hospitable but no more anxious to join his army than those along the Deep River. His march from Cross Creek to Wilmington was extremely difficult with many of the inhabitants unfriendly. When he arrived at Wilmington he still did not know that Greene was marching to South Carolina. But even had he known, he could not have followed Greene for days for his men were worn out and his supplies exhausted.

By this time, however, he had decided not to follow Greene but to proceed to Virginia. He thought there was a chance that Greene would follow him even after he heard that the latter was marching for South Carolina. However, if he did not, it would only make the conquest of Virginia that much easier. Unlike Clinton, Cornwallis placed little importance in the control of up-country South Carolina. If Camden and Ninety-Six and adjacent forts were abandoned, it would only be a case of evacuating those posts which were too exposed. Virginia and not South Carolina, he declared, was the key to the control of the South. With Virginia conquered and Charleston in British hands, resistance in the back country must wither and die, he reasoned. Furthermore, Virginia was easier to conquer than the Carolinas if the British controlled the Chesapeake and the deep rivers which divided the coastal areas and rendered difficult communication for the rebels.

Greene did not disagree with Cornwallis on the strategic importance of Virginia. In May he wrote: "Much is to be done in Virginia, and without great prudence on our part, matters may be reduced to great extremity there; and depend upon it, the enemy's great push will be against that State, as it may be said, in some sort, to sever the Continental interest assunder."[18] But with the center of British power in April in South Carolina and Georgia and with Cornwallis at least temporarily out of the way, Greene did not hesitate.

Four days after setting out for South Carolina he wrote Lee of the plans maturing in his mind. Sumter, supported by Pickens, would take position on the west side of the Wateree to prevent Lord Rawdon from getting reinforcements from Granby, Ninety-Six, or Augusta. Lee was to find Marion and then proceed to Fort Watson on the Santee, capture it, if possible, but above all prevent help from coming to Camden from the south. To provide the army with provisions, Greene had already sent a party of horse to make collections in the rich farming areas along Lynches' Creek and the Black River.[19]

After marching ten days through long stretches of pine barrens, swamps and countless streams, Greene arrived at May's Mill on the Pee Dee on April 15th. Camden was still sixty miles away and until the plantations on the east branch of Lynches' Creek were reached, the country was a desolate waste. By expresses, Greene kept Sumter informed of his progress. In all likelihood, the army would have to lay siege to Camden, Greene told Sumter, as its cannon were not heavy enough to reduce it and the army was too small to attempt an assault. However, as the post was reported to be low on food, the siege, Greene thought, should not last long. As Greene wanted everyone to feel that he came as their deliverer, he instructed Sumter to take nothing from the inhabitants without giving certificates. Whigs and Tories should be treated alike, and the government, when it was formed, could decide whether or not the recipient had a right to be paid.[20]

Greene arrived at Camden on April 20th. Upon examining the works, he found, as expected, the place too well fortified to be stormed. To the west and south the town was protected by the Wateree River and Pine Creek and on the other two sides by strong redoubts. Around the whole was a high palisade of heavy timber in front of which were abatis with their sharp points facing the enemy. Though strong, the town, as Greene had thought, was low on food, partly because the British were not expecting the return of Greene to South Carolina and partly because of the vigilance of Marion and Sumter in pouncing upon supplies coming up the Wateree.

Soon Greene had the disappointment of learning that a corps of South Carolina Tory militia from Ninety-Six had bypassed Sumter and gotten through to Camden a day or so after he arrived. The garrison contained about 900 troops and if Colonel Watson, who was reported to be on his way to Camden from the south, got through, Lord Rawdon would be stronger than Greene in numbers. Because of the strength of the enemy, Greene did not dare divide his army by surrounding the town. The first day he camped at Logstown, a short distance to the north of Camden. The next day he fell back to Hobkirk's Hill but hearing that Watson was drawing near, he marched his army to the south side of the town and sent his baggage and cannon toward Lynches' Creek. But Watson, it was soon learned, was not near and Greene returned to his former position on Hobkirk's Hill on the evening of April 23rd. Camping in battle formation at the top of a low sandy ridge, Greene hoped that Rawdon would attack him and give him a chance to destroy his enemy as Morgan had at Cowpens.

Lieutenant Colonel Francis Rawdon (later to become the Marquis of Hastings and second Earl of Moira) was twenty-six years of age, tall, dark, and attributed to be the ugliest looking man in the British Army. He was a competent officer and commanded a force of veterans made up of British and American regulars and some equally good South Carolina militia. Against such as these, Greene surely was counting a great deal on the fighting qualities of his veterans who had destroyed Tarleton at Cowpens and humbled Cornwallis at Guilford Court House.

Greene was fully aware that his invasion of South Carolina was having the effect he had counted upon. The Tories were astounded as the news traveled through the state and many sought hiding places in the swamps and forests. The Whigs, although jubilant, were still generally unwilling to come out and join Greene for fear of what might happen to their families at the hands of the Tories. Moreover, this was the planting season and as most of the inhabitants of the up-country were yeoman farmers without slaves, they must get in their crops or face starvation.[21]

While Greene was on his way to Camden, Lee had found Marion and together they had laid siege to Fort Watson, setting thirty feet or more high on an ancient Indian mound at Wright's Bluff on the Santee. At the base of the mound was a strong palisade surrounded by three rows of abatis bristling like porcupine quills. In the absence of Lieutenant Colonel John Watson, the garrison consisted of sixty regulars and forty of the most resolute Tories in the state, commanded by Captain McKay.

Lee and Marion at once cut off the garrison's water supply at Scott's Lake lying a few yards from the fort. Fearing the return of Watson who had gone hunting for Marion, Lee sent an express to Greene requesting a cannon. With a cannon, Lee said, he could reduce the fort in five minutes but with only small arms it was extremely dangerous to approach very near the palisades by day as the fort rested upon a treeless plain. Greene sent the cannon but it arrived after the fort had surrendered.

For some time the besiegers appeared undecided as to what to do. At night the attackers might have worked their way through the abatis and over the palisade but it was impossible to climb the perpendicular sides of the mound and get over the walls circling the top. Soon, too, Lee and Marion learned that thirst would not compel the garrison to surrender as they had sunk a well within the stockade.

Determined to take the fort if at all possible before a relief force arrived, Lee and Marion seized upon the idea of building a tower proposed by Colonel Hezekiah Maham. Under the latter's direction five days were spent in cutting logs and making joints for a forty-foot tower. On the night of April 22nd while Greene was maneuvering south of Camden in anticipation of the arrival of Watson, the tower was erected and pulled into position overlooking the fortress on the Indian mound. A flooring with breastworks of logs rested on top of the tower. When day broke the garrison found there was no place in the fort where one could escape from the rifles of the men on Maham's tower. After a few shots McKay raised the white flag. Thereupon, after demolishing the works and leaving only the old Indian mound standing, Marion and Lee moved north a few miles to Richard-son's plantation to be in a better position to head off Watson should he attempt to reach Camden. The next day, however, they moved to the Black River area to the eastward where they could more easily get to Greene and still keep watch for Watson. With their prisoners sent off to North Carolina, here they waited unaware of the battle being fought at Hobkirk's Hill, thirty miles away.[22]

Greene did not have to wait long at Hobkirk's Hill for the attack he was hoping for. About 9:30 on the morning of April 25th (the day Cornwallis set out from Wilmington for Virginia) Lord Rawdon's little army marched out of Camden and silently headed for Greene's camp through the woods to the right of the road leading over Hobkirk's Hill to the Waxhaws. Rawdon had heard that Fort Watson had fallen and had resolved to attack before Greene was reinforced by Marion and Lee. He had also been informed by a deserter that Greene was ill-prepared for an attack for want of supplies and because his cannon, sent off when the Americans moved temporarily south of Pine Tree Creek, had not yet returned. Rawdon, moreover, was getting low on provisions and he must either defeat his enemy or give up Camden and retreat to the region south of the Santee.

About 10 o'clock Greene's pickets saw the enemy coming and fired the alarm guns. Captain Robert Kirkwood, the veteran leader of the Delaware light troops, was immediately sent forward while Greene marshalled his army for battle. Fortunately, military stores had just arrived with Lieutenant Colonel Carrington and the cannon were back in their places. When the signal guns were heard, Greene was having breakfast after waiting for his portion from the supply of provisions brought by Carrington. Some of the troops were still eating while others had finished and were attending camp duties. Quite a number were washing their clothes at a nearby stream when the drums called them to their stations.

Although Greene had hardly expected an attack that morning he was ready whenever it came. As his troops were camped in battle formation along the ridge it took but a few minutes to have the whole army ready and waiting for the enemy to appear. To the right of the road Greene's line consisted of the Virginia

Continentals led by Lieutenant Colonels Campbell and Hawes under the command of General Huger. To the left were Colonel Gunby and Lieutenant Colonel Ford with the Marylanders, commanded by Otho Williams. In back of the Continentals stood about 250 North Carolina militia who this time, instead of running away, were to give a good account of themselves. On the extreme left was Washington and his dragoons with orders to circle and get behind the enemy to prevent their retreat to Camden. In the center just behind the line of men, Greene had his three six-pounders loaded with grapeshot.

As soon as Greene perceived that the enemy was advancing in a compact column with a narrow front, he ordered his center to open and his artillery to fire. The blast of grapeshot ripped the front of Rawdon's column to shreds, whereupon Greene sent the regiments of Gunby and Hawes charging at the enemy with fixed bayonets. Simultaneously, Campbell and Ford moved forward to close in on the enemy's flanks while Washington's horse went racing through the pines to get in the rear of the British. Having the advantage of ground and slightly superior numbers, Greene thought victory was certain as he rode close to the enemy where Hawes was pushing through the woods. The battle, Greene could see, would be bloody for both sides, but having gained the initiative, victory should be as complete as at Cowpens.

Rawdon, however, was a fighter, and before Campbell and Ford could close in upon his flanks he succeeded in extending his line. The battle was not won as yet, but Greene had no cause to doubt its outcome until he learned that the Marylanders, his celebrated veterans on whom he counted most, had fallen back with the enemy, now reorganized, pushing hard upon them. Colonel John Gunby, instead of pressing relentlessly forward, had ordered his regiment to fall back when three companies had become disordered. The mistake was fatal. Seizing the advantage they had gained, the British came at the Marylanders with a shout that completely unnerved the flower of Greene's army and sent them scrambling up and over the ridge. The rout spread to Campbell's men and soon Greene found himself all but stranded with Hawes and his plucky Virginians. The latter, inspired no doubt by Greene's presence, would have held their ground, but seeing that they would soon be surrounded, Greene ordered a retreat. Hawes's men now not only covered the rout but on one occasion advanced upon the enemy until Greene called them back.

Only by great daring and good luck did the Americans save their cannon on this unfortunate day. When the American line broke and fled, Greene's artillerymen pushed the cannon down an incline into a thicket where the guns remained unobserved by the British as they pushed after Gunby's men. Soon after, the cannon were pulled out of the underbrush and dragged through the woods around the main scene of the fighting. Greene, it is said, came upon the men struggling with the ropes and dismounted to give them a hand. When others joined them, Greene rode on to see what could be done toward bringing the rout to a halt. However, they were again all but lost when a party of Coffin's horse cut down or scattered the men drawing the cannon. But just in time Washington's cavalry appeared to send the British dragoons scurrying for cover. Horses were then hitched to the cannon and they were soon out of reach of the enemy.

Greene was not able to collect his army or bring it to a stand nearer than three miles from Hobkirk's Hill. When this was finally accomplished it was all too apparent that the army was too disorganized and unnerved to attempt an advance upon the enemy who because of Greene's superiority of horse had not followed far beyond the scene of the battle. In the afternoon, therefore, Greene retired three miles farther to Sander's Creek (the place where Gates met his great disaster) and made camp.[23]

Naturally, Greene was very vexed by the outcome of the battle of Hobkirk's Hill. Perhaps he should have blamed Colonel Washington for the defeat as much as Colonel Gunby. Washington had made so wide a circuit that he wound up far behind the scene of battle. Falling upon a motley throng of wagoners, surgeons, sightseers, and others in the rear of the enemy, instead of bypassing them, he stopped to take prisoners. When his men finally arrived at the battle area each carrying a prisoner behind his saddle, the battle was lost and all the cavalry could do was to help cover the retreat.

In general orders Greene congratulated all but Gunby's corps, much to the anger of the Marylanders. They had only obeyed orders, they declared, and were not to blame for what happened. Greene at once recognized his mistake and the next day told the army that although Colonel Gunby had displayed great bravery and spirit his order to retire was improper and the cause of the day's misfortune. A court of inquiry chosen at Gunby's request decided that although Gunby had exhibited great bravery, his "order for the regiment to retire, which broke the line, was extremely improper and unmilitary, and in all probability the only cause why we did not obtain a complete victory."[24]

Greene at first was inclined to excuse Gunby for what he termed "an error of judgment." "War is a critical business," he told Governor Nash, "and the fate of the day after every possible precaution depends upon the most trifling incident." The more he thought about it, however, the more he came to blame Gunby. In August, he told Reed that he had found Gunby "much more blameable afterwards," than at the time of the battle.[25]

Cornwallis was jubilant over the battle at Hobkirk's Hill which he called "by far the most splendid victory of the war" for the British. Clinton, too, thought Hobkirk's Hill "was perhaps the most important victory of the whole war, for defeat would have occasioned the loss of Charleston (in the then open state of the works of that capital), the Carolinas, and Georgia." Clinton and Cornwallis both exaggerated the significance of Greene's defeat for it was far from being a great victory for the British and if Greene had won, it is unlikely that Charleston would have fallen as a result of it. Lafayette summed up the battle at Hobkirk's Hill correctly when he said that like all of Greene's reverses it would, in the end, contribute only to the ruin of the enemy.[26]

With both armies losing approximately 250 men each in killed, wounded, and missing, the comparative strength of the antagonists remained essentially unchanged. Though Greene felt that he had been deserted by North Carolina and Virginia in the hour of need and that he might soon find himself crushed by the power of the enemy in South Carolina, he had no intention of relinquishing his pressure upon Lord Rawdon. To Baron Steuben, he wrote, "This repulse, if repulse it may be called, will make no alteration in our general plan of operations." To La Luzerne, Greene showed his determination to win or perish in the attempt. "We fight, get beat, rise, and fight again," he laconically wrote the French minister.[27]

The thing for the Americans to do now, Greene told Lee, was to act fearlessly with all the power within them. Otherwise the Tories would take heart and the Whigs feel that the enemy was too powerful to be overcome. Lee, therefore, was directed to cross the Santee with Marion and, if possible, lay siege to Fort Motte, about thirty miles northwest of the demolished Fort Watson. This was music to Lee's ears as he was most happy when off upon some daring undertaking.

Greene had barely sent off the letter directing Lee and Marion to cross the Santee when rumors reached camp that Cornwallis was on his way to South Carolina and that Tarleton could be expected momentarily to make an appearance. Perhaps at no time in Greene's military career did he feel so low in spirit as then. With the enemy in South Carolina and Georgia already numbering three or four times his little army, what chance would he have with no reinforcements in sight and Cornwallis to fight as well? Greene felt abandoned by the rest of the country and especially by Congress. In letters to Jefferson, Nash, La Luzerne, Washington, Reed, and members of Congress, he described the overwhelming odds against him and the seeming hopelessness of it all. To the Board of War in Philadelphia, he graphically pictured the plight of the Southern Whigs. "The well effected have struggled to the last, but they are inevitably ruined and cannot continue their exertions much longer." The guerrilla warfare raging so fiercely in the Carolinas, and especially in South Carolina, was "truly shocking to humanity." The war "rages like a fire and devours everything before it," wrote Greene. To Reed he described the hazardous game he was playing in trying to keep up an appearance of strength until help arrived.[28]

Greene did not want to call in Lee and Marion who were still endeavoring to head off Watson until the reports of Cornwallis' coming were verified. He was satisfied for the present to warn them to keep a sharp lookout for the enemy and to be prepared to join the army on the shortest possible notice. Fearing that Tarleton might soon appear, however, Greene crossed to the

west side of the Wateree on May 3rd. His fears had risen during
the last day or two and he sent an order for Lee to join
him. If worse came to worse he could retreat into North Carolina
and hope that this time the militia would join him. However, he
intended to keep up an appearance of strength and confidence.
Marching down the right side of the Wateree, he took position
on Twenty-Five Mile Creek only a short distance above Camden
Ferry. Thanks to Colonel Wade Hampton, who commanded
Sumter's cavalry, forage and provisions were waiting for the
army at nearby places. Greene brought an abrupt halt to deserting by summarily hanging five deserters in one day. When
Lord Rawdon's troops, one third of whom were deserters from
the American side since Gates's defeat, heard of it, they were
filled with consternation. Rawdon feared they might all run away
at the first opportunity.

Although Lee and Marion must have received Greene's order
to cross to the west side of the Santee in time to have prevented
Watson from getting over McCord's Ferry, they apparently expected him to come up along the east side of the river. They
therefore waited, and when Watson did not come they finally
crossed the Santee, leaving a small guard behind. By this time
Watson had crossed the Congaree as well as the Wateree. He
reached Camden on May 7th, the day before Lee and Marion
laid siege to Fort Motte and about the time Greene pitched camp
on Twenty-Five Mile Creek. "This is rather an unfortunate circumstance," Greene wrote to Marion, "as the enemy will begin
to be impudent.—Our forces divided, and the enemy collected,
put matters upon an unmilitary footing." But disappointing as
was this development, Greene felt easier. Having received no
further word about Cornwallis, he was quite certain he was
invading Virginia and not returning to South Carolina. Greene
therefore reversed his order for Lee to join him and directed him
to stay with Marion and help in the siege of Fort Motte.[29]

Greene was right in thinking that Rawdon would make another
attempt upon him as soon as Watson arrived. On that very night,
Rawdon crossed the Wateree at Camden Ferry with the intention
of attacking Greene from the rear. But the latter had wisely withdrawn his main force to Colonel's Creek, leaving Washington's
cavalry and some light troops as a rear guard. When Rawdon

learned that Greene had retired to much stronger ground nine miles to the north, he abruptly returned to Camden.

Upon reaching Camden, Rawdon at once set about preparing for its evacuation. He had received orders from Cornwallis to retire within the Santee and give up all the territory north of the Santee which could not be held with Greene in South Carolina. He had done his best to destroy Greene, and failing, there was nothing to be gained by remaining longer. Rawdon knew that Major Maxwell at Granby was being watched by Sumter from the opposite side of the Congaree. If he moved swiftly he might not only save Maxwell but lift the siege at Fort Motte. Just before leaving Camden, Rawdon sent expresses ordering Maxwell to abandon Granby and retire to Orangeburg and for Lieutenant Colonel Cruger to destroy the works at Ninety-Six and join Colonel Browne at Augusta. None of these messages ever got through so well were the roads and byways patrolled by the men under Sumter and Pickens.[30]

With the evacuation of Camden, Greene was again in high spirits. All the interior posts would be in American hands in a week or ten days, he declared. If possible, he hoped to surprise the posts and capture the occupants before they could get away. In any event, until the final campaign for Charleston began, the war in South Carolina, he thought, would be no more than a "war of posts." After the fall of Ninety-Six and Augusta he would, therefore, leave matters in South Carolina with subordinates while he hurried to Virginia to confront Cornwallis again. Lee argued against his leaving South Carolina but Greene was convinced it was "his interest and duty" to do so, as the "enemy's great push will be against that State."[31] Events, however, soon occurred which caused Greene to change his mind and decide that the country would best be served by his staying in South Carolina.

Although Cornwallis was undisturbed by the prospect of losing all of the interior posts in South Carolina, his fellow officers thought of it as a great blow to British prestige and power in the South. From Charleston, Balfour informed Cornwallis that Greene's coming had lifted the lid off a hornet's nest. A few short weeks before he had thought that all the British had to do in South Carolina was to destroy the guerrillas with Marion, Sumter, and Pickens, and the subjugation of the state would be complete. Now he was worried for the safety of Charleston itself. He wrote to Cornwallis:

> I must inform Your Excellency that the general state of the country is most distressing [and] that the enemy's parties are everywhere. The communication by land with Savanah no longer exists; Colonel Brown is invested at Augusta, and Colonel Cruger in the most critical situation at Ninety-Six. Indeed, I should betray the duty I owe Your Excellency did I not represent *the defection of this province [as] so universal that I know of no mode short of depopulation to retain it.*[32]

Fort Motte, which the forces of Marion and Lee had surrounded, stood on the south side of the Congaree about a mile from McCord's Ferry and not far from the confluence of the Congaree and the Wateree. The fort, a large house resting on a hill and surrounded by a high palisade, a ditch, and an abatis, was garrisoned by 165 troops under Lieutenant McPherson. As the defenders had a cannon, the Americans were compelled to resort to the erection of parallels.

After a day or two of hard digging, the besiegers came close enough to shoot firebrands at the house but as it belonged to Mrs. Rebecca Motte, a good patriot, Lee and Marion continued the work on the parallels. On the night of May 11th, however, signal fires from the hills across the Santee announced the approach of Lord Rawdon from Camden. There was no time to be lost. Mrs. Motte, who had helped nurse the sick in camp, offered a quiver of arrows for setting fire to her house. When the flaming missiles burst upon the roof, the defenders tried to knock off the burning shingles but a shot from Lee's cannon discouraged all effort to put out the fire. Lieutenant McPherson then surrendered and let the Americans in to help put out the fire and save Mrs. Motte's house.

The fire had barely been put out when Greene rode up with a detachment of horse. He had left General Huger with orders to level the works at Camden and then march for Granby at Friday's Ferry on the Congaree. At Fort Motte, Greene met for the first time the wiry Francis Marion and shook him by the hand. Then Mrs. Motte gave a sumptuous dinner for all the American officers as well as the British. But pleasant as was the little interlude at Mrs. Motte's, Greene could not tarry for long. After seeing to the paroling of the prisoners according to the cartel he had just made with the British, Greene set off to join his army, leaving Lee with instructions to move at once against Fort Granby. Before he left, there was more good news. Lord Rawdon had decided not to march to the relief of Granby or Ninety-Six, having blown up his works at Nelson's Ferry and retired to Monck's Corners, about thirty miles from Charleston.[33]

While Lee and Marion were besieging Fort Motte, Sumter, by Greene's orders, was racing from Ancrum's plantation at Friday's Ferry on a fifty-mile ride to Orangeburg. A strong fort thirty miles southwest of Fort Motte, Orangeburg would have been difficult to take if stubbornly defended. But to Sumter's surprise, the eighty-two men defending the post surrendered without offering much resistance.

Leaving Marion to watch Rawdon and be ready to hinder his march should he try to rescue the garrison at Granby, Lee struck out for the fort on the Congaree by the road up the west side of the river. Arriving on May 14th, Lee found Granby much stronger than either Fort Watson or Fort Motte. Situated on the high banks of the Congaree, the town, like Camden, was surrounded by a strong palisade and a formidable abatis. In the fort, Major Maxwell had 350 troops supported by five cannon.

During the night, Lee set up a battery and in the morning his two cannons began firing point blank range at the fort. After a few shots, Maxwell offered to discuss terms of surrender. Not wishing to share laurels of taking the fort with the main army which was drawing near, Lee entered into negotiations whereupon it was agreed that upon surrendering the British could keep the booty they had plundered from the Whigs of the surrounding country.

While his army was making camp at Ancrum's plantation, Greene crossed the river to see Lee and Maxwell. Upon landing, he found the militia Sumter had left behind infuriated by Lee's pledge. Lee, never popular with any but his own men, on this occasion found the Continentals as well as the militia angry over his conduct. Greene made no comment on Lee's deal, but as the pledge had been given he threatened to hang anyone who mo-

lested the enemy's baggage. This ended the matter. The fall of
Fort Granby brought the total of prisoners taken since Greene
entered South Carolina to nearly 800. If Ninety-Six and Augusta
could be taken next and the garrisons captured, Greene's fame
would soar to new heights.[34]

After sending Lee to join Pickens who was besieging Augusta
and its companion forts, Greene marched for Ninety-Six. On the
way he spent much time turning over in his mind his plans for
the future. If Ninety-Six and Augusta fell, in a few weeks he
would be in Virginia to confront his old antagonist. Cornwallis,
he thought, might very well find himself in a trap if the French
fleet could be persuaded to station itself in the Chesapeake
again. It would be a great opportunity for the allies to end the
war, Greene wrote to Lafayette and La Luzerne whom he hoped
would use their influence upon the French admirals. Inside the
bay, he assured them, the fleet would be safe against any force
that could be sent against it. Certainly had Cornwallis some of
Greene's foresight and genius he would not have gotten himself
into a trap at Yorktown.[35]

Reports of Greene's successes in South Carolina soon were
circulating throughout the North and in due time carried to the
kingdoms of Europe. At New Windsor, Washington heard the
news with joy and congratulated Greene and the Southern army
in his general orders. "These brilliant repeated successes which
reflect so much glory on the Southern Army will be attended
with the most important Consequences," declared Washington.
From Philadelphia, Joseph Reed wrote Greene that he had won
the admiration of the whole country. People, he wrote, say that
if Greene "cannot preserve the Country it is because it cannot
be preserved." Reed, however, cautioned his friend against criticizing the militia as it offended the multitude and made the
people no more ready to support the kind of army Greene wanted.
Speak of the militia therefore, wrote Reed, as "Prior of a Wife.
Be to their Faults a little blind and to their Virtues very kind."[36]

Soon Congress was discussing striking a medal for Greene
to be sent to the colleges of Europe and America. Jefferson approved but thought ones should also be made of Washington,
Rochambeau, d'Estaing, de Grasse, and Lafayette. Gold ones, he

said, should be sent to kings and rulers, silver ones to distinguished persons, and copper ones to colleges. For want of money, however, the idea was abandoned.

As much of South Carolina was falling into American hands, Greene wrote to Governor Rutledge who had gone to Philadelphia to help get supplies and money for the army, that he thought it was time to take up the work of re-establishing civil government in the state "as it is of importance to have the minds of the people formed to the habits of civil rather than military authority." Greene also mentioned his approval of using Negroes taken from Tories to pay for the raising of state troops. Any expedient, he knew, which would put soldiers in the field had to be utilitized.[37]

Although everything so far had worked out surprisingly well, Greene was not without his troubles. Sumter and Marion had both asked to be relieved of their commands and to lose either would be unfortunate. Sumter was suffering great pain from rheumatism and before leaving Orangeburg had sent in his resignation. Greene returned it with an urgent plea for him to stay on. Sumter did so even though he was as much pained by Lee's capture of Granby as by his rheumatism. Sumter had held Granby in a state of siege for many weeks and then to have it fall to Lee was most irritating to a man of his nature. He was the more provoked when he found that he could have reached Granby before Lee as Orangeburg fell the day before Fort Motte. But he had no one to blame but himself for this. Instead of returning to Friday's Ferry, he had ridden off to do what he could to embarrass the enemy in the lowlands. It was a commendable operation but one not productive of the laurels he coveted.[38]

Unlike Sumter, Marion was not sick in body but he was sick and disgusted with his role as a militia officer. He complained of the men's coming and going and of their greater concern for plundering than fighting the enemy. Marion's frame of mind is revealed by his answer to Greene's request for dragoon horses for Washington's cavalry. He had none, Marion said, unless he took them from his militia. This he would about as soon do, he declared, for he did not much care if some of the men stayed or went home.

With Greene's permission, Marion wanted to resign from the militia and go to Philadelphia to get his commission as a Continental officer. Greene could appreciate his desire to leave the militia but he could not afford an interruption of his services at this critical time. He therefore appealed to Marion's patriotism and sense of duty. If Marion left, Greene reminded him, others would follow his example and there was no telling what might result from his going. "Your state is invaded, your all is at stake, what had been done will signify nothing, unless we persevere to the end," must have been words that brought Marion to a realization of how much his country needed him.[39] With Marion placated to the point of continuing in the service, Greene left instructions for him to operate below Orangeburg. Sumter was to demolish the fortification at Granby and be prepared with Marion to delay Lord Rawdon should he attempt to relieve Ninety-Six.

As Greene crossed the Broad River to the north side of the Saluda on his march to Ninety-Six, he had high praise for the way in which Pickens' militia had intercepted all messages from Balfour and Rawdon going to Augusta and Ninety-Six. The garrisons at these forts, Greene was convinced, could only be rescued by a large force from Charleston and as there was no word that one was on its way, success seemed almost certain. Greene's army arrived at Ninety-Six on May 22nd, after a march of about sixty miles from Friday's Ferry.

Ninety-Six, a fortified town on what was still the Indian frontier, derived its name by virtue of being ninety-six miles from Fort George on the Keowee River. The village with its closely packed cabins occupied several acres on a flat plain. Around the whole town was a stout stockade protected by a ditch and an abatis. At the west corner of the quadrangle stood the town jail, used as a fort overlooking a stream from which the village obtained its water. On the bank opposite the jail and connected with the town by a covered way were two blockhouses each surrounded by a stockade and an abatis.

Although the fortifications which guarded the water supply were formidable, the principal works consisted of a star fort at the eastern corner of the town. Star Fort, erected by the British engineer Lieutenant Haldane, had a diameter of about 200 feet and consisted of ten large star points. The sides of the points facing outward were twelve feet high from the bottom of the surrounding ditch. In front of the ditch was an abatis. Inside the fort, covered ways and trenches protected the defenders should the enemy raise batteries for shooting over the banks. Commanded by a resolute officer, Lieutenant Colonel John Cruger, a New York Loyalist and son-in-law of Oliver de Lancey, Ninety-Six would be no easy fort to take. Cruger's force consisted of about 600 veteran troops recruited from among the Loyalists of New York and New Jersey. In addition, there were quite a number of South Carolina Tories and a force of Negro slaves all of whom could be depended upon to help defend the fort. For a distance surrounding the town the land was treeless. Three cannon mounted on wheels made it possible to have artillery at any point in a few minutes.

Although Greene's army of 1,000 Continentals and several hundred North and South Carolina militia was double the number in the fort, Greene saw at once that Ninety-Six, like Camden, was too strong to be carried by assault. As the stockade was too heavy to be knocked down by his light field pieces, he decided to try to reduce the fort by the use of parallels. But instead of keeping his army together as at Camden, he divided it into four camps at equal distances around the town. He had little fear that Cruger would sally forth in strength and if he did it would furnish an opportunity for rushing the fort. By ringing the fort with his army he would keep it in a tight siege.

On the first night, Greene reconnoitered the enemy's works with Kosciuszko and Pendleton. It was dark and rainy but at one point they were fired on by the guards from within. After some discussion, Greene took Kosciuszko's advice and ordered parallels to be commenced opposite the star. The blockhouses overlooking the stream were less strong, but as a well had once been dug in the town with success, it did not appear proper to expend effort on the blockhouses.

Having decided upon their plan of operation, Greene displayed an amazing lack of respect for the enemy by having Kosciuszko start a parallel during the night within 200 feet of the star. By morning they had enough work done to afford the workers protection and the digging went on. Then suddenly a party from the fort fell upon the workmen with the bayonet. Many were killed or wounded and the rest fled amid the whistling of bullets from the fort. Cruger's men returned with all the entrenching tools, losing only one man in the sally.

After this Greene prudently started a new parallel well out of gunshot from the fort. Day and night the work was pushed by men with pick and shovel while others stood guard. Nearly every night fierce attacks were made by suicide squads from the fort but the work still went on. After a week they got up to where Kosciuszko had started his first parallel. Three days later, June 1st, Greene told Pickens that in one more day they should be within a few feet of the ditch and abatis. From there they hoped to dig a tunnel under the enemy's works and blow a hole in the redoubt through which the fort could be rushed. To do this he needed more powder and Pickens was directed to send several barrels from the stock just captured by Captain Michael Rudolph at Fort Dreadnought.

In spite of the progress being made on the parallel, Greene feared with each passing day that it would end in failure. If the reinforcements promised by North Carolina and Virginia had come, victory would have been assured. But only a small part of the army was available for digging as great numbers were required to forage and stand guard.

Greene estimated that in the Ninety-Six area the Tories outnumbered the Whigs five to one. As food was scarce, what little could be found required a heavy guard to bring it in. One body of Tory militia that hid in the swamps was estimated to be over 500 in number. Thus with enemies both within and without the fort, Greene's manpower was taxed to the limit. No doubt without Washington's fearless dragoons who kept the Tories confined to the swamps the siege could not have been long maintained.[40]

Some of the Tories, Greene discovered, wanted to give up and return to their homes if they could with safety. He therefore had the word spread that all people with peaceful intentions would be protected. If something were not done to stop the bloodshed between Whigs and Tories, he feared the interior of South Carolina and Georgia would become practically depopulated. Hearing that militia with Colonel Hammond were murdering Tories near Augusta, Greene sent orders to Pickens to put a stop to it. The worthless element among the Whigs, he declared, must be punished if they killed unarmed civilians. As the surest protection for Tories was to allow them to join the Continental Army, Greene made this offer to the men of the Saluda on June 6th. Those who had committed crimes must be answerable, he said, but every effort would be made to end the civil war and establish law and order. To facilitate this work in Georgia, he directed John Williams to form a council of six or seven prominent citizens to act as a governing body until constitutional government could be established.[41]

During the siege of Ninety-Six Greene's lieutenants in other areas, confronted by less formidable objectives, gained more laurels. Marion, with Greene's permission, attacked and captured Georgetown. Fort Dreadnought, a stockade farmhouse at Silver Bluffs near Augusta, was taken by Lee's Legion. The latter then joined Pickens for the reduction of Augusta, defended by Creek Indians, Tories, and some British troops. After hot fighting, the commander, Colonel Thomas Browne, surrendered, leaving only the territory in Georgia between Ebenezer and Savannah in British hands.

Not long after the surrender of Augusta someone rode up and murdered Colonel Grierson, one of the prisoners. Like Browne, he was the author of many barbarities committed on Whigs, and feeling against both men was boundless. However, they were prisoners of war and Greene was highly incensed by the murder. The act, he said, would add fuel to the flames of civil war and encourage reprisals. But though he offered a reward of 100 guineas for the capture of the murderer, he was never apprehended. For fear that Browne might suffer a like fate, Greene had him paroled to Savannah. The rest of the prisoners were led by Lee to Ninety-Six after which they were sent to prison camps in North Carolina.

Up until June 3rd, Lord Rawdon despaired of being able to do anything to help Ninety-Six, 200 miles from Charleston. But that day a fleet arrived from Cork bearing three regiments and a corps of the Guards, numbering in all nearly 2,000 men. At once Rawdon prepared to march and soon he was on the road to Ninety-Six with 2,000 infantry and 150 dragoons.

When Greene heard that Rawdon was coming he did not abandon hope of reducing the fort as it would take a week or more for the British to reach Ninety-Six. So far, however, no dent had been made in the enemy's defenses. After giving up trying to blow a hole through the sides of the star, a Maham tower was built but Cruger's men shielded themselves from the bullets of the riflemen by raising the walls of the fort to fifteen feet with sandbags. Two batteries on twenty-foot mounds within 100 feet of the star likewise proved ineffective. In the town Cruger took the roofs off the houses so they could not be set afire by flaming missiles. For days not a man on either side showed his head above his works without being shot down.

For a time after Greene heard that Rawdon was coming, he was not sure he would actually come all the way to Ninety-Six. The second division of the French fleet was reported to be near Charleston and it did not seem that Rawdon would risk getting so far from the city. But if he did come, Greene hoped to meet and defeat him on the road. Marion, Sumter, and Pickens were ordered to round up their militia and join Greene who, if Ninety-Six did not fall, would leave enough troops behind to hold Cruger. Greene relished nothing more than an opportunity to give his Lordship a beating to make up for the embarrassment at Camden.[42]

On June 11th, Greene received a message from Sumter which removed all doubt about Rawdon's intentions. Greene gave Rawdon time to get a little closer and then on the 14th sent Washington with part of the cavalry to help Sumter slow down the enemy. By the time Washington reached the oncoming British, however, it was too late. Sumter had had his cavalry cut to pieces at one blow by the British dragoons and had retired to Granby leaving the road open to Ninety-Six. Hundreds of Sumter's militia had deserted and at Granby he found Marion with only a few men. Pickens never arrived as he was still waiting for the Georgia militia as well as his own to collect.

As late as June 17th, however, Greene was unaware of what had happened and was still hoping that the fort would fall and that he could draw his forces together for a battle with Rawdon. But that day occurred an incident which made it certain that Ninety-Six would hold out to the very last. A rider who looked like one of the curious who rode in and out of camp, jogged along the road until he came opposite the main gate of the town. Then all of a sudden he put spurs to his horse and went racing for the gate. A hail of bullets flew after him but the gate swung open and he entered unharmed. Thus Cruger learned that Rawdon was within sixty miles of Ninety-Six and should reach the fort in three or four days.[43]

Convinced that Rawdon could not be stopped, Greene decided to make one last attempt to take Ninety-Six before lifting the siege. It was the opinion that the fort could be taken by a mass attack if Greene were willing to lose 200 men. But Greene would not think of it although his officers and men would have made the sacrifice if he had requested it. Instead, Greene decided upon an attack by a select number of troops while his riflemen covered "the forlorn hope" as best they could. Captain Rudolph and Captain Kirkwood volunteered to lead the daredevils against the blockhouses while Lieutenant Isaac Duval and Lieutenant Samuel Seldon undertook the still more hazardous assignment against the Star Fort.[44]

At the signal gun at noon on June 18th, the heroic assailants leaped from their parallels as a barrage of bullets and cannon shot whizzed over their heads. In a few minutes the axe-men had hacked a way through the abatis to let the men with the pole-hooks into the ditch below the star. Meanwhile, Rudolph's men beat their way into the blockhouses as the defenders made for the safety of the town through the covered way. His men then waited for word from Greene before launching an attack upon the jail inside the main stockade.

But things went otherwise with the attack on the Star Fort. After the poleman got into the ditch it looked as though they might succeed in pulling enough sandbags off the wall to expose the men in the fort to the rifles on the Maham tower. Both sides were losing many brave men as the troops within the fort exposed themselves to shoot at the Americans in the ditch. Sensing that his foe might soon force his way into the fort, Cruger put a body of men with fixed bayonets into the ditch. From both sides they fell upon their assailants by surprise and turned the ditch into a scene of savage hand-to-hand fighting.

Perhaps, had Greene sent in another company at this critical moment, the day might have been won. But he decided against it and instead sent orders for the survivors to give up and return. Both Duval and Seldon were severely wounded and fully two-thirds of the participants were killed or wounded in the desperate half-hour battle.[45]

The siege of Ninety-Six had lasted twenty-eight days and had cost Greene 150 men. It was a high price for a siege that ended in failure. The troops, however, had fought valiantly and Greene congratulated them for their courage and perseverance. To Congress, he wrote:

> The troops have undergone incredible hardships in the siege; and though the affair was not successful, I hope their exertions will merit the approbation of Congress. Their behavior on this occasion deserves the highest commendation; both the officers that entered the ditch were wounded, and the greater part of their men either killed or wounded. I have to lament that such brave men fell in an unsuccessful attempt.[46]

Admittedly, Ninety-Six was a difficult fort to take and one hesitates to pass judgment on Greene's generalship on this occasion. However, it may be asked if he were right in concentrating his efforts on the Star Fort, the strongest part of the enemy's defenses. On the day of the final attack, Lee took the forts by the stream on the other side of Ninety-Six. If this had been done earlier would it not have been possible for Greene's troops to have scaled the stockade to open the gate into the village? Would this have taken any more lives than the unsuccessful assault on the Star Fort? With the village in his hands, the Star Fort could not have held out for long.

After the American army left Ninety-Six and headed for the Broad River someone is reputed to have suggested to Greene that he might as well give up South Carolina and return to Virginia. Greene, who had decided that with the rise of British power once again in South Carolina the interests of Virginia and the nation would be best served by his staying in South Carolina, replied, "I will recover the country, or die in the attempt." He knew that the military scene in South Carolina, although it had taken a turn for the worse, was not as dark as it seemed. Rawdon, he believed, could not stay long in the interior with his communications with Charleston constantly menaced by the American cavalry and militia. Unless Rawdon could force Greene into a battle and win it, nothing much would be gained by his march to Ninety-Six except the saving of the garrison.[47]

Though nearly overcome by the heat, upon reaching Ninety-Six Rawdon waited but a few hours before beginning the pursuit of Greene. The latter, however, had swept the country clean of provisions and before long the British were brought to a halt as they waited for supplies to arrive. At Bush Creek, Greene was able to wait two days in the hope that militia would arrive and he could give battle. But again he was disappointed. Instead of joining him, everywhere the Whigs seemed to think of nothing but getting away and the roads were filled with fleeing men, women, and children. Greene was always touched by this sad sight. How he wished he could turn upon the cause of their misery and deliver Rawdon a smashing blow.

On June 23rd Greene received word that Rawdon had crossed the Saluda and was but twelve miles away. If he kept coming as Cornwallis had in February and the South Carolina militia did not arrive, there would remain nothing to do but retreat into North Carolina again. That night Greene crossed the Broad where he left Colonel Williams with a detachment of light troops with orders to hold the enemy at the river as long as possible. Greene then set off for the Catawba. Rawdon, however, never came any farther than the Enoree some miles west of the Broad. Spent by the heat and half-starved, his army slowly retired toward Ninety-Six with Lee's dragoons hanging upon their heels. Many of the men dropped in the road from the heat and exhaustion and some fell dead.

Upon reaching Ninety-Six, Rawdon ordered Cruger to prepare for its evacuation. Leaving 1,400 men with Cruger, Rawdon set out the following day for Granby with 1,200 infantry, sixty dragoons, and four cannon. At Granby he was to meet Lieutenant Colonel Alexander Stewart with supplies and reinforcements from Charleston and provisions collected along the Congaree. Cruger was to demolish the stockades at Ninety-Six, collect all the Tories who wished to seek the safety of the British lines, and meet Rawdon at Orangeburg.

On July 1st, while camped at Tim's Tavern between the Broad

and the Catawba, Greene got word that Rawdon was marching toward Granby with about half his army. Although Greene was wrong in thinking that the Briitsh intended to re-establish themselves at Granby and stay at Ninety-Six, he at once decided to take advantage of the division of the enemy. He therefore immediately broke camp and marched south for Granby.

Upon reaching Winnsborough, Greene sent orders for Pickens, Marion, and Sumter to hurry to Friday's Ferry. Leaving the army to follow with General Huger, Greene raced ahead with all the cavalry. He hoped to slow Rawdon down sufficiently to allow the American forces to collect for a battle before Stewart arrived. But Rawdon, he found, was already below Granby and marching toward Orangeburg. Greene followed, and soon his horsemen were harassing any of the enemy who strayed from the main column. On July 8th, Captain Egleston surprised a foraging party supported by sixty dragoons and without loss of a man, overpowered the enemy almost in sight of Rawdon's army. Forty-five of the British dragoons were killed or captured, thus eliminating at one blow Rawdon's horse as a source of danger. Greene then tried to get in ahead of Rawdon to pounce upon Stewart but by the time his horsemen had made the necessary circuit, the British forces had joined. "We made a rapid march with the whole of our cavalry to intercept them," wrote Greene, "but unfortunately we were too late. However, Col. Horrye [Horry] took three of the wagons, loaded with a variety of goods."[48]

General Huger reached Friday's Ferry with the army in the cool of the morning of July 6th. From the westward, Pickens had just arrived with his militia and Sumter was drawing near in his march from the Waxhaws. Intent upon pursuing the British in the hope of forcing an engagement before Cruger arrived, Greene ordered Huger to march and cross the Congaree at Howell's Ferry (a little-used crossing halfway down the river near Beaver Creek) as Rawdon had destroyed all the boats at Friday's Ferry.

On July 8th, by the use of three canoes and a flatboat, General Huger began crossing the Congaree. With so few conveyances it took two or three days to get the army over the river to join Greene and the cavalry waiting nearby at a camp at Beaver Creek. Marion, coming from the Santee, was the last to arrive with men and horses almost overcome by the stifling heat. On July 11th, with all assembled, Greene began marching on Rawdon at Orangeburg, twenty-five miles to the south. Cruger, Greene learned, had burned Ninety-Six and was approaching by the road west of the Edisto. As Cruger had vowed he would burn every building from Ninety-Six to Orangeburg, Greene sent Pickens to the threatened area although he felt that it was an empty threat as the heat was so intense the British would have all they could do to get to Orangeburg before their horses gave out.

With his 2,000 troops, 800 of which were Continentals, Greene pitched camp on strong ground four miles from Orangeburg. On reconnoitering, he found that Rawdon could not be attacked in the town without exposing his men to heavy losses. In the center of the village was a solid brick prison, impregnable against Greene's cannon. Rawdon, moreover, could not be trapped in Orangeburg for back of him was a bridge over the Edisto. But Greene was hoping he would come out and fight as he did at Camden. In this he was disappointed and after waiting a day, Greene lifted the siege and marched his army slowly toward McCord's Ferry. That day Cruger joined Rawdon with troops almost prostrate from the intense heat.[49]

As it was folly to think of fighting Rawdon's combined forces, Greene had decided to retire to the High Hills of the Santee to rest his tired army and await reinforcements. But he did not intend to release the tension on the enemy down in the sultry and debilitating lowlands where life in summer became insufferable. On breaking camp, he detached Sumter and Marion and most of Lee's and Washington's cavalry with orders to invade the region below Orangeburg and attack the posts at Dorchester, Goose Creek, Monck's Corners, and elsewhere. The thrust into the lowlands, Greene felt, would compel Rawdon to give up Orangeburg as well as any thought of re-establishing posts at Granby and along the Santee.

Although the cavalry and militia did not accomplish quite as much as Greene had hoped, the raid succeeded in throwing the enemy into a virtual state of panic. Captain Egleston again reaped laurels by capturing a large supply train on the way from Charleston to Orangeburg. The principal action, however, occurred when the combined forces, with Sumter in command, reached the British post at Biggin's, a mile from Monck's Corners. Here they found St. John's Church, used as a fort, and the enemy's stores in flames and the garrison fleeing down the road toward Quimby's Bridge. On reaching the bridge, Lieutenant Colonel James Coates made a stand with his 500 infantry and 100 horse. Led by Lee, the Americans tried desperately to dislodge the enemy who had taken cover in a brick house. After three hours of fierce fighting, however, the Americans, who had no cannon, were obliged to give up and retire with their prisoners as Balfour at Charleston had dispatched a relief party of 700 under Colonel Gould.[50]

Balfour wrote Sir Henry Clinton that the future never looked darker for the British in South Carolina. Greene's raiders, by the time they retired, took 150 prisoners, killed or wounded 100 more, and destroyed or carried off large quantities of stores. American horse seemed to be everywhere—at Goose Creek, at Dorchester, and at innumerable plantations. Rawdon's cavalry, now thoroughly cowed, scarcely showed itself. Colonel Peter Horry of the South Carolina state cavalry dared to raid right down to the Quarter House, only six miles from Charleston.

While his lieutenants were terrorizing the lowlands, Greene crossed the Congaree at McCord's Ferry after resting at Thompson's plantation near Mrs. Motte's. From here the march to the High Hills of the Santee was about twenty-five miles which the army made by easy stages, traveling mostly in the cool of the evening and early morning.

Although Greene had not won a major battle since he took command in the South, both of the Carolinas and Georgia, except a narrow belt around Charleston and Savannah, had been recovered. Cornwallis was by this time in Virginia but Greene was confident he had made no mistake by letting him go. General Washington, supported by the army of Rochambeau in Rhode Island, should be able to reinforce Lafayette in Virginia, while Greene could help most by holding his gains in the Carolinas and preventing another rise of British power in that quarter.

CHAPTER FIFTEEN

At Eutaw Springs the Valiant Died

When Greene retired to the High Hills of the Santee he was aware of the great possibilities the second half of 1781 held for the American Army. A decisive victory might be won in Virginia if the French fleet acquired control of the Chesapeake. Greene would, therefore, not be surprised when he heard of what was shaping up in Virginia as a result of the march of Washington and Rochambeau and the appearance of Admiral de Grasse. The Battle of Eutaw Springs, however, was the result of Greene's fear that Cornwallis might break through Lafayette's lines and take the road to Charleston before the armies from the north could reach Virginia. This did not happen and perhaps the war would have ended just as soon had the Battle of Eutaw Springs not been fought.

The High Hills of the Santee, to which Greene had retired to rest his army and await reinforcements, parallel the left bank of the Wateree for fifteen miles or more. Below the High Hills, rising 200 feet above the river, was a trackless wilderness of swamp three or four miles wide. Like others, the swamps of the Wateree often furnished a hiding place for Marion and Sumter when followed too closely by the enemy. The rich sandy-loam soil which covers the greater part of the High Hills as well as the equally fertile lands of the Black River area to the eastward were drawn upon to furnish food and forage for a hungry army.

Although by no means free from the fever, the air at the High Hills was cooler and more salubrious than that of the damp and stifling lowlands from whence the army had just emerged. The army camped at Richardson's plantation at Bloom Hill along the ridge of hills facing the Wateree. Here the army found cool springs and giant oaks for shade, where mosquitoes, though by no means absent, were few compared with the myriads in the

lowlands. Besides furnishing the army with a most enticing retreat, the High Hills afforded strong ground against sudden attack
by the enemy. At the same time the hills were near enough to the
lowlands south of the Santee for Greene's army to be a constant
threat to the enemy and support to any detachment operating
there.[1]

Life at the High Hills of the Santee after what Greene and his
army had been through for the past four months was one of ease
and quiet. Greene had time to write more and longer letters
and give the people up north a better understanding of what had
happened in far off South Carolina. He told Kitty that she could
be thankful she had not come south. The war in the Carolinas,
he explained, was barbarous in comparison to anything in the
North except on the New York Indian frontier. Even in Virginia
she would have found conditions hard with little security. Martha
Washington, for instance, had been obliged to flee from Mount
Vernon at midnight to escape being taken by the enemy. To
Henry Knox, Greene wrote that he thought he had proved John
Trumbull wrong in saying he was deficient in the art of retreating.
"There are few generals," wrote Greene, "that has run oftener, or
more lustily than I have done, But I have taken care not to run
too far, and commonly have run as fast forward as backward, to
convince our Enemy that we were like a Crab, that could run
either way."[2]

From the High Hills, Greene turned again to the problem of
establishing law and order for war-torn South Carolina and
Georgia. Everywhere the frenzy and bitterness between Whigs
and Tories continued unabated. It would take time for the hatred
to subside, Greene knew, but little could be done until civil government was re-established. Greene had given up the idea of a
seven man council for Georgia, and he advised its leaders to go
ahead and have a legislature elected but not to attempt to make
a constitution as yet. Greene appointed Dr. Nathan Brownson
governor of Georgia and directed him to repair to Augusta to
organize the government.[3]

Governor Rutledge arrived at the High Hills of the Santee soon
after Greene got there and together they worked on plans for
re-establishing civil government for South Carolina. It was decided, for one thing, that Loyalists who had not borne arms

against the state or nation would be pardoned but the others must stand trial or suffer exile. With the departure of Colonel Cruger from Ninety-Six, parties of bandits posing as Whig militia were terrorizing the Loyalists of the area who had stayed behind hoping to make peace with their neighbors. "Here, turn what way you will," wrote Nathanael to Kitty, "you have nothing but the mournful widow and the plaints of the fatherless child; and behold nothing but houses desolated and plantations laid waste. Ruin is in every form and misery in every shape."[4]

Greene sent orders to Pickens directing him to do all in his power to stop the outrages in his area and to protect both the Whigs and the Tories from the outlaws. When any of the latter were caught, Greene wanted them sent to him for trial and punishment, the threat of which might make some pause in their path of crime. As countless families were reduced to beggary, Greene commanded Pickens to take from those who had plenty and give to the destitute, paying for the food with receipts which would be redeemed by the government. As a newspaper would be an aid to the solving of Southern problems, Greene urged Thomas Walters who owned a press to start publishing one at Charlotte or Salisbury.

Through his correspondence with Jefferson, Steuben, Lafayette, and others, Greene had kept himself informed of the military picture in Virginia. After Cornwallis entered Virginia, Greene directed Steuben to turn over all the Continentals he raised to Lafayette instead of sending them to South Carolina, even though the odds against Lafayette were not as great as Greene faced in South Carolina. By July, Lafayette, who had the North to draw from for supplies and reinforcements, had 2,300 Continentals and fully as many militia to pit against the 7,200 men under Cornwallis. In South Carolina and Georgia, Rawdon had upwards of 7,000 well-equipped soldiers while Greene could not put half that number of troops of any description in the field.[5]

Regardless of Lafayette's strength, Cornwallis' cavalry was overrunning much of Virginia and doing great damage. Jefferson appealed to Greene for cavalry to save the state. Greene replied by reminding Jefferson that had Virginia sent him horses and men as promised when he invaded South Carolina the war would be all but over in South Carolina and the army would be on its way to Virginia to fight Cornwallis. Greene felt sorry for Virginia, he told Jefferson, but by consulting local interest and not the welfare of the nation, the state had brought the condition upon herself.[6]

Although Greene lectured Jefferson, it was not from spite that he refused to send help to Virginia. Lafayette had been reinforced with troops from the Northern army and if more were needed they should be sought after in the North. Greene, at least, had none to spare from his slender Southern army. Virginia itself, Greene knew, was capable of putting more militia in the field.

Jefferson, of course, felt that Greene should give up South Carolina and march for Virginia. This would be a great mistake, Greene believed. If he should set out for Virginia, he told Washington, his army would be worn out by 300 miles of marching through the heat of the summer, making it unlikely that half his men would ever reach Virginia. The British meanwhile would be free to dispatch troops from South Carolina and send them to Virginia by sea. In the end, it would only serve to make the British stronger in Virginia and give them a free hand in re-establishing their power in South Carolina and Georgia.[7]

Criticism of Thomas Jefferson in Virginia itself, now that the state was invaded, had indeed risen to great heights. Some talked of having a dictator appointed and Greene was mentioned as a person to whom the state could be entrusted until the crisis was past. No dictator was appointed but the agitation led to Jefferson's defeat and the election of Thomas Nelson as governor. In August, Robert Burnet, on his way to Philadelphia to lay before Congress the plight of Greene's army, reported that he found Nelson determined to raise more troops as well as several hundred dragoon horses for Greene.[8]

Though Nathanael Greene was the conquering hero and the idol of America, there were persons other than Jefferson who found occasion to criticize him. In Philadelphia talk was that he was unpopular with his officers. There was a story that he had used strong language and heaped words of abuse upon an officer. Edmund Randolph, a member of Congress, believed the tale untrue as it was contrary to Greene's temperament and seemed "incredible" even under great provocation. Greene, it is true, would lecture his officers if he thought they deserved it but it seems unlikely that he ever actually abused a man. Afterward, when he had the trouble with Captain Gunn, he declared that he had never abused an officer during his whole career in the United States Army.[9]

For one thing, Greene thought he had altogether squelched Thomas Mifflin and others like him who had told the world in former years that he lacked enterprise, if not courage. Nevertheless, Greene assured Joseph Reed that he did not aspire to great fame. It was "far more difficult to support than acquire a great reputation," which often was acquired by accident, he told Reed. For himself, Greene believed he had earned his laurels in the South. With the Northern army, he wrote, "you have support from every side, here is it remote and uncertain. There you have resources of every kind, here you have none but what are within yourself." In brief, in the North the campaigns were relatively simple but in the South they were extremely complicated and fraught with the greatest difficulties.[10] To Benjamin Rush, with whom Greene retained a friendship regardless of the doctor's criticism of Washington and Greene in the days of the Conway cabal, Greene wrote that he hoped the Southern campaign, notwithstanding its shortcomings, was understood in the North. "Had I the pen or the eloquence of a Fox or a Rush," wrote Greene, "bad as our materials are in this Country, they would reflect no disgrace upon us."[11]

In a letter to Robert Morris, head of Congress' Finance Department, Greene explained his long-standing embarrassment for want of money:

> To conduct a war which is carried on so much at arm's-end as the operations here are, so remote from supplies of every kind, and where the enemy can be reinforced with such facility, and we with such difficulty, and the whole service attended with so many contingencies, and all this to be done without money, and with a force little more than one third equal to the enemy's, is an unenviable task, and requires more experience and greater abilities than I possess. I find myself frequently ready to sink under the load of difficulties that oppress me where all our resources depend upon expedients. Hitherto we have combated them with some degree of success, but this cannot be expected to continue without more effectual support.

As on many former occasions, Greene deprecated Congress' lack of power to tax for the war. "It is a maxim in republican government never to despair of the commonwealth; nor do I," he told Morris. But with a boat which seemed about to sink at any time, he appealed to Morris for any help he could render: "If I have any opportunity of obtaining money and drawing bills on you, I shall embrace it. But 'tis a very uncertain source, and therefore I leave you to judge of the prudence of exposing an army to such contingencies."[12]

While at the High Hills of the Santee, Greene had the unpleasant experience of having to criticize a court-martial decision. Captain Conway Oldham, a Virginian and one of Greene's best field officers, was charged with insubordination and disrespect to a superior. The court, contrary to the evidence, found him not guilty. Although Greene had the highest respect for Oldham as a brave soldier, he felt that the verdict endangered army discipline. In general orders, therefore, Greene declared his disapproval of the court's decision.

Subordination and respect from inferior to superior officers is so necessary in the very existence of an army, that the General is surprised that an officer should betray the least symptoms of a want of either. . . . No army can hope to be useful or honorable where subordination is wanting. Nor can any officer flatter himself of being crowned with military glory, while connected with an army defective in the essential of discipline, however meritorious his conduct may be as an individual.[13]

One day at the High Hills, Greene received word that Colonel Balfour had, against the protest of Tories as well as Whigs, executed a South Carolina militia officer named Colonel Isaac Hayne. As a captive Hayne had been practically forced into taking an oath of allegiance to the King and after securing his release had again taken up arms against the British. After Hayne's recapture, Balfour resolved to make an example of him. Greene had threatened that if Hayne were executed he would hang the first British officer who fell into his hands but neither threats nor the supplications of friends or family had the least effect on the British.

Upon hearing the fate of Colonel Hayne, Greene was terribly

angry, exclaiming, "by heaven, I will retaliate." But he kept his head and sent orders to Marion not to retaliate by hanging a Tory officer, as Greene wanted to save the hanging for one of the British—preferably Balfour or Rawdon if fate should cast either into his power. The British, he told Marion, would like them to retaliate on a Loyalist as it would further incite the bitterness between Whigs and Tories and cause many of the latter to join the British Army.[14]

Greene stopped all exchange of prisoners and issued a proclamation declaring that the American Army would retaliate for the inhuman execution of Hayne. If he had not done this, Greene explained to Lafayette, all the militia would have deserted in a body, so great was the outcry against Hayne's execution. Greene blamed Lord Rawdon more than Balfour for the deed and was sorry to hear his Lordship had left for England as there was no man in American he desired more to see hanging at the end of a rope.[15]

The Hayne case agitated the country for a long time and was not finally dismissed until the coming of peace. After Cornwallis was captured, Arthur Middleton and some other Southern members of Congress wanted to hang the Earl in retaliation but were voted down. Greene told Thomas McKean, who followed Samuel Huntington as President of Congress, that he never intended to hang an innocent man for the crime committed by Rawdon and Balfour. His proclamation, he said, had for its purpose the prevention of future acts of the same nature by the British as well as quieting the clamor for revenge.[16]

When Greene marched his army to the High Hills of the Santee in July, he thought that Rawdon might try to re-establish posts at Nelson's, McCord's, and Friday's ferries as soon as possible. Therefore, he had ordered Marion to take post on the north side of the Santee near Nelson's Ferry and for Sumter to repair to Friday's Ferry on the Congaree. A little later he sent Lee with the Legion to Howell's Ferry, about fifteen miles above McCord's. Each officer was ordered to do all in his power to carry off or destroy grain and cattle south of the Congaree and Santee as the enemy would find it difficult to locate in a region stripped of food and forage.[17]

General Thomas Sumter was not long at Friday's Ferry before

Greene received word from Lieutenant Colonel John Henderson, second in command, that Sumter had furloughed a good part of his militia until the first of October. Greene, who after resting his army planned to march against the enemy as soon as reinforcements arrived from North Carolina, was put out by Sumter's presumptuousness. In answer he ordered all furloughs canceled and none issued in the future without his consent. It was little less than madness, Greene declared, for Sumter to take it upon himself to disband most of his force with the enemy threatening to strike at any time. He generally had given Sumter a free hand but if he thought this entitled him to do as he pleased he would soon learn otherwise, Greene told Henderson.

Sumter was a hard man to manage and often deserved reprimanding. But on this occasion he was not so blameable as Greene imagined. He was still ailing and had left the militia in charge of Henderson with instructions to apply to Greene for permission to furlough the men. Sumter apparently thought that Greene would immobilize the militia during the hot season and therefore he let men go home before hearing from Greene. Although Sumter was too independent for the kind of teamwork and warfare demanded by Greene, his shortcomings were often unintentional or mere thoughtlessness.[18]

Although North Carolina was promising large numbers of men for Greene's army, as usual those that actually showed up were far less than promised. A thousand mountaineers under Colonel Shelby had gathered, it is true, but upon being erroneously told by Pickens that they were not needed until later, they had gone home. During August, however, a regiment of Continentals commanded by General Sumner as well as about 400 militia arrived at the High Hills from North Carolina. Before marching to engage the enemy, Greene had officers drilling and training the new recruits every morning from daylight until the heat of the day drove them from the field.

From Howell's Ferry on August 13th, Lee reported that the British, suffering from the intolerable heat and humidity of the lowlands, were in no mood to fight and that many would desert if given an opportunity. It was a good time, he said, to attack the enemy. If Greene waited, the British might be stronger as they were making a drive to force the Tories into the army.

Greene learned, too, that Stewart, who had succeeded Rawdon in command, had moved the greater part of his army to Thompson's plantation near McCord's Ferry to cover the country below and be in a position to attack Greene's army or its detachments. Soon Lee warned Greene to be on the alert as a Negro spy had offered to lead Stewart over the Santee and through the swamps by a secret trail to Greene's army at Bloom Hill, fifteen miles away.[19]

Greene relied a great deal on Lee whom he often referred to as his "right eye" and his decision to march against the enemy was no doubt predicated on the information and advice received from Lee. On August 17th Lee wrote that he thought Cornwallis would try to reach Charleston and that Greene should attack before he joined forces with Stewart.[20] Although heavy rains had driven the rivers over their banks and filled the swamps, Greene issued marching orders about the time the last of the North Carolina troops arrived. The rains and the swollen rivers, he thought, would put the enemy off his guard. In any event, the British were not likely to learn of his movement until it was too late to send reinforcements from Charleston.

As it was impossible to get through the swamp and over the Wateree at any point near the High Hills, Greene had to march by a long and circuitous route. On August 23rd, the army left its encampment at 5 p.m. for a night march to Camden, thirty miles to the north. When the army reached Camden it crossed the Wateree and marched toward Friday's Ferry where it was joined by Henderson's militia. Expresses were sent to Pickens and Marion to hurry forward and join the army at the old campsite on Beaver Creek from whence Greene had marched against Rawdon in July. Lee was directed to get over the Congaree at Howell's Ferry to cover the army's crossing. "Depend upon it," Greene told Lee, "we must have victory or ruin." This, indeed, was to be the battle for South Carolina.[21]

Before crossing the Congaree, Greene learned that at Thompson's plantation Stewart had heard that the Americans had left the High Hills whereupon he had retired thirty-five miles to Nelson's Ferry to await supplies and reinforcements from Charleston. The report, however, did not deter Greene who continued to push on by easy stages. Greene crossed the Congaree at Howell's Ferry on August 28th and soon arrived at Mrs. Motte's plantation.

Many of his men had already succumbed to the heat or the fever, though most of the marching was done during the night or early morning. Colonel Williams could not but wonder how the poor soldiers could possibly bear up long enough to meet the enemy and fight a battle.

Marching south by a road running parallel to the Santee, Greene reached Stoutemire's plantation on Maybrick's Creek on September 5th. From here he directed Marion (who had just returned from a successful raid on an enemy post on the Pon Pon) to cross the Santee at the widow Richardson's plantation where he would find the army waiting. Greene's commissary was out of beef but the soldiers supplemented their rations by catching frogs and shooting alligators in the swamps along the way.

On the night before the bloody battle of September 8th, Greene camped at Burdell's plantation, seven miles from the enemy. Pickens had joined him with the militia from the Saluda and Marion arrived that afternoon. Altogether Greene had 2,500 men to pit against Stewart's 2,300 regulars. Stewart, camped at Eutaw Springs, a mile from Nelson's Ferry, was unaware of Greene's approach, so diligent had been the American cavalry in preventing anyone from getting through to warn the enemy.

While events were shaping for a decisive battle in South Carolina, great events were also happening in the North. Admiral de Grasse had arrived from France with twenty-eight ships of the line and six frigates to establish naval supremacy in American waters long enough to seal the fate of Cornwallis. Washington, knowing that Cornwallis could not be rescued by sea, was already marching his best troops from the Hudson to Virginia. Rochambeau with the French army was following from Newport. The victory at Yorktown was fast unfolding.

It was with a confident and high-spirited army that Nathanael Greene began the seven mile march from Burdell's plantation to Eutaw Springs at four in the morning. As usual, Greene counted much on the superiority of his cavalry, although so far the dragoons had not been as successful in general battles as in skirmishing and attacking detachments. Greene's army advanced rapidly upon the British who still had no knowledge of its approach. So unconcerned was Stewart that in the early morning he sent out 200 unarmed soldiers to dig sweet potatoes for his army. But the potato diggers had not been out long before two deserters who had eluded the American scouting parties arrived at Eutaw Springs to warn Stewart of his danger. Stewart was inclined not to believe them but for precaution's sake he sent out 150 infantry and 50 dragoons under Major John Coffin to take a look.

It was about eight o'clock on a cloudless day, already growing hot, when Coffin saw a party of American horse. At once the latter galloped back to tell Lee of their discovery. Lee quickly drew his Legion up on one side of the road with Henderson's militia on the other and waited for Coffin. The latter, believing it was only a corps of militia, soon came charging recklessly down the road, his cavalry flanking the infantry on either side.

Coffin's mad rush was stopped short by a hail of bullets. Taking advantage of the confusion and consternation among the enemy, Lee sent his Legion charging with the bayonet while his dragoons sped to cut down all in their way. Few of Coffin's infantry waited long enough to fire. They threw away their muskets and went flying through the woods toward camp with their cavalry in the lead. About forty prisoners were taken, many badly wounded, and not a few of the enemy lay dead. Soon the potato detail was discovered and most of them made prisoners. The victory over Coffin, without loss to the Americans, naturally exhilarated Greene's whole army which now pushed triumphantly on toward Eutaw Springs. This little hamlet, which was soon to see one of the bloodiest battles of the war, was the site of an all but forgotten battle between the white men and the Indians in early colonial days. It was still marked, however, by a mound in which the Indians had buried their dead.

Among the pines about a mile from Eutaw, Greene's men encountered a thin line of skirmishers sent forward by Stewart to delay the Americans while he prepared his army for battle. The infantry under Lee and Henderson moved to the flanks where the cavalry was waiting while the militia with Marion, Pickens, and Malmedy moved up to fill the center. The British made little attempt to stop the American advance as Greene's line pressed forward through the open forest.

Upon coming in sight of the main body of the enemy, Greene,

who was riding in front with the militia, saw that Stewart had drawn up most of his army in one solid line in front of a clearing where his tents were still pitched. On the left his line was anchored by the steep banks of Eutaw Creek while on the right was Coffin's cavalry, now collected after its early morning rout. In the center, though Greene may not have recognized them, were his old enemies of Ninety-Six, the New York and New Jersey Loyalists with Colonel Cruger.

Stewart, an able officer, like Rawdon, was planning on a speedy victory at the point of the bayonet in the manner of the initial charge at Guilford Court House. But this time it was different. Though militia, the men with Marion, Henderson, Pickens, and Malmedy had seen a great deal of fighting. Perhaps in no general battle in the whole war did the militia fight so valiantly and successfully as at Eutaw Springs.

In a moment, as the gap between the two armies narrowed to a few hundred feet, the whole area became a deafening inferno as cannons thundered amid the roar of musketry. To the astonishment of the British, the American militia held firmly in line, loading and firing. Confronted by so stubborn an array of fighters, Stewart did not dare rush the Americans with the bayonet. After firing round after round, however, the militia gave ground and to Stewart it seemed he would soon have his opportunity for the grand charge. But Greene quickly sent forward General Sumner from the second line with his North Carolina Continentals. Again the front line held fast and the muskets and cannon roared as loudly as before. It was not long, though, before Henderson was badly wounded and had to be carried from the field. Without his leadership, his men on the left soon fell into disorder and once again Stewart, with his reserves in line, waited for the right moment for his charge.

Sensing that the critical moment had arrived, Greene ordered forward his whole second line—the Maryland, Delaware, and Virginia Continentals. As they stepped in front of the militia, Greene gave the order to charge and in one great wave the Continentals came down upon the enemy with fixed bayonets. Simultaneously the cavalry fell on the shortened flanks of the enemy. To Greene, riding with the charging Continentals, it looked as though Stewart's army would be rolled up and annihilated. The whole line of the enemy was breaking and many already were in full flight through the camp.

Contrary to orders, Richard Campbell's Virginians paused to fire a volley at the enemy. What did he think he was doing! shouted Lee as he came galloping down to Campbell. Didn't he know that Lee's Legion pressing upon the enemy's flank was practically in the line of fire? But Lee received no answer. A bullet had struck Campbell in the chest and he fell speechless over the saddlebow and was only kept from falling from his horse by his son at his side.

By this time, the British were in full flight with the main body running down the road toward Charleston and others through the woods in any direction that seemed to offer escape. On the extreme right, however, a corps under Major John Majoribanks found protection in a dense thicket of blackjack where they seemed determined to stay and fight it out. Several hundred others managed to get into a three story brick house and some smaller buildings not far from the thicket bordering the creek.

The American army in the hour of victory became disorganized. Some went after the fleeing enemy. Others tried to dislodge Majoribanks. Many, however, went rummaging through the camp and not a few were soon too overcome by the rum they found to be of much use in the field. Whether or not this alone caused Greene to lose the victory within his grasp is difficult to say. In his letters he never mentioned this as a cause of the misfortune which he said was due alone to a brick house that withstood every means to subdue it.[22]

In spite of all the Americans could do, Majoribanks succeeded in drawing close to the brick house under cover of the thicket. Lieutenant Colonel Washington, whose cavalry had been held in reserve, was ordered to try to dislodge Majoribanks. Failing in a frontal attack, Washington, supported by Hampton's South Carolina cavalry, attempted to get around behind the thicket. The move brought his riders under the guns of the men in the brick house and before they could get out of range, many were shot from their saddles. Washington, his horse shot from under him, was wounded and saved from being bayoneted by the intercession of a British officer who took him prisoner.

By this time the artillery was getting placed before the

house for point-blank delivery of their six-pounders. The shot, however, made little impression on the solid brick walls. The brave and resolute artillerymen then pushed their pieces closer to deliver more force to their cannon's blows. But still the building stood fast while the gun crews melted away under the hail of musket bullets from the house and the thicket.

Seeing an opportunity to cut down hundreds of American infantry rifling the tents and baggage, Coffin came charging out from behind the house. Captain Egleston with part of the Legion cavalry intercepted him, but Coffin still had the upper hand with Majoribanks' men crowding at the heels of his horse. Then Colonel Hampton came from somewhere to join in the fray with his South Carolina dragoons. Coffin fled, but Hampton's men in full chase were swept by a volley from the enemy infantry that emptied an appalling number of saddles. At this instance, the British seized two of the four American cannon (around which lay the gun crews, dead or wounded) and dragged them under the walls of the house.

Greene, who had a horse shot from under him, apparently stayed near the brick house after that phase of the battle developed. To a striking degree the battle of Eutaw Springs resembled Germantown where the Chew house robbed Washington of his victory in 1777. With both Majoribanks and the force in the house holding out, Greene could not go on against the main force collecting down the road. Very likely, too, the accounts of the disorder in the American ranks were exaggerated as Greene was able to retire in fair order and carry off over 400 prisoners.

With the failure of each desperate effort to dislodge the enemy in the house, Greene decided that more would be lost than gained by continuing the battle. Stewart had reorganized his men down the road and was approaching to resume the contest. Greene's ammunition was very low and his men, after four hours of fighting and a long march, were exhausted. He therefore sent orders for a general retreat. Stewart followed only to the edge of the clearing as Greene's cavalry took up the rear to cover the retreat.[23]

The long march back to Burdell's plantation was a nightmare for Greene's battered and weary army. What portion of the troops left Eutaw Springs with empty canteens one will never know, but there were apparently hundreds who had been too busy fighting to get them replenished with either water or rum during the battle. Between Eutaw Springs and the plantation there was no water save a muddy pond into which hundreds of men fairly flung themselves to gulp up the water. The suffering, of course, was greatest for the wounded who lay groaning on the litters which carried them. By the time the army finally reached the plantation, Greene thought that there were few who were not on the verge of fainting.

Thus ended the battle of Eutaw Springs. "It was," wrote Greene, "by far the most bloody and obstinate" battle of the whole war. Colonel Williams and others who had seen so many engagements fully agreed.[24] The American losses were nearly 500, or about twenty per cent of the men engaged. Perhaps in no battle of the war did the Americans lose so many officers, with sixty of one hundred killed or wounded. Richard Campell died of his wounds. Of the Continental regimental officers, only Lee and Williams came out unscathed. Philip Freneau mourned for the dead in his poem on Eutaw Springs.

> At Eutaw Springs the valiant died;
> Their limbs with dirt are covered o'er—
> Weep on, ye springs, your tearful tide;
> How many heroes are no more!

Though Greene's losses were far from trifling, Stewart's were staggering. Some estimated his losses as high as a thousand. This is probably too high, but there could very well have been 900, forty per cent of the men engaged. The results of the battle of Eutaw Springs were not unlike that of Guilford Court House. The British, though keeping the field, were woefully crippled, making their hold on the country outside of Charleston most tenuous. Both sides claimed a victory, but if Eutaw Springs were a victory for the British it was of the kind that led to certain ruin.[25]

Eutaw Springs raised Nathanael Greene's fame to new heights. News of the battle traveled swiftly through the country. Everywhere people were soon to be found drinking to the health of General Greene, the commander in chief of the Southern army. Greene's aide, William Pierce, sent to Congress with the report on the battle, wrote that no man in the army stood as high with Congress as Greene, save only General Washington. Eutaw Springs, it was said, was one of the world's great battles. Some compared Greene with Julius Caesar and Congress voted him a gold medal. In Europe, according to Joseph Reed, Greene was looked upon as one of the world's great generals. Henry Knox wrote to John Adams in Holland that "the exalted talents of General Greene have been amply displayed in North and South Carolina—without an army, without Means, without anything he has performed Wonders." Adams, who once said that Greene lacked activity, wrote John Jay that Eutaw Springs was "quite as glorious for the American arms as the capture of Cornwallis."[26]

Although the British could hardly see the genius in Greene that the rest of the world acknowledged, they gave him credit nonetheless. Lieutenant Mackenzie wrote that he believed Greene's account of the battle of Eutaw Springs was false. The American general was, however, entitled to great praise for his matchless exertions; "the more he is beaten, the farther he advances in the end. He has been indefatigable in collecting troops, and leading them to be defeated," he wrote.[27]

The day after the battle of Eutaw Springs, Stewart broke camp and started slowly for Charleston. Many, too sick or too badly wounded to travel, were left behind. The same day, Greene dispatched Lee and Marion to hinder the British march and try to cut off reinforcements on the way from Charleston. The next day Greene followed, hoping that the army would find an opportunity to deal the enemy a final blow. Upon reaching Martin's Tavern, twelve miles from Monck's Corners, Greene learned that in spite of the exertions of Lee and Marion, the reinforcements had reached Stewart. As it was too dangerous to follow further, Greene retired to Eutaw Springs where after providing for the wounded, both American and British, he set out again for the High Hills of the Santee.

As Greene rode along the hot and dusty roads his mind often dwelt on the course of the war in Virginia. It was quite possible, he thought, that Cornwallis might yet try to escape by a march to Charleston. If he should try, Greene felt confident he could bag him on the way. But he would need more troops and he wrote to Colonel Shelby to hurry forward with his riflemen. If we have a chance to lock horns with Cornwallis, he told Shelby, "it will put a finishing stroke to the war in the Southern States."[28]

Greene crossed the Congaree at McCord's Ferry and the Wateree at Simmon's Ferry and brought his army to James's plantation at Statesborough, "a beautiful spot but now deserted," wrote William James in 1821. Greene may have had his headquarters (as tradition holds) amid the giant oaks at Thomas Hooper's spacious mansion, known as the Borough House.

A few days later when Greene heard that Washington and Rochambeau had Cornwallis hopelessly surrounded with an army twice the size of the all but beaten enemy, he thought Washington would surely let him have the 700 Maryland and Delaware recruits on their way to South Carolina. Greene's Virginians would be going home at the end of the year and without replacements he would be in a bad way should the enemy launch an offensive. But Washington ordered the Maryland and Delaware troops to join the grand army at Yorktown. Henry Lee, who had gone to Virginia to try to get reinforcements for the Southern army, tersely wrote Greene: "No troops coming on to you, but a perfect monopoly has taken place of men and supplies to fight a decreased small army."[29]

On September 21st Marion reported to Greene from his post near Nelson's Ferry that the British, after getting their wind, had returned to the posts they had abandoned after Eutaw Springs. Major Archibald McArthur was at Fair Lawn with 300 troops, several hundred others were at Dorchester and Monck's Corners, while the main body, numbering 2,000 troops, was with Major John Doyle (Stewart was recovering from a wound received at Eutaw Springs) at Mrs. Fludd's plantation on the Santee, two or three miles from Eutaw Springs. The enemy, Greene knew, had to protect his source of provisions. Moreover, the move was soothing to the wounded vanity of the British. That the movement was by no means prompted by a feeling of strength and confidence can be seen by Balfour's letter to Germain appealing for help to save the South from the relentless American general.[30]

At this time, Marion, who was sick with the fever though still managing to attend his duties, was desperately short of men. A new outbreak between the Whigs and the Tories on the upper

Pee Dee and the Deep River had caused many to leave Marion
to go home to protect their families. As Greene depended on
Marion to watch the crossings of the Santee and guard the roads
leading to the High Hills, he was deeply concerned about the
smallness of his force. In a month or so Greene would have some
riflemen to send him, but the only thing he could do at this time
was to have Governor Rutledge order all the indigo previously
seized from the Tories sold for raising and equipping horsemen
for Marion.

The Loyalist uprising in North Carolina was led by Hector Mc-
Neil whose men raided Hillsborough and carried off Governor
Burke, some members of the council, and several military officers, all of whom were taken to Charleston. Alexander Martin,
speaker of the house, was chosen governor in place of Burke
but the situation looked so ominous that Greene was ready to
send a detachment into North Carolina to help put down the
Tories and drive the British cavalry back to Wilmington.[31]

The North Carolina Whigs, however, soon got the upper hand
again. Hector McNeil was killed and the Tories fled to the
swamps or followed the British into Wilmington. Presently reports reached Greene that the Whigs were persecuting the
Tories in a barbarous manner. As this had a direct bearing upon
the course of the war, Greene did not hesitate to intercede. The
practice was not only inhuman, Greene told Governor Martin,
but alien to the interests of the state and nation. Persecuting
Tories without discrimination, he wrote, will make them desperate and convert them from feeble to firm and determined
enemies. This was the very policy the British wished the
Americans to pursue. It would afford the enemy with a pretense
for burning and plundering, an excuse for which they had long
been waiting. Furthermore, Greene thought that no state had a
right to adopt a policy which would endanger the welfare of
others. The British would not retaliate upon North Carolina alone
but upon any and all of the states. Lastly, Greene reminded
Martin that persecution always strengthens the cause it intends
to destroy. As the problem of the Loyalists was the same for all
the Southern states, Greene asked the governors to get together
to work out some common program. Governor Rutledge, he told
Martin, had issued a proclamation offering pardons to Tories who

would serve six months in the army, and the other states might well do the same.[32]

When Nathanael Greene and his army were not absorbed in the heat of campaigns or battles, it seemed that he must be forever patching up quarrels between his officers. Marion accused Colonel Horry of allowing his men to take horses from his militiamen at gunpoint. Greene pleaded with both men not to quarrel but to work together for the common cause. To Horry, he wrote, "The General is a good man. Few of us are without our faults, let his virtues veil his if any he has. Let neither pride, possession, or resentment hurry you with anything that may widen the breach between you. Your bleeding Country demands a sacrifice of little injuries and your own good sense will point out the best mode of avoiding them." Later he told Horry that he judged most differences originated from misunderstanding. "A generous and a liberal way of thinking is the best foundation for human happiness," he declared.[33]

Next Greene had to lecture Captain Egleston on charges raised by an inhabitant. When one of Egleston's young blades threatened to slice an ear off the man when he protested against taking his horse, Egleston, declared the man, insulted him when he entered a complaint. "You cannot treat the inhabitants with too much delicacy," Greene told Egleston, "nor should the least encouragement to be given to the soldiers, either to invade the property of the people, or offer them any personal insults.—This conduct it is which has made the British so very odious."[34]

Not long after the army settled down again on the High Hills of the Santee, Greene made a hurried trip to Charlotte. Ammunition was critically low and Marion's operations were stymied for lack of it. At Charlotte, Greene got ammunition moving toward the High Hills as well as some North Carolina recruits, among them two regiments of hardy mountaineers under Shelby and Sevier.

While Greene was at Charlotte, the army at the High Hills succumbed to an epidemic of dysentery and fever. In some companies everyone was sick and all the doctors in camp were stricken. Colonel Williams, whom Greene left in charge of the army, hoped that the "dreadful season" would soon end. With no alcohol or quinine in camp, the wounded suffered most. "Num-

bers of our brave fellows who have bled in the cause of their
country," wrote Greene, "have been eaten up with maggots, and
perish in that miserable situation." During the sickness the
Americans had some consolation in knowing that the enemy was
suffering fully as much from the epidemic and was powerless to
attack.[35]

By the time the news arrived of Cornwallis' surrender at
Yorktown on October 19th, the army at the High Hills of the
Santee was recovering from its siege of sickness. Reinforcements
and supplies, too, had arrived from North Carolina. Everyone
was exhilarated by the news from Virginia and the army staged
a great celebration with parading and firing of salutes. The troops
were given an extra ration of food and Greene and his officers
were entertained by the ladies from the neighboring plantations.

On November 1st the Pennsylvania line with a detachment of
artillery left Virginia under the command of Anthony Wayne
and headed for South Carolina. A little later the Maryland and
Delaware recruits that Washington had detained followed under
the command of St. Clair. This was good news for Greene but he
was sorry to learn that Admiral de Grasse found that his orders
did not admit of his sailing for Charleston. Greene was indeed
disappointed for with but a few British warships at Charleston,
it seemed to him that this was the time to strike from land and
sea and end the war in the South.

Pleasing as was the news of Cornwallis' surrender, the report
which elated Greene most was that Kitty, his wife, was on her
way south! Major Blodget, Greene's aide of former years,
was escorting Kitty to Philadelphia where Robert Burnet would
take over for the rest of the journey. Kitty planned to leave
Philadelphia in December but a great snowstorm and cold
weather intervened and forced her to wait until February before setting out in her two-horse phaeton for the High Hills of
the Santee.

With British power in the South fast ebbing away, Wilmington
was evacuated on November 14th and its garrison transported
to Charleston. With the arrival of the North Carolina mountaineers, Greene felt strong enough to move against the enemy
without waiting longer for the reinforcements from Virginia. He
was not sure but what the British might try to escape from

Charleston to Savannah by land, and he wanted to get his army west of the Edisto to block the way.

Preparatory to marching, Greene ordered Sumter to take post at Orangeburg where he was to collect provisions and ferret out the Tories hiding in the swamps. To Marion, Greene sent a corps of riflemen and orders to protect Greene's left flank when he started toward Orangeburg. The British had retired from their advanced position at Mrs. Fludd's to Monck's Corners, leaving the way open for Greene to get over the ferries and on to Orangeburg.[36]

Greene marched his army from the High Hills of the Santee on November 18th after waiting ten days for more ammunition to arrive. It took nearly three days for the troops, the artillery, and a long train of supply wagons to get over the Wateree at Simmon's Ferry. Colonel Williams, in charge of the crossing, stayed at Mrs. Huger's plantation where he was entertained by a bevy of ladies from Charleston. If Greene had not the hospitality of Mrs. Lazier, declared Williams, he surely would be envious.[37]

After crossing the Wateree, the army marched slowly down the west side of the river, crossed the Congaree at McCord's Ferry, and pitched camp on Buck Head Creek on or near Mrs. Motte's plantation. It was here that Greene learned that the riflemen sent to Marion would presently leave for home as they (as was the way with militiamen) counted their time from the date of leaving home. This was a severe blow, for Greene had marched on the assumption that they would stay until he was reinforced. He thereupon rushed an express to St. Clair directing him to leave his baggage and march as rapidly as possible.

Although General Alexander Leslie, who had arrived to take command in South Carolina, had twice as many troops as Greene, the British were greatly alarmed by his bold move into the lowlands. More pressure was put on the Tories to join the army and Negroes were enlisted for military duty and for work on the defenses.

While Greene was considering what to do with his depleted force, he was surprised to hear from Marion that the enemy, instead of advancing, had withdrawn from Monck's Corners to the vicinity of Goose Creek, fifteen miles from Charleston. This move left exposed the enemy's garrison at Dorchester, thirty miles north of Charleston on the Ashley. At once Greene decided he would strike. Leaving Colonel Williams to follow with the army toward Four Holes, he selected a "flying party" of horsemen and mounted infantry for a surprise attack on Dorchester. In all he took with him 400 men, consisting of Lee's Legion, the Continental cavalry, Hampton's South Carolina cavalry, and a detachment of Maryland and Delaware Continentals.

Unfortunately, Dorchester was warned of Greene's approach. On December 1st, after skirmishing, the British came out in force. A sharp battle ensued during which nearly fifty of the British were killed and the rest driven back into the town. There they reported that they had seen General Greene at which it was concluded that the whole rebel army had descended upon them. In great haste the British burned their stores, threw their cannon into the river, and fled in the night toward Charleston.[38]

In a few days Greene learned that the enemy had withdrawn from Goose Creek and all places beyond the Quarter House and Stono. Here, within five or six miles of Charleston, Leslie had all the men he could command working day and night on fortifications. The British were also busily stocking Johns Island with cattle and everywhere, to all appearances, battening down for what looked like the final siege.

With the enemy giving up all their posts and rushing into a narrow circle around Charleston, Greene boldly marched his army over the Four Holes Bridge to the Edisto. He was headed for Round O, west of the Pon Pon, and from the Four Holes the march led through interminable swamps, dark and forbidding beneath towering cypress trees. The army had seen many swamps in South Carolina but nothing to compare with those through which it now fought its way. "The black Jack bogs of Buffalo [Creek] are not more difficult to pass than the swamps we marched through yesterday," wrote Colonel Williams on December 6th. With the best of guides, the army, he said, could make but a few miles a day.

On December 7th the army finally reached Round O between the Pon Pon and the Ashepoo rivers where Greene set up camp on Roger Saunders' plantation. His army lay straight across the land communication between Charleston and Savannah. Charleston was only thirty-five miles away and the nearest British

outpost, that on Johns Island, but twenty-five miles from Round
O. For observation purposes and to protect the army against
surprise attack, Greene sent most of his cavalry with some light
troops over the Pon Pon toward Charleston. At Round O were
fewer than 1,000 men but this position was strong and difficult
for the enemy to reach. To the east, Marion guarded the region of
the Cooper River with headquarters at Monck's Corners. Sumter
remained at Orangeburg still hunting Tories, while Hampton's
cavalry patrolled the region below the Four Holes Bridge and
kept in touch with Marion and Sumter.[39]

This was the first time Greene's army had been far down in the
lowlands—the land of live oaks and grey Spanish moss. Along the
rivers they saw the large rice plantations, many now abandoned
or in a sad state of disrepair. Here, however, the army fattened in
"the luxury of the rice plantations" which besides rice, furnished
the troops with poultry, wild game, vegetables and fruit. Indeed,
one of Greene's reasons for moving to the Pon Pon was to take
advantage of its food supply. Greene's soldiers soon perceived
that there were other attractions, too. Lewis Morris made note
of the "fine girls, the patriotic fair of the country" and he was
not alone in taking an interest in the young ladies of the Pon Pon.
From the start, Greene made it clear that nothing was to be
taken from the inhabitants except by men authorized to make
purchases for the army. To Governor Rutledge he wrote asking
him to send warrants for the commissary as he wanted the
people to realize that civil government was being re-established
and they would have the protection of the law.[40]

Although Sumter at Orangeburg and Hampton at Four Holes
were preventing the Tories from escaping to Charleston, Greene
learned that fully 1,500 Loyalists were still hiding in the swamps
along the Edisto. This was disquieting and Greene instructed
Sumter to have the word spread through the swamps that the
Southern army would presently be heavily reinforced from the
North and that the British fate would soon be sealed in the
South. Therefore they should come out and give themselves up
and Greene would give them protection. Sumter did as told, and
as a result some came, but most of them were women and children, unable any longer to endure the swamps. Those that remained came out at night looking for food and other necessities,

some swimming in and out of their hideouts on logs. Sumter had Catawba Indians tracking them down but though some were caught, most of them were too elusive. Some of the Tories who gave themselves up enlisted in Sumter's corps and helped hunt for the others. In December, Sumter told Greene that he thought most of the Loyalists would give up if they could be convinced that they would not be harmed. Some, however, he was sure, would never submit until crushed with fire and sword.[41]

Concerned for the safety of the garrison at Savannah with Greene at Round O, General Leslie soon sent 500 troops to Georgia in small boats as he had no regular transports at Charleston. This was encouraging, thought Greene. Happy, too, was the thought that when St. Clair arrived with his 1,000 Continentals and 200 dragoons, his army would be about as large as Leslie's and he should be able to tighten the siege of Charleston. Already Lieutenant Colonel Lee was back from Virginia and in the field with his Legion between the Edisto and Charleston. Greene cautioned the impetuous Lee not to allow his men to mistreat the Negroes as they were the principal source of information about the enemy.[42]

While Greene was still congratulating himself on the bright prospect facing his army, word leaked through from Charleston that Leslie was expecting large reinforcements—perhaps as many as 5,000 troops—from New York and Ireland. If this were true, the Americans would be almost hopelessly outnumbered and perhaps driven from South Carolina, a sorry prospect after so much toil and bloodshed to regain the state. In desperation, Greene wrote for help to Rochambeau who was wintering in Virginia with part of his army. It looked, he told the French general, as if Leslie would soon have 8,000 troops to throw against Greene who with St. Clair's division, would barely have one-third as many. With his Virginia Continentals leaving for home the last of December, he also wrote to everyone who might have influence in Virginia. "For God's sake, my dear sir," he exclaimed to Colonel Davie, "give no sleep to your eyes, nor slumber to your eyelids, until you get the troops on the march."

But Rochambeau declined to send any troops save a corps of cavalry under de Lauzun. Washington explained to Greene that it was probably best not to weaken the army in Virginia as it was believed the enemy was planning to re-enter the state. Greene was unconvinced by Washington's reasoning or Rochambeau's excuses. The best way to defend Virginia, he declared, was to prevent the rise of British power again in South Carolina. Colonel Davie's reply, too, was discouraging. Virginia was war weary and apathetic and without money the recruiting officers were finding it impossible to raise troops for Greene's army.[43]

Fortunately, the rumor of heavy British reinforcements was false. The Cork fleet brought only sixty artillerymen and when the troops from New York arrived the corps proved to be only a contingent of 500. Greene breathed a sigh of relief when he heard the good news. "I have not been frightened," he wrote, "but as Doctor Skinner says, I have been confoundedly scared."

Early in January, Anthony Wayne arrived at camp with the Pennsylvania line. A little later St. Clair reached camp but he came with only the Maryland and Delaware troops as the Virginia officers had refused to march until they were paid for past services. Worse, still, St. Clair had felt compelled to march so fast that nearly half fell sick and had to be left behind. Not all could be retained in South Carolina either. On January 9th Greene sent a corps of dragoons, some artillery, and a body of South Carolina militia and state troops to Georgia with General Wayne. With the British still up along the Savannah and the Tories and Indians active, conditions in Georgia were most chaotic and the Whigs in desperate need of help. Wayne's orders were to drive the British into Savannah, force the enemy to evacuate the city, bring peace between the Whigs and the Tories, and protect the latter when they surrendered.[44]

In Georgia Wayne made steady progress against the enemy. At Ebenezer, where he set up headquarters, Wayne enlisted Tories as well as Whigs into his little army. Within a short time he drove the British from Mulberry Grove (soon to be Greene's plantation and home) and other points outside Savannah. He likewise broke the power of the Indians whose warriors when captured were held as hostages for the good behavior of their tribesmen.

At the time when Greene thought Leslie was to be heavily reinforced he had asked Governor Rutledge to lay before the assembly a proposition for raising 2,000 Negro troops for the

Southern army. When the report of the size of the British reinforcements proved false, Greene did not withdraw his request for Negro troops as white men everywhere were fearful of service in the deep South during the hot season. The natural strength of South Carolina, Greene said in his letter to Rutledge, "appears to consist much more in the blacks, than the whites. Could they be incorporated, and employed for its defense, it would afford you double security. That they would make good soldiers I have not the least doubt, and I am persuaded the State has it not in its power to give sufficient reinforcements without incorporating them." The Negroes should be given their freedom and treated "in all respects as other Soldiers," Greene felt.[45]

Sentiment in the army was strong for abolishing slavery in America. There was no time more proper for restoring rights to the Negroes, declared John Laurens, than when the country was fighting for liberty. "I have long deplored the wretched state of these men, and considered their history, the bloody wars excited in Africa to furnish America with Slaves—the groans of despairing multitudes toiling for the luxuries of mercilous tyrants," wrote Laurens to his father. Lewis Morris, Greene's aide and friend of Laurens, wrote of the South at this time: "I envy everything I see, except the poor unhappy blacks who, to the disgrace of human nature, are subject to every species of oppression while we are contending for the rights and liberties of mankind."[46]

In 1778 John Laurens had written to his father, then President of the Continental Congress, asking that 5,000 Negro troops be raised to give America superiority over the British in the South. The next year Congress resolved that 3,000 Negro soldiers should be raised in South Carolina and Georgia and their masters paid $1,000 per recruit as all were to be freed. South Carolina turned down the proposal declaring that the enemy would follow the example and enlist Negroes to the ruin of Southern agriculture.[47]

Although the argument used against the use of Negro troops earlier was no longer very convincing with the enemy confined to Charleston, prejudice against Negro troops was too strong in South Carolina and Greene's proposal was turned down. Failing to get Negro soldiers, Greene asked and obtained 500 Negroes for wagoners, laborers, and servants who were paid like regulars.

For some time Congress had been considering making one of

the generals Minister of War. Some members wanted Philip Schuyler while others spoke of Henry Knox, John Sullivan, or William Heath. Most everyone, however, agreed that Nathanael Greene was the best man for the office if he could be spared from the army. Sullivan and Schuyler were now in Congress as was Greene's old friend James Varnum, and they were all in favor of having Greene. Finally Congress undertook to sound out Greene only to find that he decidedly did not want the post. In a letter to Gouverneur Morris, Greene said that he was too much a stranger to the work of the war office, even if he had no other objections. But there were other reasons. Greene said he did not like politics nor did he relish the thought of working with an impotent Congress. "That Congress have not proper Powers, I see, I feel, and I lament," he wrote. As for political life, " the more I am in an army, the more I am acquainted with human nature [and] the less fond I am of political life." Greene envied, he declared, the anonymous people of the world who live as they please in pleasant obscurity. The soldier and politician, he thought, "die living, to live after death." After receiving Greene's answer, Congress appointed Benjamin Lincoln Minister of War.[48]

As weeks passed during the winter it became ever more apparent that a stalemate had come over the southern scene. The British were not strong enough to attempt anything against Greene, and the latter could not attack Charleston with any reasonable hope of success. In January, however, Greene undertook to drive the enemy from Johns Island as the South Carolina Legislature would soon convene at Jacksonborough and he did not care to have the British in a position to disrupt the meetings. On January 3rd the attempt was made with detachments under Lee and Laurens who were to cross at a place which could be forded at low tide and converge on Colonel Craig encamped on the island with 500 troops. Lee's corps got across but Laurens took a wrong road and arrived too late. Perceiving that Lee was in danger of being trapped, Greene, who had approached the fording place with the main army for support, recalled Lee while he could still get back. The British, nonetheless, were frightened and when Laurens crossed to the island a few days later to reconnoiter he found it evacuated.

On January 18th the South Carolina General Assembly met at Jacksonborough, a little town on the Pon Pon about ten miles south of Round O. Greene had persuaded Governor Rutledge to hold the meeting at Jacksonborough both to humiliate the British by convening within a few miles of Charleston and to impress the people of South Carolina with the strength of American arms. Two days prior to the meeting, Greene moved his army to Skirving's plantation, a few miles to the east of Jacksonborough and about thirty from Charleston. Greene was going to be sure that the South Carolina Legislature remained undisturbed during its deliberations.

Among those who attended the assembly were Francis Marion, Thomas Sumter and John Laurens. During the session much progress was made toward organizing the government and establishing law and order. On January 22nd the assembly turned to other business. It was resolved that Greene's achievements in the South entitled him to be ranked with the greatest of generals, ancient or modern. His name and fame, read the resolve, should be engraved on the hearts of every friend of America. Lieutenant Colonel John Laurens, who headed the committee, then proposed that the state of South Carolina give Greene an estate worth 10,000 guineas. The measure was at once adopted and a committee appointed to find a plantation for Greene among those confiscated by the state.[49] Greene thanked the assembly for its generosity and high opinion of his services. "No people," he wrote Reed, "ever felt a stronger impulse of gratitude." The grant, Greene told his friend, would help make up for his losses and give him a new start after the war.[50]

Not long after Johns Island fell to the Americans, Lee asked and obtained Greene's permission to leave the army. Lee was not well, a condition which doubtlessly contributed to his growing discontent. He told Greene that people did not appreciate him and insinuated that his commander was one of them. Some of Greene's reports, he said, distressed him "because some officers & corps were held out to the world with a lustre superior to others, who to say the least deserved equally." Lee, never liked by many outside his own Legion, was thought by some to lack bravery as he usually took care to keep himself out of the thick of battle. Greene looked upon this as an exercise of prudence and restraint on Lee's part and not lack of fortitude. Greene assured Lee that he had the highest regard for him and the Legion and had never intentionally minimized their great services. He pleaded with Lee not to leave the army for good, but even if he did, he would always be his friend. When Lee left in February never to return, Greene wrote to Congress: "I am more indebted to this officer than to any other for the advantages gained over the Enemy in the operations of last Campaign."[51]

As Greene had relieved himself of the touchy Hayne case by handing it over to Congress, he again entered into negotiations with the British for an exchange of prisoners. Unfortunately, new complications arose to embarrass the proceedings. Governor Burke, after being taken prisoner to Charleston, was paroled to James Island. On the island were many lawless persons, some of whom were old enemies of Burke who had fled to the British for protection. When some of the Tories tried to kill him without a show of interference by the British, Burke broke his parole and escaped. General Leslie demanded his return. Greene did not approve the breaking of paroles but under the circumstances he refused to order Burke to return. Back in North Carolina, Burke promised Greene he would not resume the governorship until arrangements were made for his exchange. But he did not keep his promise as North Carolina needed his leadership and the people urged him to resume as governor. Greene was not pleased. The decision hurt Burke's reputation and embarrassed Greene's negotiations with Leslie. However, as Burke was a useful man he did not labor the point but turned to consider what Burke could do for the Southern army.[52]

Greene's effort to negotiate an exchange was further complicated by action in North Carolina. Reports reached Leslie that North Carolina had condemned to death some Tory officers on charges of treason. Leslie countered by threatening to execute an equal number of North Carolina prisoners in his hands. Greene finally brought the issue to a close by persuading North Carolina to class all Tories who had borne arms as prisoners of war. As for the question of the confiscation of Tory property, Greene disclaimed any jurisdiction on the grounds that it was purely a state question. Leslie, however, in an effort to force South Carolina to cease confiscating the estates of Tories, sent troops out to seize all the slaves they could find belonging to Whigs. Exasperating as it was, Greene and Leslie finally came to terms and exchanges were soon made.[53]

For a time neither Greene nor Marion could understand the reason for Leslie's excursions which looked like preparations for an attack. But had they known the plight of the enemy they would not have been concerned for the safety of the American Army. Transports were coming and Leslie had orders from Clinton to turn over 2,000 troops for duty in the West Indies. On April 15th, Leslie laid his orders before his officers. All agreed that no more than 1,000 troops could be spared if Charleston were to be defended any longer. This was an unexpected development for Greene who would have been less surprised had the enemy reinforced Charleston in the belief that their foe was too weak to hold his gains in the South.[54] Cornwallis had surrendered six months before but it took Greene a long time to realize that the fight was all out of England and the war was really won.

CHAPTER SIXTEEN

The Dawn of Peace

The coming of peace posed new problems for soldiers of the Revolutionary Army long out of contact with civilian life. Greene hardly knew what to do or where to turn as he pondered over his future. Should he try to pick up where he left off or should he strike out on an entirely new path, perhaps as a southern planter? Thoughts like these continued to flit through his mind as he labored to keep his army together during the trying weeks following the close of hostilities. No doubt the perplexities of these days were quite as exhausting as the old campaigns.

Notwithstanding the favorable turn of events, occasioned by Leslie's loss of troops, Greene's army remained too small to attempt an assault upon Charleston. Furthermore, it was not likely that he would have more strength later as North Carolina and Virginia were making little headway in recruiting. But more serious than the size of his army during the winter of 1781-1782 was the wretched condition of the men's clothing and the shortage of blankets, tents and other essentials. During the winter practically nothing arrived from the North. "Indeed, I think it is pushing an army to desperation to leave them in such a situation," Greene wrote to General Lincoln.[1]

By April Greene estimated that one-third of the army was confined to quarters for want of enough clothing to cover nakedness. It would have been even worse had not a collection of clothing been made from among the nearly destitute people of South Carolina. Additional aid had also been found when Governor John Mathews and the South Carolina authorities secretly arranged for an exchange of rice for clothing through Charleston merchants. Greene did not allow this without first securing Secretary Lincoln's approval and he appointed Lee and Laurens to supervise the transaction to see that the enemy got no more rice than warranted by the terms of the agreement.[2]

Although the army could not actually starve in a land of rice
plantations, for long periods it was without meat, rum or salt.
Greene sent urgent letters to the governors of North Carolina and
Virginia asking them to send cattle to South Carolina where the
animals could be fattened on rice. Both states took steps to supply several thousand head but the work of rounding up the animals and driving them to the army went on so slowly that it was
late in the spring before they began to reach South Carolina.
Meanwhile, Governor Mathews managed, in spite of the ravages
of war, to find some cattle for Greene's army. The need for meat
was so great that usually the animals were slaughtered without
waiting for them to be fattened. One story was that a soldier
upon meeting a friend coming from the slaughtering pens inquired
how the cattle were doing that morning. The friend replied "that
it took two men to hold up the creature until the butcher knocked
it down." Upon hearing this the first soldier asked "why didn't
he knock it down as it lay?"

Before Greene was able to relieve his naked and hungry troops,
the army was threatened by mutiny and desertion. Greene found
it hard to punish men driven to desperation, but discipline had
to be maintained if the army were to survive. On April 22nd
Greene wrote to Benjamin Harrison: "All the public stores are
delayed on the road. Our army literally naked, badly fed, and
altogether without spirits. Certainly this is pushing an army to
desperation. Mutiny appears in many forms."[3] Greene knew that
men in the Pennsylvania line were inciting mutiny among the
Marylanders who had not been paid in two years. He waited
his chance to catch some of the ringleaders in the act. They were
the men, he knew, who had engineered the mutiny at Morristown where the troops in January, 1781, had defied their officers,
killed some of them, and marched off to Philadelphia to demand
their pay. None of the mutineers were punished and the Pennsylvania line, consisting mostly of foreigners recruited in Philadelphia, found that demands could be satisfied by mutiny when
all else failed. On the way south they tried it again but this time
Wayne nipped the mutiny in the bud by summarily executing the
ringleaders.

Like Wayne, Greene only waited long enough to catch some
of the plotters red-handed. The moment came when they were

discovered plotting to turn Greene and their officers over to the enemy if their demands were not met by an appointed time. "It was talked pretty freely among the men," explained Greene, "that if pay and clothing did not arrive by such a day they would march their officers to Dorchester and allow them only a few days more before they would deliver them up to the enemy unless their grievances were not redressed."[4]

One ringleader, a Sergeant Gornell of the Pennsylvania line, "was pitched upon—as one who used those mutinous expressions."[5] He had been one of the plotters at Morristown, and Greene had no qualms about making an example of him. He was hanged before the whole army. But instead of executing the others, he sent them under guard to work in the laboratory at Salisbury making cartridges. This had a better effect on the army than hanging, Greene declared. Soldiers who knew they could not be hanged on suspicion became aware that they could be sent to the laboratories, the disgrace of which was "little less than death." Two months after, Greene told Reed that there was "not a murmur or complaint uttered in the army," so effective had been the measures taken. If something like this had been done in New Jersey at the first outbreak the spirit of mutiny would have been crushed at the outset, Greene thought.[6]

During the spring of 1782, Greene had more correspondence with Robert Morris regarding the latter's plan for taxing the states for the support of the war. Greene was skeptical about its application in the South, ravaged by war and with civil government barely re-established. There were still thousands of Loyalists hiding in this vast region and until a reconciliation with these people could be made, conditions would remain chaotic. But Robert Morris' plan was something to grab at and Greene let nothing go by which might offer relief. Writing to Governor Burke, Greene said he would try to make contracts with merchants for the delivery of supplies to the army if his state would levy taxes according to Morris' plan. If the states, however, did not cooperate by raising the taxes, all might yet be lost in the South after so much bloodshed and expenditure, warned Greene.[7]

Although Greene's cares were never heavier than in the spring of 1782, the thought that Kitty was on her way to South Carolina and should soon arrive made it easier to bear his daily burdens. After the big snowstorm had forced Kitty to change her plans for leaving Philadelphia in December, she continued on with the Pettits until a thaw in January made it possible to start for the South. George, age seven, was left with the Pettits to continue his schooling. Soon after, however, Pettit sent George to Princeton, believing he would be better off if tutored by Dr. Witherspoon and away from the corrupting influences of the city.

Accompanied by Major Burnet and a Mrs. Kingston, Kitty Greene had a triumphant journey through the South. In Virginia she was waited on and admired wherever she went. Her only disappointment was in not seeing General Rochambeau whom she had met in Rhode Island. Early in March Kitty reached Salisbury where Otho H. Williams, on his way home because of ill health, entertained the company with the news from camp. Not long after that Kitty was ill for awhile. But she was soon on her way again and late in March reached the High Hills of the Santee where she was warmly received by the many friends Greene had made there. Crossing the Wateree at the ferry, Kitty's driver took the road to McCord's Ferry. Arriving at Colonel Thompson's plantation in her sturdy phaeton, Kitty rested a few days before starting out on the last lap of her long journey.

Hearing that Kitty would arrive that day, Nathanael mounted his horse on the morning of April 5th and set out with aides and a guard to meet her. After riding ten or twelve miles, about noon he saw her phaeton in the distance and setting spurs to his horse, came galloping down the road to clasp his wife in his arms. After the tender greeting Nathanael got into the carriage and rode back to camp with Kitty. He still wore the cockade that Mrs. McDougall had given him at West Point before starting out for the South. Although her husband seemed his old cheerful self, Kitty was struck by how much the war in the South had aged him. It was a joyful party, however, which rode into headquarters at a plantation house near Bacon's Bridge that evening. From this time on, Kitty Greene, like Martha Washington in the North, would be the first lady of the South. Her coming was a morale builder for the whole Southland and a symbol of the advent of peace to a devastated land.[8]

About the time Kitty arrived, Greene heard that General Leslie was plotting to take him prisoner. Although warned to be on his guard, Greene was not careful enough. Leslie, as it happened, persuaded a lady living near the Ashley River to invite the Greenes to dinner. When her invitation was accepted she notified the British, but fortunately some friends in Charleston heard of what was afoot in time to warn him. Greene and Kitty had arrived at the plantation and were about to sit down to dinner when a messenger delivered him the warning. Greene and his party left at once and within twenty minutes the house was surrounded by a troop of British dragoons.[9]

In the spring of 1782 North Carolina and Georgia followed the example of South Carolina by making Greene a gift in appreciation of his services to the South. North Carolina voted him 25,000 acres along the Cumberland River or its branches. Finally laid out on the south side of Duck Creek, a branch of the Tennessee, the land brought handsome returns to Greene's grandchildren, thirty or more years after he was gone. Though Greene himself would never realize anything from his North Carolina grant, the estate voted him by Georgia became his home for a few short months before his death. Mulberry Grove, the plantation appropriated by Georgia, comprised 2,000 acres of some of the best rice lands of the South. Once the proud possession of the Loyalist John Graham, a former governor of Georgia, the plantation, with its elegant house and gorgeous gardens, was somewhat run-down though still valued at 7,000 guineas.[10]

Naturally, Nathanael Greene was criticized by some for accepting such lavish gifts from the Southern states. Greene, however, was not the only beneficiary of Southern generosity as Anthony Wayne was soon the recipient of an estate not far from Mulberry Grove, Furthermore, Greene did not allow the grants to influence his decisions as commander in chief. Before the South Carolina grant was confirmed by a deed he found cause to differ rather violently with its authorities over the question of impressment and other issues. His friends, indeed, called it madness to jeopardize his grant by taking so firm a stand against the South Carolina Legislature. In Philadelphia, Pettit thought Greene entitled to all his benefactors were pleased to give him and did not let the opportunity pass to joke about it. As South Carolina had given Greene an estate worth 10,000 guineas and

Virginia had given him a pair of horses, North Carolina, he thought, could not do less than give him a carriage and Georgia a "barrel of Tar to grease the wheels."[11]

With negotiations for peace under way in Paris, in May General Leslie sent Greene a proposal for a truce. There was no need, he thought, for the shedding of more blood and with a few concessions by both sides the two armies could be better cared for until Charleston was evacuated. Leslie wanted, especially, Greene's permission to collect provisions and forage along the lower Santee. But Greene refused. Although there were rumors of peace, he had heard nothing definite. Anyhow, he felt that he could not agree to a truce without the consent of Congress. To Congress Greene made known that he thought peace was not near and in his opinion Great Britain was trying to break up the alliance between France and America after which the British would return with fire and sword. Greene had heard of Admiral de Grasse's defeat by Admiral Rodney, and he could not believe England would make peace after winning a great naval victory. Rodney's victory, in fact, might enable the British to send reinforcements to Charleston, thought Greene. Washington entertained the same fears and wrote that he only hoped Greene could hold out in the South until more reinforcements arrived.[12]

Congress approved of Greene's declining to enter into a truce with General Leslie. The states, however, continued to view matters complacently. Few reinforcements came to Greene and many troops left for home, their time having expired. With all the states dragging their feet, Greene sent appeal after appeal for troops. At no time did the states actually turn him down but it became ever more clear that they had no intention of filling their quotas. In desperation, Greene asked Georgia to raise a regiment of Negroes but he might as well have saved himself the effort.

Greene's army camped at Round O and at Skirving's plantation from December, 1781 to March, 1782. Then, after the legislature had adjourned, Greene moved the army to John Waring's plantation in a well-stocked neighborhood near Bacon's Bridge on the Ashley River near Dorchester. This was a strong position and it was easier to move the troops than transport provisions. Here, as at the former campsites, the army built huts of logs and bark as the number of tents available was far from enough to cover the troops. In July, with sickness again ravaging the army, Greene moved his camp to Cattel's plantation at Ashley Hill about six miles south of Dorchester on the south side of the river. Here was good water, dry ground and what in general appeared to be the best campsite in the area.

Kosciuszko tells an amusing story of the time the army moved to Bacon's Bridge. At an inn five or six "pretty" girls urged him to draw their pictures. When he answered that it would be impossible to make them beautiful, they chased him all over the place with shovels, firetongs, and firehooks. Finally they cornered him and made him draw their pictures whereupon they showered him with kisses. In an effort to free himself from their embraces, Kosciuszko undertook to draw their pictures again. This time before he had finished the girls were all drunk, thus allowing him to make his escape.

As the weeks passed, Greene lost officers as well as privates. Many, such as Colonel Howard, went home because of wounds received at Eutaw Springs. More recently Henry Lee had left, then Otho Williams. Next St. Clair found reason to go back to Pennsylvania. So far he had kept his aides together and in a letter to Williams he gave some hints on how they were faring. Nat Pendleton and William Pierce were as polite as ever. Lewis Morris was as careless as ever. Robert Burnet was as cross as ever, and Thomas Shurbrick was as independent as ever. William Washington, paroled by the British and now married to Jane Elliott, the owner of a spacious plantation not far from camp, was indeed doing fine.[13]

As there was little to do but watch Charleston, the officers as well as the men were harder than ever to manage. Greene had the most trouble with Lee's Legion. The officers, especially John and Michael Rudolph, objected to the appointment of John Laurens to succeed Lee. Bringing in an outsider instead of elevating the senior officer in the Legion, who happened to be John Rudolph, was considered a slight by all the officers. It was about this time, too, when the officers of the Legion, led by the Rudolphs, threatened to resign if Greene insisted on using the infantry and horse separately and with any unit of the army. Hoping to placate the Legion, Greene put Colonel Laurens, an infantry officer, in charge of the Legion infantry and Lieutenant Colonel George Baylor in command of the cavalry. But this did not please them either. When the officers made a formal protest against using the infantry and horse separately Greene argued with them for two hours, and then, to their astonishment, accepted their resignations. If need be, he said, he would have taken the resignations of all the officers in the army rather than give in on the vital principle that the commander in chief had the right to use any unit as he saw fit. A little later Greene reinstated the officers with the understanding that the dispute would be placed before Congress. When it answered, Congress, of course, agreed thoroughly with Greene and that ended the dispute.[14]

Not many days after Greene turned down Leslie's offer for a truce, he learned that Sir Guy Carleton had arrived to take over the command of the British Army from Clinton. He heard, too, that Lord North's Ministry had fallen and that the party demanding peace with America had come to power. Soon after that he learned from his informers in Charleston that Leslie had orders from Carleton to evacuate Savannah and St. Augustine. He did not know, however, that the garrisons of those towns were ordered to New York and were not coming to Charleston. Carleton was a better general than Clinton and Greene was taking no chances regardless of peace talks. To Wayne he sent orders to march his troops to South Carolina immediately upon the evacuation of Savannah. He also advised Wayne to dispatch a troop of Georgians to Florida to take possession of St. Augustine before the Spanish arrived. If only to safeguard the boundary of Georgia, it would be a useful move, he wrote. Wayne agreed and wrote that he would take St. Augustine in the name of the United States as soon as the British were gone. An attempt on St. Augustine, however, was never made.[15]

While the main army remained inactive, Marion's corps was defeated in February by a detachment from Charleston under Colonel Benjamin Thompson (later to win fame as Count Rumford of Bavaria). At the time Marion was attending the meeting of the legislature and his troops were left in charge of Colonel Horry. Greene sent Laurens to try to cut off the British but by the time he arrived in the area they had retired.

In May Greene found it necessary to call upon Marion and all the South Carolina militia to join him to make up for the loss of several hundred North Carolina militia and other troops who were going home. Marion, however, had no sooner started for the Ashley than the Tories of the Little Pee Dee under Major Ganey took up arms again. Greene thereupon ordered Marion to turn about and march against the Tories. This he did with great success. On July 8th he wrote Greene that he had just returned from the Pee Dee, having settled the Tory problem in that quarter once and for all. He had left 150 men to "dig out" the Tories who still remained in the swamps. Those who had given up and wanted to leave with the British were going to be given the opportunity, said the government of South Carolina with Greene's concurrence. Not a few of the Loyalists seized the opportunity to join Marion's militia, the safest place for them until passions subsided. These Marion soon found to be his best fighters as they knew the British would shoot them as traitors if they were captured.

Having failed to get a truce, Leslie was soon compelled to send out large foraging expeditions. Greene was warned that Leslie would send a fleet of small vessels to the Pee Dee to plunder the plantations and perhaps Georgetown. Marion was alerted and in a short time he arrived at Georgetown. But the British stayed down the river, contenting themselves with raiding the rice plantations from which they took more than 600 barrels of rice. Lieutenant Denny, one of Greene's soldiers sent with a party to Georgetown to get a load of rum from Marion, noted in his diary that the countryside along the way was nearly deserted. At one place, he wrote, in the road they shot a twelve foot alligator. The few people they met looked worn and dejected. Most of them, however, fled at the sight of the soldiers. The plantations were all run down as nearly all the Negroes had been seized and taken to Charleston.

On August 2nd General Leslie received orders for the evacuation of Charleston as soon as ships could arrive. In a day or two the news was brought to Greene. Soon Leslie confirmed the report by asking again for a truce as the city would soon be evacuated. Again Greene refused without permission from Congress. Greene was still afraid the British would reverse themselves and return to the attack throughout America. The country, he thought, should take no chances and not relax until the enemy was gone. He, at least, was not going to risk his reputation on British promises or peace moves. If Leslie needed food badly enough, he could surrender.

Greene's refusal to make a truce was surprising to Leslie who was entirely honest in desiring to avoid further suffering. Having no alternative, Leslie again sent out a large foraging expedition— this time to the plantations along the Combahee River. Greene sent General Gist, who had joined him from Maryland, to do what he could to frustrate the enemy. In spite of all, however, the British collected 300 barrels of rice and not a few head of cattle. During the maneuver Gist and most of his men, after running out of quinine, came down with the fever. What grieved Greene most, however, was the death of the talented Lieutenant Colonel John Laurens in the Combahee operations. Laurens lost his life in an unwise skirmish with the enemy, a thing Greene had often warned him against as he was too daring and covetous of military glory. In John Laurens, the South lost a man of great promise.[16]

With talk of peace in the air, Nathanael Greene's mind often turned upon what he would do after the war. It seemed ages since he had been a businessman and he hardly knew how or where to begin life over again as a civilian. There would be opportunities in the South after the war, he knew, and already he had written to his brother Christopher about opening a trade with Charleston. For himself, more and more he liked the thought of becoming a rice planter. South Carolina had purchased the large Boone Barony on the Edisto for him which with Mulberry Grove would make him a big planter. The value of Mulberry Grove had turned out to be a little over £7,000 and as Georgia had appropriated but £5,000, Greene asked Richard Howley, a commissioner in charge of the purchase, if the state cared to make an additional grant so that he would receive the property free of any incumbrance. Georgia graciously complied with his wish and deeded the whole property to him. Still, the cost of getting started as a rice planter would be great as neither property had enough slaves. Greene knew that most of his investments in the North were of little value. Whether he could get the money or credit necessary to put his plantations into operation remained for the future to decide.[17]

Whatever the future held, it would be a joyful day when Greene was united with his whole family. His elder children, George and Martha, would remember their father, but to the little ones, Cornelia and Nathanael, he would be a complete stranger. In August Greene wrote to Dr. John Witherspoon thanking him for taking care of George and seeing to his schooling. The fond father in Greene compelled him to ask Witherspoon to give Mr. Smith, one of the masters at Princeton, some hints about George's temperament. George, said Nathanael, was of a gentle nature and could not bear severity. Some temperaments wrote Greene, require severity on occasions while with others mildness is essential.

Nathanael Greene assured Dr. Witherspoon that he admired him more than any educator in America. He remembered well the conversation they had at New Windsor when Witherspoon visited camp as a member of a committee from Congress. Both had agreed, he recalled, that a government which did not have a regard for private property would have no respect for liberty. Greene thought that American leaders should keep this well in mind as the war had loosened the fibers of law and morality upon which civilization was founded.[18]

During the summer of 1782, though the days were very hot and humid and the "sickly season" was upon the land, Greene found little time for relaxation. He was at his desk from sunrise until late at night, only taking time out for eating and taking his quinine, he told Charles Pettit. One day during a violent thunder storm a tremendous bolt of lightning crashed into the house in which Nathanael and Kitty were living but no one was harmed.

By August the fever was spreading rapidly in camp. "The camp is thin, the hospitals crowded, and deaths are so frequent that funeral services" are omitted, wrote Lieutenant Denny in his diary. Although most persons recovered from the illness, 1782 became the sickliest season in thirty years in South Carolina and by November 200 soldiers had died. So far Greene was keeping well but Kitty showed signs of succumbing to the fever in August. With some of his aides and officers down with the fever, Greene applied to General Leslie for permission for his wife and the officers to go to Kiawah Island for their health. Leslie kindly consented to their going.

A fair-sized reef facing the ocean not far from Charleston, Kiawah was a beautiful island covered with scrub oak intermixed with tall palmettoes. The woods abounded with deer and the shores were dotted with wild fowl. Nat Pendleton, Lewis Morris, and Dr. Johnson, all affected with the fever, accompanied Kitty and her companion, a Miss Fenwick, to Kiawah. With them went books, cards and a backgammon table to help pass the time away. At their lodging on the island they fared sumptuously on a great variety of fine food including fish, crabs and wild fowl as well as oranges, figs and other fruit apparently grown on the island. Surf bathing as well as riding along the sandy beach was found enjoyable and invigorating.

Before long William Washington, his wife Jane, William Pierce and others joined the party on Kiawah Island. On September 14th Pierce wrote Greene that all were feeling better or had recovered thanks to the sea air and liberal doses of "bark." Colonel Washington, he reported, looked "again like the Hercules of the Day, His dear Partner is by his side, and cherishes him with Smiles. Mrs. Greene who is the very picture of health, sits, observes, and laughs at all about her." Nat Pendleton was amused to see Jane making cigars for her William to smoke. "I wish," he declared, "they would employ themselves more in this way, and less in kissing."

Late in September, accompanied by Nat Pendleton and Lewis Morris, Kitty returned to headquarters at Ashley Hill. She had heard that Nathanael had succumbed to the fever and she had hurried back to take care of him. When she arrived, however, she found him already recovering after a very violent attack of the sickness. Though weak and with his eyes infected again, Greene was back at his desk at intervals during the day much to Kitty's disapproval. Anthony Wayne was also down with the fever which he dreaded more than the devil or British bullets. For a delicacy, Pierce, who had stayed at Kiawah, sent Greene two "palmeto cabbages" with instructions to boil them in clear water until soft and serve in slices with vinegar, butter and pepper.[19] As Nat Pendleton's fever came back and Kitty seemed again on the verge of getting it, both returned in October to Kiawah where they stayed until cold weather put an end to the disease on the mainland.[19]

Transports for the evacuation of Charleston began to arrive in the harbor after the first of October. Already the British had taken over 1,000 Tories from Georgia to Florida, New York and the West Indies. Toward the last of October, 1,000 South Carolina Tories with 2,000 slaves set sail from Charleston to make a home in Florida. One need not wish them a greater punishment than banishment to Florida, wrote Greene. Those that had gone there from Georgia were in a most deplorable condition, in want of food and shelter and wandering about in search of relief from their misery. Greene wished that America could forgive and forget and let her erring sons stay in the land but the voice of humanity was too weak, he told his friend George Weedon.[20]

Desertion from the British Army in Charleston averaged thirty a week. Many more would have escaped but for the constant patrolling of Charleston Neck by Leslie's corps of Negro dragoons. After the patrol cut up two Hessians trying to get away, practically all the German troops would have taken leave of the British if they could have escaped. Not only deserters but whole families, "battered and starved," were coming out of the city to throw themselves upon the mercy of American troops guarding the roads. Not having the facilities to care for them and fearing for their lives should they attempt to return to their former homes, Greene ordered all to be sent back into the city.[21]

Came the 13th of December and all the Loyalists who chose to leave were on transports in Charleston harbor. On other ships were thousands of Negroes from the plantations of both Tories and Whigs. Other ships were waiting at the docks to receive the British troops. Not wishing to be charged with firing the city should someone put a torch to it, Leslie had asked Greene to agree to a peaceful evacuation. Greene acquiesced and it was arranged that the incoming Americans would march at a distance of 200 yards behind the retiring British who would be allowed to embark undisturbed.

On the morning of December 14th one regiment after another of the British marched to Gadsden's dock and filed into the waiting transports. At about 11 o'clock Leslie's rear guard started marching down the King's road to the music of fife and drum.

Behind them followed Anthony Wayne with a corps of light infantry, artillery and dragoons. As the Americans advanced with music playing and colors flying, hardly a soul turned out to greet them. All the windows and doors were closed and bolted and except for the British up ahead the city seemed deserted. As agreed, Wayne kept away from the docks until all the British were aboard and the ships had sailed out into the harbor.

At about three in the afternoon, General Greene and Governor Mathews led a column of Continental troops followed by a throng of citizens into the city. General Gist and General Moultrie, the latter long a prisoner in Charleston, rode just behind them. Kitty rode in her carriage with other ladies of prominence. Governor Mathews took over the governor's mansion with a wagon load of records and state papers long in hiding during the years of British occupancy of Charleston. Greene made his headquarters at John Rutledge's elegant house on the invitation of the Rutledges who were pleased to have the Greenes as their guests.

By the third day after the Americans took over Charleston, people began to make an appearance. Within a week the city was bustling with activity with inhabitants from all over the state "flocking down like jews to the temple," as Greene said. The city was not as large or pretentious as Greene had imagined, yet there were not a few handsome buildings, he thought. Not many days after Greene had established himself at the Rutledges he came home to the find the room he used as headquarters on fire. After giving the alarm, he fought the flames until help arrived and the fire was extinguished. Many of Greene's books were ruined, among them his *Journals of the Continental Congress* which he asked Secretary Lincoln to replace if possible.

Kitty liked Charleston, and she was no sooner there than she was making plans for a grand ball to celebrate its freedom. Presently the city was the scene of gay festivities with Kitty the center of attraction. Greene, busy most of the time from morning until late at night, was willing to leave social affairs to Kitty. She was extremely happy and that was all that mattered to Nathanael. "Her flowing tongue and cheerful countenance," he wrote to Pettit, "quite triumphs over my grave face. I bear it with great philosophy as I gain on one hand what I lose on the other."[22]

When word of the evacuation reached Philadelphia, Congress appointed a committee to thank Greene and the Southern army. Dr. David Ramsay, a distinguished delegate from South Carolina, "went into lavish praises of G'l Greene, and threw out the idea of making him a Lieutenant General." But the war was ending and some members thought this was "somewhat singular and unnecessary," whereupon Ramsay withdrew his motion.[23]

Pleasing as were the reports of the praise he was receiving in the North, Greene seemed to get fully as much pleasure out of hearing from such old friends as Sammy Ward and David Howell whom he had not heard from in years. Sammy had risen to become a lieutenant colonel and had married Phoebe Greene, a daughter of Kitty's uncle, Governor William Greene. Sammy, Greene assured himself, would still have an ear as in the old days for a bit of philosophizing. "The more I am acquainted with this world," Nathanael wrote to Sammy, "the more I am convinced that the virtuous are only happy." David Howell, who used to visit Coventry in Greene's bachelor days, was now in Congress and doing his best to frustrate every attempt to strengthen the union. In political views no two men could be farther apart in 1782 than Nathanael Greene and David Howell.

In November Congress resolved that Greene should stay in South Carolina with what was left of his army until peace was ratified. Greene, naturally, was entirely in accord with this resolve. He was, in fact, in favor of sending part of the Northern army against Canada if New York were evacuated before peace was made. An American force in possession of Canada, he knew, would give Benjamin Franklin something tangible to back up his claims for the St. Lawrence Valley at the peace table in Paris.[24]

Late in December Greene ordered the 1,400 troops remaining in the Continental army under his command to James Island near Charleston where they were to set up winter quarters. James Island was a good site for the camp, being dry, sandy and well supplied with good water. The troops cleared a large area and used the brush to build a high barrier around the camp. Fortunately, the weather during the winter was so mild that the soldiers seldom needed a fire to keep warm. Though from the first there was little beef for the army, the men were content for awhile by adding fish, oysters, crabs and wild fowl to their diet.

In January Greene made a trip to Savannah to see Governor Hall. This was his second visit to Georgia as he had made a short one to Augusta to see Wayne and the Georgia Legislature before Savannah fell. After examining the fortifications which Carleton had ordered to be left standing, Greene decided that they were not worth saving as the city could not be defended against a strong fleet. Greene left Savannah thinking perhaps his visit had been of some value to the state and nation. He had strongly urged Governor Hall to do all in his power to get Georgia to levy the five per cent tax for the United States treasury. Each state, no matter how poor, must bear its share of the burden if the nation were to survive, Greene told his friends in Georgia.[25]

Not long after Greene returned to Charleston the South Carolina Legislature repealed its five per cent impost for the United States upon which Greene was relying for paying for provisions when a contract was negotiated. Thoroughly disappointed, he sent a protest to the governor and assembly in which he said that if the states would not raise money, the army must be disbanded and the confederation in turn would soon dissolve.[26]

To Greene's great surprise, he found that the South Carolina authorities were much offended by his letter which they considered dictatorial in tone and disrespectful of civil powers. Having had no desire to offend anyone, Greene immediately wrote Governor Benjamin Guerard disclaiming any thought of invading the rights of the government. All he had tried to do was to furnish information and if his "expressions were less guarded than might have been expected," it proceeded from a belief that he had and merited the confidence of the good people of South Carolina. Greene, in truth, was not without sympathy for South Carolina. In a letter to Washington, he explained that the state felt neglected by Congress. It had probably suffered more than any state in the union and had received but little help in its long struggle with the enemy.

Nathanael Greene's trouble with the South Carolina authorities was soon followed by another of a more serious nature. In April a British officer, Captain Kerr, came to Charleston under a flag of truce from St. Augustine and with him were two Loyalists inimical to the people of South Carolina. By order of Governor Guerard the sheriff of Charleston jailed all three, regardless of their flag of truce. Greene, of course, considered the men under his protection and at once ordered them to be released. "The Articles of Confederation," Greene told Guerard, "vests in Congress the sole power in all matters relating to War and Peace." Consequently, Guerard was infringing upon "the sovereign Authority of the United States," declared Greene.

The Governor answered Greene by insisting that his interpretation of the Articles of Confederation was "very improper and alarming." With no enemy within the borders of South Carolina, flags of truce, Guerard maintained, became internal affairs, subject to the sovereign power of the people of South Carolina. Guerard told Greene that he was startled by his calling the arrest an insult to himself as commander of the army.

Apparently Greene's dander was up for he did not mince words in replying to the Governor's letter: "If it is the intention of this state to adhere to the terms of the Union, and you mean to govern yourself upon the principles of the Confederation, my Letters can neither alarm nor offend you." Furthermore, Guerard might profit, wrote Greene, by studying the Articles of Confederation. Greene admitted that he did not know all that went on when Rutledge and Mathews were governors, but if they assumed the authority over flags of truce, they were in error. It was as illegal for the sheriff to seize men under a flag, Greene told Guerard, as to break into the house of an ambassador.

Greene put his dispute with Governor Guerard before a council of war consisting of Wayne, Gist, Kosciuszko and others. The council agreed that Greene was altogether in the right. Greene thereupon sent the proceedings of the council to Guerard with some rather acid comments. The Governor, Greene charged, meant to "treat with contempt those acting under the authority of Congress, in order to prove you owe no subordination" to that body. The dispute was reaching the breaking point. Greene flatly declared he would not tolerate any longer the flouting of his authority. None but a "lunatick," explained Greene, would think of interfering with the army in this way.[27]

Guerard and his council decided that they would not push

matters any further with a man who apparently would not hesitate, if need be, to use his army to uphold the rights of the United
States. He therefore ordered the prisoners to be released with
the understanding that they would leave town in forty-eight
hours. Not wishing to carry the dispute farther, Greene sent the
men back to Florida soon after they were released.[28] Greene took
great pains to apologize to Governor Patrick Tonyn of Florida
for the treatment received by the men under the flag of truce.
He should have given them full protection, he told the governor,
but he wanted to avoid a showdown with South Carolina, if
possible, as such encounters tended to weaken further the little
attachment the state had for the Union.[29]

However, Greene did not let his dispute with the Governor
and Council of South Carolina rest here. He sent all the papers
relating to the controversy to Secretary Lincoln with a request
that they be presented to Congress. "It is a matter," he wrote,
"which concerns their sovereignty which I as their representative
in my military standing did not think myself at liberty to give up
or even be silent upon." To Joseph Reed, Greene wrote that he
thought the South was taking the road to complete separation
from the Union. The South, he believed, was more suited to a
monarchy than to the republican form of government upon
which America had embarked.[30]

Greene's disputes with South Carolina, although annoying and
perhaps even jeopardizing his gift from the state, worried him
far less than troubles that suddenly burst upon him from another
quarter. The storm broke over alleged speculation with government funds on the part of Greene. This was, indeed, the most
painful and perilous episode of his whole life. The story is long
and involved. With winter coming on in 1782, the clothing
situation once again threatened to break up the army. Most of the
shipments received during the summer from the North had gone
to clothe regiments going home as they had to have protection
during their long march. Apparently Greene could expect no more
from the North before winter set in and in South Carolina only
the merchants in Charleston had any clothing for sale.

While Greene was pondering what to do for his ragged army,
John Banks who had been in Charleston with a flag of truce
issued by Colonel Lushington, a militia officer at Georgetown,

came to camp and offered to furnish the army with clothing on very favorable terms. If Greene could give him a sizable sum in specie, he could get the goods at savings of up to 30 per cent, he declared. It was about this time that Greene learned that George Abbott Hall, Robert Morris' secret agent in the South, had money for use of the army. Morris had instructed Hall not to part with any of it except at times when the army must have it or suffer certain ruin. Greene called Hall and apparently against his will compelled him to give him 1,200 guineas. This sum, with bills for $8,000 on Robert Morris, Greene turned over to Banks who was soon sending shipments of clothing out of Charleston to the American Army. In this way, as General Wayne said, the troops were better clothed than at any time since Greene took over the Southern command.[31]

In January after the evacuation of Charleston, the army ran very low on provisions. South Carolina, which previously had allowed Greene to impress provisions, passed a law prohibiting it after January 10th. Greene had the choice of defying South Carolina, disbanding the army or, if possible, securing some other means of supplying the army. For several weeks he had been endeavoring to make a contract for provisioning the army but none but John Banks would make any offer whatsoever. Banks offered to provision the army at the rate of 13¼ pence per ration. He believed this was not too high as he would have to accept bills on Robert Morris for payment and no one knew when or how the United States would get the money to satisfy the demands. Greene had opened the contract on the strength of South Carolina's having passed the five per cent duty for the United States, but the legislature had turned about and repealed the law. Colonel Carrington, in charge of making the contract, left it open for three months and when no one but Banks cared to supply the army on the credit of the United States, Greene put the question of what to do before the South Carolina Legislature. Banks, meanwhile, had come down to about 11 pence per ration and as Hugh Rutledge, Speaker of the House, reported that the legislature favored accepting the terms, Greene went ahead and executed the contract.

Soon Banks found that his credit had run out with the merchants and unless Greene could guarantee the payment, no more supplies could be delivered. After thinking it over, Greene decided he would sign Banks's notes as there seemed no other way. Banks promised to send the bills Greene gave him on Robert Morris to his agent in Philadelphia who was Charles Pettit. With Pettit handling the bills, Greene felt that he had nothing to fear.[32]

With the army clothed and a contract signed for provisioning the troops, Greene was congratulating himself that his men would not have to suffer through another winter when he first heard that he was suspected of speculating with government funds. Two of Greene's trusted officers, Robert Burnet and Robert Forsyth, had been discovered to be secret partners of John Banks and Company. But worse still, Greene was suspected of being a member of the company also.

When John Banks made the agreement to supply the clothing he had talked with Burnet who wanted to become affiliated with a mercantile establishment after the war. As Burnet had been a loyal and devoted aide, Greene, of course, highly recommended him to Banks. Unknown to Greene, however, Burnet took a one-fourth interest in the contract for supplying the clothing and agreed to become a full member of the company if he could get sufficient backing from his friends and relatives. For this purpose he had asked and obtained leave to go North where he was at the time Greene learned of his connection with John Banks and Company.[33]

Robert Forsyth, Commissary of Purchases since Davie resigned in June, 1781, had met Banks at Georgetown. Like Burnet, he agreed to become a partner in the firm and also took one-fourth interest in the clothing contract. When Greene gave the bills for $8,000 to Banks, the latter had Forsyth send them through the army mails with a letter to James Hunter, Banks's partner in Virginia. As it happened, a Captain Shelton, who was waiting to take the mail, looked over Forsyth's shoulder while he was making up the package and perceived Forsyth's connection with the company. In Virginia Shelton tipped off General Charles Scott who thought it his duty to open and examine the contents. Banks's letter disclosed that Forsyth and Burnet were partners. But most astonishing was the statement: "I find General Greene an exceedingly agreeable man; and from hints dropt already, expect his proposals for an interest in a house we may establish in Charleston." Believing it his duty to disclose what he had learned, Scott sent the papers to Governor Harrison of Virginia.

It was Harrison's message informing Greene of Banks's letter that had reached Greene on February 1st. The governor's letter read: "The enclosed copies of letters from Mr. John Banks and Major Forsyth discovers a dangerous partnership entered into by those gentlemen with others, to carry on an illicit trade within the southern states." Furthermore, "Mr. Banks has endeavored to involve you in this business, by hinting, a desire on you to become a partner, and that he had liberties granted him by your connivance, that could not be obtained by any other person."[34] Harrison declared that he did not believe Greene was involved at all as he had too high an opinion of his character.

But there were others who were ready to believe and spread the rumor, and by the time Greene received Harrison's letter, the story was spreading like wildfire that the American general was using public funds in a lucrative trade with Charleston. Soon the rumor was heightened by others. As Greene's officers were in desperate straits having had no pay for a long time, he decided to relieve their wants by drawing bills for $4,000 on Robert Morris. As Banks and Company was the only party which would cash the bills for merchandise, Greene considered it really generous of them. Although Banks upped the prices, the bills which he took had a very uncertain value. Apparently the officers were satisfied until the scandal broke about the army contracts. Then the gossip arose that Greene had not only speculated with government funds but had profited on "the necessities of his own officers."[35]

This was not all. Greene was having a great deal of trouble from men and officers appropriating army property to themselves. Horses and cavalry gear especially were objects of purloining soldiers. When he learned that Captain James Gunn had exchanged an army horse and a slave, he decided to make an example of him. Gunn claimed that he had lost a horse in the service and that he had a right to take one in its place from the army. When a court of inquiry found in Gunn's favor, Greene denounced the court and severely reprimanded Gunn in general orders. After that he sent the papers of the proceedings of the court to Congress which upheld his contention that officers had no right to sell army property without orders.[36]

Many officers, especially Gunn's companions in the cavalry, whether guilty or not of like practices, sided with Gunn. When they heard the rumor that Greene had speculated with army funds and the bills paid the officers, they became sour and bitter against the man they had looked up to with such admiration. Virginia, it was said, "rung with complaints against the arbitrary and ungrateful conduct of a general, who, after taking care of himself, had deprived his officers of the only indemnity they had ever been able to get for their losses." Soon it was noised about that Robert Morris, too, was one of the speculators as well as Greene.[37]

All this was damaging enough, but when it became known that Greene had signed notes for Banks guaranteeing payment to his creditors, it seemed undeniable proof to many that he was a partner of John Banks and Company. Though Pendleton, Carrington, Wayne and others who understood the situation rallied to Greene and swore that he was compelled to guarantee payment or disband his army, many remained unconvinced. The evidence, they felt, was too much against Greene.[38]

Greene, to be sure, had no reason to believe Banks dishonest or unreliable. Nat Pendleton and others who knew Banks assured him that the merchant could be trusted. However, it was otherwise. Soon his obligations on Banks's account plunged Greene into a debt that haunted him to his dying day. Banks was a great speculator and his vast undertakings soon brought him to financial ruin. After suffering heavy losses on cargoes of tobacco and pork, Banks wrote Pettit directing him to return the bills on Robert Morris. Not knowing they were pledged to protect the notes endorsed by Greene, Pettit complied. Soon after, bankruptcy overtook the house of John Banks and Company and Greene was left with a debt of £30,000 sterling.[39]

Finding his reputation at stake and public opinion rising against him, Greene moved fast to squelch the rumors. John Banks was brought before Associate Justice Henry Pendleton of South Carolina where he swore that Greene had no connection with his company.

Before my return to Charleston, in conversation with the General, on the commerce of this country, he told me Major Burnet had thoughts of leaving the army, and going into trade after the evacuation; and that if he should, as he had been long in his family, and as he felt a friendship for him, should be much obliged to me for such services as I might have it in my power to afford him. It was from this conversation, I took the liberty of hinting to my partner the probability of the General's taking a concern with us, not considering his peculiar situation, and how dangerous a measure of this kind would prove to public confidence. . . . I am only sorry in this whole business, that I took an improper liberty with General Greene's name, but cannot suppose that an idle surmise can effect a reputation so permanently established; especially, as I have already published to the world, under the solemnity of an oath, that he neither has, or ever had, any commercial connection with me, of a private nature, or intimated a wish or desire of the kind,—.[40]

Greene also took an oath before Judge Pendleton that he had no connection of a private nature with the house of John Banks and Company. Next General Wayne and Colonel Carrington were brought in to examine all the records and papers relating to the transactions with Banks. Both declared under oath that they could discover nothing irregular and that in their opinion General Greene was blameless. All the papers were then forwarded to Governor Harrison for his examination. Commenting upon the strange plight he was in, Greene declared, "I am not conscious of having done anything in my whole life, that should render a measure of this sort necessary."[41]

But suspicion dies hard after it is once aroused. Even after Greene's death the campaign went on to try to clear his name from all suspicion. In 1790 Carrington told Knox he was sure Greene signed the notes for Banks solely to get goods for the army. Banks was under oath, he said, to use the bills on Morris to pay the debts guaranteed by Greene. If Greene had not signed them the army would have mutinied and disbanded he stated in his affidavit.[42]

Besides Carrington, Greene's defense was continued by Wayne, Knox, John and Henry Rutledge, Williams, Pendleton, Pierce, Hamilton and others. George Washington never doubted Greene's integrity. "Persuaded as I always have been of Gen'l Greene's integrity and worth," he wrote not long after Greene's death,

"I spurned those reports which tended to calumniate his conduct in the connection with Banks, being perfectly convinced that whenever the matter should be investigated, his motives for entering into it would appear pure and unimpeachable."[43]

The testimony of the men working closely with Greene at the time the contracts with Banks were made seems good evidence that he was innocent of the charges against him. Other factors support this conclusion. In the letter discovered by General Scott, Banks had written that by "hints dropt" he thought Greene desired to have an interest in the business. As this was written after the contract for clothing was signed, it is clear Greene was not a partner at the time. Neither do the notes he signed later necessarily indicate a connection with the company. Greene, it would seem, simply undertook to back the credit of the United States with his own. There seemed to be no risk involved and the act constituted no outlay of funds on his part. The fact that both Banks and Hunter later gave bonds of indemnity to Greene when they faced bankruptcy seems further proof that he was not a member of the Company.[44]

Although it appears that Greene had no business connection with John Banks, it may be that Banks had some grounds for mentioning to Hunter that Greene was interested in trade. In letters to Griffin Greene, Nathanael had discussed the possibilities of trade with the South after the war: "This Country affords a fine field for making a fortune, and if the war terminates soon which I don't much expect, I think it will be worth your improving."[45] After the war the Greenes, in fact, sent several ships to Charleston to trade—ships in which Nathanael, apparently, had an interest.[46] Burnet must have heard Greene talk about the prospects for trade at Charleston and Savannah and knew that his chief was thinking about it. Burnet could have mentioned this to Banks and left the impression that Greene might like to become a partner. In the letter to Hunter, Banks wrote that "from hints dropt already, expect his proposals for an interest in a house we may establish in Charleston." That, of course, could have meant after the war. With negotiations going on at Paris and the preliminaries already signed, peace could be expected at any time.

Though the evidence seems to clear Greene of speculating as a partner with John Banks and his associates, there still may be some doubters. Skeptics will remember his connection with Jacob Greene and Company and suspect that there was something more than meets the eye in it all. It resembles too much, they will say, his apparent connection at this time with Wadsworth and Carter in the contracts with the French forces and the Northern Department of the American Army. Banks's letter, it is true, makes it clear that Greene had no connection with the company at the time the clothing contract was made. But he could have thereafter become involved, as it was several months more before the scandal broke. It was during this period that Greene signed the notes for Banks.

While Greene was struggling to counteract the ugly rumors afloat, a messenger arrived early in April bearing the glad tidings that the preliminary articles for peace with Great Britain had been signed at Paris. To celebrate the occasion Greene had a grand parade with fireworks in the evening. After that came the dancing and merrymaking. So great was the crowd attending the festivities on James Island that it seemed that all Charleston had come out to join in the celebration.

Now that peace was at hand, Greene's troops wanted to pack up and start for home. For weeks it had been common talk among the men that they would not serve through another summer in South Carolina. They had seen their comrades die by the hundreds the summer before and they could see no reason why the local militia could not take care of things. Greene sympathized with his soldiers but he made it clear that all who left before they were discharged or furloughed would be treated as deserters. If they would be patient, he assured them, boats would soon arrive to take them to Philadelphia where they would be mustered out of service with honors.

With the coming of spring, Kitty was anxious to get back to Rhode Island as she had been away from the children for well over a year. Little Nat was with Jacob Greene while the other children except George were with their grandparents on Block Island. As it was so uncertain when Nathanael could leave, Kitty took the first ship to set sail with troops for Philadelphia. With

her went Kosciuszko and William Pierce. Kitty arrived at Philadelphia about the middle of June. She stayed this time with the
Clement Biddles where she was "pestered to death with cere-
mony and civility," said Pierce.[47]

Kitty stayed at Philadelphia for about a month waiting for a
phaeton to be made for her. Pettit was also having a heavy
carriage made for Nathanael which would cost twice as much
as Kitty's $700 phaeton. However, the phaeton was by no means
all that Kitty bought, and before she left Greene was in debt
nearly £600 for her purchases. Greene complained of her extravagance but what bothered him more was that she had not
written a line to him during her stay in the Quaker town.

On her way to Rhode Island in her new phaeton, Kitty stopped
at Princeton to get George. By this time, Nathanael and Kitty
were angry with Dr. Witherspoon because he had charged 100
guineas for boarding and schooling George. Kitty declared that
George would have learned just as much in Philadelphia, judging
by the results. The only one who seemed entirely satisfied was
George, who had a good time at Princeton, even if he did not
learn as much as was expected of him.[48]

Nathanael Greene was also getting homesick for Rhode Island
with Kitty gone and friends leaving every day for home. He told
John Collins that he longed to get home to see all his old friends.
Rhode Island, declared Nathanael, must have been made for
local attachments. Greene worried a great deal about his state
doing its part to uphold the Confederation and to support Congress. Like South Carolina, Rhode Island, he knew, was too
provincial and self-contained. Congress had requested each state
to pay what was due their officers in the Continental army. Did
Rhode Island claim him, he asked Collins? If so, he would like
to have some money as he had had no pay since 1777. Greene's
friends, he thought, were getting tired of lending him money to
live on. Greene soon found that if Rhode Island had to pay him
she did not care to own him. Reed wrote in August that the
old adage still held: a man is honored less in his own country
than abroad. Indeed, Reed had heard more criticism of Greene
from Rhode Islanders of late than from all others put together.[49]

Although Greene was opposed to slavery, he felt compelled to
alter his views somewhat after living in the South. Without

slaves, the rice plantations could not be operated, and Greene had decided to become a Southern planter. There is evidence, however, that he hoped in time to experiment with a plan whereby the slaves could earn their freedom and become free workers on his plantations.[50] In 1783 when questioned about his views on slavery by a Philadelphia Quaker, Greene answered: "On the subject of slavery, nothing can be said in its defence." However, he went on to say, "The generosity of the southern states has placed an interest of this sort in my hands, and I trust their condition will not be worse but better. They are, generally, as much attached to a plantation as a man is to his family, and to remove them from one to another is their great punishment."[51]

Greene rented out his rice lands at Mulberry Grove for the year 1783. He rented "for a song," he said, receiving only 50 guineas, the most he could get. However, he had his South Carolina plantation, the Boone Barony on the Pon Pon, in operation that year. Like Mulberry Grove, the Boone Barony was found to be worth half again as much as the legislature had appropriated. However, as with Georgia, South Carolina magnanimously granted the whole estate to Greene. In 1796 when Kitty lost the plantation through debts, it was found to contain over 7,000 acres and to be worth $72,395.[52]

Nathanael Greene found the expense of putting his Boone Barony under cultivation taxed his resources and credit to the limit. The plantation was in charge of Roger Saunders, the owner of a nearby plantation, who was paid £58 for supervising the Barony. On Saunders' advice, Greene bought a large number of Negroes who had been sold from the plantation and who wanted to return. As more slaves were needed, others were also purchased. Besides the slaves, there were livestock, seed, tools, and provisions to buy for the plantation. By May, Saunders had 155 acres of rice planted and a large area in corn. From this Greene expected a crop of 250 barrels of rice and 1,500 bushels of corn but he was destined to be disappointed with the yield.[53]

Before the ships arrived to take home what remained of the Southern army, mutiny broke out. In May the first regiment of Virginia cavalry, stationed at Friday's Ferry, rode off for home. Led by Sergeant Dangerfield, they left to lay their grievances before the Virginia Legislature and demand their pay. When

Greene heard of the mutiny, he sent an express after the corps with an offer of pardon if they returned to their post. Believing that Dangerfield would pay no attention to his order, Greene sent a letter to Governor Harrison asking that the mutineers be punished when they reached Virginia. To Greene's disgust no attempt was made to arrest the men who brazenly went about selling the horses they had ridden home. People in Virginia were still aroused over the Banks affair and few cared to censure soldiers for mutinying and appropriating to themselves their horses and gear.[54]

About the same time that the Virginia cavalry mutinied, Greene had more trouble with the Legion dragoons stationed at George-town. Captain Egleston told Greene he was sure the Legion would refuse to stay later than June 1st because of their determination to leave South Carolina before the hot season began. They were also very disgruntled over Greene's ruling against keeping their horses. Desiring to do what he could for the dragoons in appreciation of their inestimable service, Greene ruled that they could bid on their horses with the purchase money coming out of their pay. This put the dragoons in a better temper but it angered the Legion infantry by not having the privilege extended to them. Fearing the infantry might mutiny, Greene ordered a month's pay for all the Legion and thereafter there was no more trouble.[55]

About the first of June a great commotion arose among the Maryland troops who seemed on the verge of packing up and marching off. The Pennsylvania troops, who remembered their recent encounter with Greene, murmured but made no move to mutiny. The trouble, however, spread to the Virginia Continentals, whereupon Greene put the ringleader in jail and drew up the rest of the army in battle formation whereby discipline was restored. Greene surely was sitting on a powder keg, but he somehow managed to keep it from exploding.[56]

Even Greene's aides were more or less disgruntled, although their loyalty to their commander was unshaken. Robert Morris, they charged, had ordered the cost of their clothing to come out of their pay, something not done to the officers in the Northern army. Nat Pendleton, apparently without success, wrote to Secretary Lincoln about it after seeking Greene's advice. All these worries, big and little, were wearing on Greene who already was struggling to ward off the fever.

The days of June passed slowly with the fear of the fever continuously on the minds of the soldiers. Each day the men watched and waited for the transports. Dread of the fever, Greene told Lincoln, "operates so powerfully that they will listen to nothing and are deserting in great numbers and I am really afraid if the transports don't arrive in a few days they will go off in a body.[57] Finally the long wait ended. On July 11th Greene wrote that Commodore Nicholson had arrived and all the ships should be in the harbor in a few days. As he was soon to part with the soldiers who had stayed with him to the end, Greene praised them in general orders for their loyalty and devotion.

> The American Army is doubly illustrious, but the Southern Army is more peculiarly so. No army ever displayed so much obedient fortitude, because no Army ever suffered such variety of distresses. . . . The General cannot take leave of the Army without assuring them, that he has the most perfect confidence in the gratitude, honor, and justice of his Country and he is entirely convinced that every Soldier who serves out his time with Fidelity, will be paid with Justice, if not rewarded with liberality, and that this will be done as soon as the nature of our unsettled Country, and the State of its Finances will admit.[58]

On July 29th Greene wrote Pettit that all the troops had embarked and sailed away. "I am left like Sampson after Delilah cut his locks," was the way he described it to Pettit. Greene hoped that his army when it arrived at Philadelphia would not join in the rioting of some of the northern troops who had forced Congress to flee to Princeton. He was sorry that such things should occur but perhaps, he thought, it would wake the people up and spur the states to do something to strengthen the government of the United States.[59]

On August 11, 1783, Nathanael Greene left Charleston in his carriage for the long trip home. With him were two of his aides, Major Edmund Hyrne and Major Evan Edwards. Colonel Carrington, too, would catch up with them and accompany them as far as Richmond. Why Greene chose to ride 800 miles through the summer's heat he does not say but there is a clue in Robert Forsyth's testimony given in 1791. Greene, he declared had become uneasy about the notes he had endorsed for Banks as he had learned of great losses suffered by the company following "some extraordinary speculation." Forsyth said that Greene made Banks sign a bond of indemnity to him, apparently before leaving Charleston. Greene, it seems, wanted to get the same from James Hunter in Virginia and this very likely was his main reason for undertaking the tedious journey overland to Philadelphia.[60]

Greene and his companions made their way by easy stages along the road to Georgetown. On August 15th they stayed at Colonel Horry's beautiful plantation on the Santee. The next day they crossed the Santee and reached Georgetown about noon where they were "very politely received and entertained" by Mr. Tucker and his wife, who was Major Hyrne's sister. After enjoying themselves at Georgetown for two days, Greene and his aides got into a fast sailing canoe which took them up the Pee Dee to Mr. Allston's plantation. Here they were joined by their drivers with the horses, carriage and baggage wagon. When Greene and his aides arrived at Allston's they were quite tired, having stopped along the way to see Colonel Hamit's indigo plantation where they almost melted under the scorching sun. But Mr. Allston gave them a cordial welcome and "regaled" them with "fine old wine" until their fatigue was all but gone.

On the 20th "we set out for Wilmington," wrote Greene in his interesting and witty diary, "having poverty before us and leaving plenty behind us." Most of the day they traveled over roads of loose sand but in crossing Long Bay the beach was hard "and the riding easy and delightful." While traversing the sixteen-mile stretch of beach a heavy thunder shower came up. "To behold," wrote Greene, "the sea rolling in on one side upon the beach in all the majesty of the ocean, and on the other hand to see the forked lightning play, and hear the boisterous thunder roar, filled the mind with admiration." It took two days to get to Wilmington, North Carolina, after passing through a desolate country where accommodations were mean and the people slovenly.

Nathanael Greene's arrival in Wilmington was celebrated by bonfires in the streets and the firing of cannon. After spending two days there, Greene and his party started for Halifax. The first night they stayed at the home of General Lillington and the next day rode forty-five miles before stopping for the night. The following morning they rode to General Caswell's home where he and his pretty wife gave them "a polite reception." Caswell, indeed, "was so liberal to our servants," wrote Greene, "and fed our horses so plentifully, that the first got drunk and the last got foundered." With Colonel Blount's son for a guide they should have made the colonel's house for dinner but the youth "either from the effects of cherry bounce and morning bitters or from the charms of Mrs. Caswell, found his head so like uncle Toby's smoke-jack that he missed the way where he was as well acquainted with it as with his bed-chamber, and led us at least seven miles out of the road, which prevented our arriving till within the evening."

Colonel Blount amused his guests with anecdotes while they sipped his wine and lingered at the dinner table. So great was the aversion to military service in his neighborhood, he said, that fifty-six men out of fifty-eight had been found with self-inflicted hernias. He told also of a seventh son of a seventh son who was reputed to be able to cure any disease by touching the patient. "Marvels in North Carolina thicken apace," wrote Greene. "Prodigies of every kind are propagated and believed. Hundreds of people are encamped round about this child, who is but eight years old, and will take nothing for the cures he performs. There are things in nature far above our comprehension. This may be one of them; but in this enlightened age, when science and philosophy have banished all those wonderful tales which formerly amused the world, I am not apt to be credulous."

Greene and his party arrived at Halifax, a village of about sixty houses on the banks of the Roanoke, on the last day of August. In the evening of their second day in town, the citizens gave a ball for Greene which was announced by the firing of cannon. "The room was very decent and the supper genteel," thought Greene. Most fascinating, however, were the sparkling ladies who "enlivened every soul and sweetened every pleasure."

While the dance went on, Major Edwards "took himself to a gaming table," much to Greene's displeasure, where he won back most of the money he had given a man for a pair of bay horses.

Gambling and idleness as well as the low ebb of morality and religion, thought Greene, would long retard the economic and political growth of the South. The principal barrier against a continued deterioration of the South, in his opinion, was the upper class which generally clung to standards above those of the common people. Great pains, however, were being taken in the South, said Greene, "to ruin the influence of what is called the aristocratic interest. It may appear strange, but I fear it will prove true the sooner their influence is lost the sooner monarchy under some form will begin."

At the next stop, Edwards "got to reading *Pilgrim's Progress* and got as far as Flash Lane and went to church." During the trip Major Hyrne argued much with Edwards who had a hankering for strange doctrines and "singular sentiments." Edwards expected Carrington to take his part but after he arrived, the two fairly flew at each other like "gamecocks" leaving Hyrne and Greene "at liberty to philosophize." At Petersburg, Virginia, Greene and his young officers visited Saint George Tucker who had served under Greene and had "a great turn for poetry." After seeing Tucker, the party headed for Richmond.

Just before reaching Richmond, Greene and his aides had dinner with Colonel Cary although Greene would have preferred to have hurried on to the town. But as Greene explained it he had little choice. "Col. Cary being an old bruiser, and swearing by God I should dine with him to-day, and doubling his fist at the same time, I did not care to contradict him for fear of a blow," said Greene.

Though detained at Colonel Cary's, Greene made Richmond that evening and the town turned out to give him a big reception. Greene gave an answer to a public address but did not stay for a banquet which the town fathers wanted to give him the next day. On the way to Fredericksburg, Greene and his aides lodged with John Baylor, "a great macaroni in dress, and—once the head of the Macaroni Club in London." Near Fredericksburg they dined with General Spottswood and then pushed on to the town where General Weedon received them "with open arms" at his tavern. While at Fredericksburg Greene visited Hunter's iron works, "a great curiosity to a mechanical genius." Whether or not he secured a bond of indemnity from Hunter at this time is not known. After a public dinner "and a very polite address," General Greene and his aides set out for Mount Vernon.

On the way to Washington's home, Greene upset his carriage, broke the top and bruised himself considerably. "If I had not lifted up the carriage and let it pass over me," wrote Greene, "it is probable I might have got killed or badly wounded, for the horse started upon a run and drawed the carriage after him until the harness gave way." At a nearby hamlet the carriage was repaired and on September 13th the party reached Mount Vernon. George and Martha Washington were at Princeton but Lund Washington and his wife were there to receive and entertain them.

After dining at Mount Vernon, Greene and his aides bid goodby to their hosts and started for Alexandria. When they arrived that night, Greene was sick with a fever. He was taken to the home of Colonel Fitzgerald where he lay for eight days desperately ill. Dr. Brown, a graduate of Edinburgh, attended him during his sickness during which he did not eat a thing for six days. Many prominent men, among them Richard Henry Lee, visited him but he was too weak to enjoy their company. While he lay sick, Alexandria held a public dinner in his honor. "You Sir," said the chief speaker, "have had the honor of proving to the World that circumstances of the greatest distress and a Situation surrounded with danger and with difficulty can be nobly surmounted by brave Men, animated with the spirit of liberty and under the command of wise, virtuous, and persevering Leaders."

After Greene recovered he visited Mr. Custis' plantation, six miles from Alexandria. The Custises were not at home but Greene was rewarded by a magnificent view of the Potomac. Greene left Virginia thinking "that the ladies appear to be brought up and educated with habits of industry and attention to domestic affairs, while the gentlemen attend to little but pleasure and dissipation." With all its population the state was weak and poor. As in North Carolina, he thought the common people had too much influence in politics. "The dignity of government or the faith of the nation has too little weight with this order of people," he wrote.

Reaching Maryland, Greene stayed with Mr. Degg where he

was visited by Governor Thomas Lee and many other people of note. At Annapolis Greene had the pleasure of seeing "the celebrated Mrs. Loyd" whose poise and grace was "not less remarkable than her beauty." Annapolis put on a celebration for Greene but the weather being good, Greene excused himself before the ball began and started out for Baltimore. Annapolis, Greene noted, would make a fine site for the national capital now under discussion.

At Baltimore Greene and his aides were welcomed by General Otho Williams and Colonel John Howard, two of his most celebrated officers of the southern campaign. "The pleasure of meeting [them] is easier felt than described," wrote Greene in his diary. The people of Baltimore kept him there four days during which they had a great celebration." I will not attempt to recite the honors belonging to General Greene," said the principal speaker. "They are already written indelibly on the hearts of his countrymen. We trust," he continued, "they will be faithfully transmitted to Posterity, in the brightest pages of that History, which shall record the important Circumstances of the glorious Revolution, to which your services have so greatly contributed."[61] At Baltimore Major Hyrne was wounded by Cupid's arrow and though it "penetrated the heart," wrote Greene, "he still survived."

At Philadelphia where he arrived the first of October, Greene found the whole city awaiting his coming. But though the public ovations were pleasing, he found the most happiness in seeing his old friends again. And in Philadelphia he had many friends— Joseph Reed, Clement Biddle, Charles Pettit, Robert Morris and a host of others. Happy as were his hours in Philadelphia, he soon felt compelled to set out for Princeton where Congress was sitting after fleeing from angry and mutinous Continental troops demanding their pay.

Greene arrived at Trenton on October 7th where he found Washington at the home of John Cox preparing to leave for Princeton. It was a joyous meeting after three long years since they had parted at Colonel Dey's. Greene accompanied Washington to Princeton where he probably stayed at his headquarters at nearby Rocky Hill. Elias Boudinot, President of Congress, announced Greene's arrival and presented Congress with his request for permission to repair to Rhode Island to see his family and attend some business. His request was granted and as a symbol of its appreciation of his services to America, Congress voted him two brass cannons captured in the South.[62] Upon receiving his permission to leave, Greene bid farewell to Washington and his friends in Congress and set out for Philadelphia before returning home. Thus ended his nine years in the Revolutionary army—he was once again a civilian.

CHAPTER SEVENTEEN

The Last Years

Upon leaving Princeton, Greene returned to Philadelphia with money problems uppermost in mind. From this time until his untimely death three years later there would be practically no let-up in his struggle to get out of debt and make a new start in life. Greene stayed long enough in Philadelphia to find he would salvage little from his investment with Pettit and Cox. The old quartermaster accounts, too, were still unsettled and it would be fortunate if Congress did not find some claims upon Greene and his associates in the department. But this was not all. He was shocked to learn from Pettit that John Banks had speculated with the bills he had given him for the army contracts and was bankrupt. Greene's creditors accordingly were calling upon him to satisfy the notes signed for Banks. At first Greene did not realize the seriousness of it as he believed erroneously that Banks and his associates had property enough to cover the debts.[1]

If he were to be a man of much consequence in the postwar world, Greene believed he would have to be a man of wealth. This he was resolved to become. In the coming year he would operate both his South Carolina and Georgia plantations. Before leaving Charleston he had made arrangements for expanding production on the Boone Barony and for getting Mulberry Grove operating under a manager. Already, however, outlays for slaves, livestock, seed, tools and provisions were straining his credit to the utmost. Pettit, with the Batsto Iron Works still on his hands and with funds tied up in a languishing foreign trade, could lend him very little. Greene therefore turned to Robert Morris who agreed to loan him money on the assurance that rice growing would pay handsome dividends. Later when there appeared no end to the need of money he also borrowed from Jeremiah Wadsworth.

When Greene finally left Philadelphia he rode to New York where he found passage on a vessel for Newport. Arriving there on November 27th, he was recieved at the dock by a great throng including the town fathers. Soon a public ovation was held in one of the churches at which Greene was praised for all he had done for the state and nation. "In this mighty Revolution," declared the principal speaker, "which regards the Rights of Humanity for its Base, we feel a Pride, peculiarly interesting to our Felicity that a Citizen of this State has brightened the Paths of Glory which display the Greatness of our illustrious Commander-in-Chief."[2]

At Newport Greene rented the stately Crary mansion on Mill Street near the old stone tower. As Kitty soon would have her fifth child, Nathanael decided not to collect the children right away. Little Nathanael was with his grandparents on Block Island where he drank "his dram every morning with his grand Papa." He was a great "pet" around the house which he roamed as ragged as a Continental. Martha and Cornelia were with other relatives but George, apparently, came with Kitty and went to school in Newport. After the baby, Louisa Catherine, was born, Martha and Cornelia came to live with their parents but the baby was given to Barbara Bently to nurse, and in her care she remained until the time Greene took the family to Mulberry Grove to live.[3]

Greene was still a partner with his brother Jacob and cousin Griffin and the three were soon making plans for opening a trade with Charleston and other promising commercial centers. Greene no longer owned the house he had built at Coventry as this property had fallen to Jacob with the division of their father's estate. However, he still owned the farm at Westerly acquired by the division. Here Kitty had lived before her trip to South Carolina in 1782. The farm, rented, was rather run down and Greene set about having it repaired. Though it was soon attached for debts like the rest of his property, Greene apparently held on to Westerly until his death.

Kitty's condition during the weeks before the birth of her baby was such that Greene found it inadvisable to leave Newport for long. He had hoped to attend the assembly at Providence and join with James Varnum and Henry Marchant in opposing

David Howell, William Ellery and others who were out to defeat
the five per cent impost for the Continental treasury. Until the
last, Greene was confident the bill would pass. When it was defeated, words could not express his mortification.[4]

Greene had planned on returning to South Carolina and
Georgia early in the spring to superintend operations on his plantations. But Kitty did not improve rapidly after Louisa was
born and he did not want to leave her. Furthermore, Greene
was not well himself. On a visit to Providence he had slipped
on the ice and in endeavoring to keep from falling, had wrenched
himself so badly that he suffered great pain for many weeks.

In March Congress named Greene to be one of several commissioners for making a treaty with the Indians for a cession of
a large tract of land in the upper Ohio Valley. However, with
his health poor and his family and business needing him at home,
he declined to serve. He was also urged by Washington and
others to attend a meeting of the Cincinnati in Philadelphia at
which important questions pertaining to the future of the organization were to be considered. Greene had been elected president
of the Rhode Island chapter but he had to decline going for the
same reasons for not serving on the Indian mission. James Varnum, Rhode Island's most illustrious war hero next to Greene,
went in his place.

At Philadelphia there were indeed important questions for the
Cincinnati to consider as a great storm had arisen throughout
the country against the society which was thought to be attempting to establish a hereditary aristocracy endangering the
republic itself. "There had been great commotions respecting the
commutation [pardoning of Loyalists]," wrote Greene to Reed.
"That is now subsiding and the current of public prejudice is
directed against the Cincinnati. The people in the Northern
States are much enraged against it. General Washington is much
alarmed at it. The order is now sitting at Philadelphia.—Many
want an alteration of the idea but more a dissolution. Honorary
members are much objected to and the hereditary descent more
so." Congress, continued Greene, had said nothing about the
society "but they are not less displeased with the order than
other citizens."[5]

Having been long out of touch with civilian life, and especially

New England, Greene did not at first see the need for changing the rules of the Cincinnati. 'The public," he declared, "seems to want something in New England to quarrel with the officers about, remove one thing and they will soon find another." However, when he got to Charleston that summer he found agitation against the order as strong as in New England. He then wrote Washington that he was glad he had not taken his advice against changing the rules of the society. With almost everyone in America, outside of the Revolutionary officers, opposed to the order, Washington did right, said Greene, by showing the people that the members claimed no special privileges.[6]

At Newport Greene had many visitors, among them Lafayette, von Steuben, Kosciuszko and the historian William Gordon. On one occasion late in 1784 Greene took Lafayette on a visit to his birthplace at Potowomut and to East Greenwich, Coventry and Providence. Along the way they were entertained by James Varnum, William Greene and many others. Great throngs, including many of their former soldiers and their families, turned out to greet them whenever they stopped for a day or two.

It was not until July that Greene set sail for Charleston in a new ship in which he had an interest with Jacob and Griffin. Why he invested in shipping at a time when commerce was very slow and he needed so much money for his plantations may seem mysterious. However, he believed business would soon revive and that quick profits might be made in the Charleston–West Indian trade. Greene surely needed the money for already there were judgments against him on the notes he had signed for Banks. This, indeed, was the reason for his going south in the middle of the summer instead of waiting for cooler weather in the autumn.

Altogether Greene had signed notes to the amount of £30,000 sterling which were held by Harris and Blackford, Newcomer and Collet, and James Warington. "You know," Greene wrote to Banks, "what you have done in the affair of Mr. Patten's signature. Free me from my embarrassment and you are safe but if you neglect to do me this justice you must abide the consequences."[7] But when Greene arrived at Charleston there was no answer from Banks who had gone to Virginia.

With Banks's creditors growing daily more pressing, Greene

decided to go to Virginia to see Banks and Hunter. He set out on his 400-mile journey early in September with a servant, traveling over the same roads he had taken with majors Edwards and Hyrne the year before. When he at last arrived at his destination, he found to his dismay that Banks was dead and buried. After conferring with Colonel Carrington whom Greene had made his attorney in Virginia, he wrote to Robert Forsyth, who had become a lawyer in Charleston asking him to send Carrington a statement of how much Banks had paid his creditors. "The lawyers of this State tell me," wrote Greene, "a Court of Chancery will relieve me to the amount of what ever they relinquished." Further instructions to Forsyth were to "Tell Mr. Blackford to urge his suit against Ferris and desire Mr. Rutledge to press Lushington to an agreement to bring forward the action if he continues to refuse to give a bond of indemnity. I pray you to give Mr. Primecos [Peronneau?] Mr. Collet's attorney an assignment of all the remaining funds for outstanding Debts upon the books. I am ruined if you do not exert yourself to save me."[8]

At Petersburg, after conferring again with Carrington, Greene wrote to William Blount regarding papers for suing the administrator of the Banks's estate. Blount answered that he thought there was little left of John Banks's property but he would try. Blount apparently was wrong in his assumption, for within a year Greene obtained an attachment on a huge tract of western land belonging to the Banks's estate. But this may have meant little as Forsyth thought much money might be needed to perfect the deeds. Apparently nothing was ever realized by Greene from this claim.[9]

Of more promise than the lien on Banks's western land was an attachment Carrington made for Greene on the property of James Hunter, another of John Banks's partners. Greene promised Hunter that if he had to foreclose he would pay him back should he be reimbursed by Congress. Hunter, who within a few weeks became bankrupt by an avalanche of judgments, assured Greene that there was not the slightest reason for anyone to believe Greene had had a business interest in the army contracts.[10]

In 1785, Greene kept Banks's creditors at bay by signing new notes to cover his debts. In May Collet also asked Greene to list all the property he had in the North. He would go north and examine the holdings, he said, and let Greene know how much he could allow for them. Meanwhile, through Richard Henry Lee, Greene had entered a claim in Congress for his debt in behalf of the army. He was compelled to do this, he told Lee, out of consideration for his family who would have to suffer if he were financially ruined.[11]

Nathanael Greene died without knowing if Congress would come to his rescue or what would be the outcome of his financial embarrassment. But Congress did finally pay all his debts to the creditors of John Banks and Company. In 1792, four years after Greene's death, Newcomer and Collet were paid $27,504. In 1796 Congress satisfied the remaining claim of $20,000 held by Harris and Blackford. This no doubt saved Kitty Greene from bankruptcy. However, private debts continued to mount and in 1804 Kitty lost the Boone Barony to satisfy judgments against Greene's estate.[12]

Although the Banks case was the only serious law suit that confronted Greene, he had signed a note for a foreign officer during the last year of the war which had also rebounded. The officer was Baron de Glusbeck, a hero of Cowpens, who proved to be an impostor as to title and fortune. After having his suspicions aroused about de Glusbeck, Greene asked Chevalier La Luzerne, the French Minister to the United States, to look into the matter. It was too late though, for in December, 1783, the bills were returned to Charleston protested by the Bordeaux firm on which they were drawn. With interest and damages, Greene was called upon to pay £331. Surely Nathanael Greene was learning to be careful about the papers on which he put his signature![13]

Greene's debts seemed to multiply overnight. A committee of Congress headed by Jefferson found that he had overdrawn $6,000 on his allowance for personal expenses while Kitty was in South Carolina. The committee, however, magnanimously recommended that in consideration of the high prices in the South at the time, the debt be cancelled. This was not done at the time and Greene presently received a bill, with the privilege of voicing objections, from the Comptroller's office for $6,229 in specie. It is unfortunate that Greene did not live to see Congress cancel all the debt except for $319 in September, 1786. It would have been most reassuring to know that his services in the war were still appreciated.[14]

As in 1783, Greene's rice crop did not come up to expectations in 1784. Misfortune this time came in the form of a hurricane which destroyed half the crop on the Boone Barony. The rice birds also raised havoc with the crop although the high price of rice that year helped to make up somewhat for the small yield. Greene had added 200 acres to Mulberry Grove by buying a tract of swampland on an island in the Savannah River near his plantation. More slaves were also added to his plantations. Out of a lot purchased by Saunders at St. Augustine, Greene took fifty-eight. The rest went to Anthony Wayne who, like Greene, was going deeply in debt to operate his Georgia plantation. In the gang which Greene purchased were sixteen sawyers, two coopers, one carpenter, two tanners and some who qualified as cooks and seamstresses. Altogether they cost him £3,700 of which £700 was in cash and the rest in annual installments over a period of three years. The slaves were all sent to Mulberry Grove where by Greene's instructions, they were to be well fed and clothed. They were mostly small Negroes but not a bad lot, Greene told his superintendent, William Gibbons. Saunders, however, did not like the deal and accused the merchant who supplied them with giving Greene and Wayne a picked-over lot.[15]

Besides his plantations, Greene had acquired 7,000 acres in the twenty-mile-long Cumberland Island and the smaller Little Cumberland Island off the lower coast of Georgia. This was a purchase and not a gift, and included 2,000 acres on Crooked River on the mainland opposite the islands. Although Greene went in debt £5,000 for the Cumberland property, it was a very valuable investment. The land was not only fertile but it was covered with a magnificent stand of live oak and pine of which Greene's share alone was estimated to be worth £40,000.

Before Greene left Newport he had learned that there were two or three hundred trespassers, all former Loyalists, cutting timber on Cumberland Island. He at once appealed to Governor Houston of Georgia for a suit to recover losses and for protection of his property. When Greene arrived at Charleston he again wrote to the Governor as no action had yet been taken against the trespassers. This apparently brought results as Greene did not pursue the matter further.

Not long after Greene returned to Charleston from Virginia he took passage for Newport. After spending a few crowded weeks with his family and attending to a multitude of business and social affairs, January found him again sailing back to Charleston. This time he left Kitty with the promise that when he returned it would be to take all the family to live at Mulberry Grove. But first he must do what he could to market some of his timber on Cumberland Island to make up, if possible, for the small returns thus far on his rice. For a time while on the Atlantic, Greene thought he would never live to see his family again. Tossed by mountainous seas, his ship barely escaped destruction. At least one man was washed overboard before the terrible ordeal was past and the ship safe at Charleston.

When Greene arrived at Charleston he found he must borrow more money if he intended to keep his Cumberland Island property and get operations under way with the logging. With his first installment due on his mortgage and no funds available, he offered to sell part interest in the islands to Jeremiah Wadsworth. With him for a partner the problem of finding the capital for logging would be solved. If Wadsworth did not want to go in with him there was still the prospect of getting a loan from Dutch bankers. Through Robert Morris, Greene was trying to negotiate a loan of £5,000 from Wilhem and Van Willink, reputedly a firm of vast resources.[16]

In March Greene made a trip to Mulberry Grove with Anthony Wayne who had just arrived from Pennsylvania. At Mulberry Grove Greene saw his overseer, William Gibbons. To his surprise he was told that a neighbor, also named Gibbons, claimed a section of Mulberry Grove which he declared had not been properly surveyed. Greene tried to convince him that he was mistaken but failing, he asked Nat Pendleton, who had opened a law office in Savannah, to try to get Gibbons to drop the claim.[17]

While at Mulberry Grove, Greene received from Savannah a follow-up of some disquieting letters which had been coming to him. The notes came from James Gunn, the officer with whom Greene had had the difficulty over the army horse in 1782. Gunn insisted that Greene had abused him in a way no gentleman could ignore and demanded a duel. Greene emphatically denied the charge. "No man while I was in the Army ever heard me use language indelicate or that would disgrace a gentleman," he declared. Gunn asked Greene to fight the duel at Mr. Campbell's plantation on the South Carolina side of the Savannah as the sheriff in town had "interferred" on Greene's part. He had had to wait, he said, until after the war when they were on "an equal footing" to find satisfaction. "Permit me sir," wrote Gunn, "to remind you of the personal abuse I received from you at Mr. Waring's. The ungenerous letter you wrote the president of the Court Martial and the letter of abuse I received after being acquitted by the Court—the last complained of as cruel, ungenerous, and unjust by your greatest friends."[18]

Greene, who thought Gunn was little less than a madman, saw fit to decline the challenge. Friends agreed that this was the proper thing to do as no general could be answerable to every and any man he might have offended during the war. "Conscious of having done nothing respecting you or any other Officer while in command but what my public duty imposed upon me," Greene wrote to Gunn, "I cannot think myself accountable to every individual who may put a different interpretation upon it." To this Gunn answered that he would attack Greene whenever he might find him. Greene remarked to his friends that Gunn would not find him without a pistol in his pocket.[19]

When Washington heard of how Greene had handled Gunn's challenge, he wrote Nathanael an approving letter. "Your honor and reputation," he declared, "will not only stand perfectly acquitted for the non-acceptance of his challenge, but that your prudence and judgment would have been condemnable for accepting it, in the eyes of the world, because if a commanding officer is amenable to private calls for the discharge of public duty, he has a dagger always at his breast, and can turn neither to the right nor the left without feeling its point."[20]

From Savannah Greene took passage in a ship for St. Augustine to see if he could persuade some former Loyalists to colonize Cumberland Island and engage in the logging. Greene found the Spanish Governor Don Vincent Emmanuel de Zespedes cordial and willing to help as much as possible. "My stock [of Spanish] was soon exhausted," Nathanael told Kitty. But what he lacked in conversation, he made up in bowing. The governor's wife and daughters, thought Greene, "were not beautiful" but judging by their "sweet languishing eyes" he supposed "they could make love with great violence."

Returning to Charleston without much success in getting colonizers from Florida for Cumberland Island, Greene settled down to a session of long and involved conferences with his lawyers regarding the Banks affair. At the time there seemed some promise of getting free from this nightmare of debts. "If I can get clear of this . . . it will nearly make me whole," wrote Greene to Pendleton. Greene also had good news from Griffin Greene who had a prospect of selling a ship at a profit, this being a ship in which Nathanael had an interest. As his affairs appeared to be improving, Greene informed Wadsworth in his next letter that he would not sell more than a fourth interest in Cumberland Island.[21]

Greene gave Wadsworth in the "ninth year of our Independence" power of attorney with instructions to sell most of his property in the North. Years before, Greene had bought land along the Passaic River from Abraham Lott, which he thought he could sell for £1,000 sterling. He also would sell his share of some land at Claverick near Catskill, New York, which he owned with Pettit and Biddle. Greene soon heard Pettit had put the New York land up for sale in lots of two or three hundred acres but it looked as though they could get no more than one dollar per acre. About this time Greene received word from Wadsworth that he had closed out Greene's account with Barnabas Deane and Company. Greene's share of £960 represented a great loss as he had invested £10,000 in the Company in 1779. All of the balance Greene signed over to Wadsworth from whom he had borrowed several thousand pounds since the war.[22]

In August Greene set sail for Newport with a company of South Carolina people seeking to escape the heat and the sickly season. Upon arriving, Greene found that Kitty had had her sixth child but the baby became sick during an epidemic in the summer and died. It was therefore with a sadness of heart that Nathanael thrust himself into all the last minute preparations for moving to Georgia. Through Wadsworth and Dr. Stiles (Greene's old friend and mentor of his youth), he hired Phineas Miller to accompany them to Georgia to tutor the children for thirty-five guineas a year and his board. Nathanael spent many hours endeavoring to track down books missing from his library which he was taking to Georgia. He had lost his list and could not remember to whom he had loaned them. After checking with James Varnum and others with whom he used to exchange books, he found a few, but most of the missing volumes could not be located.

Before sailing for Georgia, Greene made his will which provided that most of his property would be divided equally between his wife and the five children. The will also stipulated that his sons should have a liberal education: the kind that Nathanael Greene had wanted so much after he came to realize its value. His daughters were to have an education suitable to their station. Above all, Greene wanted his children taught moral values, "that best legacy of a Fond Father."[23]

Toward the last of October, Nathanael Greene and his family took passage for Georgia. When they arrived Nat Pendleton was on hand to take them to his house, where they stayed a few days before going on to Mulberry Grove. Kitty had never seen Mulberry Grove, the *plus belle* of the Savannah, but it was all that Nathanael had said in its praise, and she loved it from the first. The house, standing among moss-covered oaks, was a two-story Georgian with a double door set off by a panel of glass on each side and a graceful fan window above the door. A large brick chimney at each end of the house served the fireplaces needed to take the chill off during the winter months. Standing near the house was a building that served an as out-kitchen. Back of the house was a courtyard surrounded by stables, a coach house, a large poultry house and other buildings.

In April Nathanael described the beauties of Mulberry Grove and how the family was enjoying life in the South.

This is a busy time with us, and I can afford but a small portion of time to write. We are planting. We have got upwards to sixty acres of corn planted, and expect to plant one hundred and thirty of rice. The garden is delightful. The fruit trees and flowering shrubs form a pleasing variety. We have green peas almost fit to eat, and as fine lettuce as ever you saw. The mocking-birds surround us evening and morning. The weather is mild, and the vegetable kingdom progressing to perfection. But it is a great deduction from the pleasure we should feel from the beauties and conveniences of the place, that we are obliged to leave it [for Cumberland Island] before we shall have tasted of several kinds of fruit. We have in the same orchard apples, pears, peaches, apricots, nectarines, plums of different kinds, figs, pomegranates, and oranges. And we have strawberries which measure three inches round. All these are clever, but the want of our friends to enjoy them with us renders them less interesting.[24]

But though Nathanael and Kitty missed their old friends of the North, they had many friends in the South who soon were dropping in on the Greenes in their new home. Mrs. Pierce and Mrs. Pendleton with some of the other Savannah ladies were of the first to make a visit. The children, too, were happy with their new home and with their tutor, Master Miller. Long years after, Nathanael's youngest boy could remember his father holding him on his knee and teaching him "funny songs."

Not long after the family got settled at Mulberry Grove, Nathanael had all the children inoculated against smallpox by a Dr. Briskel. When Greene protested against being charged five guineas for the service, the doctor replied that that was the fee paid by people of "fashion" in Georgia. Others paid two guineas. But if Greene were dissatisfied, the doctor assured him he could pay whatever sum he desired.

Although Nathanael Greene could not help but feel somewhat isolated from the world on his Georgia plantation, letters came from time to time to show that he was not forgotten. From far off Warsaw, Kosciuszko wrote that he was homesick for America. He would gladly return, he told Greene, if he could get a commission in the American Army. Kosciuszko did not want his lady friends to forget him either. He asked Greene to humor Mrs. M. in Charleston by telling her that he was planning to marry her as soon as her husband died. "And if he is in Life, which would be the most surprising thing to live so long in that Country," added Kosciuszko, "my best Compliments to him."

Nathanael Greene heard that prints of himself and of Washington were on sale in the northern cities. Greene's picture had been made from a half-length painting for which he had posed one time in Philadelphia. The painting had been taken to London by Joseph Reed after the war where Joseph Brown, an engraver, had had an artist make a full-length picture from it. Soon hundreds of these engravings were adorning the walls of American homes. Greene presently received a complimentary copy at Mulberry Grove, while Congress was given the pictures of both Washington and Greene to hang on its walls.

As in 1783 and 1784, Nathanael Greene's rice crop in 1785 was disappointing. The crop was a third short owing to a wet season, and in addition, ninety-five barrels were lost through accident, fifty barrels having been burned in a Savannah warehouse and forty-five lost when a flatboat sank in the Savannah River. This was most exasperating, with the demands of his creditors growing louder by the day. In January, Greene had to raise £655 to give to William Pierce, one of his attorneys, to keep the "wolves from the door." Collet, for his part, was satisfied for the time being when Greene signed a new note to cover his obligation for Banks's account.[25]

Nathanael Greene's efforts to get more money, especially for logging operations on Cumberland Island, had thus far been unsuccessful. Robert Morris had done his best to get a loan from Wilhem and Van Willink but with money very scarce, they were cautious. In July, 1785, the Dutchmen had written Greene that although they could not hazard a loan they might make a contract for oak and cedar if Greene's timber was of the best quality. Greene answered that he would be glad to furnish them with timber but before a reply came, Greene was dead.[26]

In 1785, Greene also wrote to Lafayette asking him if he would see if the French Navy was interested in buying some of his timber. Greene found Lafayette most obliging, and soon arrangements were made for Greene to send a small cargo of live oak to France as a sample of what he could supply the French Navy. Late in 1785 a ship put in at Cumberland Island for the timber but as it was not ready the vessel did not wait. Greene assured Lafayette shortly after he arrived in Georgia that by the next autumn a shipment would be ready as he was taking the family to Cumberland Island for the summer at which time he would be on hand to supervise the work.[27]

Nathanael Greene renewed his efforts to get a laboring

force together for the logging on Cumberland Island. Twenty white men had been sent to the island during the summer of 1785 but labor remained very scarce and the work on the island progressed slowly. For a time Greene thought of getting a force of German indentured servants but the idea was abandoned as they were not experienced enough with the ax. If Greene had lived, he probably would have turned to slave labor as the only recourse if the timber was to be marketed. Pendleton already was offering to raise some money for slaves if Greene wanted to operate with partners.[28]

In April Greene wrote his last observation regarding the future of the Union and the new nation. Nationalism, he thought, was gaining ground and the forces of political disintegration weakening. "If you can keep the Ship [of state] afloat a few years," he assured Charles Thomson who since 1775 had served as Secretary for the Continental Congress, "the navigation will be less difficult."[29]

Greene's last letter of a public nature was probably the one he sent to Joseph del Pozo y Sucre of St. Augustine apologizing for the way Sucre was used by Savannah officials on a recent visit to Georgia. In contrast, Greene had been treated with every mark of respect and courtesy on his visit to St. Augustine not long before. "Individuals in free Governments," explained Greene, "have it but too much in their power sometimes to insult strangers under the sanction of authority, which may be easily prevented under Governments where power is less in the hands of the people." Greene hoped Sucre would not judge Georgia by the acts of a few.[30]

One of Greene's last friendly letters was to Henry Knox. He thanked Knox for getting the inscription engraved on the cannon and only wished that he had peace of mind to enjoy his public trophies more. He was so overwhelmed with difficulties, he told Knox, he knew not which way to turn. He worked hard and lived poor and his family was actually distressed for want of money. Kitty was transformed from a gay lady to a sober housewife and was not too well. In closing, he asked Knox for his advice about sending little George to Lafayette to be educated in France as the latter had requested.[31]

On June 12th Nathanael and Kitty went to Savannah where

Greene had to see Nat Pendleton about the debt owing Collet. They stayed, as usual, with the Pendletons and the next morning started back for Mulberry Grove. On the way they stopped to see William Gibbons and rest the horses. Though the day was very hot, Nathanael went out with Gibbons to see his rice fields. Apparently Greene felt no ill effects from his tour of the plantation. After dinner Nathanael and Kitty bid good-by to the Gibbons and drove off toward Mulberry Grove.

On the way home while jogging along in the carriage, Nathanael's head began to ache. By the time he got to Mulberry Grove it was worse and he went right to bed. In the morning his head was still aching and he remained in bed. But the condition did not improve and by the next morning the pain was intense over his eyes where there appeared to be some swelling. That night Nat Pendleton arrived from Savannah and noted that the general seemed to be falling into a stupor. Alarmed by Greene's appearance, he sent for Dr. Brickel. When the physician arrived he took some blood and departed with the comment that he thought he would show improvement soon.

But the next day Nathanael was much worse. His whole head was now swollen and inflamed. Dr. M'Cloud was called in for consultation. More blood was taken and blisters applied. Two days more came and went without much change. Then during the night it became apparent that he was dying. About six o'clock on Monday morning, June 19th, 1786, he breathed his last. He had lived just a few weeks short of forty-five years. Anthony Wayne who was at his bedside when he died could hardly express his grief. "My dear friend General Greene is no more," he wrote to Colonel Jackson who was asked to prepare for the funeral services in Savannah.

Nathanael Greene's remains were brought down the river Tuesday morning and carried to the home of Nathanael Pendleton. In the afternoon the funeral was held with the whole town turning out for the mournful occasion. The funeral procession was led by a corps of artillery followed by the light infantry after which came the militia of Chatham County. Next in the procession came state officials and other men of prominence. They were followed by a band playing the *Dead March of Saul*. Then came the hearse and pallbearers escorted by a company of dragoons. After the hearse rode the family and principal mourners in carriages. A long line consisting of members of the Cincinnati, public officials and most of the citizens of the city and surrounding country ended the procession. As the procession slowly advanced, minute-guns were fired by the cannon at the fort. At the vault the Honorable William Stevens read the funeral service of the Episcopalian Church. As the casket was placed in the vault, salutes were fired by the infantry and militia. Then a thirteen-gun salute was fired from the cannon and the funeral ended.[32]

On August 8th, 1786, Congress resolved to erect a monument to the memory of Nathanael Greene at the seat of the Federal Government. Two years later Congress struck a medal in his honor. Not until 1877, however, did Congress redeem its pledge by erecting a bronze equestrian statue of Greene made by the sculptor Henry Kirk Brown. It stands in Stanton Square in the city of Washington. Not forgetting the man who had delivered the South from the hands of the enemy and had afterward made his home in Georgia, the citizens of Savannah in 1820 erected by private subscription a monument to Nathanael Greene. Under this monument in the center of the city of Savannah were later placed the remains of Nathanael Greene.

In the War for Independence, wrote Thomas Jefferson in 1822, Nathanael Greene was "second to no one in enterprise, in resource, in sound judgment, promptitude of decision, and every other military talent."[33] Looking back from our own time the verdict of history would appear to bear out Jefferson's opinion and confirm the observation of Francis Kinloch, an officer in the Revolution and Congressman from South Carolina, that Greene was "the greatest military genius" produced by the American Revolution.[34]

Notes

NOTES FOR CHAPTER I*

1. With some exceptions, the material for Chapter I has been sifted from George Washington Greene's *Life of Major General Nathanael Greene*, Vol. I, and from William Johnson's *Sketches of the Life and Correspondence of Nathanael Greene*, Vol. I, which contain most of what is known of Greene's early life.

2. Greene to Samuel Ward, Jr., dated only 1772, Greene Papers, RIHS.

3. *Idem*, Oct. 9, 1772, *ibid.*

4. *Loc. cit.*

NOTES FOR CHAPTER II

1. David S. Lovejoy, *Rhode Island Politics and the American Revolution, 1760-1776*, p. 152.

2. Greene to Samuel Ward, Jr., Sept. 24, 1770, Greene Papers, RIHS.

3. *Idem*, Sept. 26, 1771, *ibid.*

4. *Idem*, Aug. 29, 1772, *ibid.*

5. *Idem*, Oct. 9, 1772, *ibid.*

6. *Idem*, Potowomut, 1772, *ibid.*

7. *Idem*, Aug. 29, 1772, *ibid.*

8. *Idem*, Oct. 9, 1772, *ibid.*

9. *Idem*, no date, *ibid.*

10. *Idem*, Jan. 25, 1773, *ibid.*

11. *Idem*, July 21, 1773, *ibid.*

12. *Idem*, May 30, 1773, *ibid.*

13. S. G. Arnold, *History of the State of Rhode Island*, II, 310-311.

14. Greene to Ward, Jr., Jan. 25, 1773, *op. cit.*

15. *Loc. cit.*

16. *Idem*, Coventry, no date, *ibid.*

17. Minutes of the East Greenwich Monthly Meeting, Aug. to Dec., 1773.

18. William Johnson, *Sketches*, II, 451.

19. Greene to Ward, Jr., Jan. 17, 1774, *op. cit.*

20. George W. Greene, *Life of Nathanael Greene*, I, 75.

21. Greene to Ward, Jr., July 10, 1774, *op. cit.*

22. John Richard Alden, *General Gage in America*, pp. 212-221.

23. Papers of the Kentish Guards, RIHS; Rhode Island *Acts and Resolves, 1773-1774*, pp. 88-110.

---

* Additional bibliographical information pertaining to references cited in the footnotes will be found in the Bibliography.

24. Frederick Mackenzie, *Diary*, I, 10-11.
25. G. W. Greene, *op. cit.*, I, 46-49.
26. Rhode Island, *Acts and Resolves*, p. 145.
27. Rhode Island, *Acts and Resolves*, p. 149; Arnold, *op. cit.*, II, 340; Lovejoy, *op. cit.*, p. 176.
28. Edmund Field, ed., *State of Rhode Island and Providence Plantations*, III, 612.
29. G. W. Greene, *op. cit.*, I, 80-81.

NOTES FOR CHAPTER III

1. Rhode Island, *Acts and Resolves*, p. 8.
2. John Barker, *The British in Boston*, p. 40.
3. Thomas to his wife, May 24, 1775, Thomas MSS, MHS.
4. Greene to Thomas, May 23, 1775, Greene Misc. Papers, NYHS; James Abercrombie to Lord Loudoun, May 12, 1775, Loudoun Papers, Box 134, # 6484, HL.
5. Bancroft Transcripts, American Papers, II, 447, NYPL.
6. Greene to Kitty (his wife), June 2, 1775, Greene Coll., I, WCL.
7. George W. Greene, *Life of Nathanael Greene*, I, 94.
8. Abercrombie to Loudoun, May 22, 1775, *op. cit.*, Box 134, # 6484.
9. Abercrombie to Loudoun, June 12, 1775, *ibid.*, Box 134, # 6487.
10. Greene to Cooke, June 22, 1775, Greene Letters, Houghton Lib.
11. Abercrombie to Loudoun, June 20, 1775, *op. cit.*, Box 134, # 6488; Allen French, *The First Year*, p. 254.
12. *Massachusetts Historical Society, Proceedings*, XIV, 287.
13. Greene to Cooke, June 28, 1775, *op. cit.*
14. Greene to Cooke, Aug. 12, 1775, MSS, VI, 117-118, RIHS; Lee to Rush, July 20, Oct. 10, 1775, Lee to Robert Morris, Nov. 22, 1775, *Lee Papers*, I, 196, 212, 219; Allen French, *op. cit.*, p. 506; Alexander Graydon, *Memoirs*, pp. 154-155.
15. H. T. Wade and R. A. Lively, *This Glorious Cause*, p. 171.
16. J. Wilkinson, *Memoirs*, I, 19.
17. G. W. Greene, *op. cit.*, II, 417.
18. Henry Belcher, *The First American Civil War*, II, 4-6.
19. Mary A. Greene, *Gen. Nathanael Greene*.
20. *Ibid.*; Lee to Rush, July 20, 1775, *op. cit.*, I, 196.
21. G. W. Greene, *op. cit.*, I, 94, 95.
22. Alexander Garden, *Anecdotes of the American Revolution*, I, 65.
23. G. W. Greene, *op. cit.*, I, 93.
24. John Sullivan to the New Hampshire Committee of Safety, Aug. 5, 1775, Sullivan Papers, NHHS; William Gordon, *History of the Rise, Progress and Establishment*, II, 67-68.
25. G. W. Greene, *op. cit.*, I, 109-111.
26. William B. Reed, *Life and Correspondence of Joseph Reed*, I, 243.
27. Bernhard Knollenberg, *Washington and the Revolution*, pp. 112-115.
28. Joseph Reed to Charles Pettit, Sept. 11, 1775, Reed Papers, NYHS; Lee to Benjamin Rush, Oct. 1, 1775, *Lee Papers*, I, 212.
29. *Mag. of Am. Hist.* (July-Dec., 1890), p. 189; James Thacher, *Military Journal*, p. 31.

30. *Am. Hist. Rec.*, (Dec., 1872), I, 547-548.

31. Charles K. Bolton, *The Private Soldier under Washington*, p. 43.

32. G. W. Greene, *op. cit.*, I, 109.

33. Kenneth Rossman, *Thomas Mifflin*, p. 53; T. S. Anderson, *The Command of the Howe Brothers*, p. 11.

34. G. W. Greene, *op. cit.*, I, 141.

35. Greene to Governor Ward, Oct. 16, 1775, *Correspondence of Governor Samuel Ward*, pp. 102-106.

36. Gov. Ward to Henry Ward, Nov. 21, 1775, *ibid.*, pp. 124-126.

37. Greene to Gov. Ward, Oct. 16, 1775, *ibid.*, pp. 102-106; Greene to Jacob Greene, Dec. 20, 1775, P. Force, *Am. Arch.*, 4th Ser., IV, 368; G. W. Greene, *op. cit.*, I, 118.

38. Greene to Gov. Ward, Dec. 10, 1775, *ibid.*, pp. 137-139.

39. *Loc. cit.*

40. *Idem*, Dec. 31, 1775, *ibid.*, pp. 152-157.

41. Lee to Gov. Ward, Jan., 1776, *ibid.*, pp. 169-170.

42. Greene to Gov. Ward, Oct. 23, 1775, *ibid.*, pp. 108-110; Greene to Cooke, Oct. 24, 1775, Force, *op. cit.*, III, 1145, 1168.

43. G. W. Greene, *op. cit.*, I, 125-126.

44. Greene to Gov. Ward, Dec. 31, 1775, *op. cit.*; Lee to Rush, Dec. 12, 1775, *Lee Papers*, I, 226.

45. *Lee Papers*, I, 246.

46. William Heath, *Memoirs*, p. 49; Ebenezer David, *A Rhode Island Chaplain*, p. 13.

47. Christopher Ward, *The War of the Revolution*, I, 126-130; Douglas S. Freeman, *George Washington*, IV, 163.

48. John Barker, *The British in Boston*, p. 70; James Thacher, *Military Journal*, pp. 40-41; J. C. Fitzpatrick, ed., *Writings of George Washington*, IV, 373; G. W. Greene, *op. cit.*, I, 148; French, *op. cit.*, p. 672.

49. Frank Moore, *Diary of the American Revolution*, I, 225.

NOTES FOR CHAPTER IV

1. Mitchell's Orderly Book, April, 1776; G. W. Greene, *Life of Nathanael Greene*, I, 154; J. C. Fitzpatrick, ed., *Writings of George Washington*, IV, 479-480.

2. Lee to Washington, Feb. 19, Mar. 3, 1776, *Lee Papers*, I, 308, 343.

3. *Idem*, Feb. 19, 1776, *ibid.*, I, 308; N. J. Prov. Congress, March 2, 1776, Stirling Papers, IV, 61, NYHS.

4. Greene's Orders, Aug. 3, 1776, NYPL.

5. Letter from New York, April 2, 1776, H. P. Johnston, "The Campaign of 1776," p. 132.

6. *New York Gazette and the Weekly Mercury*, April 18, 1776.

7. Greene to Washington, May 21, 1776, Peter Force, *Am. Arch.*, 4th Ser., VI, 536.

8. Greene to Adams, May 26, June 2, 1776, Greene Coll., I, HL.

9. Adams to Greene, June 22, 1776, *Works of John Adams*, IX, 402-403; Greene to Adams, June 2, 1776, *op cit.*, Emmet Coll., # 5688, NYHS.

10. Reed to Catherine Reed, Aug. 7, 1776, Reed Papers, III, NYHS; William Heath, *Memoirs*, p. 58.

11. Reed to Pettit, Aug. 29, 1775, Reed Papers, II, NYHS.

12. Charles Lee to Richard Henry Lee, Sept. 2, 1775, Correspondence of Richard Henry Lee and Arthur Lee, I, 151, APS.

13. Greene to Gov. Cooke, Sept. 12, 1775, Greene Misc. Papers, NYHS.

14. Greene to Governor Ward, Oct. 23, 1775, *Correspondence of Governor Samuel Ward*, p. 111.

15. Account of his journey to distribute donations, by Moses Brown, entry for Dec. 12, 1775, Moses Brown Papers, Vol. XII, RIHS.

16. Greene to Jacob Greene, Dec. 20, 1775, Force, *op. cit.*, IV, 367.

17. Greene to Gov. Ward, Jan. 4, 1776, *Correspondence*, pp. 166-167.

18. Pettit to Reed, March 25, 1776, Reed Papers, IV, NYHS.

19. Theodore Thayer, *Pennsylvania Politics and the Growth of Democracy, 1740-1776*, p. 181.

20. Lee to Rush, Feb. 25, 1776, *Lee Papers*, I, 325; Stirling to Putnam, March 10, 1776, Stirling Papers, IV, 69, NYHS.

21. Gov. Cooke to Stephen Hopkins, May 7, 1776, N. Cooke, "Revolutionary Correspondence," *Proc. of the Am. Antiq. Soc., New Ser.*, V, 34, pp. 323-324; G. W. Greene, *Life of Nathanael Greene*, I, 182.

22. G. W. Greene, *ibid.*, II, 424.

23. W. Gordon, *History of the Rise, Progress and Establishment*, II, 278.

24. Reed to Catherine Reed, July 16, 1776, Reed Papers, IV, NYHS.

25. E. J. Lowell, *The Hessians in the Revolutionary War*, p. 56.

26. *New York Packet*, Aug. 1, 1776.

27. F. Mackenzie, *Diary*, I, 44; Gordon, *op. cit.*, II, 322; Edmund C. Burnett, *The Continental Congress*, p. 204.

28. Henry P. Johnston, *Battle of Harlem Heights*, p. 213; A. Serle, *American Journal of Ambrose Serle*, p. 47.

29. Greene to Washington, July 25, 1776, Fitzpatrick, *op. cit.*, V, 338n; G. W. Greene, *op. cit.*, I, 186.

30. Adams to Greene, Aug. 4, 1776, *Works of John Adams*, I, 251-253; G. W. Greene, *op. cit.*, II, 425-427.

31. Reed to Catherine Reed, Aug. 4, 1776, Reed Papers, IV, NYHS.

32. John Montresor, "Journals," NYHS Coll. (1881), p. 121; Henry Clinton, *The American Rebellion*, p. xxiii.

33. Gordon, *op. cit.*, II, 311, sets the American losses at 1,500.

34. A. Graydon, *Memoirs*, p. 179.

35. G. W. Greene, *op. cit.*, I, 207; Knox to Adams, Sept. 25, 1776, *Proc. of the Am. Antiq. Soc.*, V, 56, p. 217; *Works of John Adams*, IX, 437-438.

NOTES FOR CHAPTER V

1. T. S. Anderson, *The Command of the Howe Brothers*, pp. 71, 136.

2. Ellery to Cooke, Oct. 15, 1776, Letters to the Governors, VIII, 76, State Archives, R. I.

3. Greene to Washington, Sept. 5, 1776, Peter Force, *Am. Arch.*, 5th Ser., II, 182.

4. G. W. Greene, *Life of Nathanael Greene*, I, 212.

5. *Ibid.*, I, 220.

6. Caesar Rodney, *Letters*, p. 63.

7. Lee to Gates, Oct. 14, 1776, Lee to Rush, Nov. 2, 1776, *Lee Papers*, II, 261-263.

8. William Heath, *Memoirs*, p. 70; G. W. Greene, *op. cit.*, I, 216; W. B. Reed, *Life and Correspondence*, I, 236; Douglas S. Freeman, *George Washington*, IV, 193.

9. Reed, *op. cit.*, I, 237-238.

10. Tilghman to Duer, Oct. 14, 1776, Force, *op. cit.*, III, 870; H. P. Johnston, "The Campaign of 1776," p. 267.

11. G. W. Greene, *op. cit.*, I, 222-225.

12. Reed to Catherine Reed, Nov. 6, 1776, Reed Papers, IV, NYHS.

13. Freeman, *op. cit.*, IV, 237.

14. Greene to Washington, Nov. 5, 10, 11, 1776, Force, *op. cit.*, III, 523, 556, 629, 638; G. W. Greene, *op. cit.*, I, 261-268.

15. Greene to Kitty, Nov. 2, 1776, Smith Coll., MNPL; G. W. Greene, *op. cit.*, I, 253; Reed, *op. cit.*, I, 323.

16. Washington to Greene, Nov. 7, 8, 1776, J. C. Fitzpatrick, ed., *Writings of George Washington*, VI, 254, 258; G. W. Greene, *op. cit.*, I, 242-246.

17. Greene to Washington, Nov. 8, 1776, Fitzpatrick, *op. cit.*, VI, 258; Force, *op. cit.*, III, 618; Anderson, *op. cit.*, p. 99.

18. Magaw to Greene, Nov. 12, 1776, Greene Coll., I, WCL; Greene to the President of Congress, Nov. 12, 1776, Force, *op. cit.*, III, 652-653.

19. Johnston, *op. cit.*, p. 284; G. W. Greene, *op. cit.*, II, 436-474. Freeman attributes Washington's failure on this occasion to a tired mind caused by the excessive strain undergone since Howe's arrival. (Freeman, IV, 245 ff.). Also see B. Knollenberg, *Washington and the Revolution*, for a critical evaluation of Washington. Some historians have attempted to exonerate Washington on the assumption that he felt governed by his council of war on military decisions. Washington, however, had not submitted the question to his staff. Neither was he governed by orders from Congress that the fort should be held. For a detailed account see E. F. DeLancey, *The Capture of Mount Washington*.

20. Greene to Washington, Nov. 15, 1776, Magaw to Greene, Nov. 15, 1776, Johnston, *op. cit.*, pp. 278-279; Force, *op. cit.*, III, 699, 700. Force, *op. cit.*, III, 699, 700.

21. Lee to Reed, Nov. 16, 1776, *Lee Papers*, II, 283.

22. F. Mackenzie, *Diary*, I, 95-102.

23. A. Graydon, *Memoirs*, pp. 189-191.

24. Greene to Knox, Nov. 17, 1776, Knox Papers, III, MHS.

25. Johnston, *op. cit.*, pp. 101, 284.

26. *Loc. cit.;* G. W. Greene, *op. cit.*, II, 136, 431.

27. Graydon, *op. cit.*, pp. 211-212; G. W. Greene, *op. cit.*, II, 431 ff.

28. *Journal of Nicholas Cresswell*, pp. 257-258; Ambrose Serle, *Journal*, p. 143.

29. Tench Tilghman to Robert Livingston, Nov. 17, 1776, Force, *op. cit.*, III, 740.

30. Mifflin to Robert Morris, Nov. 21, 1776, "Letters," *NYHS Coll.*, (1878), p. 405.

31. Reed to Charles Lee, Nov. 21, 1776, *Lee Papers*, II, 293-294.

32. Lee to Reed, Nov. 24, 1776, *ibid.*, II, 305.

33. Reed to Lee, Nov. 21, 1776, *ibid.*, II, 293.

34. Lee to Washington, Nov. 19, 1776, Force, *op. cit.*, III, 767; Washington to Lee, Nov. 21, 1776, Fitzpatrick, *op. cit.*, VI, 298.

35. G. W. Greene, *op. cit.*, I, 278, II, 454; Leonard Lundin, *Cockpit of the Revolution*, p. 142.

36. Mackenzie, *op. cit.*, I, 113; Greene to Cooke, Dec. 21, 1776, Force, *op. cit.*, III, 1342; Fitzpatrick, *op. cit.*, VI, 295; G. W. Greene, *op. cit.*, II, 451-454.

37. Heath, *Memoirs*, pp. 98-99.

38. Fitzpatrick, *op. cit.*, VI, 299.

39. *Ibid.*, VI, 305, 306, 309.

40. Anderson, *The Command of the Howe Brothers*, p. 214; G. W. Greene, *op. cit.*, I, 285, 295, 300.

41. Fitzpatrick, *op. cit.*, VI, 315, 318-319, 397.

42. Greene to Governor Cooke, Dec. 21, 1776, G. W. Greene, *op. cit.*, I, 293-295.

43. Greene to Cooke, Dec. 4, 1776, G. W. Greene, *op. cit.*, I, 280-282; C. K. Bolton, *Private Soldier under Washington*, p. 52.

44. Fitzpatrick, *op. cit.*, VI, 336-339; Freeman, *op. cit.*, IV, 276; Emmet Coll., # 1584, NYPL.

45. Freeman, *op. cit.*, IV, 291, *passim*.

46. Emmet Coll., # 1575, NYPL; Mifflin to Reed, Nov. 26, 1776, Reed Papers, IV, NYHS; Fitzpatrick, *op. cit.*, VI, 324, 364-365; K. R. Rossman, *Thomas Mifflin*, p. 73; Reed, *op. cit.*, I, 266; F. Moore, *Diary*, I, 352.

47. Lee to Gates, Dec. 11, 1776, *Lee Papers*, II, 345; Heath, *op. cit.*, pp. 113-114; Fitzpatrick, *op. cit.*, VI, 407.

48. Lee to Washington, Dec. 4, 8, 1776, *Lee Papers*, II, 329-330; Fitzpatrick, *op. cit.*, VI, 326, *passim*.

49. Lee to Heath, Dec. 9, 1776, *Lee Papers*, II, 340.

50. Greene to Washington, Dec. 7, 1776, Force, *op cit.*, III, 1197-1198.

51. Fitzpatrick, *op. cit.*, VI, 340-341.

52. Lee to Gates, Dec. 13, 1776, *Lee Papers*, II, 348.

53. J. Wilkinson, *Memoirs*, I, 109-110; *Lee Papers*, II, 345.

54. Fitzpatrick, *op. cit.*, VI, 378; Force, *op. cit.*, III, 1247; G. W. Greene, *op. cit.*, I, 284-285.

55. Fitzpatrick, *op. cit.*, VI, 352, 398.

56. Greene to Hancock, Dec. 21, 1776, Greene Coll., I, WCL. Also in Force, *op. cit.*, III, 1342; Fitzpatrick, *op. cit.*, VI, 461-462; G. W. Greene, *op. cit.*, I, 289-290.

57. E. C. Burnett, *Continental Congress*, p. 233; G. W. Greene, *op. cit.*, I, 291.

58. *Pa. Mag. of Hist. and Biog.*, IV, 145-146.

59. Greene to Cooke, Dec. 21, 1776, Force, *op. cit.*, III, 1342; G. W. Greene, *op. cit.*, I, 284-286.

60. Fitzpatrick, *op. cit.*, VI, 366.

61. Greene to Cooke, Dec. 21, 1776, Force, *op. cit.*, III, 1342.

62. Fitzpatrick, *op. cit.*, VI, 427n.

63. *Ibid.*, VI, 366.

NOTES FOR CHAPTER VI

1. Howe to Lord George Germain, Nov. 30, Dec. 20, 1776, Peter Force, *Am. Arch.*, *5th. Ser.*, III, 826, 1317-1318.
2. William Stryker, *Trenton and Princeton*, p. 94.
3. *Ibid.*, pp. 323-324, 326; von Jungkenn MSS, I, 26, WCL.
4. G. W. Greene, *Life of Nathanael Greene*, I, 300.
5. J. C. Fitzpatrick, *Writings of George Washington*, VI, 444. Washington actually had nearly 1,000 more troops than von Donop.
6. D. S. Freeman, *George Washington*, IV, 323.
7. W. Gordon, *History of the Rise, Progress and Establishment*, II, 396.
8. Greene to his wife, Jan. 10, 1777, Greene Coll., V, 88, WCL.
9. Fitzpatrick, *op. cit.*, VI, 446.
10. *Ibid.*, VI, 448.
11. Greene to Governor Cooke, Jan. 10, 1777, Sparks Coll., Vol. 59, p. 109; Houghton Lib.; Fitzpatrick, *op. cit.*, VI, 458, 461; Freeman, *op. cit.*, IV, 332-334.
12. Stryker, *op. cit.*, p. 482.
13. Catherine Williams, *Biography of Revolutionary Heroes*, pp. 193-194.
14. James Wilkinson, *Memoirs*, I, 140.
15. T. J. Wertenbaker, "The Battle of Princeton," *The Princeton Battle Monument*, pp. 52-63.
16. Alfred H. Bill, *The Campaign of Princeton*, pp. 100-122.
17. B. Rush to R. H. Lee, Jan. 7, 1777, Lee Correspondence, I, 265, APS; Fitzpatrick, *op. cit.*, VI, 469; Gordon, *op. cit.*, II, 402; Wilkinson, *op. cit.*, I, 148; Freeman, *op. cit.*, IV, 365; C. Ward, *War of the Revolution*, I, 316. General Mercer died on January 12.
18. Greene to Cooke, Jan. 10, 1777, *op. cit.*; Fitzpatrick, *op. cit.*, VI, 469.
19. John Chilton, "Diary," *Tyler's Quarterly*, XII, p. 285.
20. Fitzpatrick, *op. cit.*, VI, 471-473; Freeman, *op. cit.*, IV, 384.
21. Fitzpatrick, *op. cit.*, VII, 160, 182, 189; L. Lundin, *Cockpit of the Revolution*, pp. 231-233; William P. Tuttle, *Bottle Hill and Madison*, pp. 19-26; E. Boudinot, *Journal of Historical Recollections*.
22. G. W. Greene, *op. cit.*, I, 310-311.
23. Freeman, *op. cit.*, IV, 361; K. R. Rossman, *Thomas Mifflin*, p. 791.
24. Wilkinson, *op. cit.*, I, 153. Gordon believed the army at one time was reduced to as low as 1,500. Gordon, *op. cit.*, II, 422.
25. Greene to Adams, May 2, 1777, Greene Coll., II, HL.
26. *Pa. Mag. of Hist. and Biog.*, Vol. 62, p. 497; Fitzpatrick, *op. cit.*, VI, 482, 489; Freeman, *op. cit.*, IV, 388, 406; G. W. Greene, *op. cit.*, I, 328.
27. Greene to Cooke, Jan. 23, 1777, Greene Coll., HL; G. W. Greene, *op. cit.*, I, 315-319.
28. G. W. Greene, *op. cit.*, I, 314-321.
29. Greene to Col. Waldon, Feb. 24, 1777, Greene to Weedon, Feb. 24, 1777, Greene Coll., II, HL; Dickinson to Washington, Feb. 19, 1777, Gates Papers, Box 6, # 36, NYHS; G. W. Greene, *op. cit.*, I, 325, 332.

30. G. W. Greene, *op. cit.*, I, 334-336.

31. Thomas Jones, *History of New York*, I, 173-175.

32. Fitzpatrick, *op. cit.*, VII, 224.

33. Greene to Adams, March 3, 1777, Greene Coll., II, HL; T. Tilghman to Robert Morris, March 2, 1777, *NYHS Coll.* (1878), pp. 423-424; Adams to Greene, March, 1777, E. Burnett, *Letters*, II, 299; Fitzpatrick, *op. cit.*, II, 226n; G. W. Greene, *op. cit.*, I, 339.

34. J. R. Alden, *General Charles Lee*, pp. 169, 171, 174-179; *Lee Papers*, II, 365-366.

35. Fitzpatrick, *op. cit.*, VII, 294, 299-301.

36. G. W. Greene, *op. cit.*, I, 349; E. C. Burnett, *The Continental Congress*, pp. 300-301.

37. Freeman, *op. cit.*, IV, 395; Fitzpatrick, *op. cit.*, VII, 352-353; *Pa. Mag. of Hist. and Biog.*, XXVII, 139-140.

38. Burnett, *Letters*, II, 299.

39. John Adams, *Familiar Letters*, p. 276.

40. Greene's letter, May 20, 1777, Greene Papers, RIHS.

41. Greene to Lincoln, April 19, 1777, Greene Coll., II, HL; G. W. Greene, *op. cit.*, I, 362-364; Freeman, *op. cit.*, IV, 408; Lundin, *op. cit.*, p. 255; Fitzpatrick, *op. cit.*, VIII, 6n.

42. G. W. Greene, *op. cit.*, I, 355-356.

43. Fitzpatrick, *op. cit.*, VIII, 51-52; G. W. Greene, *op. cit.*, I, 369; George Clinton, *Public Papers*, I, 828-829; Greene to Clinton, May 14, 1777, *Proc. of the N. J. Hist. Soc.*, Vol. 61, p. 181; E. M. Ruttenber, *Obstructions to the Navigation of Hudson's River*, pp. 70 ff.

44. G. W. Greene, *op. cit.*, I, 371-376; *Pa. Mag. of Hist. and Biog.*, Vol. 70, p. 294.

45. G. W. Greene, *op. cit.*, I, 374.

46. *Ibid.*, I, 375.

47. Greene to Kitty, April 5, 1777, Greene Coll., Vol. 88, WCL; G. W. Greene, *op. cit.*, I, 377.

NOTES FOR CHAPTER VII

1. G. W. Greene, *Life of Nathanael Greene*, I, 389-391; J. C. Fitzpatrick, ed., *Writings of George Washington*, VIII, 175-181.

2. Greene to Sullivan, May 31, 1777, Greene Coll., I, WCL.

3. Fitzpatrick, *op. cit.*, VIII, 143, 181.

4. T. S. Anderson, *The Command of the Howe Brothers*, p. 238.

5. Fitzpatrick, *op. cit.*, VIII, 243-244, 248; Frank Moore, *Diary*, I, 446-447.

6. Moore, *op. cit.*, I, 450; Fitzpatrick, *op. cit.*, VIII, 263, 266-267, 353, 358, 360.

7. Fitzpatrick, *op. cit.*, VIII, 281-296; H. Knox to Lucy Knox, June 23, 1777, *Proc. of the N. J. Hist. Soc.*, Vol. 61, p. 23; G. W. Greene, *op. cit.*, I, 393-394.

8. Fitzpatrick, *op. cit.*, VIII, 298-299, 307-308; John Montresor, "Journals," pp. 424-425; Moore, *op. cit.*, I, 449-451; L. Lundin, *Cockpit of the Revolution*, pp. 323-324.

9. Fitzpatrick, *op. cit.*, VIII, 336, 340; Greene to James Abeel, July 5, 1777, Greene Folder, NYHS; G. W. Greene, *op. cit.*, I, 399.

10. Fitzpatrick, *op. cit.*, VIII, 407; G. W. Greene, *op. cit.*, I, 398.

11. G. W. Greene, *op. cit.*, I, 398-399.

12. K. R. Rossman, *Thomas Mifflin*, p. 97; Fitzpatrick, *op. cit.*, VIII, 427. See also Greene to Jacob Greene, Feb. 7, 1777, Greene Coll., HL.

13. Greene to Kitty, July 23, 1777, Greene Coll., I, WCL.

14. Fitzpatrick, *op. cit.*, VIII, 460-461, 472.

15. Fitzpatrick, *op. cit.*, VIII, 501-502. Part of the army under Stephen marched through Sussex County to the right of the route followed by Greene's divisions.

16. Greene to Cooke, July 29, 1777, Greene Coll., I, WCL.

17. Fitzpatrick, *op. cit.*, VIII, 499n.

18. Knox to Lucy Knox, Aug. 2, 1777, Knox Papers, MHS.

19. Fitzpatrick, *op. cit.*, IX, 13, 43-44.

20. Montresor, *op. cit.*, pp. 434-444.

21. Fitzpatrick, *op. cit.*, IX, 70.

22. Greene to Varnum, Aug. 17, 1777, Greene Coll., II, HL; G. W. Greene, *op. cit.*, I, 439.

23. G. W. Greene, *op. cit.*, I, 431.

24. *Ibid.*, I, 435-436; A. Graydon, *Memoirs*, p. 143.

25. Fitzpatrick, *op. cit.*, IX, 109-110; G. W. Greene, *op. cit.*, I, 441.

26. Fitzpatrick, *op. cit.*, IX, 114-116; Montresor, *op. cit.*, p. 441.

27. Fitzpatrick, *op. cit.*, IX, 128n.

28. D. S. Freeman, *George Washington*, IV, 463-464; Graydon, *op. cit.*, p. 291.

29. Fitzpatrick, *op. cit.*, IX, 129-130; Montresor, *op. cit.*, pp. 442-445.

30. G. W. Greene, *op. cit.*, I, 416-417.

31. Adams to Greene, June 25, 1777, *Rhode Island History*, Vol. 1 (July, 1942), No. 3.

32. G. W. Greene, *op. cit.*, I, 417; Louis Gottschalk, *Lafayette Joins the American Army*, p. 25.

33. Fitzpatrick, *op. cit.*, VIII, 75-76.

34. Gottschalk, *op. cit.*, p. 16.

35. Fitzpatrick, *op. cit.*, VIII, 149, 159, 187-190.

36. G. W. Greene, *op. cit.*, I, 420.

37. E. C. Burnett, *Letters*, II, 403-406, 408.

38. Adams to Greene, July 17, 1777, Burnett, *op. cit.*, II, 404-405.

39. G. W. Greene, *op. cit.*, I, 422-423; Freeman, *op. cit.*, IV, 455-456; Burnett, *op. cit.*, II, 403-406, 408. Apparently neither Knox nor Sullivan made a reply to Congress. Freeman, *op. cit.*, IV, 456n.

40. Anderson, *op. cit.*, pp. 221, 224-225.

NOTES FOR CHAPTER VIII

1. Marquis Lafayette, *Memoirs*, I, 21; J. C. Fitzpatrick, ed., *Writings of George Washington*, IX, 132, 136; G. W. Greene, *Life of Nathanael Greene*, I, 443-444.

2. G. W. Greene, *op. cit.*, I, 444; Fitzpatrick, *op. cit.*, IX, 179-180; A. Graydon, *Memoirs*, p. 292.

3. Fitzpatrick, *op. cit.*, IX, 146; G. W. Greene, *op. cit.*, I, 446.

4. G. W. Greene, *op. cit.*, I, 446; C. L. Baurmeister, *Journals*, pp. 103-104.

5. Fitzpatrick, *op. cit.*, IX, 197-203; Graydon, *op. cit.*, p. 292.

6. G. W. Greene, *op. cit.*, I, 446-447.

7. *Ibid.*, I, 447; Fitzpatrick, *op. cit.*, IX, 143-144; C. Ward, *War of the Revolution*, I, 342; J. Montresor, "Journals," p. 517.

8. John Sullivan, *Letters and Papers*, I, 475-476; D. S. Freeman, *George Washington*, IV, 475-479; Ward, *op. cit.*, I, 346.

9. Montresor, *op. cit.*, pp. 449, 516-517.

10. Fitzpatrick, *op. cit.*, IX, 207.

11. Robert Bruce, *Brandywine*, pp. 24-25; G. W. Greene, *op. cit.*, I, 449-453, II, 462; Freeman, *op. cit.*, IV, 480; Ward, *op. cit.*, I, 349-350.

12. Freeman, *op. cit.*, IV, 488.

13. Fitzpatrick, *op. cit.*, IX, 209.

14. G. W. Greene, *op. cit.*, I, 457; W. Gordon, *History of the Rise, Progress and Establishment*, II, 514.

15. Fitzpatrick, IX, 220, 229; Baurmeister, *op. cit.*, pp. 113 ff.

16. Baron de Kalb to Duc de Broglie, Sept. 4 to Oct. 11, 1777, B. F. Stevens, *Facsimiles*, # 755.

17. *Loc. cit.*

18. G. W. Greene, *op. cit.*, I, 465; Fitzpatrick, *op. cit.*, IX, 238.

19. Fitzpatrick, *op. cit.*, IX, 246-247; Montresor, *op. cit.*, p. 457; Diary of John Miller, Sept., 1777, Reed Papers, NYHS.

20. Fitzpatrick, *op. cit.*, IX, 309; Ward, *op. cit.*, I, 365-366; Walter Stern's Account, Gates Papers, Box 8, NYHS.

21. Wayne to his wife, Oct. 6, 1777, Wayne Papers, HSP; Account of the Battle of Germantown, McDougall Papers, III, NYHS; Stearns to Gates, Oct. 14, 1777, Gates Papers, Box 8, NYHS; G. W. Greene, *op. cit.*, I, 477-479.

22. B. Knollenberg, *Washington and the Revolution*, p. 69; Gordon, *op. cit.*, II, 525; W. B. Reed, *Life and Correspondence*, I, 322-323; Fitzpatrick, *op. cit.*, IX, 398.

23. Reed, *op. cit.*, I, 321; Wayne to his wife, Oct., 1777, Wayne Papers, HSP.

24. Gordon, *op. cit.*, II, 527; G. W. Greene, *op. cit.*, II, 483-485.

25. *Pa. Mag. of Hist. and Biog.*, XVIII, 5-11.

26. Fitzpatrick, *op. cit.*, IX, 326-327, 345, 376, 380-381; G. W. Greene, *op. cit.*, I, 485-486.

27. *Pa. Mag. of Hist. and Biog.*, XLI, 251.

28. Greene to one of his brothers, Oct. 27, 1777, Smith Coll., MNPL; Fitzpatrick, *op. cit.*, IX, 413.

29. G. W. Greene, *op. cit.*, I, 506-507, 533.

30. Fitzpatrick, *op. cit.*, X, 96.

31. G. W. Greene, *op. cit.*, I, 521.

32. *Ibid.*, I, 523-524.

33. Fitzpatrick, *op. cit.*, X, 103; Wayne to Richard Peters, Nov. 18, 1777, Wayne Papers, HSP; Reed, *op. cit.*, I, 341.

34. Baurmeister, *op. cit.*, p. 145; Fitzpatrick, *op. cit.*, X, 143-144; Reed, *op. cit.*, I, 350-351.

NOTES FOR CHAPTER IX

1. Greene to Marchant, Nov. 17, 1777, Greene Coll., II, HL.

2. Greene to McDougall, Jan. 25, 1778, McDougall Papers, III, NYHS; Lux to Greene, May 26, 1778, Greene Coll., II, WCL; A. Graydon, *Memoirs*, p. 299.

3. Wayne to Gates, Nov. 21, 1777, Lovell to Gates, Nov. 17, 1777, Gates Papers, Box 8, NYHS.

4. Clark to Greene, Jan. 10, 1778, Greene Coll., II, WCL; G. W. Greene, *Life of Nathanael Greene*, II, 33.

5. H. Lee, *Memoirs*, p. 582; J. Laurens, *Army Correspondence*, p. 21; Greene to McDougall, Jan. 25, 1778, McDougall Papers, III, NYHS.

6. H. Lee, *op. cit.*, I, 260; G. W. Greene, *op. cit.*, II, 15; D. S. Freeman, *George Washington*, IV, 605.

7. Lovell to Gates, Nov. 17, 1777, Gates Papers, Box 8, NYHS; G. W. Greene, *op. cit.*, II, 7-8.

8. Lovell to Gates, Nov. 27, 1777, Gates Papers, Box 8, NYHS.

9. J. Adams, *Letters*, I, 264; G. W. Greene, *op. cit.*, II, 4-5.

10. Rush MSS, XXIX, 136, Ridgway Lib.

11. Freeman, *op. cit.*, IV, 551, 598; G. W. Greene, *op. cit.*, II, 8-9.

12. Wilkinson to Gates, Nov. 8, 1777, Gates Papers, Box 8, NYHS; J. Wilkinson, *Memoirs*, I, 330-332, 339; Tilghman to Robert Morris, Dec. 2, 1778, "Letters," *NYHS Coll.* (1878), pp. 434-435.

13. Greene to Jacob Greene, Jan. 3, 1778, Greene Coll., III, HL; Greene to McDougall, Jan. 25, 1778, McDougall Papers, III, NYHS; Clark to Stirling, Jan. 15, 1778, Stirling Papers, IV, 94, NYHS; G. W. Greene, *op. cit.*, II, 31.

14. G. W. Greene, *op. cit.*, I, 547-548.

15. Greene's letter, Feb. 25, 1778, Greene Misc. Papers, NYHS; Knollenberg, *Washington and the Revolution*, pp. 78-91; E. Burnett, *Letters*, p. 295; G. W. Greene, *op. cit.*, II, 38-39.

16. Lux to Greene, May 26, 1778, Greene Coll., II, WCL.

17. Knollenberg, *op. cit.*, p. 70; J. Thacher, *Military Journal*, pp. 127-129.

18. K. R. Rossman, *Thomas Mifflin*, p. 137; Letter of Richard Peters, Jan. 29, 1778, Wayne Papers, HSP.

19. Wayne to Peters, Dec. 30, 1777, Wayne Papers, HSP; J. C. Fitzpatrick, ed., *Writings of George Washington*, X, 170-171, 180; G. W. Greene, *op. cit.*, I, 538-539.

20. Thacher, *op. cit.*, p. 126; Wayne to Peters, Dec. 30, 1777, Wayne Papers, HSP; G. W. Greene, *op. cit.*, I, 543-545; Freeman, *op. cit.*, IV, 570-571; W. B. Reed, *Life and Correspondence*, I, 361.

21. Reed's letter, Jan. 7, 1778, Reed Papers, V, NYHS; Freeman, *op. cit.*, IV, 614; *Pa. Mag. of Hist. and Biog.*, XXI, 314-315.

22. Fitzpatrick, *op. cit.*, X, 454; Freeman, *op. cit.*, IV, 575.

23. Knox to his wife, Dec. 2, 1777, Knox Papers, MHS; Greene to McDougall, Feb. 5, 1778, McDougall Papers, III, NYHS.

24. H. Swiggett, *The Forgotten Leaders of the Revolution*, pp. 49-51.

25. J. M. Palmer, *General Von Steuben*, pp. 103 ff.

26. G. W. Greene, *op. cit.*, II, 47; Reed, *op. cit.*, I, 363.

27. Burnett, *op. cit.*, III, 83; *Am. State Papers*, Class IX, Claims, p. 245.

28. G. W. Greene, *op. cit.*, II, 49, 466, 505-506; W. Johnson, *Sketches*, I, 138-141.

29. George Washington Greene quite naturally rules out the money motive entirely. G. W. Greene, *op. cit.*, II, 474, 503-504.

30. Greene to Laurens, May 1, 1778, Greene Coll., II, WCL; G. W. Greene, *op. cit.*, II, 51-52, 66-67.

31. *Pa. Mag. of Hist. and Biog.*, XLII, 310-311; G. W. Greene, *op. cit.*, II, 43-47, 53; Reed, *op. cit.*, I, 361; Greene to Biddle, March 23, 1778, Greene Coll., III, HL.

32. Greene Coll., LXXXVII, WCL; Washington Papers, Vol. 161, p. 77n, LC.

33. G. W. Greene, *op. cit.*, II, 59-60, 83; *Journals of the Cont. Congress*, XXXIII, 643; Greene to Laurens, April 3, 1778, Greene Coll., II, WCL.

34. Greene to Griffin Greene, Feb. 9, 1779, Oct. 22, 1780, Greene Papers, MCL.

35. *Idem*, May 25, 1778, *ibid*.

36. Jacob Greene to Greene, April 12, 1778, Griffin Greene to Greene, May 24, 1778, Greene Coll., II, WCL; Greene to Griffin Greene, May 25, 1778, Greene Papers, MCL.

37. Griffin Greene to Greene, May 24, 1778, Greene Coll., II, WCL; G. W. Greene, *op. cit.*, II, 77.

38. Griffin Greene to Greene, April 13, 1778, Greene Coll., III, WCL; Greene to Griffin Greene, April 30, 1779, Greene Papers, MCL.

39. *Journals of the Continental Congress*, XXXIII, 643; Greene to Duane, April 16, 1779, Greene Coll., IV, HL.

40. Greene to Calhoun, April 18, 1778, Greene Coll., III, WCL.

41. Pettit to Greene, April 8, 1778, Greene Coll., III, WCL.

42. Greene to Griffin Greene, Sept. 18, 1779, Greene Papers, MCL.

43. Griffin Greene to Greene, Jan. 13, 1780, Greene Papers, LC; Jacob Greene to Greene, May 7, 1780, Greene Coll., VII, WCL; Greene to Gov. Greene, Sept. 3, 1780, Greene Coll., VIII, WCL. See also the letters of Nathanael and Griffin Greene in the Marietta College Library.

44. Articles of Agreement between Greene, Wadsworth, and Deane, 1779, Greene Coll., V, WCL; Wadsworth to Greene, Oct. 17, 1782, Wadsworth Papers, WA; Freeman, *op. cit.*, V, 507n.

45. Deane to Wadsworth, Dec. 8, 1779, Wadsworth Coll., CHS; Cash Book # 148, Wadsworth Coll., CHS; Greene to Wadsworth, Dec. 19, 1779, Wadsworth Coll., # 130, CHS; Wadsworth to Greene, Sept. 16, 1779, April 27, 1780, July 6, 1780, Sept. 3, 1780, Wadsworth Papers, WA; Greene to Wadsworth, Feb. 19, 1782 May 8, 1780, Greene Papers, YUL.

46. Greene to Wadsworth, April 30, 1779, Wadsworth Coll., CHS.

47. Greene to Wadsworth, April 14, 1779, Wadsworth Coll., CHS.

48. See letters from Wadsworth to Greene, 1780-1783, WA.

49. Wadsworth to Greene, December 12, 1782, Wadsworth Papers, WA.

50. Webb to Greene, Sept. 1, 1779, Greene Coll., V, WCL; Otis to Greene, Sept. 3, 1779, Greene to Otis, Sept. 17, 1779, Greene Coll., V, WCL.

51. Greene to Pettit, Nov. 29, 1778, Reed Papers, VI, NYHS; Pettit

to Greene, Jan. 5, 1780, Pettit to Greene, June 11, 1780, Pettit to Greene, May 5, 1779, Greene Coll., III, V, VI, WCL.

52. Greene to Griffin Greene, March 20, 1779, Greene Papers, MCL.

53. Pettit to Greene, May 5, 12, 1779, Pettit to Greene, Jan. 5, 1780, Greene Coll., IV, VI, WCL.

54. Pettit to Greene, May 24, 1781, Aug. 23, 1781, Dec. 14, 1781, Greene Coll., XXXIII, XLII, XLI, WCL.

55. Fitzpatrick, *op. cit.*, XI, 351.

56. F. Moore, *Diary*, II, 48-49.

57. Fitzpatrick, *op. cit.*, XI, 362.

58. B. F. Stevens, *Facsimiles*, V, 500, 508; G. W. Greene, *op. cit.*, II, 79.

59. Charles Lee to Congress, May 13, 1778, *Lee Papers*, II, 392-393; J. R. Alden, *General Charles Lee*, p. 83.

60. Lux to Greene, May 26, 1778, Greene Coll., II, WCL; Alden, *op. cit.*, pp. 199-200.

61. G. W. Greene, *op. cit.*, II, 84-85, 89, 93-94.

NOTES FOR CHAPTER X

1. J. Montresor, "Journals," p. 497; W. B. Wilcox, "British Strategy in America," *Journal of Modern History*, XIX, No. 2 (June, 1947), 110-111.

2. J. C. Fitzpatrick, ed., *Writings of George Washington*, XII, 75n, 83, 85-86, 91; J. R. Alden, *General Charles Lee*, p. 207.

3. Fitzpatrick, *op. cit.*, XII, 90-91, 105-106, 277; Orderly Book, No. 2, June 21-22, 1778, HL.

4. Greene to Washington, June 24, 1778, Washington Papers, Vol. 78, p. 35, LC. By his words one may believe Greene wanted a general action but had to hedge a bit in presenting his case to Washington for fear he might think him too bold.

5. J. Sparks, *Correspondence*, IV, 553; Fitzpatrick, *op. cit.*, XII, 140; W. W. Stryker, *Battle of Monmouth*, pp. 75-77; D. S. Freeman, *George Washington*, V, 19-20; Alden, *op. cit.*, pp. 209-210; H. C. Lodge, ed., *Works of Alexander Hamilton*, VIII, 68; L. Gottschalk, *Lafayette Joins*, pp. 210-211.

6. Fitzpatrick, *op. cit.*, XII, 119n; Lee to Washington, June 25, 1778, *Lee Papers*, II, 417-418.

7. Stryker, *op. cit.*, pp. 75 ff; E. J. Lowell, *The Hessians*, p. 213.

8. Clinton to Germain, July 5, 1778, *Lee Papers*, II, 461-466.

9. Alden, *op. cit.*, pp. 224-225; Freeman, *op. cit.*, V, 27 ff; F. V. Greene, *The Revolutionary War*, pp. 144-145; see *Lee Papers*, III, 174, for Lee's defense of his withdrawal.

10. See Gottschalk, *op. cit.*, p. 228 for an interpretation which makes Lee out to be a traitor and a leader of the cabal against Washington.

11. Stryker, *op. cit.*, p. 205; C. L. Baurmeister, *Revolution in America*, p. 487.

12. Desertions from Clinton's army have been estimated as high as 1,000. Freeman, *op. cit.*, V, 40.

13. F. V. Greene, *op. cit.*, p. 147; Baurmeister, *op. cit.*, pp. 185-186.

American estimates of British losses were usually too high. See Wayne to Peters, July 12, 1778, Wayne Papers, HSP; Fitzpatrick, *op. cit.*, XII, 164; William Watson to Joseph Lyman, July 4, 1778, MSS, # 650, MNPL.

14. Fitzpatrick, *op. cit.*, XII, 148-150, 160, 163; Orderly Book, No. 2, HL.

15. Montresor, *op. cit.*, p. 504; Gottschalk, *op. cit.*, pp. 237-240; Fitzpatrick, *op. cit.*, XII, 187.

16. G. W. Greene, *Life of Nathanael Greene*, II, 93-94.

17. *Ibid.*, II, 95-96.

18. Fitzpatrick, *op. cit.*, XII, 199-200.

19. G. W. Greene, *op. cit.*, II, 98-101.

20. Fitzpatrick, *op. cit.*, XII, 232-233; J. Sullivan, *Papers*, II, 171.

21. W. B. to his father, Aug. 22, 1778, Reed Papers, V, NYHS.

22. B. F. Stevens, *Facsimiles*, # 845; Gottschalk, *op. cit.*, p. 249; Wilcox, *op. cit.*, pp. 114-117; C. Ward, *War of the Revolution*, II, 590.

23. Greene to Pettit, Aug. 22, 1778, Reed Papers, V, NYHS; Stevens, *op. cit.*, # 848; Gottschalk, *op. cit.*, p. 253; G. W. Greene, *op. cit.*, II, 119-120; J. Sullivan, *op. cit.*, II, 264-265.

24. Sullivan, *ibid.*, II, 246.

25. W. Gordon, *History*, II, 163.

26. *Loc. cit.*; Freeman, *op. cit.*, V, 71.

27. Fitzpatrick, *op. cit.*, XII, 386-387.

28. G. W. Greene, *op. cit.*, II, 148-150; Freeman, *op. cit.*, V, 75-76; Gottschalk, *op. cit.*, pp. 254-255, 261-262; Fitzpatrick, *op. cit.*, XII, 389; *Lee Papers*, III, 234-235.

29. G. W. Greene, *op. cit.*, II, 121-122, 125-126. The French fleet eventually sailed for Martinique as the naval warfare had gravitated to the West Indies.

30. G. W. Greene, *op. cit.*, II, 132-133; S. G. Arnold, *History of Rhode Island*, II, 428; Ward, *op. cit.*, II, 592.

31. This refers to Lieutenant Colonel William Smith Livingston, formerly Greene's aide but then second in command of Webb's Connecticut regiment. See Fitzpatrick, *op. cit.*, XII, 397n; G. W. Greene, *op. cit.*, II, 129.

32. Sullivan, *op. cit.*, II, 404.

33. G. W. Greene, *op. cit.*, II, 142-143, 151.

34. *Ibid.*, II, 145-146, 156.

NOTES FOR CHAPTER XI

1. Greene to Washington, Nov. 30, 1778, Greene Coll., III, HL; Peter Angelakes, "The Army at Middlebrook," *Proc. of the NJHS*, LXX, No. 2 (1952); Pettit to Greene, Dec. 4, 1778, Greene Coll., II, WCL; Greene to Pettit, Dec. 12, 1778, Reed Papers, V, NYHS; J. C. Fitzpatrick, ed., *Writings of George Washington*, XIII, 395; G. W. Greene, *Life of Nathanael Greene*, II, 166.

2. Greene to Jay, April 15, 1778, Reed Papers, VI, NYHS; Greene to Hubbard, April 30, 1778, *Proc. of the NJHS*, LXI, 182-183.

3. Sarah Bache to Franklin, Jan. 17, 1778, Emmet Coll., # 5856, NYPL; G. W. Greene, *op. cit.*, II, 166, 169.

4. Greene to McDougall, Feb. 11, 1779, McDougall Papers, IV, NYHS; Greene to Washington, Jan. 5, 1779, Greene Coll., IV, HL; Fitzpatrick, *op. cit.*, XIV, 3-12, 26-32, 35-42.

5. Greene to Hooper, April 29, 1779, Greene Coll., IV, WCL; Greene to Cox, April 6, 1779, Greene Coll., III, WCL; Greene to Hay, April 20, 1779, Greene Coll., IV, WCL; Pettit to Greene, May 7, 1779, Greene Corresp., VII, 43, APS; McDougall to Benson, May 12, 1779, McDougall Papers, V, NYHS.

6. Greene to Hay, April 27, 1779, Greene Coll., IV, WCL; Pettit to Greene, May 11, 1779, Greene Corresp., VII, 67, APS; Washington to Reed, May 22, 1779, Reed Papers, VI, NYHS; Fitzpatrick, *op. cit.*, XIV, 439-440.

7. Peck MSS, V, # 36, RIHS; Greene Corresp., VI, 73, APS; Peters to Greene, Oct. 21, 1779, Greene Corresp., II, 7, APS; Greene to Hubbard, July 21, 1779, Greene Coll., IV, WCL.

8. E. C. Burnett, *Letters*, IV, 292-293; Greene to Hay, June 24, 1779, Greene Corresp., VI, 96, APS; Greene to Pettit, July 29, 1779, Greene Corresp., XI, 4, APS.

9. Hooper to Greene, May 27, 1779, Greene Corresp., V, 82, APS; G. Clinton, *Public Papers*, V, 103-104; Stewart to Wadsworth, July 6, 1779; Stewart Papers, Houghton Lib.

10. Howe to Greene, Aug. 3, 1779, Greene Coll., II, WCL; Greene Papers, 1775-1781, I, 29-30, LC.

11. Greene to Arnold, Dec. 16, 1779, Greene Coll., IV, HL; Fitzpatrick, *op. cit.*, XVII, 300-301.

12. *N.J. Arch, 2nd. Ser.*, IV, 143-144, 467; Washington to Stirling, Jan. 13, 14, 1780, Stirling Papers, V, 2, NYHS; *Pa. Mag. of Hist. and Biog.*, XV, 61; J. Lewis Transcripts, Letters of Jan. 15, 17, 22, 1780, MNPL.

13. *Pa. Mag. of Hist. and Biog.*, LXV, 363-369.

14. Greene to Huntington, Jan. 13, 1780, Greene Coll., V, HL; Greene to Reed, Feb. 20, 1780, Reed Papers, VII, NYHS; Pettit to Greene, Jan. 16, 1780, Bancroft Coll., NYPL; Greene to Wadsworth, Feb. 8, 1780, Greene Papers, YUL.

15. Reed to Greene, Feb. 14, 1780, Greene Papers, I, LC; Pettit to Greene, Feb. 15, 1780, Greene Coll., VI, WCL; Cox to Greene, Feb. 16, 1780, Bancroft Coll., NYPL.

16. Schuyler to Greene, March 22, 1780, Burnett, *op. cit.*, V, 90-91; Fitzpatrick, *op. cit.*, XVIII, 185n.

17. Greene to Washington, March 22, 1780, Burnett, *op. cit.*, V, 99n; Fitzpatrick, *op. cit.*, XVIII, 157.

18. Greene to William Greene, May 27, 1780, Greene to the Committee, May 26, 1780, Greene to Reed, May 20, 1780, Greene Coll., V, HL; Burnett, *op. cit.*, V, 170-171n; Committee's Report, May 25, 1780, Reed Papers, VII, NYHS.

19. G. W. Greene, *op. cit.*, II, 187-188.

20. Martha Lamb, *History of the City of New York*, II, 239-240; Greene to the Rev. William Gordon, 1785, Smith Coll., MNPL; *NJ Arch., 2nd. Ser.*, IV, 417, 445-448.

21. Washington to Stirling, June 8, 1780, Stirling Papers, V, 8, NYHS; Armstrong to Gates, June, 1780, Gates Papers, Box 14, NYHS; D. S. Free-

man, *George Washington*, V, 172; Fitzpatrick, *op. cit.*, XVIII, 490-491, XXX, 34 ff; F. Moore, *Diary*, II, 297-298.

22. Clinton to Germain, July 4, 1780, G. Clinton, *Public Papers*, V, 876-877n.

23. Maxwell to Gov. Livingston, June 24, 1780, Greene Coll., V, HL; Lewis to Furman, June 23, 1780, J. Lewis Transcripts, MNPL; L. Morris to Brig. Gen. Morris, June 24, 1780, *NYHS Coll.*, VIII, 458.

24. O. H. Williams, *Papers*, p. 211; Greene to Washington, June 24, 1780, *NJ Arch.*, *2nd. Ser.*, IV, 481-482; Cox to Reed, June 25, 1780, Reed Papers, VII, NYHS; G. W. Greene, *op. cit.*, II, 197-201; H. C. Lodge, *Works of Alex. Hamilton*, VIII, 69.

25. Peck MSS, VI, # 19, RIHS; Greene to the Committee, July 24, 1780, Greene to Huntington, July 26, 1780, Greene to Washington, Aug. 3, 1780, Greene Coll., V, HL; Greene to Congress, July 26, 1780, Greene Papers, LC.

26. Cornell to Greene, Aug. 1, 1780, Greene Coll., VIII, WCL; Burnett, *op. cit.*, V, 300-306.

27. Burnett, *op. cit.*, V, 307, 315-316n, 323; Pettit to Greene, Aug. 11, 1780, Greene Coll., VIII, WCL; Fitzpatrick, *op. cit.*, XIX, 366-367.

28. Greene to Kitty, Aug. 14, 1780, G. P. Richmond, ed., *Letters by Nat. Greene*; Greene to Wadsworth, Aug. 12, 1780, Greene Papers, YUL; Burnett, *op. cit.*, V, 323, 339n; Reed to Greene, Aug. 19, 1780, Reed Papers, VIII, NYHS.

29. Greene to Arnold, Sept. 7, 1780, Greene Coll., V, HL; Irvine to Armstrong, Sept. 5, 1780, Greene to Reed, Sept. 8, 1780, Reed Papers, VIII, NYHS; B. F. Stevens, *Facsimiles*, # 733; Greene to Colonel Peabody, Sept. 16, 1780, Greene Coll., VIII, WCL; Greene to G. Morris, Sept. 14, 1780, Greene Coll., V, HL; Greene to L. Morris, Sept. 14, 1780, *NYHS Coll.*, VIII, 467-469; Washington to Reed, Aug. 20, 1780, Reed Papers, VIII, NYHS; Fitzpatrick, *op. cit.*, XIX, 431-432; *Pa. Mag. of Hist. and Biog.*, XV, 73, XX, 6-8.

30. Wayne to Johnston, Sept. 29, 1780, Wayne to Robinson, Oct. 1, 1780, Wayne Papers, HSP.

31. Fitzpatrick, *op. cit.*, XX, 608; G. Messam to Armstrong, Sept. 11, 1790, Gates Papers, Box 15, NYHS; Greene to Colonel Peabody, Sept. 6, 1780, Greene Coll., VIII, WCL.

32. S. Shaw, *Journals*, pp. 82-83; G. W. Greene, *op. cit.*, II, 374-375, 377-378.

33. Fitzpatrick, *op. cit.*, XX, 181-182; G. W. Greene, *op. cit.*, II, 378-379.

NOTES FOR CHAPTER XII

1. Greene to Congress, Nov. 2, 1780, Greene to Washington, Nov. 2, 1780, Greene to Wilkinson, Nov. 2, 1780, Greene's Letter Book, LC.

2. Greene to Reed, Nov. 1, 1780, Greene to Pickering, Nov. 2, 1780, Greene to Febiger, Nov. 2, 1780, Pickering to Greene, Nov. 5, 1780, *ibid.*

3. Greene to Congress, Nov. 2, 1780, *ibid.*; G. W. Greene, *Life of Nathanael Greene*, III, 43 ff.

4. H. Clinton, *The American Rebellion*, pp. 467-470.

5. *Maryland Archives*, XLV, 175-176.

6. G. W. Greene, *op. cit.*, III, 51.

7. Greene to Rodney, Nov. 10, 1780, Greene to Lee, Nov. 10, 1780, Greene to the Board of War, Nov. 10, 1780, Greene's Letter Book, LC.; Greene to Gist, Nov. 10, 1780, Steuben Papers, NYHS.

8. T. Jefferson, *Papers*, IV, 133.

9. Greene to Matlack, Nov. 20, 1780, Greene's Letter Book, LC; Greene to Kitty, Nov. 18, 1780, G. P. Richmond, ed., *Letters by Nat. Greene;* G. W. Greene, *op. cit.*, III, 56-62.

10. G. W. Greene, *op. cit.*, III, 61-62.

11. Greene to Steuben, Nov. 22, 1780, Steuben Papers, NYHS.

12. Greene to Steuben, Nov. 27, 1780, Stevens to Washington, Nov. 24, 1780, Steuben Papers, NYHS; G. W. Greene, *op. cit.*, III, 65-66.

13. E. Watson, *Memoirs*, p. 297; H. Lee, *Memoirs*, I, 244-245.

14. Washington to Gates, Oct. 22, 1780, Gates Papers, Box 5, 162, 164, NYHS; Greene to Gates, Dec. 6, 1780, Gates Papers, Box 15, NYHS; Greene to Gates, Dec. 4, 1780, Greene Papers, LC; J. C. Fitzpatrick, *Writings of George Washington*, XX, 238-240.

15. Greene to Marion, Dec. 4, 1780, Greene's Letter Book, LC.

16. *Mag. of Am. Hist.*, XXVIII, 419-420; G. W. Greene, *op. cit.*, III, 119-122; B. P. Robinson, *William R. Davie*, pp. 90 ff.

17. Greene to Marbury, Dec. 16, 1780, Greene to Gunby, Dec. 30, 1780, Greene's Letter Book, LC; Greene to Rowson, Dec. 26, 1780, Greene Coll., XIII, WCL.

18. Greene to the N.C. Board of War, Dec. 7, 1780, Greene Coll., XI, WCL. See Robinson's *Davie*, pp. 101-103, for the method of taxing and collecting provisions.

19. Lux to Greene, April 22, 1780, HSP; Lux to Greene, May 6, 1780, Greene Coll., II, WCL; Greene to Steuben, Dec. 28, 1780, Steuben Papers, NYHS.

20. Jefferson, *op. cit.*, IV, 183-184; Greene to Huntington, Dec. 28, 1780, Greene Coll., XIII, WCL; Greene to Jefferson, Dec. 14, 1780, Greene Coll., XII, WCL.

21. G. W. Greene, *op. cit.*, II, 438; W. Johnson, *Sketches*, II, 159.

22. Greene to Morgan, Dec. 16, 1780, Greene Coll., XII, WCL.

23. Greene to Sumter, Dec. 15, 1780, *Charleston Year Book*, 1899, p. 73.

24. Greene to Sumter, Jan. 19, 1781, Greene Papers, Bancroft Coll., NYPL; H. Lee, *op. cit.*, I, 165-166; G. W. Greene, *op. cit.*, III, 122-123.

25. G. W. Greene, *op. cit.*, III, 131-132.

26. Greene to Marion, Jan. 4, 1781, Greene Papers, Bancroft Coll., NYPL.

27. Morgan to Greene, Dec. 31, 1780, Greene Coll., XIII, WCL; G. W. Greene, *op. cit.*, III, 135-136.

28. Greene to N. C. Board of War, Dec. 7, 1780, Greene Coll., XI, WCL.

29. Greene to Morgan, Dec. 29, 1780, Greene to Luzerne, Dec. 29, 1780, Greene Coll., XIII, WCL.

30. Greene to Morgan, Jan. 3, 1781, Greene Papers, Bancroft Coll., NYPL.

31. Morgan to Greene, Jan. 4, 1781, Greene Coll., XIV, WCL.

32. Greene to Morgan, Jan. 8, Jan. 19, 1781, Greene Papers, Bancroft Coll., NYPL.

33. Greene to Huntington, Dec. 28, 1780, Greene Coll., XIII, WCL; Lewis Morris to his father, Dec. 21, 1780, *NYHS Coll.*, VIII, 473-474.

34. Morgan to Gates, Jan. 26, 1781, Gates Papers, Box 16, NYHS; H. Lee, *op. cit.*, I, 253-254.

35. The cannon were the ones captured by Morgan at Saratoga, lost by Gates at Camden, and finally presented to Greene after the war by Congress. For his masterful generalship (General Washington and some others thought good luck accounted for the victory as much as anything) Congress awarded Morgan a gold medal. Colonels Howard and Washington received silver medals and Pickens a sword. Morgan to Greene, Jan. 19, 1781, Greene Papers, LC; Greene to Washington, Jan. 24, 1781, Greene Papers, Bancroft Coll., NYPL; B. Tarleton, *History*, pp. 217-221; B. F. Stevens, *Clinton-Cornwallis Controversy*, I, 319-320; O. H. Williams, *Papers*, p. 36.

NOTES FOR CHAPTER XIII

1. Greene to Steuben, Jan. 23, 1781, Greene Coll., XVI, WCL; Greene to Varnum, Jan. 24, 1781, Greene Coll., LXXXVIII, WCL.

2. Lee to Greene, Jan. 27, 30, 1781, Lewis Morris to Nash, Jan. 28, 1781, Greene Coll., XVII, WCL; W. D. James, *Francis Marion*, pp. 90-91.

3. Greene to Marion, Jan. 25, 1781, Greene Papers, Bancroft Coll., NYPL; Marion to Greene, Jan. 28, 31, 1781, Greene Papers, LC.

4. Greene to Stevens, Jan. 25, 1781, Greene Coll., XVI, WCL; Greene to Jefferson, Jan. 26, 1781, Greene Papers, Bancroft Coll., NYPL; Greene to Nash, Jan. 26, 1781, Greene Coll., XVII, WCL.

5. Greene to Mathews, Jan. 23, 1781, Greene to Harrison, Jan. 26, 1781, Greene Papers, Bancroft Coll., NYPL.

6. Greene to Huntington, Jan. 31, 1781, Greene to Huger, Jan. 31, 1781, Greene Coll., XVII, WCL.

7. W. Gordon, *History*, IV, 39.

8. Morgan to Greene, Jan. 25, 1781, Greene Coll., XVI, WCL; Morgan to Jefferson, Feb. 1, 1781, T. Jefferson, *Papers*, IV, 495-496; Morgan to Gates, Jan. 26, 1781, Gates Papers, Box 16, NYHS.

9. Greene to Huger, Jan. 31, 1781, Greene Papers, Bancroft Coll., NYPL.

10. G. W. Greene, *Life of Nathanael Greene*, III, 159. See Greene to Washington, Feb. 9, 1781, Greene Papers, Bancroft Coll., NYPL, and Greene to Steuben, Feb. 3, 1781, Greene Coll., XVIII, WCL. It is certain that George Washington Greene is wrong in saying that Greene first heard of Cornwallis' crossing the Catawba while waiting at the place of rendezvous. Greene sent letters from Oliphant's Mills that morning telling about the crossing.

11. G. W. Greene, *op. cit.*, III, 159; *North Carolina Booklet*, Vol. 12, No. 2.

12. G. W. Greene, *op. cit.*, III, 161.

13. Greene to Butler, Feb. 6, 1781, Greene to Gunby, Feb. 8, 1781, Greene to Marbury, Feb. 8, 1781, Greene Coll., XIX, WCL.

14. Greene to Pickens, Feb. 3, 1781, Greene to Huger, Feb. 5, 1781, Greene to Patrick Henry, Feb. 10, 1781, Greene Coll., XVIII, WCL;

Greene to Preston, Feb. 24, 1781, SC State Arch.; Greene to NC militia, Feb. 5, 6, 1781, Greene to Washington, Feb. 9, 1781, Greene Papers, Bancroft Coll., NYPL; Balfour to Germain, Feb. 18, 1781, Emmet Coll., # 15502, NYPL; T. Jefferson, *op. cit.*, IV, 546.

15. Greene to Washington, Feb. 9, 1781, Greene Papers, Bancroft Coll., NYPL; Greene to Nash, Feb. 9, 1781, Greene Coll., XVIII, WCL; Greene to Steuben, Feb. 10, 1781, Steuben Papers, NYHS.

16. Greene to S. Ward, Dec. 23, 1782, Greene Papers, RIHS; *Rhode Island History*, Vol. 17, No. 1, p. 20.

17. Lee, *Memoirs*, I, 275 ff., 289-290.

18. Greene to Jefferson, Feb. 15, 1781, Greene Coll., XIX, WCL; Greene to Steuben, Feb. 15, 1781, Steuben Papers, NYHS; B. Tarleton, *History*, p. 229.

19. Lee, *op. cit.*, I, 294.

20. Greene to Jefferson, Feb. 15, 1781, Greene Coll., XIX, WCL; Greene to N. C. Legislature, Feb. 16, 1781, Greene to Washington, Feb. 15, 1781, Greene Papers, Bancroft Coll., NYPL.

21. Greene to Nash, Jan. 13, 1781, Greene to N. C. Leg., Feb. 17, 1781, Greene to Lawson, Feb. 17, 1781, Greene to Caswell, Feb. 18, 1781, Greene to Butler, Feb. 17, 1781, Greene Papers, Bancroft Coll., NYPL; Greene to Nash, Feb. 17, 1781, Greene to Caswell, Feb. 16, 1781, Greene to Polk, Feb. 16, 1781, Greene Coll., XIX, WCL; *N. C. St. Rec.*, XV, 424.

22. Greene to Steuben, Feb. 16, 1781, Steuben Papers, NYHS; Greene to Burr, Feb. 17, 1781, Greene to Campbell, Feb. 18, 1781, Greene Papers, Bancroft Coll., NYPL; Preston to Greene, Feb. 18, 1781, Greene to Martin, Feb. 17, 1781, Steuben to Greene, Feb. 17, 1781, Weedon to Greene, Feb. 17, 1781, Greene Coll., XXI, WCL; T. Jefferson, *op. cit.*, IV, 634-638; O. H. Williams, *Papers*, p. 40; H. Clinton, *Observations*, pp. 65-66.

23. Balfour to Clinton, Feb. 24, 1781, March 3, 1781, Emmet Coll., # 15503, NYPL; Greene to Sumter, Feb. 21, 1781, Greene Papers, Bancroft Coll., NYPL; Greene to Washington, Feb. 28, 1781, Greene Coll., XXI, WCL.

24. Greene to Reed, March 18, 1781, Reed Papers, XI, NYHS. Gordon is right in placing Greene's visit to Lee and Pickens after the army crossed the Dan and not on the day Lee crossed as George Washington Greene does in his life of Greene. It could not be otherwise as Pickens was near Guilford Court House on February 19th and Greene wrote him as late as February 21st to hurry forward. Gordon, *op. cit.*, IV, 48; G. W. Greene, *op. cit.*, III, 179.

25. C. Ward, *War of the Revolution*, II, 798-799; Lee, *op. cit.*, I, 307-313; G. W. Greene, *op. cit.*, III, 181-182; Gordon, *op. cit.*, IV, 48-49; C. Stedman, *History*, II, 334. Accounts of the massacre differ. Gordon's differs from that told by G. W. Greene which is nearer to the above. Most historians believe that Lee's story of his good intentions was an afterthought and that the bloodshed was deliberate on his part.

26. Greene to Campbell, Feb. 26, 1781, Williams to Greene, Feb. 26, 1781, Crocket to Greene, Feb. 26, 1781, Rowland to Greene, Feb. 26, 1781, Greene Coll., XXI, WCL; Greene to Campbell, Feb. 24, 1781, Greene Papers, Bancroft Coll., NYPL; Jefferson, *op. cit.*, V, 20.

27. Pierce to Butler, March 4, 1781, Greene Coll., XXII, WCL.

28. Greene to Washington, March 9, 1781, Greene Coll., XXIII, WCL; Lee, *op. cit.*, I, 323; Gordon, *op. cit.*, IV, 52-53; G. W. Greene, *op. cit.*, III, 187-188; Stedman, *op. cit.*, II, 336.

29. G. W. Greene, *op. cit.*, III, 186-187.

30. Greene to Jefferson, March 10, 1781, Greene Coll., XXIII, WCL; L. Morris to his father, March 10, 1781, *NYHS Coll.*, VIII, 483.

31. Greene to Pickens, March 8, 1781, Greene Coll., XXIII, WCL; Pickens to Greene, March 5, 1781, Greene Coll., XXII, WCL.

32. Ward, *op. cit.*, II, 784, places these troops under Colonel John Greene. The latter, however, was already with Nathanael Greene and had been with him since he joined the army at Cheraw. Greene's letter made it clear that Richard Campbell brought these troops. See Greene to Jefferson, March 10, 1781, Campbell to Greene, March 8, 1781, Greene Coll., XXIII, WCL.

33. The Campbells are difficult to distinguish as Richard, Arthur, and William were usually addressed as Colonel Campbell. Greene, however, makes it clear that William Campbell was "the famous" one who commanded at King's Mountain. Greene to Morgan, March 20, 1781, Greene Coll., LXXXVIII, WCL; Greene to Rev. William Gordon, no date, Smith Coll., MNPL.

34. Greene to Steuben, March 11, 1781, Steuben Papers, NYHS; Richard Campbell to Greene, March 8, 1781, Greene Coll., XXIII, WCL; Steuben to Greene, March 5, 1781, Greene Coll., XXII, WCL; Gordon, *op. cit.*, I, 54; Lee, *op. cit.*, I, 354; G. W. Greene, *op. cit.*, III, 190; Ward, *op. cit.*, II, 784.

35. G. W. Greene, *op. cit.*, III, 93; Gordon, *op. cit.*, IV, 54; Tarleton, *op. cit.*, p. 277; Stedman, *op. cit.*, II, 337.

36. Greene to Reed, March 18, 1781, Reed Papers, X, NYHS; Anthony Singleton's letter, March 21, 1781, Steuben Papers, NYHS; Gordon, *op. cit.*, IV, 55; Stedman, *op. cit.*, II, 339.

37. Cornwallis to Germain, March 17, 1781, B. F. Stevens, *Clinton-Cornwallis Controversy*, I, 365.

38. *Mag. of Hist.*, XXVIII, 422; G. W. Greene, *op. cit.*, III, 201, 208.

39. E. Giles to Hawley, March 27, 1781, R. W. Gibbes, *Documentary History*, III, 43-44.

40. Greene to Jefferson, March 21, 1781, Greene to Sumter, March 16, 1781, Greene Coll., XXIV, WCL; Greene to Morgan, March 20, 1781, Greene Coll., LXXXVIII, WCL; Greene to Jefferson, March 23, 1781, Brown Memorial, Providence; Greene to Huntington, March 16, 1781, J. Almon, *The Remembrancer*, 1781, II, 38; Morris to his father, March 16, 1781, *NYHS Coll.*, VIII, 484; Williams to E. Williams, March 16, 1781, O. H. Williams, *op. cit.*, pp. 42-43; Tarleton, *op. cit.*, pp. 276-278; Lee, *op. cit.*, I, 343-358; Greene to Reed, March 18, 1781, Reed Papers, NYHS.

41. Tarleton, *op. cit.*, p. 277; G. W. Greene, *op. cit.*, III, 200. Cornwallis gave a lack of provisions as his reason for not following Greene the next day. Other letters, however, show that he could not risk another battle if he had all the provisions in the country. Stevens, *op. cit.*, I, 396; Stedman, *op. cit.*, II, 344.

NOTES FOR CHAPTER XIV

1. Greene to Reed, March 18, 1781, Reed Papers, IX, NYHS.
2. *Loc. cit.*
3. L. Gottschalk, *Lafayette and the Close*, pp. 215-218; *Letters of Richard Henry Lee*, II, 218-219.
4. T. Jefferson, *Papers*, V, 541.
5. After Greene's death the admirers of Henry Lee tried to make out that he was the author of the plan to invade South Carolina. Furthermore, they insisted that Lee was author of practically all of Greene's brilliant moves. Greene's letters, however, prove that this is untrue. Realizing that a wrong was being done to a great strategist, Henry Rutledge, General Williams, Colonel Carrington, and others came forth to defend Greene before Congress and the nation. See Rutledge's letter, June 26, 1822, Greene Coll., LXXXVI, WCL; Greene to Steuben, April 3, 1781, Greene Coll., XXVI, WCL; Greene to Sumter, March 30, 1781, Greene Coll., XXV, WCL; Rawdon to Germain, March 23, 1781, J. Almon, *The Remembrancer*, 1781, I, 331; Greene to Burnet, April 5, 1781, Smith Coll., MNPL; Balfour's letter, April 7, 1781, Leslie's Letter Book, Emmet Coll., NYHS; Greene to Lafayette, April 3, 1781, Morgan Lib.; G. W. Greene, *Life of Nathanael Greene*, III, 214; H. Lee, *Memoirs*, II, 31-54; H. Clinton, *The American Rebellion*, p. 273; W. Johnson, *Sketches*, II, Postscript, pp. 3-5.
6. Clinton, *op. cit.*, p. 512; C. Stedman, *History*, II, 354.
7. Clinton, *op. cit.*, pp. 512-513; B. F. Stevens, *Clinton-Cornwallis Controversy*, I, 428.
8. Clinton, *op. cit.*, pp. 523-524.
9. Jefferson, *op. cit.*, V, 277, 312n.
10. Clinton, *op. cit.*, pp. 482-495.
11. Greene to Lafayette, April 3, 1781, Greene Coll., XXXVI, WCL; Gottschalk, *op. cit.*, pp. 205-207.
12. Greene to Steuben, April 2, 1781, Steuben Papers, NYHS; Clairborne to Greene, May 2, 1781, Greene Papers, LC.
13. Greene to Lafayette, June 9, 1781, Greene Papers, LC.
14. Greene to Steuben, April 6, 1781, Steuben Papers, NYHS; Greene to Jefferson, April 6, 1781, Greene Coll., XXVI, WCL; Jefferson, *op. cit.*, V, 312n; Gottschalk, *op. cit.*, p. 234.
15. Jefferson, *op. cit.*, V, 313, 405; Greene to Jefferson, April 6, 1781, Greene Coll., XXVI, WCL; Greene to Steuben, April 4, 1781, Steuben Papers, NYHS.
16. Greene to Nash, April 12, 1781, Greene Coll., XXVII, WCL; Greene to Jefferson, April 28, 1781, Greene Coll., XXIX, WCL; Reed to Greene, June 6, 1781, Reed Papers, IX, NYHS; Johnson, *op. cit.*, II, 112.
17. Greene to Lee, April 4, 1781, Greene Coll., XXVI, WCL.
18. Clinton, *op. cit.*, pp. 508-510; Stevens, *op. cit.*, I, 417; G. W. Greene, *op. cit.*, III, 275.
19. Sumter to Greene, April 17, 1781, Greene Coll., XXVII, WCL; Greene to Lee, April 10, 1781, Greene Papers, LC.
20. Greene to Sumter, April 15, 1781, Greene Coll., XXVII, WCL.
21. Greene to Congress, April 22, 1781, Weare Papers, NHHS; Greene to Sumner, April 21, 1781, Greene Coll., XXVIII, WCL.

22. Marion to Greene, April 23, 1781, Lee to Greene, April 19, 1781, Greene Coll., XXVIII, WCL; Stedman, *op. cit.*, II, 360; Greene to Marion, April 25, 1781, Greene Coll., XXIX, WCL; G. W. Greene, *op. cit.*, III, 236; Johnson, *op. cit.*, II, 100-104.

23. Greene to Steuben, April 27, 1781, Steuben Papers, NYHS; Greene to Butler, May 2, 1781, Greene Papers, LC; Rawdon to Cornwallis, April 26, 1781, Clinton, *op. cit.*, pp. 513-515; W. Gordon, *History*, IV, 83-84; C. Ward, *The War of the Revolution*, II, 804 ff.

24. It seems wrong to blame Sumter for the defeat as William R. Davie does in his *Memoirs*. General Greene did not order Sumter to join him as Davie maintains but rather to guard the approaches to Camden from the west which he attempted to do. See Davie's Account of the Campaign of 1781, Greene Coll., XIII, WCL; G. W. Greene, *op. cit.*, III, 378 ff; Johnson, *op. cit.*, II, 111.

25. Greene to Nash, May 2, 1781, Greene Papers, LC; G. W. Greene, *op. cit.*, III, 252.

26. Clinton, *op. cit.*, p. 295; Gottschalk, *op. cit.*, p. 230.

27. G. W. Greene, *op. cit.*, III, 251-253; Stedman, *op. cit.*, II, 358.

28. Greene to the Board of War, May 2, 1781, Greene Coll., XXX, WCL; Johnson, *op. cit.*, II, 118-119.

29. D. Ramsay, *History of the Revolution in South Carolina*, II, 232; Johnson, *op. cit.*, II, 110; Greene to Marion, May 4, 1781, Greene Coll., XXX, WCL; Greene to Lee, May 4, 1781, Greene Papers, Illinois State Hist. Soc.

30. Clinton, *op. cit.*, pp. 513-514.

31. G. W. Greene, *op. cit.*, III, 275.

32. Clinton, *op. cit.*, pp. 284-285, 520-522.

33. Pendleton to Marion, May 11, 1781, Greene to Marshall, May 11, 1781, Surrender Terms, May 15, 1781, Greene to Rutledge, May 14, 1781, Greene Coll., XXXI, WCL; G. W. Greene, *op. cit.*, III, 279-281; Johnson, *op. cit.*, II, 427-428.

34. Lee to Greene, May 15, 1781, Greene to Sumter, May 23, 1781, Greene Coll., XXXI, WCL; Johnson, *op. cit.*, II, 121, 460.

35. Greene to Lafayette, May 23, 1781, Greene Papers, LC; Greene to La Luzerne, June 22, 1781, Greene to Varnum, June 22, 1781, Greene Coll., XXXV, WCL; Johnson, *op. cit.*, II, 423.

36. G. Clinton, *Public Papers*, VII, 29; Reed to Greene, June 6, 1781, Reed Papers, IX, NYHS.

37. Greene to Rutledge, May 14, 1781, Greene Coll., XXXI, WCL.

38. Sumter to Greene, May 6, 1781, Greene Coll., XXX, WCL; Greene to Sumter, May 7, 17, 1781, Greene Coll., XXXII, WCL; Sumter to Greene, May 15, 1781, Greene Coll., XXXI, WCL; G. W. Greene, *op. cit.*, III, 295-298; Johnson, *op. cit.*, II, 121-122.

39. Greene to Marion, May 9, 1781, Greene Coll., XXXI, WCL; Marion to Greene, May 6, 1781, Greene Coll., XXX, WCL. About this time, Lee told Greene he was disappointed in Marion whom he thought rather inadequate due to his nature. Lee, who was seldom very generous in his opinion of his fellow officers, thought Sumter in most every way worse than Marion. Lee to Greene, May 8, 1781, Greene Coll., XXX, WCL.

40. Greene to Lee, May 29, 1781, Greene Coll., XXXIII, WCL; Greene to Huntington, June 29, 1781, Greene Papers, DUL; Greene to Huntington, June 20, 1781, Greene Coll., LXXXVIII, WCL.

41. Greene to Pickens, June 5, 1781, Greene to Williams, June 13, 1781, Greene to the Inhabitants of the Saluda, June 6, 1781, Greene Papers, DUL; Greene to Davie, May 23, 1781, Greene Coll., XXXII, WCL.

42. Greene to Marion, June 10, 1781, Greene to Sumter, June 12, 1781, Greene Coll., XXXIV, WCL; Greene to Clark, June 12, 1781, Greene Papers, DUL.

43. Burnet to Rudolph, June 14, 1781, Burnet to William Washington, June 14, 1781, Sumter to Greene, June 14, 1781, Greene to Pickens, June 18, 1781, Sumter to Greene, June 19, 1781, Greene Coll., XXXV, WCL; Greene to Marion, June 25, 1781, Greene Coll., XXXVI, WCL; Sumter to Greene, June 14, 16, 17, 1781, *Charleston Year Book*, 1899, pp. 22-23; Sumter to Marion, June 16, 1781, Greene to Sumter, June 17, 1781, R. W. Gibbes, *Documentary History*, III, 97.

44. L. Morris to J. Morris, June 22, 1781, *NYHS Coll.*, VIII, 488-489.

45. G. W. Greene, *op. cit.*, III, 314-315; Ward, *op. cit.*, II, 821-822; Johnson, *op. cit.*, II, 150. Johnson believed that Cruger did not send men into the ditch as described herein.

46. Greene to Huntington, June 22, 1781, Greene to La Luzerne, June 22, 1781, Greene Coll., XXXV, WCL; O. H. Williams, *Papers*, p. 47.

47. Greene to Pickens, June 28, 1781, Greene Coll., XXXVI, WCL; Greene to Huntington, June 22, 1781, Greene Coll., XXXV, WCL.

48. Johnson, *op. cit.*, II, 160.

49. Williams to Greene, July 8, 1781, Pierce to Greene, July 8, 1781, Sumter to Greene, July 8, 1781, Greene to Marion, July 10, 1781, Marion to Greene, July 10, 1781, Greene Coll., XXXVII, WCL; L. Morris to his father, July 21, 1781, *NYHS Coll.*, VIII, 490; Johnson, *op. cit.*, II, 162-165.

50. Lee to Greene, July 15, 1781, Greene Coll., XXXVIII, WCL; Sumter to Greene, July 17, 1781, *Charleston Year Book*, 1899, pp. 41-44; Balfour to Clinton, July 20, 1781, Leslie's Letter Book, NYPL; Marion to Greene, July 19, 1781, Greene Coll., XXXVIII, WCL; Greene to McKean, July 26, 1781, Greene Coll., XXXIX, WCL; Clinton, *op. cit.*, pp. 550-551; Johnson, *op. cit.*, II, 170-173; G. W. Greene, *op. cit.*, II, 332; Lee, *op. cit.*, II, 157; W. D. James, *Francis Marion*, pp. 124-125.

NOTES FOR CHAPTER XV

1. W. Johnson, *Sketches*, II, 178; W. D. James, *Francis Marion*, p. 124. Johnson puts Greene's camp on John Singleton's plantation near Stateburg. This, however, was the site of Greene's second camp on the High Hills after the battle of Eutaw Springs.

2. Greene to Knox, July 18, 1781, Greene Papers, CHS.

3. Greene to the Georgia delegates in Congress, July 18, 1781, July 25, 1781, Greene Papers, DUL.

4. G. W. Greene, *Life of Nathanael Greene*, III, 351.

5. Febiger to Bland, July 3, 1781, R. Bland, *Papers*, II, 71; C. Ward, *The War of the Revolution*, II, 872 ff.; Clinton, *The American Rebellion*, p. 356.

6. Greene to Lafayette, June 9, 1781, Greene Papers, LC; Greene to Jefferson, June 27, 1781, Greene Coll., XXXVI, WCL; Johnson, *op. cit.*, II, 423.

7. Greene to Washington, July 17, 1781, pamphlet, RIHS.

8. Burnet to Greene, Aug. 20, 1781, Greene Coll., XLI, WCL; Greene to Nelson, Aug. 10, 1781, Greene Coll., XL, WCL; T. Jefferson, *Papers*, VI, 106; M. C. Tyler, *Patrick Henry*, p. 386.

9. Randolph to Madison, Aug. 16, 1781, E. C. Burnett, *Letters*, VI, 485n.

10. Greene to Reed, Aug. 6, 1781, Reed Papers, IX, NYHS.

11. Greene to Rush, Aug. 8, 1781, Greene Coll., XL, WCL.

12. Greene to Morris, Aug. 18, 1781, Greene Coll., XLI, WCL; G. W. Greene, *op. cit.*, III, 371-372.

13. G. W. Greene, *op. cit.*, III, 352.

14. Greene to Marion, Aug. 10, 1781, Greene Coll., XL, WCL; Johnson, *op. cit.*, II, 457.

15. Greene to Lafayette, Aug. 26, 1781, Greene Coll., XLII, WCL; Greene to Balfour, Sept. 19, 1781, Greene Coll., XLIV, WCL.

16. Greene to McKean, Oct. 25, 1781, Greene Coll., XLVI, WCL; E. Boudinot, *Recollections*, p. 59.

17. Greene to Marion, July 21, 1781, Greene to Sumter, July 21, 1781, Greene Coll., XXXVIII, WCL.

18. Greene to Henderson, Aug. 6, 1781, Greene Papers, LC; George Washington Greene, the biographer, censures Sumter severely, as do many other authors. G. W. Greene, *op. cit.*, III, 377-381.

19. Lee to Greene, Aug. 20, 1781, Greene Coll., XLI, WCL.

20. Lee to Greene, August 17, 1781, Siege of Yorktown Papers, II, 10, ML.

21. Greene to Lee, Aug. 24, 1781, Greene to Henderson, Aug. 24, 1781, Greene Coll., XLII, WCL; H. Lee, *Memoirs*, II, 276.

22. Lee blamed the American cavalry for the misfortune. If it had stayed near the center of the battle and been on hand at crucial moments, the enemy would have been utterly destroyed, he declared. Lee, *op. cit.*, II, 290-291, 377. Johnson blames the infantry for stopping to rifle the baggage. Johnson, *op. cit.*, II, 424.

23. Greene to Person, Oct. 24, 1781, Greene Coll., XLVI, WCL; Lee, *op. cit.*, II, 284-292; James, *op. cit.*, pp. 134-135.

24. Lee to Greene, Oct. 28, 1781, Siege of Yorktown Papers, ML.

25. Greene to McKean, Sept. 11, 1781, Greene Coll., XLIV, WCL; Williams to E. Williams, Sept. 11, 1781, Williams to E. Giles, Sept. 23, 1781, O. H. Williams, *Papers*; *Pa. Mag. of Hist. and Biog.*, XXX, 359-361; Lee, *op. cit.*, II, 291-292; C. Stedman, *History*, II, 278-289; Clinton, *op. cit.*, p. 355.

26. Reed to Greene, Nov. 1, 1781, Reed Papers, IX, NYHS; Pierce to Greene, Oct. 24, 1781, Greene Papers, LC; Giles to Williams, Sept. 2, 1781, Williams, *op. cit.*, p. 49; Knox to Adams, Oct. 21, 1781, *Proc. of the Am. Antiq. Soc.* XVI, 225; Greene to Adams, Jan. 28, 1782, Greene Coll., LIII, WCL; J. Adams, *Works*, VII, 487.

27. F. Mackenzie, *Diary*, II, 373.

28. Greene to Shelby, Sept. 16, 1781, Greene Coll., XLIII, WCL.

29. G. W. Greene, *op. cit.*, III, 417; Lee to Greene, Sept. 28, 1781, Siege of Yorktown Papers, ML.

30. Marion to Greene, Sept. 21, 1781, Greene Coll., XLIV, WCL; Greene to Marion, Sept. 19, 1781, Marion to Horry, Sept. 23, 1781, Marion's Letter

Book, State Arch., S. C.; Balfour to Germain, Oct. 12, 1781, Leslie's Letter Book, NYPL; Johnson, *op. cit.*, II, 243.

31. Greene to Horry, Sept. 24, 1781, Marion's Letter Book. State Arch., S. C.; Lee to Greene, Sept. 25, 1781, Siege of Yorktown Papers, ML.

32. Greene to Martin, Oct. 9, 1781, Greene to Rutherford, Oct. 18, 1781, Greene Coll., XLV, WCL; Rutledge's Proclamation, Sept. 27, 1781, Marion's Letter Book, State Arch, S. C.; Johnson, *op. cit.*, II, 250.

33. Greene to Horry, Nov. 6, 1781, Horry to Rutledge, Oct. 31, 1781, Horry to Greene, Oct. 31, 1781, Marion's Letter Book, State Arch., S. C.; Greene to Horry, Feb. 14, 1782, Greene Coll., LIV, WCL.

34. Greene to Egleston, Oct. 21, 1781, Greene Coll., XLVI, WCL.

35. Greene to Martin, Nov. 11, 1781, Greene Coll., XLVII, WCL; Johnson, *op. cit.*, II, 261.

36. Hampton to Greene, Nov. 13, 1781, Marion to Greene, Nov. 17, 1781, Greene to Sumter, Nov. 2, 1781, Greene Coll., XLVII, WCL; Greene to Marion, Nov. 5, 1781, Marion's Letter Book, State Arch., S. C.; Johnson, *op. cit.*, II, 260.

37. As it is difficult to read Williams' handwriting, the name of the woman who entertained Greene may be misspelled. Williams to Greene, Nov. 19, 1781, Greene Coll., XLVIII, WCL; G. W. Greene, *op. cit.*, III, 419.

38. Greene to Lee, Dec. 9, 1781, Siege of Yorktown Papers, ML.

39. Greene to Rutledge, Dec. 3, 1781, Greene to Lee, Dec. 2, 1781, Greene Coll., XLIX, WCL; Johnson *op. cit.*, II, 265.

40. Greene to Rutledge, Dec. 3, 1781, Greene Coll., XLIX, WCL.

41. Greene to Sumter, Nov. 25, 1781, Sumter to Greene, Nov. 22, 23, 1781, Greene Coll., XLVIII, WCL; *Charleston Year Book*, 1899, pp. 57-66; Sumter to Greene, Dec. 9, 1781, Greene Coll., XLIX, WCL; Sumter to Greene, Dec. 16, 1781, Greene Papers, LC; Sumter to Greene, Jan. 2, 1782, Greene Coll., LI, WCL.

42. Greene to Marion, Dec. 6, 1781, Greene to Twiggs, Dec. 12, 1781, Greene Papers, DUL; Greene to Lee, Dec. 7, 1781, Greene Coll., XLIX, WCL.

43. Greene to Rochambeau, Dec. 27, 1781, Greene Papers, LC; Washington to Greene, Feb. 1, 1782, J. C. Fitzpatrick, ed., *Writings of George Washington*, XXIV, 1-2; Greene to Rochambeau, March 12, 1782, Greene Papers, Bancroft Coll., NYPL; G. W. Greene, *op. cit.*, III, 425; Johnson, *op. cit.*, II, 269-272, 276.

44. Greene to Washington, Jan. 24, 1782, Greene to Wayne, Jan. 9, 1782, Greene Papers, Bancroft Coll., NYPL.

45. G. W. Greene, *op. cit.*, III, 426 ff.; Greene to Rutledge, Dec. 9, 1781, Greene Coll., XLIX, WCL.

46. W. G. Simms, *Correspondence of John Laurens*, pp. 117-118; L. Morris to J. Morris, Dec. 10, 1781, "Letters," *NYHS Coll.*, VIII.

47. Letter of John Armstrong, April 3, 1779, Box XI, Gates Papers, NYHS; C. K. Bolton, *Private Soldier*, pp. 21-25.

48. Greene to G. Morris, Nov. 21, 1781, Greene Coll., XLVIII, WCL; G. Morris to Greene, Dec. 24, 1781, Greene Papers, LC; Greene to Christopher Greene, Greene Papers, # 834, RIHS; C. Biddle to Greene, Nov. 11, 1781, Siege of Yorktown Papers, ML.

49. The Assembly listed 118 estates which should be considered for confiscation. House Journals, pp. 26, 31-32, 69-70, State Arch., S. C.

50. Greene to Rutledge, Feb. 26, 1782, Greene Papers, Bancroft Coll., NYPL; Greene to Reed, Feb. 27, 1782, Reed Papers, X, NYHS.

51. Lee was especially piqued because Greene put Laurens in command of the raid on Johns Island. Laurens, however, not only out-ranked Lee but knew the country well. Johnson, *op. cit.*, II, 328, 460-461; Greene to Lee, Jan. 26, 1782, Greene to Congress, Feb. 18, 1782, Greene Papers, Bancroft Coll., NYPL; Lee to Greene, Jan. 29, 1782, Greene Coll., LXXXVIII, WCL.

52. Burke to Greene, Jan. 19, 1782, Greene Papers, LC; Leslie to Greene, Jan. 27, 1782, Greene Coll., LIII, WCL; Greene to Burke, Jan. 21, 1782, April 8, 1782, Greene Papers, Bancroft Coll., NYPL; Greene to Burke, March 9, 1782, Greene Coll., LVI, WCL.

53. Greene to Burke, March 13, 1782, Greene Coll., LIV, WCL; Leslie to Greene, April 4, 1782, Greene to Leslie, April 5, 1782, Greene to Marion, April 12, 1782, Greene Coll., LVII, WCL; Marion to Greene, March 29, 1782, Greene Coll., LVI, WCL; Burnet to Reed, April 12, 1782, Reed Papers, X, NYHS.

54. Greene to Knox, May 20, 1782, Knox Papers, VIII, MHS.

NOTES FOR CHAPTER XVI

1. Greene to Lincoln, March 9, 1782, Greene Papers, Bancroft Coll., NYPL.

2. Greene to R. Morris, Aug. 13, 1782, HM, 22719, HL; Greene to Washington, March 9, 1782, Greene to Harmar, March 11, 1782, Greene Coll., IX, WCL; Greene to R. Morris, March 7, 1782, Greene Papers, Bancroft Coll., NYPL.

3. Greene to Harrison, April 22, 1782, Greene Coll., LVIII, WCL.

4. Greene to Hanson, May 18, 1782, Greene to Washington, May 19, 1782, Greene Coll., LX, WCL.

5. Harmar to Greene, April 20, 1782, Siege of Yorktown Papers, II, 2, ML.

6. Greene to Reed, July 10, 1782, Reed Papers, X, NYHS; G. W. Greene, *Life of Nathanael Greene*, III, 451.

7. Greene to Davie, March 5, 1782, Greene Coll., LV, WCL; Greene to Burke, March 5, 1782, Greene to Harrison, Feb. 8, 1782, Greene to R. Morris, March 7, 1782, Greene Papers, Bancroft Coll., NYPL; C. L. Ver Steeg, *Robert Morris: Revolutionary Financier*, pp. 158 ff.

8. Mathews to Greene, Jan. 24, 1782, Greene Coll., LII, WCL; Williams to Greene, Feb. 23, 1782, Pettit to Greene, Feb. 10, 1782, Greene Coll., LIV, WCL; Pettit to Greene, March 15, 1782, Greene Coll., LV, WCL; Burnet to Greene, March 21, 1782, Greene Coll., LVI, WCL; Burnet to Reed, April 12, 1782, Reed Papers, X, NYHS.

9. *Pa. Mag. of Hist. and Biog.*, VII, 390.

10. Wadsworth Coll., # 152, CHS; W. Johnson, *Sketches*, II, 463; Wayne to Greene, June 15, 1782, Greene Coll., LXII, WCL; Clay to Greene, May 13, 1782, Greene Coll., LX, WCL.

11. Pettit to Greene, March 15, 1782, Greene Coll., LV, WCL; Williams to Greene, July 20, 1782, O. H. Williams, *Papers*, p. 68.

12. J. Almon, *The Remembrancer*, May 21, 1782, Part II, 324-325;

Greene to Congress, May 23, 1782, First Overtures for the Cessation of Hostilities, WCL; Greene to Martin, May 18, 1782, Greene Coll., LX, WCL; J. C. Fitzpatrick, ed., *Writings of George Washington*, XXIV, 408; Greene to Knox, May 20, 1782, Knox Papers, VIII, MHS.

13. Greene to Williams, June 6, 1782, Williams, *op. cit.*, p. 66; G. W. Greene, *op. cit.*, III, 486.

14. Greene to Lee, June 6, 1782, Greene Coll., LXI, WCL; Laurens to Greene, June 20, 1782, Legion protest to Greene, June 18, 1782, Greene Papers, LC; Greene to Hanson, July 10, 1782, Greene Coll., LXIII, WCL; Greene to Lee, Sept., 1782, Greene Coll., LXIX, WCL.

15. Carleton to Leslie, May 23, 1782, Leslie's Letter Book, NYPL; Greene to Washington, May 31, 1782, Greene Coll., LXI, WCL; Wayne to Greene, June 30, 1782, Greene to Wayne, June 18, 1782, Greene Coll., LXII, WCL; Wayne to Greene, July 17, 1782, Greene Coll., LXIV, WCL.

16. Greene to Pettit, Aug. 14, 1782, Reed Papers, X, NYHS; Mathews to Greene, Aug. 5, 1782, Greene Coll., LXV, WCL; Leslie to Carleton, Sept. 8, 1782, Leslie's Letter Book, NYPL; Gist to Greene, Sept. 11, 1782, Greene Coll., LXVII, WCL; Greene to Hanson, Aug. 29, 1782, Greene Coll., LXVI, WCL; Williams, *op. cit.*, p. 70; G. W. Greene, *op. cit.*, III, 442-445.

17. Greene to C. Greene, April 14, 1782, Greene Papers, # G-834, RIHS; Greene to Howley, Oct. 13, 1782, Greene Papers, DUL; Clay to Greene, Aug. 6, 1782, Greene to Rush, Aug. 14, 1782, Greene Coll., LXV, WCL.

18. Greene to Witherspoon, Aug. 28, 1782, Greene Coll., LXVI, WCL; Greene to Pettit, Aug. 14, 29, 1782, Reed Papers, X, NYHS.

19. Pierce to Greene, Sept. 14, 1782, Greene Coll., LXVII, WCL; Pendleton to Greene, Sept. 20, 1782, Greene Coll., LXVIII, WCL; Wayne to R. Morris, Sept. 29, 1782, "Letters," *NYHS Coll.*, (1878), p. 482; Greene to Trumbull, Sept. 29, 1782, Pierce to Greene, Sept. 30, 1782, Greene Coll., LXVIII, WCL; Pendleton to Greene, Oct. 15, 1782, Greene Coll., LXIX, WCL.

20. E. C. Burnett, *Letters*, VI, 497-498; Leslie to Tonyn, Sept. 30, 1782, Leslie's Letter Book, NYPL; Wayne to R. Morris, Sept. 29, 1782, "Letters," *NYHS Coll.*, (1878), p. 482; Greene to Weedon, Oct. 24, 1782, Weedon, Correspondence, p. 143, APS.

21. Wilmot to Burnet, Oct. 19, 1782, Greene Coll., LXX, WCL; Intelligence, Nov. 6, 1782, Greene Coll., LXXI, WCL; *Pa. Mag. of Hist. and Biog.*, VII, 293; E. Denny, *Journal*, Oct. 1, 1782, pp. 252-253.

22. Greene to Pettit, Aug. 29, 1782, Reed Papers, X, NYHS; Greene to Williams, Nov. 12, 1782, Williams, *op. cit.*, pp. 71, 74-75; Greene to Boudinot, Dec. 19, 1782, Greene Coll., LXXIII, WCL; L. Morris to his father, Dec. 19, 1782, "Letters," *NYHS Coll.*, VIII, 509; Wemyss to Simonds, Dec. 13, 1782, Greene Coll., LXXII, WCL.

23. J. Madison, *Writings*, I, 315; *Journals of the Cont. Congress*, XXIV, 47-48, XXV, 855, 857.

24. Greene to Washington, Dec. 19, 1782, Greene Coll., LXXIII, WCL.

25. Greene to Hall, Jan. 20, 1783, Greene Letters, XIII, HL; Greene to Habersham, Jan. 20, 1783, Greene Papers, DUL.

26. Greene to Guerard, March 8, 1782, Greene Letters, XIII, HL.

27. Greene to Williams, April 11, 1783, Williams, *op. cit.*, p. 80.

28. S. C. Council Journal, No. 59, pp. 27-29; G. W. Greene, *op. cit.*, III, 474-475.

29. Greene to Tonyn, April 14, 1783, Greene Coll., LXXVI, WCL.

30. Greene to Lincoln, April 19, 1783, Greene Coll., LXXXVI, WCL; Greene to Reed, April 23, 1783, Greene Coll., XIII, HL.

31. Johnson, *op. cit.*, II, 318, 358-360.

32. *Ibid.*, II, 374. *See also* Testimony, *Am. State Papers*, pp. 189-191; Robert Forsyth's Testimony, Greene Coll., LXXXVI, WCL; Knox Papers, XXV, MHS.

33. *Ibid.*, II, 380. Burnet died within a few months.

34. *Ibid.*, II, 359-360, 363-364.

35. *Ibid.*, II, 373.

36. The Gunn Case, Greene Coll., LXXXVII, WCL; Johnson, *op. cit.*, II, 326-327.

37. Johnson, *op. cit.*, II, 365.

38. Pendleton to Mrs. Greene, Dec. 30, 1789, Greene Coll., LXXXVI, WCL.

39. Forsyth's Testimony, Nov. 5, 1781, Greene Coll., LXXXVI, WCL; Johnson, *op. cit.*, II, 404-405.

40. G. W. Greene, *op. cit.*, III, 562.

41. Johnson, *op. cit.*, II, 372-379; Greene to Williams, July 2, 1783, O. H. Williams, *op. cit.*, pp. 81-85; Greene to Scott, Feb. 18, 1783, Greene Coll., LXXIV, WCL; Greene to R. H. Lee, Aug. 2, 1785, Greene Coll., LXXXIV, WCL; Misc. Rec., WW, pp. 225-227, State Arch., S.C.

42. Carrington to Knox, Feb. 4, 1790, Carrington's Affidavit, Feb. 4, 1790, Knox Papers, XXV, MHS.

43. Washington to Wadsworth, Oct. 22, 1786, Fitzpatrick, *op. cit.*, XXIX, 25-26.

44. Forsyth's Testimony, Nov. 5, 1791, Greene Coll., LXXXVI, WCL.

45. Greene to Griffin Greene, April 14, 1782, Greene Papers, MCL.

46. Greene to Hazelhurst, June 26, 1784, Greene Coll., LXXXI, WCL.

47. Jacob Greene to Greene, May 4, 1783, Greene Coll., LXXVII, WCL; Pierce to Greene, June 19, 1783, Greene Coll., LXXVIII, WCL; Greene to Pettit, April 3, 1783, Reed Papers, X, NYHS; Williams, *op. cit.*, p. 80.

48. Pettit to Greene, July 26, 1783, Greene Coll., LXXVIII, WCL.

49. Greene to Collins, April 22, 1783, Greene Papers, DUL; Reed to Greene, Aug. 3, 1783, Greene Coll., LXXVIII, WCL.

50. G. W. Greene, *op. cit.*, III, 519-520.

51. Johnson, *op. cit.*, II, 451.

52. Greene to Pettit, April 3, 1783, Reed Papers, X, NYHS; H. A. M. Smith, *The Baronies of South Carolina*, pp. 80-82.

53. Saunders to Greene, May 26, 1783, Greene Coll., LXXVII, WCL; Saunders to Greene, June 7, 1783, Greene Coll., LXXVIII, WCL.

54. Pendleton to Greene, July 1, 1783, Greene Coll., LXXVIII, WCL; Greene to Harrison, May 20, 1783, Greene Papers, LC; Greene to Lincoln, May 17, 1783, Greene Coll., LXXVII, WCL.

55. Egleston to Greene, May 12, 1783, Greene Papers, LC; Greene to Egleston, May 17, 1783, Greene Coll., LXXVII, WCL.

56. Greene to Lincoln, June 3, 1783, Greene Coll., LXXVIII, WCL; Johnson, *op. cit.*, II, 384.

57. Greene to Lincoln, June 18, 1783, Greene Coll., LXXVIII, WCL.

58. General Orders, June, 1783, Pendleton Papers, NYHS; Greene to Lincoln, July 11, 1783, Greene Coll., LXXVIII, WCL.

59. Greene to Pettit, July 29, 1783, Reed Papers, X, NYHS.

60. Greene to Pettit, Aug. 9, 1783, Greene Coll., LXXXVIII, WCL; Carrington to Greene, Sept. 21, 1783, Greene Coll., LXXIX, WCL; Forsyth's Testimony, Nov. 5, 1791, Greene Coll., LXXXVI, WCL.

61. Testimonials, Greene Papers, VII, 327-330, LC.

62. A few years later when the cannon were delivered to him at Charleston, Greene took them to Mulberry Grove where they stood for many years. They are now at West Point. Greene to Boudinot, Oct. 7, 1783, Greene to Washington, Nov., 1783, Greene Coll., LXXXIX, WCL; Burnet, *op. cit.*, VII, 337; *Journals of the Cont. Cong.*, XXV, 101-102; Johnson, *op. cit.*, II, 403; Knox Papers, XVI, 90, MHS.

NOTES FOR CHAPTER XVII

1. Pettit to Greene, Feb. 7, 1784, March 6, 1784, Greene Coll., LXXX, WCL; W. Johnson, *Sketches*, II, 402.

2. Greene to Malgine, Channing and Goodwin, Nov. 29, 1783, Greene Coll., LXXXIX, WCL.

3. W. Littlefield to Greene, March 22, 1784, Greene Coll., LXXX, WCL; B. Bently's bill for nursing and caring for Louisa Catherine, July, 1785, Greene Coll., LXXXVIII, WCL.

4. Greene to R. Morris, July 3, 1784, Greene Coll., XIII, HL; Greene's letter, Feb. 24, 1784, Greene Papers, RIHS; G. W. Greene, *Life of Nathanael Greene*, III, 526.

5. Greene to Reed, May 4, 1784, Reed Papers, XI, NYHS; Knox to Greene, March 4, 1784, Greene Coll., LXXX, WCL; Greene to Washington, Feb. 16, 1784, Greene to Olney, April 15, 1784, Greene Coll., LXXXVIII, WCL.

6. *William and Mary Quarterly*, X, No. 1, p. 14; Greene to Washington, Aug. 29, 1784, Greene Coll., LXXXIV, WCL.

7. Greene to Banks, undated, Greene Coll., LXXXVII, WCL.

8. Lushington was also one of Banks's partners. Greene to Forsyth, Oct. 2, 1784, Greene Coll., LXXXII, WCL.

9. Forsyth's Testimony, Greene Coll., WCL.

10. Greene to Hunter, Aug. 29, 1785, Annmary Brown Memorial, Providence; Hunter to Greene, Sept. 2, 1785, Greene Coll., LXXXIV, WCL.

11. Collett to Greene, June 13, 1785, Greene Coll., LXXXVI, WCL; Greene to R. H. Lee, Aug. 22, 1785, Greene Coll., LXXXIV, WCL.

12. Misc. Rec., VV, pp. 42-43, State Arch., S. C.; Johnson, *op. cit.*, II, 436-437n; *Am. State Papers*, Class IX, Claims, pp. 189-191.

13. Greene to La Luzerne, May 20, 1783, Greene Coll., LXXVII, WCL; Lacase and Mallet's letter, Dec., 1783, Greene Coll., LXXXVIII, WCL; Greene to Lacase and Mallet, Jan. 14, 1784, Greene Coll., LXXX, WCL.

14. *Journal of Cont. Congress*, XXVI, 189-199; Comptroller's Office, Aug. 30, 1784, Greene Coll., LXXXII, WCL.

15. Saunders to Greene, Nov. 25, Dec. 3, 1783, May 29, 1784, Greene Coll., LXXXI, WCL; Greene to Wadsworth, June 7, 1784, Greene Coll., LXXXI, WCL; Greene to R. Morris, June 9, 1784, Greene Coll., LXXX,

WCL.; Saunders to Greene, Jan. 30, 1784, Greene Coll., LXXX, WCL; Jervais to Saunders, Sept. 3, 1784, Greene Coll., LXXXII, WCL; L. Morris to Greene, July 17, 1784, Greene Coll., LXXXI, WCL; Greene to Hewson, Edwards & Co., Aug. 6, 1784, Greene Coll., LXXXII, WCL; Greene to Saunders, Jan. 4, 1784, Greene Coll., LXXX, WCL.

16. Greene to Wadsworth, Feb. 3, Feb. 17, 1785, Greene Papers, YUL; Greene to Marbois, April 15, 1785, Greene Papers, YUL; Tates to Greene, April 6, 1785, Greene Papers, LC.

17. Greene to Pendleton, May 15, 1785, Pendleton Papers, NYHS; Greene to W. Gibbons, Aug. 29, 1784, Misc. Papers, XVII, MHS.

18. The Gunn Case, Greene Coll., LXXXVII, WCL; Gunn to Greene, Feb. 23, 1785, Greene Coll., LXXXIII, WCL.

19. Greene to Wadsworth, March 8, 1785, Wadsworth Coll., CHS; G. W. Greene, *op. cit.*, III, 527-528.

20. J. C. Fitzpatrick, ed., *Writings of George Washington*, XXVII, 144-145.

21. Greene to Pendleton, April 29, 1785, Pendleton Papers, NYHS; Greene to Wadsworth, May 11, 1785, Greene Papers, YUL.

22. Pettit to Greene, June 30, 1785, Greene Coll., LXXXIII, WCL; Greene to Wadsworth, March 26, July 13, Sept. 7, 11, 1785, Greene Papers, YUL.

23. Last Will and Testament, Oct. 11, 1785, Greene Papers, LC; Greene to Wadsworth, Sept. 7, 13, 1785, Greene Papers, YUL.

24. G. W. Greene, *op. cit.*, III, 532.

25. Greene to Ward, April 14, 1786, Greene Papers, RIHS; Pierce to Greene, March 24, 1786, Greene Coll., LXXXV, WCL; Greene to Knox, March 12, 1786, Knox Papers, XVIII, MHS.

26. Wilhem and Van Willink to Greene, July 8, 1785, Greene Coll., LXXXIII, WCL; Greene to Wilhem and Van Willink, Jan. 7, 1786, Greene Coll., LXXXV, WCL.

27. Lafayette to Greene, Dec. 3, 1785, Greene Papers, LC; Lafayette to Greene, Dec. 29, 1785, Greene Coll., LXXXIV, WCL; Greene to de Castries, Dec., 1785, Greene Coll., LXXXIV, WCL.

28. McLane to Greene, July 3, 1786, Greene Coll., LXXXIII, WCL; Hillhouse to Greene, Oct. 4, 1785, Greene Coll., LXXXIV, WCL.

29. Greene to Thomson, April 24, 1786, *NYHS Coll.*, (1878), p. 207.

30. Greene to Sucre, June, 1786, Greene Coll., LXXXVI, WCL; G. W. Greene, *op. cit.*, III, 530-531.

31. Greene to Knox, March 12, 1786, Knox Papers, XVIII, MHS. After Greene died Kitty took George to France where he was left with Lafayette. Washington also offered to take care of George and give him an education. G. W. Greene, *op. cit.*, III, 529n.

32. G. W. Greene, *op. cit.*, III, 534-535; *The Columbian Magazine or Monthly Miscellany*, pp. 59-80; Wayne to his daughter, June 20, 1786, *Pa. Mag. of Hist. and Biog.*, XXX, 492-493; Article by Charles Jones, Pub. Aug. 26, 1885, Augusta, Georgia.

33. *The Works of Thomas Jefferson*, ed. by P. L. Ford, XII, 246.

34. F. Kinloch, *Letters from Geneva and France*, II, 142.

Bibliography

MANUSCRIPT SOURCES

Moses Brown Papers. Rhode Island Historical Society (RIHS*).
Deane Papers. Connecticut Historical Society (CHS).
East Greenwich Monthly Meeting Minutes. Moses Brown School, Providence, R. I.
Emmet Coll. New York Public Library (NYPL).
Gates Papers. New York Historical Society (NYHS).
Greene Coll. William Clements Library (WCL).
Greene Correspondence. American Philosophical Society (APS).
Greene Letters and Transcripts, Greene Coll. Huntington Library (HL).
Greene Letters. Houghton Library, Harvard University.
Greene Misc. Papers. New York Historical Society (NYHS).
Greene Papers, Bancroft Coll. New York Public Library (NYPL).
Greene Papers. Connecticut Historical Society (CHS).
Greene Papers. Duke University Library (DUL).
Greene Papers, Knollenberg Coll. Yale University Library (YUL).
Greene Papers. Library of Congress (LC).
Greene Papers. Marietta College Library (MCL).
Greene Papers. Rhode Island Historical Society (RIHS).
Greene Papers. Yale University Library (YUL).
Heath Papers. Massachusetts Historical Society (MHS).
Kentish Guards Papers. Rhode Island Historical Society (RIHS).
Knox Papers. Massachusetts Historical Society (MHS).
Lee Correspondence (Richard, Henry, and Arthur). American Philosophical Society (APS).
Leslie's Letter Book. New York Public Library (NYPL).
Letters to the Governors. State Archives, Providence, R. I.
Joseph Lewis Transcripts. Morristown National Park Library (MNPL).
Loudoun Papers. Huntington Library (HL).
McDougall Papers. New York Historical Society (NYHS).
Marion's Letter Book. State Archives, S. C.
Mitchell's Orderly Book. New York Historical Society (NYHS).
Peale's Diary. Huntington Library (HL).
Peck MSS. Rhode Island Historical Society (RIHS).
Pendleton Papers. New York Historical Society (NYHS).
Reed Papers. New York Historical Society (NYHS).

---

* Abbreviations indicate the form used in the footnotes.

Rush MSS. Ridgway Library.
Schuyler Papers. New York Public Library (NYPL).
Siege of Yorktown Papers. Morgan Library (ML).
Smith Coll. Morristown National Park Library (MNPL).
South Carolina, State Archives:
 Journal of the Assembly
 Council Journal
 Misc. Records
Sparks Coll. Houghton Library, Harvard University.
Steuben Papers. New York Historical Society (NYHS).
Stewart Papers. Houghton Library, Harvard University.
Stirling Papers. New York Historical Society (NYHS).
Sullivan Papers. New Hampshire Historical Society (NHHS).
Thomas MSS. Massachusetts Historical Society (MHS).
Trumbull Papers. Massachusetts Historical Society (MHS).
Von Jungkenn MSS. William Clements Library (WCL).
Wadsworth Coll. Connecticut Historical Society (CHS).
Wadsworth Papers. Wadsworth Atheneum (WA).
Washington Papers. Library of Congress (LC).
Wayne Papers. Historical Society of Pennsylvania (HSP).
Weare Papers. New Hampshire Historical Society (NHHS).
Webb MSS. Yale University Library (YUL).
Weedon Correspondence. American Philosophical Society (APS).

PRIMARY PUBLISHED SOURCES

ADAMS, JOHN. *Familiar Letters of John Adams and his Wife Abigail Adams during the Revolution*, ed. Charles Francis Adams. Boston: 1875.
————. *The Works of John Adams*, ed. Charles Francis Adams. 10 vols. Boston: 1856.
ALMON, JOHN (ed.). *The Remembrancer*. 17 vols. London: 1775-1784.
American State Papers. Class IX, Claims. Washington: 1834.
ANDRÉ, JOHN. *Minutes of a Court of Inquiry upon the Case of Major John André*. Albany: 1865.
ARMAND, CHARLES. "Letters of Colonel Armand, 1777-1791," *New York Historical Society Collections*, XI (1878). New York: 1879.
BARKER, JOHN. *The British in Boston, Being the Diary of Lieutenant John Barker*. Cambridge: 1924.
BAURMEISTER, CARL L. *Revolution in America: Baurmeister Journals*, ed. B. A. Uhlendorf. New Brunswick: 1957.
BLAND, RICHARD. *The Bland Papers*, ed. Charles Campbell. 2 vols. Petersburg: 1840.
BOUDINOT, ELIAS. *Journal of Historical Recollections of American Events during the Revolutionary War*. Philadelphia: 1894.
BURNABY, ANDREW. *Travels Through North America*. New York: 1904.

BURNETT, EDMUND C. *Letters of Members of the Continental Congress.* 8 vols. Washington: 1921-1936.

CHILTON, JOHN. "Diary," *Tyler's Quarterly Historical and Genealogical Magazine,* XII (1931).

CLINTON, GEORGE. *Public Papers of George Clinton.* 10 vols. New York: 1899-1914.

CLINTON, HENRY. *The American Rebellion,* ed. W. B. Willcox. New Haven: 1954.

————. *Narrative of the Campaign in 1781. Answer to Sir Henry Clinton's Narrative. Observations on Earl Cornwallis's Answer.* Philadelphia: 1865-1866.

COOKE, NICHOLAS. "Revolutionary Correspondence—1775-1781," *Proceedings of the American Antiquarian Society,* XXXVI (Oct., 1926).

CORNWALLIS, CHARLES. *Correspondence of Charles, first Marquis Cornwallis.* 3 vols. London: 1859.

CRESSWELL, NICHOLAS. *The Journal of Nicholas Cresswell, 1774-1777.* New York: 1924.

DAVID, EBENEZER. *A Rhode Island Chaplain in the Revolution: Letters of Ebenezer David to Nicholas Brown, 1775-1778,* eds. J. D. Black and W. R. Roelker. Providence: 1949.

DEANE, SILAS. "The Deane Papers," *New York Historical Society Collections,* XIX-XXIII (1886-1890). New York: 1887-1891.

DENNY, EBENEZER. "Military Journal of Ebenezer Denny," *Memoirs of the Historical Society of Pennsylvania,* Vol. III. Philadelphia: 1860.

FITHIAN, PHILIP VICKERS. *Journal, 1775-1776,* eds. R. Albion and L. Dodson. Princeton: 1934.

FORCE, PETER. *American Archives.* 9 vols. Washington: 1837-1853.

GAGE, THOMAS. *The Correspondence of General Thomas Gage with the Secretaries of State—1763-1775,* ed. Clarence E. Carter. New Haven: 1931-1933.

GAINE, HUGH. *The Journals of Hugh Gaine, Printer,* ed. P. L. Ford. 2 vols. New York: 1912.

GIBBES, ROBERT W. *Documentary History of the American Revolution.* 3 vols. New York: 1853-1857.

GRANGER, DANIEL. "A Boy Soldier under Washington: the Memoir of Daniel Granger," *Mississippi Valley Historical Review,* XVI (March, 1930).

GRAYDON, ALEXANDER. *Memoirs of His Own Times,* ed. John S. Littell. Philadelphia: 1846.

GREENE, NATHANAEL. *Letters by and to Gen. Nathanael Greene with some to his wife,* ed. George P. Richmond. New York: 1906.

————. "Greene Papers from the Ely Collection," *Proceedings of the New Jersey Historical Society,* Vol. 61 (1943).

HAMILTON, ALEXANDER. *The Works of Alexander Hamilton,* ed. Henry Cabot Lodge. 9 vols. New York: 1885-1886.

HEATH, WILLIAM. *Memoirs of Major-General Heath.* New York: 1904.

HOWE, WILLIAM. *Howe's Orderly Book,* ed. B. F. Stevens. London: 1890.

HUNTINGTON, EBENEZER. *Letters Written by Ebenezer Huntington during the American Revolution.* New York: 1914.

JEFFERSON, THOMAS. *The Papers of Thomas Jefferson.* Vols. 4-6. Princeton: 1951-1952.

Journal of each Provincial Congress of Massachusetts—in 1774 and 1775. Boston: 1838.

Journals of the Continental Congress, 1774-1789. 34 vols. Washington: 1904-1937.

LAFAYETTE, MARQUIS. *Memoirs, Correspondence and Manuscripts of General Lafayette.* 3 vols. London: 1837.

LAMB, RICHARD. *Memoirs of His Own Life.* Dublin: 1809.

LAURENS, JOHN. *The Army Correspondence of John Laurens in the Years 1777-1778,* ed. W. G. Simms. New York: 1867.

LEE, CHARLES. *Lee Papers, New York Historical Society Collections.* 4 vols. New York: 1871-1874.

LEE, HENRY. *Memoirs of the War in the Southern Department of the United States.* 2 vols. Philadelphia: 1812.

————. *The Campaign of 1781 in the Carolinas with Remarks Historical and Critical on Johnson's Life of Greene.* Philadelphia: 1824.

LEE, RICHARD HENRY. *Memoirs of the Life of Richard Henry Lee and his Correspondence.* 2 vols. Philadelphia: 1825.

————. *The Letters of Richard Henry Lee.* 2 vols. New York: 1912-1914.

MCHENRY, JAMES. "The Battle of Monmouth," *Magazine of American History,* III, (1879).

MACKENZIE, FREDERICK. *Diary of Frederick Mackenzie.* 2 vols. Cambridge: 1930.

MADISON, JAMES. *The Writings of James Madison,* ed. G. Hunt. 9 vols. New York: 1900-1910.

Maryland Archives and Correspondence of the State Council of Maryland, 1780-1782. Vols. XLV-XLVII. Baltimore: 1929-1930.

MONTRESOR, JOHN. "Journals of Capt. John Montresor," *New York Historical Society Collections* (1875). New York: 1876.

MOORE, FRANK. *Diary of the American Revolution from Newspapers and Original Documents.* 2 vols. New York: 1860.

MORRIS, LEWIS. "Letters to General Lewis Morris," *New York Historical Society Collections* (1875). New York: 1876.

MORRIS, ROBERT. "Letters to Robert Morris, 1775-1782," *New York Historical Society Collections* (1878). New York: 1879.

NELSON, THOMAS. "Letters of Thomas Nelson, Jr., Governor of Virginia," *Publications of the Virginia Historical Society,* New Series, No. 1. Richmond: 1874.

New Jersey Archives, Second Series. Vols., III, V. Trenton: 1906, 1917.

NEW YORK. *Documents Relative to the Colonial History of the State of New York.* 15 vols. Albany: 1856-1887.

New York Gazette and the Weekly Mercury, ed. Hugh Gaine.

New York Loyal Gazette, 1777, ed. James Rivington.

New York Packet, 1776, ed. Samuel Loudon.

New York Royal Gazette, 1777-1783, ed. James Rivington.

North Carolina State Records. 16 vols. Goldsboro: 1895-1907.

North Carolina Colonial Records. 10 vols. Raleigh: 1886-1890.

PAINE, THOMAS. *The Writings of Thomas Paine,* ed. Moncure D. Conway. 4 vols. New York: 1894-1896.

REED, WILLIAM B. *Life and Correspondence of Joseph Reed.* 2 vols. Philadelphia: 1847.

Rhode Island Acts and Resolves, 1773-1774. Newport: 1773-1774.

————. *Records of the Colony of Rhode Island and Providence Plantations,* ed. J. R. Bartlett. 10 vols. Providence: 1856-1869.

RODNEY, CAESAR. *Letters to and from Caesar Rodney, 1765-1784.* Philadelphia: 1933.

ROWE, JOHN. *Letters and Diary of John Rowe, Boston Merchant,* ed. Anne Rowe. Boston: 1903.

RUSH, BENJAMIN. *The Autobiography of Benjamin Rush,* ed. G. W. Corner. Princeton: 1948.

RUTLEDGE, JOHN. "Letters of John Rutledge," *South Carolina Historical and Genealogical Magazine,* XVIII (1917).

SERLE, AMBROSE. *The American Journal of Ambrose Serle, Secretary to Lord Howe, 1776-1778,* ed. E. H. Tatum. San Marino: 1940.

SHAW, SAMUEL. *The Journals of Major Samuel Shaw,* ed. Josiah Quincy. Boston: 1847.

SIMCOE, J. G. *Simcoe's Military Journal.* New York: 1844.

SPARKS, JARED. *Correspondence of the American Revolution: Being Letters of Eminent Men to George Washington.* 4 vols. Boston: 1853.

STEVENS, B. F. *Facsimiles of Manuscripts in European Archives Relating to America, 1773-1783.* 25 vols. London: 1891-1898.

————. *The Clinton-Cornwallis Controversy.* 2 vols. London: 1888.

SULLIVAN, JOHN. *Letters and Papers of Major-General John Sullivan,* ed. O. G. Hammond. 3 vols. Concord: 1930-1939.

SUMTER, THOMAS. "Official Correspondence between Brigadier-Genreal Thomas Sumter and Major General Nathanael Greene," *Charleston Year Book, 1899,* Appendix, pp. 3-135.

TARLETON, BANASTRE. *History of the Campaign of 1780 and 1781 in the Southern Provinces of North America.* Dublin: 1787.

THACHER, JAMES. *A Military Journal during the American Revolutionary War.* Boston: 1827.

THOMSON, CHARLES. "The Thomson Papers," *New York Historical Society Collections*, (1878). New York: 1879.

TUCKER, ST. GEORGE. "The Southern Campaign, 1781—Narrated in the Letters from Judge St. George Tucker to his wife," *Magazine of American History*, VII (July, 1881).

WALDO, A. "Valley Forge, 1777-1778: Diary of Surgeon Albigence Waldo," *Pennsylvania Magazine of History and Biography*, XXI (1897).

WARD, SAMUEL. *Correspondence of Governor Samuel Ward*, ed. B. Knollenberg. Providence: 1952.

WARREN, JAMES. *Warren-Adams Letters, being chiefly a Correspondence among John Adams, Samuel Adams, and James Warren, 1743-1814. Massachusetts Historical Society Collections*. Vols. 72-73. Boston: 1917-1925.

WASHINGTON, GEORGE. *Letters to Washington and Accompanying Papers*, ed. S. Hamilton. 5 vols. Boston: 1898-1902.

————. *Writings of George Washington*, ed. J. C. Fitzpatrick. 39 vols. Washington: 1931-1944.

WATSON, ELKANNAH. *Men and Times of the Revolution*, ed. W. C. Watson. New York: 1857.

WEBB, SAMUEL B. *Correspondence and Journals of Samuel Webb*, ed. W. C. Ford. 3 vols. New York: 1893-1894.

WHARTON, F. *Revolutionary Diplomatic Correspondence of the United States*. 6 vols. Washington: 1889.

WILD, EBENEZER. "The Journal of Ebenezer Wild," *Massachusetts Historical Society Proceedings*, Second Series, VI.

WILKINSON, JAMES. *Memoirs of My Own Times*. 3 vols. Philadelphia: 1816.

WILLIAMS, OTHO H. *Calender of the General Otho Holland Williams Papers in the Maryland Historical Society*. Baltimore: 1940.

WISTER, SALLY. "Sally Wister's Diary," *American Historical and Literary Curiosities*. New York: 1860.

SECONDARY PUBLISHED SOURCES

ABBOTT, WILBUR C. *New York in the American Revolution*. New York: 1929.

ALDEN, JOHN R. *General Charles Lee: Traitor or Patriot?* Baton Rouge: 1951.

————. *General Gage in America: Being Principally a History of His Role in the American Revolution*. Baton Rouge: 1948.

ANDERSON, TROYER S. *The Command of the Howe Brothers during the American Revolution*. New York: 1936.

ANDREWS, JOHN. *History of the War with America, France, Spain, and Holland, 1775-1783*. 4 vols. London: 1785-1786.

ARNOLD, S. G. *History of the State of Rhode Island.* 2 vols. New York: 1860.

BELCHER, HENRY. *The First American Civil War.* 2 vols. London: 1911.

BILL, ALFRED H. *The Campaign of Princeton, 1776-1777.* Princeton: 1948.

BOLTON, CHARLES K. *The Private Soldier under Washington.* New York; 1902.

BOWMAN, ALLEN. *The Morale of the American Revolutionary Army.* Washington: 1943.

BOYNTON, E. C. *History of West Point and Its Military Importance During the American Revolution.* 8 vols. New York: 1864.

BRUCE, ROBERT. *Brandywine.* Clinton, N. Y.: 1922.

BURNETT, E. C. *The Continental Congress.* New York: 1941.

CALDWELL, CHARLES. *Memoirs of the Life and Campaigns of the Hon. Nathanael Greene.* Philadelphia: 1819.

CALLAHAN, NORTH. *Henry Knox, General Washington's General.* New York: 1958.

CARRINGTON, H. B. *Battles of the American Revolution, 1775-1781.* New York: 1888.

CURTIS, EDWARD. *The Organization of the British Army in the American Revolution.* New Haven: 1926.

DABNEY, WILLIAM. *After Saratoga: The Story of the Convention Army.* Albuquerque: 1954.

DAVIS, WILLIAM E. "The Society of the Cincinnati in New England, 1783-1800," *William and Mary Quarterly,* Ser. 3, V (Jan., 1948).

DELANCEY, E. F. *The Capture of Mount Washington.* New York: 1877.

DRAKE, F. S. *Life and Correspondence of Henry Knox.* Boston: 1873.

DRAPER, LYMAN C. *King's Mountain and Its Heroes.* Cincinnati: 1881.

DUER, WILLIAM A. *The Life of William Alexander, Earl of Stirling.* New York: 1847.

FIELD, EDMUND (ed.). *State of Rhode Island and Providence Plantations at the End of the Century.* 3 vols. Boston: 1902.

FIELD, THOMAS. *The Battle of Long Island.* Brooklyn: 1869.

FLEXNER, JAMES T. *The Traitor and the Spy: Benedict Arnold and John André.* New York: 1953.

FORD, W. C. "The Defenses of Philadelphia in 1777," *Pennsylvania Magazine of History and Biography,* XVIII (1894).

FORTESCUE, J. W. *A History of the British Army.* 14 vols. New York: 1899-1930.

FREEMAN, DOUGLAS S. *George Washington, a Biography.* 5 vols. New York: 1948-1952.

FRENCH, ALLEN. *The Day of Concord and Lexington.* Boston: 1925.

————. *The First Year of the American Revolution.* Boston: 1934.

————. *General Gage's Informers.* Ann Arbor: 1932.

FROTHINGHAM, RICHARD. *Life and Times of Joseph Warren.* Boston: 1865.

GARDEN, ALEXANDER. *Anecdotes of the American Revolution.* 3 vols. Brooklyn: 1865.

GORDON, WILLIAM. *History of the Rise, Progress and Establishment of the Independence of the United States of America.* 4 vols. London: 1788.

GOTTSCHALK, LOUIS. *Lafayette and the Close of the American Revolution.* Chicago: 1942.

———. *Lafayette Comes to America.* Chicago: 1935.

———. *Lafayette Joins the American Army.* Chicago: 1937.

GRAHAM, JAMES. *Life of General Daniel Morgan.* New York: 1856.

GREENE, FRANCIS V. *General Greene.* New York: 1893.

———. *The Revolutionary War and the Military Policy of the United States.* New York: 1911.

GREENE, GEORGE W. *Life of Nathanael Greene, Major-General in the Army of the Revolution.* 3 vols. New York: 1867-1871.

GREENE, MARY A. *General Nathanael Greene.* (Pamphlet, RIHS).

HATCH, LOUIS C. *The Administration of the American Revolutionary Army.* New York: 1904.

HUMPHREYS, MARY C. *Catherine Schuyler.* New York: 1897.

JAMES, WILLIAM D. *A Sketch of the Life of Brig. Gen. Francis Marion.* Charleston: 1821.

JOHNSON, WILLIAM. *Sketches of the Life and Correspondence of Nathanael Greene.* Charleston: 1822.

JOHNSTON, HENRY P. *The Battle of Harlem Heights.* New York: 1897.

———. "The Campaign of 1776 around New York and Brooklyn," *Memoirs of the Long Island Historical Society,* Vol. III. Brooklyn: 1878.

———. *The Storming of Stony Point.* New York: 1900.

JONES, CHARLES C. *The History of Georgia.* 2 vols. Boston: 1883.

JONES, THOMAS. *History of New York during the Revolutionary War.* 2 vols. New York: 1879.

KINLOCH, FRANCIS. *Letters from Geneva and France.* 2 vols. Boston: 1819.

KNOLLENBERG, BERNHARD. *Washington and the Revolution: A Reappraisal.* New York: 1940.

LAMB, MARTHA J. *The History of the City of New York.* 3 vols. New York: 1877-1896.

LEFFERTS, CHARLES M. *Uniforms . . . in the War of the American Revolution, 1775-1783.* New York: 1926.

LIBBY, O. G. "A Critical Examination of Gordon's History of the American Revolution," *Annual Report of the American Historical Association.* (1899). 2 vols. Washington: 1900.

LOSSING, BENSON. *The Pictorial Field-Book of the Revolution.* 2 vols. New York: 1851-1852.

LOVEJOY, DAVID S. *Rhode Island Politics and the American Revolution, 1760-1776.* Providence: 1958.

LOWELL, EDWARD J. *The Hessians . . . in the Revolutionary War.* New York: 1884.

LUNDIN, LEONARD. *Cockpit of the American Revolution: The War for Independence in New Jersey.* Princeton:1940.

McCRADY, EDWARD. *The History of South Carolina in the Revolution. 1775-1783.* 2 vols. New York: 1901-1902.

MARTYN, CHARLES. *The Life of Artemas Ward, the First Commander-in-Chief of the American Revolution.* New York: 1921.

MILLER, JOHN C. *Triumph of Freedom, 1775-1783.* Boston: 1948.

MONTROSS, LYNN. *Rag, Tag and Bobtail: The Story of the Continental Army, 1775-1783.* New York: 1952.

MOOK, H. T. "Training Day in New England," *New England Quarterly,* XI (Dec., 1938).

NELL, WILLIAM C. *The Colored Patriots of the American Revolution.* Boston: 1855.

NEVINS, ALLAN. *The American States during and after the Revolution, 1775-1789.* New York: 1924.

PALMER, JOHN McAULEY. *General Von Steuben.* New Haven: 1937.

PARTRIDGE, BELLAMY. *Sir Billy Howe.* London: 1936.

PAULLIN, C. O. *The Navy of the American Revolution.* Cleveland: 1906.

RAMSAY, DAVID. *History of the American Revolution.* 2 vols. Trenton: 1811.

————. *The History of the Revolution of South Carolina from British Province to an Independent State.* 2 vols. Trenton: 1785.

ROBINSON, BLACKWELL P. *William R. Davie.* Chapel Hill: 1957.

ROSSMAN, KENNETH R. *Thomas Mifflin and the Politics of the American Revolution.* Chapel Hill: 1952.

RUTTENBER, E. M. *Obstructions to the Navigation of Hudson's River.* Albany: 1860.

SIMMS, WILLIAM G. *Army Correspondence of Colonel John Laurens.* New York: 1867.

————. *The Life of Francis Marion.* New York: 1857.

SMITH, HENRY A. M. *The Baronies of South Carolina.* Charleston: 1931.

STEDMAN, CHARLES. *History of the Origins, Progress and Termination of the American War.* 2 vols. London: 1794.

STEINER, B. S. *Life and Correspondence of James McHenry.* Cleveland: 1907.

STRYKER, WILLIAM W. *The Battle of Monmouth.* Princeton: 1927.

————. *The Battle of Trenton and Princeton.* Boston: 1898.

SWIGGETT, HOWARD. *The Forgotten Leaders of the Revolution.* New York: 1955.

————. *The Great Man.* New York: 1953.

THAYER, THEODORE. *Pennsylvania Politics and the Growth of Democracy, 1740-1776.* Harrisburg: 1953.

TOWNSEND, JOSEPH. "Some accounts of the British Army and the Battle of Brandywine," *Bulletin of the Historical Society of Pennsylvania,* I, No. 7 (1846).

TYLER, MOSES C. *The Literary History of the American Revolution, 1763-1783.* 2 vols. New York: 1941.

——. *Patrick Henry.* New York: 1898.

VAN DOREN, CARL. *Mutiny in January.* New York: 1943 .

——. *Secret History of the American Revolution.* New York: 1941.

VAN TYNE, CLAUDE. *The Loyalists in the American Revolution.* New York: 1902.

——. *The War of Independence: American Phase.* Boston: 1929.

VER STEEG, CLARENCE L. *Robert Morris: Revolutionary Financier.* Philadelphia: 1954.

WADE, HERBERT T. and LIVELY, ROBERT A. *This Glorious Cause.* Princeton: 1958.

WALLACE, WILLARD M. *Appeal to Arms: A Military History of the American Revolution.* New York: 1951.

——. *Traitorous Hero: The Life and Fortunes of Benedict Arnold.* New York: 1954.

WARD, CHRISTOPHER. *The War of the Revolution.* 2 vols. New York: 1952.

WEELEN, JEAN-EDWARD. *Rochambeau.* New York: 1936.

WERTENBAKER, THOMAS J. "The Battle of Princeton," *The Princeton Battle Monument.* Princeton: 1922.

——. *Father Knickerbocker Rebels.* New York: 1948.

WILDES, H. E. *Anthony Wayne.* New York: 1941.

WILLCOX, W. B. "The British Road to Yorktown: A Study in Divided Command," *American Historical Review,* LII (1946).

——. "British Strategy in America, 1778," *Journal of Modern History,* XIX, No. 2 (June, 1947).

——. "Rhode Island in British Strategy, 1780-1781," *Journal of Modern History,* XVII (1945).

WILLIAMS, CATHERINE. *Biography of Revolutionary Heroes.* Providence: 1839.

Index

487